PRINCIPLES of MACROECONOMICS

PEARSON
Education

PRINCIPLES of MACROECONOMICS

Joseph G Nellis

Professor of International Management Economics
School of Management
Cranfield University

David Parker

Professor of Business Economics and Strategy
School of Management
Cranfield University

An imprint of Pearson Education
Harlow, England • London • New York • Boston • San Francisco • Toronto • Sydney • Singapore • Hong Kong
Tokyo • Seoul • Taipei • New Delhi • Cape Town • Madrid • Mexico City • Amsterdam • Munich • Paris • Milan

Pearson Education Limited
Edinburgh Gate
Harlow
Essex CM20 2JE
England

and Associated Companies throughout the world

Visit us on the World Wide Web at:
www.pearsoned.co.uk

First published 2004

ISBN 0 273 64614 1

British Library Cataloguing-in-Publication Data
A catalogue record for this book is available from the British Library

10 9 8 7 6 5 4 3 2 1
09 08 07 06 05 04

Typeset in 9.5/12 pt Stone Serif by 35
Printed and bound in Great Britain by Henry Ling Ltd., at the Dorset Press, Dorchester, Dorset

The publisher's policy is to use paper manufactured from sustainable forests.

To

Helen, Gareth, Daniel and Kathleen
Megan, Michael and Matthew

CONTENTS

LIST OF APPLICATIONS

LIST OF FIGURES AND TABLES

List of figures

Appendix

List of tables

PREFACE

Target audience

This book is intended for students studying macroeconomics on a wide range of degree and professional programmes, at both undergraduate and postgraduate levels. It should also prove useful to managers attending continuing studies courses in which an understanding of the dynamics of the macroeconomy and the importance of changes in macroeconomic policy represent an integral part. The book will be particularly attractive to those studying for a wide range of academic qualifications such as the Master of Business Administration (MBA), MScs in Business and Finance, Diploma in Management Studies (DMS), and BA Business Studies. In addition, the material should be relevant to those taking professional accountancy and banking examinations in which macroeconomics is a core element.

Our aim in writing this book is to provide a text that will be accessible not only to specialist economics students and tutors but to managers from the business world. The rationale for the book lies in the belief that, armed with a clear understanding of the core *Principles of Macroeconomics*, managers are better equipped to appreciate and react appropriately to changes in the national and global business environment in which their organisations operate and compete.

Structure of the book

The book has been structured to provide a comprehensive treatment of the *Principles of Macroeconomics*. After an introductory chapter that provides an overview of the key terms and concepts, the text turns to the measurement of economic activity and then to the dynamics of production, income and expenditure flows around the economy. This discussion is followed by a detailed explanation of the determination of economic activity, including the key concepts of aggregate demand and aggregate supply. We also examine in detail the causes, consequences and possible policy responses to inflation and unemployment. The later chapters of the book are concerned more centrally with international macroeconomic issues, namely international trade, the balance of payments and exchange rate determination. We also provide an overview of the roles of the major institutions in the international economy, such as the International Monetary Fund (IMF) and World Bank.

Finally, the last two chapters of the book study the causes of business cycles as well as the significance of market forces in macroeconomic management.

Key features of the book

We have endeavoured to make the book as user-friendly as possible both to the student and the course tutor. To this end a number of key features have been incorporated. Each chapter contains the following sections:

- aims and learning outcomes
- a discussion of the core principles of the subject
- applications
- concluding remarks
- key learning points
- topics for discussion.

All of the key principles, including definitions and formulae, are highlighted throughout the text for easy reference and revision. The book is designed for an international readership. Consequently, throughout the text we use the US dollar (denoted $) as the normal unit of account. We have intentionally minimised the use of technical jargon and mathematical treatment throughout the book, relying instead on clear discussion augmented by graphical analyses. This supports the user-friendly approach adopted in the book. We have included details concerning IS-LM analysis separately, as an appendix after Chapter 5. The inclusion of applications within each chapter is intended to reinforce and test the reader's understanding of key concepts. A detailed glossary of macroeconomic terms is also included at the end of the book for easy reference.

Website material

Access to supplementary material is available from the following website address:

www.booksites.net/nellisparker

This material is designed to support the work of tutors and students. The website includes the following:

- *Overhead transparency masters*
  These provide for each chapter a full set of visual aids, using Powerpoint slides, covering:
  - the structure of each chapter
  - the learning outcomes
  - highlighted text in the book including formulae and definitions
  - all tables and diagrams used in the book
  - key learning points
  - topics for discussion.
- *Guidance notes*
  These provide brief notes to tutors and students with respect to answering each of the *topics for discussion* questions that are included at the end of each chapter.

Feedback

Our aim has been to make this book as user-friendly as possible and to serve the needs of a wide range of readers. However, we recognise that there is always room for improvement in any textbook and therefore we would appreciate feedback from readers concerning areas for further improvement and development of the text. Such feedback should be directed through the publishers via the above website address.

Acknowledgements

We would like to acknowledge the important contributions made to the content of this book by the current and former students whom we have taught, in various institutions around the world. Their questions, insights and experience have helped to shape and improve our own thinking on and understanding of the *Principles of Macroeconomics*. In addition, we would like to thank Chris Williams, Dawn Richardson and Liz Blackford for their many hours of hard work devoted to typing and retyping drafts of the manuscript. Any remaining errors are, of course, solely our responsibility! Finally, and once again, this book could not have been written without the support and patience of our families. We thank them.

Joseph G. Nellis
David Parker

PUBLISHER'S ACKNOWLEDGEMENTS

We are grateful to the following for permission to reproduce copyright material:

National Statistics for Application 4.1 figure, Application 4.2 figure, Application 10.1 figure and Application 11.1 figure, Crown copyright material is reproduced with the permission of the Controller of Her Majesty's Stationery Office and the Queen's Printer for Scotland; Thomson Financial for Application 10.2 figure from *Privatisation International*, October 2000, issue 145; European Communities for Application 12.1 figure from *Employment in Europe 2002: Recent Trends and Prospects*; World Bank for Application 13.2 figure from *Global Economic Prospects 2003*. Copyright 2002 by World Bank. Reproduced with permission of World Bank conveyed through Copyright Clearance Center, Inc.; International Monetary Fund for Figure 16.1 from http://www.imf.org/external/about.htm.

The Dallas Morning News for an extract from 'Group offers another way to account for ourselves' by Scott Burns published in *Dallas Morning News*, 22nd October 2002; International Monetary Fund for extracts from *World Economic Outlook: Recessions and Recoveries – World Economic and Financial Surveys*, April 2002, and *World Economic Outlook: Trade and Finance – World Economic and Financial Surveys*, September 2002; Lloyds TSB plc for extracts from 'The economic outlook – global recovery remains fragile' published in *Lloyds TSB Economic Bulletin*, June 2003, and 'Debt crisis in Latin America – the lessons from Asia' published in *Lloyds TSB Economic Bulletin*, November 2003; Confederation of British Industry for extracts from *Economic Bulletin*, May and July 2003; Bank of England for an extract from 'The velocity of narrow money' published in *Inflation Report*, 13th November 2002; Federal Reserve Bank of Philadelphia for an extract from 'How inflation hawks escape expectations traps' by S. Leduc published in *Business Review*, First Quarter 2003; Penguin Books Limited and WW Norton Inc. for an extract from *Globalization and its Discontents* by Joseph Stiglitz, 2000; Federal Reserve Bank of Boston for an extract from 'Beyond shocks: what causes business cycles? An overview' by Jeffrey C. Fuhrer and Scott Schuh published in *Conference Series*, No.42, July 1998.

Every effort has been made by the publisher to obtain permission from the appropriate source to reproduce material which appears in this book. In some instances we have been unable to trace the owners of copyright material, and we would appreciate any information that would enable us to do so.

Chapter 1

MACROECONOMICS – CONCEPTS, AIMS AND POLICY

Aims and learning outcomes

Macroeconomics is a field within economics concerned with the study of total, or aggregate, economic activity. The study of macroeconomics investigates the workings of the wider economy, including the measurement and determination of national income, output and expenditure and the consequences for employment and prices. The field is also concerned with developments in the international economy with implications for the flow of exports and imports between countries and international flows of capital. In contrast, *microeconomics* involves the study of the individual parts of the economy – rather than the economy as a whole – with respect to individual market prices, individual firms' revenues and costs of production and the employment of factors of production at the individual firm level. The core elements of microeconomics are covered in our companion volume, *The Principles of Business Economics*.

In this chapter we introduce the key concepts and terms which underpin the study of the macroeconomy and which are analysed in greater detail in the subsequent chapters of this book. This chapter covers the following:

- the macroeconomy and business;
- macroeconomic policies;
- the economic problem;
- government and the economy;
- government economic objectives;
- policy targets, instruments and policy goals.

The aim of this book is to provide a clear and concise picture of the way in which an economy 'works', i.e. the determination of economic activity, and why different governments adopt different economic policies in their efforts to influence or manage economic activity. It is important to appreciate at the outset that 'policy is a function of time and place'. In other words, while the fundamental principles of macroeconomics used to explain economic activity develop slowly over time, policy decisions may be subject to considerable revision as domestic and international economic events unfold and government objectives change.

Learning outcomes

After studying this material you will be able to:

- Appreciate the key variables and features concerned with the macroeconomy.
- Recognise the importance of developments in the macroeconomy for business performance.
- Identify the main policies available to governments and other official bodies to manage the macroeconomy.
- Understand the fundamental challenges facing economies with respect to the attainment of optimum economic growth – the so-called 'economic problem'.
- Analyse the role of government in an economy.
- Appreciate the key macroeconomic objectives which governments may pursue.

The macroeconomy and business

The success or failure of a business is, to a large extent, dependent upon how its managers perform in terms of financial controls, marketing strategies, product design, research and development, etc. A great deal of time and effort is spent by successful firms in ensuring that the right decisions are made in a competitive environment with the greatest attention being paid to the immediate environment in which the firms are operating – to the workforce, to the production line, to the marketplace for products, to direct competitors. This immediate environment is described as the *microeconomic* environment of a firm and involves a firm's prices, revenues, costs, employment levels and so on.

There are, however, other facets of a firm's environment of which the most notable comprise the general social and economic conditions of the larger economic system of which each firm forms a part. Changing social values (e.g. with regard to the natural environment) combined with changes in the international economic environment powerfully condition economic activity at the firm level and, hence, the way in which organisations are managed. The political and legal institutions of a country also have a significant impact upon the business sector and the way in which firms attempt to carry out their activities. In this book our attention is focused on the firm's wider economic environment, that is the *macroeconomy*. In contrast to the microeconomy, this refers to the factors which are external to the immediate environment of the firm: these involve changes in general inflation and employment, for example, rather than changes in the firm's own product prices and workforce. Macroeconomics, therefore, refers to the national and, increasingly, international economy of which the firm is a subunit.

Macroeconomics is a field of economics which deals with the economy as a whole and the determination of national output, income and expenditure and the implications for employment and prices.

By definition, since each firm is a subunit of the larger economic system, it is unable to exercise control over the macroeconomic environment in the way that it has control (though perhaps limited) over its microeconomic environment. Yet a plain truth stares every firm in the face: failure to adapt to a changing, dynamic macroeconomy inevitably results in business failure. Nevertheless, how many managers actively seek to keep themselves informed of the key developments within the wider economy? One thing is certain: successful firms pay considerably more attention to these external economic factors than those firms that struggle to survive. Ultimately, the changing macroeconomy determines the growth in the nation's income and the ability to expand demand for products and services.

It is not difficult to identify which aspects of the macroeconomic environment are of greatest importance to business decision making: *all* aspects are important. This is readily confirmed by asking a group of managers to decide whether or not changes in each of the following macroeconomic variables are likely to have an impact upon their businesses (recognising that some variables will have a more immediate and direct impact than others):

- economic growth;
- the general level of prices and inflation;
- interest rates;
- availability of credit and liquidity;
- total investment;
- public expenditure plans;
- personal and corporate taxation;
- total consumer expenditure;
- total savings;
- wages and earnings at the national economy level;
- national employment trends;
- exchange rates;
- imports, exports and the balance of payments.

The list could be extended but the message is that firms operate within an environment that is extremely complex and dynamic.

In addition, all of these economic variables are interrelated to some extent. For example, changes in liquidity (i.e. monetary growth) affect interest rates; changes in taxation have implications for the level of public expenditure as well as consumer spending and investment; changes in the exchange rate affect the price of imports and exports and hence can have an impact on the volume (and value) of goods and services traded. Furthermore, most of these variables are either directly

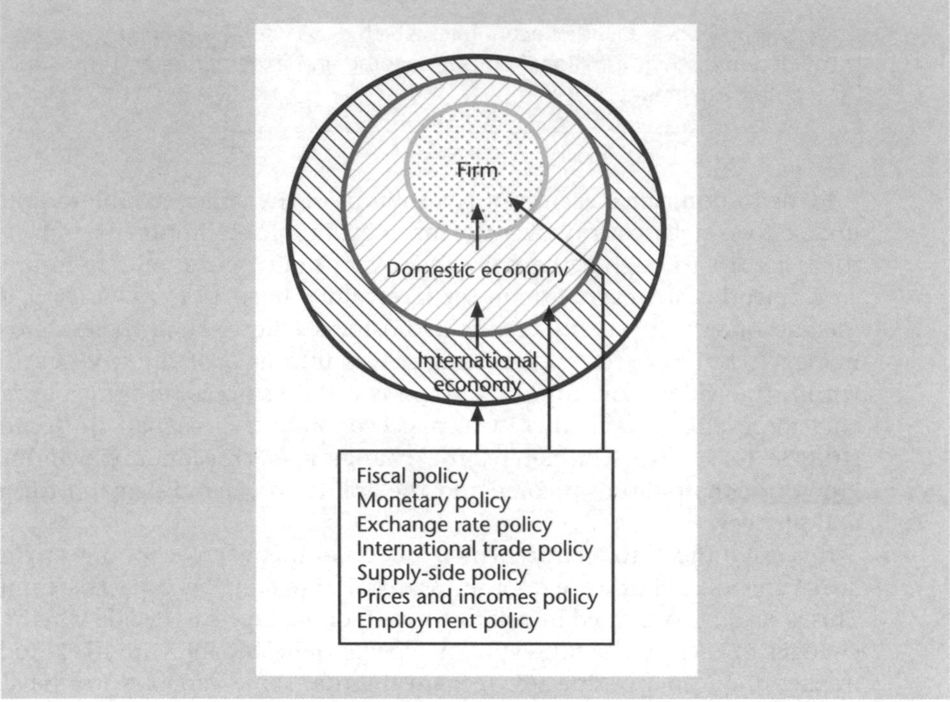

Figure 1.1 The macroeconomy and business

controlled by the government or indirectly affected by government economic policies.

The extent to which firms are vulnerable to both domestic and international macroeconomic policies is summarised in Figure 1.1. In this figure, the most prominent macroeconomic policies at the disposal of governments (including central banks) are listed. We now explain briefly each of these in turn.

Macroeconomic policies

The economic policy options available to governments (including central banks) are summarised below.

Fiscal policy

> *Fiscal policy* is concerned with the composition of and changes in the levels of government expenditure and taxation.

Changes in fiscal policy are generally announced once a year in most countries. Given the scale of government spending (both central and local) in economies and the corresponding scale of taxation (both personal and corporate), fiscal policy may be used as a powerful tool to directly influence national expenditure and, therefore, the level of economic activity. In this context, fiscal policy is an important instrument of *demand management*.

Monetary policy

Monetary policy is defined as measures taken by governments and central banks to influence the cost of borrowing (i.e. the rate of interest) and availability of credit and liquidity in the economy, thereby affecting the overall demand for and supply of money.

While fiscal policy changes are usually announced annually in national budget statements, monetary policy changes are more continuous. For example, interest rate changes may be announced by the authorities at any time, and these rapidly affect the level and structure of competing interest rates generally (such as bank lending and savings rates).

Exchange rate policy

Exchange rate policy refers to government and central bank intervention in the foreign exchange markets to influence the level and direction of the external value of a country's currency.

The degree of intervention in the foreign exchange markets depends upon the country's specific exchange rate objective: whether to have a fixed, freely floating or managed rate and, where the exchange rate is fixed or managed, at what level to 'peg' the rate. Exchange rate policy has important implications for international trade and capital flows in and out of a country, i.e. for the current and capital accounts of the balance of payments. It also has an impact upon domestic monetary policy because interest rate levels may have to be set to influence international capital flows with the objective of supporting the exchange rate.

International trade policy

International trade policy involves measures taken by government, in addition to exchange rate policy, to influence the magnitude and direction of foreign trade.

There may be many reasons for these measures, notably correction of balance of payments problems (i.e. deficits or surpluses), preserving domestic employment, encouraging economic growth and promoting foreign cooperation (e.g. within trade blocs such as the North American Free Trade Agreement (NAFTA) and the Single Market of the European Union). The measures may take the form of subsidies for exports, tariffs (duties) on imports and other protectionist measures such as import quotas and embargos.

Supply-side policy

Supply-side policy arises out of what is often termed *supply-side economics.*

> *Supply-side economics* refers to those government measures that are directed at tackling problems involving the growth and sustainability of a nation's *total* or *aggregate supply* (i.e. national production) of goods and services in the economy over time.

Supply-side policy, therefore, contrasts with the policies described above, especially fiscal and monetary policies, which are usually concerned with affecting the level of *total* or *aggregate demand* for goods and services, i.e. the demand side of the economy. Supply-side measures are directed specifically at influencing a country's productivity and output. These may involve the introduction of new technology, the encouragement of competition and enterprise, privatisation of state-owned assets, efforts to increase labour efficiency and mobility and other measures to improve competitiveness in the international market economy.

Prices and incomes policies

> *Prices and incomes policies* are examples of direct intervention by government in the working of a market economy concerned with the setting of prices for goods and services and wage settlements.

These policies have two fundamental aims: control over general inflation and the protection of jobs in the domestic economy. In addition, prices and incomes policies can have a significant impact upon the distribution of national income between the owners of land, capital and labour (i.e. the workforce). There is a general view among economists, however, that prices and incomes policies should be regarded only as temporary or emergency measures since, by definition, they distort the operation of markets by undermining wage and price levels and therefore the demand for and supply of goods, services and labour.

Employment policy

Employment policy is concerned with government efforts to create jobs and thereby reduce unemployment.

The policy may be implemented either indirectly, via stimulation of aggregate demand in the economy, or directly through supply-side measures such as job creation schemes and the provision of training programmes.

There is a large degree of overlap between the various policies defined above and their impact upon the macroeconomic variables listed earlier. These interrelationships are emphasised and explored throughout the book. We now consider the overriding economic problem that faces governments, individuals and firms from which the study of economics has evolved.

Application 1.1

Macroeconomic challenges

For a decade now, the British economy has grown at an average rate of close to 3 per cent a year, just above its long-run trend rate. The spare capacity created by the recession of the early 1990s has gradually been used up. Unemployment has more than halved from over 10 per cent in early 1993 to around 5 per cent now, on the internationally standardised measure. And growth has been more stable than for decades. But overall this stability has concealed the contrasting fortunes of different sectors in the economy.

Since 1997 household spending on consumption has risen, on average, by 4 per cent a year in volume terms. It is most unlikely that consumer spending can continue to rise at this rate. The trade deficit has widened sharply in recent years, reaching some 3 per cent of GDP at the end of last year. And the increase in the trade deficit would have been even larger had it not been for an improvement in the terms of trade, the ratio of export to import prices, which rose by 8 per cent over the past five years. The result of the widening trade deficit, and the improvement in the terms of trade, is that domestic demand has been able to grow faster than output. Over the past five years, domestic demand has risen by over 6 per cent more than output – slightly more than the excess of demand over output in the late 1980s. In turn, net trade has made a negative contribution to output growth for six years in succession. A continuation of that trend would be unprecedented in Britain's modern economic history.

Application 1.1 continued

The strength of consumption and the weakness of net exports have led to an imbalance between manufacturing and services. Manufacturing profitability has fallen by more than half over the past five years, while in less easily traded services profitability has been broadly unchanged.

The need to rebalance the British economy is clear. Domestic demand is likely to be able to grow at no more than the rate of growth of total output; indeed, if the trade position is to improve it will have to grow by less. And within that figure, we need to allow room for the growth of public services.

How will this rebalancing of demand come about? That is not yet clear.

Source: Extract from a speech entitled 'Monetary Policy in the UK: Challenges Ahead', delivered to the British Chamber of Commerce National Conference, London 23 April 2002 by Mervyn King, then Deputy Governor of the Bank of England, now Governor of the Bank of England.

Activity

This extract is typical of pieces that you will find in the quality financial press summarising key developments in the economy. At the outset of your study of macroeconomics, attempt to set out what you consider to be the key challenges facing the British economy, as described.

The economic problem

At the heart of the study of economics is the problem of how countries attempt to match the demands on their resources with the available supply. Despite a phenomenal growth in production since the Industrial Revolution, there is no evidence that, even in the richest countries, people's wants are satisfied. Although most people in the industrialised world are well fed, clothed and housed, new wants are continuously being created: stores continue to be crowded with people wanting the latest fashions and electronic gadgets. Even the nature of the desirable home has changed. Thirty years ago house buyers in many Western countries looked for inside lavatories, but today they increasingly seek en-suite bathrooms and double garages. At the same time, however, for over one-half of the world's population – those in developing countries – life remains harsh. Here, the need for basic sanitation replaces the en-suite bathroom as a priority. Indeed, in these countries there often remains a desperate need for the most basic of foodstuffs and other necessities of life to ward off malnutrition and disease.

The message is clear enough: wants are limitless, but the resources to satisfy them are scarce. Therefore, all societies – from the richest to the poorest – share a common economic problem involving the allocation of scarce resources to meet the needs and demands of consumers and producers. How should resources be

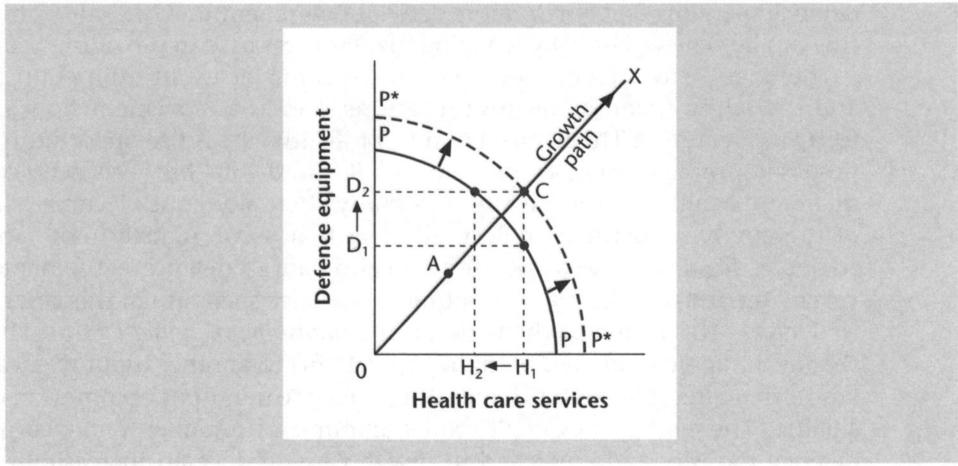

Figure 1.2 Production possibility curve

allocated when satisfying one set of wants inevitably means another set is not met? This is equally true for individuals, firms and governments, who all face the same kind of economic problem. The individual who buys a larger house may have to forgo an annual foreign holiday or the purchase of a new car. The firm that pays more to its workforce may have to reduce its investment in new machinery. When the government buys more school books out of the education budget, there may be a shortage of money available to employ teachers. In other words, every decision involving the satisfaction of wants using scarce resources involves a choice. Each use of resources means forgoing some other use.

When discussing resource use, economists use the term *opportunity cost* to describe the *next best option* or *alternative forgone*. The concept of opportunity cost can be usefully illustrated in a simple diagram. The curve PP in Figure 1.2 represents what is called a *production possibility curve* or *frontier*.

> *A production possibility curve* shows the maximum output of two goods or services that can be obtained given an economy's current level of resources and assuming maximum efficiency in production.

The underlying concept of this curve can be extended to any number of goods or services, though only two can be neatly represented on a two-dimensional diagram. The assumption of maximum efficiency means that resources are not wasted in producing the goods and services. To illustrate the concept of opportunity cost, assume that the two goods are defence equipment and health care services. It should be appreciated that if there are no more resources available, then to produce one unit more of something means producing less of another good (there is an opportunity cost). Therefore, if a country should decide to raise defence spending and obtain more defence equipment then the curve shows that this can be achieved only by reducing the resources used in providing health care.

The increase in defence spending is represented by a shift from point D_1 to D_2 and the fall in spending on health care services as a movement from point H_1 to H_2 in Figure 1.2. The reduced output of health care is the opportunity cost of producing more defence equipment. Similar trade-offs between defence equipment and health care services are shown anywhere along the PP curve. The shape of the curve, incidentally, reflects the fact that as we transfer more and more resources from one use to another – health care to defence equipment or vice versa – the resulting increase in output (of defence spending in this case) is likely to decline. This relates to the concept of *diminishing marginal returns*. This states that as we apply more of one input (e.g. labour) to another input (e.g. capital or land) then after some point the resulting increase in output becomes smaller and smaller. Therefore, for example, equal amounts of resources removed from the defence industry and employed in health care produce an increasingly smaller addition to the health care output.

It should be noted that since the PP curve shows the maximum production of defence equipment and health care possible with the available resources, any production combination below the curve (e.g. point A) represents an inefficient use of resources. In contrast, any point above the curve, which of course we should prefer since it implies we can have both more health care and defence equipment (e.g. point C), cannot be achieved given the current level and

Application 1.2

Venezuela in crisis

In the first quarter of 2003 the Venezuelan economy contracted by an astonishing 29 per cent. Unemployment rose to 20 per cent and many were reported to be going short of food.

Much of the decline in national output resulted from a two-month general strike aimed at ousting the Venezuelan president, Hugo Chávez. A major casualty of the strike was the oil industry, vital to the Venezuelan economy – it shut down. This economic collapse followed a year of more gradual economic contraction resulting from the global recession.

Activity

Explain, using a production possibility frontier diagram, what has been happening to the Venezuelan economy. Although at an early stage of your study of macroeconomics, outline what policy measures you think could be adopted to reverse the economic decline in Venezuela and how you believe they would impact on the economy.

productivity of the country's economic resources. The obvious solution to the trade-off between defence and health care, as implied by the production possibility curve, is to increase the capacity of the economy to produce more of both. This is what is meant by *economic growth* and would be illustrated by an outward shift of the PP curve, as shown in Figure 1.2, by the broken P*P* curve. One objective of government, therefore, is to stimulate economic growth and hence raise economic welfare by moving the economy along a growth path such as 0X. Whether governments should attempt to do this by active intervention in the economy (e.g. through planning and investment subsidies), or whether they should simply maintain an economic and political environment in which private enterprise can flourish, continues to divide economists, much as it has done for centuries.

Government and the economy

All societies face the economic problem outlined above but they may attempt to solve it in different ways. One approach is to have a central planning body which makes all of the decisions about what is produced, whose wants are met and how. The former Soviet Union was a good example of a *planned* or *command economy* before its break up in the early 1990s. There, resource use was directed through a powerful hierarchy of state agencies headed by the USSR State Planning Committee (called Gosplan). Along with the Ministry of Finance and around 900 ministries and departments scattered across the Soviet Union, in principle Gosplan controlled the entire national economy of that country. The planners decided what to produce, how the goods and services should be supplied, where production should take place and to whom the goods and services should be distributed.

An alternative approach, favoured in the West and recently adopted in much of the former Soviet bloc, is a reliance on prices and markets to allocate resources. A *free market economy* is associated with the private ownership of resources and the profit motive – an economic system known as *capitalism*. Instead of the allocation of resources through central planning, a capitalist economy uses prices as a signal to both producers and consumers exchanging goods and services in the free market. Prices indicate what and how much firms should produce to maximise their profits and they regulate how much consumers will buy to satisfy their wants. If a price is set too low, demand will exceed supply and prices will therefore tend to rise. In contrast, if a price is set too high supply will exceed demand and prices will be forced down.

In this way the price mechanism allocates resources according to consumer demand reflected in the prices that consumers are willing and able to pay. A major objection to capitalism, however, is unfairness in the distribution of resources, and it is this which led to the rise of socialism as a political and economic alternative to capitalism in the nineteenth century – socialism is associated with a planned economy. In the free market economy, those with the highest incomes have more influence on the distribution of resources than those on low incomes. Each unit of money spent in the marketplace acts like a vote for goods and services. Those with the largest incomes and wealth therefore have the largest number of votes. This is not an equal 'franchise' so, therefore, central planning in which everyone (in principle) receives a more equal amount would seem fairer. In practice, however, planning has often been associated with economic waste and inefficiency as well as the production of poor quality goods and services (i.e. with production well inside the production possibility curve in Figure 1.2). For example, at one time the former Soviet Union produced two-and-a-half times more shoes than the USA but shortages of footwear continued. The shoes produced were generally of poor quality and did not last long. Wasting economic resources is equivalent to moving the production possibility curve in Figure 1.2 inwards towards the origin – fewer of all goods are produced and the general economic well-being of society declines as a result.

In practice, all economies fall somewhere between the two extremes of central planning and completely free, capitalist markets. They are known, therefore, as *mixed economies*. In the former Soviet Union, while most resources were allocated by the state, there still remained a small market sector. In contrast, in the USA (generally recognised as the leading capitalist economy), there is considerable state involvement in the provision of welfare services, law and order and defence. In all capitalist economies, governments to varying degrees aim to make the 'votes' in the marketplace more equal through taxation and the provision of welfare benefits. The extent to which this should and can be done without creating economic disincentives remains controversial.

There are many reasons why governments may want to intervene in markets, even in capitalist economies. These come under a number of headings described below.

Reasons for government intervention

- provision of essential services;
- transfer payments;
- natural monopolies;
- social costs and benefits;
- support for industry and commerce;
- management of total demand in the economy.

Each of these reasons for government intervention is discussed briefly.

Provision of essential services

Governments may provide certain services such as health, education, policing, sanitation, etc. for everyone regardless of their ability to pay. Such services are sometimes referred to as *merit goods*, in the sense that governments may regard it as meritorious or morally right to secure equality of access to such goods and services for every citizen.

Transfer payments

Transfer payments are payments by the state for which no goods or services have been offered in return and are intended (usually) as a means of maintaining living standards for those in society who are in most need. They are paid out of taxation receipts. Examples of transfer payments include unemployment benefits and pensions for retired workers provided by the state.

Natural monopolies

Generally, economists believe that free market competition is beneficial because it provides consumers with the maximum choice of suppliers and provides maximum incentives for firms to produce efficiently. However, governments may decide to intervene directly in certain sectors of the economy where, for technical reasons, competition cannot occur. For example, governments are likely to intervene where there are large investments in distribution systems so that it is prohibitively expensive to lay down more than one system, such as in parts of the gas, water and electricity sectors (the so-called *public utilities*). These are commonly referred to as *natural monopolies*. In many countries after World War II such natural monopolies were state-owned: governments felt that private ownership of natural monopolies was socially and economically unacceptable. Today, however, may countries have privatised or are in the process of privatising their gas, water and electricity industries. This diminishes the role of the state but does not remove it altogether. The newly privatised public utilities normally remain state-regulated in terms of their pricing policies and service levels.

Social costs and benefits

Governments intervene to control or prohibit certain goods and services which are considered to have a detrimental effect on society, for example drugs and pornography. In addition, governments may also intervene to protect society from the side-effects of others' actions, for instance the control of pollution and the prosecution of polluters. Such side-effects (or spillover effects) are called *social costs* or *external costs*. Equally, governments often promote the supply of goods and services which are considered to have appreciable *social* or *external benefits*, for example the provision of free inoculations against infectious diseases. Government intervention with regard to control of these *externalities* may take many forms including laws and regulations, fines and compensation payments, as well as taxes and subsidies aimed at reducing or encouraging supply. Goods and services with appreciable externalities and where it is difficult or impossible to exclude non-payers from their consumption, and where consumption by one person does not restrict consumption by another (e.g. defence services), are usually referred to by economists as *public goods*.

Support for industry and commerce

Just as governments provide support for individuals so they may also choose to support individual firms or entire industries. This may take the form of industrial and regional aid – notably grants, subsidies, tax concessions and planning exemptions. Governments support firms for a variety of reasons – social and political as well as economic. The economic reasons include a desire to increase investment, to finance risky research and development, to redistribute employment, to increase total employment and to benefit exports.

Management of total demand in the economy

Government may intervene to control and stimulate the level of total (i.e. aggregate or national) economic activity. This is based on the view that, left to its own devices, the free market does not necessarily lead to full employment of the nation's scarce resources and therefore operation on its optimum or highest potential production possibility curve. Equally, the free market might lead to high and unacceptable inflation. Government intervention for much of the second half of the twentieth century in many Western nations was directed mainly at regulating the level of total demand in the economy to influence employment and prices. More recently, attention has switched towards stimulating the economic supply of goods and services in the private sector (*supply-side economics*) and away from *demand management*. Whether governments should aim to control demand, especially through changes in taxation and public spending, is a subject which has attracted considerable debate amongst economists and policy makers – and is one which we explore throughout this book.

Government economic objectives

Governments have a number of economic objectives, although the importance of each and the trade-offs between them vary from time to time. Several of these have been mentioned already.

Government economic objectives

- a high and sustained level of economic growth;
- full employment of economic resources, including labour;
- low and stable inflation;
- a sound balance of payments coupled with a stable currency value in the foreign exchange markets.

From time to time other objectives may be emphasised, such as a reduction in regional imbalances, a redistribution of income and wealth, more or less state ownership, and promotion of competition and private enterprise. The pursuance of these objectives is made all the more difficult by the existence of policy conflicts or what are often called policy *trade-offs*. Trade-offs may arise, such as between having a lower rate of inflation and a higher rate of employment, in the policy measures adopted by government. Subsequent chapters explore many of these policy conflicts.

Policy targets, instruments and goals

In attempting to understand the ways in which governments manage economies, it is important to appreciate the distinction between *policy targets, policy instruments* and *policy goals*. The relationship can be summarised as follows:

Policy targets ➜ Policy instruments ➜ Ultimate policy goals

Targets may be defined as quantifiable aims set out by governments and which governments (and other official bodies, in particular central banks) attempt to achieve using policy instruments. Examples of policy targets might be: economic growth in *real* terms (allowing for inflation) of say 3 per cent per annum; reduction of unemployment by 250,000 per annum; restriction of inflation to no more than 2 per cent per annum, and so on. Once the policy targets are set, governments may choose from a range of policy instruments in their efforts to achieve them. Instruments may include, for example, changes in the level and structure of interest rates, credit restrictions and other monetary controls, exchange controls and changes in taxation. A policy goal is what the government is ultimately attempting to achieve, for example stable prices over time, full employment or strong and sustainable economic growth. This distinction between policy targets, instruments and goals features in later chapters, such as Chapter 6 and especially in the discussion of fiscal and monetary policies in Chapters 7 and 9.

Concluding remarks

In this chapter we have provided a foundation for the more detailed and structured analysis of the macroeconomy which follows. The next chapter deals with the technical aspects of the measurement of economic activity, formally referred to as *national income accounting*. Chapters 3, 4 and 5 represent the core of the theoretical framework used to develop an understanding of the interrelationships within an economy, involving the key sectors which contribute to economic flows. These sectors are: the household, firms, financial services, government and foreign trade sectors. The framework is referred to as the *circular flow of income* model. This is developed to consider the impact of changes in certain macroeconomic variables upon the economy and the determination of the level of national output, income and expenditure.

Chapters 6 through to 12 focus on the major policy measures at the disposal of governments in their efforts to manage the economy. The policies covered include: fiscal policy, monetary policy and the role of banking, as well as supply-side economics. In addition, we provide a detailed treatment of the key economic challenges facing policy-makers with respect to managing economic growth, inflation and unemployment.

The international aspects of the macroeconomy are covered in Chapters 13 to 16, involving the theory of international trade and the balance of payments, exchange rate regimes and institutions in the international economy.

Finally, Chapters 17 and 18 deal with two further aspects of the macro-economy, namely the dynamics of business cycles and the role of market forces in the context of macroeconomic management.

Key learning points

- *Macroeconomics* is concerned with the workings of the wider economy, including the measurement and determination of national income, output and expenditure, and the consequences for employment and inflation.
- *Microeconomics* involves the study of the individual parts of the economy with respect to individual market prices, individual firms' revenues and costs of production and the employment of factors of production at the individual firm or market level.
- The *economic policy options* available to governments include: fiscal policy, monetary policy, exchange rate and trade policies, supply-side policy, prices and incomes policy, as well as employment policy.
- *Fiscal policy* is concerned with the composition of and changes in the level of government expenditure and taxation.
- *Monetary policy* is defined as measures taken by governments and central banks to influence the cost of borrowing (i.e. the rate of interest) and availability of credit and liquidity in the economy, in order to affect the overall demand for and supply of money.
- *Exchange rate policy* is concerned with the degree of government and central bank intervention in the foreign exchange markets to influence the level and direction of the external value of a country's currency.
- *International trade policy* involves measures taken by government, in addition to exchange rate policy, to influence the magnitude and direction of foreign trade.
- *Supply-side economics* refers to those government policies that are directed at tackling problems involving the growth and sustainability of a nation's total or aggregate supply (i.e. national production) of goods and services in the economy over time.
- *Prices and incomes policies* are examples of direct intervention by government in the working of a market economy and are concerned with directly influencing the setting of prices of goods and services and wage settlements.

- *Employment policy* is concerned with government efforts to create jobs and thereby reduce unemployment.
- The *economic problem* refers to the existence of scarce resources alongside insatiable demand for these resources; this leads to the concept of opportunity cost.
- *Opportunity cost* is the economic cost of using resources in one use rather than another and is defined as the *next best* or *alternative use forgone.*
- A *production possibility curve* or *frontier* shows the maximum output of two goods or services that can be obtained given the current level of resources and assuming maximum efficiency in production.
- The concept of *diminishing marginal returns* states that as we apply more of one input (e.g. labour) to another input (e.g. capital or land), then after some point the resulting increase in output becomes smaller and smaller.
- *Government intervention* in market economies may take place for a number of reasons involving: the provision of essential services; transfer payments; natural monopolies; social costs and benefits; support for industry and commerce; and the management of aggregate demand in the economy.
- The main *economic objectives* of governments include a high and sustained level of economic growth; full employment of resources, including labour; low inflation; and a sound balance of payments coupled with a stable currency value.
- *Policy targets* may be defined as quantifiable aims set by governments and which governments (and other financial bodies, in particular central banks), attempt to achieve using policy instruments.
- *Policy instruments* include changes in the level and structure of interest rates, credit restrictions and other monetary controls, exchange controls, changes in taxation and government expenditure.
- *Policy goals* are what the government is ultimately attempting to achieve, such as stable prices, full employment or strong and sustainable economic growth.

? Topics for discussion

1. What do you understand by the terms macroeconomics and microeconomics?
2. What are the main subjects covered in the study of the macroeconomy?
3. Outline the main sectors of the macroeconomy. In what ways would you expect changes in exchange rate policy and international trade policy to affect the macroeconomy?
4. What do you understand by the following terms:

   (a) fiscal policy
   (b) monetary policy

(c) supply-side policies
(d) economic growth
(e) opportunity cost?

5. Using an appropriate diagram, explain the nature of 'the economic problem' faced by all economies.
6. Explain the shape of the production possibility curve.
7. What role can government play in the macroeconomy?
8. Distinguish between policy targets, policy instruments and policy goals in government management of the macroeconomy.

Chapter 2

THE MEASUREMENT OF ECONOMIC ACTIVITY

Aims and learning outcomes

Accurate measurement of economic activity is important as a basis for sound decision making. No-one would sensibly attempt to drive a car without reliable information about its direction and speed. Likewise, governments and others (especially businesses) affected by economic information would be unwise to make decisions in the absence of sound information about the state of the economy. Clearly, decisions will be different according to whether the economy is in a boom period or in a recession, or whether it is growing or declining in size.

In this chapter we provide a detailed guide to the standard methods used throughout the world to measure and track the level of economic activity. While slight differences in terminology and conventions exist between the methods used in some countries, all have the same underlying principles and general construction for arriving at estimates of economic activity at the national or aggregate level. The procedures involved are commonly known as *national income accounting*.

In the sections below we discuss a number of important aspects concerning the measurement of economic activity, namely:

- national income accounting methods;
- adjustments to national income statistics;
- problems in measuring economic activity;
- uses of national income statistics;
- factors influencing the size of national income;
- real versus nominal values;
- other indicators of economic activity.

At the outset, it is important to appreciate the key relationships between the *flow* of *national income* within an economy, a nation's *stock of wealth* and a nation's *capital stock*. National wealth is a stock concept which represents all of the physical assets or things that have value and are owned by the citizens of a country. The capital stock of a nation is the part of national wealth that can be used to generate more wealth. This will include all the capital goods and raw materials within the country – as well as *social capital* representing the general physical infrastructure such as roads, schools, hospitals, etc. which are usually mainly owned by the state. Note that capital does *not* include consumer goods which are a subset of national wealth but not of the capital stock.

In contrast national income is a *flow* concept. It measures statistically the financial value of the flow of new wealth resulting from the productive use of the nation's capital stock, i.e. the output of goods and services produced. As a continuous flow, national income is measured per time period.

Learning outcomes

After studying this material, you will be able to:

- Understand how economic activity is measured, based on *national income accounting* methods.
- Appreciate the importance of the various sectors of the economy and their contribution to economic activity.
- Identify the uses of national income statistics.
- Recognise the problems associated with the measurement of economic activity and the limitations of national income accounts.
- Distinguish between *real* and *nominal* values in the context of economic measurement.
- Discuss what other indicators of economic activity should be monitored in addition to the standard ones included in the national income accounting procedures.

National income accounting methods

By economic activity, we mean the level of production of goods and services over a particular time period, usually measured quarterly and annually. Changes in the level of economic activity from one time period to another thus provide estimates of the growth of the economy.

Figure 2.1 highlights a number of key questions which surround the measurement and interpretation of information on economic activity. The answer to these questions will have different implications for different sectors within the economy. For example, a sustained rise in economic activity will lead to an increase in household incomes and a resultant rise in consumer spending. This will directly impact on corporate sales, production and profitability as well as future capital investment expenditure. At the same time, government tax revenues can be expected to rise because of higher household incomes and spending as well as larger corporate profits. Decisions by the government about how and where this tax revenue should be spent will have important implications for future growth of the economy. In addition, changes in economic activity can be expected to influence as well as be affected by 'official' policy measures taken by the government (and the central bank). Measurement of economic activity is also important in order to determine the trend rate of growth over a long time period which can be used as a benchmark against which to assess any short-run volatility – giving rise to 'booms' and 'recessions'. Finally, international comparisons will have particular significance, for example for international investment decisions by corporates as well as for foreign aid contributions.

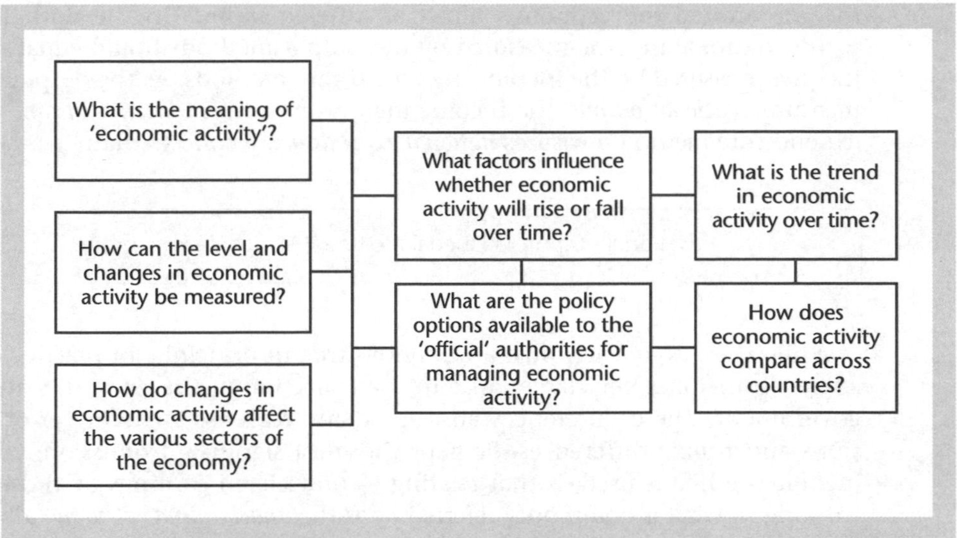

Figure 2.1 Interpreting economic activity information – key questions

> *National income* is a statistical measure of the total money value of the output of goods and services produced by an economy over a specified period of time.

Calculation of the size of the national income provides the basis for comparing changes in economic activity although, of course, we need to adjust *nominal* money values to allow for inflation if we are to arrive at what has happened to *real* national income between different years. This distinction between nominal and real values will be dealt with later in this chapter.

Since the total value of goods and service produced is ultimately translated into incomes for the factors of production that produced the output, and since total income ultimately is either spent or saved we can measure the flow of national income around the economy in any one of three ways. Collectively, these methods of measuring the flow of economic activity are referred to as *national income accounting*.

National income accounting

- output (or production) method;
- income method;
- expenditure method.

In theory, each method of measurement should provide the same money value for the size of economic activity because they each measure the same flow of income around the economy, albeit at different points in the flow. In other words, national income measured by the output method should equal national income measured by the income or expenditure methods. As the output method measures *national output*, the income method measures *national income* and the expenditure method measures *national expenditure*, it follows that:

National output = National income = National expenditure

While these equalities must always hold true in principle, in practice discrepancies (sometimes very large) arise in the collection of the relevant statistics by government. These differences arise for many reasons, including errors, omissions and timing differences. Perhaps the most significant omission, when the income method is used, is that relating to undeclared earnings by those people working in what is commonly referred to as the *underground economy* (alternative terms used include the *hidden*, *shadow*, *informal*, *parallel* or *black economy*). Consequently, statistical discrepancies or *residual errors* feature in countries' national income accounts to make the three totals balance. These residual errors would not exist in a world of perfect statistics. For practical purposes, given that errors will inevitably exist in all three methods of measurement, an *average* of all three totals is sometimes used as the appropriate indicator of economic activity. The importance of residual errors is diminished if it can be assumed that they are relatively stable over time as a proportion of the total and if we are mainly concerned with changes in, rather than levels of, economic activity. A fuller discussion of the problems associated with measuring economic activity is covered later in this chapter.

Before describing each of the three methods of measuring national income, we identify the sectors of the economy in which economic agents are responsible for generating economic activity, in terms of output, income and expenditure. There are five such sectors.

Sectors of the economy

- the household sector;
- the firm sector;
- the government sector;
- the financial sector;
- the foreign sector.

In the next chapter we shall describe in detail, using the so-called *circular flow of income* model, how these five sectors of the economy are interrelated and how they jointly contribute to the determination of economic activity.

We now return to the three methods of measuring the national income –the so-called *national income accounting methods* – noted above. The key details are highlighted in Box 2.1.

Box 2.1

National income accounting

The output method

The output method calculates the total value of the final output of goods and services produced in the economy over a specified period of time, giving rise to the *gross domestic product* (*GDP*). It is important to note that all final goods and services must be included regardless of whether they are sold to consumers, government, foreigners or to other firms in the form of capital equipment. To avoid the problem of *double-counting*, and hence overestimation of the country's total output, intermediate production of goods and services (e.g. components and materials) must not be included in the final total. Alternatively, the problem of double-counting can be avoided by summing only the *value added* by each firm at the different stages of production, rather than the final outputs (see Box 2.2).

The income method

Since national income arises from the production of goods and services by the factors of production, another way of calculating the value of total output is to sum all of the incomes that these factors receive for their services – wages and salaries, rent, interest, profits and dividends. This method is referred to as the *income method* of measuring the level of economic activity in any time period. It is important to note that only incomes that have been received in return for productive services should be included. Transfer payments, therefore, must be excluded because they merely represent a redistribution of income, for instance from taxpayers to pensioners. Including these payments would lead to double counting and therefore overestimation of national income. In other words, if transfer payments were not excluded, raising pensions, unemployment benefits or similar welfare payments would lead to a statistical increase in national income when the actual (real) output of the economy had not changed.

The expenditure method

By adding up all the money values of expenditures on final goods and services produced in an economy, we arrive at the measurement of *national expenditure*. It should be noted that this will only be equal to national output if we allow for net changes in the value of the physical increase in stocks (inventories) and work in progress. Therefore, national expenditure is the sum of the consumption of domestically produced goods, investment expenditure (including an allowance for changes in stocks and work in progress), expenditure by government and net receipts from foreign trade. As before, to avoid double-counting, only expenditure on *final* goods and services (i.e. sold to final consumers or as investment goods to firms) should be included.

It is important to appreciate fully the danger of double-counting when using the output method for calculating economic activity. An example will readily illustrate this danger (see Box 2.2).

Box 2.2

Danger of double-counting

Consider a situation in which Firm A supplies components valued at \$10m to Firm B, which in turn sells its output valued at \$14m to Firm C, that then sells its output valued at \$17m to the final consumer. Schematically:

Firm A $\rightarrow$ *Firm B* $\rightarrow$ *Firm C* = *Total output*

Output \$10m $\rightarrow$ \$14m $\rightarrow$ \$17m = \$41m.

Double-counting gives a total output for the economy (i.e. GDP) of \$41m.

However, using the value added *or* final output method produces a very different total:

Value added method:

\$10m + \$4m + \$3m = \$17m

Final output method:

– – \$17m = \$17m

In other words, the accurate figure for total output is \$17m by either the value added or final output methods – and not \$41m.

Adjustments to national income statistics

A number of adjustments are required when calculating the economy's total flow of national income using the above three methods: These involve:

- the inclusion of net income from abroad;
- allowance for capital depreciation and stock appreciation;
- valuation of output at market prices or factor (i.e. production) costs.

Net income from abroad

Part of an economy's measured output may have been produced by foreign-owned firms. Likewise, some domestically-owned firms may be contributing to the production of output in other countries. How much of the income resulting from these activities should be included when measuring output depends upon the purpose for which we are calculating national income. Do we wish to measure only *domestic* output (literally produced within the country), or do we wish to measure the output of the economy's factors of production wherever they are located? In the former case we arrive at measurements of gross *domestic* output, gross *domestic* income and gross *domestic* expenditure. In the latter case, we can allow for *net income from abroad*. This represents the difference between the income (i.e. earnings) received by the domestic economy from the production of its firms located overseas minus that income paid to overseas residents from their production in the domestic economy. For instance, profits earned by IBM outside the USA and remitted back to the USA would be included to arrive at the US gross *national* product and gross *national* income. Similarly, profits earned by Nissan from producing cars in the USA and remitted to Japan would be excluded from US national income. Therefore we can write:

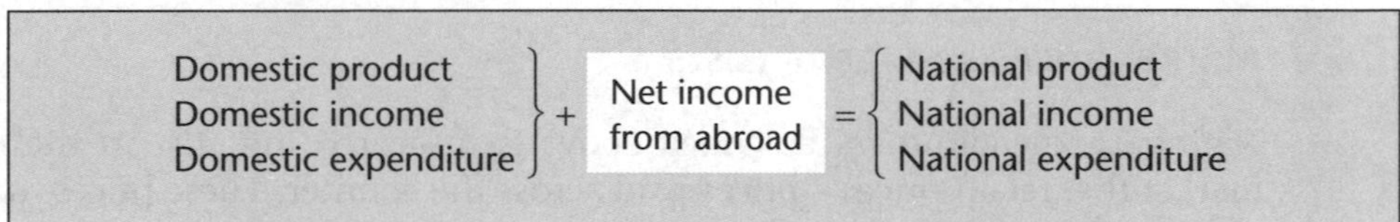

Capital depreciation and stock appreciation

During any given period some investment expenditure will merely be replacing capital, both equipment and buildings, that has worn out during the production of income and output in that period. Therefore, some allowance should be made for depreciation or capital consumption when calculating national income since this investment expenditure does not represent an increase in the economy's productive capacity or wealth. Only *net* investment (i.e. investment expenditure after depreciation) represents the true increase in the country's capital stock during the period. Where no allowance is made for depreciation the resulting totals are referred to as *gross* output, income or expenditure; when depreciation is deducted from the gross sum we arrive at the corresponding *net* figures. We can therefore define the following terms:

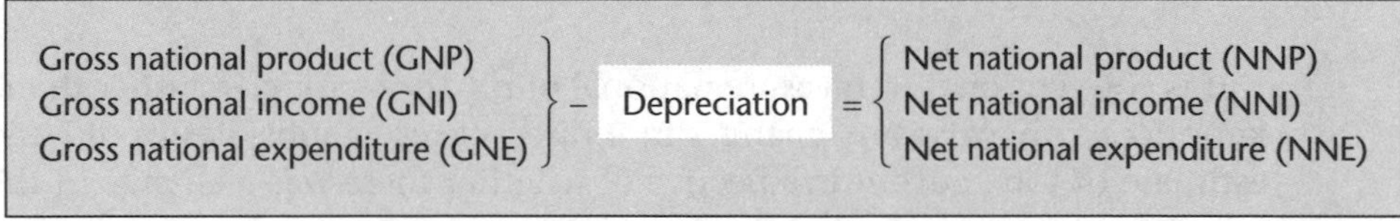

Official estimates of depreciation in the economy are made when adjusting national income figures from gross to net. Nevertheless, when discussing national income it is common to use the gross rather than the net amounts even though the latter provide a more accurate reflection of the growth in national well-being. This is done for two reasons: first, because depreciation tends to change relatively slowly over time and hence gross and net figures move closely together and, second, because it is difficult to make an accurate estimate of depreciation at the national level. In other words, the gross figures are usually more accurate than the net figures.

Just as the government statisticians take account of depreciation or capital consumption when calculating national income figures, so they also adjust their estimates to take account of stock appreciation. It is conventional to subtract from national income totals any increase in the value of the net change in stocks of unsold goods arising from a general increase in prices. The reasoning is similar to that which lies behind adjusting for depreciation. Stock appreciation does not represent a *real* increase in a nation's output. When stock appreciation occurs it is not physical (i.e. real) output that grows, as reflected in higher stocks in the economy – it is merely that the stocks have a higher monetary (i.e. nominal) value reflecting a general rise in prices, or inflation.

Market prices and factor costs

National expenditure as described above is measured initially on the basis of market (i.e. retail) prices – prices paid across the counter. These prices, however, may be distorted by the inclusion of indirect taxes and subsidies. Indirect taxes, such as sales tax and excise duties, increase the prices of goods and services, while subsidies have the opposite effect. At the same time, national income and national product are both measured at factor costs, that is, with respect to the amounts paid to factors of production for their services excluding indirect taxes and subsidies. In order to ensure equivalence across the three methods of measuring economic activity, market prices must be converted to factor costs by subtracting indirect taxes and adding subsidies. Therefore we can write:

Gross national expenditure at factor cost =		Gross national expenditure at market prices
	–	Indirect taxes
	+	Subsidies

It is conventional to measure national output at factor cost rather than at market prices, otherwise any changes in indirect taxes or subsidies would distort the estimate of total output irrespective of whether there was a change in the actual quantity of goods and services produced.

Problems in measuring economic activity

We have already noted the main problems associated with the estimation of economic activity based on national income accounting as we have discussed each measurement method in turn. We bring these and other difficulties together in this section for completeness. The calculation of economic activity is a complicated statistical process and general difficulties arise for a number of reasons:

- *Arbitrary definitions* must be made involving a number of activities. For example:
  - output estimates include goods and services sold and paid for but exclude work done by a person for him or herself (such as personal home maintenance and home-grown produce);
  - goods which have a serviceable life of several years are included in national income at their full value in the year they are bought (with the exception of owner-occupied houses, where an annualised value is estimated).
- Data from which the national income figure is estimated (e.g. income tax returns) are likely to be full of errors and are often incomplete.
- Official statistics do not take account of the value of the unmeasured *underground economy* which is kept hidden from officialdom and which might be very high in value (see Application 2.1).
- As noted earlier, there is a danger of *double-counting*. If a firm buys vegetables from a farmer in order to produce soup, the output of the farmer (vegetables) will be included in the output of the firm (soup) although the vegetables, of course, are produced only once. A firm's output should be valued after excluding the value of bought-in materials, otherwise double-counting results.
- *Transfer payments*, that is the transfer of income from one person to another (e.g. pensions and social security payments), do not affect national income and must not be included.
- Services provided 'free' to the public by the government, such as policing, health services and much education are valued at factor cost, whereas the output of private firms includes profit in its valuation. A country with a strong government-services sector might therefore arguably be undervaluing the level of national output and income because so much activity would be valued at cost.

For all of the reasons above associated with the problems of accurately measuring economic activity, it is important that caution is exercised with respect to the use and interpretation of the derived estimates.

Application 2.1

Economic activity and the underground economy

The importance of the underground economy

The existence of a so-called *underground economy* is of great concern to many governments. It represents undeclared incomes and hence a loss of tax revenue. It also creates a distortion to the official statistics relating to economic activity, which may make it more difficult to identify current and future trends upon which to base policy decisions. A precise definition of the underground economy, however, is quite difficult. The underground economy develops all the time adjusting to changes in taxation and regulations. The following table highlights the main types of activities which comprise the underground economy:

Application 2.1 continued

Types of underground economic activities

Type of activity	*Monetary transactions*		*Non-monetary transactions*	
Illegal activities	Trade in stolen goods; drug dealing and manufacturing; prostitution; gambling; smuggling; fraud		Barter of drugs, stolen, or smuggled goods. Producing or growing drugs for own use. Theft for own use	
	Tax evasion	*Tax avoidance*	*Tax evasion*	*Tax avoidance*
Legal activities	Unreported income from self-employment. Wages, salaries, and assets from unreported work related to legal services and goods.	Employee discounts, fringe benefits.	Barter of legal services and goods.	All do-it-yourself work and neighbour help.

Structure of table from Lippert and Walker, *The Underground Economy: Global Evidence of its Size and Impact*. Vancouver, B.C., The Frazer Institute, 1997.

Some economists argue that the relative size of the underground economy grows when the tax burden becomes heavier, all things being equal.

Estimating the size of the underground economy

In some countries the size of the underground economy is enormous. For example, in the USA it is estimated to be larger than the economies of many countries – somewhere within the range of 5 per cent to 12 per cent of America's GNP. If we take an average figure of 9 per cent as a reasonable estimate, then this amounts to well over $800bn in 2003. This is larger than the GNP of Belgium, Denmark, Greece, Ireland, Luxembourg, Portugal, Spain, Austria, Finland, Norway, Sweden, Switzerland, Australia, New Zealand and many more countries! Estimates of the underground economy vary greatly from country to country and there is no consistent approach to measurement. Some estimates are based on the assumption that there is a strong correlation between the amount of cash individuals use in making payments (relative to other forms of payment such as cheques) and the scale of the underground economic activity. This would seem to be quite a natural approach to measurement since underground economic activity is generally conducted on a cash basis, leading some economists to argue that the more cash that is demanded relative to other forms of monetary payment, the larger the size of undeclared economic activity and income.

There is no 'best' method for estimating the size of the underground economy; each approach has strengths and weaknesses, and yields its own insights and results. The following table describes common methods. The *currency demand* and the *latent variable* approach are the most widely used.

Application 2.1 continued

Ways of measuring the underground economy: different methods*

Method	*Main features*
DIRECT APPROACHES	
Sample survey	Estimates size of shadow economy from survey data
Tax audit	Estimates size of shadow economy from audit measurements of undeclared taxable income
INDIRECT APPROACHES	
National accounting statistics	Estimates size of shadow economy on basis of the discrepancy between income and expenditure statistics in national accounting or in individual data
Labour force statistics	Estimates growth in shadow economy on basis of decline in labour participation in the official economy, assuming the labour force has a constant participation rate overall
Transactions	Uses data on the overall volume of monetary transactions in the economy to calculate total nominal (unofficial plus official) GDP, then estimates size of shadow economy by subtracting official GDP from total nominal GDP
Currency demand	Estimates size of shadow economy from the demand for cash, assuming shadow transactions are undertaken in cash and that an increase in the shadow economy will raise demand for cash
Physical inputs (electricity consumption)	Estimates growth of shadow economy from electricity consumption, assuming that electricity consumption is the single best physical indicator of overall economic activity. Subtracts the growth rate of official GDP from the growth rate of total electricity consumption and attributes the difference to the growth of the shadow economy
MODELS	
Latent variable approach	Estimates the size of the shadow economy as a function of observed variables that are assumed to influence the shadow economy, for example the burden of taxation, the burden of government regulation, for and of variables where shadow economic activities leave traces, like cash, official working time, unemployment, etc. Advantageous method because it considers multiple causes and effects simultaneously.

*For a detailed description of the different methods, see Friedrich Schneider and Dominik Enste, 'Shadow Economies: Size, Causes and Consequences, *The Journal of Economic Literature*, 2000, 38/1, pp.77–114.

Activity

Consider the importance of the underground economy when computing national income figures. Why do changes in the economic composition of an economy have a bearing on the size of the underground economy?

Uses of national income statistics

National income statistics are calculated for many purposes, the most important ones being:

- to measure the total income (standard of living) of a country – for this purpose national income is commonly measured in terms of national income per head (per capita) of population;
- to measure the improvement (deterioration) in national wealth and the standard of living over time;
- to compare the economic activity of different countries;
- to identify trends in consumer expenditure;
- to identify trends in industrial production;
- to assist central government in its economic planning.

While national income is commonly used in discussions and analyses of the standard of living within a country, the question arises as to whether or not it is *a reliable* measure of economic well-being. A few cautionary notes must be made in this context.

National income as a measure of economic well-being

A high standard of living means that individuals enjoy a large amount of economic wealth, and also economic welfare. However, although popular usage tends to associate standard of living with material wealth, it properly refers to both wealth and well-being.

National income may be high even when a government spends much of its own income on defence and other items of expenditure which do not have any immediate relevance to the economic wealth of individuals in the society. In other words, if a government spends, say, two thirds of its income on armed forces, national income might be high but the general standard of living low.

National income is a monetary measure, and in a country where much trade is done by barter, or leisure activities not related to payments are pursued, figures for national income would not reflect the contribution of the barter economy or leisure activities to the standard of living.

A country might have a considerable stock of existing wealth, but a low national income. Wealth earned in the past is not apparent from current figures for national income. Similarly, national income figures do not indicate whether a country has potential wealth-earning resources for the future. For example, a country with large amounts of unexploited natural resources would have a potentially strong economy, but current national income figures may not show this.

The 'standard of living' might be considered from a purely 'material' point of view. It is more appropriate, however, to measure what a country has in terms of its more general welfare.

There is a difference between economic wealth and economic welfare. Economic welfare is a measure of the well-being or quality of life of society's members, and takes account of matters such as the amount of leisure time for individuals, pollution levels and the quality of the environment, what items people purchase as well as income and wealth. If the state of the economy is taken to include the quality of life, national income would be an inadequate economic indicator.

Comparisons between different countries

We have to be careful when comparing the national incomes of countries like the USA with a small Middle Eastern oil producer which may have a very high per capita income. We cannot conclude that, on average, people in the USA have a lower standard of living. The income in the Middle Eastern state may not filter through to the majority of the population, i.e. it may not be equally or fairly distributed.

When comparing countries there is also the problem of converting national income calculated in one currency to that of another. This is not necessarily as straightforward as it sounds and may make conclusions about such comparisons difficult to reach. For example if Country X has a national income valued at US$200bn and Country Y has a national income valued at US$100bn, it might seem that Country X is twice as rich as Country Y and so the standard of living in X is twice as high as in Y. However, if the population of X is 40 million people and the population of Y is 8 million, the national income per head of the population would be:

Country X: US$5,000 per capita
Country Y: US$12,500 per capita

Income per capita is two and a half times higher in Y than in X.

The relative standard of living of different countries is therefore better compared by means of national income per capita than by means of total national income. Other difficulties in making comparisons between countries relate to the size of the underground economy as well as to people's needs and defence spending. For example:

- A country with a strong underground economy will be much wealthier than its official income per head of population might suggest. Given differences in the scale of the underground economy from country to country, figures for national income will not be readily comparable.
- The needs of people in one country may differ widely from the needs of people in another country. This may be due to differences in social attitudes, customs and habits, religious beliefs, climate, density of population or other factors. One country might have thriving industries for tobacco and alcoholic goods, for example, whereas another country might ban these entirely. A country with a hot climate might spend large sums on air conditioning and other similar products, whereas a country with a cold climate will want central heating and insulation products instead. When people in different countries want entirely different things, it is not really possible to presume that their comparative standards of living can be measured on a single monetary scale.

- Countries may produce items that are of little or no relevance to their immediate standards of living: defence is the obvious example. The figures of income per capita of a country with high defence spending and one with little such spending are therefore not directly comparable.

These drawbacks to using income per head of population for international comparisons mean that simpler and more direct comparisons may have to be used instead. One way of doing this is to select a number of products which are universally in demand in every country (or at least most countries). Examples might be television sets and motor cars. Measurements can then be obtained of:

- the average number of cars or televisions per household or per head of the population;
- how long it takes an 'average' worker to earn enough in wages to buy a car or a television.

Factors influencing the size of national income

The overall size and rate of growth of national income and output – and thus economic activity – depend on several factors which include:

- the natural resources of the country (mineral deposits, fertility of the soil, etc.);
- the nature of the labour force (its size in relation to the total population, its energy, skill, ability and mobility, etc.);
- the amount of capital investment (which may depend on the sophistication of a country's banking system, and money and capital markets);
- whether resources, i.e. the factors of land, labour and capital, are combined and utilised in an efficient way;
- the ability of the country to produce innovative ideas (e.g. new technologies);
- political stability;
- the availability of foreign direct investment flows.

These will all affect the potential size of national income. We comment on each of these points below.

Availability of natural resources

A country with more natural resources has more potential wealth to exploit, whereas a country with few natural resources (e.g. a desert country with no oil) may be very poor. Natural resources might be only partly exploited, but in some countries environmental considerations might result in conscious decisions by the government not to exploit certain resources.

Nature of the labour force

The size, energy and skills of the workforce affect potential national income, because a more productive workforce will be capable of producing a greater gross domestic product. Technical training and education are important ingredients contributing towards labour skills.

Amount of capital investment

Greater amounts of expenditure on investment will contribute immediately to gross domestic product but the investment capital will then be used to produce more output for consumption in future years. Some countries attract capital investment more easily than others and an efficient financial services sector will ensure that funds supplied by savers are channeled into worthwhile investments.

Efficient utilisation of resources

The efficient combination of land, labour and capital contributes towards greater productivity and thus higher gross domestic product. Poor countries of the world are unable to achieve such an efficient combination, most noticeably because of inadequate capital investment and lack of entrepreneurial skills.

Innovation

Innovation is a key to growth of output and expansion of industry. Successful innovation usually occurs in countries with a good educational system as well as significant investment in research and development.

Political stability

Countries which are politically unstable will probably have difficulty in attracting new investment, domestically or from overseas. Social unrest, perhaps manifesting itself in widespread strike action, might also directly affect the workforce and the day-to-day operations of corporates.

Foreign direct investment

Investment from aboard will help to boost gross domestic product and national income, even though the foreign investors will want to receive financial returns on their investment.

It should now be clear that national income includes many items that are of central concern to governments. The output of the economy as a whole or by sector, the growth in personal and corporate incomes and expenditure within the economy both on domestic output and on imports are all matters in which governments take a keen interest. The overall level of activity in an economy, as indicated by the statistics, must imply a certain level of employment or unemployment.

In conclusion then, although the calculation of national income is not easy or perfect, it is essential that governments gather this type of information if they

Application 2.2

Economic activity and the 'genuine progress indicator'

The following edited extract from *The Dallas Morning News* by Scott Burns questions the validity of official estimates of economic activity and suggests the need to adjust national product statistics to include a wide range of factors which impact on an economy's general well-being and progress.

> We measure the wrong stuff. We add things that should be subtracted. We forget to add (or subtract) other things because they don't go through a cash register . . . That's the nutshell message from Michel Gelobter, the new executive director of Redefining Progress, a non-profit think-tank [concerning the accuracy and relevance of accounting for the US economy].
>
> When I first visited the organisation seven years ago, I learned that real economic progress had stopped in 1973. We were in a broad economic decline.
>
> A measure that Redefining Progress had created, the 'genuine progress indicator' (GPI) gave a very different message from our conventional measures such as gross domestic product. Today things haven't changed very much, but the GPI has turned upward.
>
> 'This is all about the three E's – environment, economy and equity. I would add a fourth E – engagement,' Mr Gelobter said.
>
> I asked him to give me a synopsis of the genuine progress indicator. 'It's a great encapsulation of the three E's. It's the GNP (gross national product) – but with prison time, heart attacks and clear-cut forests taken out.
>
> 'We also put back in volunteerism and time spent with families. It's our attempt to measure real progress. If we don't make those changes, we get errors.' I asked for an example. 'Like the error in the '90s when prison building was one of our fastest-growing sectors . . . The trouble with conventional economic accounting is that it doesn't account for the foundations we're laying for the future. Indiscriminately adding up our economic activity is a way to send the wrong signals. We have to measure what we want.'
>
> That's how the genuine progress indicator came about. Starting with a broad measure of the general good – personal consumption – statisticians at Redefining Progress subtract net foreign lending or borrowing. Then they subtract an amount if the distribution of income has become more unequal. They add it if the distribution of income has become more equal. After that they subtract social costs such as the cost of crime, automobile accidents, commuting, family breakdown, lost leisure time and underemployment. For the year 2000 these losses would have taken 18.5 per cent off the general good of personal consumption.
>
> The biggest losses, however, aren't social costs. They are environmental costs. Here, they estimate items such as the depletion of non-renewable

Application 2.2 continued

resources, the cost of long-term environmental damage, and the cost of ozone depletion, lost farmlands and lost wetlands.

Fortunately, conventional economic accounting also ignores a lot of really good things. Among the positives not counted is value of housework and parenting. Not to mention the value of volunteer work.

Using the same methodology, Redefining Progress found the 1950s and 1960s were good periods for genuine progress. In the 1970s, however, a major gap developed. Genuine progress slowed dramatically. Progress turned negative in the 1980s. In the 1990s the trend reversed again – but our real progress is only a fraction of what conventional indicators tell us.

Needless to say, this is not a perfect science. But when it comes to measuring broad national welfare, Redefining Progress is on the right track.

Activity

China's economy is growing rapidly and is expected to overtake Japan's sometime in the next 20 years. In the context of the 'genuine progress indicator' does this imply that people in China will be more affluent than the Japanese?

want to understand what is going on in the economy – and whether or not policy actions are required.

Real versus nominal values

To identify changes in the scale (i.e. volume) of economic activity it is necessary to remove the effects of inflation. Activity indicators are therefore expressed in *real* – or volume – terms. Thus, real gross domestic product (GDP) statistics are expressed at *constant prices* (i.e. with respect to prices in some base period). Failure to remove the effects of inflation would lead to gross exaggeration in estimates of economic activity in times of rapidly rising prices – such *nominal* values, therefore, would be inappropriate as indicators of growth in the volume of output.

Figure 2.2 below highlights the importance of the effects of inflation. In order to deflate nominal GDP (measured at current prices), we need to use an appropriate estimate for inflation. The most comprehensive measure is the *GDP deflator* – an economy wide estimate of price changes, defined as follows.

The *GDP deflator* is the weighted average of prices of all goods and services produced in an economy and purchased by households, firms, government and foreigners.

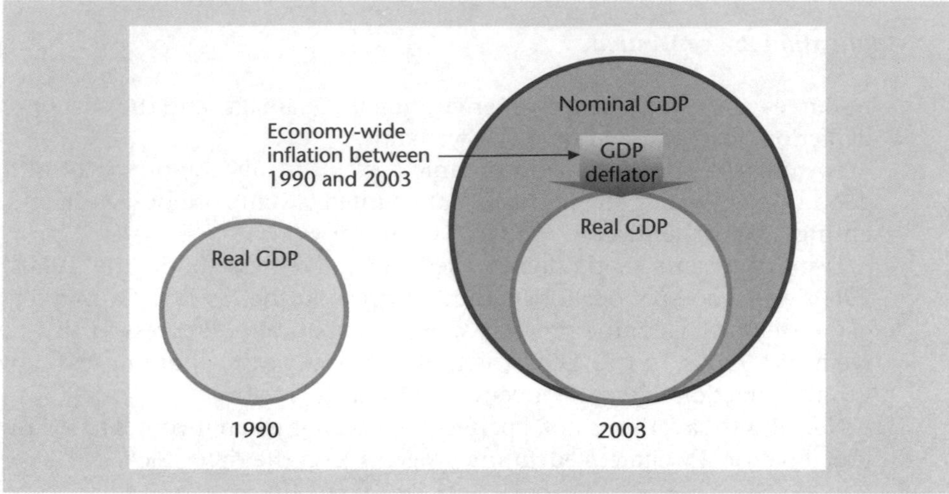

Figure 2.2 Real versus nominal GDP

For example, if *nominal* GDP in a particular year (say, 2003) is $4bn, and the GDP deflator for that year is 115 (i.e. 15 per cent above the general price level of the base year, say 1990, set at 100), then *real* GDP in 2003 is $3.478bn, expressed in base year (1990 prices). Hence:

$$\text{Real GDP}_{2003} = \frac{\text{Nominal GDP}_{2003}}{\text{GDP deflator}} \times \text{Base year price level}$$

$$= \frac{\$4\text{bn}}{115} \times 100$$

$$= \$3.478\text{bn}$$

Other indicators of economic activity

Indicators of economic activity are not confined to the direct components of output and income discussed above. They can take almost any form if they throw some light on the state of demand and the general level of economic activity. Even the rate of price inflation may provide some useful information – rising inflationary pressures may given an early warning that demand is growing faster than the economy's ability to produce extra output.

We briefly discuss the following additional indicators in turn:

- monetary aggregates;
- business survey data;
- labour market statistics;
- cyclical indicators.

Monetary aggregates

One important group of indicators relates to *monetary aggregates*. With the help of economic theory we can extract messages from the growth of the money supply about the pressure of demand and thereby infer the level of economic activity in the economy. It is important, of course, to remember that movements in the monetary aggregates reflect both movements in the rate of inflation as well as in the level of economic activity, i.e. both price and volume fluctuations.

The role of monetary aggregates as an economic indicator – and particularly their relationship with the level of prices – has long been the subject of debate. The 'velocity of circulation' of money, measuring the relationship between the stock of money in an economy and the level of economic activity, may change over time, thus making movements in the monetary aggregates difficult to interpret over the longer term. We discuss this subject in detail in Chapter 8.

In most countries monetary figures are timely and regular, normally published on a monthly basis. There are usually also monthly figures on the amount of credit taken out by consumers, which can be taken as an indirect indicator of consumer spending.

Business survey data

In many countries the traditional type of economic statistics referred to above are complemented by surveys of business opinion. Such surveys are generally frequent and may, therefore, provide a more up-to-date picture of activity than the official economic statistics relating to national output which are reported after inevitable time-lags. These surveys take a qualitative approach, asking respondents to compare the state of business from one period to the next. The focus may be in terms of general confidence about the economic outlook or on items specifically related to activity such as expectations about the levels of output and stocks (planned or unplanned) or order books. In essence, such information provides predictions as to whether activity will increase or decrease relative to an earlier period. There are also surveys of consumers' confidence which can act as useful indicators of the future spending patterns by individuals and households.

Labour market statistics

Generally, labour market statistics represent another pointer to the state of the economy. The information includes figures for unemployment and job vacancies each month, as well as estimates of the number of people employed in the whole economy. The release of such information is especially important in times of economic recovery, signalling perhaps a potential shortage of labour and the threat of inflationary pressures arising from higher wage demands. Such information can often lead to quite volatile movements in stock market prices.

The significance of labour market statistics as an indicator of economic activity is diminished, however, by the fact that they tend to react some months later than changes in output. This is because companies tend to wait for changes in output to become more firmly established before acting to take on more workers or to make existing workers redundant. Consequently, employment (and unemployment) statistics are often described as *lagging indicators* of economic activity.

Cyclical indicators

It should be clear to the reader that there is really no end to the range of information that may tell us something about the current and future states of the economy. Apart from those discussed already, there is a myriad of indicators for individual sectors of the economy – ranging from new construction orders and housing starts, to the weekly sales figures of a single department store chain. In addition, there is always our own 'gut instinct'.

Typically, there will be no consistent picture emerging from these various sources, especially at turning points, such as the peak or trough of the *business cycle*. The chances are that some series will be pointing upwards and others downwards. It requires a considerable amount of judgement to interpret and explain such diverse indicators.

Generally, governments' statistical departments consolidate the information from a number of data series into several distinct composite indicators of the state of the economic cycle, giving rise to the following indexes:

- longer leading index;
- shorter leading index;
- coincident index;
- lagging indexes.

The methodology behind such indexes is often quite complex – the components are smoothed, and de-trended, and then amalgamated, using sophisticated techniques of time-series analysis. While such indexes do not give any new information on the economy, they are a useful means of combining the information from a number of individual series. Details concerning these indexes are given later in Chapter 17 which deals with business cycles.

Application 2.3

When is a recession not a recession?

The most conventional rule of thumb for defining a national recession is at least two consecutive quarters of negative GDP growth. Unfortunately, this simple rule does not translate well to the global context. First, quarterly real GDP data are not always available – for a number of major emerging market countries, quarterly output data do not exist before the mid-1990s, and there are still many countries that only report GDP annually rather than on a quarterly basis. Even among those that do report quarterly, national methods for seasonally adjusting output data differ to such an extent that meaningful aggregation is difficult. Second, while we cannot measure it exactly, it is likely that quarterly global growth does not turn negative nearly as often as does GDP within the typical country. Indeed, annual global growth has never been negative for any year in recent history – but this should not be interpreted as evidence that the world has not experienced a recession.

The principal reason that global growth is rarely negative is that world output is more diversified than national output. For example, the USA, Europe, and Japan do not always experience downturns at the same time. Data on annual real GDP indicate that the current slowdown has a similar level of synchronisation as earlier episodes in the mid-1970s and early 1980s, even though growth in China (in particular) has remained relatively robust during this slowdown. The lower level of synchronisation in the early 1990s was an exception – largely reflecting specific regional events, including the asset price bubble in Japan and the consequences of German unification activity in continental Europe. It is also the case that trend growth for the world is higher than for most advanced economies because developing countries grow faster on average, so it takes a steeper dip to hit negative territory.

While global output may rarely decline, it is useful to have a simple benchmark for identifying slowdowns that could be labelled as global recessions. One reasonable solution to this conundrum is to adjust world output growth for growth in world population, and declare that a sufficient (although not necessary) condition for a global recession is any year in which world per capita growth (measured on a comparable basis) is negative. In the figure overleaf, the first bars show unadjusted world GDP growth during the major recent slowdowns, 1975, 1982, 1991 and 2001. In no case did world growth dip below 1 per cent, much less turn negative.

In 1975, GDP growth of 1.9 per cent was almost exactly offset by world population growth, so that per capita GDP growth was about zero. However, per capita GDP growth actually turned negative in 1982 and, to a lesser extent, in 1991. By contrast, per capita GDP growth in 2001 was over 1 per cent, well ▶

Application 2.3 continued

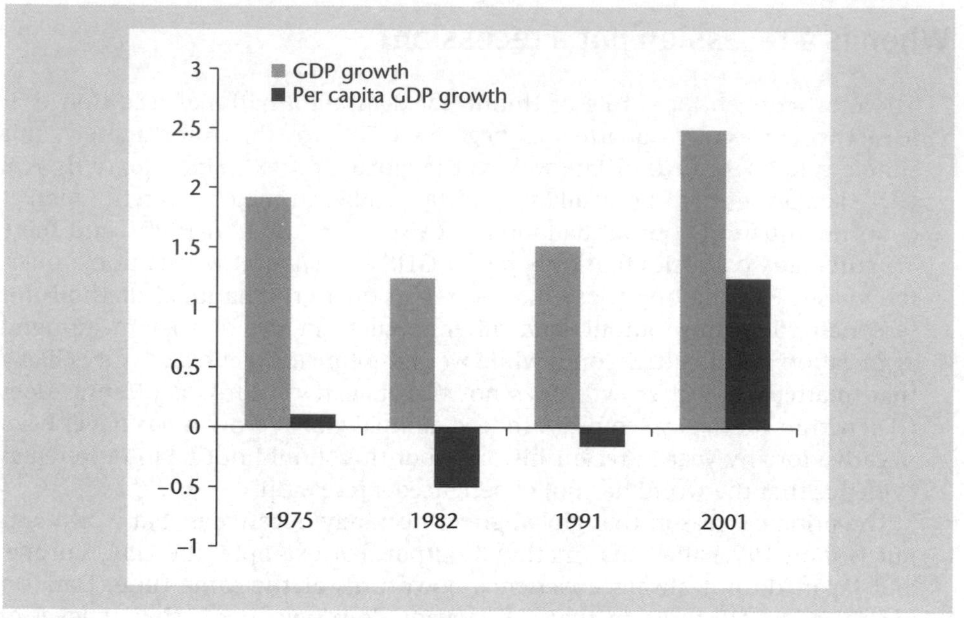

Comparison of global slowdowns

above zero. Compared with the earlier episodes, unadjusted growth was stronger at 2.5 per cent, instead of dipping below 2 per cent as in the previous episodes. Also, world population growth is lower today (1.3 per cent) than it was a decade earlier. Thus, the current slowdown has not come close to meeting the hurdle of negative per capita annual GDP growth, which would automatically qualify it as a recession. This partly reflects the relatively high weight of China, which has continued to grow strongly.

Can we declare that the world is not in recession simply because annual global per capita growth is positive? No, not necessarily. Whilst negative per capita GDP growth is a sufficient condition to identify a global recession, by itself it would probably be unduly conservative. As in the case of individual recessions, one cannot rely absolutely on any mechanical rule, but instead some element of judgement is required. That is how recessions are identified in the USA by the National Bureau of Economic Research (NBER), for example. The NBER defines a recession as a significant decline in activity spread across the economy and lasting more than a few months, and focuses on economy-wide monthly series (especially non-farm employment and real personal income less transfers). It also looks at data from manufacturing (real manufacturing and trade sales and industrial production), although – as the NBER notes – this is a relatively small part of the US economy whose movements

Application 2.3 continued

often differ from those of other sectors. The rule of thumb of at least two quarters of negative growth often referred to by commentators is simply a useful way of approximating this system. Indeed, in a downturn, the NBER committee chose to identify the US slowdown as a recession even though, based on current information, GDP growth was only negative in the third quarter.

Source: Edited extract from *World Economic Outlook*, April 2002, International Monetary Fund: Washington, DC.

Activity

What other approaches could be considered with respect to identifying whether or not an economy is in recession?

Concluding remarks

This chapter has been concerned with the measurement of economic activity based on national income accounting methods. As we have discussed, the output, income and expenditure methods should, in theory, provide the same estimates of economic activity – but, in practice, a number of measurement problems are inevitable. It is important, therefore, to be cautious in comparing and interpreting national income statistics and to be aware of the inherent shortcomings and pitfalls. However, such statistics are nevertheless of considerable value to all of us – individuals, firms and governments – since they impact directly on decisions concerning corporate investment, government expenditure and taxation, interest rates, household savings etc.

At the same time, the information from national income accounts should be used alongside other indicators of economic performance and standards of living to provide a more comprehensive picture of an economy's well-being. These additional indicators include monetary aggregates, business survey data, labour market statistics and cyclical indicators. We shall be dealing with all of these in various chapters throughout this book.

In the next chapter, we show how the five sectors of the economy listed earlier – households, firms, financial services, government and foreign sector – interact to determine the level of economic activity. The approach adopted is based on the *circular flow of income model* – a framework which lies at the heart of understanding the dynamics of an economy.

Key learning points

- *National income* is a statistical measure of the total money value of the output of goods and services produced by an economy over a specified period of time.
- *National income accounting* is based on three methods of measuring economic activity: output (or production) method, income method and expenditure method.
- In principle, estimates of national output, income and expenditure should be the same – but, in practice, discrepancies arise resulting from errors and omissions.
- Five sectors are responsible for generating economic activity: the household sector, the firm sector, the government sector, the financial sector and the foreign sector.
- *Transfer payments* represent a one-way flow of funds (payments) from the government for which there is no provision or exchange of goods or services in return.
- The *output method* calculates the total value of the final output of goods and services produced in the economy over a specified period of time, giving rise to the *gross domestic product (GDP)*.
- The *income method* measures the sum of all of the incomes received by the factors of production for their services.
- The *expenditure method* represents the sum of all the money values of expenditures on final goods and services produced in an economy.
- *Gross national product* equals gross domestic product *plus* net income from abroad.
- *Net national product* equals gross national product *minus* depreciation of the nation's capital stock.
- *Gross national expenditure at factor cost* equals gross national expenditure at market prices *minus* indirect taxes *plus* subsidies.
- *The size and rate of growth of national income* depends on: availability of natural resources, the nature of the labour force, amount of capital investment, efficient utilisation of resources, innovation, political stability and foreign direct investment.
- *Real GDP* represents an indicator of growth in the volume of output produced in the domestic economy – after the effects of inflation have been removed.
- The *GDP deflator* is the weighted average of prices of all goods and services produced in an economy and purchased by households, firms, government and foreigners.
- Other indicators of economic activity include: monetary aggregates, business survey data, labour market statistics and cyclical indicators.

? Topics for discussion

1. Describe briefly the methods of measuring national income.
2. Explain why national income accounts systematically underestimate the true value of goods and services produced each year.
3. Explain why comparing the GDP of the USA with that of China is unlikely to provide an accurate indicator of the relative economic status of people in the two countries.
4. What do you think the growth of the underground economy is dependent on? Explain your answer.
5. Critically comment on the following statement: 'It has just been reported that the value of the economy's output grew by 4 per cent over the past year.'
6. What factors influence the size of national economies?
7. Describe in detail the difference between real and nominal GDP.
8. Apart from official GDP statistics, what other information might suggest that an economy is heading towards a recession (defined as more than two consecutive quarters of falling output)?

Chapter 3

MODELLING THE ECONOMY – THE CIRCULAR FLOW OF INCOME

Aims and learning outcomes

In the last chapter we examined how the level of economic activity can be measured and the problems associated with this. In this chapter we introduce the dynamics of national income flows and their impact on the level of economic activity. The analysis will demonstrate the interrelationships between the sectors of the economy that, collectively, contribute to the determination of national income. At the heart of this analysis lies the so-called *circular flow of income* model which represents a simplified picture of an economy. In Chapter 4, we delve deeper into the workings of the economy to examine how changes in the income flows between sectors impact on the level of national output, income and expenditure, and hence the overall performance of the economy.

The following topics are discussed in the chapter:

- the sectors of the economy;
- the circular flow of income model;
- the concept of equilibrium in the economy;
- leakages and injections;
- the circular flow of income and aggregate demand;
- the concept of disequilibrium.

At the outset, it should be appreciated that the approach to understanding the macroeconomy described below – as encapsulated by the circular flow of income model – is the fundamental basis of the more detailed analysis provided in subsequent chapters. These chapters build on this model and explore in detail its underlying mechanics and implications for economic policy, inflation, unemployment, international trade and economic growth.

A clear understanding of the circular flow of income model may be likened to a description of the internal workings of a car engine and the determination of motion. Economic policy options and decisions, discussed in later chapters, are akin to the various styles that may be adopted when driving a car. Remember that not all drivers are equally 'good' and some may even get lost – hence, it should not be surprising that economists and policy makers frequently disagree about how the economy should be managed!

Learning outcomes

After studying this material, you will be able to:

- Appreciate the nature and role of each of the main economic sectors that contribute to the generation of economic activity over time.
- Understand how these sectors interact through the circular flow of income model to determine the level of economic activity.
- Comprehend the meaning of *equilibrium* in the economy and its significance.
- Recognise the importance of the various *leakages* from and *injections* into the circular flow that lead to disequilibrium in economic activity.
- Appreciate the link between the circular flow of income and the concept of *aggregate demand.*

Sectors of the economy

Economies are made up of a multitude of economic agencies, performing varied roles within the economy in terms of both the production of goods and services and their consumption. Within the economy as a whole, economic agents may be aggregated into one of five broad groups or sectors.

Sectors of the economy

- the household sector;
- the firm sector;
- the government sector;
- the financial services sector;
- the foreign sector.

In the study of economies, these sectors and their roles are usually described as follows.

The household sector

At the most basic level, this sector represents the total population in an economy. It is usual to think of the population as being made up of 'units' or 'households'. Households provide all of the resources (factors of production) that firms need to produce goods and services. These resources take the form of labour, land and capital (both physical and financial). In return, households receive from firms payment for these factor services in the form of wages and salaries (including benefits in kind), rents and interest, profits and dividends. At the same time, these 'incomes' generate expenditure on the goods and services produced by firms: this is referred to as final consumption expenditure (or simply, *consumer spending* or *consumption*). This expenditure is final in the sense that it is not intended to generate further production – goods purchased by households are consumed. Any income that is not spent is saved by households. Note that expenditure may be on domestically-produced goods and services or on imported goods and services. Also, some income will be paid in the form of various taxes – both direct and indirect – to the government.

The magnitude of savings, taxes and imports is of critical importance to the determination of economic activity, as will be explained below and in Chapter 4.

The firm sector

All those organisations that use resources to produce goods and services are collectively referred to as the 'firm sector'. In contrast to the household sector, firms employ and reward the factors of production provided by households. The employment of these resources gives rise to the many different types of goods and services produced in an economy, which are then bought by households, by other firms (as intermediary goods, e.g. machines and components), by the government and by foreigners. Firms also perform a vital role in the determination of economic activity arising from their investment expenditure in the form of new plant and machinery, land and buildings and other productive capacity. This process of creating capital is known as *fixed investment*. However, some of the goods produced by firms may not be sold but may instead be held as *stocks* of unsold goods (alternatively referred to as *inventories*). A rise in stock levels may be intentional (i.e. *planned*) in order to satisfy expected future demand or unintentional (i.e. *unplanned*) due to an unexpected fall in demand. In either case, we refer to a rise in stocks as *stock* (or *inventory*) *investment*. Thus, gross investment expenditure by firms is made up of two components: fixed investment plus stock investment.

The government sector

The government sector (central and local) performs a number of key roles in the determination of economic activity. It raises revenue through *direct taxes* levied on incomes (wages, rents, interest, profits and dividends, as noted above) and through *indirect taxes* or expenditure taxes such as value added tax, petrol duties, property taxes, etc). The collection of taxes is necessary to meet two kinds of expenditure carried out by the government. First, the government spends on physical goods and services, including the wages of government employees such as teachers, soldiers, civil servants, etc., the purchase of military equipment, desks, personal computers, etc., and investment in the nations' infrastructure such as in roads, schools and hospitals. Second, governments also spend money financing *transfer payments* and *welfare benefits*. These cover a wide range of expenditures including pensions for retired workers, unemployment benefit as well as subsidies to private sector firms and to state-owned enterprises. Thus, it will readily be appreciated that:

Transfer payments represent a one-way flow of funds (payments) from the government for which there is no provision or exchange of goods or services in return.

Such transfer payments do *not* represent an addition to the nation's total output of products and services. There is no corresponding value creation or output produced. They merely redistribute existing income and spending power away from those who are responsible for paying tax to those who are being subsidised. Given this fact, transfer payments as part of government spending are *excluded* from the totals for government expenditure and are not included for the purposes of national income accounts which measure the money value of national output.

The financial services sector

Financial institutions, such as banks and insurance companies, play a vital role in the economy by providing transmission services that channel money from savers to borrowers. These institutions do not produce any physical goods but they influence the workings of the 'real' economy by acting as intermediaries in directing surplus funds to those who require funds for investment purposes. Without a financial sector, the economic system would quickly grind to a halt.

The foreign sector

Foreigners buy some of the goods and services produced by the economy (i.e. a nation's exports). They also satisfy some of the demand in the economy by selling goods and services (i.e. a nation's imports). In addition, foreigners also make a contribution to economic activity via the flow of capital into and out of countries. These international capital flows may be in a number of forms, namely direct foreign investment (in plant and machinery, new factories, etc.), debt financing and equity capital (share purchases). Such flows have increased in recent decades with the globalisation of capital markets and the growth of foreign trade, investment and international aid programmes.

Macroeconomics involves the study of the interrelationship between these five sectors and the determination of economic activity by these sectors. Inevitably, aggregation of the activities of economic agents in this way conceals information about individual behaviour. For example, a rise in the economy's total output or income tells us nothing about who receives this increased output or who earns the additional incomes. Sometimes in economic analysis it is useful to disaggregate and consider individual decision making: for instance, the individual firm's competitive strategy. In this chapter, however, we are concerned only with understanding the nature of the broad economic flows in economies. Therefore, we can make useful progress by referring to the five broad sectors above. The purpose of this chapter is to present the principles of macroeconomic activity through a simplified version of how actual economies function.

The circular flow of income model

Let us first make a few simplifying assumptions in order to make our task of describing economic activity in the macroeconomy more straightforward. These assumptions will be relaxed later.

- All income is spent. (If you are a student you will probably find this assumption quite easy to accept!)
- There are only two sectors in the economy – households and firms.
- There are no government or financial services sectors.
- The economy is 'closed' in the sense that there is no trade with other countries or international capital flows.

> *The circular flow of income model* describes the way in which income flows backwards and forwards between households and firms in the economy.

Based on this simplistic representation of the economy, we can readily appreciate that:

- the income of firms is the revenue received from the sales of goods and services to households;
- the income of households is the income arising from the ownership of the factors of production: namely, wages or salaries for labour, rent for owners of land, interest for lenders of capital, and profits and dividends for owners of businesses.

Firms must pay households for the use of the factors of production, and households must pay firms for the consumption of goods and services. This creates a circular flow of income in this closed economy, as shown in Figure 3.1. It will be seen from this figure that factors of production 'pass through' the marketplace for their services, thereby determining the level of payments to each factor – as shown at the bottom of the diagram. For example, the labour market reflects the demand for and supply of labour giving rise to the level of employment and the going wage rate for each skill. Similarly, the price and quantity of goods and services bought by consumers are determined in the corresponding marketplace, shown at the top of the diagram. These 'markets' represent any situation which brings about an interaction between buyers and sellers – shops, markets themselves, telephone deals and so on.

Figure 3.1 shows the flow of goods and services (in volume terms) along with the flow of factor services of production in the clockwise direction with the equivalent monetary flows in the anti-clockwise direction. From now on, however, we will only show the monetary flows for clarity of exposition as we extend our discussion of this model of the circular flow of income. This is obviously appropriate because we are dealing with the circular flow of *national income*. This income represents the total monetary value of the physical output produced

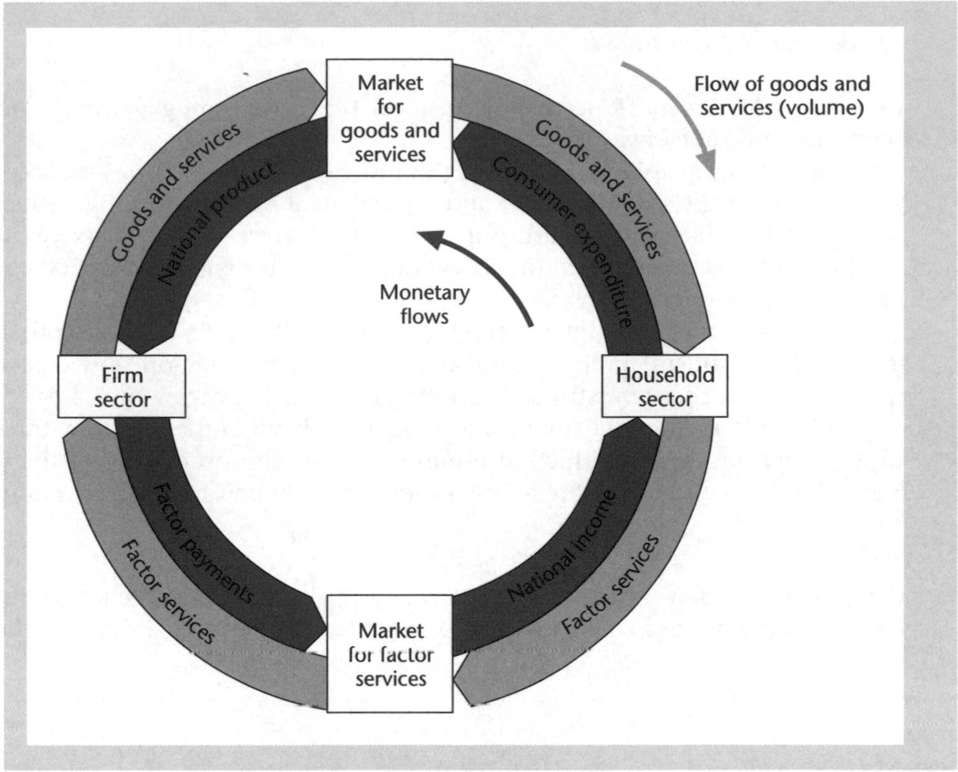

Figure 3.1 Circular flow of income – simple model

(*national product*), the monetary reward to the factors of production employed (*national income*) and the total monetary expenditure (*national expenditure*), as explained in Chapter 2.

Application 3.1

Changes in the US circular flow of income

In the second quarter of 2003, US GDP was revised up to an annualised rate of 3.1 per cent. This is more than double the growth rate in late 2002. Much of this increase is due to a large spurt in government spending due to the Iraq war: federal defence expenditure added an estimated 1.75 percentage points to the growth rate. However, other parts of the US economy also seem to have improved. Led by continued spending on equipment and software, private investment rose at its fastest rate since early 2000, indicating an upturn in capital

Application 3.1 continued

spending. The Federal Reserve now believes that the turning point in the US economy came as early as May.

In the second quarter of 2003, a big fall in stocks or inventories reduced the growth rate for the second quarter and the Federal Reserve thinks that reduction continued into July and August. But with factory stocks now at a six-year low, most economists expect them to recover in the remaining months of 2003, leading to faster economic growth.

In July 2003, orders for durable goods rose at a healthy rate, suggesting that the increased investment in the second quarter was not a one-off and consumer spending in the shops outstripped expectations in July, growing by 1.4 per cent.

Some of this additional demand continues to leak out of the economy through expenditure on imports, which also jumped in the second quarter of the year. Nevertheless, the additional retail sales should further boost the US economy.

Activity

Using a circular flow of income diagram explain how the above changes in the US macroeconomy can be expected to impact on the overall level of national income.

The concept of equilibrium in the economy

The 'simple' economic system illustrated in Figure 3.1 involves no foreign trade, no government sector and no financial sector. We have also assumed that households spend *all* of their income and therefore there are no savings taking place. For example, if the household sector receives \$100bn in factor payments, households will spend \$100bn purchasing goods and services from the firm sector. In the figure, income is circulating around the economy and the flow at the bottom (representing all forms of income – i.e. national income) will be equal to the flow at the top (representing expenditure on all goods and services produced – i.e. national product). When this balance exists in a system we usually describe it as an *equilibrium*. Equilibrium will exist in the economy unless something happens to disturb it. Thus, for this 'simple' economy, we can describe the equilibrium condition as:

Equilibrium: national income = national expenditure

We have said nothing yet, however, about the size of the national income flow or the national expenditure flow. It is important to appreciate that equilibrium can exist at any level of activity – the determination of equilibrium simply refers to the situation in which total income is spent and generates a particular level of economic activity. Thus, equilibrium can exist if the flow is \$50bn, \$100bn or \$500bn, etc., provided that total income equals total expenditure. A low level of economic activity (relative to the potential productive capacity of the economy) implies underemployment of one or more of the factors of production, spare capacity within firms and a relatively small flow of goods and services to households: the economy is not operating on its production possibility frontier (see p.9). A high level of activity relative to potential productive capacity could imply full employment of factor services, with factories and firms working at full capacity and a large volume of goods and services being produced: the economy is on or near to its production possibility frontier.

Leakages and injections

Introducing the financial sector

So far we have illustrated only a very simple model of the economy. Let us now introduce the financial sector into this model and restate our underlying assumptions. Let us assume again that we have a closed economy (no foreign sector) and there is no government sector. Households now receiving income dispose of it in two ways:

- they either spend the income on consumer goods and services (denoted as C); or
- they save a proportion of their income (this proportion is referred to as the *savings ratio*, denoted as S).

The only part of national income (denoted as Y) not directly received by households will be that part of profits which firms retain as reserves. However, since these reserves belong to shareholders, who themselves are ultimately households, they are part of total savings in the broadest sense of the term. Thus, it follows that:

National income = Total consumption expenditure + Total savings

Symbolically:

$$Y = C + S$$

Savings represent a reduction in the circular flow which can be counterbalanced by firms borrowing and spending these funds for investment purposes, channelled through the financial sector (e.g. banks). Thus, investment is that part of total output which is not currently consumed.

In other words:

$$Y = C + I$$

where:

I represents investment expenditure, including stocks (inventories) of materials, work in progress and finished but unsold goods.

We have now extended the simple circular flow model and instead of just income and consumer expenditure flows, we also have savings and investment expenditures flows – as shown in Figure 3.2. This now allows us to introduce two key concepts in the context of the circular flow, referred to *leakages and injections*.

Leakages and injections

- A *leakage* from the circular flow of income is defined as that part of national income that is not spent by households on the consumption of domestically produced goods and services. This is also sometimes referred to as a *withdrawal* from the circular flow.
- An *injection* into the circular flow of income represents any expenditures on domestic goods and services originating from outside the household sector.

Thus, net savings (after allowing for household borrowing) represent a leakage since it means that some part of the incomes paid out by firms is not being returned in the form of spending on current output (as shown by a 'thinner' consumer expenditure flow in Figure 3.2). Investment expenditure represents an injection since it is expenditure that does not arise *directly* from the household sector.

It should be clear from Figure 3.2 that as long as the leakage from (net) savings is matched by an equal injection through investment expenditure decisions by firms, equilibrium in the economy will exist.

Planned and realised values

It is important to appreciate fully the meaning of the equilibrium condition for the (simplified) economy that we have just described. In a sense, the actual value of savings always equals the value of investment expenditure in the economy. Since total saving is defined as that part of national income which is not spent, then by definition:

$$\text{National income} = \text{Consumer expenditure} + \text{Savings}$$

Likewise, since total investment is defined as that part of national production that is not consumed, then:

$$\text{National product (output)} = \text{Consumer expenditure} + \text{Investment spending}$$

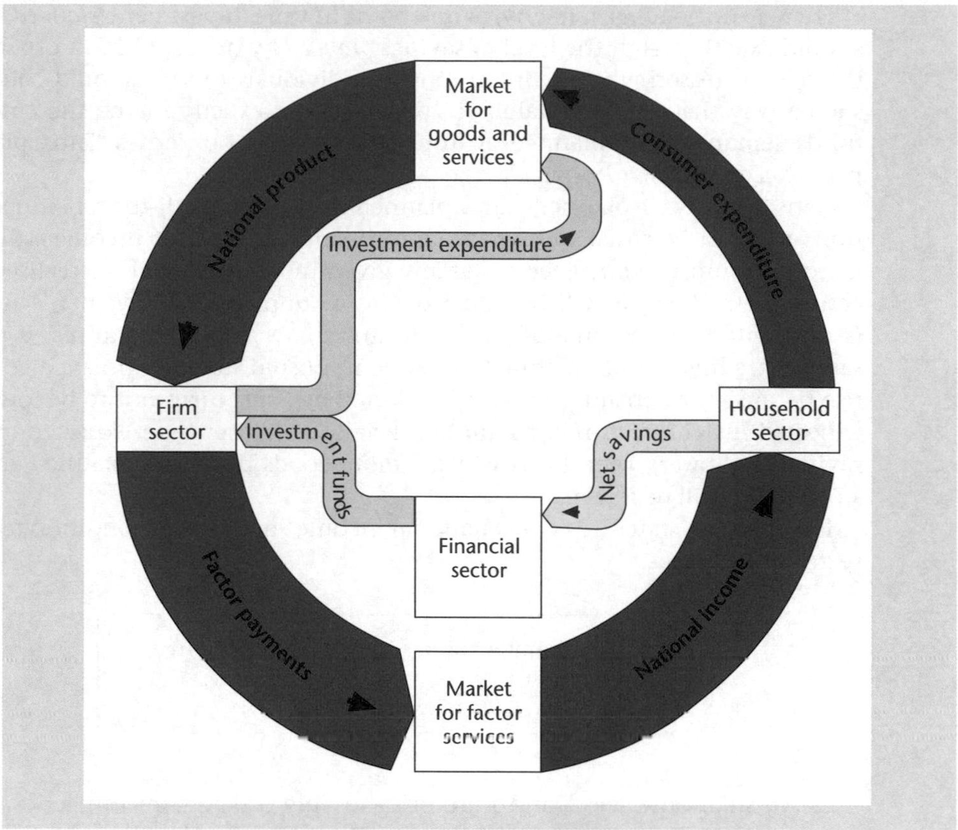

Figure 3.2 Circular flow of income – with a financial sector

Since national output is, by definition, equal to national income, then these equations imply that:

$$\text{Savings} \equiv \text{Investment}$$
$$S \equiv I$$

Note the use of '≡' to signify that S and I must, by definition, be equal.

The $S \equiv I$ identity, however, provides no information about what *causes* changes in economic activity over time. All we have demonstrated so far is that, over time, *actual* or *realised* savings will be identical to *actual* or *realised* investment.

The key to understanding the dynamics of the economy rests with the analysis of why the actual values of S and I are what they are. This is explained by the relationships between *planned* or *intended* levels of savings by households and investment expenditure by firms.

There is no good reason why, at any point in time, investment *planned* by firms should exactly match the level of savings *planned* by households. In other words, there is no reason why the intentions of individuals to save should coincide in such a way that the total value of savings should exactly match the amount of funds demanded and planned by firms for investment purposes. Thus, planned S may exceed planned I or vice versa.

Consequently, if planned I and planned S are not equal, then planned injections will not be equal to leakages and the circular flow of income will not be in equilibrium, *ex ante*. Even so, at any given moment, actual (or realised) I and actual (or realised) S will be equal owing to unplanned movements in stocks (stocks will either be building up or declining), *ex post*. For example, if planned savings are higher than planned investment, unsold stocks of finished goods will rise because the consumption level expected by firms turns out to be lower than expected. By contrast, if consumption levels are higher than expected (planned savings are lower), then firms will sell more goods than they planned and their stock levels will be lower.

Thus, we can state the *ex ante* national income equilibrium condition for a two-sector economy as:

National income equilibrium condition

Planned S = Planned I

As we shall now see, S and I are not the only leakages and injections in the economy. Other leakages and injections into the circular flow arise from the activities of government (in the form of taxes and expenditure decisions respectively) and from foreign trade (in the form of expenditure on imports and revenue from exports respectively). We now introduce each of these in turn into our model.

Introducing the government sector

In a modern, mixed economy the government is a key player in the generation of economic activity. The government has several functions and so plays several different roles in the circular flow of income.

- The government acts as the producer of certain goods and services instead of privately-owned firms – thus the 'production' of public administration services, education and health services, the police force, armed forces, fire brigade services, and public transport are all aspects of its output. The government in this respect acts, like firms, as a producer, and must also pay wages to its employees and rewards to the owners of the other factors of production it employs (such as capital).
- The government acts as a purchaser of goods and services. National and local government obtain funds from the firms and households of the economy (in

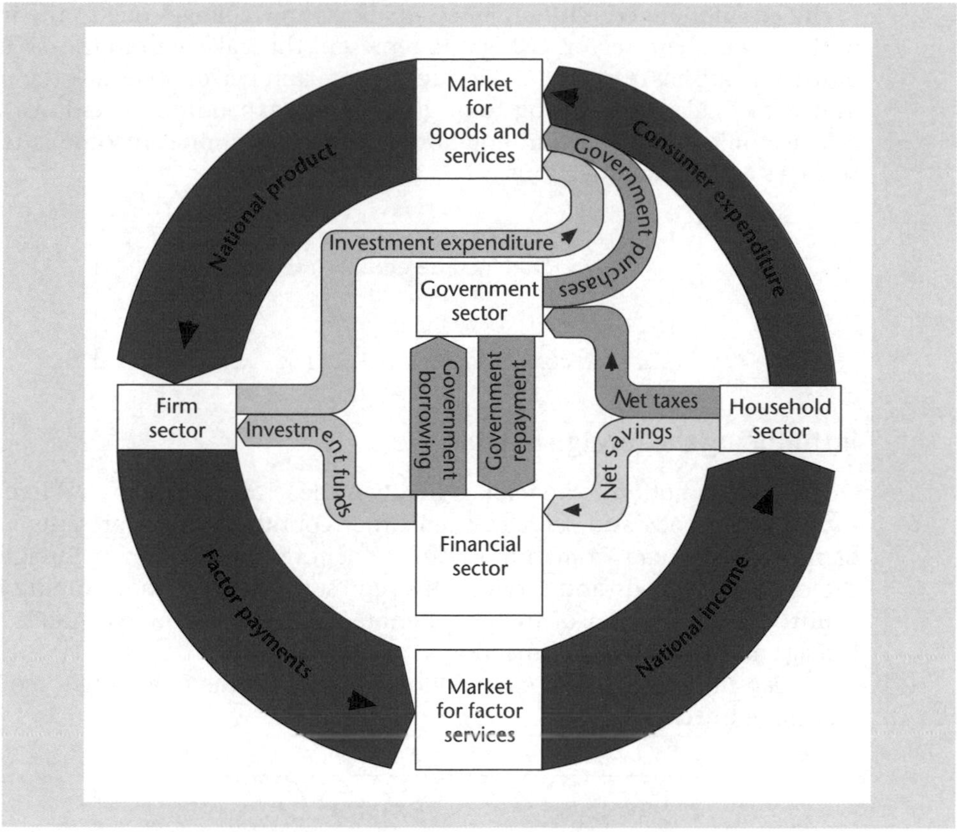

Figure 3.3 Circular flow of income – with a government sector

the form of corporate and personal as well as indirect taxation) and then use these funds to buy goods and services from firms.

- The government acts as a means of transferring wealth or income from one section of the economy to another, for example by taxing workers and paying transfer payments, such as pensions and unemployment and social security benefits, to other members of society.

The effect of introducing the government into the circular flow of income model is that we have another leakage of income from the system in the form of taxation and another injection of income in the form of government spending. These are shown in Figure 3.3.

Note that the government may also borrow or repay funds to the financial sector. The value of borrowing during the course of a financial year is commonly referred to as the *budget deficit*, while the accumulated total stock of debt outstanding represents the *national debt*. Net repayment of debt in the course of any year is the result of a *budget surplus*.

The equilibrium condition expressed above now changes due to the inclusion of the government sector. Using T to represent the leakage from the circular flow of income arising from all taxation (corporate and personal) and G the injection into the circular flow arising from government expenditure decisions, then, as before, the condition for an equilibrium level of national income is that total leakages equal total injections.

National income equilibrium condition

$$S + T = I + G$$

Introducing the foreign sector

Our final assumption to be relaxed involves the 'closed economy'. When a country imports goods and services from other countries, this represents a leakage of national income from the economy (denoted as M). When foreigners buy the exports of goods and services this represents 'new' money coming into the country – an injection of income (denoted as X). We now have an additional leakage and an additional injection.

We can illustrate the full circular flow model with the following three leakages and three injections.

Leakages	*Injections*
Savings (S)	Investment (I)
Taxes (T)	Government Expenditure (G)
Imports (M)	Exports (X)

These are illustrated in Figure 3.4.

Equilibrium in the full circular flow of income model is now given by:

National income equilibrium condition

$$\underbrace{S + T + M}_{\text{Total leakages}} = \underbrace{I + G + X}_{\text{Total injections}}$$

The model is now complete in the sense that we are describing the equilibrium conditions under which there will be no tendency for national income to change.

Thus the *total value* of realised, actual or *ex post* leakages from the economy in the form of savings, taxes and imports will always equal the *total value* of realised,

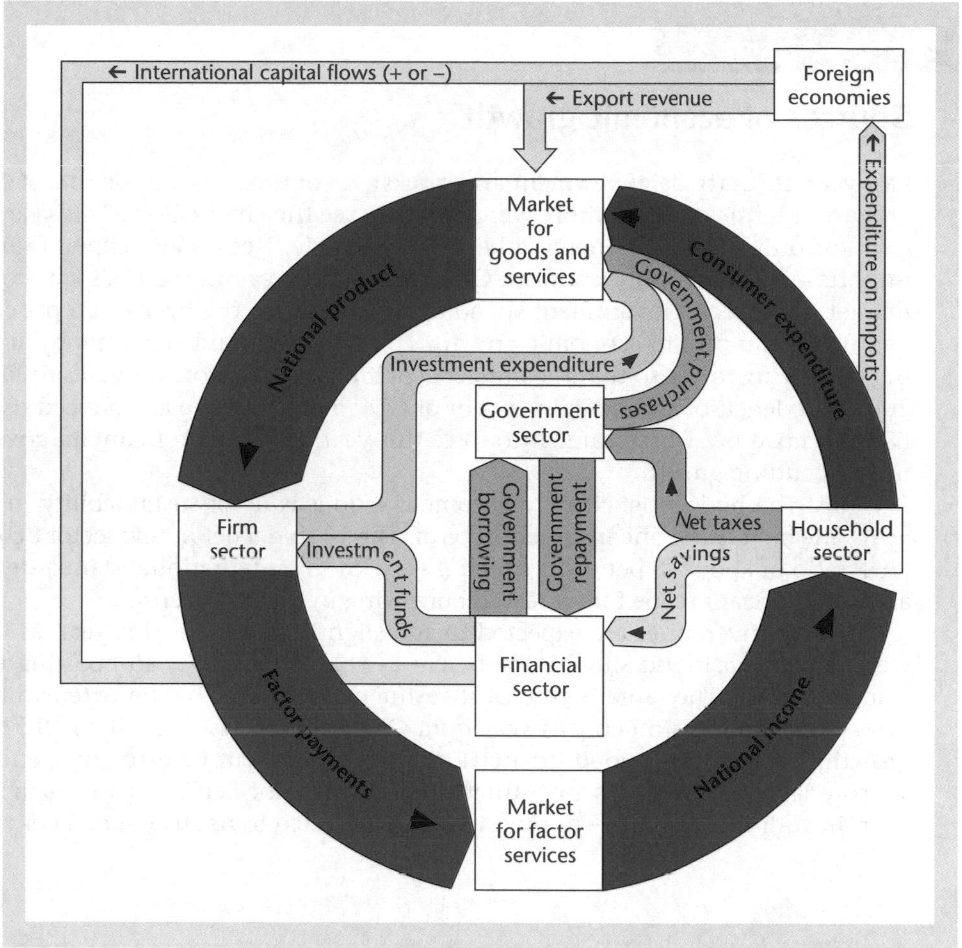

Figure 3.4 **Full circular flow of income model**

actual or *ex post* injections into the economy in the form of investment, government expenditure and exports. But, as we indicated earlier, it does not follow that the total of *planned* or *ex ante leakages* and the total of *planned* or *ex ante injections* equal each other because decisions regarding leakages and injections are made by different people.

As we shall see in the next chapter, a difference between total planned leakages and total planned injections in the circular flow of income will result in a change in the level of activity in an economy. The economic flow which will vary up and down to maintain equilibrium will be the national income itself.

Note that in Figure 3.4, *international capital flows* are shown. These arise as a result of a number of factors including overseas borrowing and investment decisions. It will be appreciated that international capital flows are captured within the domestic expenditure flows insofar as they affect consumption and investment.

Application 3.2

Sources of economic growth

Last year, three (trade, investment and stocks) out of the five components of GDP growth in terms of expenditure were negative, see the chart below. This year, we look for only one component to be negative, trade. Net trade – exports minus imports – is likely to subtract from GDP growth this year, as the UK's key export market stays weak. Government spending is expected to rise by about 5 per cent, adding 0.7 per cent to economic growth. This has been funded mainly by allowing borrowing to rise so that the budget deficit has moved from a small surplus in 2001 to a deficit of around 3.3 per cent of GDP in 2003. A pre-announced rise of £8bn in taxation, which came into force this year, will help to maintain government spending growth.

Whilst the budget deficit may become a serious issue of sustainability in the years ahead, it is not one in the short term. The UK has a net public sector debt to GDP ratio of about 30 per cent, which is very low by international standards and allows significant scope for increased borrowing in the short term.

Stocks or inventories are expected to add slightly to growth this year, as they were cut last year and should not be cut as sharply this year so boosting economic growth. The same is true of investment spending. To the extent that it does not subtract as much this year from GDP as it did last year, it should help growth. Firms are in a good financial position having cut investment spending sharply last year. Business investment is therefore not being cut as much this year. In addition, government investment is projected to rise by over 25 per cent.

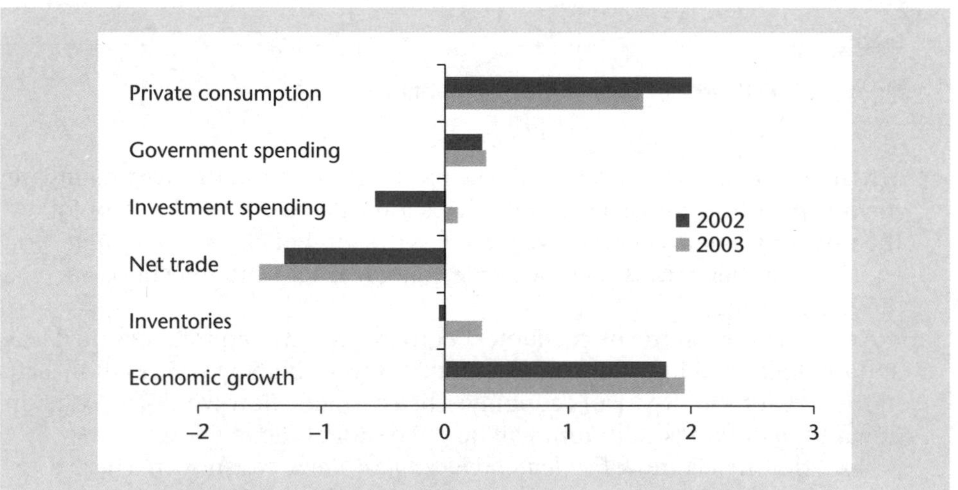

Sectoral contributions to GDP growth

Application 3.2 continued

Although we expect a 1.3 percentage point slowdown in consumer spending this year from 4 per cent in 2002 to 2.7 per cent, it will still contribute some 2 per cent to 2003 economic growth. With government and investment spending and stocks helping, GDP growth by our calculation could rise by around 2 per cent in 2003. Next year, the composition of GDP will change again, and investment spending and net trade should add to economic growth, so leading to its acceleration to 2.8 per cent.

Source: Lloyds TSB *Economic Bulletin*, no. 45, June 2003, pp.4–5.

Activity

In the context of the circular flow of income and with reference to a circular flow of income diagram show how the movements in sectoral spending for 2003 shown in the chart are likely to affect the level of national income.

The circular flow of income and aggregate demand

Before we leave the concept of the circular flow of income, we can establish an important link between the measurement of national income, the concept of the circular flow and *aggregate demand*.

We mentioned earlier that the level of activity in our circular flow can be measured by total income, total expenditure or total output or at different 'points' in the flow itself. The measurements should all give the same result since they are measuring the same thing – namely the magnitude of economic activity. Let us concentrate on total expenditure.

Total spending in the circular flow of income must consist of payments for goods and services by the domestic sector – denoted by consumer spending (C), investment spending (I), government spending (G) and the net addition to spending brought about by foreign trade (i.e. net exports denoted by $X - M$). We have, then, the identity established in the previous chapter for the calculation of national income via the expenditure method:

$$\text{Total spending} = C + I + G + (X - M)$$

Another name for this identity is *aggregate demand* (denoted AD) because it represents total spending or demand in the economy. We shall return to this subject in Chapters 4 and 5. An equilibrium level of national income exists in an economy when:

National income equilibrium condition

Aggregate supply (*AS*) = Aggregate demand (*AD*)

where:

aggregate supply represents the total output of the economy or real GDP; aggregate demand represents total spending.

Only when this condition is met can we state that the total value of domestic goods and services that households, firms, government and foreigners want to buy is matched by the total value of goods and services firms want to supply. Note that this refers to the demand for and supply of *domestic* goods and services (that is, including the value of exports and after deduction of expenditure on imports).

It should be appreciated that aggregate supply represents the amount of goods and services that firms are willing to produce, given the general level of wages and prices. Hence, an equilibrium national income relates to the situation where the production *plans* of firms match the *actual* supply of goods and services needed to satisfy aggregate demand in a particular time period. When this condition is satisfied there is no tendency for the economy to move away from equilibrium.

From this discussion of equilibrium it is easy to understand the meaning of a disequilibrium level of national income. But first, to clarify our discussion so far, we provide an alternative approach to explaining a national income equilibrium – based on (the less sophisticated) concept of a water barrel (see Box 3.1)!

Box 3.1

An alternative model of the economy

In simplistic terms, the productive capacity of an economy can be likened to a water barrel. Over time, a growing economy can be thought of in terms of a barrel which increases in volume – see Figure 3.5 which shows an expanding barrel representing an economy with an increasing productive capacity over the ten-year period from 1993 to 2003.

At any given point in time, the actual output of an economy, as measured by the value of gross national product, represents a certain utilisation of this productive capacity. When the level of national product is distributed in the form of payments to the factors services which contributed to it, a circular flow commences as described earlier in the chapter. The size of the national product and national income are illustrated in Figure 3.6 – note that the levels in the first two barrels are equal, indicating that national product is equivalent to national income.

The third barrel in this figure highlights the leakages and injections listed above. It is now easy to appreciate why, in equilibrium, the sum of *realised* or *ex post* leakages must equal the sum of the *realised* or *ex post* injections.

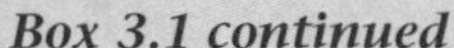

Box 3.1 continued

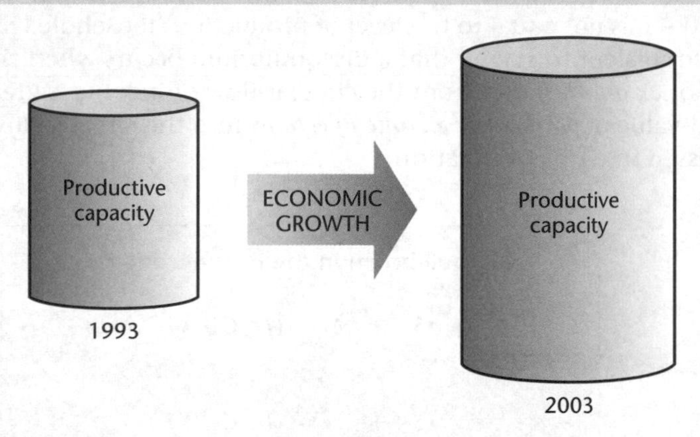

Figure 3.5 Growth in productive capacity

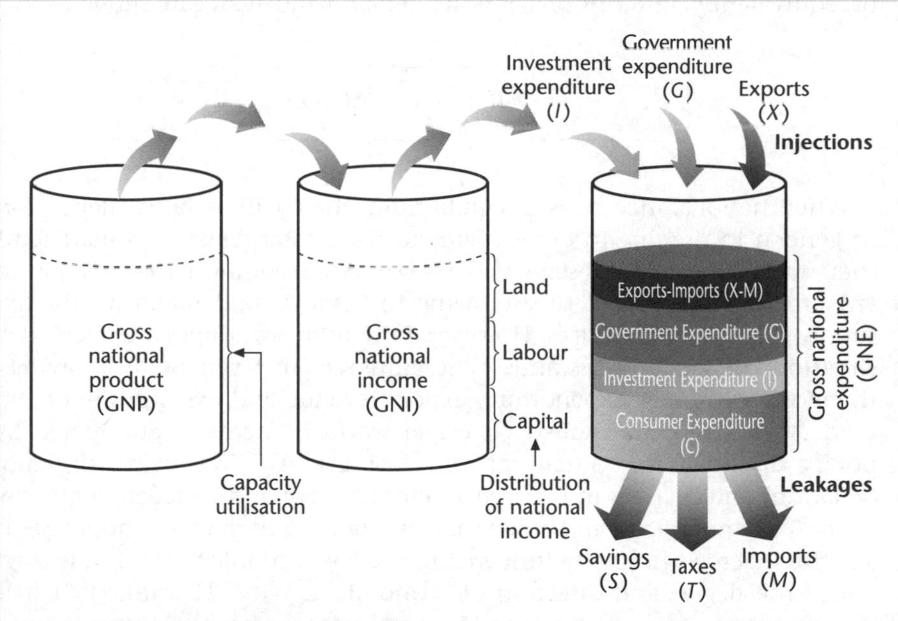

Figure 3.6 An alternative model of the economy

But, of course, if the *planned* or *ex ante* leakages and injections are not equal then the total level of water in the barrel will change, i.e. there will be a change in the level of economic activity, signifying a disequilibrium situation until equilibrium is once again restored. We discuss this in more detail later (see pp.133–4).

The concept of disequilibrium

A *disequilibrium* in the macroeconomy occurs when the output firms plan to produce and sell is not equal to the level of production households plan to purchase. This is equivalent to saying that a disequilibrium occurs when the total value of *planned* or *ex ante leakages* from the circular flow of income is greater or less than the total value of *planned* or *ex ante injections* into the circular flow.

Expressed in terms of notation:

Disequilibrium in the macroeconomy

$$(S + T + M) > (I + G + X)$$

or

$$(S + T + M) < (I + G + X)$$

or, equivalently, in terms of aggregate demand and aggregate supply:

$$AD < AS \quad \text{or} \quad AD > AS$$

When national income is in equilibrium, there will be no tendency for prices in general to rise due to excess demand since total demand is matched by the total supply of goods and services (i.e. $AD = AS$). In addition, there will be no tendency for unemployment to rise owing to inadequate demand for the available supply of goods and services. However, long-term economies are rarely, if ever, in situations of stable prices and stable employment levels because savings (and, therefore, consumer expenditure, export revenue and expenditure on imports) tend to change continuously. The real world is therefore dominated by temporary disequilibrium situations with rising and falling prices (inflation and deflation) and changes in the level of employment and hence unemployment.

Many economists would argue that the role of government should be to manage the macroeconomy by influencing the levels of injections and leakages and hence the degree and direction of economic activity. This may be carried out using a range of policy measures focusing upon either the demand side of the economy (adjusting the level of aggregate demand) or the supply side of the economy (affecting the capacity of the economy to produce goods and services). This gives rise to *demand management* policies and *supply-side* policies respectively. These policies were introduced on p.14, and are detailed in later chapters. A controversial issue in policy making today is the extent to which governments should emphasise either demand-side or supply-side measures in influencing the level of economic activity.

Concluding remarks

In this chapter we have considered the concepts of both equilibrium and disequilibrium in national income or economic activity. We have done this by focusing on the circular flow of income model, beginning with a simple two-sector model of just firms and households, and later introducing three other major sectors of the economy, namely the financial, government and foreign sectors. Using this model we were able to identify the circumstances under which national income equilibrium and disequilibrium situations can occur. We saw that there is an important distinction to be made between *planned* or *ex ante* and *realised* (actual) or *ex post* savings and investment decisions. The same applies to the other leakages from the circular flow of income – taxes and expenditure on imports – and the other injections into the circular flow – government expenditure and export revenues. Only when planned savings plus taxes plus import spending equals planned investment plus government spending plus export revenue will there be no tendency for the level of national income and therefore economic activity to alter.

In the next chapter we turn to look in much more detail at the determination of economic activity in the macroeconomy, thereby completing our explanation of the 'mechanics' of the economy, before we turn to discussing the 'driving' or policy options in later chapters (recall the analogy with the car described earlier in this chapter).

Key learning points

- The *circular flow of income model* represents a simplified exposition of the way in which income flows around the economy in exchange for goods and services between the various sectors that contribute to overall economic activity.
- The sectors which contribute to the determination of economic activity are: *households*, *firms*, the *financial sector*, the *government* and the *foreign sector*.
- *In equilibrium*, total income is equal to total expenditure, and this can take place at any level of economic activity. For a simple economy, with no government or foreign sector, equilibrium will exist when:

  Planned or *ex ante savings* = *Planned* or *ex ante investment expenditure*

- A *leakage* from the circular flow of income is defined as that part of national income that is not spent by households on the consumption of domestically produced goods or services.
- *An injection* into the circular flow of income represents any expenditures on domestic goods and services originating from outside the household sector.
- *Leakages from the 'full' circular flow model* of the economy are: savings (S), tax receipts (T) and expenditure on imports (M).
- *Injections into the 'full' circular flow model* of the economy are: investment expenditure (I), government expenditure (G) and export revenue (X).

- *Equilibrium in the full circular flow model* of the economy is given by:

$$S + T + M = I + G + X$$

i.e. Total leakages = Total injections

- A difference between total *planned* leakages and total *planned* injections will result in a change in the equilibrium level of activity in the economy – leading to a change in national income.
- Total spending or *aggregate demand* in the circular flow of income model is given by:

$$\textit{Total spending} = C + I + G + (X - M)$$

where C represents consumer (or household spending), I represents investment spending (including stock investment), G is government spending (both current and capital expenditure), X represents revenue from exports and M represents expenditure on imports.

- The *equilibrium level of national income* may also be shown by:

Aggregate supply (AS) = Aggregate Demand (AD)

- A *disequilibrium in the macroeconomy* occurs when the output that firms plan to produce and sell is *not* equal to the level of production that households plan to purchase. In terms of leakages and injections, disequilibrium occurs when:

$$S + T + M > I + G + X$$

or

$$S + T + M < I + G + X$$

or, equivalently

$$AS < \text{or} > AD$$

- When national income is in equilibrium, there will be no tendency for prices in general to rise (or fall) because total demand is matched by the total supply of goods and services. Likewise, there will be no tendency for unemployment to rise (or fall).
- In reality, the world is dominated by temporary disequilibrium situations because planned savings (and therefore consumer spending), taxes, investment expenditure, government expenditure, export revenue and expenditure on imports all tend to change.
- Many economists argue that the *role of government* should be to manage the macroeconomy by influencing the levels of injections and leakages and hence the degree and direction of economic activity. Measures used to achieve this may be described as *demand management* policies.
- Governments may also choose to focus on influencing the output or supply side of the economy – resulting in *supply-side* policies.

? Topics for discussion

1. Why must *realised* or *ex post* savings equal *realised* or *ex post* investment in an economy with only firms, households and a financial sector (no government and no foreign sector)? Explain your answer using a circular flow of income diagram.
2. Why, in such an economy, is it not necessary for planned savings to equal planned investment? If planned savings exceeded planned investment, explain the process by which the level of national income adjusts.
3. In a full, circular flow of income economy (with households, firms, financial, government and foreign trade sectors), why is it not necessarily the case that realised investment will equal realised savings but that realised injections must equal realised leakages in total?
4. Explain how equilibrium would be restored in the circular flow of income if there was a reduction in the overall level of planned investment expenditure.
5. What are the policy choices available to governments with respect to the management of aggregate demand? (*Hint*: consider the leakages and injections shown in Figure 3.6.)

Chapter 4

THE DETERMINATION OF ECONOMIC ACTIVITY

Aims and learning outcomes

In Chapter 3 we illustrated the flows of outputs, incomes and expenditures around an economy in the form of the circular flow of income model, which is a useful diagrammatic summary of economic activity. We now turn to discuss the determination of these flows, i.e. the underlying dynamics of the macroeconomy. We are essentially interested in understanding what *causes* the level of economic activity to rise or fall in the short term around an economy's long-term growth path. Such fluctuations in economic activity give rise to what are known as *business cycles,* in which the rate of growth in production periodically rises and falls. A full treatment of the determinants of long-term economic growth and the causes of business cycles is presented later, in Chapters 10 and 17 of the book.

This chapter considers the causes of fluctuations in economic activity employing a framework developed by economists over many years based on principles set down by John Maynard Keynes. Within this so-called Keynesian approach to the determination of economic activity, a useful simplifying assumption is that all prices (including interest rates, wages and prices of goods and services generally) are fixed in the short term. This may seem to be an unrealistic assumption, but it reflects the fact that, in reality, it takes time for economic agents (firms, markets, banks, etc.) to adjust their prices in response to changing market conditions. The significance of this assumption will become clearer as we proceed through the chapter and explore the determinants of aggregate (total) expenditure in the economy. In the next chapter, Chapter 5, we discuss the impact of changes in aggregate expenditure on price levels.The following aspects relating to the determination of economic activity are covered in the current chapter:

- the meaning of equilibrium national income;
- components of aggregate planned expenditure;
- consumer expenditure and savings;
- investment expenditure;
- government expenditure;
- expenditure on exports and imports;
- determination of equilibrium national income;
- deflationary and inflationary gaps;

- multiplier effects;
- the accelerator principle.

Keynesian versus monetarist schools

Views on what determines aggregate expenditure and hence the level of economic activity are sometimes broadly divided into two schools of thought: the *Keynesian* and the *monetarist* schools. The division between these two schools was particularly sharp in the 1970s and 1980s, at a time of economic instability in many parts of the world. Today, however, it could be argued that most economists' views draw from both schools.

The Keynesian school evolved from the work of the British economist John Maynard Keynes, as set out in his book *The General Theory of Employment, Interest and Money* published in 1936. His ideas had a profound impact upon economists and governments after 1945 and led to the concept of *Keynesian demand management*. Keynes and his followers argued that the levels of total output (*aggregate supply*) and employment in an economy are determined by the level of aggregate expenditure or *aggregate demand* for goods and services. Their views were concerned largely with short-run measures to affect the level of economic activity focusing on changes in aggregate demand. Today, economists who incline towards a Keynesian approach to the economy still believe that when an economy has spare productive capacity and unemployment, investment and output can be stimulated so as to increase employment without necessarily creating inflationary pressure. They argue that this can be achieved primarily through changing government expenditure and/or taxes – that is, by what are known as *fiscal policy* measures (fiscal policy is discussed in detail in Chapter 7).

The monetarist approach stems largely from the work of the American economist Milton Friedman developed mostly in the 1960s and 1970s. Based partly on empirical research, initially into the historical relationship between the growth of the money supply and inflation in the USA, and partly on a theoretical study of the relationship between changes in the money supply and money GDP (the value of domestic output), Friedman argued that controlling the growth of the money supply is essential in order to prevent inflation. Monetarist economists also argue that controlling inflation is a prerequisite to reducing unemployment because inflation in market economies, they believe, is harmful to private sector investment decisions and therefore detrimental to economic growth.

Monetarist policy prescriptions, like the prescriptions of Keynesian policy, are directed at aggregate demand in the economy. However, unlike Keynesians, monetarists tend to shun positive state action to increase employment, especially through the use of fiscal measures. Instead, they prefer to rely upon private sector initiative and investment and free markets. Insofar as government has a role to play in the economy, monetarists argue that it is to protect private property rights and ensure that the growth in the money supply is controlled to prevent inflation and unexpected fluctuations in aggregate demand. Monetary policy measures are discussed in detail in Chapter 9; while the debate on the relative roles of markets and state intervention to the solution of macroeconomic problems is the focus of Chapter 18 in particular, although the debate surfaces at a number of points in the book.

Learning outcomes

After studying this material you will be able to:

- Appreciate the meaning of national income equilibrium.
- Understand the components of aggregate planned expenditure.
- Distinguish between planned (*ex ante*) and realised (*ex post*) expenditures.
- Recognise the factors that impact on consumer spending (consumption) and savings levels.
- Understand the factors that lead to changes in investment expenditure.
- Understand the roles of government expenditure as well as monetary flows from exports and imports in the determination of national income equilibrium.
- Appreciate the nature of 'deflationary gaps' and 'inflationary gaps'.
- Understand the importance of 'multiplier' and 'accelerator' effects when there are changes in any components of aggregate expenditure.

The meaning of equilibrium national income

The starting point for an analysis of fluctuations in economic activity is the concept of an *equilibrium national income*, as introduced in the previous chapter.

> By the term *equilibrium*, economists mean a state of affairs in which the forces that are influencing change in opposite directions are perfectly balanced so that there is no tendency to change.

A national income equilibrium occurs when the planned expenditure on goods and services in the economy is just equal to the actual supply of goods and services available for purchase. There is then no tendency for economic activity to rise or fall. If planned expenditure exceeds the output of goods and services, however, either output or prices, or both, will tend to rise, leading to a higher nominal (monetary) value of national income. A rise in the *nominal* value of national income does not necessarily mean that the *real* value (i.e. the physical volume of output) will rise: this will depend upon the economy's ability to increase output. Where output cannot be increased, or increased as fast as aggregate demand is increasing, inflation will tend to result. Similarly, if output exceeds planned expenditure either prices or output, or both, will tend to fall, leading to a decline in the nominal value of national income. Again, the real value of national income will depend upon the relative changes in output and prices. In other words, a national income equilibrium occurs when:

National income equilibrium

Aggregate supply = Aggregate planned expenditure

Aggregate supply is the total output of the economy (i.e. national income) and is commonly denoted by the letter Y. Aggregate planned expenditure (denoted as AE) is made up of a number of components, as we saw in the circular flow diagrams in Chapter 3.

These are:

- planned consumer expenditure (C);
- planned investment expenditure (I);
- planned government spending (G);
- planned expenditure on exports *minus* planned expenditure on imports ($X - M$).

Note that in order to calculate the aggregate planned expenditure for *domestically* produced goods and services, we must *subtract* planned expenditure on imports (M) because the goods bought by domestic households, firms and government as well as exports sold overseas are likely to include a foreign component (e.g. imported raw materials).

Therefore, the national equilibrium condition income can be expressed as:

$$Y_e = AE = C + I + G + (X - M)$$

where Y_e represents the equilibrium level of national income (output)

Before proceeding, it is crucial to grasp the significance of *planned* and *actual* expenditure with respect to the determination of national income equilibrium (see Box 4.1).

Box 4.1

Distinction between planned and actual expenditure

Planned expenditure is also referred to as *intended* or *ex ante* expenditure. This expenditure is made up of planned spending by consumers, the investment plans of firms, planned spending by government as well as export and import spending plans. These plans will be based on a host of factors including the current (and perhaps expected) level of incomes of consumers, business confidence and employment levels, government objectives, the government's budgetary position, foreign exchange rates, etc.

Actual expenditure is also referred to as *realised* or *ex post* expenditure and refers to the consumption, investment, government spending and net exports actually achieved. This outcome may differ from the planned amounts, i.e. planned expenditure may differ from actual expenditure.

Components of aggregate planned expenditure

In order to understand how changes in national income (Y) may be determined by changes in aggregate planned expenditure, it is necessary to examine each of the components of aggregate planned expenditure in turn.

Following on from the discussion concerning the distinction between planned and actual expenditures, it is worth noting that, in the short-term, we would expect planned investment expenditure , planned government expenditure and planned expenditure on exports to be *independent* of the level of national income. This should not be difficult to appreciate since in the case of firms and government, planned investment and government spending are generally based on prior strategic decisions and take time to alter. Planned expenditure on exports is obviously independent of a country's national income and is determined instead by the propensity of *other* countries to import.

Planned investment, government and exports expenditure are, therefore, described as *exogenous* variables – in the sense that any change in any of them is *independent* of the level of and any change in domestic national income.

In contrast, planned consumer expenditure and planned expenditure on imports *do* tend to vary with changes in national income, even in the short term. These variables are, therefore, described as *endogenous* – that is, any change in them is *dependent* on the level of and any change in domestic national income.

Consumer expenditure and savings

Domestic consumer expenditure is the dominant component of aggregate demand in all economies, dwarfing the other expenditures. For example, around two thirds of the total domestic expenditure in developed countries is accounted for by consumers. In poorer economies, this figure tends to be even higher reflecting, in particular, low levels of investment spending. Therefore, any changes in spending plans by consumers are likely to have a significant impact upon the level of economic activity in an economy. More spending in stores raises aggregate demand, while a fall in consumer confidence will deflate domestic spending plans, with obvious implications for firms' sales, investment and production. Since consumers can spend or save their income, it follows that for any given post-tax income level, when the percentage of income that consumers intend to spend on goods and services rises, the level of planned savings fall. In contrast, a decline in consumer spending out of post-tax income raises the percentage of planned savings.

In addition to income, a number of other factors may affect consumption, such as consumer confidence, the wealth of consumers (as reflected in accumulated savings, etc.), the cost and availability of credit, government taxation and subsidies, advertising of goods and services and so on. Nevertheless, economists tend to single out *disposable income* as the most important influence. Disposable income (Y_d) is the amount of income that consumers have left over after paying direct taxes to the government and receiving direct state subsidies (e.g. welfare benefit). One way of expressing the relationship between planned consumer expenditure and disposable income is to state that an individual's total planned consumption (C) is dependent upon (or, to use the mathematical term, is *a function of* – denoted by the letter f) disposable income. This is written as:

$$C = f(Y_d)$$

It also follows that as disposable income can be spent or saved, planned savings (S) are also a function of disposable income, i.e.:

$$S = f(Y_d)$$

Propensities to spend and save

Important concepts in the determination of economic activity may be derived from the relationships between consumer spending, savings and disposable income.

These are:

- the average propensity to consumer (apc);
- the average propensity to save (aps);
- the marginal propensity to consume (mpc);
- the marginal propensity to save (mps).

These concepts may be referred to in the context of both planned and actual expenditures.

The proportion of disposable income that goes towards consumer spending is referred to as the *average propensity to consume (apc)*. Similarly, the proportion of disposable income saved is known as the *average propensity to save (aps)*. In notation form:

Average propensity to consume

$$apc = \frac{\text{Total consumption expenditure}}{\text{Total disposable income}} = \frac{C}{Y_d}$$

Average propensity to save

$$aps = \frac{\text{Total savings}}{\text{Total disposable income}} = \frac{S}{Y_d}$$

By definition, the numerical values of the average propensities to consume and save must sum to 1, because household disposable income is either spent (consumed) or saved, i.e.:

$$apc + aps = 1$$

When total disposable income rises in an economy, and since consumer spending and savings are related to income, total consumer spending and savings will also increase. Similarly, when total disposable income falls, spending and savings will decline. The proportion of any *change* in disposable income which is spent on consumer goods and services is known as the *marginal propensity to consume (mpc)*, while that part of any change which is absorbed by extra savings is referred to as the *marginal propensity to save (mps)*. More formally:

Marginal propensity to consume

$$mpc = \frac{\text{Change in consumption expenditure}}{\text{Change in disposable income}} = \frac{\Delta C}{\Delta Y_d}$$

Marginal propensity to save

$$mps = \frac{\text{Change in savings}}{\text{Change in disposable income}} = \frac{\Delta S}{\Delta Y_d}$$

where Δ is a shorthand notation for 'a small change in' or increment.

Once again, since any change in household disposable income can only be used for consumption or savings, it follows that the numerical values of the marginal propensities to consume and save must sum to 1, i.e.:

$$mpc + mps = 1$$

An example might help to clarify the meaning of the terms *apc, aps, mpc* and *mps*. Suppose, for instance, that an individual household plans to spend 72 per cent of its weekly disposable income of $500 on consumer goods (i.e. C = $360) and save the rest (S = $140). If the household's disposable income now rises to $600, it might decide to spend $60 of the extra $100, saving the remainder of the additional disposable income. Initially, the *apc* was 0.72 (i.e. $360/$500) and the *aps* was 0.28 (i.e. $140/$500) but now the *apc* is 0.7 (i.e. $420/$600) and the *aps* is 0.3 (i.e. $180/$600). The *mpc* and *mps* can also be calculated. The *mpc* is 0.6 (= $60/$100) and the *mps* 0.4 (= $40/$100).

This example illustrates a tendency that, as disposable incomes rise, people tend to save a larger proportion of any increase in income. In other words, the *mpc,* and therefore the *apc,* tend to fall. By similar logic we can deduce that different income groups in society at any given time can be expected to have different propensities to consume and save. In general, we would expect richer social groups to save a larger percentage of any increase in disposable income than poorer groups.

As mentioned earlier, the magnitudes of the propensities to consume and save will, of course, be influenced over time by a whole range of factors, such as changes in the distribution of income (the impact of taxes and state welfare payments), the cost and availability of credit, interest paid on savings, and the age distribution of the population (the young and the retired tend to spend a larger proportion of their incomes on consumption, whereas middle-aged people usually have a relatively higher propensity to save). Note that some rich economies, such as the US, have relatively low domestic savings rates as a percentage of national income, underlining that propensities to consume and save are affected by a large number of economic and social variables and not simply the level of income.

Many economists question whether consumption and savings are directly linked to current disposable incomes. Planned consumer spending and savings may not react immediately to changes in income. For instance, people may draw on past savings to maintain consumption when current disposable incomes fall, say in the early stages of an economic recession, particularly if they believe that their incomes will subsequently recover. This leads to the idea that consumption is dependent upon people's perceptions of their *permanent* incomes rather than their *current* disposable incomes. If this is the case, consumption may not react immediately to changes in income during cyclical fluctuations in economy activity. In economic upturns, planned consumption will tend to lag behind the rise in income, while in economic downturns, the growth rate of consumption will not fall as quickly as the fall in the growth rate of disposable incomes.

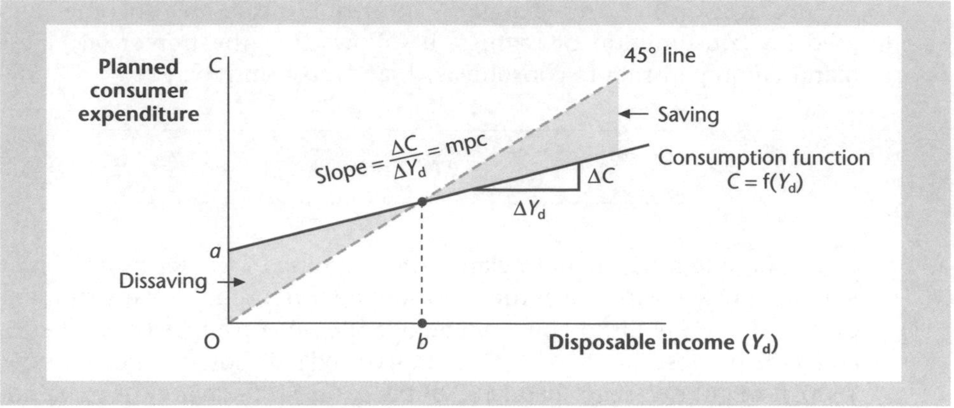

Figure 4.1 Consumption function

An alternative approach relates consumption to some perception of *lifetime* income. For example, a young trainee professional may spend at a relatively high rate anticipating a larger income later in his or her career. The exact nature of the relationship between consumption and current income continues to be researched. Nevertheless, current income is usually a significant influence on consumption. Hence, to assume that consumption is dependent simply upon current disposable income is satisfactory for the analysis of national income determination that we are developing in this chapter.

The relationship between total planned consumer spending and disposable income (measured in real, i.e. inflation-adjusted, terms) can be shown diagrammatically – see Figure 4.1. This relationship is commonly referred to as the *consumption function*. We are usually concerned with the consumption function for the entire economy, which is the aggregate of all the individual consumption functions in the economy.

It should be noted that, for simplicity, we have assumed that planned consumer spending for the entire economy has a *constant* relationship with total disposable income and is thus shown as a straight line (the *mpc* is therefore assumed to be constant, given by the slope of the consumption function). The height of the consumption function above the horizontal axis denotes the level of spending planned by consumers corresponding to different levels of disposable income.

Also note that, as drawn in Figure 4.1, planned spending is positive even when disposable income is zero, as shown by the positive intercept at *a* on the vertical axis. This reflects the fact that consumers may still decide to spend, financing consumption from past savings and loans. This level of planned consumption is referred to as *autonomous consumption*.

Figure 4.2 shows a 'mirror image' of the consumption function, namely the *saving function*. The distance O*a* in both Figures 4.1 and 4.2 is the same, of course, illustrating the level of *dissaving* when disposable income is zero.

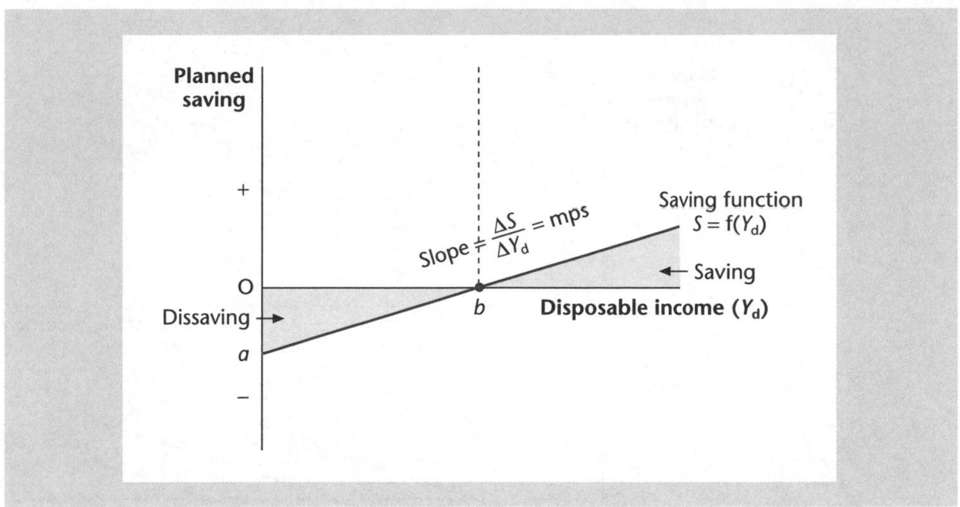

Figure 4.2 **Saving function**

Note that at point *b* in Figure 4.2, planned saving is zero reflecting equality between planned consumer expenditure and disposable income. At disposable income levels below point *b*, planned dissaving occurs, while above *b*, positive planned saving exists.

The level of planned saving and dissaving can also be identified on the consumption function diagram, Figure 4.1. Assuming the same scales on both axes of this diagram, a line drawn at 45° from the origin (O) will show all the points at which disposable income and planned consumer expenditure are equal (i.e. no planned saving or dissaving occurs). This line of equality is shown as a dotted line in Figure 4.1. With the consumption function as drawn, the only point at which $C = Y_d$ is where the consumption function crosses the 45° line, i.e. at disposable income level *b*. Hence, the areas shaded to the left and right of this intersection denote planned dissaving and planned saving respectively.

Movements along and shifts in consumption and saving functions

Changes in disposable income (in real terms) will lead to changes in planned consumer expenditure and saving – resulting in movements *along* the *C* and *S* functions in Figures 4.1 and 4.2, respectively. By contrast, changes in other factors that might impact on *C* and *S*, such as changes in borrowing costs, wealth effects, future income expectations, consumer confidence, etc., will cause *shifts* in the *C* and *S* functions. The term 'wealth effects' is a catch-all phrase relating to savings and investments of individuals. For example, stock market booms and slumps will lead to rises and falls in an individual's personal wealth with likely consequent effects on their plans to spend and save. Shifts in the *C* and *S* functions are illustrated in Figure 4.3.

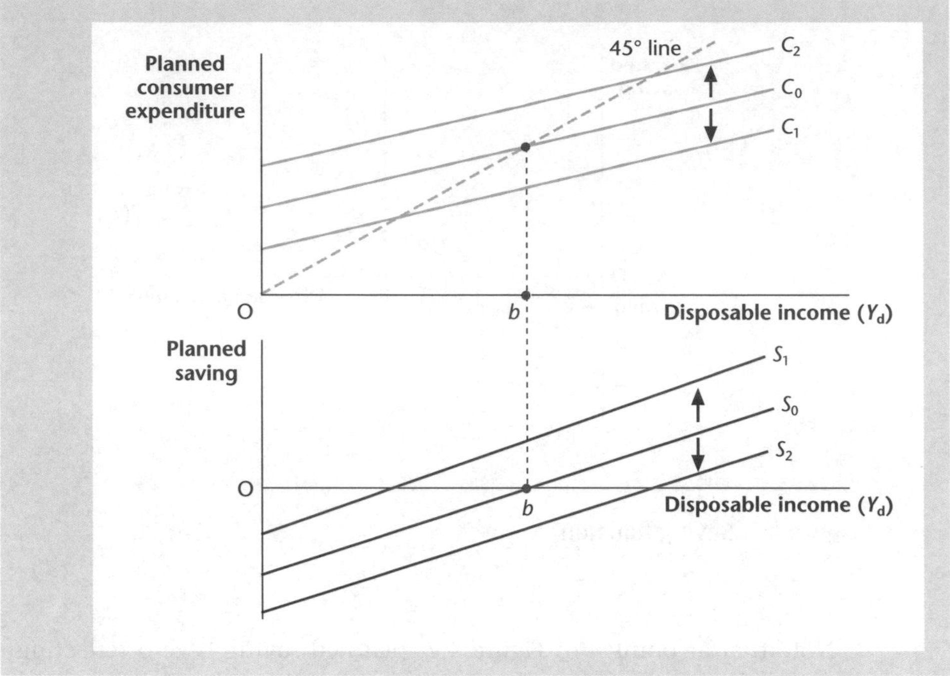

Figure 4.3 Shifts in consumption and saving functions

When the level of (real) interest rate rises, for example, and saving becomes more attractive and borrowing for consumer spending becomes less attractive at any given level of disposable income, the result is an upward shift in the saving function from S_o to S_1 and a downward shift in the consumption function from C_o to C_1. Likewise, a surge in stock market valuations can be expected to shift upwards the consumption function from C_0 to C_2, leading to a corresponding downward shift in the saving function from S_0 to S_2.

So far, we have discussed planned consumer spending (and saving) as a function of (real) disposable income (Y_d). However, it will be appreciated that disposable income changes when either real GDP alters or when personal taxes and welfare payments change. Assuming that in the short-term taxes paid and government welfare payments received are fixed, C and S are then *directly* determined by real GDP (i.e. the level of real national income, Y). In the remainder of this chapter, and indeed for much of this book, we use this relationship between planned spending and real GDP to develop our analyses of the determination of economic activity.

Investment expenditure

Investment expenditure is another major component of aggregate expenditure. By the term 'investment' in the context of the determination of economic activity, economists mean capital expenditure on the purchase of physical assets such as plant, machinery and equipment (referred to as *fixed investment*) and stocks (referred to as *inventory investment*). Physical investment expenditure creates *new* assets thereby adding to the country's capital stock and hence its production capacity. The term 'investment' is also used in a financial context to describe the purchase and change in ownership of financial assets (e.g. shares, bank accounts). It is very important to understand that this is *not* the kind of investment referred to in this chapter, which is purely concerned with the creation of 'physical' capital.

The relationship between investment expenditure and national income (i.e. real GDP) is more complex than the relationship between consumption expenditure and national income. In practice, investment expenditure decisions by firms are likely to be dependent upon a host of factors such as interest rates, return on capital, the state of technology, the growth in consumer demand, taxation and investment incentives, business confidence and expectations, as well as the level of and changes in national income itself. Given this complexity, it does not seem unreasonable to argue, as many economists have done as a simplifying assumption, that investment (I) is largely *independent* of the level of national income. In Keynesian analysis of economic fluctuations, in particular, the emphasis tends to be more upon the effects on investment of changes in business confidence rather than on changes in national income, as such.

Distinction between autonomous and induced investment

- *Autonomous investment* refers to the level of investment expenditure that is not determined by the level of national income. Such investment is therefore independent of the level of economic activity, i.e. real GDP. This is also sometimes referred to as *exogenous investment*.
- *Induced investment* is the level of investment brought about by changes in the level of national income. This is alternatively known as *endogenous investment* because it is brought about by a change from *within* the model itself, i.e. a change in the level of economic activity (real GDP).

If planned investment is treated as being independent of national income levels then we can illustrate this by graphing the level of planned investment as a straight line parallel to the national income (real GDP) axis, as in Figure 4.4. The amount of planned investment, I, is determined by the other possible factors affecting investment already referred to, such as when any of these change, planned investments rises or falls, i.e. the investment line shifts up or down. Moreover, if we add the level of planned investment in the economy, I, to the consumption function as shown in Figure 4.1, we can derive a $C + I$ line, as also illustrated in Figure 4.4.

Government spending

The third component of aggregate planned expenditure is planned government expenditure, denoted by G. This represents the current spending and capital

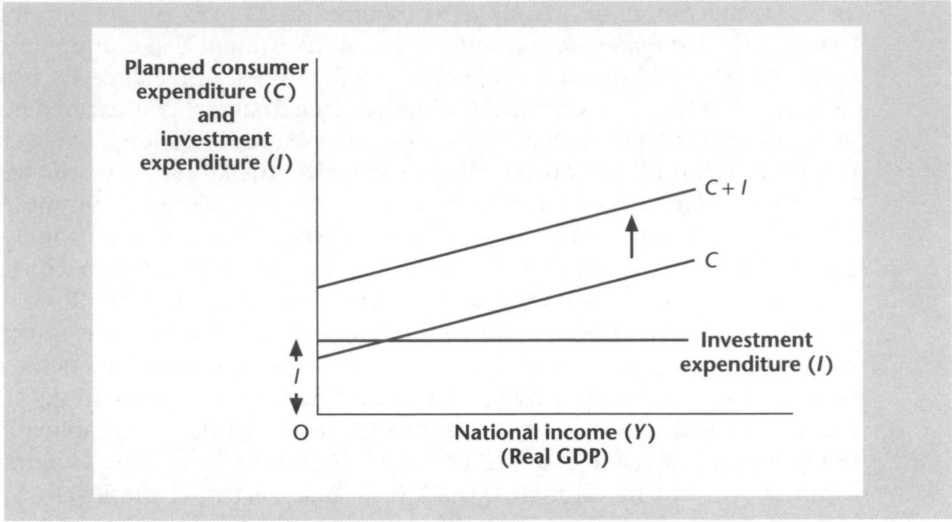

Figure 4.4 Consumer spending and investment

spending (i.e. investment) by central and local government on the provision of *social* goods and services, such as health, roads, education and defence, and marketed goods and services, including, for example, state postal services and the output of other state industries. It should be noted that in the context of the circular flow of income model (Chapter 3) and the approach to the determination of economic activity being developed in this chapter, transfer payments by government (i.e. unemployment benefits, state pensions and other welfare payments) are excluded from the government expenditure component because such transfer payments are not made in return for productive services – no addition to total output arises. Transfer payments merely move taxation receipts from one household to another.

Government current and capital spending, like firms' investment, is affected by many factors – in this case political and social as well as economic. As with firms' investment expenditure, therefore, it is difficult to predict a stable and reliable relationship between national income (real GDP) and planned government expenditure. For example, the planned introduction of a new road-building or school-building programme is much more likely to be influenced by expected traffic density and the numbers of schoolchildren than national income. In addition, short-term changes in government expenditure may be difficult to achieve because of political constraints on altering spending plans and administrative timescales. It is not clear either what will happen to government spending when national income fluctuates. On the one hand, when the national income falls, governments might attempt to rein back their spending so as to avoid a rise in the tax burden. On the other hand, economic recessions lead to higher unemployment and more social deprivation, which tend to increase public spending.

Given the uncertainty about how government spending will change as national income changes, we shall assume that G, like firms' investment expenditure, is

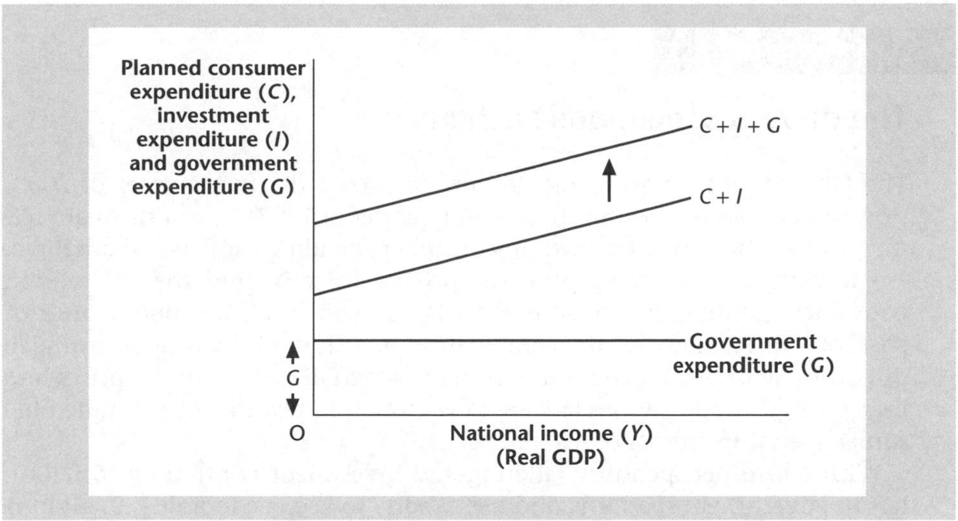

Figure 4.5 Consumer spending, investment and government expenditure

independent of national income or *autonomous*. It is therefore shown as a horizontal line in Figure 4.5, with G representing the total value of planned government spending. Should planned government expenditure rise or fall for whatever reason, unrelated to a change in real GDP, this will be reflected in the diagram by a parallel shift upwards or downwards in the line, respectively. Moreover, adding G to C and I gives the line $C + I + G$ in Figure 4.5.

Expenditure on exports and imports

We can now complete our analysis of aggregate planned expenditure by adding the difference between planned expenditure on exports (X) and imports (M) to $C + I + G$. When foreigners buy our exports, take holidays in our country or travel using our national airline, for example, the amount remitted to our economy becomes part of the total demand for our goods and services. Similarly, when we buy foreign goods, take holidays abroad and use foreign airlines income leaks out of our circular flow of income (in the way explained in Chapter 3) and is lost to our economy (except that these funds in turn permit people in other countries to buy our exports). In the same way, any flows of funds into the country for investment purposes, including investments in stocks and shares, bank accounts and more tangible investments such as the building of new offices and factories, add to demand here by boosting consumption (C) and investment (I). In contrast, when residents of our economy invest overseas this takes funds out of the country, thereby adding to demand abroad but reducing it here.

We shall assume for convenience that X and M, like I and G, are independent of national income – although this is a gross simplification. Planned expenditure on exports of goods and services are usually more related to the level of incomes in export markets than domestic national income, but increasing demand at home

Application 4.1

The drivers of economic activity

The UK economy grew by just 0.1 per cent over the first quarter of 2003, the slowest pace of growth since the second quarter of 1992. One of the main reasons for this was the weakest growth in consumer spending for five-and-a-half years.

The consumer has long been the driving force behind the UK economy – consumer spending has outstripped GDP growth in all but one quarter of the past four years. However the combination of a slump in consumer confidence – caused by worries over the war with Iraq, uncertainty over house prices and the impending tax rise – and relatively slow growth in real incomes, resulted in consumer spending growth of just 0.2 per cent.

With consumer spending faltering and investment continuing to fall, it was left to government spending and net exports to keep economic growth in positive territory for a forty-third successive quarter. Government spending rose by 2.5 per cent over the first quarter, following a sharp increase in military expenditure, while net exports made a significant positive contribution to growth. The Gfk Consumer Confidence indicator has shown signs of recovery following the end of the war, averaging –3 over the second quarter compared with –7 in the first quarter, but it remains well below the levels of last year. Similarly the CBI Distributive Trades Survey has reported a slight pickup in retail sales growth since the start of the year, but the CMI/Grant Thornton Service Sector Index for May reported that consumer services firms experienced the fastest quarterly decline in business volumes for a year.

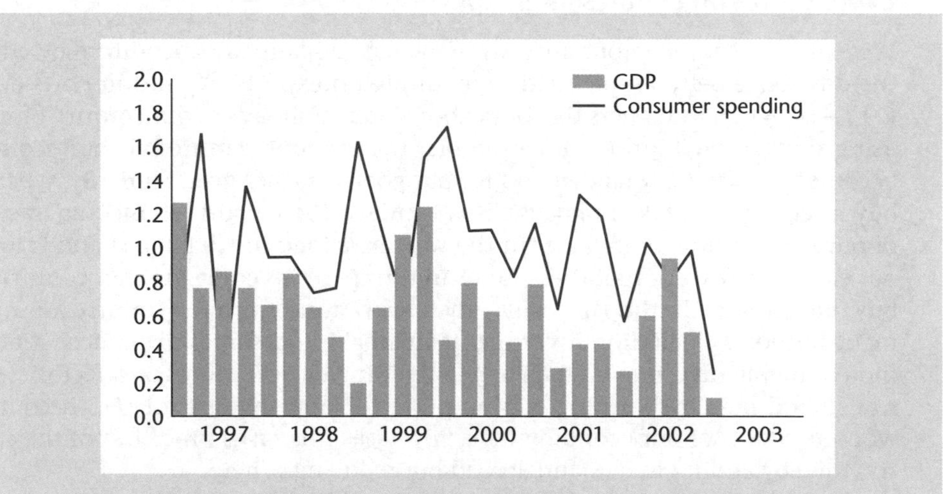

GDP and consumer spending (three-month percentages)

Source: Office of National Statistics

Application 4.1 continued

The manufacturing sector has shown no signs of a pickup. Official data for April and May show manufacturing output 0.2 per cent down on January and February. Survey evidence has not signalled any turnaround in capital expenditure either and official data have shown the goods trade deficit widening in May. Hence the economy is again set to rely on strong government spending to achieve growth in the second quarter.

A pickup in growth in the second half of the year is largely reliant on the USA leading a recovery in global demand. US bond yields have remained low which, in combination with continued loosening of monetary policy, is allowing firms and consumers to refinance cheaply. In conjunction with tax cuts, equivalent to over 0.5 per cent of US GDP growth this year, this should underpin growth. However as Alan Greenspan recently remarked, 'businesses focused on strengthening their balance sheets and [have been] reluctant to ramp up their hiring and spending' despite progressive loosening of monetary policy in recent years. Therefore a strong US pickup is by no means certain.

Source: Edited extract from CBI *Economic Bulletin*, July/August 2003.

Activity

On the basis of the above analysis, discuss the factors that are driving economic growth upwards and those that are inhibiting growth. Explain the relationship between the different economic variables you identify as being important.

may lead to potential exports being diverted to the home market, producing an inverse relationship between domestic national income and exports. Turning to planned expenditure on imports, we tend to buy more imported goods and services as our incomes rise. In general, although exports and imports may be affected by changes in national income, the precise relationship is quite complex. Rather than pursue this further we shall assume that X and M are independent of national income. Once again, such a simplifying assumption allows us to make progress without detracting seriously from the economic significance of the discussion.

The difference between X and M can be positive or negative depending upon whether the value of planned exports is greater or less than the value of planned imports. Assuming that it is positive, adding $X - M$ to C, I and G gives the aggregate schedule, denoted AE, as shown in Figure 4.6. The result illustrates the relationship between total planned expenditure in the economy and real GDP (i.e. national income). In this figure the vertical distance between the lines $C + I + G$ (as derived above) and $C + I + G + (X - M)$ represents the net value of exports and imports. Therefore, if planned expenditure on imports was greater than planned expenditure on exports, the $C + I + G + (X - M)$ line would lie below the $C + I + G$ line.

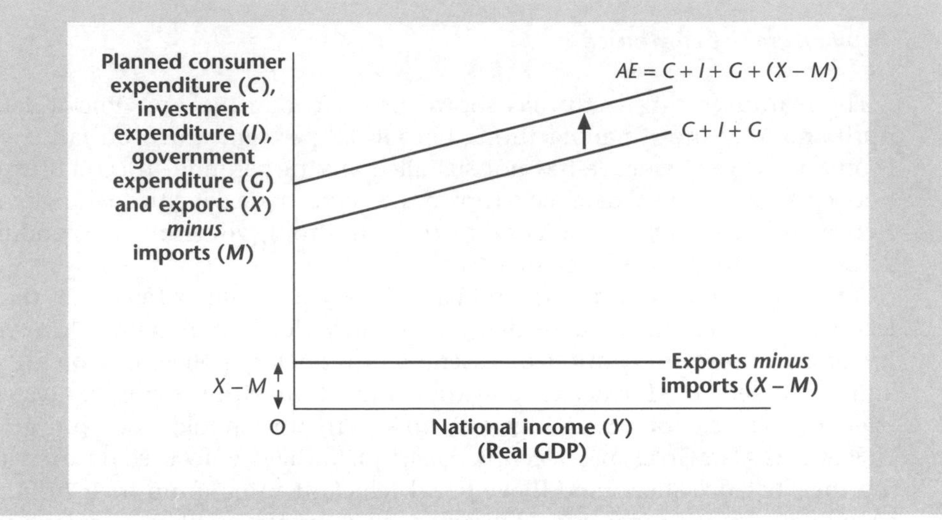

Figure 4.6 Aggregate planned expenditure schedule

Determination of equilibrium national income

Having considered each category of aggregate planned expenditure and its relationship to real GDP, we can now develop the analysis further and, in particular, look at the circumstances in which an equilibrium national income equates with unemployment or inflation. It will be recalled from the above discussion, and Chapter 3, that equilibrium in an economy exists when aggregate planned expenditure in the economy equals total output so that there are no forces making for a change in the level of national income. We have shown that aggregate planned expenditure (AE) is given by $C + I + G + (X - M)$. Therefore, as the condition of equilibrium expenditure we can write:

Equilibrium expenditure

$$Y = AE = C + I + G + (X - M)$$

If values of Y and AE are graphed together, then the locus of all possible equilibrium expenditure positions of the economy will be shown along the 45° line of Figure 4.7 (assuming the same scales are used on both axes). In other words, any point along this 45° line represents an equality between the level of national income (which is the same as real GDP or aggregate supply) and the level of aggregate planned expenditure.

Superimposing the aggregate planned expenditure schedule (AE) in Figure 4.6 onto this diagram allows us to identify what level of equilibrium activity in

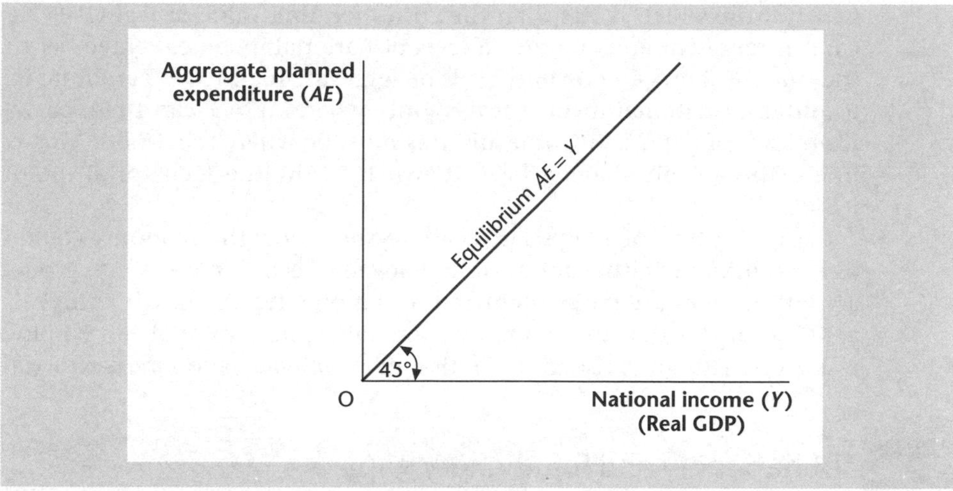

Figure 4.7 The line of equilibrium (45° line)

the economy will exist at any particular point in time. An example is given in Figure 4.8, where the equilibrium level of national income is Y_e. This is the only level of national income equal to aggregate planned expenditure so that the economy is in equilibrium. Other levels of aggregate planned expenditure would lead to a rise or fall in national income and therefore a fall in output.

For example, point *A* on the *AE* line in Figure 4.8 indicates a level of aggregate planned expenditure greater than national income (real GDP) and is therefore not an equilibrium point. Similarly, point *B* indicates an aggregate planned

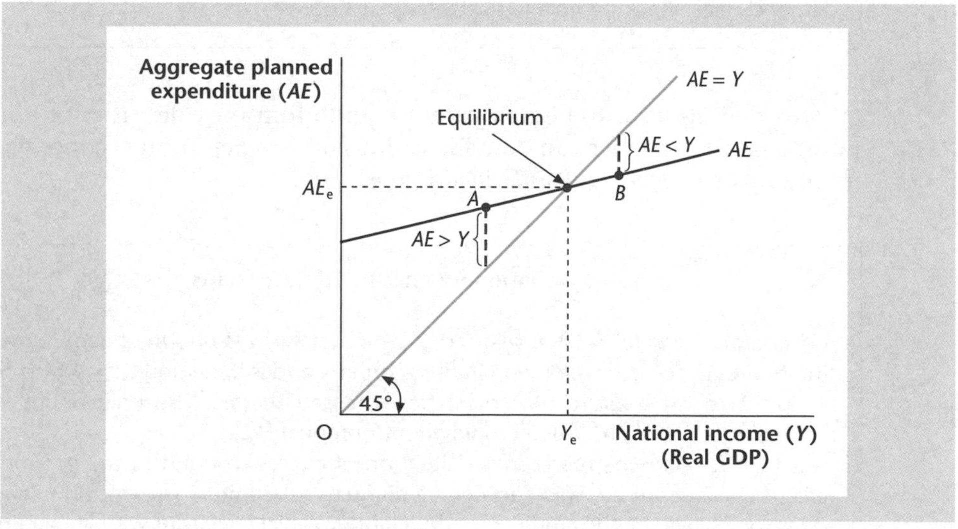

Figure 4.8 Aggregate planned expenditure and equilibrium level of national income

expenditure which is less than the corresponding value of real GDP. Again, this cannot represent an equilibrium level of national income. Remember that while the line *AE* shows all possible levels of aggregate planned expenditure in relation to different national income levels, only where $AE = Y$ can there be an equilibrium level of national income and this must be where the *AE* line crosses the 45° line – the 45° line having been drawn to show the locus of all points where $AE = Y$.

Using this type of analysis it is easy to show how the economy could be stable or in equilibrium either at low or high levels of economic activity. Low economic activity implies unemployment of the nation's resources, while high economic activity implies that the economy is operating near to or at full employment of resources. This gives rise to the notion of *deflationary* and *inflationary gaps*.

Deflationary and inflationary gaps

It is important to appreciate from the analysis above that the equilibrium level of national income (Y_e) is not necessarily the level of income (i.e. economic activity) at which all resources (factors of production) are fully utilised. In other words, Y_e in Figure 4.8 is not necessarily associated with a position of *full employment* (which we shall denote as Y_{fe}). An equilibrium level of national income can occur at *any* level of economic activity.

Full employment equilibrium

A *full employment equilibrium* is a special case where aggregate planned expenditure exactly coincides with the economy's productive capacity (i.e. potential GDP), with no demand deficiency and no excess demand arising.

This definition of full employment equilibrium provides us with a reference point against which we can describe various other states of the economy, namely involving *deflationary and inflationary gaps*.

Deflationary and inflationary gaps

A *deflationary gap* (also often referred to as a *capacity gap* or *output gap*) represents a situation of deficiency in demand in the economy and is the amount by which aggregate planned expenditure (*AE*) must be increased to raise the equilibrium level of national income (Y_e) to its full employment potential (Y_{fe}).

An *inflationary gap* represents a situation of excess demand in the economy and reflects the amount by which aggregate planned expenditure (*AE*) must be *reduced* in order to achieve the full employment equilibrium level of output with stable prices.

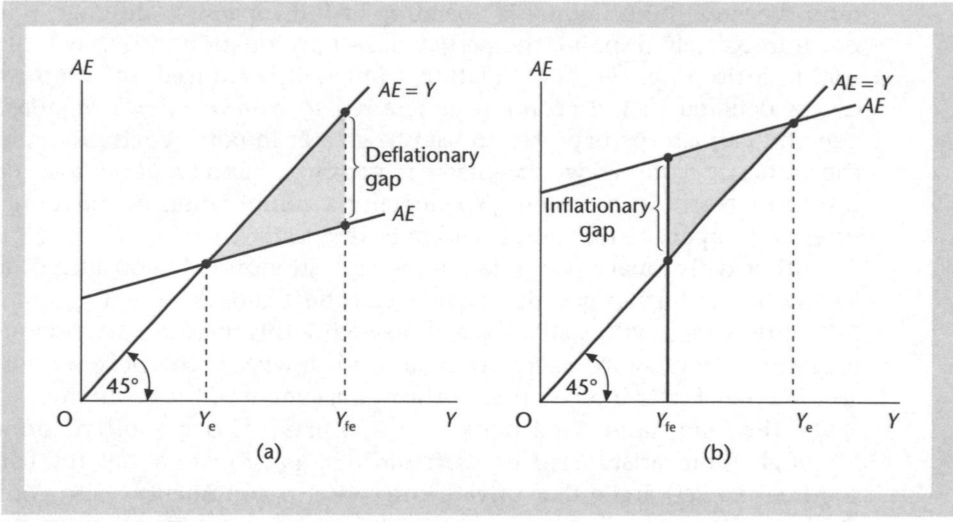

Figure 4.9 Deflationary and inflationary gaps

Both of these situations are shown in Figure 4.9. In the case of Figure 4.9(a), the equilibrium level of national income is Y_e. Aggregate planned expenditure is less than the country's potential output (Y_{fe}) if all resources were fully employed. The economy is therefore suffering from unemployment or underutilisation of people and other resources because of a deficiency in demand. While in the short-term all prices are fixed (as discussed earlier), the persistence of a deflationary gap is likely to lead, eventually, to a fall in prices, i.e. to *deflation*. (Note that the term deflationary gap, as explained here, represents a situation of demand deficiency which *may* lead to falling prices, while deflation refers to an *actual* fall in prices.)

The deflationary gap is similar to that which faced many Western economies in the early 1930s and which so influenced Keynes when he put forward his theory on the cause of general unemployment and the so-called Great Depression. According to Keynes, the problem lay with insufficient aggregate expenditure to generate enough economic activity to provide full employment. In other words, economies were suffering from a deflationary gap between the existing level of aggregate planned expenditure and the full employment supply of goods and services (Y_e was less than Y_{fe}). His policy prescription at that time, therefore, was that economies should 'spend, spend, spend' their way out of recession. As it would prove difficult to encourage the private sector, both households and firms, to spend at a time of economic recession, it was proposed that the lead should be taken by the government – hence the growth in significance of fiscal policy as a demand management tool after 1945 (see p.67).

In the case of Figure 4.9 (b), the equilibrium national income (Y_e) is to the right of the full employment level (Y_{fe}). That is to say, the required level of aggregate planned expenditure exceeds the value of output that is possible to achieve at full employment with stable prices. Since output cannot be increased in the short term (because the economy is operating at full capacity), although prices may not immediately respond, the persistence of an inflationary gap will ultimately lead to a rise in prices – i.e. inflation – unless it is reduced. Inflation caused by excess demand in the economy is referred to as *demand-pull inflation*. Excess demand can also be expected to lead to greater import penetration, given that the domestic economy will be unable to satisfy demand for goods and services in the short term. An economy experiencing a combination of inflationary pressures and import penetration is said to be *overheating*.

Neither deflationary nor inflationary gaps are normally considered desirable, so an obvious further question is: how can these gaps be closed so as to achieve full employment with stable prices? Answering this question arguably raises the biggest controversy in macroeconomics today: what is the necessary or acceptable degree of state intervention in the management of the economy?

On the one hand, free market economists (who are often monetarists, although monetarists need not *necessarily* be passionate about the benefits of the free market) argue that private enterprise in conjunction with competitive markets will eventually restore an equilibrium level of national income with full employment and low or zero inflation. The free market is self-regulating, therefore state intervention is at best unnecessary and at worst hampers the operation of market forces. On the other hand, Keynesians (incidentally along with other groups, notably Marxist economists, whose views are not explored in this book) dispute that the market economy can be relied upon to adjust to full employment with stable prices. Either the process will not occur at all or, if it does, it will take too long and have unacceptable economic, social and political consequences. Writing at a time of protracted unemployment, Keynes dismissed the idea of waiting for market adjustments, observing succinctly, 'In the long run we are all dead.'

Adopting a Keynesian stance (we consider monetarist and free market views in more detail in Chapters 9 and 18), if free market forces are not capable of regulating the level of economic activity, then there is a case for state intervention. This leads to a subsidiary question concerning how governments might attempt to influence economic activity in order to close deflationary and inflationary gaps in aggregate planned expenditure. In other words, how can aggregate expenditure be changed in an economy to reverse deflationary pressures or to squeeze out inflation?

Keynesian economists assign the responsibility for managing aggregate spending to government, using *fiscal policy* measures especially, which may involve either, or both, of the following:

- Changes in personal and corporate taxation to influence consumer spending and business investment expenditure plans and therefore aggregate expenditure.
- Direct changes in government spending plans, again to influence aggregate expenditure.

In addition to using fiscal policy to influence consumer spending and to change government spending plans, other possibilities recognised by Keynesians involve affecting the level of private sector investment other than through tax changes, as well as measures affecting the flow of exports and imports. For example, various governments around the world under the influence of Keynesian precepts have at different times introduced investment incentives, changed interest rates in a countercyclical fashion, offered export inducements, and have resorted to import controls of various kinds to limit spending on imports. Such attempts by governments to moderate economic activity in a Keynesian fashion have been commonly referred to as either 'stop-go' or economy 'fine-tuning' policies.

Keynesian economists stress that initial changes in investment expenditure, government expenditure and expenditure on exports and imports have a multiple impact upon changes in national income (and thus real GDP) and that this effect can be broadly estimated. This gives rise to one of the most important concepts in Keynesian macroeconomic analysis with regard to the measurement of the impact of changes in aggregate expenditure, namely the *national income multiplier*.

Multiplier effects

Changes in any of the components of aggregated planned expenditure will have an effect on the equilibrium level of national income (Y_e). For example, a change in any of the *injections* into or *leakages* from the circular flow of income will bring about a change in the level of economic activity. As we have already discussed (see p.56), injections refer to either government spending (G), investment spending (I) or expenditure on exports (X), which *add* to the circular flow of income; while leakages refer to taxation (T), savings (S) or expenditure on imports (M), which *reduce* the amount of income circulating around the economy.

Let us consider a change in one of the injections. For example, if the government decided to raise its level of expenditure then, by definition, aggregate planned expenditure in the economy would increase, as shown in Figure 4.10. The increase in G is depicted as a vertical movement in aggregate planned expenditure from AE_1 to AE_2. Therefore, an initial increase in government expenditure has given rise to a new equilibrium level of national income Y_e^*. It is important to notice, however, that the initial increase in government expenditure is less than the consequent increase in national income ($\Delta G < \Delta Y$). This is a fundamental argument of Keynesian analysis. In general, an initial increase in aggregate expenditure leads to a larger total increase in national income. The extent to which Y changes as a result of a change in an injection or leakage is measured by the *multiplier effect*.

Definition of the multiplier effect

The *multiplier effect* is defined as the ratio of the resultant change in national income with respect to the initial change in injections or leakages.

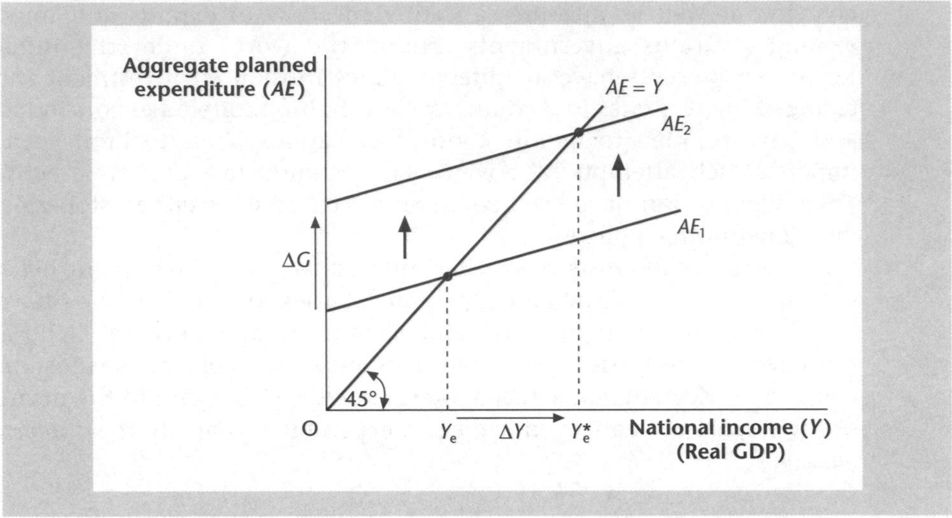

Figure 4.10 Impact of increasing government expenditure on aggregate expenditure

This gives rise to measures such as the *government expenditure multiplier* ($\Delta Y/\Delta G$), *investment expenditure multiplier* ($\Delta Y/\Delta I$) and the *export multiplier* ($\Delta Y/\Delta X$), where, as before, Δ means 'change in' or increment. Similarly, we can measure the multiplier effects of changes in any of the leakages, i.e. $\Delta Y/\Delta T$, $\Delta Y/\Delta S$ and $\Delta Y/\Delta M$. In more general terms:

Calculating the size of the multiplier

$$\text{Size of the multiplier} = \frac{\text{Change in national income}}{\text{Initial change in aggregate expenditure}}$$

From Figure 4.10, it should be clear that the value of the multiplier is dependent upon the slope of the aggregate expenditure (*AE*) line. In our example, this slope is equal to the marginal propensity to consume (*mpc*) since the other components of aggregate expenditure (*G*, *I* and *X* – *M*) have been assumed to be unrelated to national income (as discussed earlier in the chapter). To discover how the value of the multiplier is derived, let us take a simple case in which the only leakage from the circular flow of income is saving – that is, all income is either spent (consumed) or saved. Thus, it follows directly that for any change in national income:

$$mpc + mps = 1$$

In this simple case, therefore, the impact of any change in aggregate planned expenditure will depend upon the size of the leakages from the circular flow of income in the form of savings. That is, the multiplier will depend upon the *mps* and may be measured as follows:

Simple case: leakage due to savings

$$\text{Multiplier} = \frac{1}{mps} = \frac{1}{(1 - mpc)} \quad \text{since } mpc + mps = 1$$

The above case is, clearly, a gross (but useful) simplification of reality. In addition to savings, the other two leakages from the circular flow (taxation and expenditure on imports) generally affect the size of the multiplier. To understand this, consider what happens as a result of an increase in investment expenditure (*I*) by firms. This will increase the level of national income (output or real GDP) which, in turn, will stimulate consumer spending (*C*). But part of the increase in *I* and *C* will be spent on imported goods and services, not domestically produced goods and services. Thus, the larger the marginal propensity to import, the smaller is the final change in the level of domestic economic activity resulting from an injection into the circular flow.

Similarly, income taxes also reduce the size of the multiplier effect. As before, assume there has been an injection into the economy due to an increase in *I*, resulting in an initial higher level of national income. If income taxes are raised, disposable income will rise by less than gross income and hence *C* will rise by less than it would have done if taxes had not changed. The larger the marginal rate of tax, the smaller the change in disposable income and real GDP arising from an injection into the circular flow.

In reality, therefore, the marginal propensity to save combined with the marginal rate of tax (*mrt*) and the marginal propensity to import (*mpm*) determine the size of the multiplier. Thus, in the more general case, we can define the multiplier as follows:

General case: leakage due to savings, taxes and imports

$$\text{Multiplier} = \frac{1}{\text{total leakage}}$$

where the total leakage is composed of:

mps = the marginal propensity to save, $\Delta S/\Delta Y_d$;
mrt = the marginal rate of tax, $\Delta T/\Delta Y$;
mpm = the marginal propensity to import, $\Delta M/\Delta Y_d$;
Y_d = disposable income (i.e. after tax).

With reference to the aggregate expenditure schedule, *AE*, shown in the figures above, this expression is equivalent to 1/(1 – slope of *AE* line).

A 'demultiplier' effect will also arise when we have a reduction in any of the injections I, G and X. A reduction in aggregate planned expenditure will lead to a multiplied reduction in national income, based on the analysis as set out above.

Recalling the circular flow of income model, summarised diagrammatically in Figure 3.4 of Chapter 3, we can visualise an initial addition to aggregate expenditure going around the economy – but as it does so some of the additional spending is lost to the circular flow because it leaks out through savings, expenditure on imported goods and services, and to the government in the form of taxation. In other words, the amount of extra spending circulating around the economy for a second time is smaller (than that which was injected initially) and by the amount which leaked out in the first round. Similarly, the amount circulating in the third round is less than that which circulated in the second, by the amount which leaked out in the second round, and so on. Therefore, the amount of additional expenditure circulating around the economy declines continuously until it becomes negligible. If we add up the amount of extra expenditure and income generated in each round we would find that it is a multiple of the initial injection – this multiple being smaller the larger the leakages from the circular flow in the form of savings, spending on imports and taxation. The total increase in income in relation to the initial increase in expenditure is the multiplier. So that, for instance, if national income rises in total by an amount that is twice the initial increase in expenditure then the multiplier has a value of two.

The multiplier effect is often likened to throwing a stone into the centre of a lake, causing ripples which spread throughout the water. Figure 4.11 depicts this ripple effect in the context of the multiplier process.

Consider the impact of a \$1bn public works road building programme announced by government. For simplicity, assume that we are dealing with a closed economy (i.e. one with no foreign trade and therefore no leakage effect due to imports) and that there are no taxes (an extreme situation, one we might consider to be nirvana!). The only leakage from the circular flow arises from savings – the marginal propensity to save, *mps*, which we shall assume is 10 per cent. The expenditure of \$1bn by the government will, initially, raise the level of national income, Y, by \$1bn. But only 90 per cent of this increase will be spent subsequently since there will be a leakage of 10 per cent from the circular flow in the form of savings. Thus, \$900m of extra spending will arise, increasing the level of national income by a further \$900m. As national income rises, there will be a further stimulus to spending, again leading to a rise of AE (and Y) by 90 per cent of \$900m (i.e. \$810m).

This process will continue with each subsequent stimulus to the level of aggregate expenditure and economic activity being smaller than the previous one. In principle, the total rise in national income resulting from the initial \$1bn injection will be \$10bn if the *mps* is 10 per cent. Thus:

$$\text{multiplier} = 1/mps = 1/0.10 = 10 \text{ times the initial injection}$$

The concept of a 'ripple' effect also gives rise to the notion of 'regional' as well as national multiplier effects, with the leakage of income into imports now

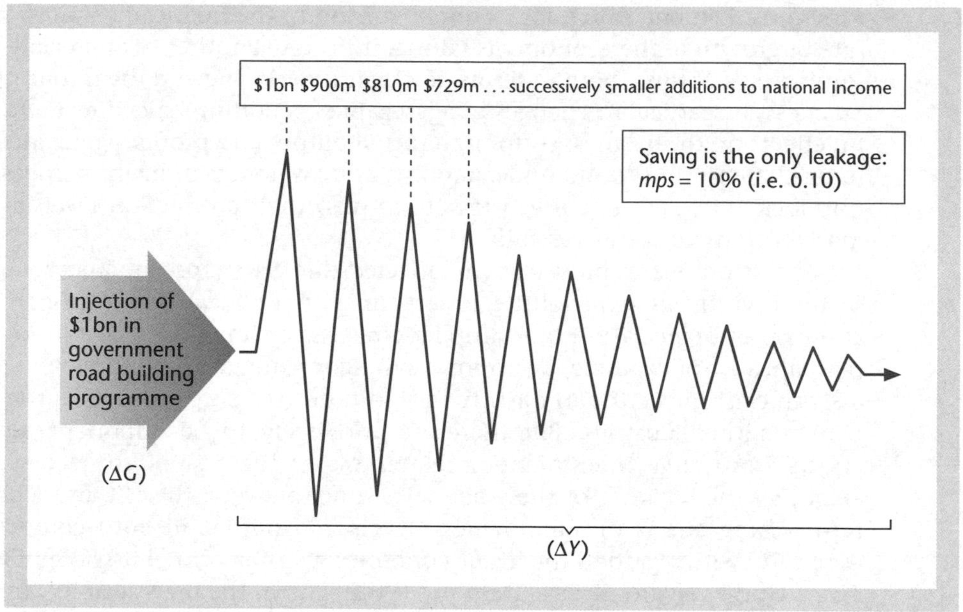

Figure 4.11 The multiplier process

defined as spending outside a particular geographic region of the economy in question. For example, a new government shipbuilding order would probably have its greatest impact upon the levels of income in the region in which the shipbuilding industry is based, especially in terms of increased employment and therefore expenditure in local shops and on local services. However, other regions further afield would also benefit from the new shipyard orders and the increased spending power of the shipyard workers, for example steel producing areas. The larger the spending on goods and services outside the shipbuilding region, the smaller the regional multiplier effect of the new shipbuilding order. Since 'imports' include all spending outside of the region, generally the smaller the regional economy, the smaller will be the multiplier. For this reason, *national* multiplier effects can be expected to be larger than regional multiplier effects, except where the term 'region' is used to cover a group of countries (e.g. the European Union).

Importance of the national income multiplier

The analysis so far may seem somewhat remote from the real world of business. Diagrams with 45° lines, consumption functions, equilibrium national incomes and national income multipliers are not part of the normal vocabulary of business; nor do they appear often in press reporting of economic events. However, they are important concepts if we are really to understand how an economy functions. It is one thing, for example, to read in the financial columns that the rate of growth of the economy is falling, it is quite another to appreciate the full significance of this – both in terms of why it is declining and the implications for business. In particular, changes in aggregate expenditure have direct and powerful effects on the business sector in terms of output and profits, aggravated by the multiplier effect. A sound understanding and awareness of likely changes in economic activity is essential if firms are to plan their production levels and their marketing strategies successfully.

In addition, many industries are affected directly by private and government sector investment expenditure programmes, both local and national. In this context, an appreciation of multiplier effects is of immense value in helping to plan ahead. For example, decisions by the government to build new roads have a significant impact upon directly related industrial sectors, such as the various construction industries. But there are also likely to be important additional effects from large investment programmes for the rest of the economy. For example, the building of the Channel Tunnel between the UK and France had far-reaching effects on employment levels and output in both countries, and especially with regard to the local economies near the tunnel itself. Similarly, the Three Gorges Hydro-Electric Dam project in China, the biggest of its kind in the world, will have far-reaching economic implications for China and surrounding countries for many years ahead.

Not only can businesses gain from an understanding of the multiplier process, it also provides a simple but useful quantitative guide for the government in assessing the impact of policy measures upon the economy. Government economic policies may even be directed at influencing the size of the multiplier itself, and hence aggregate expenditure, through effecting changes in the rate of taxation, the level of savings and the flow of imports.

Governments usually resort to demand management when the economy is in danger of 'overheating'; that is, when domestic spending exceeds the ability of the economy to supply goods and services, thereby aggravating inflation and attracting imports. Similarly, in the case of downturns in economic activity, the government may decide to intervene and stimulate aggregate spending to boost output. In both cases, in deciding by how much demand should be lowered or raised in order to reduce or increase national income to the desired level, account must be taken of the multiplier effects.

For example, if the government estimates that demand should decline by \$3bn to close an inflationary gap and hence to reduce inflationary pressures, and the multiplier effect of government spending is estimated accurately to be 2, then government spending needs only to be reduced by \$1.5bn for the target to be achieved. Indeed, if government spending was reduced by the full \$3bn and the multiplier remained at 2, the result would be a severe and unintended collapse in aggregate spending and national income of \$6bn. The result might well be an unintended deflationary gap leading to rising unemployment and recession.

Application 4.2

Business investment and the economy

Business investment plays a key role in economic wealth creation, but in the UK it grew by an average of just 1.7 per cent per annum between 1999–2001. Last year it fell by 8 per cent, the worst outturn since the recession in 1991. This decline could be viewed as a correction of overcapacity following the late 1990s boom that was driven by information technology and communications (ICT). The world economic slowdown, and the large fall in stock markets, led by ICT shares, have also contributed to the investment downturn.

However, business investment has fallen more sharply compared with other major economies, despite the UK having a better overall growth record. Why should this be? Much of the explanation lies with the decline in profitability and associated rise in the business cost and tax burden.

Addressing this issue, the Confederation of British Industries (CBI) recently unveiled a six-point plan for boosting investment, including measures to raise investment returns and reduce regulatory obstacles. The need for action is clear, as recent CBI survey evidence points to a further fall in business investment across a broad range of sectors over the next 12 months.

Source: CBI, *Economic Bulletin*, May 2003.

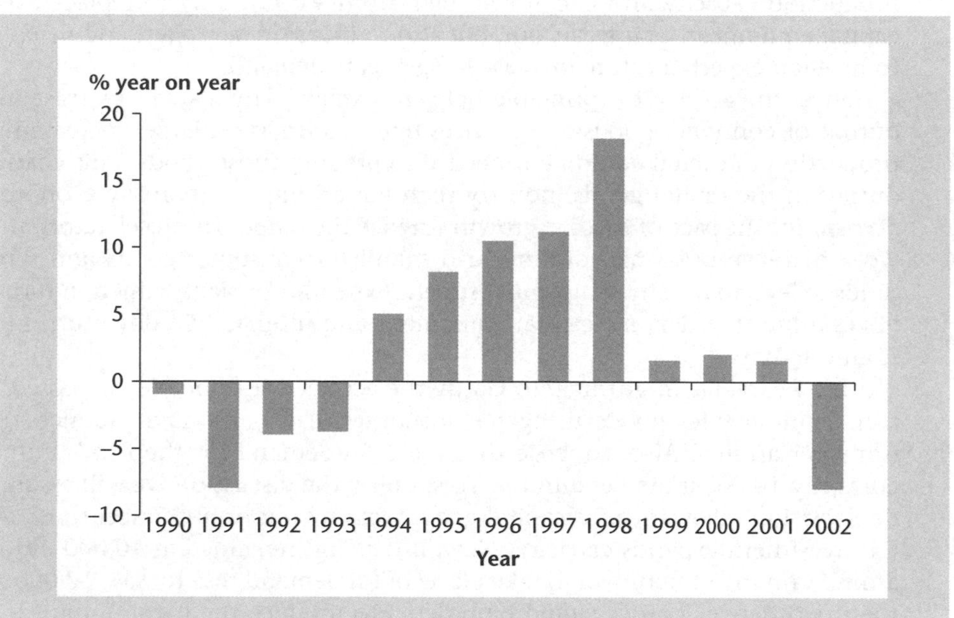

Business investment growth

Source: Office of National Statistics

Application 4.2 continued

Activity

Explain the economic circumstances under which business investment is likely to rise or fall. Research the sorts of measures that might raise investment returns.

The accelerator principle

The discussion set out in this chapter has been concerned with explaining why an increase (or decrease) in an injection into the circular flow of income will lead to an increase (or decrease) in the level of the national income. The final change in the level of economic activity will depend on the size of the corresponding multiplier effect, after allowing for leakages. But in the case of an increase in net investment expenditure (i.e. gross investment minus an allowance for depreciation or replacement investment), another important principle must be considered, referred to as the *accelerator principle*.

The *accelerator principle* relates to the relationship between the amount of net investment and the *rate of change* of national income, whereby a rapid rise in income (and thus consumer spending) will stimulate firms to increase existing production capacity and encourage them to invest not only to replace existing capital equipment, as it wears out, but also to invest in *new* plant and machinery to meet an expected future increase in aggregate demand.

Hence, the accelerator principle helps to explain why a small increase in the output of consumer goods and services tends to lead to a larger increase in the production of capital equipment needed to produce those goods. This change in output in the capital goods industry then has an impact upon the economy by *accelerating* the pace of income growth – hence the name. The accelerator can also work in reverse. A small decline in demand for consumer goods and services tends to lead to the shelving of investment expenditure plans, which in turn provokes a fall in orders for capital equipment and ultimately a downturn in economic activity.

A brief example might help to clarify the accelerator principle. Suppose that a firm manufactures goods using ten machines, each of which produces 1,000 units per annum. Also, suppose that the total demand for the firm's output is currently 10,000 units per annum. To simplify the discussion we will assume no depreciation (allowance for capital goods wearing out or obsolescent), therefore all investment expands capacity. Now, if demand remained at 10,000 units per annum, no investment would take place; but if demand rose to, say, 12,000 units then two new machines would be ordered to produce the extra output. If subsequently demand rose again, this time to 15,000 units, a further three machines would be purchased and so forth. Note that the 3,000 rise in demand represents a 25 per cent increase in the output of goods (i.e. from 12,000 to 15,000 units that year) while the purchase of an extra three machines amounts to a 50 per cent rise in the production of the machine manufacturing industry (i.e. from two to three machines that year). Hence the rise in consumer demand has caused an *accelerated* increase in the production of new machines. Equally, of course, if at some stage consumer demand ceased to grow, then the firm would cease investing and a small fall in consumer demand would trigger a much larger proportionate fall in the demand for machines. For example, if demand subsequently stagnated or if it shrank from 15,000 units in the above example, new investment that year would fall to zero.

This process by which investment jumps as consumer demand rises and then collapses when the growth in demand ends can be observed in all economies and makes the state of new orders for the engineering industry a good barometer of changes in the overall level of economic activity. Specifically, the accelerator principle highlights the following:

- Net investment by a firm will be maintained only if the demand for the firm's output *continues to rise at a steady rate*.
- Demand for consumer goods and services must increase *at an increasing rate* if net investment is to rise.
- When demand ceases to grow then *net* investment becomes zero.

In practice, the accelerator principle does not work quite so mechanically as set out above. In particular, investment decisions are also affected by business expectations: for example, businesses may continue to invest during a downturn in consumer demand if they feel it is temporary and that investment is necessary if they are to compete successfully in the future. Similarly, if a firm is working with excess capacity, an increase in consumer demand might be met out of this excess capacity rather than through new investment. Nevertheless, the accelerator effect operates in all economies to varying degrees and is important in understanding the causes of economic fluctuations. More particularly, the accelerator principle emphasises the interrelationships between output, consumer demand, investment and the business cycle. Since a change in consumer demand is largely dependent upon a change in national income (Y) from one time period to the next, and net investment (I) is affected by changes in consumer demand, the accelerator principle, in its most simple form, can be expressed as follows.

Accelerator principle

$$I = a\Delta Y$$

where:

I = current net investment expenditure or fixed capital investment
a = the accelerator effect, and
ΔY = the change in national income or output between the current and previous time period

In other words, the level of investment is related to changes in income over time by the accelerator process.

The combined effect of multiplier and accelerator forces working through an investment cycle was put forward by Keynes as an explanation for changes in the level of economic activity over time associated with business cycles. We shall be dealing with the topic of business cycles in more detail in Chapter 17, but for the remainder of this chapter we shall summarise the key aspects of the interaction of multiplier–accelerator principles and the business cycle.

If firms face an increase in actual demand (or even expected demand) that cannot be met from existing capacity, they will invest in more capital equipment. Since additional investment expenditure (I) is an injection into the circular flow of income, the level of national income (Y) will rise and by more than the initial increase in investment because of the multiplier effect. The rise in national income itself may stimulate a further rise in planned consumer expenditure, which leads to more planned investment expenditure through the accelerator process, and so on. The interrelationship between the accelerator and the multiplier effects in business cycles can be summarised as follows:

$$\underbrace{\Delta I \rightarrow \Delta Y}_{\text{Multiplier effect}} \underbrace{\rightarrow \Delta I}_{\text{Accelerator effect}} \underbrace{\rightarrow \Delta Y}_{\text{Multiplier effect}} \ldots \text{etc}$$

These interactions between multiplier and accelerator effects are the basis of *peaks* (*booms*) and *troughs* (*busts*) in economic activity, i.e. the primary explanation of the business cycle as shown in Figure 4.12 (for further details about business cycles, see Chapter 17).

An initial rise in investment expenditure leads to higher income through the multiplier effect. The rise in income in turn leads to more consumer demand and, through the accelerator effect, a further increase in the pace of investment expenditure, and so on. This process occurs in the recovery and boom phases of the business cycle. Similarly, during the recession and bust stages, a reduction in investment leads to a fall in incomes, less consumer demand, more cancelled investment programmes and so forth, with the multiplier and accelerator effects working in reverse. Together the multiplier and accelerator effects exaggerate the consequences for economic activity (real GDP) of any initial small changes in consumer demand.

Less obvious, perhaps, is why a boom, once it is underway, comes to an end or why, once an economy goes into a slump, the end result is not total economic collapse. The explanation relates to *turning points* in the business cycle. In a period of economic expansion economic bottlenecks eventually emerge, notably shortages of labour and certain labour skills, raw materials and perhaps energy. In addition, high investment may increase the cost of credit (interest rates). The overall effect is to drive up the costs of firms' inputs. The rise in costs in turn

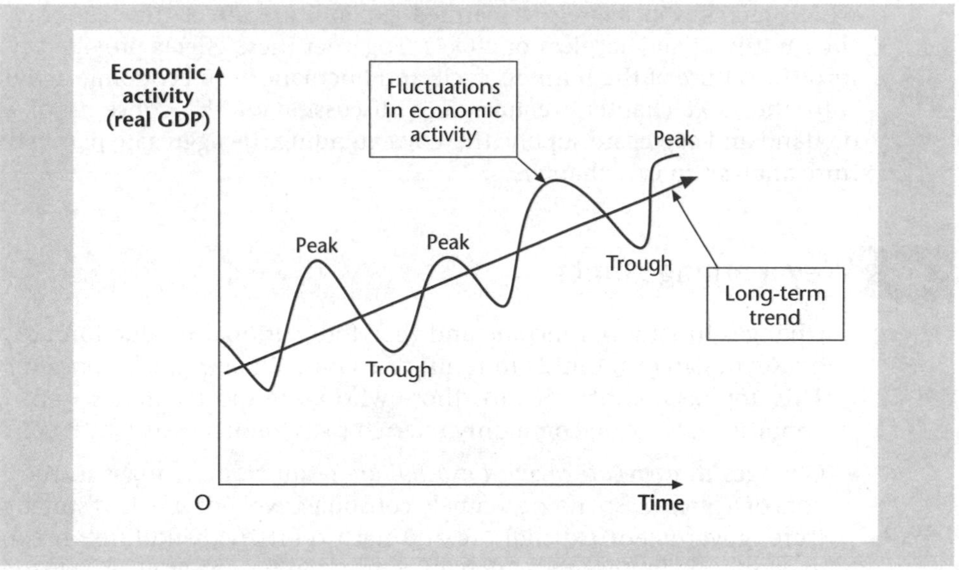

Figure 4.12 The business cycle

pushes up output prices (referred to as *cost-push inflation*) leading eventually to a fall in the rate of growth of demand for goods and services. Higher prices may also lead to government action to deflate demand through fiscal and monetary measures to prevent accelerating inflation. These deflationary pressures eventually affect demand in the economy, leading to a slowdown in planned investment expenditure.

A turning point also occurs when economies are in recession. Although businesses will initially cancel investments when trading activity slackens, it is very unlikely that investment will contract to zero. Some investment expenditure must occur if production is to continue at all over the longer term, if only to replace the existing stock of capital as it wears out (depreciates). Therefore, there will be a floor to the level of investment. In addition, after a period of economic contraction cost pressures, including the cost of capital (i.e. interest rates) and perhaps wage rates, tend to ease, leading to new business opportunities. Eventually the economic decline is reversed.

Concluding remarks

In this chapter we have considered both how an equilibrium level of national income is determined and the Keynesian notion of an equilibrium level of national income below or above the economy's full employment potential. We have looked, in particular, at the composition of aggregate expenditure and the effect of changes in aggregate planned expenditure on national income and therefore employment and inflation. Especially important is the process by which changes in aggregate planned expenditure affect the economy through the multiplier and accelerator effects. Together these effects provide key insights into the nature of the business cycle and fluctuations in economic activity.

In the next chapter we turn to a discussion of the concepts of aggregate demand and aggregate supply, thereby extending the aggregate planned expenditure analysis in this chapter.

✔ Key learning points

- Changes in national income and therefore national production are analysed by Keynesian economists in terms of changes in *aggregate planned expenditure*. This approach contrasts with those who place more emphasis on monetary conditions, who are commonly referred to as 'monetarists'.
- Changes in *aggregate planned expenditure* result from changes in the components of aggregate spending, namely consumer expenditure, investment expenditure, government expenditure and net exports (expenditure on exports less expenditure on imports, which, of course, can be a positive or negative figure).
- A *national income equilibrium* occurs when aggregate supply equals aggregate planned expenditure.
- *Consumer spending* or 'consumption' is a function of a number of factors including the current level of consumers' disposable income. Disposable income can either be spent or saved. It follows, therefore, that savings are also a function of income (in addition to possible other factors).
- The *average propensity to consume* (*apc*) equals total consumer expenditure divided by total disposable income. It is concerned with consumers' total consumption out of total income.
- The *marginal propensity to consume* (*mpc*) equals the change in consumer expenditure resulting from a change in income. It is therefore concerned with how consumer spending alters as income alters.
- The *average propensity to save* (*aps*) equals total saving divided by total disposable income. It is concerned with consumers' total savings out of total income.
- The *marginal propensity to save* (*mps*) equals the change in saving resulting from a change in income. It is therefore concerned with how household saving alters as income alters.
- *Planned* (*ex ante*) *consumption* and *planned* (*ex ante*) *saving* may be different to the actual (*ex post*) consumption and saving achieved.
- The *consumption function* shows the relationship between planned consumer spending and disposable income. Its slope is given by the marginal propensity to consume (*mpc*). Changes in disposable income lead to changes in planned consumption, as shown along the consumption function. Changes in other factors which impact on consumer spending such as *wealth effects* lead to a shift in the position of the consumption function.

- *Investment expenditure* is a product of *autonomous investment*, which is determined by factors other than the level of national income (e.g. interest rates, business confidence) and *induced investment*, which is investment brought about by changes in national income.
- *Government expenditure* is affected by many economic, political and social factors. It is therefore conventional to treat government expenditure as *autonomous* of changes in national income in introductory Keynesian analysis.
- *Expenditure on exports* is a function of foreign demand and therefore of incomes outside of the domestic economy. It is also affected by factors, such as exchange rates. *Expenditure on imports* is also affected by a number of factors, of which the level of domestic national income is but one. For convenience, we assume that exports and imports are autonomous of domestic national income, while recognising that this is a simplification.
- Changes in the levels of one or more of the components of aggregate expenditure will lead to a new national income equilibrium. The result can be a *full employment equilibrium, inflationary gaps* and *deflationary gaps*.
- A *full employment equilibrium* level of national income exists when planned expenditure exactly coincides with the economy's productive potential (i.e. potential GDP). There is, therefore, no excess demand or demand deficiency.
- An *inflationary gap* occurs when there is excess demand in the economy that cannot be met through higher production, the result over time is rising prices (inflation).
- A *deflationary gap* occurs when there is a deficiency in demand in the economy so that not all of the existing planned supply is bought. The result is economic deflation leading to higher unemployment, downward pressure on prices in the economy, and recession.
- Keynesian economists assign the responsibility for managing aggregate expenditure primarily to government *fiscal policy*. Government can affect the level of aggregate planned expenditure by altering its own spending and by changing taxation.
- Changes in expenditure (such as government expenditure) lead to *multiplier effects* on the level of national income. An initial injection of extra spending leads to a multiple change in the level of national income, depending upon the size of the leakages from the circular flow of income.
- A change in income leads to a larger percentage change in investment through what is known as the *accelerator effect*.
- The *multiplier–accelerator interactions* can help to explain the nature of *business cycles*.

? Topics for discussion

1. You read in your newspaper that economists predict a sharp rise in consumer spending. The current level of unemployment is historically low at 3 per cent. What advice would you give the government on the policies it should adopt?

2. The predicted sharp rise in consumer spending is attributed by economists to lower planned savings. In the last few weeks interest rates have fallen and consumer confidence to borrow and spend has risen. Using a consumption function diagram illustrate the expected effect.

3. Draw an appropriate diagram to show how a change in disposable income is likely to impact on aggregate planned expenditure.

4. Assume that the *apc* is 0.9 and the *mpc* is 0.8. The current level of a consumer's disposable income is $20,000, having risen from $19,000 in the past year due to lower government taxes. Calculate:

   (a) the total level of savings from the new level of income
   (b) the change in consumption that will result from the higher income now received.

5. The government plans to raise state spending by $2bn in the next fiscal year. Economists estimate that consumers will spend on average 80 per cent of any increase in income they receive after tax and that the marginal propensity to import is 0.25. The government's marginal tax rate is 30 per cent. The government argues that this increase in spending will be sufficient to remove a deflationary gap in the economy, estimated as equivalent to a deficiency in aggregate expenditure of $4bn.

   (a) Calculate the change in national income that can be expected from the £2bn of extra government spending.
   (b) Comment on the government's forecast that the $2bn in extra state spending is sufficient to remove the deflationary gap and restore full employment.

   You should assume that there are no other relevant changes in economic conditions that might impact on income and expenditure.

6. Why is it important to take account of accelerator effects when considering changes in the macroeconomy? What does the accelerator effect imply for the stability of investment spending over time?

7. Explain how the multiplier and accelerator effects may impact together to lead to fluctuations in national income. What steps might government adopt to reduce economic instability?

8. What difficulties are associated with the estimation of multiplier effects?

Chapter 5

AGGREGATE DEMAND AND AGGREGATE SUPPLY

Aims and learning outcomes

In previous chapters we have built up the model of the macroeconomy and national income determination from first principles. This culminated in Chapter 4 in the aggregate planned expenditure (AE) and 45° line diagrams, which showed different combinations of aggregate planned expenditure and national income (real GDP). Using these diagrams we were able to identify situations of inflationary and deflationary gaps in the economy. In later chapters we will turn in detail to the different policies governments can adopt to close both inflationary and deflationary gaps. However, before we do this we shall introduce a new framework based on the concepts of *aggregate demand* (*AD*) and *aggregate supply* (*AS*). We will also use AD–AS analysis in later chapters.

This chapter discusses the relationship between aggregate demand, the price level and real GDP. It also considers the relationship between aggregate supply, the price level and real GDP. It is the interaction of aggregate demand and aggregate supply that determines the dynamics of macroeconomic changes, with implications for output, employment and inflation.

In this chapter the following topics are discussed:

- aggregate demand;
- changes in aggregate demand;
- aggregate supply;
- aggregate supply in the long run;
- aggregate supply in the short run;
- macroeconomic equilibrium.

Just as there are two sides to any market, so there are two sides to an economy – a demand side and a supply side. Aggregate demand relates to the demand side and aggregate supply to the supply side.

Learning outcomes

After studying this material you will be able to:

- Understand the nature of *aggregate demand*.
- Appreciate why aggregate demand changes.
- Recognise the importance of *aggregate supply* in the macroeconomy.
- Understand the meaning of the *aggregate production function*.
- Grasp the distinction between *short-run* and *long-run* aggregate supply.
- Understand the meaning of an economy's *potential* real GDP.
- Identify how *macroeconomic equilibrium* depends upon the matching of aggregate demand and aggregate supply.

Aggregate demand

As we have seen in the previous chapter, aggregate expenditure is composed of consumer spending (C), investment spending (I), government spending (G) and spending on exports less imports ($X - M$). It is the spending plans under each of these demand headings that gives us *aggregate planned expenditure* (*AE*). The AE schedule, along with the Keynesian 45° diagram, enables us to analyse the potential for inflationary and deflationary gaps to arise in an economy. However, let us now introduce new concepts – *aggregate demand* and the *aggregate demand curve* – which will allow us to explore the implications for the price level as well as for real GDP. Note that the AE diagrams showed changes in planned expenditure and the implications for the economy's output – but the price level was assumed to be fixed in the short term. By introducing the aggregate demand curve, we can now explore the link between price, demand and real GDP simultaneously.

At any given point in time, aggregate demand will be equal to the actual output of the economy (real GDP) and is given by:

$$AD = C + I + G + (X - M) = \text{Real GDP}$$

Assuming that the economy has sufficient productive capacity, the higher the level of aggregate demand, the higher will be GDP, particularly because consumer spending is related directly to income. We can therefore define an aggregate demand curve.

Aggregate demand curve

The *aggregate demand curve* shows the quantity demanded of real GDP at different price levels, *holding all other factors constant*.

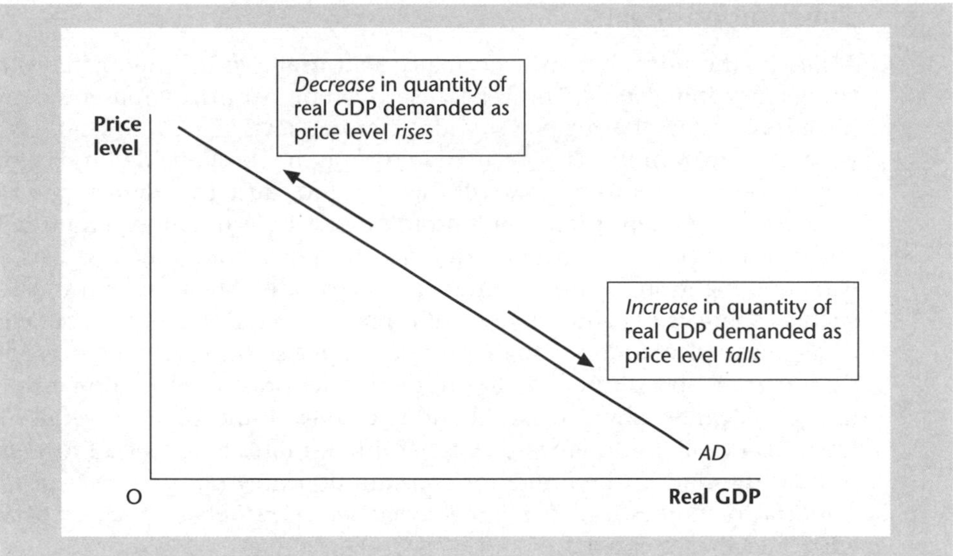

Figure 5.1 Aggregate demand curve

To construct the AD curve we hold constant all other influences on real GDP levels other than the price level. Therefore, a change in any other influence on real GDP results in a new AD curve. Figure 5.1 shows a typical AD curve with the price level on the vertical axis and real GDP on the horizontal axis and is downward sloping (for simplicity, we draw the curve as a straight line).

The AD curve is downward sloping as a result of two separate effects:

- real money balance effect;
- substitution effects.

Real money balance effect

At lower price levels the *real* purchasing power of money balances (currency and bank deposits) rises. This is referred to as the *real money balance effect* which leads to a greater quantity of goods demanded and therefore a higher real GDP. For example, if price levels fell by a half and money balances stayed the same, the real purchasing power of the money balances would double. We would be able to buy twice the volume of goods than we did before. In other words, a fall in the price level in the economy raises the real purchasing power of money and causes a movement down the AD curve. There is, however, another reason for the downward slope of the AD curve and this relates to *substitution effects*.

Substitution effects

A rise in the price level will normally lead to a rise in interest rates, all other things remaining equal. This is because given higher prices households and firms have less real purchasing power and therefore they will tend to lend less and will wish to borrow more. This decrease in the supply of loanable funds alongside a rise in the demand to borrow will then tend to cause the interest rate to rise. In turn, a higher interest rate will tend to depress investment expenditure by firms and the purchase of consumer durables by households, such as cars, that are usually bought on credit. The higher interest rate may also depress asset values such as share prices and the price of homes and land, further encouraging a fall in aggregate demand. The higher interest rate also makes saving more attractive than current spending. In addition, the higher price level for domestic goods is likely to depress export demand and encourage imports. The overall result is a lower real GDP. In other words, higher interest rates tend to lead to substitution of consumption in the future for consumption now (an *intertemporal effect) and* imports for domestic goods (an *international substitution effect*, associated also with a decline in exports).

Changes in aggregate demand

In practice, the AD curve is likely to shift over time, sometimes quite frequently. Major influences on aggregate demand include:

- government macroeconomic policy;
- expectations of firms and households;
- global trends.

Government macroeconomic policy

Changes in government expenditure and taxation or *fiscal policy* will directly and indirectly impact on aggregate demand. The undertaking of either more state spending or tax cuts will increase aggregate demand. Government spending directly affects aggregate demand, while changes in taxation indirectly stimulate consumer and investment spending through changes in disposable income, i.e. income after tax (all other things remaining constant – often expressed as *ceteris paribus* or *cet. par*). An *expansionary fiscal policy*, therefore, leads to a higher aggregate demand, as illustrated in Figure 5.2 by the shift to the right of the AD curve, from AD_1 to AD_2. The expected result will be an increase in real GDP but also some effect on the price level, depending on the economy's productive capacity. We will return to this later. By contrast, a reduction in government spending and higher taxes, or what is know as a *contractionary fiscal policy*, will shift the AD curve to the left leading to a lower real GDP; as illustrated by the movement from AD_1 to AD_3 in Figure 5.2.

A government might also use *monetary policy* to affect aggregate demand and therefore the level of economic activity. As we will see in Chapters 8 and 9, the

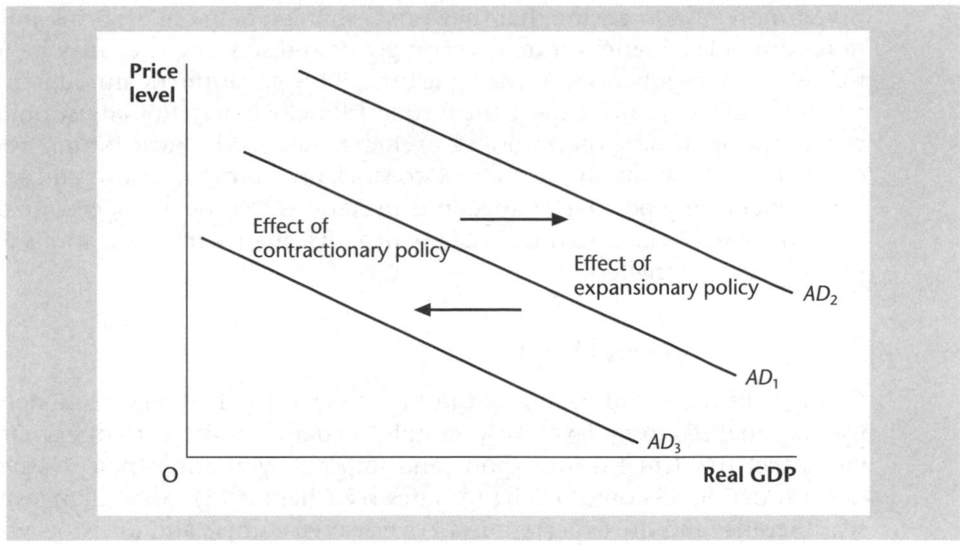

Figure 5.2 Impact of policy on aggregate demand

money supply is determined by the banking system including the country's central bank. Interest rates are set either by central banks independently of government (such as in the USA, UK and European Union) or under instruction by, or the influence of, government. Monetary policy is concerned with setting the money supply and interest rates so as to expand or contract aggregate demand. The greater the real quantity of money (the real purchasing power) the higher will tend to be aggregate demand. Similarly, with lower real interest rates, higher borrowing can be expected to finance increased investment expenditure and spending on consumer durables. A greater quantity of money and lower interest rates shift the AD curve in Figure 5.2 to the right (AD_1 to AD_2) in the same way that an expansionary fiscal policy led to a higher GDP. In contrast, a reduction in the money supply and higher interest rates has a similar effect as a contractionary fiscal policy, shifting the AD curve to the left, from AD_1 to AD_3.

The role of expectations

Expectations are extremely important in determining the state of the macroeconomy. When households and firms feel optimistic about the future they are more likely to borrow to spend and invest in new plant and machinery. When expectations are such that people and businesses feel pessimistic about the future, they are likely to cut back on their consumption and investment plans. Expectations about future income can affect spending today, as can expectations about, in particular, future price levels, taxes, interest rates and exchange rates. If we expect something to cost more in the shops in the future we are likely to buy it now. If firms expect 'better times' and higher profits in the future they may invest more now to ensure that they can cash in on a 'boom'. If firms and households anticipate higher future taxes on goods and services, they may be tempted to buy more cheaply now. At the same time, if the government announces income tax cuts but we do not expect them to last long, we may not adjust our current consumption. If we expect a lower exchange rate in the near future, leading to dearer imports, we might be inclined to stock up on imports now, and so on.

In general, any positive change in expectations that boosts aggregate demand will shift the AD curve to the right; any negative change in expectations will shift the AD curve to the left.

The impact of global trends

Changes in the world economy can be expected to affect aggregate demand at the national economy level. For example, a change in the current exchange rate will affect the demand for exports and imports by altering their relative prices (for a fuller discussion of exchange rates see Chapter 15). Also, changes in overseas incomes and the expectations of overseas customers and investors will affect the demand for national exports. More exports or fewer imports lead to a shift in the aggregate demand curve to the right; conversely, fewer exports and more imports shift the aggregate demand curve to the left. From this relationship, it should be obvious why expansions and contractions in the major world economies tend to move together. In times of world recession or 'slump', such as the 1930s, in the early 1980s and at the start of the millennium, most major economies suffer a decline in aggregate demand or at least a decline in the rate of increase of aggregate demand. In times of 'boom', such as at times in the 1960s and in the second half of the 1990s, most major economies benefit from rising world aggregate demand.

Having reviewed the nature of the AD curve, we now turn to consider aggregate supply.

Aggregate supply

Aggregate supply (*AS*) is the total of goods and services produced in the economy at any given time. The aggregate supply available will depend upon the factors of production utilised. These factors of production are *labour (N)*, *capital (K)* and *land (L)*. Also important is the *state of technology (T)* including the technical know-how available in an economy. We can represent the aggregate supply relationship in terms of an *aggregate production function* that relates output (Y) to the inputs (N, K, L, T).

Aggregate production function

$$Y = f(N, K, L, T)$$

The aggregate production function states that the greater the volume of factor inputs, the greater the economy's output. Of course, concentrating simply on the *quantity* of inputs could be dangerous because it is the *utilisation* of these inputs and their *quality* which is important; unemployed labour and unused plant and machinery add nothing to output. Unskilled labour is less productive than skilled labour; modern machines usually outperform older machines, and so on; while technology (T) is a major consideration in many leading industries. We shall look at all of these aspects in more detail in the chapter on economic growth and supply-side economics, Chapter 10. For now, we are primarily concerned with deriving the AS curve and its inter-relationship with the AD curve.

Aggregate supply in the long run

A *long-run aggregate supply curve* shows the relationship between the price level and real GDP in the long run. In a competitive market economy, at any point in time in the long run, when all short-run frictions have worked their way out, long-run aggregate supply (LRAS) should be at the level where *actual* real GDP equals the economy's *potential* real GDP given fully efficient use of all the available inputs (i.e. a state of full employment of resources). In Figure 5.3 the LRAS curve is shown as vertical at the economy's full-employment real GDP, Y_{f1}. The LRAS is unaffected by price changes. This is because an increase in the demand for goods and services cannot increase the supply, which is fixed at the potential GDP. The expected result, therefore, of a higher aggregate demand would be a higher price level. However, an increase in the price level would reduce real wages (wages divided by the price level: W/P), to which, at full employment, workers can be expected to respond by demanding a compensating money wage

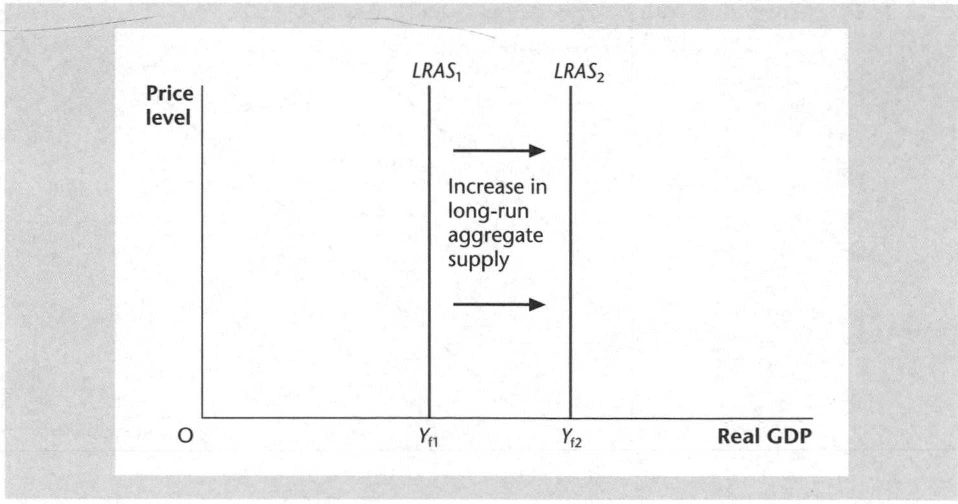

Figure 5.3 Long-run aggregate supply

increase. Unless *real* wages are restored to their previous level, fewer workers can be expected to seek employment, leading to a fall in labour inputs and therefore in output. Employers can be expected, therefore, to respond by granting the compensating wage increase. The real wage (W/P) is restored to its previous level, but at a higher price level. Real GDP is unaffected.

It is important to note that this LRAS curve is drawn for any given future time period. Over time or over the years, the LRAS curve can be expected to shift to the right reflecting *economic growth*. For example, any increase in the quantity of the factor inputs (labour, capital and land) and any changes in the quality or productivity of these inputs (e.g. improved human capital through better education and training) should shift the LRAS curve to the right. Equally, improvements in technology which are embodied in the capital stock through improved or more productive capital inputs should also shift the LRAS curve rightwards.

The movement from $LRAS_1$ to $LRAS_2$ in Figure 5.3 illustrates an increase in long-run aggregate supply from Y_{f1} to Y_{f2}. A decline in long-run aggregate supply would be represented by a movement in the opposite direction.

Aggregate supply in the short run

In the short run, real GDP may be at or below the potential real GDP at full employment. A higher aggregate demand at a time when aggregate supply is below its potential level can be expected to lead to more output produced. This is illustrated in Figure 5.4 by the *upward sloping* short-run aggregate supply (SRAS) curve. The elasticity of the short-run aggregate supply curve reflects the extent to

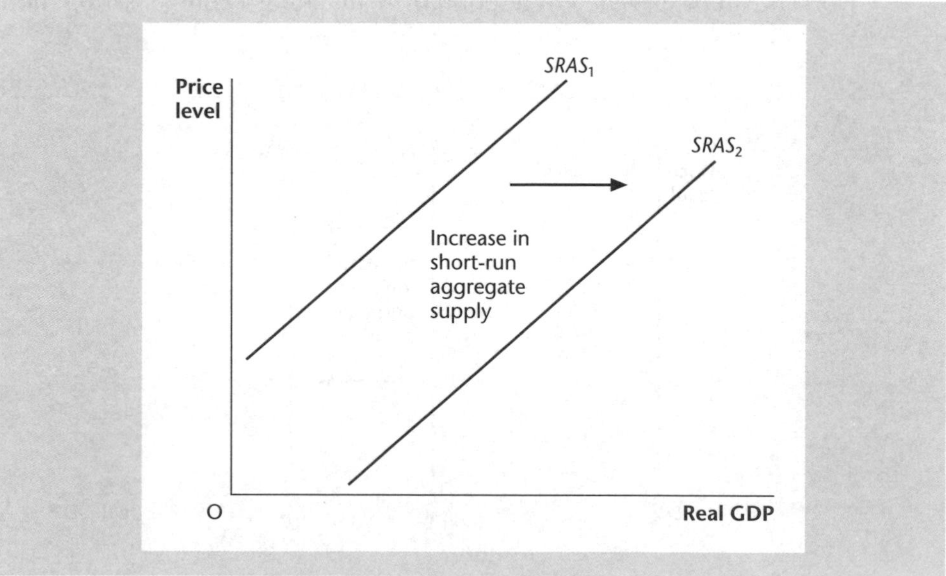

Figure 5.4 Short-run aggregate supply

which real GDP rather than the price level rises when aggregate demand increases. For example, if higher demand raises prices and causes a fall in the real wage (W/P) – the real cost of employing labour – and in the short-run workers do not respond by successfully demanding a compensating money wage (W) adjustment, there will be an incentive for employers to take on more, now effectively cheaper, employees. The result is a larger labour force (N) and therefore a higher real GDP, everything else being equal. The 'flexibility' of the labour force in terms of its response to changes in the price level and wage demands can therefore have a significant impact on the elasticity of the SRAS curve. Where compensating wage increases are obtained immediately then the SRAS will be vertical (like the LRAS curve shown earlier).

As in the case of the LRAS curve, changes in the availability of factor inputs (e.g. the willingness of the unemployed to seek work) also impacts on the

Application 5.1

The impact of oil price shocks

The Asian crisis and oil

The 1997–98 Asian economic crisis benefited consumers in the USA because of declines in oil and gasoline prices. Oil prices fell from about \$22 a barrel in October 1997 to about \$12 a barrel by mid-1998. As a consequence, gasoline prices in the USA, adjusted for general inflation, fell to record low levels.

Asia's economic fragility reduced its demand for oil in OPEC countries who, in order to prevent prices from falling, agreed to cutbacks in production. But some members of the cartel reneged on this agreement, and because the agreed-upon cuts were small in any case, oil prices still fell.

Benefits to the USA

Lower oil prices benefit the US economy in a number of areas. A 10 per cent drop in the price of oil is estimated to add 0.2 per cent to economic growth in the USA. This represents major cost savings for industries such as transportation, iron and steel, aluminium, chemicals, glass and cement. Reductions in business costs help reduce inflationary pressures and this helps to keep interest rates from rising.

However, oil price falls do not benefit everyone. The USA produces about 50 per cent of its oil consumption and so a fall in oil prices hurts domestic producers.

Although it is better for the USA to have Asia economically strong, Asia's financial weakness in the late 1990s provided some offsetting benefits to the drain on the USA economy due to the decline in American exports.

Activity

Illustrate the impact of the fall in oil prices, using aggregate demand/aggregate supply curves, on real GDP and the price level in the USA.

short-run aggregate supply curve. In addition, changes in money wage rates (*W*) can also affect the SRAS because of their impact on real wages (*W*/*P*) and therefore the willingness of employers to hire labour and produce more output. There may also be changes in the capital stock due to changes in investment expenditure (perhaps affected by business expectations or changes in interest rates). But as current investment only marginally changes the capital stock, capital inputs, along with land and technology, are more important in determining changes in long-run aggregate supply than short-run aggregate supply. In contrast, expectations can be expected to affect management decisions about how much to produce at any given time and may change quickly. In this way expectations can have a significant effect on SRAS.

An increase in SRAS is illustrated in Figure 5.4 by the movement rightwards in the curve from $SRAS_1$ to $SRAS_2$. A decrease in short-run aggregate supply would lead to a movement in the opposite direction.

Macroeconomic equilibrium

By placing the aggregate demand and aggregate supply curves on the same diagram, we are able to identify the macroeconomic equilibrium. The AD curve shows the volume of real expenditure at every possible price level and the AS curve the volume of real GDP supplied at every possible price level. The macroeconomic equilibrium occurs where there is no excess aggregate demand in the economy – demand that cannot be met by supply. Equally, it occurs where there is no excess supply – production for which there is no current demand. This occurs where aggregate demand equals aggregate supply ($AD = AS$). This equilibrium is illustrated in Figure 5.5.

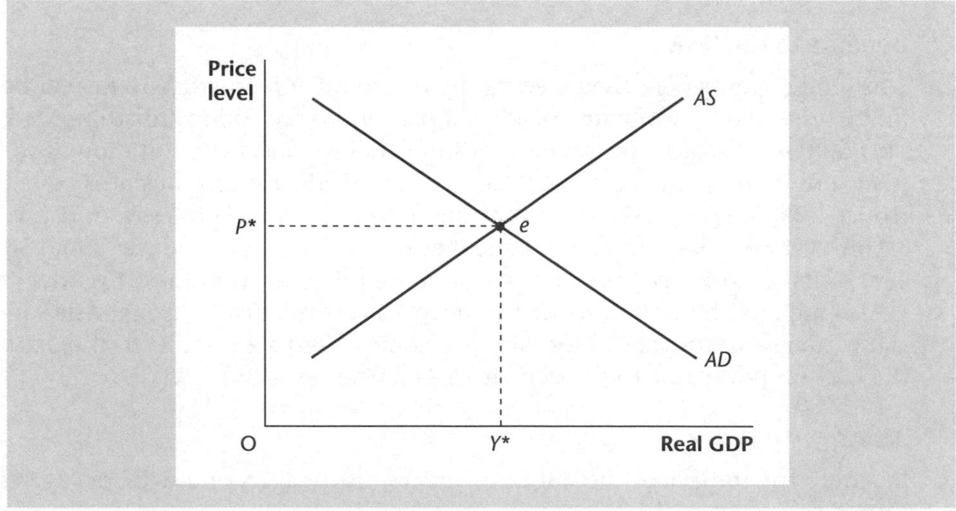

Figure 5.5 Aggregate demand, aggregate supply and macroeconomic equilibrium

The equilibrium occurs at point *e* giving a price level of P^* and a real GDP of Y^*. If, for example, the price level was higher than P^* then aggregate supply would exceed aggregate demand ($AS > AD$). As a result there would be unsold goods and services and, consequently, output and prices would be cut. This would continue until the equilibrium, *e*, was restored. Similarly, if the price level was below P^* then aggregate demand would exceed aggregate supply ($AD > AS$). This would cause prices to rise and would encourage firms to produce more until, again, the equilibrium position, *e*, was reached.

However, and this is important, in the *short run* there is no necessary reason why the AD–AS equilibrium, *e*, should be at a full employment output (full-employment real GDP). For example, in Figure 5.5, assume that the full employment real GDP is to the right of Y^*. The result would reflect the equivalent of a *deflationary gap* with real GDP below its full employment potential. Equally, it is possible that the equilibrium in the macroeconomy occurs in the short run where there are serious inflationary pressures. This would be the case in Figure 5.5 if GDP exceeded the full employment GDP (i.e. Y^*) with price stability. In this case we would say that an *inflationary gap* exists.

In reality, changes in aggregate demand and aggregate supply are continuous and cause the economy to fluctuate around its long-run growth path. For example, an increase in aggregate demand might lead to a rise in prices. The rise in prices causes a fall in the real wage rate (W/P), as discussed earlier, leading to a short-run increase in employment until compensating wage adjustments occur. Higher other input prices, such as the rise in world oil prices that occurred in the 1970s and again after 2000, will raise firms' costs of production leading to a leftward shift in the SRAS curve and a fall in real GDP, and a new short-run macroeconomic equilibrium. As shown in Figure 5.6, the leftward shift in the SRAS

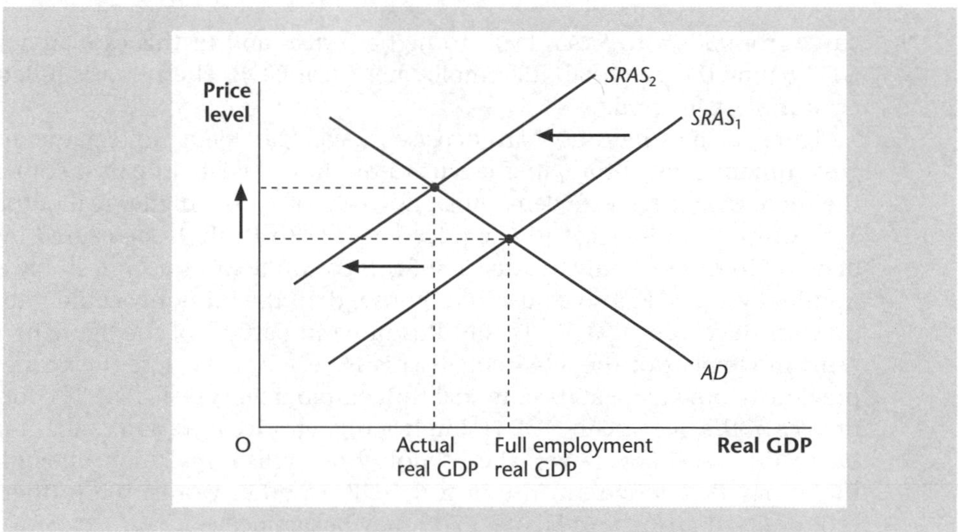

Figure 5.6 Impact of higher input costs on aggregate supply

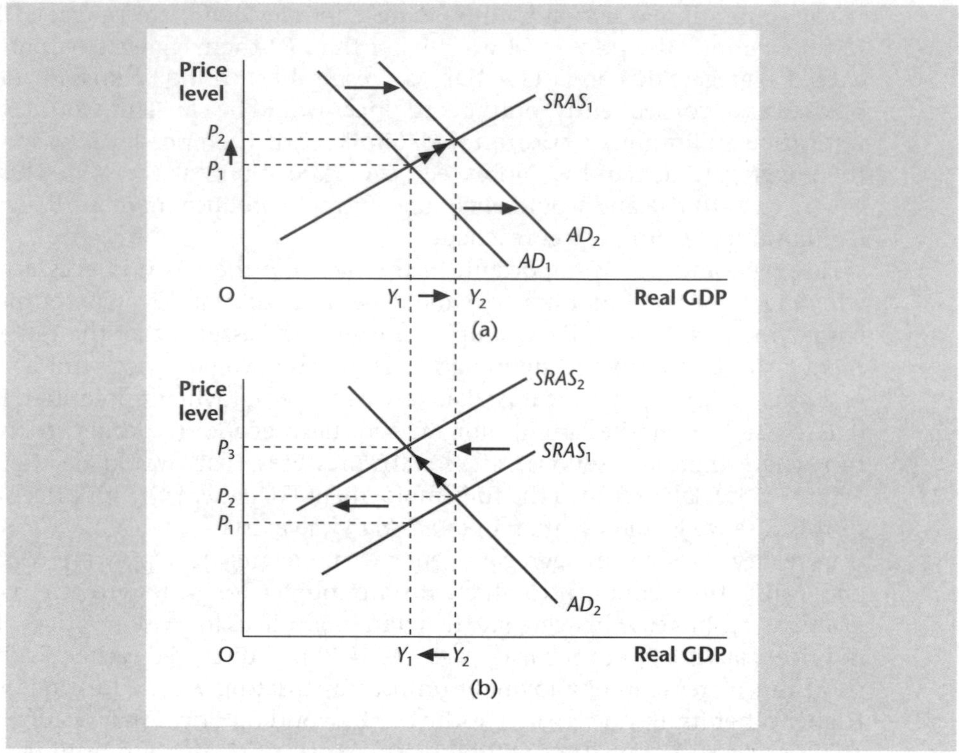

Figure 5.7 Increasing aggregate demand: new macroeconomic equilibrium

curve from $SRAS_1$ to $SRAS_2$ leads to higher prices and in this case an actual real GDP below the potential, full employment real GDP. The result is inflation and economic stagnation.

Figure 5.7 illustrates how an increase in aggregate demand (e.g. due to higher government expenditure) might cause a rise in real GDP. In part (a) of the figure the increase in aggregate demand is shown leading to a higher real output, Y_1 to Y_2, alongside an increase in the price level, P_1 to P_2. Both are caused by higher demand in the economy. However, if firms continue to adjust prices upwards and nominal wages (*W*) also adjust in response, then the economy could return to its previous level of real GDP. This is illustrated in part (b) of the figure by the leftward movement of the SRAS curve. This is very likely where the economy was previously producing at its potential (full employment) real GDP. The longer-run impact of the increase in GDP is simply a higher price level as a result of inflation (P_1 to P_3). Where, however, the economy previously had high unemployment there may be a long-term rise in real GDP. In other words, the further macroeconomic adjustment in Figure 5.7(b) may be avoided.

Application 5.2

Portugal's twin deficits

The following commentary refers to the economic environment in Portugal in 2003.

The twin deficits

The Portuguese economy is in poor shape. As economic activity slows, the imbalances are growing and look set to persist for quite some time. The fiscal deficit reached 4.1 per cent of GDP in 2001 with only a slight improvement in 2002 – despite government efforts to rebalance public accounts. With excessive deficits in two consecutive years, the European Community might bring sanctions against Portugal. The current account deficit was 9.7 per cent of GDP in 2002 (the highest in Euroland), and is expected to remain high (although declining) in the next few years. With a possibly appreciating euro, adjustment will not be easy. Moreover, robust private credit growth and low domestic savings have led to high foreign borrowing and current levels of household and firms indebtedness are high. This, together with a poor competitiveness record, poses some questions on the recovery potential of this economy and its ability to unwind the macroeconomic imbalances.

But it has not always been like that. Not so long ago – take 1998 – Portugal was growing at an impressive 4.6 per cent, although the current account deficit was already 7.0 per cent, the fiscal deficit was 2.6 per cent, inflation only 2.2 per cent and the unemployment rate remained low at 5.2 per cent. A more balanced picture altogether, even considering the better international environment and the already mounting current account deficit. What happened between 1998 and 2002 that drove the economy into such a poor state? What went wrong?

Impact of monetary union

First and foremost there was an unprecendental monetary impulse resulting from Portugal's entry into Europe's Economic and Monetary Union (EMU) and the sustained decline in interest rates. (Portugal entered the final stage of the Economic and Monetary Union on 1 January 1999, with the founding members.) This generated fast growth of credit to the private sector (the ratio of private loans to GDP is currently 142 per cent *vis-à-vis* 97 per cent in Euroland) and a moderate boom in the construction sector (productive investment growth was more limited and thus capacity utilisation and potential growth were less affected). Because national savings growth was low, banks had to finance the credit expansion through foreign borrowing; and credit continued to expand faster than income.

▶

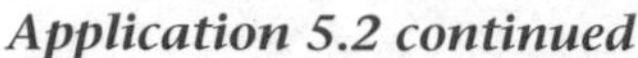

Application 5.2 continued

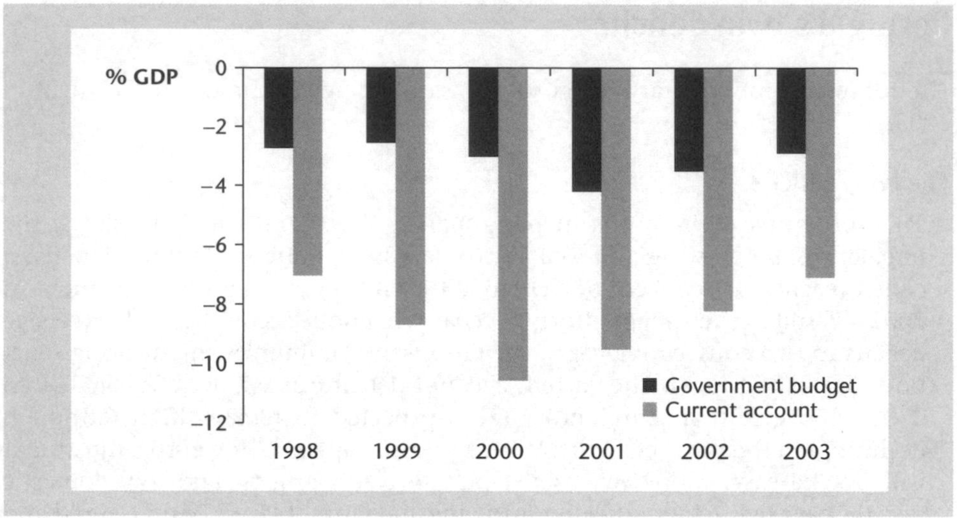

The demand impulse was exacerbated by a rather expansionary fiscal policy. The compounded impulse on domestic demand was significant and inflationary pressures started building up. Robust growth of public wages (used as a benchmark for wage negotiations in the private sector) combined with low productivity growth translated into a unit labour cost growth in Portugal well above that in Euroland; and thus the inflationary gap remained open as the economy's competitiveness was eroded. This, in turn, increased the current account deficits as shown in the figure.

Source: Edited extract from Deutsche Bank, *Focus Europe*, 3 March 2003.

Activity

Use aggregate demand and aggregate supply analysis to illustrate the economic events in Portugal during the period referred to in the above discussion.

Concluding remarks

In this chapter we have introduced the concepts of aggregate demand and aggregate supply. Aggregate demand is the total demand in the economy while aggregate supply refers to the output of the economy. Throughout the remainder of the book we will use the term aggregate demand when considering the effect of demand changes on price levels and real GDP in the macroeconomy. Indeed, henceforth, instead of using aggregate expenditure and the 45° line diagram to consider macroeconomic equilibrium and changes in macroeconomic equilibrium, we will usually use AD–AS analysis. The latter is superior in the sense that it specifically identifies the impact of changes in demand not only in terms of changes in incomes and output (real GDP) but in terms of changes in the price level (or inflation/deflation).

By also introducing the aggregate supply curve, we have highlighted the importance of production or supply in determining the macroeconomic equilibrium. In the earlier 45° line diagram, supply is simply assumed and does not feature directly in the diagram. By concentrating on supply as well as demand, AD–AS analysis identifies how changes in the macroeconomic equilibrium can be bought about by changes in both demand and supply factors. For example, achieving full employment is now no longer simply a matter of raising aggregate demand but in taking a view about supply-side responses to this higher demand.

In the next chapter we turn to consider in more detail the management of the economy using aggregate demand–aggregate supply analysis.

Key learning points

- *AD–AS analysis* is superior to the use of aggregate expenditure and the 45° line diagram because it identifies the impact of changes in aggregate demand (and aggregate supply) on prices as well as real GDP.
- The *AD curve* is downward sloping because of a *real money balances effect* and *substitution effects*.
- The *real money balances effect* states that with a lower price level the real purchasing power of the money stock in the economy rises, leading to higher demand.
- The *substitution effects* identify how changes in interest rates can lead to a substitution of current for future consumption (an *intertemporal effect*) and how price changes can affect the demand for exports and imports (an *international substitution effect*).
- *Shifts in the aggregate demand curve* reflect changes in government macroeconomic policies, expectations and global trends.
- The *aggregate production function* is the relationship between an economy's output and factor inputs (labour, land, capital as well as technology).
- The *long-run aggregate supply curve* shows the relationship between price levels and real GDP, where real GDP reflects the economy's potential to produce given full employment of factor inputs and the available technology.
- The long-run aggregate supply curve (LRAS) is vertical.
- The *short-run aggregate supply curve* (*SRAS*) shows the relationship between price levels and real GDP, where real GDP may not be at its potential full employment level. The curve is therefore more elastic than the LRAS.
- A *macroeconomic equilibrium* occurs where aggregate demand equals aggregate supply so that there is no excess demand or excess supply in the economy. In

the short run, this equilibrium may or may not be at a full-employment level of real GDP.

- The effect on output and prices of an increase in aggregate demand in the economy will depend upon the way in which short-run aggregate supply responds.
- At any particular time in the long run, the macroeconomic equilibrium in a competitive market economy will be at the potential real GDP level. In this case, higher aggregate demand can only lead to a higher price level.
- In the very long run only economic growth or shifting the long-run aggregate supply to the right can lead to a higher real GDP.

Appendix 5.1 (see pp.117–125)

- The *IS curve* shows the different combinations of real GDP and interest rates at which aggregate planned expenditure is in equilibrium, i.e. equilibrium in the 'goods' market.
- The *LM curve* shows the different combinations of real GDP and interest rates at which the money market is in equilibrium.
- *IS–LM equilibrium* represents the particular combination of real GDP and the interest rates at which the goods market and the money market are in equilibrium, simultaneously.
- The *aggregate demand curve* shows the level of total demand in the economy at different combinations of prices and real GDP corresponding to points of equilibrium in the goods market (given by the IS curve) and money market (given by the LM curve).
- An *expansionary fiscal policy* will shift the IS curve rightwards, resulting in a higher real GDP and a higher interest rate, holding all other factors constant.
- A *contractionary fiscal policy* will shift the IS curve leftwards, resulting in a lower real GDP and a lower interest rate, holding all other factors constant.
- The shape of the LM curve is crucial in determining the extent to which fiscal policy is successful in expanding or contracting the economy.
- An *expansionary monetary policy* shifts the LM curve to the right, resulting in a fall in interest rates and a rise in real GDP.
- A *contractionary monetary policy* shifts the LM curve to the left, resulting in a rise in interest rates and a fall in real GDP.

? Topics for discussion

1. Explain the composition of aggregate demand. Explain under what circumstances the aggregate demand curve might shift (a) to the right (b) to the left.
2. Distinguish between short-run and long-run aggregate supply and discuss the importance of this distinction for macroeconomic policy.

3. Using appropriate AD–AS diagrams explain how (a) a deflationary gap (b) an inflationary gap may occur.
4. How might governments attempt to influence long-run aggregate supply and therefore potential GDP?
5. Why might increases in aggregate demand simply lead to a higher price level rather than a higher real GDP?
6. Discuss the role of price and wage adjustments in understanding the macroeconomic equilibrium.
7. Illustrate the possible effects of the following policy measures on the AS and AD curves:

   (a) a cut in income tax rates
   (b) a rise in government expenditure
   (c) a decrease in the cost of borrowing by firms and households
   (d) a fall in the value of the domestic currency on the foreign exchange market
   (e) a rise in consumer confidence.

8. Illustrate the possible effects of the following policy measures using IS-LM analysis:

   (a) a rise in income tax rates
   (b) a fall in government expenditure
   (c) a fall in interest rates
   (d) an injection of liquidity into the economy by the central bank.

Appendix 5.1: IS–LM analysis

The equilibrium in the macroeconomy has been discussed so far using the aggregate expenditure (45° line) diagram and aggregate demand (AD) and aggregate supply (AS) curves.

In this appendix we deal with an alternative approach called IS–LM analysis. We relegate this discussion to an appendix because not all macroeconomics courses include coverage of IS–LM curves.

The IS curve

The first part of IS–LM analysis is concerned with the derivation and characteristics of what is called the *IS (investment–savings) curve*. The IS curve recognises that changes in interest rates impact on the level of planned aggregate expenditure. Higher interest rates can be expected to reduce borrowing by firms and therefore their planned investments in plant and machinery, industrial and commercial buildings, etc. Similarly, lower interest rates mean that firms are likely to plan to invest more. The IS curve shows the equilibrium level of real GDP associated with each given rate of interest. It shows combinations of real GDP and the interest rate for which aggregate planned expenditure equals actual national output, and

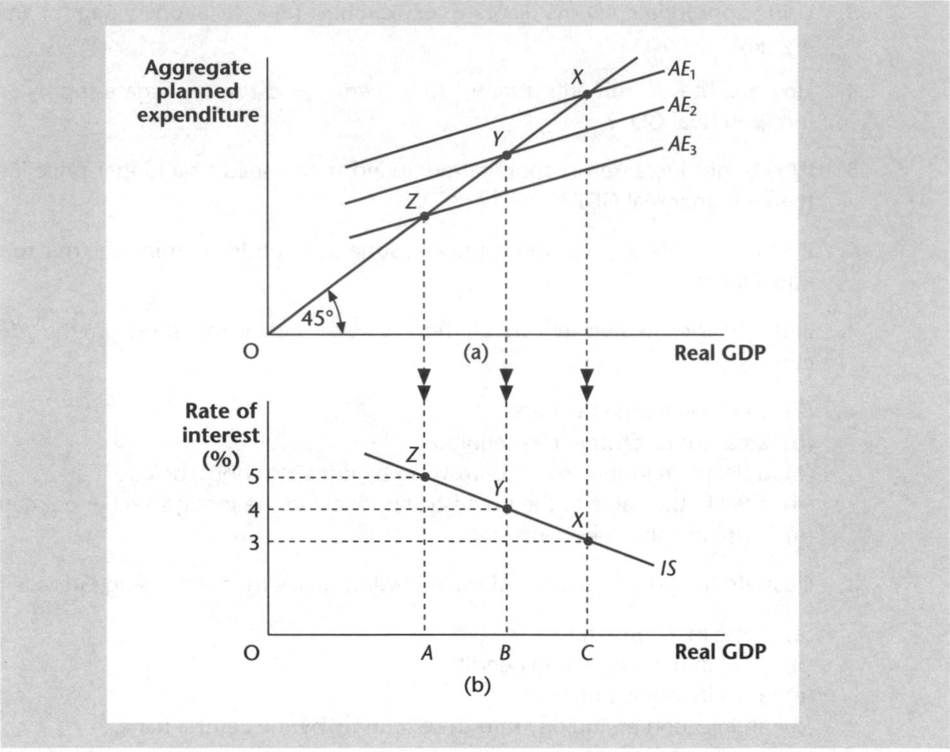

Figure A5.1 **Deriving the IS line**

for which total injections equals total leakages, i.e. equilibrium in the 'goods' market.

We can derive the IS curve as follows. In Figure A5.1, part (a), as usual the 45° line shows all the points at which aggregate planned expenditure is identical to real GDP. Any point along this line therefore represents an equilibrium position. Suppose that AE_1, AE_2, AE_3 are three possible aggregate planned expenditure curves for the economy, each reflecting different interest rates of say 3 per cent, 4 per cent, and 5 per cent respectively. The aggregate planned expenditure line AE_1 represents a higher level of economic activity than AE_2 and AE_3 and is associated with a lower interest rate than AE_2 and AE_3. AE_2 represents a lower level of economic activity than AE_1, but a higher economic activity level than AE_3. Points *X*, *Y* and *Z* represent equilibrium positions where aggregate planned expenditure equals real GDP.

In part (b) of the diagram, the relationship between interest rates and real GDP is illustrated. Points *X*, *Y* and *Z* in this part of the diagram correspond to the expenditure equilibria in part (a). Point *Z* represents an interest rate of 5 per cent and a real GDP of *A*; point *Y* an interest rate of 4 per cent and a real GDP of *B*; and *X* an interest rate of 3 per cent and a real GDP of *C*. Drawing a line through points *X*, *Y* and *Z* gives us the *IS* line. It tells us that, for example, at the interest rate of

4 per cent aggregate planned expenditure only equals real GDP if real GDP is at the level of *B*. Equally, it tells us that if real GDP is at *B* then an interest rate of 4 per cent is needed to bring about the necessary aggregate planned expenditure.

> The *IS curve* shows the different combinations of real GDP and interest rates at which aggregate planned expenditure is in equilibrium, i.e. equilibrium in the 'goods' market.

The LM curve

The other part of IS–LM analysis is concerned with the *LM (liquidity–money) curve*. The LM curve represents equilibrium in the market for money. Money is demanded for transaction, precautionary and speculative motives (see p.206 for details) by firms and households. The supply of money is determined by the banking system and especially the actions of the central bank. The market equilibrium for money occurs when the stock of real money demanded equals the quantity supplied. The concern is with *real* money because the quantity of money demanded is proportional to the price level; for example, when inflation rises, households demand more money to finance their spending.

Figure A5.2, part (a), shows the quantity of money demanded at different combinations of the interest rate and real GDP. Each of the *Md* lines represents a demand for money, with Md_3 representing the highest level of demand and Md_1

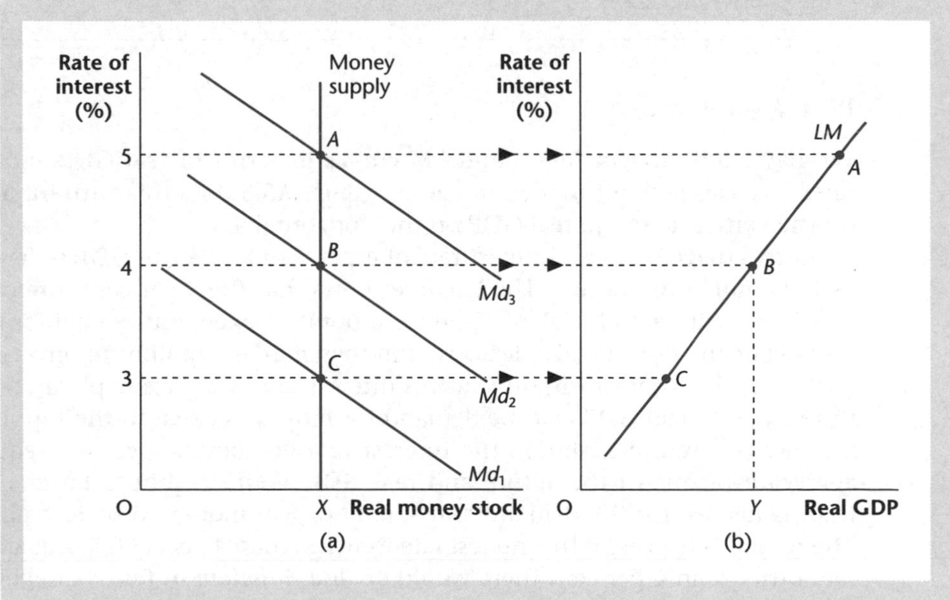

Figure A5.2 **Deriving the LM curve**

the lowest, for each level of real GDP. Thus there is a different demand for money for each level of real GDP (mainly reflecting the higher level of transactions using money in the marketplace that will occur with higher output). Equilibrium between the demand and supply of money occurs where the demand for money curves intersect the supply of money line. The supply of money line is drawn vertical, at a level of *A*, suggesting that it is unaffected by changes in interest rates. (This is a generalisation, however, and interest rates may affect the money supply – see p.205). The supply of money can be taken as given by the banking system or the central bank. Points *A*, *B* and *C* identify combinations of interest rates and real GDP at which the demand for and supply of real money are in equilibrium. Each *Md* curve is downward sloping reflecting how the quantity of money demanded rises as interest rates decline (for more on this relationship, see p.207).

Part (b) of the figure shows the LM curve. It indicates the different combinations of real GDP and the interest rate at which the demand for money equals the supply of real money. For example, the line shows us that when the real GDP is at level *Y* in (b) and the supply of real money is at level *X* in (a), then equilibrium in the market for money occurs at an interest rate of 4 per cent. It also tells us that if interest rates are currently 4 per cent and the supply of money is at level *X*, then for equilibrium in the market for money to occur real GDP must be at the level *Y*.

> The *LM curve* shows the different combinations of real GDP and interest rates at which the demand for money and the supply of money are in equilibrium, i.e. equilibrium in the 'money' market.

IS–LM equilibrium

We have derived separate IS and LM curves in terms of real GDP and interest rates. We can now bring them together. Figure A5.3 does this with interest rates on the vertical axis and real GDP on the horizontal axis.

On this diagram, at an interest rate of 4 per cent and a real GDP of level Y_e, an IS–LM equilibrium occurs. The IS curve shows that the 4 per cent interest rate is consistent with a real GDP of Y_e and is a point of expenditure equilibrium. The 4 per cent interest rate also leads to a money market equilibrium given the real GDP of Y_e. In other words, only at this interest rate is aggregate planned expenditure equal to real GDP *and* the demand for money is equal to the supply of real money. For example, should the interest rate be above 4 per cent, equality in aggregate planned expenditure and real GDP would require a lower real GDP than is needed for the demand and supply of real money to be in equilibrium. The reverse is the case if the interest rate were less than 4 per cent, i.e., at an interest rate other than 4 per cent there would be *disequilibrium* in terms of expenditure on goods and services (disequilibrium in either the 'goods market'), or in the demand and supply of real money (disequilibrium in the 'money market'), or

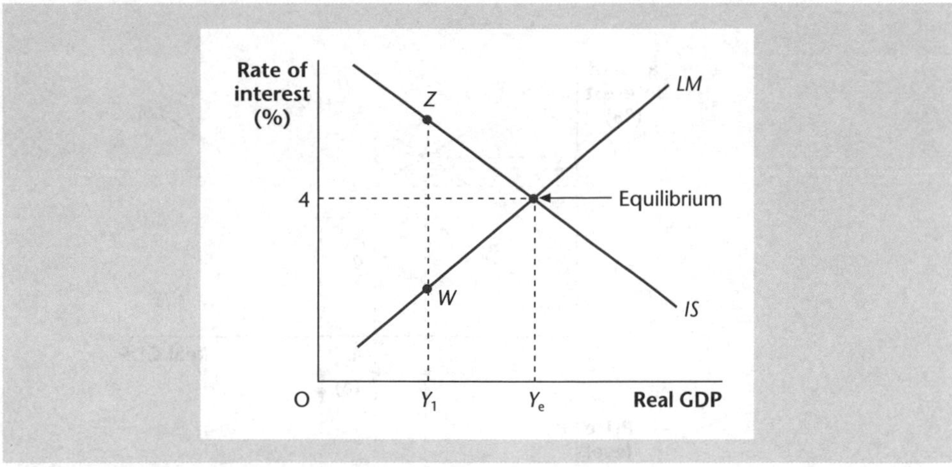

Figure A5.3 IS–LM equilibrium

disequilibrium in both of these markets. Consider, for example, point Z on the IS curve with a real GDP of Y_1. This position is unsustainable because the interest rate associated with it is too high (real GDP is too low) to achieve equilibrium in the money market. Interest rates in a competitive money market will decline to point W. However, at interest rate W aggregate planned expenditure exceeds real GDP. With planned expenditure above real GDP, real GDP will rise, assuming spare capacity. The rise in real GDP leads, in turn, to a higher demand for real money balances because of transactionary and precautionary motives to hold money and a higher interest rate. This adjustment process continues until the goods and money markets are both in equilibrium at an interest rate of 4 per cent and a real GDP of Y_e. Indeed, competitive forces in the goods and money markets mean that the economy will always move to an interest rate and real GDP where the IS and LM curves intersect.

> Thus *IS–LM equilibrium* represents the particular combination of real GDP and the interest rate at which the goods and money markets are in equilibrium, simultaneously.

IS–LM and the aggregate demand curve

Now suppose that prices, which so far are have been held constant, were to change. The effect would be to change the real demand for and supply of money. For example, if prices (P) rise by 10 per cent with the stock of money (M) unadjusted, the real stock of money (M/P) falls by 10 per cent. Similarly, if prices fall by 10 per cent the real stock of money would rise by 10 per cent. This is illustrated in Figure A5.4 part (a) with LM_1 showing the original LM curve, LM_2 a

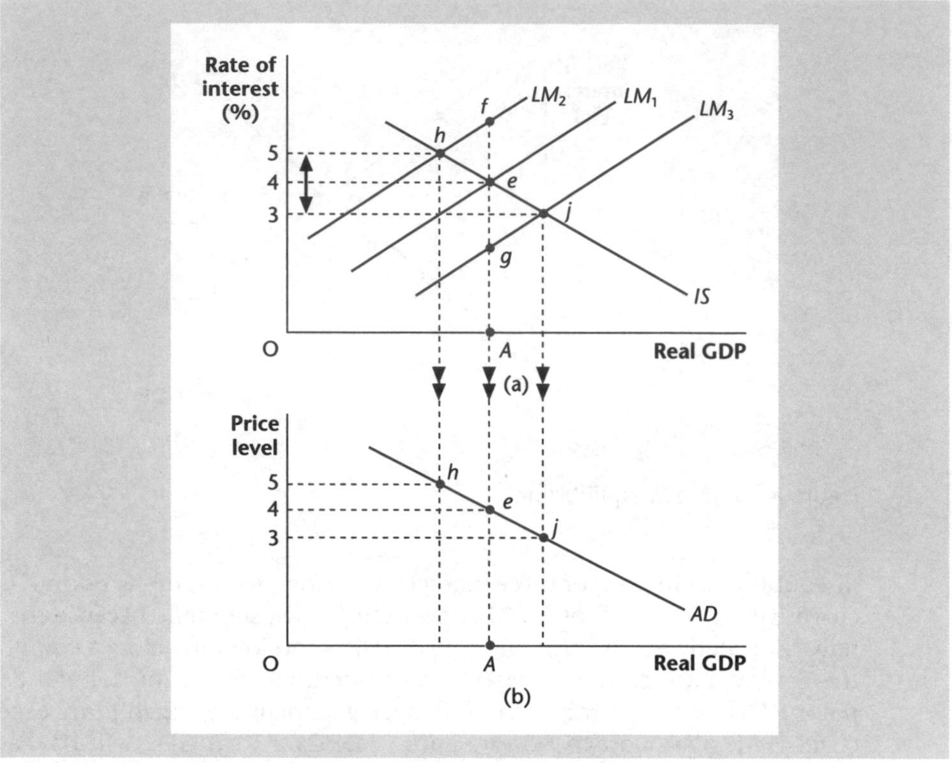

Figure A5.4 **IS–LM and the aggregate demand curve**

lower real money supply and LM_3 a higher real money supply. A decline in the real stock of money necessitates a higher interest rate to achieve equilibrium in the money market, and a higher real stock of money and a lower interest rate. In more detail, with the LM curve LM_2 and a real GDP of A, interest rates rise to level f from level e. With the LM curve LM_3 and real GDP at A, the level of interest rates falls from e to g.

In summary, there is a different LM curve for each price level leading to interest rate changes to keep the demand for money equal to the supply of real money. When prices rise, the real supply of money declines and interest rates rise leading to an equivalent decline in the demand for money. When prices fall, the real supply of money increases and interest rates fall to bring about an equivalent rise in the demand for money. In all cases, the change in interest rates leads to a different equilibrium in the goods market or in planned expenditure relative to real GDP, as shown by the IS line. Therefore, the only positions of equilibrium following the changes in prices are h, e and j in Figure A5.4, part (a). For every price level there is a different interest rate and real GDP.

Part (b) of Figure A5.4 shows the aggregate demand curve introduced earlier, indicating the levels of total demand in the economy at different combinations

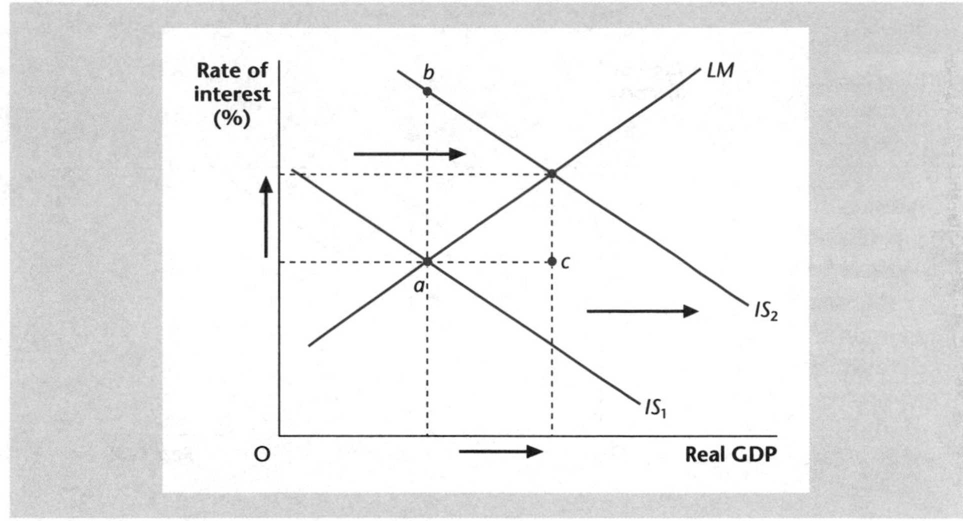

Figure A5.5 **IS–LM analysis – illustrating fiscal policy**

of prices and real GDP. Each of the points shown along the AD curve corresponds to IS–LM equilibrium points in part (a) of the diagram.

IS–LM and macroeconomic policy

We can illustrate the effects of changes in fiscal and monetary policies using IS–LM analysis

Fiscal policy

An expansionary fiscal policy resulting in an increase in government spending or a reduction in taxation will shift the IS curve rightwards, for example from IS_1 to IS_2 in Figure A5.5. The result is a higher real GDP and a higher interest rate, holding all other factors constant.

By contrast, a contractionary (or deflationary) fiscal policy will shift the IS curve leftwards, leading to a lower real GDP and a lower interest rate. It should be noted that in both cases the shift in the IS curve is greater than the change in real GDP (compare the distance *ab* to *ac* in Figure A5.5). This is because the higher interest rate leads to a decline in private investment expenditure, which partially offsets the fiscal expansion (conversely for a fiscal contraction). However, if the LM curve is horizontal then a fiscal expansion or contraction would have no effect on interest rates. By contrast, if the LM curve is vertical then fiscal policy would have no effect on real GDP, leading in the case of an expansionary fiscal policy solely to higher interest rates that 'crowd out' equivalent amounts of private investment expenditure. The shape of the LM curve (its gradient) is therefore crucial in determining the extent to which fiscal policy is successful in expanding

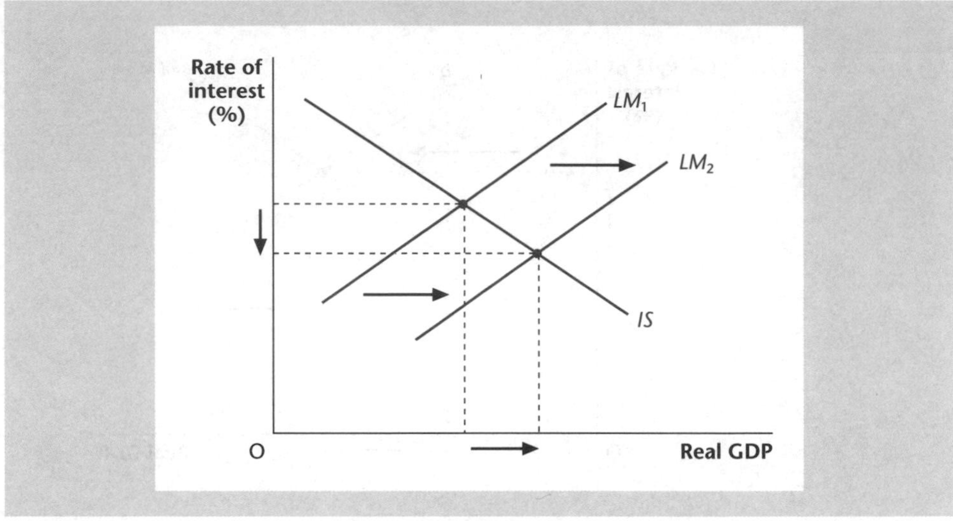

Figure A5.6 IS–LM analysis – illustrating monetary policy

or contracting the economy. A horizontal LM curve is an extreme Keynesian case, where there is a 'liquidity trap' (see p.207) so that people hold any quantity of money at the going interest rate. The vertical LM curve is an extreme monetarist case, where fiscal expansion simply 'crowds out' private spending leading to no additional real GDP.

Monetary policy

Monetary policy involving an increase in the money supply will lead to a shift in the LM curve to the right, as illustrated in Figure A5.6, where the LM curve shifts from LM_1 to LM_2. As a result, interest rates fall and real GDP rises. The lower interest rate following the increase in the money supply stimulates investment and perhaps consumer expenditure, leading to a higher real GDP.

It is worth noting that if the LM curve is horizontal – the extreme Keynesian case – monetary policy would be ineffective in stimulating the economy. The increase in the money supply would simply be held in idle money balances and interest rates would be unaffected. In such circumstances, the demand for money is perfectly elastic at the going interest rate leading to the liquidity trap. In contrast, if the LM curve were vertical, the extreme monetarist case, an increase in the money supply shifts the LM curve to the right leading to lower interest rates and a higher increase in real GDP than if the LM curve were upward sloping or more elastic. We suggest you draw the relevant diagram to test this point. Clearly, the elasticity of the LM curve is important in determining the impact of macroeconomic policy. Equally, the slope of the IS curve will influence the extent to which interest rates and real GDP alter following monetary policy changes.

Conclusion

IS–LM analysis is concerned with the relationship between interest rates and real GDP and equilibrium in the goods (IS) and money (LM) markets. It provides an alternative insight into the effects of fiscal and monetary policies on the macroeconomy than that provided by the AD–AS analysis mainly used in this book. However, to repeat, not all macroeconomics courses use IS–LM analysis and you should check the course syllabus before spending time studying it.

Chapter 6

MANAGEMENT OF THE ECONOMY – AN OVERVIEW

Aims and learning outcomes

The previous chapters have, essentially, been concerned with two major aspects of macroeconomics, namely:

- the meaning and measurement of economic activity;
- the determination of the level of economic activity.

In Chapters 7 through to 12 we turn to consider the policy options available to governments (and central banks) to manage the economy and to achieve a range of economic objectives. Policies at the macroeconomic level may be categorised into two groups:

- demand-side policies;
- supply-side policies.

Demand-side policies are concerned with management of the level of aggregate demand in the economy to maintain economic stability from year to year. In this sense they are often referred to as short-run policies.

Supply-side policies refer to those measures which are aimed at creating the conditions which support sustainable increased aggregate supply or economic growth in the long run.

Chapters 7 to 9 deal with the two fundamental approaches to demand management in terms of the domestic economy. These are:

- fiscal policy;
- monetary policy.

Chapter 10 looks at the determination of economic growth over the long run and various policy options which are collectively referred to as *supply-side policies*. Chapters 11 and 12 look at the application of economic policies with respect to two main economic objectives involving the maintenance of price stability and full employment of the economy's resources.

In this chapter we set the scene for our analysis of the various macroeconomic policies and objectives by providing a broad overview of the main issues stemming from management of the economy. In particular, we discuss the following:

- policy targets, instruments and goals;
- macroeconomic policy trade-offs;
- macroeconomic policy options;
- dynamics of the economy.

At the outset, it is important to note that there is a major debate taking place in many parts of the world concerning the extent to which governments can and should intervene in the form of discretionary (active) policies to influence the level of economic activity. Should government policy seek to directly *change* the workings of the economy or to *influence* the macroeconomic climate while leaving the determination of economic activity essentially to free market forces? So-called *Keynesian economics* is associated with active government intervention primarily through fiscal policy to maintain economic stability. By contrast, so-called *monetarist economics* is closely aligned with the maintenance of monetary stability, while leaving the determination of the level of economic activity to the free market.

The debate concerning the optimal (and desirable) role of government in the economy stems from a philosophical shift amongst economists in recent decades. At the centre of the debate today is the limit to direct demand management by individual governments in a world which is becoming increasingly interdependent.

Learning outcomes

After studying this material you will be able to:

- Understand the range of economic objectives that governments may seek to achieve.
- Appreciate the potential trade-offs that arise as a result of the various policies that may be adopted by government.
- Identify the main issues in macroeconomic management.
- Recognise the essential differences between fiscal, monetary and supply-side policies.

Policy targets, instruments and goals

In attempting to understand the ways in which governments manage economies, it is important to recall the distinction, introduced earlier (Chapter 1, p.15), between *policy targets*, *policy instruments* and *policy goals*. The relationship is summarised as follows:

Policy targets → Policy instruments → Policy goals

Policy targets

Targets in the context of the macroeconomy may be defined as quantifiable aims set by governments. Examples of policy targets might be:

- the achievement of a particular rate of economic growth each year; for example, 3 per cent per annum in the case of a mature industrialised economy (such as the USA) and, perhaps 8 per cent per annum for an emerging economy (such as China);
- reduction in the level of unemployment by, say, 250,000 over the next 12 months;
- maintenance of inflation within a target range of, say, 1.5 to 2.5 per cent, year on year.

It is important to appreciate that the achievement of such targets in a macroeconomic sense are merely steps towards the achievement of particular goals of policy which are more fundamental to the long-term prospects of a country.

Policy instruments

Once the policy targets have been set, governments are able to choose from a range of policy instruments to help them achieve the targets – of course, this does not guarantee the targets will be met. Policy instruments may include:

- changes in taxation and government expenditure;
- changes in the level and structure of interest rates and the availability of credit in the financial markets;
- manipulation of the exchange rate (such as devaluation) in order to support a country's export sector;
- direct support for the export sector through subsidies or protectionist measures to stem imports (including tariffs and volume restrictions).

Policy goals

A policy goal is what the government is ultimately attempting to achieve over the longer run. Such goals may, and often do, include:

- full employment of resources across the economy;
- long-term price stability;
- a stable economic environment that is conducive to long-term investment by corporates and high and sustainable economic growth;
- a satisfactory balance of payments position, coupled with a stable currency value in the foreign exchange markets;
- an income and wealth distribution which ensures that the fruits of economic expansion are equitably shared amongst citizens.

The distinction between policy targets, policy instruments and policy goals will be evident in the discussions of macroeconomic policies in subsequent chapters.

Macroeconomic policy trade-offs

The successful achievement of the macroeconomic targets noted above is made all the more difficult by the existence of policy conflicts or what are often called policy *trade-offs*. Trade-offs may arise, such as between a lower rate of inflation and a higher rate of employment, in the policy measures adopted by government.

Application 6.1

The macroeconomics of globalisation

Read the following extract:

> The Atlantic Age has led us to a position in 2000 where about one fifth of world output is consumed outside the nation state in which it is produced. This is a stylised fact: one fifth of world output is traded, four fifths is domestic. This means that the centre of gravity, politically, is still located *inside* the nation state. Whatever we say about globalisation, our lives are still bounded by nation states. But in 1800 the proportion of world consumption which traversed borders was less than a tenth of what is it now, say 2 per cent of world output was traded. Thus the last 200 years have represented a massive surge in both the growth, and in the internationalisation of our economy. The internationalisation of our lives is massive compared to that of our great grandparents, in 1900, and theirs was already quite different to that of their great grandparents in 1800. For instance, we now routinely travel abroad to work, sometimes permanently, we travel for pleasure over distances undreamed of even by our grandparents. We derive our lifestyle in part from investments in overseas assets, via our pension funds, our bank accounts, our dividends. The international flow of technology and know-how, of physical capital across borders, and of multinational production has expanded enormously over the last two centuries. One interesting feature of this emerging global scene is the role of the transnational business. The world economy has a trend rate of growth of about 3 per cent pa. World trade grows at about 6 per cent pa. So the world economy is growing, and as it grows, it is becoming more international. But foreign direct investment, that is investment overseas by transnational business, is growing at 9 per cent pa. It is global business not global trade which is the defining driver of our new world.

Source: Extract from a paper by Stephen Regan, 'The World Economy in 2002', Cranfield School of Management, 2002.

Activity

Given the macroeconomics of *globalisation*, consider the implications for government management of domestic economies.

For example, a country experiencing a stagnation of economic activity – evidenced by rising unemployment and falling output – alongside a higher inflation rate (a situation commonly described as one of *stagflation*) will be faced with a policy dilemma. A stimulus to economic activity stemming, for example, from a cut in direct taxation or a reduction in the cost of borrowing (short-term interest rates) is likely to add to inflationary pressures. In other words, a pick-up in output and the employment of resources may lag behind the rise in aggregate demand in the economy. In contrast, efforts to reduce inflation, by way of increasing short-term interest rates and/or imposing higher taxation will aggravate an economic slowdown and lead to still further rises in the unemployment total in the short term.

Macroeconomic policy options

At the centre of understanding the macroeconomy lies the relationship between aggregate supply and the components of planned expenditure or aggregate demand. Macroeconomic equilibrium is defined as a situation in which aggregate supply (output) equals aggregate demand. That is

Macroeconomic equilibrium

Output = Consumption expenditure + Investment expenditure + Government expenditure + Exports expenditure – Imports expenditure

Policies which focus on creating the conditions for a sustainable growth in output (Y) are referred to as *supply-side policies*. Policies that focus on controlling or influencing aggregate expenditure are referred to as *demand-side policies*.

Using the standard notation set out in previous chapters, we can summarise the policy options with examples of particular policy measures:

Macroeconomic policy options

$$Y = \underbrace{C + I + G + (X - M)}$$

Y ↓ *Supply-side policies*	$C + I + G + (X - M)$ *Demand-side policies*
■ Employment policy	■ Fiscal policy
■ Competition policy	■ Monetary policy
■ Privatisation and deregulation	■ Exchange rate policy
■ Incentives to work and invest	■ Trade policy
(for further details see Chapter 10)	(for further details see Chapters 7, 8, 9, 13 and 15)

Although each of the policies identified above is described in detail in subsequent chapters, we provide a brief overview of each here.

Supply-side policy

Supply-side policy arises out of what is often termed *supply-side economics*. This refers to the use of microeconomic policy measures that are directed at tackling problems that restrict the aggregate supply (i.e. output) of goods and services in the economy. Supply-side policies, therefore, contrast with demand-side policies, especially fiscal and monetary policies, which are concerned with affecting the level of total or aggregate demand for goods and services. Supply-side measures are directed specifically at influencing productivity and output costs. These may involve the introduction of new technology, the encouragement of competition and enterprise, and privatisation of state assets, efforts to increase labour efficiency and other measures to improve the operation of the market economy. In other words, supply-side policy is essentially aimed at raising the productive capacity of the economy over time so that a growing demand for goods and services can be met without inflationary pressures. Increasing productive capacity, from year to year, is the result of *economic growth*. Capacity may be increased either as a result of an accumulation of resources (land, labour and capital) or an improvement in the utilisation of existing resources through improved management of resources and technological progress.

The concept of productive capacity at a point in time may be likened to the volume of a barrel. As we discussed in Chapter 3, economic growth over time will increase this productive capacity as represented by a bigger barrel. Figure 6.1 illustrates this analogy showing a growth in productive capacity between the

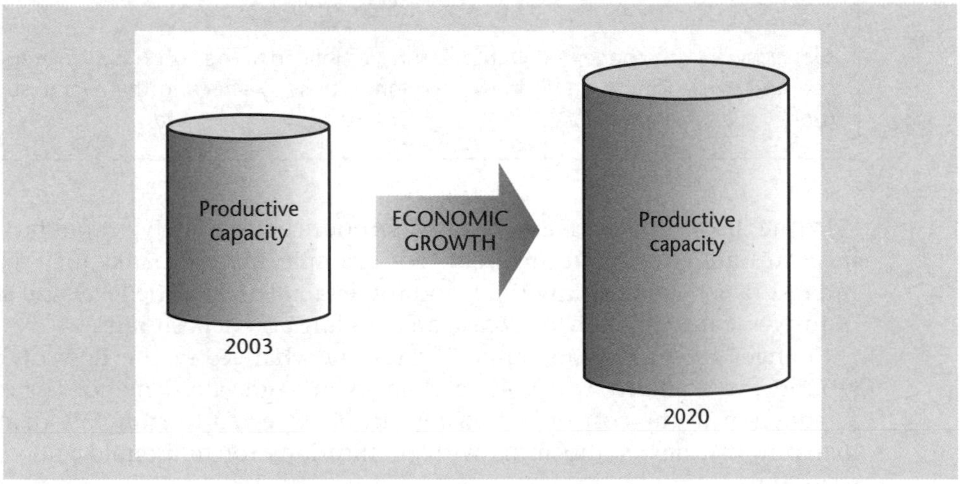

Figure 6.1 Economic growth and productive capacity

years 2003 and 2020. Of course this does not imply that an economy's full potential productive capacity is always being utilised – this will depend on many factors, not least the demand for goods and services, as discussed fully in Chapters 4 and 5.

Demand-side policies

As shown above, demand-side policy refers to any measures which are aimed at directly controlling or indirectly influencing the level of aggregate demand in an economy. These measures fall under the headings of fiscal, monetary, exchange rate and trade policies.

Fiscal policy

Fiscal policy is concerned with decisions about the composition of and changes in the levels of government expenditure and taxation.

Since government expenditure is itself a major component of aggregate demand in every economy, changes in its level will have a direct impact on the overall level of spending in the economy. Similarly, changes in taxation cause consequent changes in the spending behaviour of consumers and firms – and hence the level of total economic activity. When fiscal policy is employed by governments with the explicit aim of directly managing the level of aggregate demand, this is known as *Keynesian demand management*.

Monetary policy

Monetary policy is concerned with measures to influence the cost (i.e. the rate of interest) and availability of credit in the economy, thereby affecting the overall supply of money (i.e. liquidity).

While fiscal changes are usually announced annually, monetary policy measures are often more frequent. For example, central banks may announce interest rate changes at any time, and these rapidly affect the level and structure of interest rates generally (such as bank lending and deposit rates).

Changes in (short-term) interest rates and changes in the flow of liquidity around the economy will lead to changes in aggregate demand. For example, a reduction in the cost of borrowing can be expected to stimulate demand for loans by consumers and firms with implications for household and corporate spending.

Aggregate demand includes expenditure on exports as well as expenditure on imports. The net effect ($X - M$) may be a trade surplus (and hence a stimulus to the economy) or a trade deficit (leading to a leakage of national income overseas).

Exchange rate and trade policies

Exchange rate policy is concerned with the external value of a currency in the foreign exchange markets with implications for the price of exports in foreign economies, the price of imports in the domestic economy and international trade flows.

Changes in relative prices can be expected to lead to changes in the volumes of exports and imports demanded. The combination of price and volume changes affects the values of exports and imports and therefore aggregate demand.

Exchange rate policies range from leaving the determination of the rate (*vis-à-vis* other currencies) completely to market forces, to intervention in the foreign exchange market to influence the rate. These two extremes give rise to a *floating* exchange rate regime and a *fixed* exchange rate regime. Countries may sometimes select an intermediate policy in which the exchange rate is determined by a combination of market forces and limited intervention by the relevant authorities. This situation is sometimes referred as a *managed floating* exchange rate regime or a 'managed float'.

While the flow of exports and imports may be affected by the use of an appropriate exchange rate policy, countries may also choose to adopt particular trade policies to achieve the same outcome. Trade policies range from free trade to trade embargoes. Between these two extremes we can identify situations of varying degrees of 'protectionism' which embrace tariffs, quotas, export subsidies, etc. Trade and protectionism are discussed in detail in Chapter 13.

Dynamics of the economy

Having set out above a brief overview of the main demand and supply-side policy options available to countries, we can now illustrate the complexity of macroeconomic management by viewing the economy again in terms of the 'barrel', illustrated earlier (p.61) and in Figure 6.1. The level of aggregate spending at any time can be likened to a particular level of water in the barrel; while the capacity of the barrel determines the full potential aggregate supply (i.e. long-run real GDP). This is illustrated in Figure 6.2.

In this figure, the level of aggregate demand ($C + I + G + X - M$) is below the full capacity of the economy (i.e. the top of the barrel). As we discussed in Chapter 3, the level of spending will be affected by changes in the various injections into the circular flow of income and by changes in the various leakages. The various

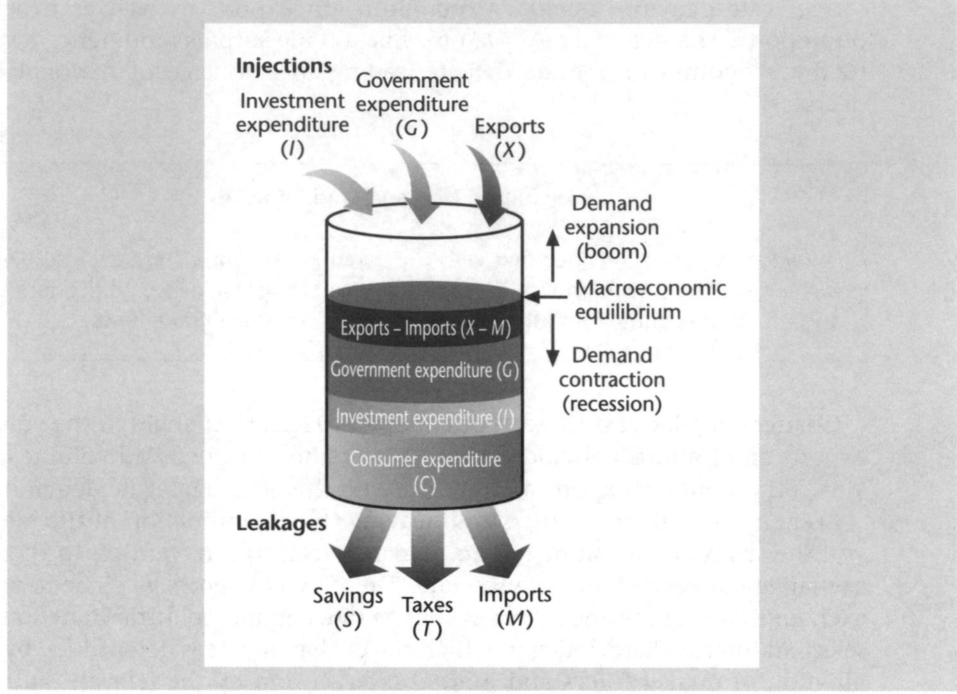

Figure 6.2 Macroeconomic policy and economic activity

injections and leakages and their effect on aggregate demand are illustrated in Figure 6.2.

At any point of time we can define *macroeconomic equilibrium* as a situation in which the total size of injections is matched by the total size of leakages, so that the level of national income and therefore economic activity (the level of water in our barrel) remains constant.

In reality, an equilibrium is likely to be extremely temporary, given the reality that decisions by firms, households, government and foreigners will be changing continuously. In the real world the total of the expenditure plans by the various economic agents are unlikely to match the actual level of output produced. A mismatch between expenditure plans and production decisions will inevitably lead to *unplanned* changes in inventories (i.e. stocks) and, hence, to changes in the level of production and economic activity.

Figure 6.2 also illustrates the various macroeconomic policy options noted above. Supply-side policy is about productive capacity – i.e. expanding the size of the barrel. Demand-side policy is about using fiscal, monetary, exchange rate and trade policies to affect the various injections and leakages and therefore the level of spending and the level of national income in the economy – or the water level in our barrel.

Application 6.2

Will cutting wages work?

In the following extract from his book *Treatise on Money* (1930), vol. 1, Keynes argued that creating unemployment and cutting wages in a recession could be self-defeating and simply lead to a further fall in demand in the economy. When planned savings exceed planned investment businesses suffer losses and entrepreneurs:

> will seek to protect themselves by throwing their employees out of work or reducing their wages. But even this will not improve their position, since the spending power of the public will be reduced by just as much as the aggregate costs of production. By however much entrepreneurs reduce wages and however many of their employees they throw out of work, they will continue to make losses so long as the community continues to save in excess of new investment.

Activity

Consider the strengths and weaknesses of Keynes' argument. What are its implications for the management of the economy?

Concluding remarks

This chapter has been concerned with setting the scene for the subsequent chapters on different aspects of the management of the economy. We have considered the range of macroeconomic goals that governments may pursue and have clarified the differences between policy targets, policy instruments and policy goals. We have also identified trade-offs between policy targets, an issue that will surface from time to time in our more detailed discussion of the different aspects of macroeconomic management in the following chapters. In addition, policies concerned with influencing aggregate demand have been distinguished from those more related to supporting long-term growth in aggregate supply. Finally, we have introduced the main policy instruments, namely fiscal policy and monetary policy, concerned with demand management.

We now turn to considering these policy instruments in detail. Chapter 7 looks at fiscal policy and Chapters 8 and 9 at money and monetary policy.

✔ Key learning points

- *Policy targets* are quantifiable aims which governments attempt to achieve using policy instruments.

- *Policy instruments* include changes in taxation and government expenditure, changes in the level and structure of interest rates, credit restrictions and other monetary controls, manipulation of the exchange rate and measures to influence or control exports and imports.
- *Policy goals* are what the government is attempting to achieve over the longer run such as stable prices, full employment, strong and sustainable economic growth, a satisfactory balance of payments position, a stable currency and an equitable distribution of income and wealth.
- *Macroeconomic equilibrium* is defined as a situation in which aggregate supply (output) equals aggregate demand.
- Policies which focus on creating the conditions for sustainable growth in output are referred to as *supply-side policies*.
- Policies that focus on controlling or influencing aggregate demand (expenditure) are referred to as *demand-side policies*.
- *Supply-side policies* include employment policy, competition policy, privatisation and deregulation as well as incentives to work and save.
- *Demand-side policies* include fiscal policy, monetary policy, exchange rate and trade policies.
- *Fiscal policy* is concerned with decisions about the composition of and changes in the levels of government expenditure and taxation.
- *Monetary policy* is concerned with measures to influence the cost (i.e. the rate of interest) and availability of credit in the economy, thereby affecting the overall supply of money (i.e. liquidity).
- *Exchange rate policy* is concerned with the external value of currency in the foreign exchange markets with implications for the price of exports in foreign economies, the domestic price of imports and international trade flows.

? Topics for discussion

1. Differentiate between demand-side and supply-side policies.
2. Provide a short report for a country of your choice highlighting the current economic situation. Suggest some economic policy responses to address any economic challenges you identify.
3. Distinguish between policy targets, policy instruments and policy goals. Give examples of each.
4. It is often suggested that there is a trade-off between unemployment and inflation. What do you understand by this?
5. A country is facing rising inflationary pressures. Identify and illustrate the policy options to deal with these pressures from both the demand-side and supply-side of the economy.

Chapter 7

FISCAL POLICY AND GOVERNMENT FINANCES

Aims and learning outcomes

The previous chapter provided an overview of the management of the economy. In this chapter we look at the nature of fiscal policy as a method of macroeconomic management. Deliberate changes in government spending and tax rates intended to stabilise the economy are referred to as *discretionary fiscal policy*. The spotlight in this chapter is on discretionary fiscal policy and the related subjects of the public finances and government budgetary policy.

The idea of using fiscal policy for demand management stems largely from the work of the British economist John Maynard Keynes in the 1930s and is concerned with manipulating taxation (personal and/or corporate) and government expenditure to influence the level of economic activity. In his book *The General Theory of Employment, Interest and Money* (1936), Keynes argued that demand deficient unemployment (see p.300) resulted from a lack of aggregate demand and that market forces alone are unable to generate sufficient jobs to remove this unemployment, in particular within the short to medium term. His solution was the use of discretionary fiscal policy to stimulate demand. *Fiscal policy* is the term economists use to describe policies directed at changes in government spending and taxation. Remember from Chapter 3 that an increase in government expenditure (G) is an *injection* into the circular flow of income. Hence, an increase in G will expand aggregate demand and, if the economy has sufficient spare capacity to meet this extra demand, physical production (i.e. *real* national income) and employment will also increase. In contrast, taxation is referred to as a *leakage* from the circular flow of income, such that an increase in taxes will reduce aggregate demand and the level of economic activity. Similarly, a cut in government expenditure or a reduction in taxation will have opposite effects on the economy.

In Chapters 4 and 5 we also identified how inflationary and deflationary gaps between aggregate demand and aggregate supply could arise. Keynes was particularly concerned with a deflationary gap when he wrote *The General Theory*. The 1930s were a time of high unemployment. From the 1950s, however, Keynesian economists were more concerned with keeping down inflation. Keynes had argued that government spending and taxation levels could be used to eliminate a deflationary gap in the economy. The resulting rise in public and then private spending through the national income *multiplier effect* (see pp.87–92) would produce a sustained rise in economic activity. Keynesians argued that an inflationary gap could be removed in a similar way, by provoking a fall in spending using discretionary fiscal policy. The term 'Keynesians' is used to describe economists who have followed and developed the ideas of Keynes.

In this chapter the following concepts are covered:

- fiscal policy, inflationary and deflationary gaps;
- problems with fine tuning aggregate demand;
- government expenditure and fiscal policy;
- taxation and fiscal policy;
- government borrowing;
- criticisms of fiscal policy and deficit financing.

In macroeconomics an understanding of fiscal policy is essential if we are to analyse macroeconomic demand management critically. That is to say, if we are to understand the nature of demand management using Keynesian techniques and the possible difficulties that may arise, we need a thorough grounding in discretionary fiscal policy. The purpose of this chapter is to provide that grounding.

Learning outcomes

After studying this material you will be able to:

- Recognise the meaning of government *discretionary fiscal policy* measures in an economy.
- Appreciate the rationale for discretionary fiscal policy in the context of *macroeconomic management*.
- Identify difficulties that may be faced when using discretionary fiscal policy measures to manage the level of economic activity.
- Appreciate the development of *public choice theory*.
- Determine a government's *budgetary stance* at any given time.
- Appreciate the important role of *government borrowing* in demand management.
- Understand the relationship between government borrowing and the *national debt*.

Fiscal policy, inflationary and deflationary gaps

A *deflationary gap* represents a situation of deficiency in demand in the economy, indicating the amount by which aggregate demand must be increased and exists when the equilibrium level of national income is below its full employment potential. To increase aggregate demand to the level required to raise national income and therefore short-run aggregate supply to the full employment level, the government could either raise government expenditure or reduce taxation levels. Either of these measures would produce a multiple rise in demand through the *multiplier effect*.

In contrast, an *inflationary gap* represents a situation of excess demand in the economy and reflects the amount by which aggregate demand must be reduced

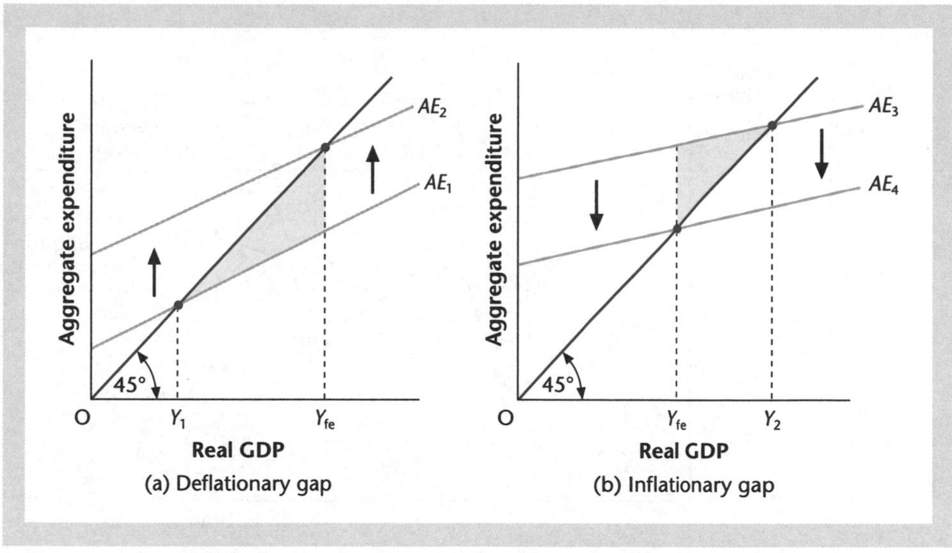

Figure 7.1 **Fiscal policy with deflationary and inflationary gaps**

in order to achieve the full employment equilibrium level of output with stable prices. To close this gap, the government could either reduce government expenditure or raise taxation levels. Again these measures would have the effect of reducing aggregate demand, this time through a negative multiplier effect. Figure 7.1 illustrates both cases for two different economic situations using the 45° line diagram introduced in Chapter 4.

In Figure 7.1(a) expansionary fiscal measures cause aggregate expenditure to rise from AE_1 to AE_2, leading to an increase in real GDP (national income) from Y_1 to Y_{fe}. In Figure 7.1(b) the level of aggregate expenditure is reduced from AE_3 to AE_4 as a result of contractionary fiscal measures. Note that in this case, the economy's full potential output is Y_{fe} – any output to the right of this, such as Y_2, cannot be produced in the short run. In contrast, Y_1 in (a) is below Y_{fe} and so an increase in aggregate expenditure will lead to an increase in real GDP. In both cases Y_{fe} represents the equilibrium level of national income with full employment and stable prices. Note also that the change in aggregate expenditure required in both figures is smaller than the resulting change in national income. The difference reflects the multiplier effect.

Fiscal policy and fine-tuning

Fiscal policy, used in this manner, is often described as a policy of *fine-tuning* aggregate expenditure to maintain equilibrium national income at full employment output without inflation.

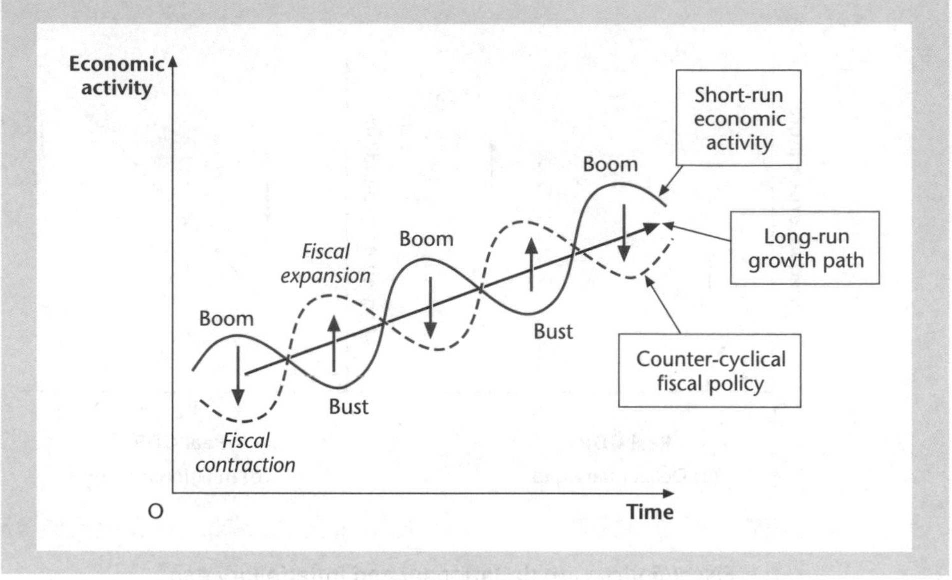

Figure 7.2 Fiscal policy and business cycles

The central message of Keynesian economics is that governments can smooth out cyclical fluctuation, in national income through fine-tuning demand using fiscal policy. To offset short-run fluctuations in the level of economic activity, known as *business cycles*, Keynesian economics identifies a continuing role for the state to monitor and influence the level of aggregate demand. This would involve contractionary fiscal policy measures during economic booms and expansionary fiscal policy measures during economic busts – as shown in Figure 7.2. Such policy decisions are often referred to as *counter-cyclical* fiscal policy. If appropriate fiscal actions are carried out at the right time, all of the time, then short-run fluctuations in economic activity should be neutralised, allowing the economy to grow smoothly along its long-run growth path. However, as we discuss in detail later in this chapter, there are many pitfalls with this approach to macroeconomic management.

The use of fiscal policy measures by the government to influence the level of economic activity gives rise to the label *discretionary fiscal policy* (or *stabilisation policy*). In contrast, there is a sense in which fiscal policy helps to stabilise economic activity *automatically*. For instance, if the level of unemployment rises, tax revenue to the government will tend to decline (income tax revenues will fall as incomes contract and less spending in the shops leads to lower receipts from sales taxes); while government expenditure on the various forms of welfare benefits will automatically rise as unemployment increases, unless the government takes positive steps to stop this happening by cutting government expenditure. The fall in tax revenue represents a reduction in a leakage from the circular flow of

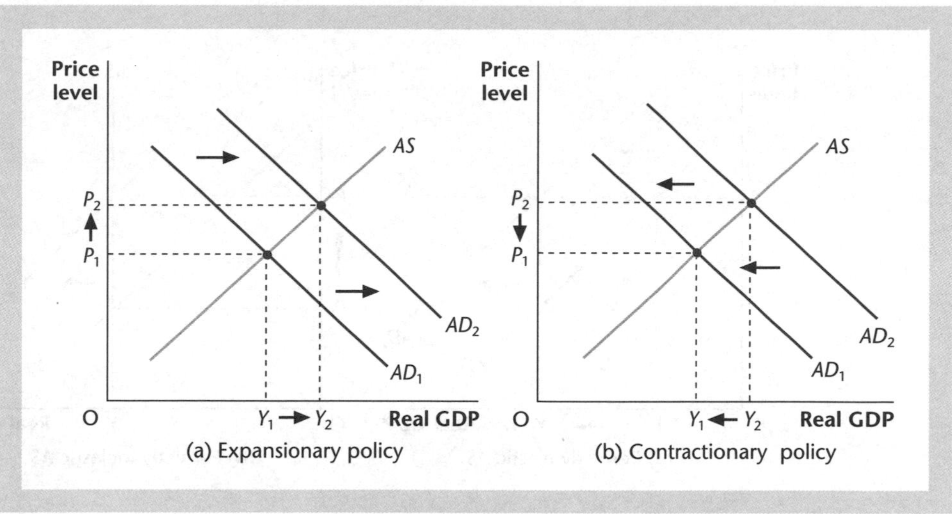

Figure 7.3 Fiscal policy and AD/AS curves

income, while the increase in government spending represents a larger injection into the circular flow. Combined, these effects result in aggregate demand falling less quickly than in the absence of government involvement in the economy. Fiscal policy, in this context, is referred to as an *automatic stabiliser*, i.e. there has been no deliberate action on the part of the government to alleviate any fall in aggregate demand due to rising unemployment. The effect occurs automatically, as the change in economic activity takes place.

Figure 7.1 shows how fiscal policy might be used to remove inflationary and deflationary gaps using one diagrammatic approach introduced earlier in the book, the aggregate expenditure or 45° line diagram. Alternatively, we can show the same effects using aggregate demand (AD) and aggregate supply (AS) curves. The AD–AS diagram was introduced and explained in Chapter 5.

In Figure 7.3(a) a reduction in tax rates or a rise in government expenditure leads to a shift in the AD curve to the right, representing an expansionary policy. This causes an increase in real national income (or GDP). Similarly, in Figure 7.3(b) an increase in tax rates or a fall in government spending causes a decrease in aggregate demand and real national income, representing a contractionary policy. Both increasing and reducing aggregate demand lead to a movement along the aggregate supply curve (AS) and an effect on the price level as well as real national income. Increasing aggregate demand using fiscal policy can be expected to lead to some rise in prices unless the AS curve is perfectly elastic. Decreasing aggregate demand can be expected to impose downward pressure on prices as spending in the economy falls.

Figures 7.4(a) and 7.4(b) show two opposite extreme cases. The first is where aggregate supply is perfectly elastic and the second where aggregate supply is

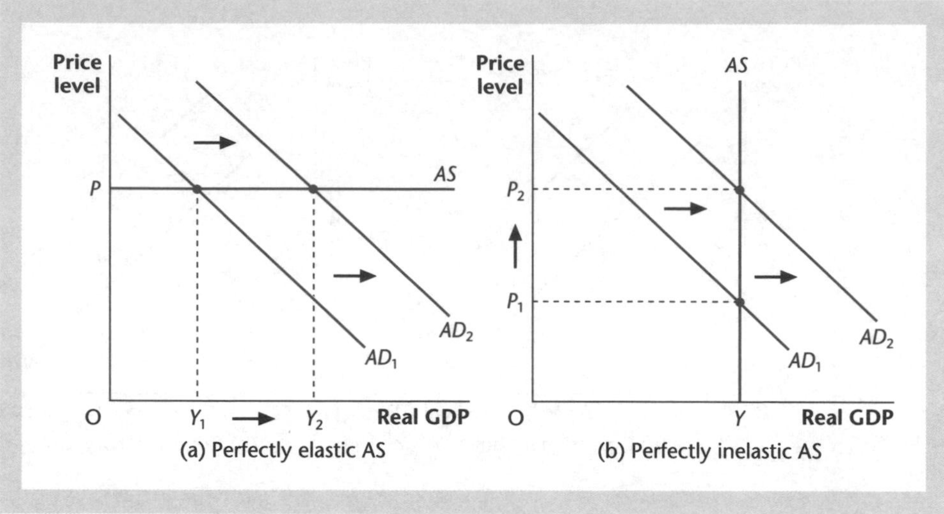

Figure 7.4 **Elasticity of aggregate supply – effectiveness of fiscal policy**

perfectly inelastic. In the first case there is no rise in prices when aggregate demand is increased from AD_1 to AD_2 by discretionary fiscal policy. All of the additional aggregate demand raises *real* national income (real GDP) from Y_1 to Y_2. This outcome is closest to a perfect Keynesian effect, in which discretionary fiscal policy aimed at raising aggregate demand benefits output and employment and has no adverse affect on the rate of inflation. This is most likely to occur when there is extensive unemployment and under-utilisation of existing resources (labour, capital and land) in the economy.

In the second case, where aggregate supply is perfectly inelastic, the increase in aggregate demand has no effect whatsoever on real GDP (and hence employment). Real GDP remains at Y while prices rise (from P_1 to P_2) leading to inflation. This outcome is the most likely to occur when there is already full employment and full utilisation of existing employed resources even before fiscal policy increases aggregate demand.

Perfectly elastic and perfectly inelastic aggregate supply curves are extreme cases and most often an upward sloping aggregate supply curve can be expected (as in Figure 7.3 (a)). In which case an increase in aggregate demand resulting from discretionary fiscal policy leads to some beneficial effects on real national income (i.e. real GDP), alongside some rise in the price level, depending upon the *elasticity* of the aggregate supply curve. A vertical aggregate supply curve will occur, however, at the full employment level of real national income. Only by shifting the long-run aggregate supply curve to the right can real national income then be increased and this is achieved through *economic growth* and *supply-side economic* measures, as detailed in Chapter 10, and not through discretionary fiscal policy impacting on aggregate demand.

Problems with fine-tuning aggregate demand

In the period following World War II through to the mid-1970s, a number of countries around the world attempted to fine-tune aggregate demand using fiscal policy (often coupled with monetary measures such as changes in interest rates – see the discussion of monetary policy in Chapter 9). On the one hand, from the late-1940s to the late-1960s unemployment remained low in Western economies, which seems to suggest that Keynesian demand management was successful. On the other hand, the reconstruction of the continental European economies after the War, alongside more international economic cooperation worldwide, for example with regard to exchange rates, and increased free trade supervised by the General Agreement on Tariffs and Trade (GATT) signed in 1947, led to an unparalleled expansion in world trade from which most countries benefited. The extent, therefore, to which low unemployment was the product of Keynesian demand fine-tuning remains uncertain. Certainly, in the 1970s both unemployment and inflation rose leading to *stagflation*, which Keynesian economics appeared unable to tackle through fiscal measures alone. Stagflation is a condition of rising unemployment and a rising price level. From a Keynesian viewpoint, to reverse rising unemployment requires reducing taxes and increasing government spending in order to stimulate total demand in the economy, while tackling inflation requires higher taxes and reduced government spending in order to reduce aggregate demand – clearly both policies cannot be pursued at the same time.

One possible solution to this dilemma, favoured by a number of Keynesian economists in the 1960s and 1970s, and pursued by some governments at that time, was the introduction of a *prices and incomes policy*. The idea was that inflation could be confined by either voluntary or mandatory limits on wage and price increases, while at the same time fiscal measures were used to support employment. For example, the government might agree that wages should be frozen or allowed to rise by a maximum of say, 3 per cent per annum, in line with the growth in labour productivity in the economy. This should, in turn, remove wage pressures on producers' costs and therefore the need for price increases. The history of prices and incomes policies is not, however, a happy one. While they often succeeded initially in restraining wage demands, they eventually broke down in country after country as workers refused to accept a reduction in real wages (i.e. wages deflated by prices) – the reduction in price increases tended to lag behind the wage freezes. This breakdown led to a subsequent wage-price explosion as workers tried to restore their real incomes and a return to high inflation, often with continued rising unemployment (for a further discussion see pp.274–278). The failure of prices and incomes policies to provide much more than a breathing space in the battle against inflation is not too surprising. Prices and incomes policies merely hold down cost increases coming from wages. They do nothing to tackle other sources of inflation, for example resulting from excess aggregate demand or from other cost increases, such as rising oil prices (a particular problem in the world economy of the 1970s).

Limitations of discretionary fiscal policy

Fine-tuning aggregate demand through changes in government spending and taxation is likely to have limited success for a number of reasons introduced below and discussed fully at the end of the chapter:

- The full impact of government spending programmes (particularly in the case of major capital projects) may take a long time to feed through into aggregate demand, reducing the ability of governments to fine-tune economic activity successfully.
- Once state expenditure is increased it may be difficult to reverse the spending. It makes no sense to the electorate to leave bridges, roads, hospitals, etc. half-built, and once pensions and other welfare provisions are increased, it is not politically easy to attempt to reduce them.
- The cost of large-scale government projects has a tendency to escalate out of all proportion to original estimates once the projects have commenced (civil engineering projects funded by governments are particularly prone to large cost overruns).
- Taxation including social security contributions as a percentage of GDP tends to drift upwards as governments raise taxes to finance higher state spending more often than they reduce them.

In general, government spending plans have become politically sensitive and therefore cannot be easily directed to fine-tune aggregate demand in the manner Keynesian economists recommend. How many governments are likely to be elected on the basis of promising to *reduce* government expenditure, even if cuts are justified from a macroeconomic viewpoint?

Public choice theory

From the 1960s some economists began to put forward an alternative view of government spending and taxation under the title of *public choice theory*. Under Keynesian economics governments are expected to operate as objective or disinterested regulators of the economy, altering taxation and public spending in the public interest to smooth out business cycles. But why should the politicians that direct policy and the civil servants who administer it be disinterested parties? Presumably politicians seek re-election and re-election is linked to winning public popularity by spending more, for instance on schools and hospitals, rather than less. Similarly, civil servants are likely to benefit directly, in terms of status, promotion prospects, continued employment, size of budgets handled, and so forth, if public spending programmes grow, not if they are curtailed. Public choice theory, which originated in the USA, dismissed the notion of disinterested fine-tuning of demand and explained the gradual increase of public spending and taxation over time in terms of politicians and government administrators pursuing their own interests (votes and big budgets) rather than the public interest. This viewpoint gained influence amongst economists and policy makers from

Application 7.1

The dangers of discretionary fiscal policy

The following story, first told by Professor Frank Paish, graphically indicates the dangers of intervention by government using discretionary fiscal policy measures.

Imagine that you are driving a car along a straight but undulating road. These undulations are not regular: some of the hills are steep, some are gentle; some are long, some are short.

You are given the instruction that you must keep the car going at a constant speed. To do this you will need to accelerate going up the hills and brake going down them.

There is a serious problem, however. The car is no ordinary car. It has the following distinctly unusual features:

- The front windscreen and side windows are blacked out, so you cannot see where you are going! All you can see is where you have *been* by looking in your rear-view mirror.
- The brake and accelerator pedals both work with a considerable and unpredictable delay.
- The car's suspension is so good that you cannot feel whether you are going up or downhill. You can only judge this by looking in your mirror and seeing whether the road behind you is higher or lower than you are.
- Finally (you are relieved to know), the car has a special sensor and automatic steering that keep it in the correct lane.

As you are going along, you see that the road behind you is higher, and you realise that you are going downhill. The car gets faster and faster. You brake – but nothing happens. In your zeal to slow the car down, you put your foot down on the brake as hard as you can.

When the brake eventually does come on, it comes on very strongly. By this time the car has already reached the bottom of the hill. As yet, however, you do not realise this and are still braking.

Now the car is going up the hill the other side, but the brakes are still on. Looking in your mirror, you eventually realise this. You take your foot off the brake and start accelerating. But the pedals do not respond. The car is still slowing down rapidly, and you only just manage to reach the top of the hill.

Then, as you start going down the other side, the brakes eventually come off and the accelerator comes on . . .

Activity

What lessons are contained in this story for government fiscal policy?

the 1970s, alongside another school of economic thought opposed to Keynesian economics called *monetarism* (see Chapters 8 and 9). Both helped to change the policy climate against Keynesian economics and discretionary fiscal policy measures.

So far we have discussed the essence of fiscal policy from the viewpoint of its role as a discretionary demand management instrument. We turn now to a more general analysis of government expenditure and taxation decisions, in terms of their overall structure and the role of the public sector finances.

There are three broad elements to government sector finance:

- expenditures at national and local levels;
- taxation to provide an income to government at all levels in order to finance these expenditure plans;
- government borrowing if expenditure exceeds income.

Government expenditure and fiscal policy

Governments spend vast sums of money on our behalf (e.g. in the fiscal year 2002, the Federal Government of the USA spent a total of $1,918bn – this *excludes* the spending carried out by individual state governments in the USA). Government expenditure represents a major injection into the circular flow of income of all industrialised economies and, as such, is an important source of changes in the level of national income. The injection takes place at three levels:

- at the national level by the central or federal government;
- at the local level through state governments (in Federal countries) and municipalities (local authorities);
- through state-owned enterprises, government agencies and trading services.

All of this expenditure takes the form of both current account expenditure (such as books for schools, notepaper for government offices, staff salaries, energy costs, etc.) and capital account expenditure (buildings, roads, etc.). In addition to current and capital account items, transfer payments are also made by central and local government, for example to pay state pensions, child benefit and housing subsidies. All of these categories of expenditure play a major role in the running of an economy in terms of the provision of public and social services, job creation and the redistribution of the national income across different sectors of society.

Government expenditure has important implications for the private sector. Some government expenditure (e.g. on law and order, education, health and transport) provides for a sound and more productive private sector. Without law and order or protection of private property rights, business trading activity and investment would undoubtedly collapse. Spending on education and spending on health improve the skills of the labour force and reduce time off work through sickness, respectively. Good road and other transport links help to reduce the costs of trading geographically. Government expenditure can therefore be of considerable benefit to the economy, provided the spending is undertaken efficiently (without waste). Also, any element of government expenditure which is not spent on imported goods and services raises the level of demand in the domestic economy for the goods and services produced. This is equally true whether the expenditure takes the form of transfer payments to the household sector to spend, subsidies or grants to the business sector, or direct government spending on goods and services. Through the multiplier effect (reinforced by the accelerator effect – see pp.94–97) the initial increase in government spending will lead to an even greater increase in the demand for the output of the private sector, boosting aggregate demand as a whole. Balanced against this, however, government spending has to be financed.

Taxation and fiscal policy

Government income comes from a variety of sources, the main one being *taxation*. Other sources, which need only a brief mention here, are:

- social security contributions;
- surpluses (profits) of state enterprises and other state trading authorities paid over to government;
- rent, interest and dividends earned by central and local governments;
- sales of public assets (e.g. privatisation proceeds);
- direct charges to users of government services (e.g. the use of beds by private patients in state-run hospitals, charges for medicines provided by the state health system, college fees, etc.).

The primary function of taxation is to raise revenue to finance government expenditure, but it may also be used to influence expenditure patterns, to redistribute income and wealth, and to reflect other social and political objectives. It is tempting to look upon taxation as an 'evil', in that it can deter companies from investing more capital when high profit taxes reduce the potential returns to private investors and may deter individuals from working and saving, perhaps encouraging the growth of the so-called *underground economy* in which people work for cash and do not declare their income for tax purposes (see pp.27–29). We return to this issue in Chapter 10, when discussing the role of tax cuts as a supply-side measure to stimulate output and employment. Figure 7.5 provides details of taxation revenues as a percentage of GDP for a range of countries in the year 2000. It is clear from the table that governments play a large role in modern economies and to do this they need to raise large sums in taxation.

The primary functions of taxation are summarised in Box 7.1.

Political debates concerning taxation are more or less continuous nowadays. These debates generally reflect differing views about what is or is not an appropriate tax level and a 'good' tax system and structure. We postpone a discussion of the appropriate tax level to Chapter 10 and consider here only the principles of a 'good' tax system.

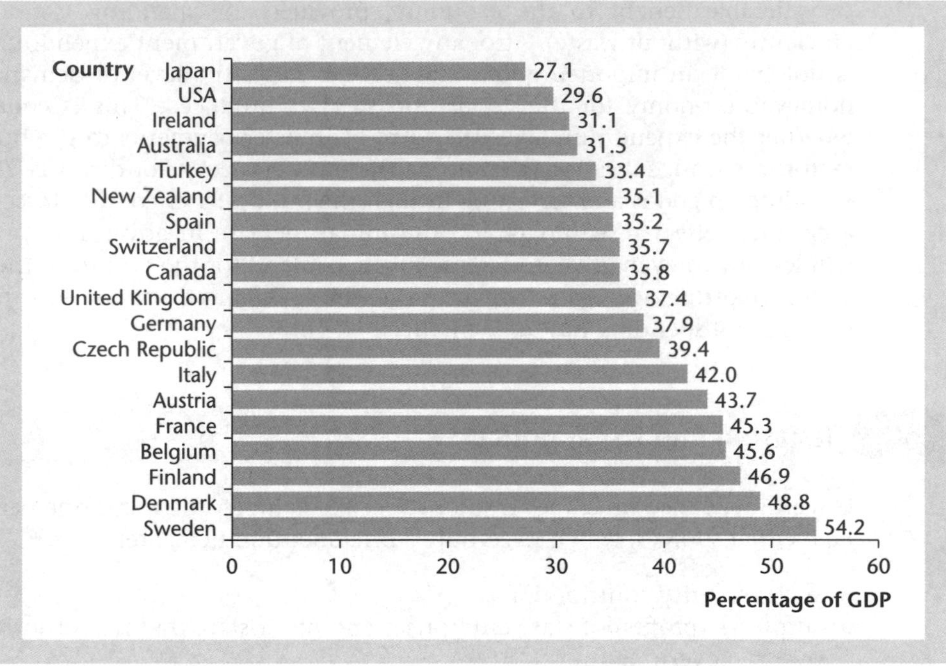

Figure 7.5 Total tax revenue for selected countries (2000)
Source: OECD

Box 7.1

Functions of taxation

- To raise revenue for government at all levels (central, federal, state, municipality, etc.) to finance its expenditures in total or in part (see the discussion of government borrowing, later).
- To redistribute wealth from the better-off to the less well-off – for example high taxes on those with high incomes or with considerable personal wealth, to finance social security payments to the less well-off in society.
- Taxes, in the form of import tariffs and duties, may be used to protect domestic industries from foreign competition (see pp.315–317 for a discussion of the use of tariffs).
- Taxes may also be levied on certain products to take account of their 'social costs'; for example, tax revenue from cigarette sales can help to offset the cost to the nation of funding health care for those suffering from smoking-related diseases, while the tax itself should act as an incentive to give up smoking. Likewise, tax on petrol may help to encourage economy with regard to petrol consumption and hence reduce the pollution from car emissions.

In general terms, a tax system may be deemed well designed if it is structured such that:

- The amount of tax to be paid is easily understood by everyone, so that uncertainty and consequent damage to the economy does not occur.
- Payment is convenient (e.g. the 'pay-as-you-earn' (PAYE) system in the UK, which collects income tax on employees' earnings from employers and before wages are paid to the employees; or sales taxes on goods and services paid for at the point of sale).
- The government's tax collection costs are minimised compared with the amount of tax collected so that net revenues are maximised; similarly, compliance costs (costs to individuals and businesses of complying with the payment of taxes, e.g. collecting taxes on behalf of the government) should be kept as low as possible.
- Tax rates can readily be adjusted up or down to reflect changing economic circumstances.
- Work, investment and enterprise are not greatly discouraged because of tax levels, otherwise economic activity and tax revenues will suffer through disincentive effects.
- Evasion and avoidance of the tax is difficult. Evasion occurs when individuals and businesses illegally fail to pay the taxes due. Avoidance involves individuals and businesses adopting strategies that legally reduce their tax bills (e.g. claiming maximum allowable expenses against tax). Both evasion and avoidance reduce the desired tax yield.

These principles are generally agreed. Some economists argue, however, that a further requirement is that people should pay taxes according to their *ability to pay*. This is far more controversial because it may conflict with the goals of minimising evasion, avoidance and collection costs, and may discourage work and enterprise. In addition, this issue has strong political undertones – consider, for example, the controversy that surrounds any attempt to take more tax from 'the rich'. Some see this as being only fair because the rich can afford to pay the extra tax. Others argue that taxing the rich damages private enterprise and therefore reduces national income and ultimately tax revenues.

The various types of tax collected by the government may be categorised in a number of ways, namely: *progressive, regressive* and *proportional* as well as *direct* and *indirect*. We describe the characteristics as well as the advantages and disadvantages of each type of tax in turn.

Progressive taxes

A *progressive tax* is one that takes a greater proportion of people's income as their income rises.

This is the type of income tax system used in most economies. There are several arguments which can be made both for and against progressive tax systems. Generally, progressive taxes facilitate a redistribution of wealth from the better off to the poorer sections of society, especially when combined with state welfare payments. Such redistribution may be an objective of government. Also, a progressive income tax may help counterbalance the regressive nature of other taxes, which may bear more heavily on the less well-off, such as sales taxes on food, drink and tobacco. In addition, progressive taxation may be more politically acceptable to society than other forms of taxation in so far as it is regarded as socially just or equitable.

At the same time, however, high and progressive taxation can act as a deterrent to investment and initiative in both the business and household sectors; while encouraging tax evasion and the use of economic resources in inventing complex tax avoidance schemes. In most countries tax accountants and lawyers are amongst the highest paid of professionals! It can also encourage a transfer of wealth to other countries as individuals and businesses attempt to avoid paying high tax rates. The result is the establishment of 'tax havens' overseas. Moreover, progressive taxation may encourage an unsustainable growth in public spending, especially if in democracies the majority vote for more spending on health, education, etc., and attempt to place the resulting costs on the shoulders of a rich but declining minority.

Regressive taxes

A *regressive tax* takes a higher proportion of income from those least able to pay.

An example of a regressive tax would be a tax on essential goods and services such as basic food stuffs and housing or taxes on household fuel bills (poorer households tend to spend a larger proportion of their incomes on food, accommodation and home heating than richer households).

Proportional taxes

Proportional taxes take a set proportion or percentage of income in tax.

For example, an income tax rate that is constant across different income levels is a proportional tax.

The difference between progressive, regressive and proportional income taxes is illustrated in Figure 7.6. Whereas the progressive tax falls more highly on higher income levels, the regressive tax does the reverse. The tax burden falls as incomes increase.

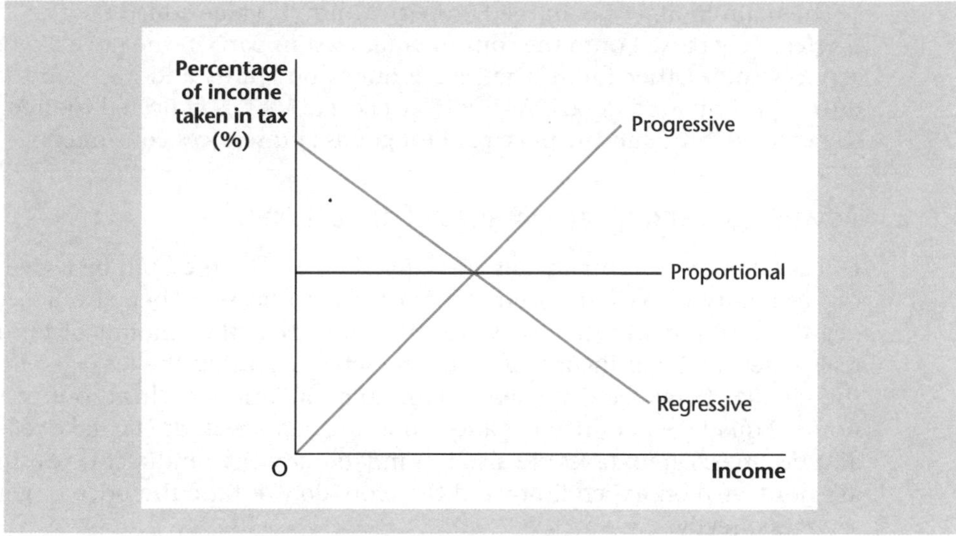

Figure 7.6 **Progressive, regressive and proportional tax rates**

Whether taxes are regressive, progressive or proportional, they can also be classified as direct or indirect taxes, depending on the method of payment.

Direct taxes

Direct taxes are paid directly to the tax collecting department by the taxpayers or their agents (e.g. their employers).

The main categories of direct taxes are income tax, profits tax (corporation tax), capital gains tax, and inheritance and wealth taxes. In addition, social security contributions, though not strictly a tax, are mainly collected directly from employees and employers. Direct taxes tend to be set by governments so as to be progressive or proportional. Their main advantages, at least from the government's viewpoint, are the generally low collection costs in relation to tax yield and the fact that payment of them is usually difficult to evade.

Indirect taxes

Indirect taxes, in contrast, are usually either regressive or proportional in nature and are applied to expenditure or the value added to production.

The main indirect tax in the European Union is value added tax (VAT), which is effectively passed onto the consumer (at least in part) in the price of goods and services sold. Other indirect taxes are duties on spirits and beers and tariffs or duties on imported goods. An indirect tax like VAT is collected indirectly from the taxpayer through the price paid for goods and services consumed.

Advantages and disadvantages of direct taxation

Direct taxes are potentially fair and equitable, in that they can be levied according to ability to pay (if governments choose to do so). They also act, to some degree, as automatic stabilisers (see p.141), in that the amount of tax revenue rises when national income is rising, thereby increasing the leakage effect from the circular flow of income and taking some inflationary 'heat' out of the economy. Equally, when incomes and profits are depressed, the tax take reflects this and declines. Direct taxes are also less inflationary than indirect taxes since they are not levied on expenditure and therefore do not raise the price of goods and services directly.

Two disadvantages of the main direct tax, namely income tax, are often stressed: these refer to the possibility of a *poverty trap* and a *fiscal drag effect.* The combination of income tax, social security contributions and the possible loss of earnings-related welfare benefits as income rises, can result in an extra \$1 of earned income leading to a decrease in an individual's disposable income of more than \$1. This represents an effective tax rate on additional income (known as the *marginal rate of tax*) of over 100 per cent for some low-income earners. This result is known as the *poverty trap* and is clearly a disincentive to working (see p.246 for a fuller discussion). It undoubtedly also encourages growth of activity in the underground (or shadow) economy representing the 'unofficial' or 'unrecorded' economy, where goods and services are provided but taxes are evaded.

An additional problem with direct taxes arises when tax-free allowances and tax thresholds (the level at which different marginal rates of tax come into effect) are not increased in line with the general rate of price inflation. In this situation, tax payments will tend to rise in real terms as people's and businesses's incomes rise (perhaps simply reflecting higher prices) and they are 'dragged' into higher income and profit tax brackets or become liable to pay tax for the first time – this process is referred to as *fiscal drag*. In turn fiscal drag could lead to higher wage demands as workers attempt to compensate for earnings lost through higher taxes and higher prices as firms try to recover some of their income lost through tax.

Advantages and disadvantages of indirect taxation

It is argued that indirect taxes are preferable to direct taxes, in that the consumer has the choice of not paying the tax (e.g. VAT) by simply not consuming the taxed good or service. Indirect taxes can also be levied on particular types of goods and services at different rates in order to encourage use (e.g. the use of public transport) or to discourage consumption (e.g. cigarettes, petrol). In this way, the allocation of the nation's resources is changed from the production of certain goods to the production of other, what government considers more 'desirable', goods. However, indirect taxes have a possible disadvantage, in that they may conceal the true tax burden that people face because they are hidden. The consumer may be unaware of the precise amount of tax that he or she is paying when consuming goods and services. By contrast, income and profits taxes are normally much more transparent to the payers.

Indirect taxation can be a flexible fiscal policy weapon because it may be possible for the rates to be altered quickly and with immediate effect. This is useful from the government's standpoint in terms of the speed with which aggregate demand may be stimulated or reduced as part of discretionary fiscal policy. At the same time, however, indirect taxes such as VAT tend to have an inflationary impact on the economy. By raising retail prices by the amount of the tax levied, there is a danger that this will tend to push up wage demands and may lead to a wage–price–wage spiral. Also, as noted above, indirect taxes tend to be regressive in nature, though a system of indirect taxes on luxury goods would be less regressive than, say, taxes on goods accepted as 'essentials' (e.g. food and accommodation) and could even be made progressive if tax fell heavily on goods and services consumed more by those with higher incomes.

As noted earlier, government expenditure is financed largely by tax revenue. However, when total expenditure exceeds tax revenue, the government, just like any firm or household, may borrow to finance the difference. We now turn to this aspect of state sector finance. Government borrowing has a major role to play in the operation of discretionary fiscal policy.

Government borrowing

The annual budget represents the government's fiscal strategy or *fiscal stance*. For example, the fiscal stance at a time of a deflationary gap may be one of *deficit financing,* whereby the government seeks to boost the economy by planning for a budget deficit (i.e. government expenditure, an injection into the circular flow of income, is planned to exceed tax revenue, a leakage from the circular flow of income). The effect of this will be an expansion of aggregate demand, leading to more income and employment and perhaps higher prices, through the multiplier effect. In contrast, if the economy is overheating (i.e. an inflationary gap is emerging combined with greater penetration of imports into the economy), the government could plan for a budget surplus or for tax revenues to exceed government spending, in order to slow down the general level of economic activity. In this way, the budget is a major policy instrument available to a government to help it achieve particular economic objectives, for example higher employment, faster economic growth and lower inflation.

The government's budget deficit or surplus

The amount of money which the government sector borrows during a given financial year when its expenditure outstrips tax receipts is referred to as the *budget deficit*.

The size of the budget deficit may be determined by a number of factors, namely:

- the size of the budget deficit of central, state and local governments;
- the size of the deficit of state industries and other state-owned corporations financed by borrowing from non-government sources;
- the amount of net lending by government to the private sector and overseas;
- the government sector's receipts from the sale of financial assets and other financial transactions;
- the government sector's receipts from the sale of real assets (e.g. the proceeds from privatisation).

When total tax revenues *exceed* total government sector expenditure there is a *budget surplus*.

A budget surplus means that the government is in a position to repay some of its accumulated borrowings from previous years.

The total of government borrowing over time makes up the country's *national debt* (and is sometimes called the *federal* or *gross public debt*). A budget deficit adds to the national debt, while a budget surplus reduces it. The manner in which government borrowing occurs is considered further, in Chapter 9.

If governments balanced their budgets every year then discretionary fiscal policy could not be used to tackle inflationary and deflationary gaps. At the same time, if governments continuously operated with budget deficits the size of the country's national debt would continuously rise. This debt would need to be financed by government borrowing, leading to an increasing amount of annual government spending allocated to paying interest on the debt. The result might be a vicious circle, in which budget deficits increase because of the need to pay more each year in interest charges on the national debt. Also, the debt would need to be serviced as government borrowing came due for repayment, as well as interest payments came due. Refinancing the national debt and paying the interest on the outstanding debt is known as *servicing* the national debt.

Continuous budget deficits are therefore unwise and in any event should not be necessary. Prudent government financing involves governments repaying debt (running budget surpluses) when the economy is prospering and borrowing because of budget deficits, to stimulate aggregate demand, when the economy is in recession.

Cyclical and structural deficits

Budget deficits caused by the business cycle, which affects the levels of tax revenues and government spending, are known as *cyclical deficits*. They disappear when the economy recovers. In contrast, budget deficits that last over a complete business cycle are known as *structural deficits*.

While government could take a relaxed attitude to a cyclical deficit, a structural deficit is far more worrying. It implies a long-run imbalance between government spending and tax receipts leading to a continuously rising national debt. If, as a consequence, the national debt were to rise faster than GDP, then the 'burden of the national debt' on the economy would increase. This burden is the cost of *servicing* the debt. It should be noted in this context that inflation reduces the effective real value of the national debt, as it does other debt in the economy. Concerns about the debt burden can rise, therefore, at times of low inflation or if prices in an economy actually fall (a situation of *deflation*).

Prudent government financing implies avoidance of structural deficits. Some governments have also operated a further prudent rule, that government long-term borrowing should only finance government capital investments (e.g. new roads, public buildings, other economic infrastructure) and not government current expenditures (e.g. welfare benefits, the pay of government staff and interest charges on the national debt).

The balanced budget multiplier

When the totals of government spending (G) and taxation (T) are the same in any year, this situation is referred to as a *balanced budget*.

It is important to appreciate that a balanced budget is not the same as a *neutral* budget. A budget stance is said to be neutral when the level of aggregate demand in the economy and hence economic activity is left unaltered by budgetary policy. At first glance it might seem that comparable expenditure and tax changes within the context of a balanced budget would have a zero effect upon aggregate demand and hence on national income because the government spending change is completely offset by the tax change. But this is not so, as the following example makes clear (see Box 7.2).

In general, allowing for savings, taxation and also imports, a balanced budget will have an expansionary effect on national income, as in this example. The impact of expenditure upon imports, another leakage from the circular flow of income, is reflected in the balanced budget multiplier in exactly the same way as savings are reflected.

Box 7.2

The balanced budget multiplier

Suppose that a government starting with a balanced budget raises its expenditure (G) by \$1bn, financed entirely by an increase in tax revenue (T) of \$1bn, leaving the overall budget balanced. Assume also that consumers spend 80 per cent of any increase in their incomes while 20 per cent is saved. That is to say, the marginal propensity to consume $mpc = 0.8$ and the marginal propensity to save $mps = 0.2$. Everything else being equal, the initial injection due to an increase in G will boost aggregate demand and will eventually result in national income (Y) rising by:

$$\Delta Y = \frac{1}{mps}\Delta G = 5 \times \$1\text{bn} = \$5\text{bn}$$

This is as a consequence of the multiplier effect which here is 1/0.2 or 5. (See pp.87–92 to review the meaning of the *mpc*, *mps* and multiplier effect.)

At the same time, however, the increase in taxation will have caused a rise in leakages from the circular flow of income, which acts to reduce the effect of injections of extra demand on the level of national income. Taking account of taxation makes the net result of the rise in government spending and taxation less straightforward because part of any increase in taxation may be financed by households reducing the rate of their *savings*. To the extent that this happens, then the increase of the leakage due to taxation will be offset by a reduction in a second leakage, savings. In other words, the *net* change in leakages is less than the change in taxation. Consequently, only that part of any increase in taxation that is financed by a reduction in consumer spending will affect the level of aggregate demand and national income. The initial impact of this in our example will be given by $0.8 \times \Delta T$ (i.e. $mpc \times$ the change in taxation) and will have a (negative) multiplier effect on aggregate demand in general, equal to:

$$\Delta Y = \frac{mpc \times \Delta T}{mps} = \frac{0.8T}{0.2} = \$4\text{bn}$$

Hence, the *net* result of an equivalent increase in G and T is that national income rises by (\$5bn – \$4bn) = \$1bn. This is known as the *balanced budget multiplier effect.*

Application 7.2

Where have all the Keynesians gone?

Read the following extract:

Do big deficits increase interest rates? There is a strange debate on this question going on between the Brookings Institution and *The Wall Street Journal* editorial page. The context, of course, is President George W.Bush's proposed $674bn tax cut.

The *Journal*, the temple of supply-side economics and advocate of the Bush plan, insists that deficits don't affect interest rates. Their editorials point to the Reagan years in the 1980s, when deficits were high and rates low. Supply-siders believe that reduced taxes on capital energise investment and growth – generating enough tax revenue to pay for the deficit. The *Journal* accuses Brookings of practicing 'Rubinomics', after the former Treasury Secretary under Bill Clinton, Robert Rubin, who made budget surpluses a fiscal Holy Grail.

The objects of the *Journal's* scorn are two Brookings economists, William Gale and Peter Orszag, authors of the recent influential paper *The Economic Effects of Long-Term Fiscal Discipline*. Gale and Orszag contend that increased deficits must hike interest rates. Despite their disclaimer that they're not troubled by short-term deficits, Gale and Orszag are essentially resurrecting the old 'crowding out' theory. Under that premise, government borrowing competes with private investment for a fixed supply of capital. Keynesians add that it all depends on whether the economy is at full employment.

But crowder-outers believe that government borrowing increases the overall demand for money; hence, the price of money – interest rates – must rise, too. Higher rates, according to Gale and Orszag, then raise the cost of capital, neutralise the benefit of the tax cut and actually reduce the net growth rate.

What's bizarre about this debate between the *Journal* and Brookings is the absence of a third party – those who believe in Keynesian economics. As several generations of Keynesians have pointed out, the actual effect of government deficits on interest rates depends on how slack the economy is and on what the Federal Reserve does. In a weak economy, government borrowing can energise consumer demand and economic growth without putting upward pressure on prices. Without a crystal ball that tells you consumer and investor confidence and Fed policy, you can't predict how deficits will affect rates, much less with the precision that Gale and Orszag suggest in their work.

The Keynesian dynamic still applies, but whatever happened to its champions? Here the story shifts from economics to politics. Moderate Democrats ▶

Application 7.2 continued

such as Rubin and Clinton were won over to the 'crowding out' theory because it fit the fiscal and political circumstances of the 1990s, when the budget was still suffering from the immense deficits bequeathed by Reagan and George Bush I. Rubin had an implicit deal with the Fed to trade lower deficits for lower rates. Centrist economists also saw the big surplus as insurance for Social Security's solvency.

Today, however, the economy is soft. Since Bush II took office, the US has shed 2.7 million jobs. We have a jobless recovery. Consumer borrowing is about at its limit. State budget deficits, now approaching a collective $80bn, will require hikes in taxes and cuts in services, further reducing consumer demand. An Iraq war will not generate much stimulus. And Bush's proposed tax cut delivers little stimulus this year.

In this political and fiscal climate, the Brookings' view is not so much wrong as unhelpful. It is axiomatic that large permanent public deficits are damaging. But it should be just as axiomatic that weak economies need significant, temporary pump priming that results in big deficits. Although Gale and Orszag concede as much, their passion is reserved for deficit reduction, and their paper is ammunition for the view that cutting deficits is virtuous policy in all seasons. Paradoxically, this leaves President Bush and the *Journal* editorial page in the anomalous role of pseudo-Keynesian apologists for deficits.

We are at precisely the phase of the business cycle when large deficits are needed. In fact, you can indeed grow your way out of huge public debt. The US did it after World War II, and interest rates stayed low. But contrary to Bush's premise that tax cuts on dividends will energise capital spending, the overhang of surplus capacity suggests the need for a Keynesian recovery led by public and private spending that stimulates demand.

In the current circumstance of stalled job creation, tapped-out consumers, and capacity overhang, the Bush/*Journal*/supply-side view is fanciful, and the Gale-Orszag resurrection of 'crowding out' is irrelevant. We need serious deficit spending this year – not tax cuts that favour dividends but spending that gives relief to consumers and state budgets and energises demand. This is the debate Brookings should be prosecuting. Yes, the long-run fiscal effects of Bush's tax cuts would be economically dubious, but as the master himself famously said: 'In the long run, we're all dead.'

Source: *'Economic Viewpoint'* by Robert Kuttner, *Business Week*, 3 February 2003, p.14.

Activity

In the light of the above discussion, consider the arguments for and against government deficit financing in times of recession. What economic changes exist if governments run fiscal deficits?

Criticisms of fiscal policy and deficit financing

Traditional Keynesian demand management techniques place considerable emphasis on the use of the government's budget to influence the level of economic activity. It was common for governments after 1945 to run a budget deficit financed by borrowing. For example, from the early 1950s UK governments ran budget deficits in all but one financial year (1969–70) until 1986. After 1986 the government had some years of budget surpluses, though years of deficits reappeared in the early 1990s.

During the 1970s, concern began to grow amongst economists about the economic effects of persistent deficit financing. This was especially true among *monetarists*. These economists had a number of criticisms to make about the way in which fiscal policy measures, via the budget, were directed at controlling aggregate demand in the economy. Essentially, monetarists expressed concern regarding the effect that government deficit financing had on the growth of the money supply and hence inflation. They criticised the management of aggregate demand and national income via discretionary fiscal policy for destabilising the economy. They also argued that discretionary fiscal policy had little impact upon the 'real' economy in the long run. By the real economy they were referring to the growth in physical output, and therefore employment, as against a rise in prices which leads to a growth only in the money value of production.

The monetarist critique of discretionary fiscal policy complements the criticisms of government spending and taxation put forward by *public choice* theorists, as reviewed earlier. Indeed, generally monetarists sympathise with the conclusions of public choice theory. In more specific terms, the monetarist criticisms of discretionary fiscal policy and government deficit financing may be summarised under the following five headings:

- intervention versus the free market;
- destabilising the economy;
- distortion of government expenditure;
- impact of deficit financing on private sector investment;
- budget deficit, money supply and inflation.

We discuss each of these criticisms in turn.

Intervention versus the free market

Keynesians and monetarists tend to disagree, sometimes fundamentally, about the appropriate role of the government in managing the economy. On the one hand, monetarists tend to favour free enterprise and competition, arguing that government intervention via demand management and fiscal policy measures hampers competitive forces and discourages the development of an enterprise culture. They also maintain that government expenditure is used as a prop for declining industries and hence fosters and perpetuates inefficient production. At the same time, high taxation to finance this expenditure, they argue, impedes the development of new industries and creates disincentives to work, save and invest. This critical view of the role of government and the use of fiscal policy can be readily associated with the approach of Mrs Thatcher's administration in the UK and President Reagan's in the USA during the 1980s.

Destabilising the economy

Keynesian economists regard fiscal policy as an effective way to dampen down the economic fluctuations associated with the business cycle. While monetarists argue that, far from dampening these fluctuations, discretionary fiscal policy has the effect of destabilising the economy by exaggerating the booms and slumps. They argue that this is due to government attempting to maintain aggregate demand at unsustainably high levels. This builds up inflationary pressures, which are further fed by more government spending and by an expansion of the money supply to ward off rising unemployment as industry becomes less price competitive. Moreover, they tend to argue that fiscal measures are often mistimed or misjudged thereby increasing rather than reducing cyclical fluctuations in the economy.

While the *direction* of the necessary discretionary fiscal policy may be obvious (e.g. the economy is slipping into recession and domestic expenditure needs 'pump priming'), the *timing* of the fiscal changes so as to have the desired effect on aggregate demand may be problematic – it could be uncertain how long it will take for tax changes and new government spending schemes to have the desired effect. Also, it may be difficult for government to estimate accurately the size of the fiscal changes needed to prevent recession (or inflation), especially if the multiplier effect is uncertain. Government fiscal measures may be associated with *information lags, decision lags* and *execution lags.*

> The term *information lag* refers to the delay between changes in economic activity occurring and the information about recessionary or inflationary developments becoming available to policy makers.

For example, government macroeconomic statistics are collected and analysed sometimes months after the events they record.

> The term *decision lag* refers to the delay between policy makers receiving information about macroeconomic changes and decisions being made in government to take counteracting fiscal measures.

For instance, the government's budget (tax and spending plans) may only be set once a year.

Finally, the *execution lag* refers to the delay between the announcement of tax and government expenditure changes and their effects on the economy.

The effect of this delay may be compounded by a failure of household expenditures to react quickly to fiscal incentives. In particular, a tax cut that households perceive to be short term only may not affect their consumption behaviour at all. This is to be expected if consumption is a function of *permanent income* rather than simply current income (see pp.73–74 for a discussion of the *consumption function* and the *permanent income hypothesis*).

Distortion of government expenditures

Most government expenditures are not quickly 'fine tuned' without damaging economic and social effects. Civil engineering schemes financed by government, such as road building programmes, cannot be quickly switched on and off. Leaving projects half-completed may not make any economic sense. Equally, varying state pensions, education spending and health care according to the state of the business cycle is not easy and in any event might be economically and socially damaging. From this prospective, government spending plans are not a useful instrument of short-term discretionary fiscal policy. In which case, more emphasis is placed on 'fine tuning' aggregate demand through the use of tax changes. But taxes can also have unintended economic and social consequences and the impact of tax changes on the economy may be delayed, especially if governments have a policy of only changing taxes and tax rates annually.

The impact of deficit financing on private sector investment

Monetarists argue that if the government borrows to finance budget deficits this forces up rates of interest in the financial markets. While the government has the ability to pay increased interest charges, either by raising taxes or by borrowing even more funds, the same does not apply to private-sector firms. Faced with higher interest rates, they may be forced to cut back on their investment spending plans. In addition, as interest rates rise, the exchange rate is also likely to rise because international capital flows are attracted by the higher interest rate (see pp.374–378 for a full discussion of this relationship). A rise in the external value of the currency can be expected to damage firms' competitiveness leading to a reduction in home sales (in favour of the now relatively cheaper imports) and exports. This in turn may be expected to cause still further cut-backs in investment expenditure as well as in employment.

This phenomenon, whereby increased government expenditure financed by increased borrowing leads to a reduction in private sector investment, is referred to by economists as *crowding out*.

> *Crowding out* refers to the decrease in private sector spending that occurs as a consequence of higher interest rates due to increased government borrowing in the capital markets to finance government expenditure.

The extent of the crowding out will depend on the extent to which interest rates rise and the extent to which private spending, especially investment, is dampened by the higher interest rates. As world capital markets become more and more integrated and as the growth of multinational companies that can tap various national capital markets continues, the relevance of crowding out is likely to diminish. It is unlikely that one government's borrowing, even when large, will have a significant impact upon the availability of worldwide capital funds for private investment expenditure.

Budget deficit, money supply and inflation

Monetarists argue that a persistent budget deficit forces the government into greater borrowing from the banking sector, causing the money supply to grow much faster than the output of goods and services, leading to inflation. The precise process by which this takes place will be discussed in Chapter 9. A common monetarist slogan to sum up this result is: 'too much money chasing too few goods causes inflation.' As the money supply and inflation grow, the international competitiveness of firms declines and unemployment rises.

Monetarists maintain, therefore, that governments should *not* try to manage aggregate demand directly but, instead, should focus their efforts on creating a stable monetary environment in which private enterprise can flourish. They argue that this is most readily achieved by reducing state intervention, balancing the government budget over the business cycle, and controlling the amount of money circulating in the economy in order to diminish inflationary pressures.

Concluding remarks

In this chapter we have studied the nature of discretionary fiscal policy and the use of discretionary fiscal policy as a countercyclical demand management tool. We have also looked in detail at the nature of government expenditure, government taxation and government borrowing.

The notion that government, by changing its expenditure and the level of taxation, can significantly influence aggregate demand and hence the level of economic activity has proved attractive at various times in the past. Up to the mid-1970s, many governments pursued policies of this type, known as Keynesian policies, after the writings of the British economist, John Maynard Keynes. However, the onset of stagflation (i.e. rising inflation and rising unemployment) coupled with the failure of prices and incomes policies led to a policy reappraisal from the mid-1970s. First, research identified failures in operating countercyclical policies – in particular there seemed to be a built-in 'ratchet effect', in which government spending and taxation rose but were rarely cut back, leading to what appeared to critics to be an ever-expanding state sector. Second, the theory that lay behind Keynesian economics, and which justified demand management by fiscal policy, was challenged by the rise of an alternative school of thought in economics, *monetarism*. The next two chapters are concerned with money and banking and the theoretical foundations as well as practical implications of monetary policy.

✔ Key learning points

- *Fiscal policy* is the term used to describe government macroeconomic policy that is concerned with changes in government expenditure and taxation.
- *Keynesian economics* emphasises the use by governments of *discretionary fiscal policy* to smooth out business cycles and remove inflationary and deflationary gaps.
- *Fine-tuning aggregate demand* using fiscal policy is, however, subject to a number of criticisms.
- Some criticisms of discretionary fiscal policy centre on a resulting rising burden of taxation, an overinflated state sector, disincentive effects on the private sector and mistimed interactions leading to economic instability.
- *Government expenditure* is the term used to cover all forms of state spending at national or federal, state and more local levels.
- *Taxes* are levied to finance government spending and influence the allocation of resources and the distribution of income and wealth.
- Taxes may be progressive, regressive or proportional. A *progressive* income tax falls more heavily on high incomes, i.e. it takes a larger proportion of the incomes of high earners than low earners. A *regressive* tax falls more lightly on those with high incomes than those with low incomes. A *proportional* tax is one that takes a constant proportion of income no matter the size of the income.
- Taxes divide into *direct taxes* (e.g. income and profits taxes) and *indirect taxes* (e.g. sales taxes including VAT).
- *Deficit financing* refers to government expenditure financed by borrowing; in other words, when the value of government spending exceeds the value of tax receipts thus adding to the country's national debt.
- The *national debt* is the total value of the stock of government debt at any given time. It is the product of the accumulated borrowing of government, less government debt repayments, over the years.
- The *budget deficit* is a term used to describe the amount of government borrowing needed to fill the gap between government spending and taxation in a given year. When governments spend less than they raise in taxation the result is a *budget surplus* and *debt repayment*.

- *Fiscal drag* refers to the automatic tendency for tax receipts to change directly with changes in the national income.
- A *balanced budget* is one where government spending and taxation receipts are equal.
- The *balanced budget multiplier* refers to the expansionary effect on national income even when government spending and tax revenues rise by the same amount.
- Other criticisms of discretionary fiscal policy, notably by so-called *monetarists*, relate to its possible failings in a market economy, including destabilising effects due to mistimed or misjudged changes in government spending and taxation, crowding-out effects on private investment, and inflationary effects through a consequent expansion of the money supply.
- *Public choice theory* complements the monetarist critique of Keynesian economics by drawing attention to self-seeking behaviour by politicians and government officials that leads to bloated government budgets and wasteful state expenditures.

? Topics for discussion

1. Under what economic circumstances might economists recommend fiscal intervention in a market economy?
2. Explain, using appropriate diagrams, how fiscal policy might be used to combat (a) an inflationary gap, and (b) a deflationary gap, in the economy.
3. What is the relationship between fiscal changes and the multiplier effect? Why does a balanced budget tend to stimulate the economy?
4. When might more government borrowing be inadvisable?
5. What is the relationship between the budget deficit and the national debt? When is the national debt likely to become more of an economic burden?
6. Why did economists tend to become more cautious about the benefits of Keynesian 'fine-tuning' of the economy from the mid-1970s?
7. What do you understand by the term 'crowding-out' and when is it likely to be most prevalent?
8. Under what circumstances might a progressive tax be more desirable than a proportional or regressive one? Give examples from your own economy of progressive, proportional and regressive taxes.
9. What is 'fiscal drag'? How might its economic effects be neutralised?

Chapter 8

MONEY, BANKING AND INTEREST RATES

Aims and learning outcomes

The purpose of this chapter is to set out the fundamental principles underlying the importance of money in a modern economy. The analysis first covers the nature and functions of money and how it has evolved over time. We then provide a detailed description of the role of the banking sector with respect to the creation of money as a basis for understanding the relationship between money, the banking system and the determination of interest rates. A central element of the chapter is the analysis of the impact of changes in the quantity of money flowing around the economy on output, employment and prices.

In particular, we cover the following topics relating to money:

- what is money?;
- measuring the money supply;
- banks and the creation of money;
- determination of monetary growth;
- determination of interest rates;
- money and economy policy.

It is important to stress at the outset that a clear and detailed understanding of the role of money and the banking system is essential in order to develop a critical appreciation of monetary policy and the principles of *monetarism* in modern economies. Monetarism represents a particular philosophy which is based on the premise that the root cause of inflation is a growth of the money supply in excess of an economy's growth of output. This philosophy lies at the heart of a proactive monetary policy approach to macroeconomic stability – in which 'money' is said to 'cause' inflation. This view contrasts with the alternative approach, held by Keynesian economists, which argues that money plays a more passive role in determining the level of economic activity and inflation. In other words, monetary growth occurs in *response* to a rising national income, output and expenditure.

Learning outcomes

After studying this material you will be able to:

- Understand what is money.
- Appreciate the different functions of money in a modern economy.
- Distinguish between 'narrow money' and 'broad money'.
- Understand the importance of the 'liquidity spectrum'.
- Recognise the different official measures of the money supply.
- Realise how commercial banks can 'create money' even when they have no legal power to print currency.
- Understand the role of money supply changes in the determination of interest rates.
- Appreciate the importance of money in macroeconomic policy.

What is money?

To most people, *money* is a collective term for the notes and coins in their immediate possession or in their bank accounts. Clearly, this is a correct interpretation of what is meant by the term 'money', but it is not a comprehensive definition, as we shall see.

In principle, anything can be classified as 'money'. For example, at various times throughout history, rare beads, precious metals and even livestock have been used as 'money'. The main precious metals employed for transactions purposes have been gold and silver but, with the passage of time, 'paper' money has developed starting as receipts for gold and silver deposited with institutions (e.g. goldsmiths) which were essentially the precursors of modern banks.

> The most general definition of money is any asset that is widely accepted for purposes of exchange, i.e. as payment for goods and services.

In this context, attempts to define and categorise money have traditionally started with identifying what functions money performs. We can identify four functions of money:

- a medium of exchange;
- a unit of account;
- a standard of deferred payment;
- a store of value.

We describe each of these functions in order to clarify the development of money.

A medium of exchange

Without money the only way of exchanging goods and services would be by means of barter. But barter requires a 'double coincidence of wants', which arises when one person wants to buy what another person wants to sell and vice versa. This situation will involve transaction costs of making exchanges, such as search costs for a willing trader. Money guarantees a double coincidence of wants because people with something to sell will always accept money in exchange, thus reducing the transaction costs of making exchanges. In this way, money is said to act as a lubricant that smoothes the mechanism of exchange.

A unit of account

Money should provide an agreed standard measure – i.e. a unit of account – by which the value of different goods and services can be compared. With the value of all goods and services denominated in money, the determination of relative prices is easy and quick. This, of course, is not the case in a barter economy in which the value of every good and service must be individually expressed in terms of all other goods and services.

A standard for deferred payment

This function of money reflects how much value will be given in return at some future date for goods and services provided or received now. Note that in order to provide an acceptable standard for deferred payments, it is important that money should at least maintain its value over a period of time, i.e. it should represent a *store of value.*

A store of value

Money is a store of value in the sense that it can be held and exchanged later for goods and services. If this were not the case then it would not be acceptable as a means of payment. In this context, inflation plays a vital role. Inflation reduces the purchasing power (i.e. value) of money and, hence, it is important for governments to maintain a relatively low inflation rate in order to ensure that confidence in the money issued is maintained.

It is a worthwhile exercise to discuss what could be classified as 'money' based on the above functions. Not surprisingly, we normally associate money with the legal tender of notes and coins in our pockets and deposited in our bank accounts which have been issued by governments. These pieces of paper and metal carry the authority of government and are therefore usually readily accepted by individuals and businesses as a means of payment (exchange) in day-to-day transactions. As such, the issue of notes and coins by governments is technically known as the *fiduciary issue* or *fiat currency* (in Latin *fiat* means 'let there be' and hence 'by decree').

Measuring the money supply

Over time, a wide range of different financial assets has evolved, making up the instruments which can be collectively referred to as 'money' in a modern economy. These instruments may be classified into one of two categories of money, referred to as *narrow money* and *broad money*.

Narrow money and broad money

> *Narrow money* reflects the medium of exchange function and thus refers to money balances that are readily available to finance current spending, i.e. balances available for transaction purposes.

> *Broad money* not only includes money balances held for transaction purposes, but incorporates money held as a form of saving. It provides an indicator of the private sector's holdings of *relatively* liquid assets – assets which can be converted with relative ease and without capital loss into spending on goods and services.

At the heart of what is meant by money and the measurement of the money supply is the concept of *liquidity*.

The concept of liquidity

> *Liquidity* is defined as the ability to transform a wealth holding into any form without loss of face value or delay.

Obviously, the most liquid asset of all is cash itself, giving us a basis for measuring what is money. However, we could also include other forms of purchasing power in a definition of money, notably deposits held in bank cheque accounts and accounts at other financial institutions that can be accessed 'without loss of value or delay' (sometimes referred to as 'sight', 'current account' or 'demand' deposits). These are very liquid assets just like notes and coins because they can be quickly converted into cash and at little if any loss. But why stop at bank and other, similar accounts in measuring money? What about savings, such as government bonds and term share accounts? All financial assets which will eventually mature and have a redemption date will increase in liquidity as they get nearer to maturity. For example, a bill of exchange can be sold at minimal discount when it is just a few days from maturity, and loan stock nearing its redemption date will be traded on the Stock Exchange at a price near its face value.

Money can therefore be defined 'narrowly', which means that financial assets have to be very liquid to be counted as money, or money can be defined more 'broadly', with less-liquid assets included as well. In other words, there is a spectrum of assets, each with various degrees of liquidity, giving rise to a spectrum of measures of what is money.

A liquidity spectrum

A convenient way of illustrating the range of various measures of money is to think of a *liquidity spectrum*, as illustrated in Figure 8.1. Imagine that an individual's total assets can be classified along a scale of liquidity ranging from the most liquid to the least liquid (i.e. illiquid) assets. Obviously the most liquid asset will be cash, while the least liquid asset might be a person's future pension entitlement or house – especially if the owner cannot sell the house quickly, raise equity against it easily, or does not wish to sell it at all. Other assets can be placed between these two extremes accordingly. For example, bank cheque accounts will fall close to the liquid end of the spectrum, while a five-year fixed-term investment would lie towards the illiquid end, as shown in the figure.

The idea of this personalised liquidity spectrum can be readily extended to the economy as a whole. For official purposes, however, governments do not measure monetary aggregates across the full range of the spectrum. Instead, governments (and the central banks which have responsibility for monitoring and regulating the financial system) focus on a limited range of assets, giving rise to various 'official' money supply measures.

These measures are commonly referred to using the letter 'M' followed by a number (0, 1, etc.) such that the bigger the number the wider the range of assets included in the definition. In the case of the USA, the terms M1, M2 and M3 are used while in the UK the terms M0, M3 and M4 are commonly adopted. For illustration, Boxes 8.1 and 8.2 provide an overview of the definitions of these monetary aggregates in the USA and UK.

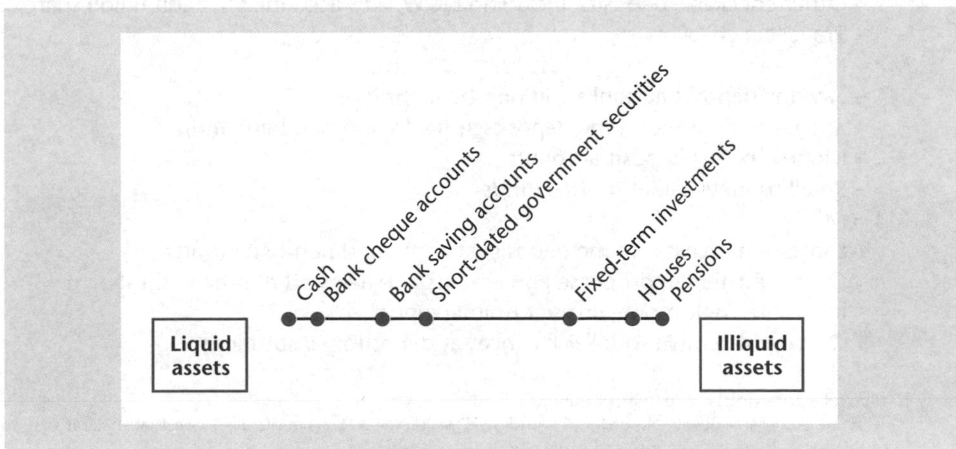

Figure 8.1 Measuring the money supply – a liquidity spectrum

Box 8.1

Main monetary aggregates: UK

M0 = Cash in circulation outside banks
 + Cash inside banks
 + Banks' balances at the Bank of England
 (M0 is referred to as the *monetary base*)
M1 = Cash in circulation outside banks
 + Retail sight deposits at banks
 + Wholesale sight deposits
M2 = Cash in circulation outside banks
 + Retail sight deposits at banks
 + Retail deposits and shares in building societies
M3 = M1
 + UK private sector time deposits and certificates of deposit (CDs)
M4 = M3
 + UK private sector deposits and shares in building societies
 – Building society holdings of cash, bank deposits and bank CDs

Box 8.2

Main monetary aggregates: USA

M1 = Currency in circulation
 + Demand deposits at banks and non-bank thrifts*
 + Other checkable deposits, including NOW, ATS accounts**, credit union share drafts
 + Travellers cheques
M2 = M1
 + Savings deposits at banks and non-bank thrifts
 + Small-denomination time deposits at banks and non-bank thrifts
 + Money market deposit accounts
 + Retail money market mutual funds
M3 = M2
 + Large-denomination time deposits at banks and non-bank thrifts
 + Overnight/term repurchase agreements at banks and non-bank thrifts
 + Institution-only money market mutual funds
 + Overnight/term Eurodollar balances at depository institutions

*Thrifts refer to savings and loan associations.
**NOW accounts are 'negotiable order of withdrawal' accounts. ATS accounts are those that make it easy to shift from savings to demand accounts and make payments as needed.

It should be noted that the Bank of England only routinely publishes statistics for M0 and M4 representing *narrow* and *broad* money respectively. With respect to M4, statistics for 'retail M4' are also monitored representing the proportion of M4 that is retail in nature, i.e. deposits in banks' and building societies' retail accounts, mainly but not solely from the household sector.

M1 represents *narrow* money, while M2 or M3 represent *broad* money in the USA.

From the description above of the meaning and measurement of the money supply, it should be clear that a major role is played by the banking system in the creation of money. We now turn to explain and clarify this role – and in so doing, lay the foundations for understanding the principles of monetary policy, which we detail in the next chapter.

Application 8.1

Monetary expansion and inflation

HANOI – Following the central bank's loosening of monetary policy and continuous expansion in bank credit, observers are waiting with bated breath for the first signs of inflation.

After the 4.2 per cent inflation of 1998, Vietnam has consistently managed to keep prices under control. In 1999, inflation was just 0.1 per cent while in 2000, it actually had deflation of 0.6 per cent.

In 2001, inflation was again a marginal 0.8 per cent against a target of 5 per cent. Prices have gone up 2.8 per cent so far this year against a targeted 3–4 per cent.

All that could change. In July 2002, the Government approved an infusion of VND10.39 trillion into five State-owned commercial banks, increasing their combined statutory capital by a quarter.

Though the Government will issue VND7.84 trillion in 20-year bonds for the purpose, the banks' books will reflect the capital infusion.

However, they can only pledge the bonds with the SBV (Vietnam's central bank) after five years to raise any money. According to Finance Deputy Minister Le Thi Bang Tam, 'This is a measure to control money supply and head off inflation.'

Meanwhile, the SBV has been given the green light to lend VND100bn to the Industrial and Commercial Bank's training credit fund.

The central bank is also set to increase the money supply via the [Treasury] bill market.

At commercial banks, the growth of loans have exceeded that of deposits so far this year.

▶

Application 8.1 continued

Following a relaxation of lending rules by the central bank at the beginning of the year, banks too have relaxed their stipulations for lending, with the result that lending has surged sharply.

By July, the balance outstanding had risen 15.4 per cent and loans in Vietnamese *dong* increased 16.1 per cent.

Experts forecast that at this rate of growth, outstanding loans will climb 30 per cent in 2002, much higher than in the last few years.

To facilitate this particular surge in lending activities, the central bank has pumped a large amount of money into the system.

Through open market operations alone, the SBV pumped in over VND5,300bn in the first six months, a huge figure considering it was just VND3,200bn in the whole of 2001.

However, most of the banks have again run out of liquidity now and hardly seem to participate in auctions of government bonds and the Development Assistance Fund.

Some still hold billions of *dong* worth of commercial paper, such as government bonds and bank drafts, and find it hard to turn them into cash because of their low liquidity.

Source: http://vietnamnews.vnagency.com.vn/2002–08/08/Stories/18.htm

Activity

What does the above review of monetary conditions imply with respect to the state of the Vietnamese economy?

Banks and the creation of money

Governments have the ability to increase the money supply by simply instructing their central bank to print more bank notes. However, commercial banks also have the ability to create money even though they generally do not have the authority to produce their own currency. They can do this by *the creation of bank deposits*. Note that it is the bank deposits which are money, not cheques as such: cheques are merely the means of transferring bank deposits from one person to another. It is the bank deposit and not really the cheque which is accepted in payment for goods and services. Deposits with commercial banks form a major part of the total spending in developed economies. Cash in circulation forms only a very small part of the money used for spending purposes. Cash is provided by the central bank or the government's mint. If the commercial banking sector as a whole could increase the volume of sight (i.e. demand) deposits without causing a reduction in the amount of cash in circulation, then the total quantity of spending money in the country would increase.

There are three ways in which new bank deposits can be created:

- when a bank receives a cash deposit from a customer;
- when a bank makes a loan to a customer and this loan is then credited to the customer's cheque account with the bank;
- when a bank purchases a security, such as a bond, leading to the deposit of the purchase price by the seller back into the banking system.

In order to demonstrate the principle by which the banking sector, through its lending behaviour, can 'create' money via expansion in the level of bank deposits, consider the example shown in Box 8.3.

Box 8.3

'Creating' money via expansion

First let us assume that:

- there is only one bank in our banking system even though it may have several branches;
- there is never any shortage of suitable borrowers;
- banks only have two assets (cash reserves and loan advances) and one liability (deposits);
- banks need only keep 10 per cent of deposits in cash in order to satisfy customer's demands for cash (or to meet the cash 'reserve requirement' ratio set by the central bank);
- cash does not leak out of the system in any way.

As our starting point let us imagine that someone deposits $1,000 in cash in a new account at the bank. An extract from the balance sheet would look like this:

Assets		*Liabilities*	
	$		$
Cash	1,000	Deposits (initial)	1,000

Given that the bank only needs to keep 10 per cent of the $1,000 deposit in cash, it will therefore have $900 available for lending to willing borrowers. If the bank lends up to this total in the form of advances, crediting these to customers' accounts, then its balance sheet will be affected as follows:

Assets		*Liabilities*	
	$		$
Cash reserve	100	Deposits (initial)	1,000
Advances	900		
Total	**1,000**	***Total***	**1,000**

Now suppose that the borrowers spend all of these advances ($900) with cash being drawn from the bank or cheques issued to meet these expenditures. Eventually this $900

Box 3.1 continued

will flow back to the bank as deposits from shopkeepers, restaurants, etc. Now 90 per cent of these new deposits ($810) can be relent by the bank, assuming a continued cash-to-deposit ratio of 10 per cent (even where there are a number of banks rather than just a single bank, provided that they are increasing their advances at the same rate, they should receive new deposits at their branches of roughly the same amount as they lend out – therefore, the process by which deposits are created remains similar to the one in this example). Once more, these new advances ($810) will be spent and again this amount, in principle, will be redeposited. The process will continue until new deposits are negligible.

It is apparent, therefore, from the above simple example, that an initial increase in bank deposits of $1,000 cash leads to a *multiple* expansion of bank deposits related to the percentage cash reserve requirement ratio. This fact introduces the concept of the *bank credit multiplier.*

Bank credit multiplier

The *bank credit multiplier* measures the amount of new deposits (money) created from an initial deposit. Ignoring any leakages from the banking system, the eventual increase in deposits following an initial deposit of cash is given by:

$$D = \frac{C}{RR}$$

where:

D = Eventual total increase in deposits

C = Initial increase in deposits

RR = Reserve requirement ratio (i.e. the proportion of new deposits required to be held as cash or as liquid assets).

$\frac{1}{RR}$ = Bank credit multiplier

In the Box 8.3 example, the initial deposit of $1,000 will lead to a $10,000 increase in total deposits ($1,000 × 1/0.1) because 10 per cent or 1/10 of each deposit is held by the bank as a cash reserve. It should be obvious, therefore, that the extent to which a bank is able to create credit and hence its impact upon the money supply is dependent upon its cash-deposit reserve ratio, RR.

The example above illustrates two things:

- the origins of the saying 'every loan creates a deposit';
- the ability of banks to create money.

While the Box 8.3 example shows a bank holding assets only in the forms of cash and advances, in practice banks may hold a wide range of additional assets, such as overnight lending to the money market and purchases of government treasury bills (regarded as liquid assets because of their short-term nature) and government long-dated securities and equities (more illiquid asset forms). The holding of such assets will restrict the ability of banks to lend in the form of loans or advances. Also, from time to time governments may impose minimum requirements on banks with regard to the assets they hold, especially cash, in order to constrain credit expansion and hence the growth in the money supply in the economy.

Turning to the impact upon the money supply of a bank purchasing a security, there are two possibilities to consider. If the security is sold by the private sector and the money received is redeposited in the banking system, then we face the same situation as described above, giving rise to a bank credit multiplier effect. However, if the security is sold by the government then the outcome is not so clear cut. The government can either spend the money which has been raised in this way (in which case the money will eventually find its way back into the banking system leading to a multiple expansion of credit, as before) or it can retain the money as cash reserves. In the latter case, this will result in a contraction in the ability of banks to lend and ultimately a contraction in total bank deposits and therefore the money supply. The purchase and sale of government securities in this manner to affect bank lending is referred to as *open market operations*. Indeed, the government can exercise its influence on the ability of banks to expand their lending by dealing across a wide spectrum of government securities with various dates to maturity, ranging from short-dated securities (e.g. 90-day government bills) to medium- and long-term government bonds. By replacing short-term government debt with longer-dated securities (a procedure known as *funding*) the authorities are able to reduce liquidity in the financial system, including the banks.

Credit creation in practice

We must be careful not to overstate the ability of banks to create credit and hence money – in practice. There are a number of practical constraints on the growth of a bank's deposit (and on the growth of the deposits across the banking sector as a whole). These constraints stem from:

(a) leakages of cash out of the banking system;
(b) the attitude of other banks towards lending policy;
(c) the nature of customer demand for loans;
(d) prudent management of lending operations by the banks themselves.

We shall touch on some of the general issues involving these constraints.

(a) Leakages from the banking system

Leakages are caused by:

- the public (firms and individuals) choosing to hold some of their extra money in cash (notes and coins in their hands);

- the purchase of government securities by the banks;
- till money held by non-banks.

The public might choose to hold a certain proportion of any extra money they obtain in the form of banknotes. For example, if the bank lends $10,000 to a customer, who then uses the money to buy a car, the car dealer who is paid the $10,000 might decide to hold some of this extra money in cash instead of depositing it all into the bank.

If banks choose to purchase securities from the government, payment will be made by means of a transfer out of the banks' deposits with the central bank. The banks will then have less cash and this will reduce their ability to create credit, as discussed above.

(b) The attitude of other banks towards lending

If there are several banks in the banking system, one bank might wish to pursue an active policy of expanding the volume of its deposits. However, if other banks in the system are more conservative, the result will be as follows:

- The expansionary bank will perhaps lend more money to customers.
- The money lent will be paid to individuals or firms who might deposit it with other commercial banks. Inter-bank settlement will be made through the banks' deposits with the central bank. Since a particular bank's customer (say of bank A) may well be transferring funds to customers of other banks, the effect will be to reduce bank A's balance at the central bank.
- With their extra deposits, the other banks will provide loans to their customers, and some of the resulting payments will be made to customers of bank A, which will relend on the basis of the deposits it receives. But because it is lending more aggressively than the other banks, it will be continually making net payments to those banks through inter-bank settlements. The result of this process will be a reduction in bank A's cash reserve base. Since its deposits at the central bank will decline, this reduction in bank A's cash reserve base will eventually put an end to the increase in its lending, unless it can continually attract new deposits. In this example, therefore, the behaviour of the other more cautious banks places restrictions on the lending policy of bank A.

(c) The demand for loans

Banks can only lend money if there is a sufficient demand for loans at the interest rate set by the banks. There is no reason why the demand for loans should be large enough to equal or exceed the volume of loans the banks would really wish to make. If this is the case, banks would have to:

- purchase other types of interest-earning financial assets, instead of making loans; or
- reduce the rate of interest charged on loans in order to increase the volume of demand for them from those who wish to borrow.

Application 8.2

German banks under pressure

The difficulties of the German banking sector have attracted considerable international attention. Economists and market participants have been concerned that the banks' problems would lead to a credit crunch, or that a major bank failure would lead to a systemic crisis. Fears of the economic consequences of weakness in the German banking sector were perhaps augmented by a lack of trust in the monetary and fiscal policy framework of European Monetary Union and in the German government's economic policies. While some of these fears seem exaggerated, there is no doubt that the German banking sector is presently facing very difficult conditions.

German banks have come under pressure from several sides. First, following an agreement between the EU Commission and the German government reached in 2001, German public sector banks will effectively lose their government guarantees by 2005. This is raising their funding costs and forcing them to pay more attention to the quality of their loan books. Second, owing to insufficient risk controls and management mistakes in the past, the cooperative and private banks are presently engaged in repairing their balance sheets by writing off an unusually large amount of bad loans and cutting costs. These problems have been exacerbated by the continuing weakness of general economic conditions.

Still ordinary balance sheets but rapidly deteriorating profits

The aggregate balance sheet of the German banking sector does not reveal unusual weaknesses. However, German banks have a dismal record of profitability, which is likely to deteriorate even more this year. An improvement in operating results is urgently needed to avoid a dangerous erosion of the equity capital base.

German bank balance sheet and profitability indicators (per cent of total assets)

	1999	*2000*	*2001*	*2002*
Share holdings	3.02	3.42	3.22	2.84
Bond holdings	15.12	15.62	16.06	15.40
Real estate loans	17.27	16.49	16.50	16.56
General write-offs	0.39	0.32	0.30	0.17
Equity ratio	3.55	3.61	3.70	3.89
Return on equity	6.47	5.92	4.54	N.a.
Return on assets	0.23	0.21	0.17	N.a.
Cost–income ratio (%)	66.0	68.4	71.4	N.a.

Application 8.2 continued

An examination of the aggregate balance sheet of the German banking sector can only give a rough picture of the state of health of the industry. Differences between the major segments of the industry remain in the dark and worrisome weaknesses of individual banks may be offset by better data of other banks. Nevertheless, it is a good starting point for the pursuit of the question whether the banking sector in general is in a position to fulfil its role for the economy as a mediator between borrowers and lenders. The table above gives the developments of a few balance sheet indicators over the recent years. By and large, these indicators give little reason for immediate concern. Reflecting the equity bear market, direct share holdings of banks have eroded in recent years and are fairly small relative to total assets.

Moreover, the share of mortgage lending is only moderately higher than the share of bond holdings in total assets, pointing to a limited exposure of banks to the weakish housing market. General asset write-offs declined relative to total assets, and the share of equity capital increased moderately.

Against this, profitability deteriorated significantly. Income data for the aggregate banking sector are only available until 2001. In that year, the return on equity fell to only 4.5 per cent from 6.5 per cent in 1999. The main reason for the decline was a lack of cost control. Even in 2000, a year of record growth for the German economy as a whole, the cost–income ratio of German banks rose by almost 2.5 percentage points. In the following year, which brought a much weaker economic environment, costs rose by another 3 percentage points relative to revenue.

The return on equity of German banks was less than half the return recorded in 2001 for EU banks on average. The cost–income ratio of German banks was almost 5 percentage points above the EU average. The results of 2002 reported by several banks earlier this year point to another severe deterioration of profitability and increase in the cost–income ratio. Provisions for bad debts increased sharply and several banks felt the need to support their profits by realising capital gains through the sale of assets. With 'hidden reserves' now significantly diminished, a further deterioration of banks' results could jeopardise their equity capital base soon.

Source: Extract from Deutsche Bank, *Focus Europe*, 10 March 2003, pp.8–9.

Activity

What might the weaknesses in the German banking system mean for monetary conditions and in turn economic activity in Germany? Explain how these weaknesses could lead to a credit crunch.

(d) The lending policy of banks

Banks might have sufficient cash or liquid assets to increase the volume of their lending, but may decide not to do so because they consider applicants for loans to be too risky. The decision to make a loan depends largely on the following.

- *How risky the loan seems to be* – a company in danger of liquidation is obviously a more risky proposition than a flourishing business. Loans to certain individuals might also be considered a high bad-debt risk.
- *The interest rate to charge* – higher rates may be charged to higher-risk customers.

The result of all these constraints is that the bank credit multiplier, or the banks' ability to create money, will be much less than any simple numerical example may suggest.

Even taking these constraints into consideration, however, it should be clear that the banking system is a powerful force in our economy. It has the power to expand deposits if extra cash is injected into the system and contract deposits if cash is removed, for the bank credit multiplier works in reverse too. It is not surprising, then, that any government wishing to influence or control activity within the economy will need to pay close attention to what the banking system is doing and, if necessary, devise ways of regulating it. It would clearly be pointless for a government to attempt to control the supply of money without controlling bank lending – a major source of 'new' money. This leads us on to the analysis of monetary policy and the instruments used by the government in its efforts to control the money supply – see Chapter 9.

The determination of monetary growth

In the next chapter, which deals with the principles and practice of monetary policy, we shall examine the ways in which the official authorities (governments or central banks) may attempt to control the growth in the money supply. However, as a foundation to the chapter, we provide here an overview of the factors which cause changes in the money supply.

Naturally, the government has the ability to increase or decrease the *narrow* money supply by simply instructing the central bank to either print or destroy bank notes. However, since a very large proportion of a country's money supply (*broadly* defined) is made up of bank deposits, then anything which affects the volume of bank deposits will affect the money supply.

The volume of bank deposits, including cash reserve holdings, can be affected in many ways and we can group these under six main headings related to:

(a) the size of the government's (i.e. state sector) budget deficit;
(b) domestic lending by banks to the private sector (households and firms);

(c) official financing of the balance of payments current account deficit (or surplus);
(d) competition between domestic banks and other financial institutions as well as foreign banks;
(e) the government's stance on monetary policy;
(f) banks' non-deposit liabilities.

We briefly discuss each of these factors and their impact on the total size of the money supply.

(a) The government's budget deficit

The size of the budget (i.e. fiscal) deficit and the means by which it is financed by the government can significantly influence the volume of deposits within the banking system and, via the bank credit multiplier, the growth in the money supply aggregates described earlier. To understand this, consider the five different ways in which a budget deficit may be financed.

- *Borrowing from the banks directly*. If the budget deficit is financed by the government borrowing directly from the banking system, then when the borrowed sum is spent by the state sector, it creates new deposits in the banking system without any offsetting leakages. As a consequence, there will be a multiple expansion of the money supply.
- *Printing more money*. As we noted above, the government can simply instruct the central bank to print more notes in order to finance a government budget deficit. To the extent that the private sector will want to hold more cash (rather than other assets), then the money supply will increase directly. Any additional cash which is not held for transactions purposes will find its way into the banking system as new deposits, leading to a multiple expansion of deposits and hence to an increase in the money supply.
- *Sale of government securities to the non-bank public*. If the government sells securities to the public to finance its budget deficit, then the total money supply is unaffected because there will be no net injection of cash to affect overall bank deposits. There will be an initial reduction in the money supply in the form of bank deposits because of the payments by the non-bank public for the securities, but they will be offset by an equivalent amount of government spending.
- *Borrowings from overseas and in foreign currency*. Borrowings in foreign currency have no effect on domestic bank deposits and hence no effect on the money supply provided the funds are not converted into the domestic currency and spent by government.
- *Sale of government securities to overseas residents*. Financing the budget deficit by selling government securities denominated in the domestic currency to overseas residents will increase the domestic money supply when spent by government, by the value of the securities purchased. Again, there may well be a bank credit multiplier effect to the extent that the initial injection of new money affects bank deposits.

Of course the government may also try to reduce its budget deficit (as opposed to financing it) by raising taxation and/or lowering government expenditure. An increasingly important development with regard to the size of a budget deficit in recent decades across many countries has been the growing popularity of privatisation, i.e. the sale of state-owned assets. The revenue from privatisation initiatives, however, while reducing the size of a budget deficit, is not a sustainable means of financing it – since assets can only be sold once!

(b) Domestic bank lending to the private sector

Lending by domestic banks to the private sector (as well as to foreigners provided they spend the loans in the domestic economy) will increase the money supply via the bank credit multiplier as described earlier. Indeed, depending on the volume of new loans and the reserve or liquidity requirements facing the banking system, the growth in the money supply could be considerable. However, the growth will critically depend on the willingness of the private sector to borrow from the banks, i.e. on the so-called *demand for money*. This introduces the central role of interest rates in the economy and the importance of monetary policy. We shall provide a fuller account of this topic in the next chapter.

(c) Official financing of the balance of payments

Financing a balance of payments current account deficit broadly means that money is leaving the country in the form of a leakage from the circular flow of income and therefore there will be a reduction in the money supply. The reverse is true for a balance of payments current account surplus, representing an injection into the circular flow. Any increase or decrease will, again, have a multiple effect on bank deposits and the money supply, all other factors remaining constant.

(d) Competition between banks and other financial institutions

If non-bank financial institutions (e.g. insurance companies and mutual organisations) and foreign banks succeed in attracting funds away from the domestic banking sector, perhaps because of more attractive interest rates for deposits, then there will be an initial reduction in bank deposits. Some of these may be invested overseas, thus having a consequential effect on the domestic money supply, at least until the domestic banks offer more competitive interest rates again and attract funds back.

(e) The government's stance on monetary policy

As we shall see in the next chapter, the government's stance on monetary policy will affect the ability of the banks to expand lending and create new deposits. For example, a *tight* (i.e. *contractionary*) monetary policy due to high real interest rates or a higher *reserve ratio requirement* (where the banks are made to keep a higher cash-to-deposit ratio or assets in other liquid forms), or the imposition of certain qualitative and/or quantitative lending restraints on them will affect their scope to make advances. Such measures will have the effect of restricting the expansion in the money supply, unless the banks are able to get reserve funds from unrestricted sources and are able to find ways around the lending restrictions.

(f) Banks' non-deposit liabilities

The net non-deposit liabilities of a bank equal the total of its capital and reserves minus the value of its land, buildings, capital equipment, etc. An increase in these liabilities will reduce the ability of the banks to lend and hence lead to a reduction in the money supply.

The above factors which determine how much the money supply (broadly defined) grows are monitored closely by the official authorities in every country around the world (i.e. by governments, central banks and organisations such as the IMF). The factors, as described, indicate the measures that might be taken if the objective is to control the growth of the money supply in the economy – i.e. the flow of liquidity – with implications for economic activity, employment and prices. The measures to control the money supply may, therefore, be listed as follows.

Controls over the money supply

- Reduce or control the size of the government's budget deficit by raising taxes and/or reducing government expenditure.
- Finance as much government borrowing as possible by raising funds from the non-bank private sector (e.g. by encouraging domestic citizens to purchase government savings certificates) – this diverts consumer spending into government expenditure with no net effect on aggregate demand.
- Control the increase in lending by banks and other financial institutions. (There are various ways in which governments can try to do this as part of their overall monetary policy; we shall look at these in detail in the next chapter.)
- Maintain a current account balance on the balance of payments, thereby removing the impact of external and foreign currency influences on the expansion of the money supply.

The determination of interest rates

In the above analysis, much of the attention was placed on direct measures to control the money supply through the control of bank lending. However, we also noted the importance of the demand for money in this context – since banks cannot lend if no-one wants to borrow! The determination of the demand for money is central to the role of monetary policy in many economies – and a key factor in this determination is the *rate of interest*. The rate of interest represents the opportunity cost of holding cash – because the cash could alternatively be placed in an interest-bearing bank account. But what determines the rate of interest?

Short-term and long-term interest rates

It is important, first of all, to distinguish between *short-term* and *long-term* interest rates.

- The *short-term interest rate* is determined by the demand for and supply of money in the so-called money market. It is this rate which lies at the heart of monetary policy and the role of the central bank in controlling inflationary pressures in an economy. It is important to note that the short-term rate is policy determined, i.e. *set by the central bank*.
- In contrast, *long-term interest rates* are determined by the interaction of the demand for and supply of funds in the capital market. The capital market is the primary source of funds for long-term borrowing by governments and corporates.

We look at the interaction of demand and supply factors in both the money and capital markets below in order to highlight the essential features of each market.

(a) Money market and the short-term interest rate

Figure 8.2 shows the demand for and supply of money at any time in the money market. Note that the interaction of the demand for money schedule (M^D) and the supply of money schedule (M^S) determines the nominal rate of interest, i_0. At any point in time, there is a given stock (supply) of money available to the market. The demand for money (M^D) represents the willingness on the part of firms and households to hold their assets in liquid (i.e. cash) form. It will be seen that M^D is negatively sloped indicating that the higher the interest rate, the less the incentive to hold cash rather than interest-earning securities. A fall in the interest rate raises the demand for money since the opportunity cost of holding assets in liquid form is lower.

In the following discussion, for simplicity, we will talk about the choice between holding cash and investing in government treasury bills and bonds since, while other interest-bearing assets exist, the interest rate on them tends to move in line with the interest rate on government securities.

The money-market equilibrium is given at E in Figure 8.2 – and hence the short-term interest rate which clears the market is i_0.

If the policy-determined interest rate is set *above* i_0, then the supply of money exceeds the demand for money. People will use the excess money supply to purchase government securities (treasury bills and bonds), causing the prices of bills and bonds to rise, and the interest rate (i.e. yield) on them to fall. The reverse will

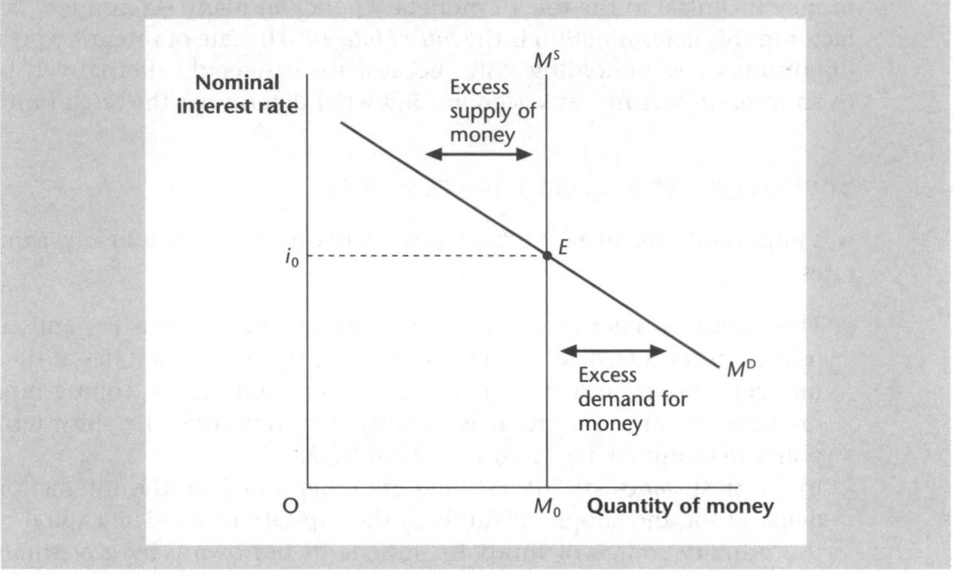

Figure 8.2 Money market equilibrium and short-term interest rates

occur if the interest rate is set *below* i_0, where an excess demand for money will exist. In consequence people would sell bills and bonds for cash, causing their prices to fall and their yields to rise. The inverse relationship between yields and the prices of financial assets is explained in more detail in Box 8.4.

Box 8.4

Link between bond prices and yields

There is an inverse relationship between the market price of bonds and the yield (i.e. interest rate) on these bonds. To illustrate this, consider that the government issues a bond that promises to pay a yield of $10 per annum until it matures. If the *issue price* of the bond is set at $100, then the interest rate is set at 10 per cent each year. The *market price* of issued bonds fluctuates.

In the financial markets, if the price of the issued bond was to fall to $50, reflecting current demand for and supply of bonds, the market interest rate would become 20 per cent to the bond holder. This is because $10 is being earned each year on an asset valued at only $50.

Equally, if the market price of the bond rose from $100 to $200, then the yield (interest rate) would halve to only 5 per cent since there is now only a $10 return on an asset valued at $200. Hence, we observe an *inverse relationship between the market price of bonds and interest rates.*

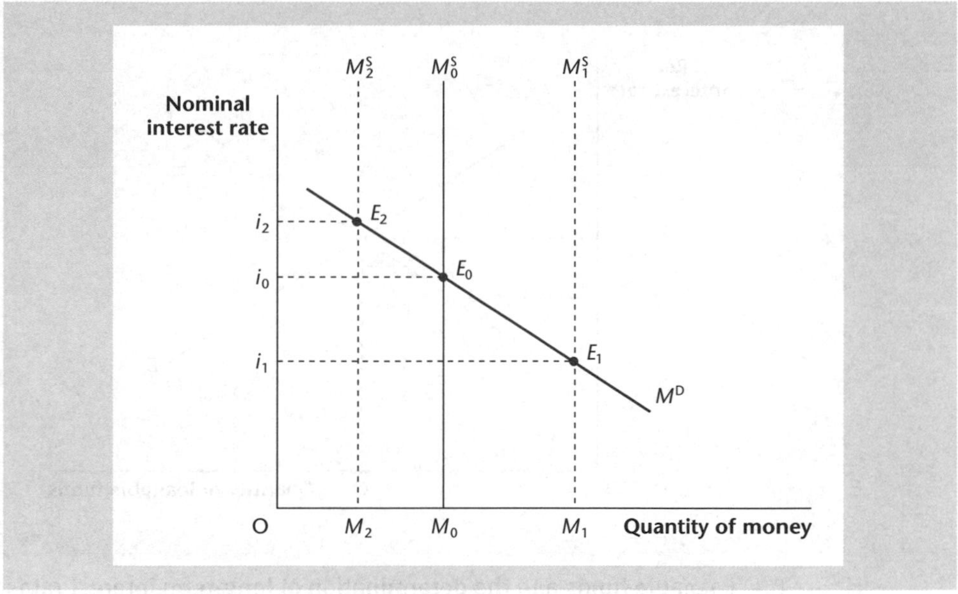

Figure 8.3 Impact of policy-determined interest rate changes

An important point to note with regards the demand for and supply of money is that in most developed countries, the central bank *sets* the short-term interest rate and allows the money supply to adjust to the demand for money. Figure 8.3 shows this point. If the monetary authorities decide to reduce the short-term interest rate from i_0 to i_1, they must automatically increase the money supply from M_0^S to M_1^S – i.e. *inject* sufficient liquidity into the money market – achieving a new equilibrium in the money market at E_1. Conversely, a rise in interest rates to i_2 will require an automatic reduction in the money supply to M_2^S to restore equilibrium in the money market.

The significance of changes in the policy determination of interest rates in the context of monetary policy is explained further in Chapter 9, where we shall see that a crucial factor is the sensitivity of the demand for money (M^D) to changes in interest rates.

(b) Capital markets and long-term interest rates

In contrast to the policy-determined interest rate explained above, long-term interest rates are market-determined, i.e. determined by the interaction of demand for (*D*) and supply of (*S*) funds by firms and households in the capital markets. In broad terms, the demand for loanable funds reflects the demand for long-term finance to meet the investment needs of the private sector. The supply of loanable funds is broadly the amount of savings households and firms are willing to make available to the financial markets. This is illustrated in Figure 8.4.

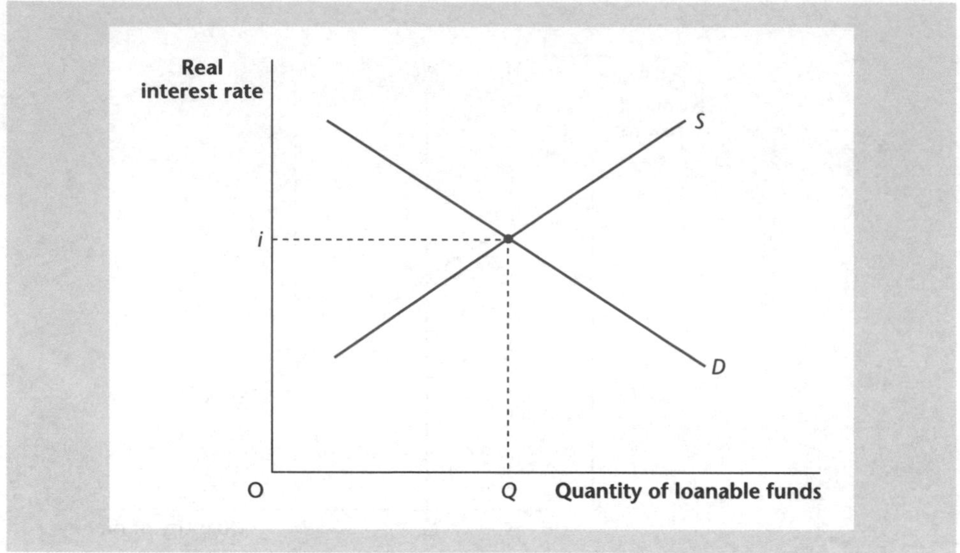

Figure 8.4 **Loanable funds and the determination of long-term interest rates**

Note that in the market for loanable funds, it is the *real* (i.e. inflation-adjusted) interest rate that is being determined. It is the real interest rate that determines the demand for loans (D) and the supply of loanable funds (S).

Expectations concerning risk, return and inflation enter into decisions in this market and hence the determination of nominal long-term interest rates. As expected risk and inflation rise, and other things being equal, the suppliers of funds will require a higher nominal interest rate on their funds.

The demand curve in Figure 8.4 slopes downwards from left to right. As the real rate of interest can be viewed as the price of borrowing, investors will want to borrow more at lower real interest rates and vice versa. The supply curve slopes upwards from left to right because the real interest rate can also be viewed as the reward for saving, and people will want to save at a higher real return on funds.

Although we have separated the discussion of short-term and long-term interest rate determination, it should be understood that the short-term and long-term interest rates normally tend to move in the same direction. This is because long-term bonds are much less liquid than short-term treasury bills. If the rate of interest on treasury bills is maintained at or above the long-term rate then investors will tend to have little incentive to buy longer-term bonds, causing the price of these bonds to fall and their interest rate (i.e. yield) to rise. However, situations may arise when long-term interest rates lie below the short-term rate. This can happen when investors expect lower inflation in the future, which will reduce the proportion of risk associated with holding bonds. In this case, holding bonds may be more attractive than holding treasury bills, thus the prices of bonds will be bid up and their yield will tend to fall.

Money and economic policy

The potential significance of money – both in terms of its supply and demand – for the state of a country's economy arises from the rate at which the quantity of money in circulation is growing. In other words, the growth in liquidity has important implications for the state of the macroeconomy with respect to:

- inflation;
- economic growth;
- employment.

Recognition of the importance of money in modern economies has led to the elevation of so-called 'monetarism' and monetary policy to the centre of macroeconomic management. This subject is the focus of attention in Chapter 9.

Concluding remarks

In this chapter we have looked at the nature and importance of money to the economy. The money supply plays an essential role as the lubricant of market exchanges. In the absence of money, barter would have to be used in market transactions and this undoubtedly would mean a very much smaller number of exchanges and therefore a very much smaller real GDP. We have also seen that, in principle, any good or asset could act as money – what is crucial is that it is accepted readily as a *medium of exchange*.

Today the money supply is composed of cash (notes and coins) plus other financial assets that are relatively liquid and therefore can be converted easily for use to purchase goods and services. Central banks monitor the growth in the money supply because of its potential effect on the level of aggregate demand in the economy for goods and services. This has led to the creation of official 'monetary aggregates', which take the form of M0, M1, M2, M3 , M4 etc. measures. Central banks monitor these measures for signals of changes in the money supply that might precipitate either recession or inflation.

To control the growth in the money supply central banks take steps to control bank lending. Bank advances (loans) through the *bank credit multiplier* lead to a multiple increase in purchasing power. Central banks may take steps such as changing short-term interest rates with a view to reducing the demand for bank loans. We discuss in detail the different policies central banks can adopt in our review of monetary policy in the next chapter.

Key learning points

- *Money* is any good that is widely or readily accepted for purpose of exchange, i.e. as a payment for goods and services.

- *Money has four main functions* in a modern economy, namely as a medium of exchange; a unit of account; a standard for deferred payment; and a store of value.
- Money is a *medium of exchange* because people will accept money in exchange for goods and services therefore reducing transaction costs.
- *Barter* is much inferior to the use of money in exchange transactions because it requires a 'double coincidence of wants'.
- Money is a *unit of account* as it provides a standard measure by which the value of different goods and services can be compared.
- Money is a *standard for deferred payments* because it indicates the value that will be given in return at some future date for goods and services received now.
- Money is a *store of value* because it can be held and exchanged later for goods and services – as long as inflation does not erode its future purchasing power.
- *Narrow money* refers to money balances that are readily available to finance current spending, i.e. balances available for transaction purposes.
- *Broad money* includes money balances for transaction purposes and money held as a form of saving, which can be converted with relative ease without capital loss into spending on goods and services.
- *Liquidity* is defined as the ability to transform an asset or wealth holding into another form without loss of face value or delay.
- The *liquidity spectrum* refers to the range of assets in an economy ranging from the most liquid to the least liquid (i.e. illiquid).
- *Central banks* measure the money supply in their country using official measures of monetary aggregates, commonly referred to as M0, M1, M2, M3 and M4.
- *Commercial banks* are able to 'create money' even though they usually do not have the discretion to print bank notes; they do this through retaining only a proportion of any bank deposit as a cash reserve in their vaults and liquid investments and lending-out or 'advancing' the rest. This leads to the concept of the 'bank credit multiplier'.
- *The bank credit multiplier* measures the amount of new deposits (money) created from an initial bank deposit.
- *Money supply growth* is determined by a range of factors, including the size of the government's budget deficit; domestic lending by banks to the private sector; official financing of a balance of payments current account deficit (or surplus); competition between domestic banks and other financial institutions, as well as foreign banks; the government's monetary policy; and banks' non-deposit liabilities.
- Interest rates are determined by the interaction of demand and supply in the money and capital markets, resulting in *short-term* and *long-term* interest rates respectively.
- Control of the money supply is a core component of 'monetarism' or monetarist economics in macroeconomic policy today.

? Topics for discussion

1. What do you understand by the term 'money supply'? Giving examples from your own country, distinguish between 'narrow money' and 'broad money'.
2. What roles are played by money in modern economies? Why might inflation undermine these roles?
3. Explain how commercial banks can 'create money' even when (as normal) they have no legal authority to print bank notes.
4. For your economy set out the main monetary aggregates published by your central bank. Draw a graph showing how these monetary aggregates have fluctuated over the last five years.
5. Explain using an appropriate diagram how changes in the money supply may affect interest rates.
6. Outline the role of money in macroeconomic policy.

Chapter 9

MONETARY POLICY

Aims and learning outcomes

Monetary policy is concerned with any measures used by the official authorities (government or central bank) to influence the availability or price of money (i.e. the rate of interest) in order to achieve particular macroeconomic goals, such as low unemployment, stable prices and faster economic growth. Growth in the importance of monetary policy as an instrument of macroeconomic management is explained to a large extent by the apparent failure of Keynesian fiscal policy measures at various times in the past to reduce the twin problems of inflation and unemployment – referred to as *stagflation*. This failure was explained by monetarist economists in terms of excessive government spending financed by spiraling budget deficits. As mentioned in the previous chapter, government budget deficits can be financed not only through borrowing, from both the banking and non-banking sectors, but also through the printing of new money. Both of these financing methods lead to an increase in the money supply.

Monetarists argue that if the money supply is allowed to grow faster than the economy's output then households and firms will find themselves holding larger money balances than they want to hold. This surplus of money balances will, therefore, be spent on goods and services leading to an increase in aggregate demand beyond the ability of the economy to supply more goods and services – resulting in an inflationary gap. According to monetarists, if measures are not taken to close this gap, the outcome will be a general rise in prices – i.e. *demand-pull inflation* – caused by excessive monetary growth. In addition, any upward pressure on prices will also fuel expectations of future inflation, resulting in higher wage demands and thus *cost-push inflation* and an ensuing danger of a wage-price-wage inflationary spiral. A related consequence of excessive monetary growth will then be rising unemployment, as the competitiveness of firms declines and as workers price themselves out of jobs. This in turn can lead to an economic recession.

In the eyes of monetarists, unemployment can be brought down in the longer term only if the productive efficiency of the economy is increased and if inflationary expectations are diminished. It should be appreciated, however, that these monetarist views are not universally accepted by economists and governments. In particular, some economists (notably Keynesian economists) do not believe that controlling the growth in the money supply is necessarily the best way of bringing down inflation. Nor do they accept that the only solution to unemployment is to reduce inflationary expectations and improve economic efficiency. This difference in policy prescriptions has, in the past, led to a division of economists into two schools of thought: Keynesians and monetarists. However, this distinction should not be exaggerated. Many economists today do not fit neatly into either camp, preferring to argue instead for a balance of policy measures, both monetary and fiscal, to influence economic activity.

In this chapter we cover the following core elements of monetarist economics and policy, namely:

- the principles of monetarist economics – sometimes referred to as *monetarism*;
- the theoretical foundations of monetary policy – enshrined in the so-called *quantity theory of money*;
- instruments of monetary policy;
- demand for money;
- effectiveness of monetary policy;
- criticisms of monetarism;
- monetary policy, economic growth and inflation;
- effects of monetary policy on business.

The development of our understanding of monetary policy owes much to one particular economist – namely Milton Friedman, formerly of the University of Chicago in the USA, who is commonly referred to as 'the father of modern monetarism'.

Learning outcomes

After studying this material you will be able to:

- Understand the principles and meaning of 'monetarism'.
- Appreciate how the money supply can impact on both output and the price level through a 'money transmission mechanism'.
- Identify the impact of interest rate changes on economic activity.
- Understand the main elements of monetary policy and monetarism.
- Recognise the role of interest rates and national income in the determination of the demand for money.
- Recognise how monetary policy can impact on the demand for and supply of money.
- Appreciate the main criticisms of monetary policy and monetarism.
- Understand the impact of monetary policy on business activity.

The principles of monetarism

At the heart of monetarist philosophy lies a series of propositions or principles. These may be summarised as follows.

The principles of monetarism

- Inflation is principally caused by 'too much money chasing too few goods', i.e. too much liquidity in the economy relative to the economy's output.
- To control inflation it is essential that growth in the flow of money around the economy is controlled.
- To ensure consistency in monetary policy decisions, control over the money supply and interest rates should be taken out of the hands of governments and conducted independently by central banks.
- Government intervention to directly control aggregate demand should be kept to a minimum to avoid the creation of economic distortions and inefficiencies.
- Governments should aim to achieve a balanced budget over the medium term or over the business cycle to avoid the possible destabilising effects of excessive budget deficits and surpluses.
- All markets should be allowed to operate freely with the minimum of government intervention and regulation (this is discussed more fully in Chapter 18).

Control over the money supply is central to the monetarist philosophy and thus the implications of monetary decisions for growth, employment and prices. At the most general level, it is not difficult to identify why money is important in the determination of aggregate demand. If the money supply is allowed to rise it will eventually mean that, first, households and firms have more money (i.e. liquidity) in their pockets and bank accounts and, second, interest rates in general will tend to fall. Consequently, consumers and investors will have the potential to affect aggregate demand through their purchasing power – that is, they can use money to buy goods and services and for savings and investment purposes, such as purchasing government bonds and stocks and shares as well as investing in physical assets such as land and buildings. Increased consumer and investment spending then feed through into higher demand in the economy, affecting production, employment and inflation. This process by which a rise in the money supply affects aggregate demand and in turn money GDP (i.e. GDP at current nominal prices) is known as the *money transmission mechanism*.

The money transmission mechanism

The *money transmission mechanism* can be readily described as operating in two stages, involving:

- a link between interest rates and investment and consumer spending decisions;
- a link between investment and consumer spending decisions and changes in the level of aggregate demand.

To explain these key linkages, we shall assume that the official authorities *set* the interest rate and allow the money supply to respond automatically. From the previous chapter, recall that only the short-term interest rate is set by the monetary authorities (i.e. is policy-determined), while long-term interest rates are market-determined via the market for bonds in the capital market.

We shall explain each of these links in turn.

Link between interest rates and spending

A change in short-term interest rates can be expected to have a direct effect on planned household borrowing to finance a wide range of consumer durables (e.g. cars, furniture, etc.) as well as non-durables (e.g. holidays, clothing, etc.). Changes in short-term interest rates may also affect the demand for mortgage loans for house purchase when mortgage rates vary in line with the policy-determined interest rate – with implications for the amount of disposable income remaining after mortgage payments are made each month. In this way, interest rates can be expected to have a *direct* effect on total planned consumer spending and hence the level of aggregate demand in the economy.

A link is also likely to exist between a change in interest rates and planned investment spending by corporates. In this context, a decrease in the real rate of interest, by making borrowing less expensive, can be expected to generate new investment expenditure. The negative relationship between investment (I) and the real rate of interest (i) is referred to as the *investment demand function*. This relationship is illustrated in Figure 9.1, which also shows the impact of a change in interest rates in the money markets – in this case a fall in the interest rate from i_0 to i_1. A policy decision to reduce the interest rate from i_0 to i_1 will mean that the official authorities (central bank) agree to buy all the extra bonds offered for sale at this new lower interest rate, i_1 – thereby injecting liquidity into the financial markets and increasing the money supply from M_0^S to M_1^S in Figure 9.1 (a). Part (b) of the figure indicates that there will be a corresponding increase in planned investment spending from I_0 to I_1 and shown as a movement down the *investment demand function* (I^D).

To summarise:

- A *fall* in the real interest rate will result in an *expansion* in the money supply and a *movement down the investment demand function*, resulting in an *increase* in investment spending.
- In contrast, a *rise* in the real interest will result in a *contraction* in the money supply and a *movement up the investment demand function*, resulting in a *decrease* in investment spending.

The increase in planned investment spending (as well as planned consumer spending) will result in a rise in aggregate planned expenditure, AE, and an

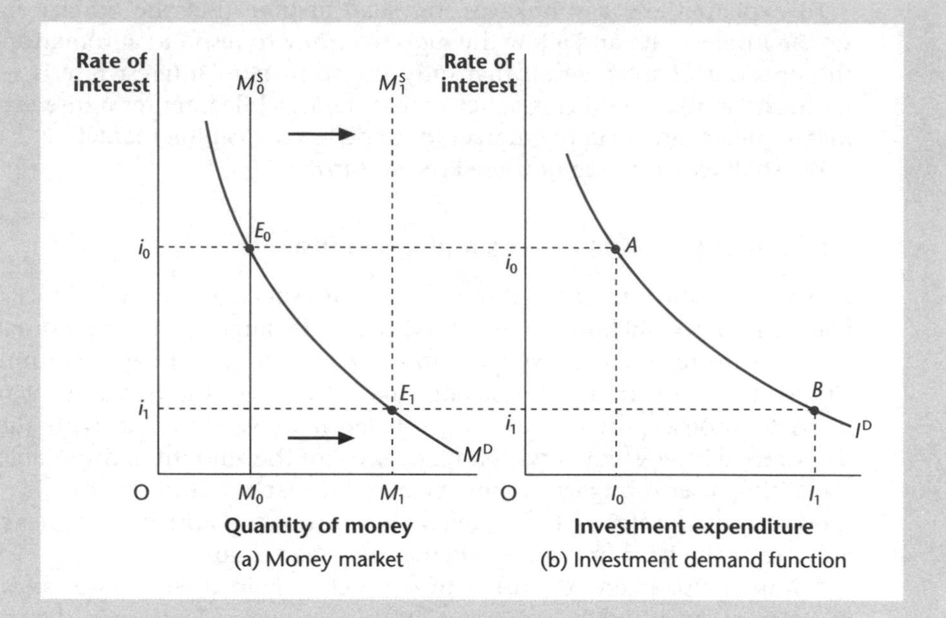

Figure 9.1 **Link between the interest rate and investment spending**

upward shift in the AE curve. We can, as before, link this shift in AE to the aggregate demand (AD) diagram, which shows the relationship between the price level and real GDP. This is explained and illustrated below.

Link between aggregate planned expenditure and aggregate demand

The relationship between aggregate planned expenditure and aggregate demand is illustrated in Figure 9.2.

In the case of a fall in the (real) interest rate, the AE curve in the top diagram will shift upwards as planned investment (and/or consumer) spending increases. This, in turn, will result in a rightward shift in the corresponding aggregate demand curve in the bottom diagram, from AD_0 to AD_1. Conversely, a rise in the interest rate will cause the AE curve to shift downwards and will result in a leftward shift in the aggregate demand curve.

Note that we have not, as yet, included an aggregate supply curve in this figure or indicated the economy's potential full employment output. The implications for inflation, resulting from a change in interest rates, crucially depend on the responsiveness of aggregate supply (AS) to changes in aggregate demand. If AS grows more slowly than the growth in the money supply (resulting from a fall in interest rates), then inflationary pressures will increase – resulting

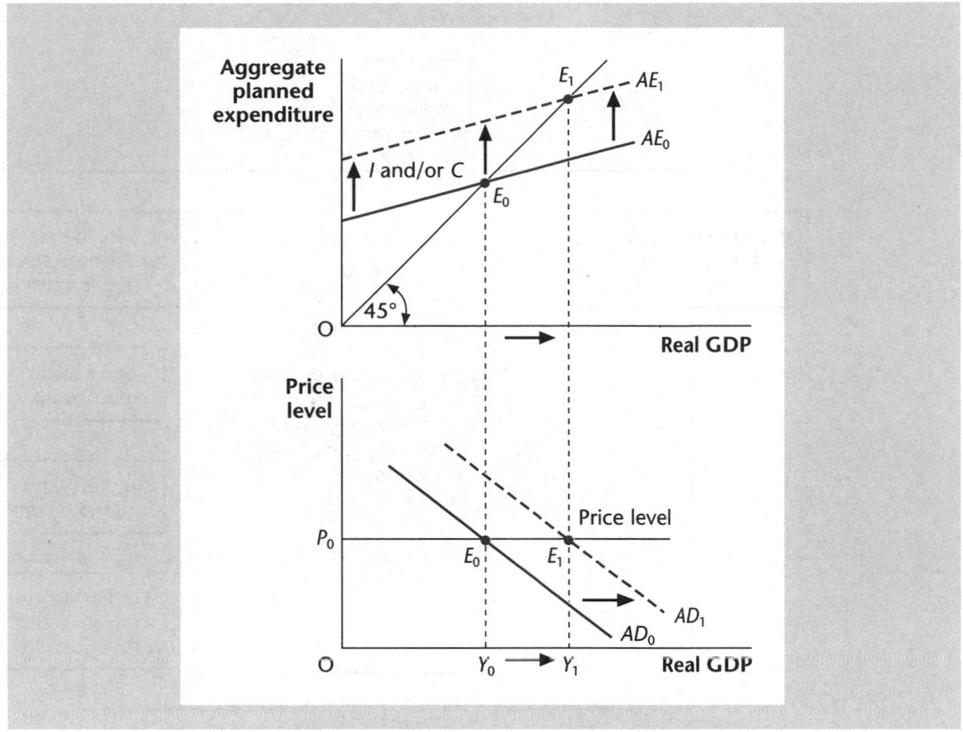

Figure 9.2 Link between aggregate planned expenditure and aggregate demand

in an actual rise in prices (inflation), everything else held constant. The extent to which the economy has spare productive capacity is, therefore, crucial, in predicting the likely impact of an expansion in the money supply on real GDP or prices.

We can bring together the above analysis of the link between changes in the money supply, interest rates, output, aggregate demand and prices in a flow chart to illustrate the transmission mechanism of money – see Figure 9.3. This indicates how an increase in the money supply affects the level of economic activity directly through an increase in the demand for goods and services and more indirectly through interest rate changes, as discussed above through the two linkages.

To conclude this section on the money transmission mechanism, it should be noted that there is a link to be considered between changes in interest rates and the external value of the currency. Monetary expansion, through an increase in the domestic money supply and a decrease in interest rates, will tend to cause a depreciation of the currency against other currencies. This, in turn, can be expected to boost exports and depress imports – depending on a number of conditions (as detailed in Chapter 15). The consequent improvement in net exports

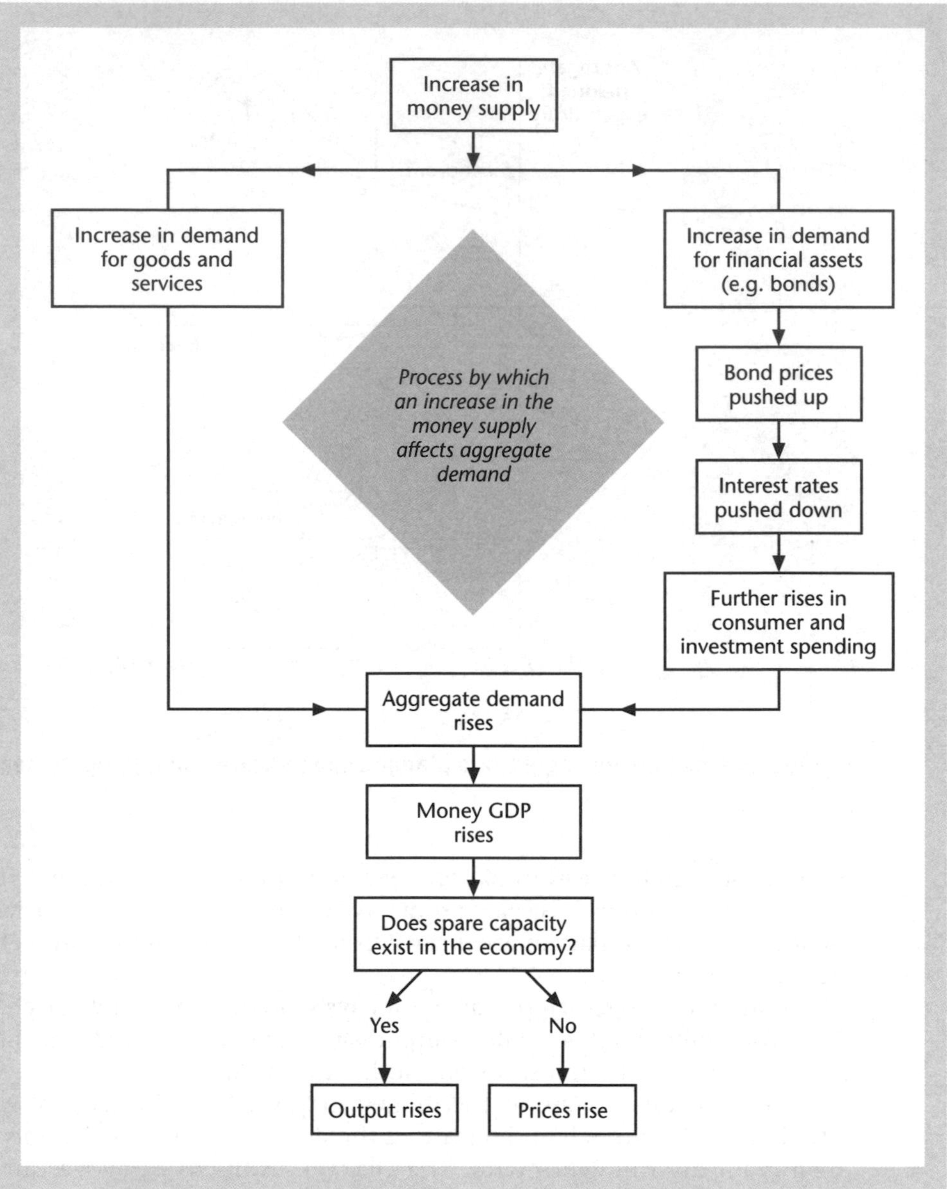

Figure 9.3 Transmission mechanism of money

will cause the AE curve to shift upwards and, hence, the AD curve to move to the right, as in Figure 9.2.

The discussion above illustrates the potential importance of monetary policy in influencing the overall level of spending and hence the rate of inflation and economic growth in the economy.

Application 9.1

Monetary policy in the Great Depression

Read the following extract:

The Great Depression of the early 1930s is the most severe recession on record. The following table provides an overview of the impact of the Depression on a range of economies across the globe.

Most countries entered recession in 1929–30 and began their recoveries in 1932–33; in France, the contraction occurred somewhat later (1932–35). Output losses in the USA, Germany, France, Italy, Japan, Canada, Sweden, and Australia exceeded 10 per cent of GNP, and were also sizable in many other countries. As the US economy was at the time by far the largest, and experienced just about the deepest contraction, the Great Depression in the USA accounted for much of the decline in global output.

Most economic historians concur that the Great Depression – at least the first stage – was caused primarily by monetary policy in the USA, propagated mostly by a series of banking panics, and then spread to the rest of the world via the international gold exchange standard. The US Federal Reserve tightened monetary policy in early 1928, in response to the stock market boom which began in 1926 and the belief that banks should confine their lending strictly to commercial bills and not finance stock market speculation. The contractions in central bank credit and the monetary base, along with a rise in the discount

The Great Depression

Country	Share of world output, 1931 (%)	Economic activity Peak	Trough	Output loss (%)[1]
United States	42.4	1929	1933	−29.4
United Kingdom	13.1	1930	1931	−0.5
Germany	9.5	1928	1932	−26.3
France	7.9	1932	1935	−10.4
Italy	5.4	1928	1933	−13.7
Japan	5.1	1930	1933	−14.9
Spain	4.2	1929	1931	−6.3
Canada	2.5	1929	1933	−29.7
Netherlands	2.1	1930	1934	−14.2
Switzerland	2.0	1930	1932	−6.5
Sweden	1.6	1930	1933	−12.1
Australia	1.4	1926	1931	−24.9
Denmark	1.1	1930	1932	−4.4
Norway	0.9	1930	1931	−8.0
Finland	0.5	1928	1931	−7.2
Portugal	0.4	1935	1936	−0.7

[1] Cumulative loss in output from peak to trough (based on annual data). The peak is defined as the year before real growth turned negative. The trough is defined as the year before real growth turned positive.

Application 9.1 continued

rate, precipitated a downturn in the US economy starting in August 1929 (before the stock market crash of October 1929).

A series of banking panics beginning in October 1930 turned an otherwise serious recession into a depression. These panics, which resulted in the suspension of 9,000 banks (more than one third of the total), exacerbated the economic contraction because they reduced broad money. The US Federal Reserve was insufficiently aggressive in trying to counter the collapse in broad money, for example via open market purchases. The collapse of broad money reduced output through several channels: (1) lower aggregate demand, which – in the face of nominal wage rigidity – decreased real output; (2) disruption of financial intermediation from the bank failures; (3) asset price deflation, whereby declining asset prices reduced the value of collateral for bank loans, inducing weakened banks to engage in a fire sale of their loans and securities, leading to further asset price deflation; and (4) debt deflation, in which falling goods prices led to rising debt burdens in an environment where contracts were not fully indexed and rising real interest rates.

The fall in broad money in the USA raised interest rates, leading to a capital inflow from the rest of the world, and reduced output, lowering US demand for the rest of the world's output. The USA ran persistent balance of payments surpluses with its main trading partners during 1929–31. In the rest of the world, the combination of the gold outflow and the fall in exports to the USA caused aggregate demand to decline. This was exacerbated by a loss of confidence in the currencies of the reserve countries, leading central banks to convert their holdings of foreign exchange into gold, which caused a contraction in the world money supply. Countries that did not adhere to the gold exchange standard, such as Spain, experienced milder contractions.

The Great Depression generally ended once countries left the gold exchange standard and adopted policies that restored confidence in the financial system and stimulated aggregate demand, including expansionary fiscal and monetary policies.

The pace of recovery from the Great Depression varied widely across countries, depending in part on macroeconomic and structural policies. In the UK which left gold early, it took only a year for output to exceed its peak level before the recession began. In the USA, recovery began in 1933 but was sluggish compared with the strength of the monetary expansion under way, and it took about three years for output to return to its previous peak level.

Source: Extract from 'Were Business Cycles in the Late Nineteenth Century Different from Modern Cycles?', *World Economic Outlook*, April 2002, International Monetary Fund, Washington DC, pp.110–111.

Activity

How likely is another Great Depression in the light of developments in monetary policy in recent decades?

The theoretical foundations of monetary policy

The significance of the role of money (and interest rates) in the economy and the underlying principles of monetarism, as described above, have a theoretical basis enshrined in what is referred to as the *quantity theory of money*. In essence, this theory relates changes in the money supply to changes in prices.

The quantity theory of money was first presented in formal terms by the American economist Irving Fisher in 1911, but the general idea that there is a link between a growth in the money supply and price rises dates back to the eighteenth century and particularly the writings of the Scottish philosopher David Hume.

The quantity theory of money

The *quantity theory of money* is based on the so-called *equation of exchange* which relates total expenditure (national expenditure) to the total value of output (national production). Various representations of this *equation of exchange* exist. Here we use one of the commonest forms, which is:

$$M^S V \equiv PY$$

where

M^S is the money supply
V is the velocity of circulation of money
P is the general price level
Y is the real value of national income or real GDP.

The *velocity of circulation* is the average number of times a unit or $ of money is used over a given time period (e.g. annually) to buy the goods and services that make up nominal GDP (or GDP at current prices). V can be derived in practice by dividing PY by M^S in each time period. It should be clear that $M^S V$ is equivalent to the amount of money available in the economy to finance national expenditure and PY is the value of national production. Since $M^S V$ *must equal* PY, the quantity theory of money is, in fact, an *identity* (denoted by $\equiv$ in the expression above).

Monetarists have traditionally made a number of assumptions which transform the $M^S V \equiv PY$ identity into a vehicle for predicting the likely impact of monetary growth upon inflation. In particular, they make two key assumptions:

- The velocity of circulation of money (V) changes very slowly over time and independently of changes in the money supply – therefore, it can be treated as a constant.
- Monetarists tend to believe that a free market economy has an in-built tendency to establish an equilibrium national income at full employment through changes in wages and prices. Therefore, it is assumed that, in the absence of

economic growth, the total real output (Y) is relatively constant (in other words, that Y is restricted by the productive capacity of the economy at full employment and changes only slowly over time).

These two assumptions relating to the constancy of V and Y have been subject to much debate and criticism by economists over the years. We return to this issue later in the chapter, but for our present purposes we need only note from these monetarist principles that *if* V and Y *are* constant then prices will vary directly with the amount of money in circulation – in effect $\Delta M^S = \Delta P$.

Moreover, on the basis of empirical testing, monetarists also argue that the direction of causation is from changes in M^S to changes in P, rather than the reverse. Hence, they are able to conclude that 'too much money chasing too few goods causes inflation'. In other words, and in very simplistic terms, if the money supply increases by 20 per cent then this should *eventually* lead to a 20 per cent increase in prices (in practice, the relationship will not be so precise, of course, if V and Y do not remain constant although their non-constancy does not negate the possibility of a direct link between monetary growth and price rises, i.e. inflation). The time taken for an increase in M^S to cause a rise in P is usually estimated to be around 18 months to two years.

In addition to the above assumptions which are necessary to create a direct link between changes in the money supply and changes in prices, there are three further propositions to which all monetarists seem to subscribe. These are:

- The money supply can be controlled by the authorities – this is necessary if the authorities are to target and control the rate of growth in the money supply to limit the growth of money GDP (i.e. PY).
- A competitive private sector economy automatically tends towards full employment. Therefore, there will be no long-term unemployment as envisaged by Keynes unless competition in markets (including the labour market) is impeded. For this reason monetarists reject Keynesian demand management policies, believing that they create uncertainty (e.g. with regard to investment expenditure). Instead, they tend to favour supply-side reforms (see Chapter 10) alongside sound money policies.
- By a sound money policy, monetarists mean that there should be a steady rate of growth in the money supply (M^S) corresponding to the growth in real output (Y) in order to achieve a stable level of prices. This gives rise to the authorities targeting either the level of inflation directly or monetary targets with a view to achieving a particular inflation rate. This is discussed further below.

The validity of monetarist principles, like most theories in economics, is fundamentally dependent on the underlying assumptions being shown to be correct over time, in particular the constancy of V and Y. However, quite apart from this, we must also be able to measure the money supply and be able to control it. Money can take many forms, as already explained in Chapter 8. Equally, the ability of the authorities to control the money supply at any given time may be problematic. We now turn to look at the methods the authorities might use to control the money supply.

Application 9.2

The velocity of narrow money

Read the following extract:

> During the past two years, the annual rate of growth of narrow M0 has averaged 8.0 per cent. By contrast, the annual rate of growth of nominal consumption has averaged just 5.0 per cent. Should policy makers be concerned by this rapid growth in the quantity of narrow money? Does it signal that inflation will soon pick up, or perhaps that consumption is being underrecorded? Not necessarily – the relationship between economic activity and M0 is complicated by changes in interest rates and the associated process of financial innovation.
>
> The chart below compares the velocity of circulation of narrow money, defined here as the ratio of nominal consumption per annum to M0, with a nominal interest rate. The nominal interest rate is a measure of the opportunity cost of holding cash. It measures the cost of the interest forgone (represented here by the return on eligible bills) when an individual chooses to hold cash in preference to other forms of wealth. When the opportunity cost of holding cash is high, then other things being equal, narrow money holdings should be low relative to consumption – in other words velocity should be high.
>
> For most of the period since 1870 the two series have moved together. During the early part of the 1970s, the nominal interest rate began to rise

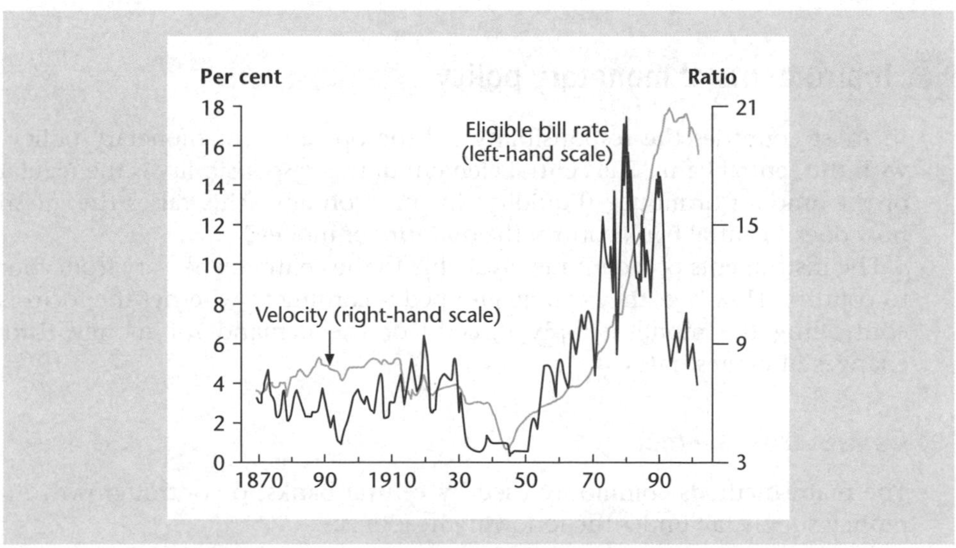

Narrow money velocity and the short-term interest rate in the United Kingdom*

*Velocity series is based on annual data before 1970 and quarterly data thereafter. Interest rate data are annual before 1975 and quarterly thereafter.

Application 9.2 continued

sharply, reaching a peak of 17.4 per cent in 1980 Q1. This unprecedented increase in the opportunity cost of holding narrow money may have contributed to the development of cash saving innovations, such as the introduction of automated teller machines (ATMs), encouraged payment of salaries by cheque, or by direct money transfer, and promoted the introduction of credit and debit cards. These innovations were associated with a significant upward shift in velocity.

But since the early 1990s, interest rates have fallen precipitously. The chart suggests the puzzle is not the current strength of M0 growth, but rather its weakness. Why has M0 not grown more quickly to bring velocity back into line with the low levels seen before the high inflation/high nominal interest rate era of the 1970s and 1980s? Part of the explanation is perhaps that people have grown accustomed to holding less cash, and that the technology enabling them to do this, while expensive to set up, is relatively cheap to maintain.

Source: Extract from Bank of England, *Inflation Report*, November 2002, p.9.

Activity

Explain why the growth rate of narrow money may not be a good predictor of the future growth of nominal GDP.

Instruments of monetary policy

In most countries the responsibility for the operation of monetary policy lies with the central bank. The central element of this responsibility is the regulation of the amount of money (liquidity) in the economy. This raises the question: how does a central bank control the quantity of money?

The instruments or techniques available to the central bank vary from country to country. However, they can be grouped according to whether the focus is on controlling the money supply directly or the demand for money through changes in interest rates.

Control over the money supply

The main methods commonly used by central banks to control growth in the money supply fall under the following headings:

- reserve requirement ratios
- open market operations
- central bank lending to banks
- funding policy

- direct controls
- control over interest rates.

We describe each of these methods in turn.

Reserve requirement ratios

The central bank may require the commercial banks and perhaps other financial institutions to maintain minimum ratios of cash and perhaps other liquid assets. An increase in these required ratios reduces the ability of banks to lend and therefore to increase the money supply through the *bank credit multiplier* (for details of the bank credit multiplier, see pp.174–175).

Open market operations

This is a common method employed by central banks to control the money supply and involves the purchase and sale of government securities (treasury bills and bonds) by the central bank in the open market. If the aim of the central bank is to *reduce* the money supply, it will *sell* more government securities. Those who buy the securities will do so using cheques drawn on their bank accounts. This in turn will reduce the banks' balances at the central bank and lead to a contraction in bank lending if the banks' reserves fall below the required reserve ratio, if one exists, or prudential levels. There will be a multiple contraction of credit and hence the money supply in circulation as a result.

The reverse applies if the central bank wishes to increase the money supply because of the resulting effect on credit expansion.

It should be noted that the effect of open market operations on the money supply will be more limited where the extra government securities brought or sold are bills rather than bonds and if some are purchased by banks. By definition, since they are shorter-dated securities, bills are more liquid assets than bonds and therefore place a smaller constraint on bank lending due to required or prudential reserve ratios.

Central bank lending to banks

In simple terms, since the central bank normally plays a special role as 'lender of last resort' to the domestic financial markets, it can lend more money to the banking sector that can be used for credit expansion. Expanding the so-called 'monetary base' in this way has a direct implication for the *broad money* supply – see Chapter 8 for details. Of course, the importance of the central bank's role in this context directly depends upon whether the banks will choose to borrow extra funds in this manner. This decision by banks will depend upon:

- the rate of interest charged by the central bank (commonly referred to as the discount rate, repo rate or lending rate);
- the willingness of the central bank to lend, which can occur through the repurchase from the banks of government securities.

The operation of monetary policy in this way varies from country to country. For example, in some countries the central bank may choose to keep its lending rate to banks below market rates, thereby encouraging banks to borrow or to sell back securities. By controlling the amount of money it is willing to supply at below-market rates, the central bank can effectively control the monetary base and therefore squeeze or increase the money supply – causing a monetary contraction or expansion, respectively. In other countries, the central bank may choose to control the interest rate on its lending rather than the amount of money available to lend to the banks. The lower this rate is compared to market rates, the more banks will be willing to borrow leading to an expansion in the monetary base and money supply, as before. Raising interest rates will have the opposite effect.

Funding policy

Whereas the previous three methods of controlling the money supply were concerned with controlling the monetary base, funding policy, in contrast, is a method by which the central bank attempts to control the liquidity of the banking system. For example, if the central bank sells more bonds and less bills to the commercial banks, not only are the banks' reserves at the central bank reduced, but the banks now holding relatively fewer bills will have reduced liquidity – bills are a more liquid asset than bonds because of their much shorter period to maturity. The banks' reduced liquidity will mean that they have less scope to make loans. The reverse applies if the central bank should sell more bills and fewer bonds.

Direct controls

Yet another way of controlling the growth of the money supply is for the central bank to impose direct controls on bank lending. Direct controls may be either *quantitative* or *qualitative* in nature.

- *Quantitative controls* might be imposed on either the growth of banking lending (assets) or bank deposits (liabilities). These would take the form of a restriction in total bank lending to the private sector without having to resort directly to higher interest rates. Quantitative controls can be either temporary or more permanent in nature, although while they might succeed in reducing bank deposits, they may not succeed in controlling the overall level of demand or expenditure in the economy if businesses redirect their borrowing to non-controlled financial instruments or non-controlled financial institutions. For example, large companies might use their own bank deposits to set up a lending scheme of their own, a process known as 'disintermediation'. This raises the question of the need for appropriate regulation of all financial service providers.
- *Qualitative controls* might be used to alter the type of lending by banks by, for example, the central bank instructing banks to restrict their lending to the private household sector and lend more to industry, or to lend less to a

particular type of firm (e.g. property companies) and more to manufacturing businesses.

Control over interest rates

Today the emphasis within monetary policy in many countries is on the direct control of interest rates. In principle, the central bank can either predetermine the quantity of money it is willing to supply to the financial markets and allow the interest rate to be determined by market forces or it can announce a particular interest rate and then conduct open-market operations to ensure that the money supply adjusts to ensure that the pre-determined interest rate is the equilibrium one in the financial markets. This is shown in Figure 9.4, in which the central bank has announced a rise in interest rates from i_0 to i_1 with open market operations ensuring that the money supply is reduced from M_0^S to M_1^S.

A tightening of monetary policy through an increase in interest rates (equivalently, a reduction in the money supply) can be expected to reduce aggregate planned expenditure and therefore aggregate demand in the economy. This particular monetary policy stance is often described as 'pulling on a string'. Of course, if a small rise in interest rates does not have the desired negative effect on spending – and therefore inflation – then the 'pull' can be increased even further with still larger increases in interest rates. In contrast, a relaxation of monetary policy through a reduction in interest rates may create a situation that can be described as 'pushing on a string'. This could arise when a fall in interest rates is viewed as a sign of a weak economy with negative effects on business and consumer confidence, such that a reduction in the cost of borrowing is ineffective in stimulating aggregate planned expenditure and aggregate demand.

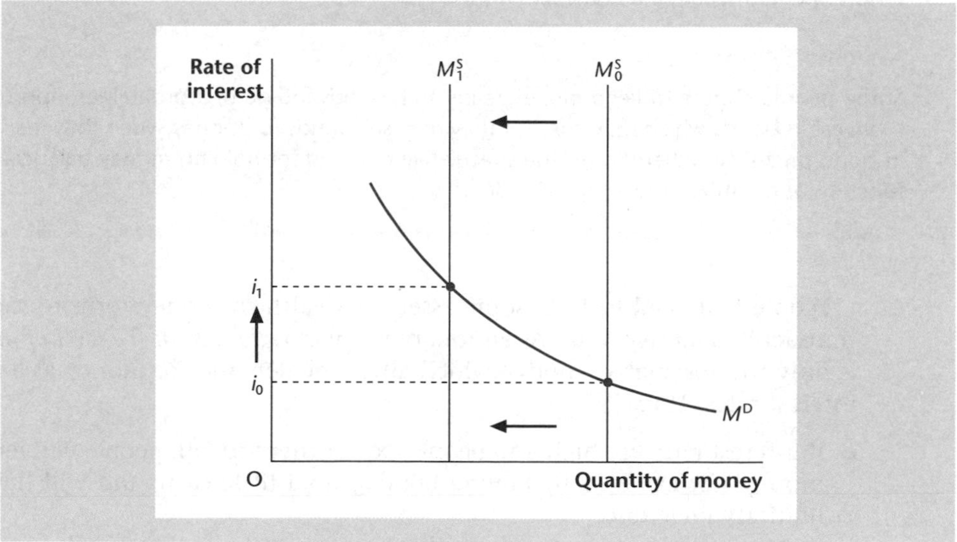

Figure 9.4 Interest rates and monetary control

The impact of interest rate changes on national expenditure, particularly consumer and investment spending, and economic growth is critically dependent on the overall responsiveness of the demand for money to interest rates. Given the importance of this, we give a full analysis of this topic below.

Demand for money

The demand for money refers to the desire to hold wealth and assets in liquid form, i.e. money balances, rather than using wealth to buy interest-bearing securities and goods and services. Keynes made an important contribution to our understanding of the demand for money and pointed to three reasons or *motives* why people would want to hold their assets in the form of money (see Box 9.1).

Box 9.1

Motives for holding money

Transactions motive

Households need money to pay for their day-to-day purchases. The level of transactions demand for money (denoted M_T^D) depends on household incomes, i.e. $M_T^D = f(Y)$.

Precautionary motive

People choose to keep money on hand or on deposit in the bank as a precaution for a 'rainy day' when it might suddenly be needed – again the amount held (denoted M_P^D) will tend to be a function of income, i.e. $M_P^D = f(Y)$.

Speculative motive

Some people choose to keep money ready to take advantage of a profitable opportunity to invest in bonds which may arise (or they may sell bonds for money when they fear a fall in bond prices). In other words, the speculative demand for holding money balances, is a function of the interest rate, i.e. $M_S^D = f(i)$.

People will need to hold some assets or wealth in money form to satisfy the transactions motive and precautionary motives *regardless of the level of interest*. It is only the speculative motive which alters the demand for money as a result of interest rates. Thus:

- if interest rates are high and people expect them to fall, people will lend more money (for example by buying bonds), hold little cash, and will have a *low* liquidity preference;
- if interest rates are low and people expect them to rise, they will hold money to satisfy the speculative motive and their liquidity preference will be *high*.

The conclusion is that the demand for money will be high (liquidity preference will be high) when interest rates are low. Note, however, the importance of expectations. It is not interest rates alone which determine behaviour.

Liquidity preference curve and liquidity trap

We can now draw a *liquidity preference curve*, LL, as shown in Figure 9.5. What does the liquidity preference curve suggest? When interest rates are high, say at i_1, people will be careful to avoid having lots of cash – holding money balances of only M_1^D, perhaps just enough for transactionary and precautionary purposes (so that $M_1^D = M_T^D + M_P^D$). At i_1 the opportunity cost of holding cash is high (since cash can earn high interest rates if invested) and thus liquidity preference is therefore low. At low interest rates, however, Keynes identified the possibility of a 'liquidity trap' situation. Once rates are very low, say at i_2, their most likely movement is up and bond prices must fall. Under these circumstances (since no-one wants to make a capital loss) people will hold their assets in the form of cash (M_2^D) and therefore sell their bonds and wait for better investment opportunities. This partly explains why even with very low interest rates in the early 1930s, investors held back and investment did not respond to ease the depression.

In the liquidity trap situation, an increase in the supply of money will *not* reduce the interest rate any further. The implication of this is that monetary policy (via monetary expansion) will have no effect on aggregate demand, real GDP and unemployment.

This view of the demand for money and the possibility of a liquidity trap, as put forward by Keynes, has attracted considerable controversy and criticism especially from monetarists, notably Milton Friedman. Given the central importance of the elasticity of demand for money with respect to interest rates as the centre

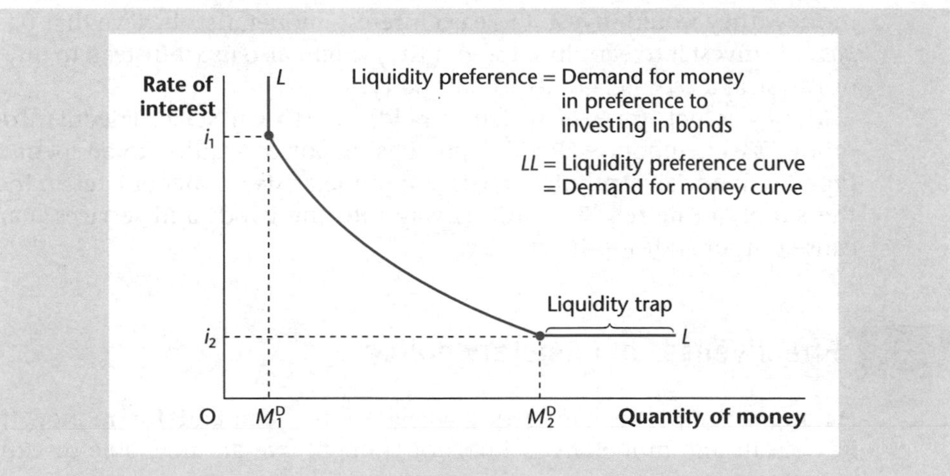

Figure 9.5 Liquidity preference curve – the demand for money curve

piece of monetary policy in many countries today, it is important that we understand the alternative monetarist view of the demand for money.

The primary criticism by monetarists of the Keynesian argument is that holding money or government bonds is only *one* choice for holding wealth – in reality, the trade-off is not a narrow one between holding cash and buying bonds. Other ways of holding wealth include:

- stocks and shares other than government bonds;
- a wide range of physical assets.

Each such method of holding wealth brings some form of return or yield to the holder. For example:

- the yield from money might include some interest, such as on bank deposit accounts, but the main yield from money is a convenience yield – this is the convenience of having ready money when it is needed instead of having to go to the bother of converting other assets into cash;
- stocks and shares are financial assets which should provide a yield (interest or dividends and capital growth) which may keep ahead of the rate of inflation providing a *real* return to investors;
- physical assets including property and consumer durables such as furniture and cars. There might be a money yield from physical assets owing to an increase in their capital value but the yield also includes a non-monetary return, for example the rewards from living in an owner-occupied house, the use of furniture, the enjoyment from owning a new car or a painting.

Friedman argued that the demand for money is related to the demand for holding wealth in its other forms. Money is a direct substitute for wealth in the form of bonds, equities or physical assets. In this respect, he argued against the Keynesian view that holding money is only a substitute for holding financial assets (bonds). Whereas Keynes believed that if people did not want to hold money, they would invest it to earn interest, monetarists believe that people will *possibly* invest it to earn interest, but they might also use it instead to buy equities or physical assets, i.e. goods and property.

Money is not an asset which is held for its own stake. Friedman described money as a 'temporary abode of purchasing power' waiting to be spent on other types of financial or physical assets. For monetarists, sooner or later an increase in the supply of money will find its way into the goods and services market and cause output and/or prices to rise.

Effectiveness of monetary policy

Having set out the contrasting views of the demand for money from the Keynesian and monetarist schools of thought, we are now able to explore the effectiveness of monetary policy on the demand for money, again setting out the monetarist and Keynesian views.

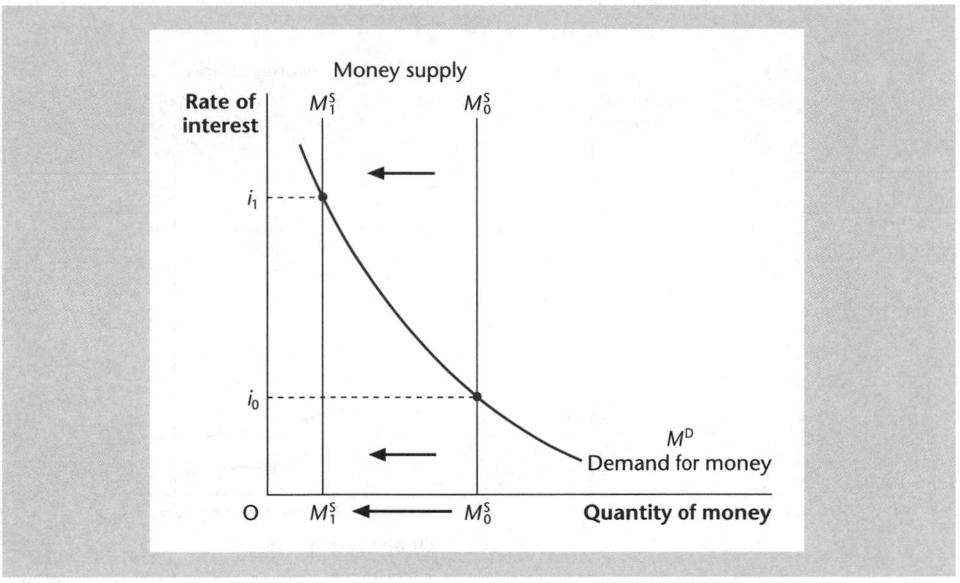

Figure 9.6 Monetarist view of the link between interest rates and changes in the money supply

Monetarist view

The effectiveness of monetary policy through policy-determined interest rates (or money supply controls) rests on the monetarists' belief that people's willingness to hold their assets in the form of money balances is relatively *insensitive* (or *inelastic*) with respect to the rate of interest. That is to say, the demand for money (M^D) is relatively unresponsive to the price of money. This view is illustrated in Figure 9.6. It is controversial and has been subject to much empirical testing, though no consensus view has emerged. The issue seems to be one of *degree of responsiveness*, in the sense that the demand for money does appear to be interest inelastic at high *real* rates of interest (i.e. allowing for inflation in calculating the cost of borrowing). If the M^D schedule is steep (inelastic) then any change in the money supply has a strong impact upon interest rate levels or vice versa. This is illustrated by a leftward shift (reduction) or rightward shift (increase) in the money supply schedule, M^S. In the case of a reduction from M_0^S to M_1^S, interest rates will be pushed up from i_0 to i_1 in Figure 9.6. It should be noted that the money supply curve is drawn for convenience as a vertical line, which suggests that the money supply is determined independently of interest rates. This may not be true in reality, but this is not crucial to the current discussion.

Keynesian view

In contrast, Keynesian economists dispute the idea that the demand for money is relatively insensitive to changes in interest rates. They argue, instead, that as

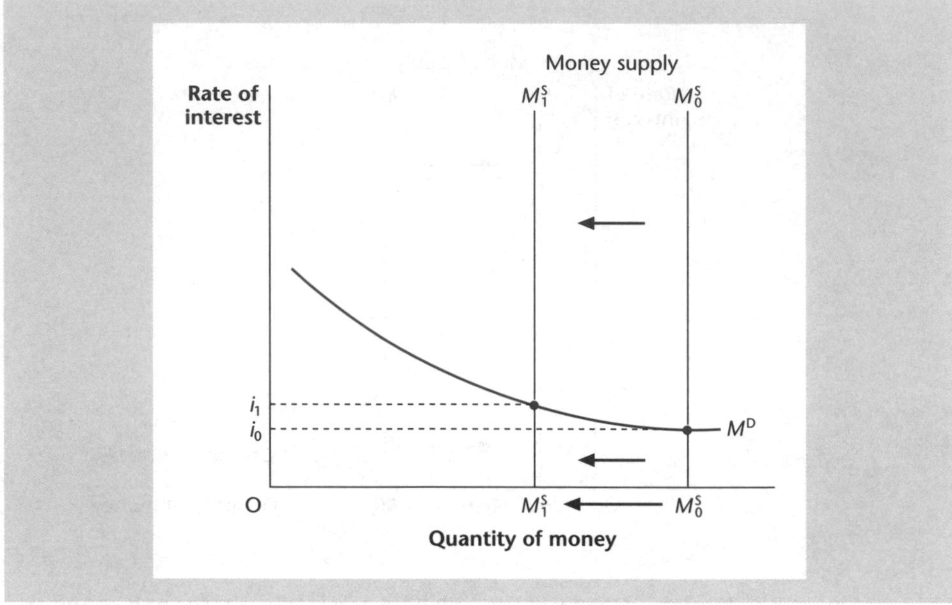

Figure 9.7 Keynesian view of the link between interest rates and changes in the money supply

interest rates vary then the demand to hold money balances will fluctuate as people move their balances into and out of various interest-bearing assets. Keynesian economists identify government bonds as the most obvious alternative to holding money balances because they are risk-free and, since they can be readily traded in the stock market, they are a liquid asset. Therefore, Keynesians argue that the willingness to hold assets in the form of money is relatively *sensitive* with respect to changes in interest rates on bonds: i.e. the demand to hold money balances is relatively *interest elastic* as shown in Figure 9.7.

Comparing the monetarist and Keynesian views

If the Keynesian view is correct then, in contrast to the monetarist conclusion above, measures taken by authorities to change the money supply will have little effect on the rate of interest. In Figure 9.7 a reduction in the money supply from M_0^S to M_1^S has only a small impact upon the interest rate, pushing i_0 only up to i_1. Monetarists also hold a fundamentally different view of the likely impact of interest rate changes upon aggregate demand from that held by Keynesians. As we saw in the discussion of national income determination in Chapter 4, Keynesian economists argue that aggregate demand in general, and investment expenditure in particular, is fairly insensitive to changes in interest rates. In other words, any given change in interest rates is believed to lead to a less than proportionate change in total expenditure in the economy. The reasoning behind this is that, even if people wish to hold extra money balances (cash) as interest rates fall, these balances may not necessarily be spent on extra goods and services (i.e. on additional transactions in the economy). Instead, it is argued, these balances may be held for other purposes associated with precautionary (unforeseen contingencies) and/or speculative motives (e.g. stock market dealings) – these motives for holding money balances were discussed earlier.

More specifically, with regard to investment expenditure, there is no doubt that changes in interest rates have some influence upon investment decisions, but Keynesian economists argue that the relationship is unlikely to be precise. The reasons for this view are as follows:

- Investment expenditure in the government sector is undertaken for a host of reasons – social, political and economic – which may not be affected by the interest rate level.
- Investment expenditure plans in the private sector commonly stretch over many years and are often large scale, so short-term changes in interest rates are unlikely to be a critical factor.
- The key determinant of investment in the private sector is the *expected* rate of return on capital (discounted to present values) relative to the cost of raising money (the interest rate or discount factor) – the volatility of expectations will have a major effect on investment decisions and interest rates are but one factor in determining expectations.

For these reasons Keynesians believe that even if changes in the money supply cause a significant change in interest rates and vice versa, the relationship between changes in interest rates and the level of investment is unpredictable. As noted above, the effect of interest rates on investment may be especially unreliable in the circumstances of an economic recession, when business expectations are depressed.

In contrast, monetarists argue that the rate of interest is a main determinant of investment decisions. The reasoning behind this view is that a fall in interest rates will make some investments profitable, which were previously unprofitable, and therefore aggregate investment should increase (and vice versa when interest rates increase). Therefore, aggregate investment in the economy is inversely related to the rate of interest.

The difference between the Keynesian and monetarist views on the impact of interest rate changes upon investment is summarised in Figure 9.8, where the curves labelled I_1 and I_2 represent levels of planned investment expenditure at different interest rates (referred to as *marginal efficiency of investment curves*). I_1 is a Keynesian representation, where investment is not particularly affected by moderate changes in interest rates. I_2 shows the monetarist position, where interest rate changes do have a significant effect on investment expenditure. Empirical evidence on aggregate investment expenditure seems to confirm that it has an

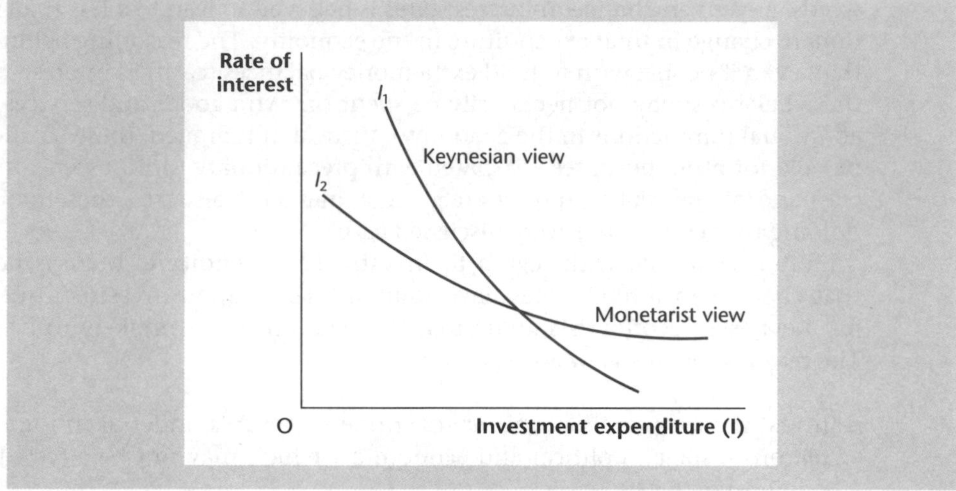

Figure 9.8 Keynesian and monetarist views compared

inverse relationship with interest rates, but that it is a fairly weak one and with varying time lags before investment responds.

Criticisms of monetarism

Just as there has been considerable controversy over the years about the foundations of Keynesian economics in macroeconomics, so too there has been heated debate surrounding the validity of monetarism and therefore the effectiveness of monetary policy in influencing output, employment and prices.

The criticisms that have been made against monetarism may be summarised under the following headings concerning:

- causality from M^S to P;
- constancy of V and Y;
- strength of linkages;
- implications for economic activity.

We summarise the criticisms concerning each of these aspects below.

Causality from M^S to P

As we have discussed, monetarists' views on the importance of money are based on the *quantity theory of money*. In essence, this implies that there is a direct and predictable relationship between growth in the money supply and inflation. Monetarists further suggest that, based on empirical research, the direction of this relationship is from changes in M^S to changes in P. Both contentions have been strongly challenged, however, and as yet there is no consensus view. Just because inflation tends to correlate with increases in the money supply, as the monetarists' empirical results show, this does not necessarily mean that the increase in the money supply *causes* inflation and in any predictable way.

Constancy of *V* and *Y*

In addition, the assumed constancy of V and Y by monetarists in the quantity theory has been challenged on empirical grounds. The assumption of an unchanged Y implies that the economy is always at full employment, but clearly this will not be the case in an economic recession. If there is substantial unemployment and the authorities choose to reflate the economy by increasing the money supply, this is likely to raise Y (i.e. the volume of transactions and hence real output) rather than P. Consequently, the link between changes in M^S and changes in P will be less predictable than argued by monetarists.

Turning to the assumed constancy of V, if in practice the frequency with which each unit of money changes hands is subject to change over time, perhaps as a result of technological innovations which affect the speed of money through the economy, this compromises the usefulness of monetary measures in relation to counterinflationary policy. For example, in the extreme case, an increase in M^S could be offset totally by a decline in the speed with which money circulates in the economy (i.e. through a fall in V) so that M^SV and therefore PY remain unchanged. Empirically, V has been shown to change over a number of years in most countries and in some periods more quickly than in others.

Strength of linkages

Apart from controversy regarding the assumptions underlying the monetarists' interpretation of the quantity theory, we have also discussed at length earlier in this chapter the controversy over the strength of two key linkages:

- the link between changes in the money supply and changes in interest rates;
- the link between changes in interest rates and aggregate demand (particularly investment expenditure) in the economy.

Monetarists believe that these linkages are strong, while their critics disagree.

Implications for economic activity

Moreover, it has been argued by the critics of monetarism that the economic effects of a tight (contractionary) monetarist strategy may be even worse than the consequences of the inflation that it seeks to remove. These suggested effects are as follows:

- There may be a sharp increase in unemployment as a result of deflationary monetary measures, i.e. a credit squeeze coupled with high interest rates.

- Rising unemployment will reduce tax receipts to the government and at the same time will put increased pressure on government expenditure and the budget deficit, making control of the money supply more difficult.
- A strict monetarist approach is likely to require a reduction in a government's budget deficit – this brings with it a conflict between economic policy and achieving a government's social objectives through expenditure on welfare programmes.
- Monetarists emphasise the favourable effects of their policy recommendations over the longer term, but in the meantime the economic suffering may lead to a change in government and a change in economic strategy – thus any long-term benefits that might accrue will never be realised.
- A sharp rise in interest rates which are then held at a high level for some time may arrest investment and reduce economic growth. This will be particularly important if the rise in interest rates is due to a fall in bond prices resulting from the need for the government to finance a growing budget deficit resulting from the monetary contraction and consequent economic recession. In this way, government expenditure, financed by borrowing may 'crowd out' private sector investment spending as interest rates are driven up – making private capital investment projects, at the margin, financially unattractive. At the same time, in an open economy with a high degree of capital mobility, businesses may also be hampered by the effect of high interest rates on the exchange rate (a subject discussed in more detail in Chapter 15).

Monetary policy, economic growth and inflation

We can now pull together the essential elements of monetary policy, set out in this chapter, to provide a clearer understanding of the wider implications of central bank policy on interest rates. In the case of a rise in interest rates – a tightening or contraction of monetary policy – we can identify three effects:

- investment and consumer spending falls, after a certain time lag;
- the value of the domestic currency rises on the foreign exchange markets (due to short-term capital inflows) with a negative impact on net exports;
- a negative multiplier process takes place, again with a time lag, due to the consequent falls in investment spending, consumer spending and net exports – and hence, an overall decline in aggregate expenditure. This decline will lead to a fall in incomes, which induces further falls in consumer spending, investment spending, and so on.

Thus, a rise in (real) interest rates can be expected to reduce real GDP growth as a result of these effects – and with it inflationary pressures.

If the central bank *lowers* interest rates, the events just described will occur in the opposite direction, ensuring real GDP growth (subject to the availability of spare capacity in the economy) and an increase in inflationary pressures (again, subject to the extent to which the economy is at or close to its full employment potential with respect to the utilisation of resources).

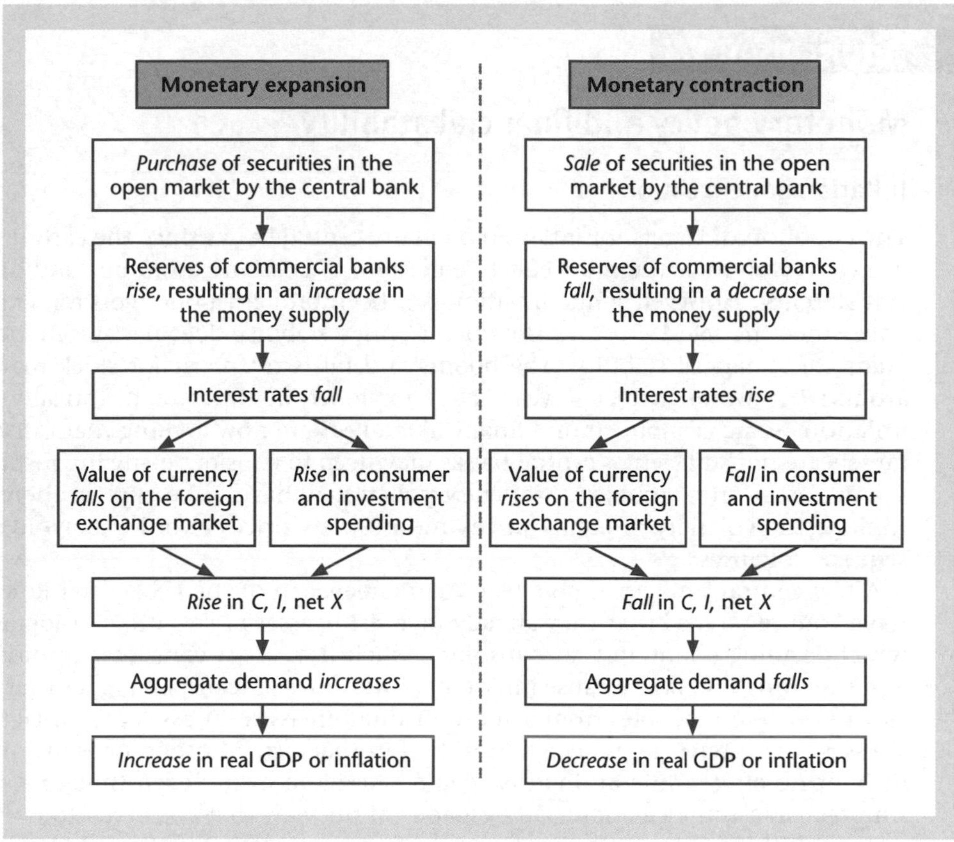

Figure 9.9 **Ripple effects of central bank monetary policy**

The flow diagram (Figure 9.9) provides a summary of the interactions between a change in interest rates and the implications for real GDP and inflation. A decision by the central bank to pursue an *expansionary* or *contractionary* monetary policy will result in a 'ripple' effect through the economy, with implications for aggregate demand, output and inflation.

Note that the left-hand side of the flow chart begins with the central bank buying securities in the open market, which results in an increase in the money supply (i.e. liquidity is injected into the banking system) and drives down interest rates. Alternatively, as explained earlier, interest rates could be policy-determined, in which case the money supply will be allowed to increase to ensure equilibrium in the money market that equates to this interest rate. Either way, the effect is the same: an increase in the money supply has a 'ripple' effect throughout the economy, resulting in real GDP growth and an increase in inflation – and vice versa when we start on the right-hand side of the flow chart involving the sale of securities by the central bank and a rise in interest rates.

Application 9.3

Monetary policy and financial stability

Inflation under control

The adoption of targets for inflation by many central banks since the early 1990s was perceived to be the most effective method of ensuring economic and financial stability. However, while inflation has been brought under control, experience since the late 1990s has shown that price stability does *not* automatically guarantee financial stability. The booms and busts of the major stock markets around the world in recent years have exploded at times of historically low inflation. Some economists and financial analysts are now arguing that inflation targets are not sufficient – central banks may need to consider using interest rates to curb asset price 'bubbles'. Monetary policy may have to be applied therefore to tame the volatility of equity prices and property prices in order to avoid subsequent collapses.

A few central bank governors (e.g. Alan Greenspan of the US Federal Reserve) have counter-argued that they already take rising asset prices into consideration when deciding on interest rates insofar as such rises boost consumer confidence and spending and hence cause inflationary pressures. Greenspan argues that you can never tell a 'bubble' from a more justified increase in asset prices. He also stresses that interest rates are a 'blunt' tool in that a small rise in rates may have little or no effect while an increase could cause a recession even though it may suppress an asset-price boom. Greenspan is of the view that it is better to wait for an asset bubble to burn itself out and then to rectify its after-effects by relaxing monetary policy, aggressively if necessary.

In retaliation, opponents of Greenspan point out that uncertainty about whether there is a bubble or not is no excuse for adopting a passive position. In addition, reducing interest rates when asset prices fall sharply, but failing to raise them when they boom, creates a moral hazard that makes speculative asset bubbles more rather than less likely. They also argue that even if a rate increase does cause a recession, this may be better than the alternative. The longer a bubble is allowed to grow, the more it encourages the build-up of other imbalances, such as an excessive growth of personal debt or over-investment by corporates resulting in excess capacity – which may lead to an economic downturn that is prolonged.

Alan Greenspan is supported by the governor of the Bank of England, Mervyn King. He has been a supporter of inflation targeting for a long time. Mr King believes that the framework of inflation targeting can deal effectively with policy dilemmas involving asset price booms. The solution is to look at inflation over a longer time period than usual. Normally, central bankers focus on the prospects for inflation up to two years ahead. But asset-price bubbles can create imbalances that might cause inflation to fall outside its target range much further into the

Application 9.3 continued

future. So there is a trade-off between deviations of inflation rates from target in the short term (a year or two ahead) and deviations from target later. It may sometimes make sense to increase interest rates now, and accept that inflation will undershoot its target in the short run, in order to avoid undershooting by rather more later.

Otmar Issing of the European Central Bank (ECB) has also put forward the view that short-run deviations from inflation targets may be acceptable in order to achieve price stability in the long run. Indeed, this is one justification for the ECB's focus on monetary growth, within its framework, for dealing with inflation. Mr Issing believes that paying particular attention to monetary (and credit) growth can help to prevent the emergence of serious financial imbalances.

Central banks cannot continue to disregard surging asset prices by arguing that monetary policy should focus solely on consumer-price inflation. Volatility in asset prices can have major long-term consequences for inflation. Some central bankers have now come to realise that they cannot afford to focus only on the short-term situation.

Activity

What are the potential implications for the household and corporate sectors arising from a change in central bank philosophy as described above?

Effects of monetary policy on business

Monetarists contend that, by pursuing a policy of strictly controlling the growth in the money supply, an economic environment will eventually be created in which enterprise and efficient firms can flourish. After the credit squeeze and recession necessary to remove inflationary pressures, firms will be left 'leaner and fitter' and therefore better able to take advantage of the available opportunities that will emerge in a post-inflationary economy. Clearly, therefore, the positive effects of monetary policy on business must be looked at from a long-term perspective – and perhaps by a government with a great deal of confidence and strong nerve!

As we have intimated on several occasions in this chapter, however, monetarist measures to reduce inflationary pressures are likely to have a number of negative effects on business, at least in the short term. Possible negative effects include the impact upon exchange rates, profits, investment and even the very survival of some firms. For example:

- *High interest rates will tend to hit exporters because high interest rates attract foreign currency causing the exchange rate to rise.* Under certain circumstances this reduces the competitiveness of exports in foreign markets. At the same time, as the value of the currency rises, domestic producers suffer as imported goods gain a competitive price advantage. These effects follow because an appreciation in the foreign exchange rate resulting from capital inflows ('hot money') makes exports more expensive in foreign markets and less expensive in the home market. There may, therefore, be unfavourable consequences for the balance of payments. Chapter 15 discusses the relationship between the exchange rate and the balance of payments.

- *High interest rates, coupled with a high exchange rate will tend to decrease aggregate demand for domestically produced goods.* This is, therefore, likely to lead to a squeeze on profits with a consequent unplanned increase in stocks (inventories) of unsold goods. To finance the costs of holding these stocks, firms may have little choice but to borrow even more money despite high interest rates (this is sometimes referred to as 'distress borrowing').
- *Ultimately, firms may not be able to survive in a high interest rate and high exchange rate environment.* The closure of firms has obvious implications for unemployment, investment and the future productive capacity of the economy. Some firms that shut down will be those that are the least efficient and least creditworthy. At the same time, however, otherwise healthy firms may be caught out by a credit squeeze that leads to cash-flow difficulties. Firms which have committed themselves to large investment programmes and those which are heavily dependent upon exporting are especially vulnerable to rising interest rates.

Concluding remarks

This chapter has focused on the important subject in macroeconomics of monetary policy. It has considered in detail the main principles and theoretical underpinnings of *monetarism*, including the *quantity theory of money*.

As we have seen, monetary policy can take a number of forms using different tools or techniques to control the growth in the money supply in the economy. Monetary policy can concentrate upon controlling the supply of money or the demand for money. Central to monetary policy is the determination of the interest rate. Interest rates affect the willingness of consumers and firms to borrow, spend and invest. The higher the real (inflation-adjusted) interest rate, the more contractionary monetary policy will tend to be. The lower the real interest rate, monetary policy will have an expansionary effect on the economy, everything else being equal.

Monetarists criticise Keynesian economics for ignoring the importance of sound money policies in favour of fiscal measures to balance the economy. Monetarists tend to favour markets free from much state intervention, balanced government budgets over the business cycle, and monetary policies that create stable conditions for private sector investment decisions. Given their support for private enterprise, and their distrust of government economic management, many monetarists argue that monetary policy should not be used actively by governments, through their central banks, to manage the level of economic activity. Rather, monetary policy should be set so as to provide stable monetary conditions, in which private businesses and households can spend, invest and save with confidence. This leads to the notion of monetary 'rules', such as money supply growth targets or inflation or interest rate targets over the longer-term, in the place of Keynesian-style 'discretionary' macroeconomic policies. It also leads to the idea of taking the day-to-day control of monetary policy, including the setting of interest rates, away from government (politicians) and placing it under the supervision of an independent central bank. This is the case today in many countries around the world such as the USA, the UK and all members of the European Union which adopted the euro (whose central banks are under the direct control of the European Central Bank).

However, monetarism has itself been subject to much controversy and criticism since the 1970s, when it first posed a serious challenge to Keynesian economics. Criticism has centred upon the theoretical foundations of monetarist beliefs; in particular, whether there is a causal relationship between changes in the money stock and changes in price levels which can be predicted. In addition, monetarist policies have proved difficult to implement effectively. Finding a measure of the money supply that captures the effect of monetary changes on inflation has proved tricky, especially one which can be used with confidence and which can define desirable money supply targets that can actually be met. For example, with the abolition of exchange controls and financial deregulation in the UK after 1979, the government felt it necessary to fall back upon manipulating interest rates to restrain the rise of credit in the economy. But high interest rates in turn proved difficult to sustain over long periods for political and economic reasons. Moreover, from time to time interest rates appeared to be set more with a view to influencing the level of the exchange rate rather than with a view to constraining the growth in the money stock. It would merely be coincidental if the interest rate needed to maintain a particular exchange rate was also the right one to achieve the money supply target. Not surprisingly, interest rate policy in this context has been described as a 'blunt instrument'. The 'bluntness' of monetary policy effectiveness in the past may be explained by the fact that changes in interest rates have generally been *reactionary* measures, i.e. efforts to reduce inflation have too often been too little and too late. This may be likened to applying brakes with full force only after the car has gone out of control!

Over the past few years, compared to the 1970s and 1980s, with inflation in Europe and North America running at low levels, monetary policy has been used to stimulate consumer demand and private investment, thorough interest rate reductions. However, it is unclear how far 'pushing the string' using monetary measures can stimulate economic activity in the face of recessionary pressures. The example of Japan with very low interest rates throughout the 1990s and a stagnant economy suggests that monetary policy may be more successful in tackling 'booms' and inflation than recessionary forces.

Key learning points

- *Monetarist economists* believe that inflation results from 'too much money chasing too few goods'.
- Monetarists argue that to control inflation it is necessary to control the growth in the economy's money supply.
- Monetarists tend to favour free markets over state intervention, monetary 'rules' over 'discretionary' policy, and, therefore, an independent central bank.
- Monetarists criticise Keynesian-style macroeconomic management for being inflationary and economically destabilising.
- Monetarists believe that governments should balance their budgets over the business cycle to prevent long-term inflationary pressures.
- The *money transmission mechanism* is central to monetarism and identifies how changes in the money supply, both directly and indirectly, through changes in (real) interest rates affect aggregate planned expenditure and therefore aggregate demand.
- Changes in interest rates affect the willingness of consumers and firms to borrow and spend or invest.
- The *quantity theory of money* is a core identity in monetary economics. It is an identity that links total expenditure (M^SV) to the total value of output (PY).
- Monetarists use the quantity theory of money to show how changes in the money supply (M^S) may lead to changes in the price level (P), depending upon the behaviour of the velocity of circulation (V) and real output (Y).
- Central banks may use a variety of instruments in an attempt to control the money supply, including setting a *reserve ratio requirement*, adopting *open market operations*, varying their *lending to the banking system*, adopting *funding policies* that affect the liquidity of the banks, and using *direct controls*.
- *Direct controls* on bank lending may take both quantitative and qualitative forms, affecting the quantity and type of bank lending, respectively.
- *Interest rate policy* can also be used to affect the demand for money.
- Monetarism is criticised for its assumptions that the velocity of circulation of money (V) and real output (Y) are constant.
- Monetary policy can affect both output, and therefore, economic growth and inflation through its effects on consumption and investment, leading to changes in aggregate expenditure and therefore aggregate demand.
- Monetary policy affects business through its effects on both the domestic and international sectors of the economy. Changes in interest rates can have an effect on exchange rates, leading to changes in the demand for exports and imports, and changes in international capital flows.

? Topics for discussion

1. In what ways may an expansion in the money supply affect the level of economic activity?
2. What monetary measures might a central bank use to control the money supply?
3. Compare and contrast measures to control the money supply and control interest rates. What do you understand by the term a 'policy-determined interest rate'?
4. How might changes in short-term interest rates affect the rate of monetary growth in an economy?
5. Under what conditions will the growth in the money supply have an equal proportionate effect on an economy's price level?
6. Compare and contrast the Keynesian and monetarist views with respect to the demand for money.
7. The central bank announces a cut in its (short-term) interest rate from 5 per cent to 4 per cent. Discuss the possible effects for (a) the economy as a whole and (b) an individual firm that has a large export business.
8. In a world which is becoming increasingly dominated by the free flow of capital, what is the likely future role of domestic monetary policy?
9. The central bank tightens monetary policy by sharply raising its short-term interest rate – to well above the rate of price inflation. Assess the implications for:

   (a) consumer spending
   (b) savings
   (c) inflationary pressures
   (d) employment
   (e) investment expenditure
   (f) the exchange rate
   (g) economic growth.

Chapter 10

ECONOMIC GROWTH AND SUPPLY-SIDE ECONOMICS

Aims and learning outcomes

In previous chapters we have been concerned primarily with the nature and composition of aggregate demand and the contributions of Keynesian and monetarist economics to understanding the causes of fluctuations in economic activity, unemployment and inflation. Keynesian economics emphasises the use of interventionist fiscal measures to tackle unemployment that results from a lack of aggregate demand. Monetarism is concerned with controlling the growth of the money supply and its impact on aggregate expenditure and therefore employment and prices. In recent years, economists have also been interested in the factors which determine economic growth and the resulting levels of production (real GDP) or *aggregate supply*. In this approach to macroeconomic policy, the key to reducing unemployment and inflation lies in improving the ability of the economy to supply goods and services efficiently. In other words, unemployment will fall permanently only if goods and services are competitive in terms of price and quality in domestic and world markets. Similarly, the reverse side of 'excess aggregate demand' as the cause of inflation is insufficient aggregate supply of goods and services to meet current demand.

In practice, many supply-side economists also favour a sound money policy to keep down inflation and to provide an economic environment conducive to long-term corporate planning and investment with implications for employment and production. Therefore, while supply-side economics is distinct from monetarism, in the sense that it is possible to support monetarist principles without favouring supply-side reforms (and vice versa), many modern monetarists are also content to be labelled 'supply-siders'.

In this chapter the following issues are considered:

- the nature of economic growth;
- growth accounting;
- technical progress and innovation.;
- models of economic growth;
- the principles of supply-side economics;
- supply-side economics in practice.

The idea that government economic policy should be concerned with supply as well as demand is not new. For example, at various times since the mid-1940s, successive governments in the UK, the USA, France, the former West Germany, Japan, South Korea and elsewhere intervened in the economy with the aim of increasing production. These initiatives were often grouped together under the title of *industrial policy*. Industrial policy measures were introduced to nationalise industry, raise investment, increase the supply of skilled labour through government-sponsored training programmes, rationalise production, redistribute industry regionally, and to assist exports. In France, for example (and even more obviously in the former Soviet Union and China), economic activity was planned from the centre through the use of what were called *national plans*. These plans set down targets for the growth in GDP and various other economic indicators often over the following five years. In Japan the Ministry for International Trade and Industry (MITI) has been credited with aiding the expansion of Japanese industry from the 1950s by planning, identifying potential markets and assisting investment programmes.

Modern supply-side economics is distinct from earlier industrial policy, however, because the emphasis is on establishing an economic environment conducive to *private entrepreneurship* rather than state planning and state investment subsidies.

Supply-side policies are aimed at creating an economic environment in which there is more incentive for individuals to work and save and for private sector firms to invest, produce and employ.

At the same time, many supply-side economists tend to assume that demand in a market economy will usually be sufficient to buy whatever the economy produces. Therefore, the role of government should not be to 'plan' demand in a Keynesian manner, but to privatise inefficient state enterprises, liberalise markets, reduce taxes and public spending, and free-up the labour market, so that wages and employment respond to market signals. The idea that 'supply creates its own demand' has a long pedigree dating back to the French economist Jean Baptiste Say in the early nineteenth century. 'Say's law of markets' suggested that production creates equivalent additional purchasing power, which will be spent on the production. As we saw earlier, however, this result depends upon having planned injections that equal planned leakages. For example, if households plan to save more than firms plan to invest, everything else being equal, there will be insufficient aggregate demand to meet aggregate supply – in which case Say's law no longer holds (at least in the short run, until output, prices and employment fully adjust to the lower demand). Nevertheless, if supply side reforms can make product and labour markets more flexible, so that they react more quickly to excess supply, falling output and employment should be temporary. Supply side economics is therefore consistent with Say's law over the longer term.

A primary objective of supply-side policies is the creation of the necessary economic conditions for an economy to achieve its potential economic growth given its resource endowment. In this chapter we look in particular at three of the policies that have been pursued to that end by governments, namely:

- changes in labour laws to make labour markets more flexible;
- the reduction of taxation and the creation of greater incentives to work and invest;
- the programme of privatisation and market liberalisation.

However, we begin by considering the nature of economic growth. Achieving higher economic growth is the objective of supply-side economics.

Learning outcomes

After studying this material you will be able to:

- Understand the nature and causes of economic growth.
- Recognise the differences between three major models of economic growth.
- Appreciate why more supply as a result of economic growth allows more expenditure to occur without inflation resulting.
- Identify the types of supply-side measures governments may adopt.
- Distinguish between different supply-side measures and their likely economic consequences.
- Contrast supply-side economics with Keynesian and monetarist economics.

The nature of economic growth

> *Economic growth* is the term economists use to describe the rate of increase in an economy's potential real output (the volume of output) in the economy over time.

Increases in output lead to equivalent increases in real income and therefore higher economic growth is associated with improvements in living standards and quality of life. For example, a sustained growth rate of 3 per cent per annum will lead to a doubling of real GDP in 23 to 24 years – and will lead to a quadrupling of real GDP in 48 years. Economic growth is illustrated in Figure 10.1 by the movement outwards in a *production possibility curve* from P_1P_1 to P_2P_2. The characteristics of a production possibility curve were detailed on p.9. The movement outwards in the curve results from economic growth in the economy leading to the supply of more goods and services – in the diagram, for convenience, summarised as more capital goods (K_1 to K_2) and more consumption goods (C_1 to C_2). The resultant higher output should mean higher living standards, on average.

Higher economic growth may, of course, also be associated with external costs, such as pollution and environmental degradation and therefore the relationship

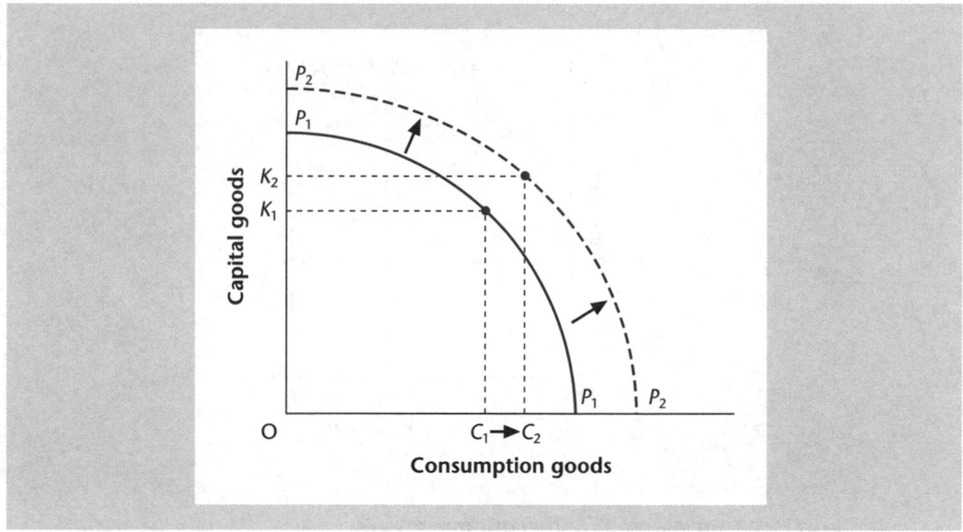

Figure 10.1 Economic growth and the production possibility curve

between economic growth and the standard of living is not necessarily straightforward. Also, individuals' standard of living depends upon *their* income, which may or may not move in line with national income. Moreover, population growth and changes in income distribution in the economy will impact on an individual's spending power. Nevertheless, as a general rule, economic growth does lead to improved economic welfare and a reduction in income inequalities, as the history of Europe and North America since the industrial revolution has demonstrated and the experiences of parts of South East Asia in more recent times underline.

Economic growth can result from either an increase in physical factor inputs in the economy or an improved quality and utilisation (productivity) of the existing level of inputs. An increase in the size of the labour force, perhaps resulting from increased immigration, should permit more production in the economy, as would a higher proportion of the population joining the workforce (or what is called the *participation rate* or the percentage of the population participating in the labour force). Similarly, increased investment in new physical capital should lead to higher economic growth and, as evidenced in North America in the nineteenth century, opening up additional lands to agricultural production and mineral exploitation leads to more output. However, modern industrialised economies tend to have low levels of population growth and there is usually little scope for an increased input of land as a factor of production. Hence, economic growth mainly depends upon new capital investment, alongside improvements in the quality and utilisation of existing labour, capital and land inputs.

In the long-run, investment raises a nation's potential GDP by adding to its capital stock. The effect of this is to move the economy's long-run aggregate supply curve rightwards in Figure 10.2, from $LRAS_0$ to $LRAS_1$ to $LRAS_2$ for example,

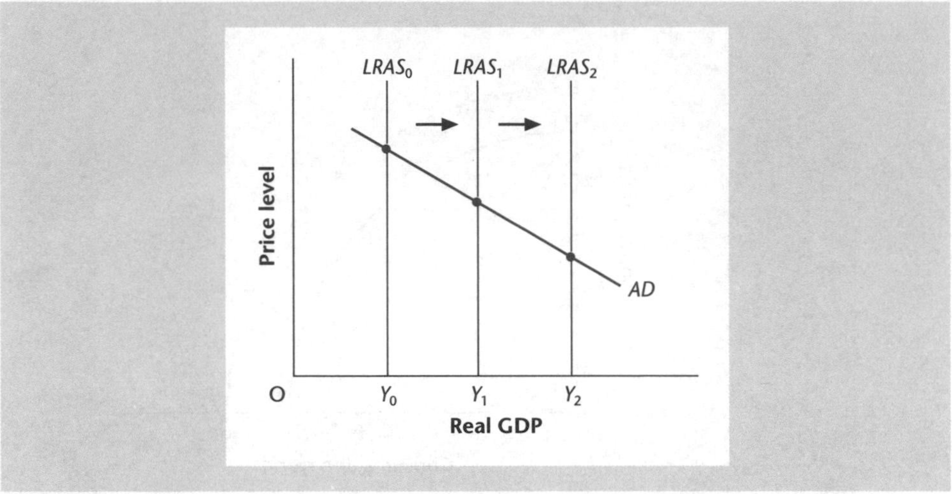

Figure 10.2 Investment and economic growth

leading to a rise in real GDP over time, equivalent to an outward shift in the PP curve. For a given AD, a rightward shift in the LRAS curve will also lead to a fall in the price level – resulting in *benign deflation* (in contrast to *malign* deflation which results from a fall in AD for a given LRAS).

Improvements in the labour force lead to higher output per unit of labour input (i.e. per worker) or what is called higher *labour productivity*. This might be brought about by improving the quality of the labour force, through more education and training – leading to the concept of investing in *human capital* – or by better management (utilisation) of the existing labour input. Similarly, existing physical capital in the form of plant, machinery, industrial and commercial buildings, etc., might be better exploited leading to higher *capital productivity* – or there might be an improved capital input due to technical progress, leading to a more productive capital stock. This will be reflected in an economy's *capital–output ratio*. Higher capital productivity leads to a lower capital-to-output ratio because more output is obtained from each unit of capital input. The same principle applies to land as an input: while the amount of land in use may be fixed in supply, the output from the stock of land is improved through better agricultural processes and superior mineral exploitation – much as occurred during the 'agricultural revolution' in Europe from the seventeenth century and has happened in Asian farming more recently.

Growth accounting

The discussion above sets out some generalisations about the causes of economic growth involving either an increase in physical factors (labour or capital), improved quality and utilisation of existing factors or technological advances.

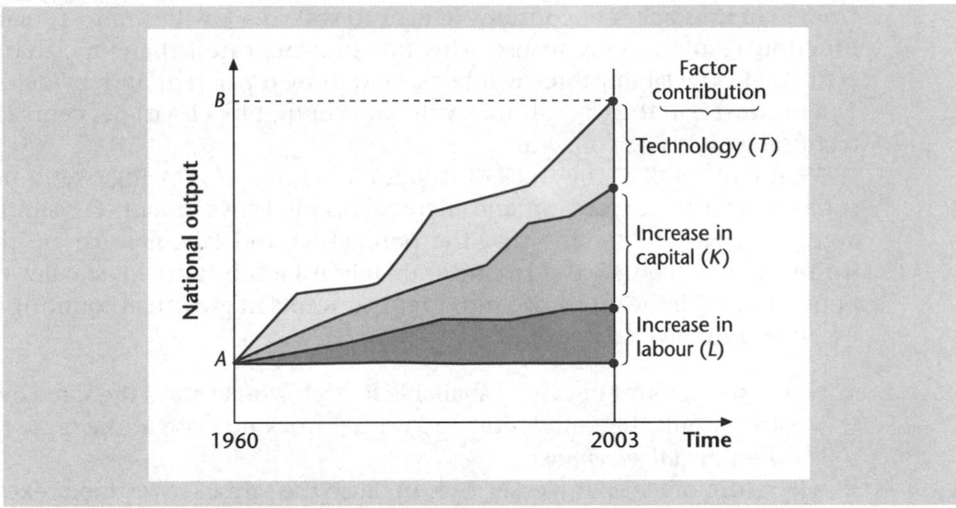

Figure 10.3 Accounting for economic growth

> *Growth accounting* seeks to *quantify* the contribution to an economy's growth in output from the factor inputs based on statistical techniques.

Consider Figure 10.3 which shows, for a hypothetical economy, growth in national output from A in 1960 to B in 2003. Growth accounting is concerned with the decomposition of this increase in output due to an increase in labour (L), an increase in capital (K) and technology (T) for a given land area.

An economy's production function

The relationship between national output and the factor inputs is expressed by economists in a mathematical form and is referred to as the *production function*. In general we can express the production function as:

$$Y = f(L, K, T)$$

A commonly used production function is the *Cobb-Douglas function,* although other forms of production function exist. The Cobb-Douglas production function shows output (Y) as dependent upon the factor inputs of labour (L) and capital (K) for a constant (fixed) state of technology:

> **Cobb-Douglas production function**
>
> $$Y = AL^{\alpha}K^{\beta}$$
>
> where α, β are parameters and A is a constant

Under circumstances of constant returns to scale $\alpha + \beta$ will sum to 1, making the function relatively easy to use. This function indicates, therefore, that a 1 per cent rise in the labour force will boost output by α per cent and, by definition, a 1 per cent rise in the capital stock will boost output by $(1 - \alpha)$ per cent, assuming technology remains constant.

We might think of the stock of labour and capital as growing over time due to some population expansion and increased capital investment. For simplicity of argument, we will assume that the population and labour force are the same (in practice, of course, the labour force might be substantially smaller than the population). This leads to two important concepts in growth accounting – *capital widening* and *capital deepening*:

- where the amount of capital available to each worker stays the same over time, in other words the population and capital stock increase at the same rate, this is called *capital widening*.
- where the capital per worker rises because the rate of investment exceeds the growth in population, this is referred to as *capital deepening* because each worker now has more capital available.

Economies starting with low levels of capital stock will need relatively low levels of investment to provide new workers with the same level of capital as existing workers, compared to economies with high levels of capital stock per worker. The remainder of the investment, therefore, leads to capital deepening or raising the average amount of capital per worker and therefore labour productivity. This means that lower-income economies with low capital stocks should grow faster than richer economies with the same rate of investment, provided that their population growth is restrained. This leads to the notion of the *convergence hypothesis* – in which growth rates between lower income and higher income economies eventually converge. However, to date the empirical evidence to support the convergence hypothesis has not been strong.

Technical progress and innovation

At any given time, an economy consists not only of a stock of factor inputs but a given state of technical knowledge. This knowledge is in the form of scientific knowledge that is written down and perhaps expressed in patents, alongside knowledge that comes from experience and may be deeply embedded in the skills and experience of the labour force. This latter form of knowledge is known as *tacit knowledge*. Because of its nature, tacit knowledge is hard to codify, but along with the existing level of *scientific knowledge* it contributes towards an economy's ability to produce more efficiently over time. An example should clarify the difference between tacit knowledge and scientific knowledge. A patent that sets out a particular process for producing a new pharmaceutical product is scientific knowledge. The experience of working in a pharmaceuticals firm over the years, which allows an 'experienced' employee to perform more productively than a new recruit, reflects tacit knowledge. It might be very difficult for this employee to write down accurately why he or she is more productive.

Technical advances leading to improved scientific knowledge occur through *inventions* or the discovery of new knowledge. However, in themselves inventions do not add to output and therefore economic growth. Inventions must be incorporated into actual production or improved production methods if output is to benefit. This incorporation of technical knowledge to increase production is termed *innovation*. It is technical innovation that stimulates economic growth. For example, during the 1960s and 1970s Japanese industry was very successful at innovating by taking products and processes invented elsewhere in the world. The same has been happening in China since the 1990s, providing a major drive to China's economic growth prospects.

Innovation can take two broad forms, both of which benefit economic growth:

- *new products and services* (e.g. DVD recorders);
- *new processes of production* (e.g. 'just-in-time' production methods).

The level of research and development expenditure as a share of GDP is sometimes used as a measure of an economy's innovativeness, but it is an imperfect measure. This is because an economy may have a strong record of spending on research and development but with poor results. Alternatively, the expenditure may lead to many new inventions but industry may fail to capitalise on them by innovating and the advantages are lost to other economies. The UK economy is often criticised for its failure to innovate, while having an impressive history of invention, for example in computers, DNA research and the creation of the hovercraft.

Total factor productivity

Technical progress is one important cause of economic growth when reflected in high levels of productive innovation. However, economies can also grow by improving their management of existing factor inputs with a *given* technology. The resulting increase in output is in effect a residual product, unexplained by changes in the volume of factor inputs. This residual is called *total factor productivity*.

For example, recall the generalised Cobb-Douglas function described above with output (Y) dependent on the quantity of labour (L), the quantity of capital (K) and technology (T):

$$Y = f(L, K, T)$$

Assuming that the state of technology is fixed in the short run (a reasonable assumption), a doubling of inputs of K and L might be expected to lead to a doubling of output (Y) under conditions of constant returns to scale. If, however, output more than doubled under the same conditions clearly there is some increase in Y that is unexplained by L, K and T or returns to scale, i.e. there is a residual. This residual is the growth in total factor productivity.

We can therefore think of economic growth as resulting from changes in the quantity and quality of factor inputs, changes in technology and changes in the management of resources. This is reflected in the main 'growth models' in economics, to which we now turn.

Models of economic growth

What causes economic growth? Why do growth rates vary between countries? Many theories have been developed over many years in an attempt to provide answers to these fundamental questions. In this section we look at three particular theoretical models. These are:

- classical growth theory;
- neoclassical growth theory;
- endogenous growth theory.

At the outset, it is important to appreciate that no theory has as yet been developed that provides all the answers to all possible questions concerning economic growth. Understanding the causes of growth and why different countries grow at different rates still poses considerable intellectual challenges for economists (and policy makers).

Classical growth theory

This theory stems from the writings of the classical economists in the late eighteenth and early nineteenth centuries and is most closely linked to the views of Thomas Malthus. The essence of the theory is that growth in a nation's output resulting from advances in technology is only temporary. It is argued that an increase in the real GDP per worker raises the subsistence level of wages per worker. This, in turn, will result in a population explosion and an increase in the available supply of labour. A greater supply of labour will depress the real wage, returning income per worker (and real GDP per worker) back to the subsistence level. The outcome is a fall in the rate of economic growth and an inevitable fall in the population itself at this subsistence level of income.

> *Classical growth theory* concludes that economic growth is only a temporary phenomenon and is dependent on population growth.

It is little wonder that this rather depressing view of economic growth and economic development led to economics being labelled as the *dismal science*!

Figure 10.4 illustrates the key points of classical growth theory. Starting at point *a*, capital per worker of $(K/L)_1$ results in an output per worker of $(Y/L)_1$, given by the production function A.

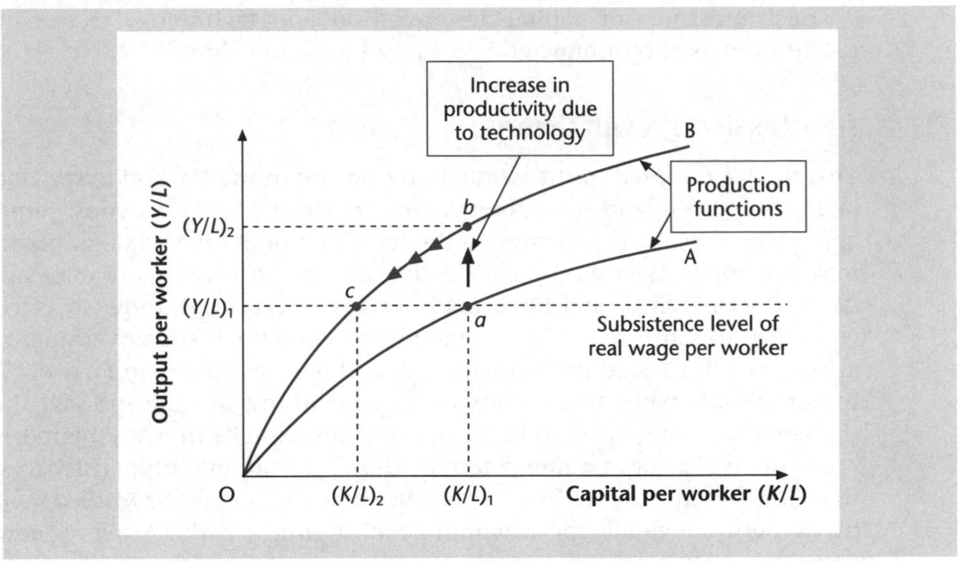

Figure 10.4 **Classical growth theory**

As outlined above, a technological advance increases labour productivity and the economy moves to point *b* on the new production function, B. Here, output per worker is now $(Y/L)_2$. This, according to the classical theory, increases the average real wage per worker to well above the subsistence level, resulting in a population explosion, i.e. economic prosperity leads to more births and longer life expectancy. But as the population grows, both capital per worker and output per worker fall and the economy tracks from *b* to *c* in Figure 10.4. The outcome is a fall in real wages per worker back to the subsistence level – and the population falls as a consequence, in line with falling living standards.

The essential message of the classical theory is that, if the capital stock (K) remains fixed, then as the population and the labour force expand, we can expect *diminishing returns to labour*, and so output per worker will inevitably fall. Today, some people are worried that the world is heading towards a Malthusian-type crisis. There are fears that population growth (particularly in developing countries) will outstrip resources. However, two vital factors are missing from the theory, which lead us to dismiss the 'gloom and doom' scenario. These are concerned with the impact on economic growth stemming from:

- technological change;
- capital accumulation.

The classical economists failed to appreciate that new and better farming techniques would increase productivity in the agricultural sector, to the extent that today the world has a plentiful supply of food – despite population growth to well over 6 billion.

The importance of capital accumulation and technology is recognised by recent models of economic growth – as we explain below.

Neoclassical growth theory

This theory is rooted in the work of Roy Harrod in the UK and Evsey Domar and later the Nobel laureate Robert Solow in the USA. At its most simple, this approach develops the Keynesian theory of national income determination and makes it more dynamic by considering *changes* in certain variables over time. Assuming only firms and households, or a two-sector economy (so as to remove complications introduced by international capital flows and government budgetary policy), firms produce and sell goods and services, invest and pay out incomes to households, while households spend some of this income and save the rest. If the level of saving is equal to the level of investment in every period then the economy will grow at a rate determined by the marginal propensity to save and the capital–output ratio. In a two-sector economy, *ex post* or *realised* savings and investment are equal (for a definition of *ex post* or *realised* savings and investment, see p.70).

Let us assume, for simplicity, that the labour force (L) is growing at a constant rate (say l) and is not influenced by the rate of economic growth (i.e. population growth is independent of the rate of economic growth, in contrast to classical growth theory). Also, assume there is no technical progress and there is a constant marginal propensity to save (e.g. 10 per cent) out of income in the economy. With zero technical progress and a constant growth in the population (which again we equate with the growth in the economy's labour force), only the growth rate of capital can affect output (Y). But capital growth depends upon savings and, through the marginal propensity to save, income – while income (output) depends in turn on the amount of capital. The system is therefore interdependent.

The productivity curve, given by $y = \mathrm{f}(k)$, is shown in Figure 10.5 and illustrates that the higher is the amount of capital available to each worker (k), the higher is the output per worker (y). As we move along the curve from left to right, its slope decreases reflecting diminishing returns to capital inputs. When *capital deepening* occurs (a rising amount of capital per worker) we expect output to rise, but more and more investment per worker is likely to lead to diminishing returns to capital applied and therefore a rise in the capital–output ratio. This is the same as saying that an increasing amount of capital per worker leads to increasing output per worker but at a diminishing rate.

Saving (s) is a constant fraction of income (output), Y, and let us assume that the rate of depreciation of the capital stock – denoted d – is also constant. Out of any new investment some of the additional capital must go to replace capital that is wearing out or becomes obsolescent (called *capital depreciation*). The net addition to the capital stock is therefore equal to saving (which is equal to investment) minus depreciation. Hence, in a *steady state*, total saving (i.e. sY) must be just sufficient to provide for enough investment to meet depreciation (dK, the

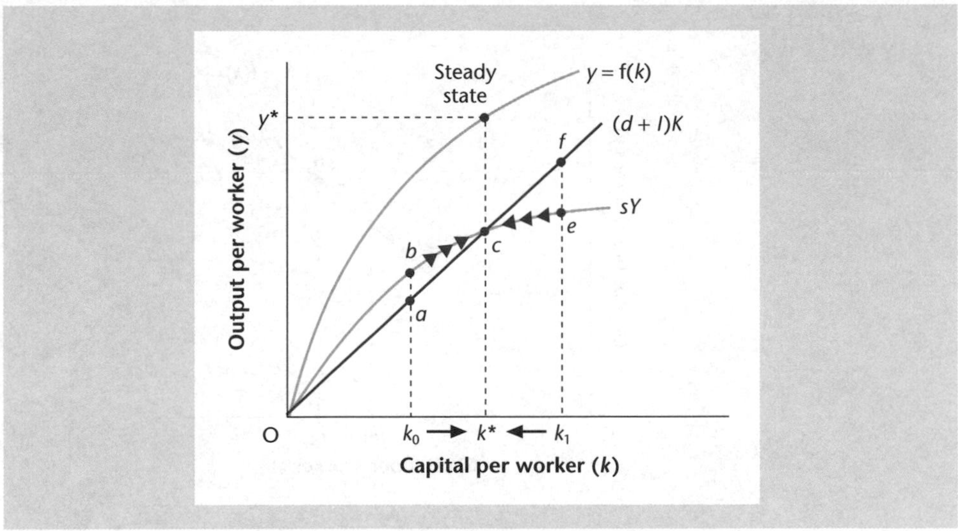

Figure 10.5 Neoclassical growth model and steady state growth

rate of depreciation (*d*) times the capital stock (*K*)) and provide an increasing labour force (growing at a constant rate *l*) with new capital (equal to *lK*) in order to retain a constant amount of capital per worker. Thus:

Steady state

$$sY = (d + l)K$$

This is shown on Figure 10.5 by the straight line $(d + l)K$. This line shows the amount of investment needed to maintain a constant amount of capital per worker or what we may alternatively call the *capital–labour ratio*. The figure also shows the savings function (sY) for each capital–labour ratio. At a low capital–labour ratio (k_0), savings could be greater than the investment needed to maintain a constant ratio and therefore output per worker would grow. By contrast, at a high capital–labour ratio (k_1) savings might be lower than the amount of investment required to maintain the capital–labour ratio and hence the ratio would fall along with the growth in output per worker.

In other words:

- when $sY > (d + l)K$, the capital–labour ratio must *rise*;
- when $sY < (d + l)K$, the capital–labour ratio must *fall*.

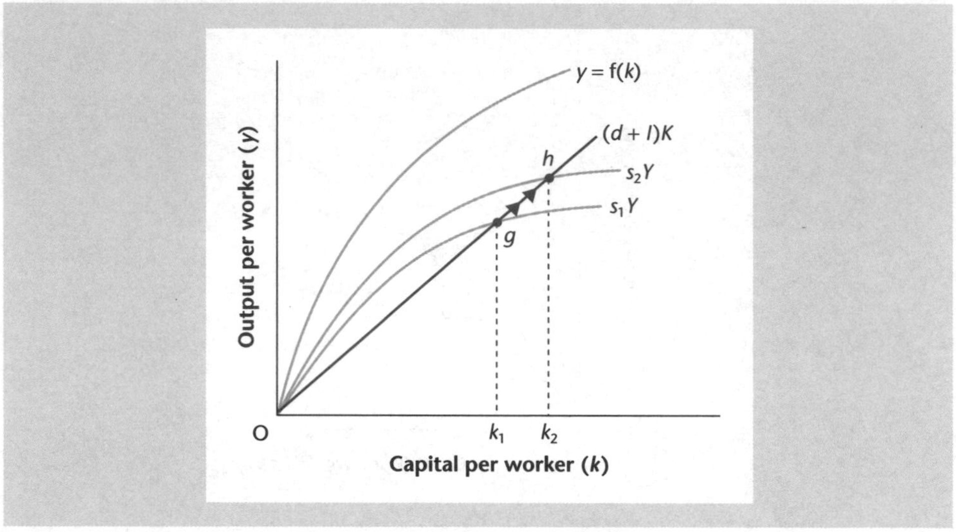

Figure 10.6 **Neoclassical growth model and the savings rate**

These situations are illustrated in Figure 10.5. The level of investment needed to keep the capital–labour ratio constant at k_0 is shown by point *a*, while saving is at the higher level shown by the *sY* function, i.e. at level *b*. Capital accumulation will therefore increase until the capital–labour ratio reaches level *c*. Now the actual and required investment are equal and the capital–labour ratio no longer rises. By contrast, if savings occurred, as shown by the savings function, *sY*, at point *e* in Figure 10.5, with the level of investment needed to keep the capital–labour ratio constant at k_1 given by point *f*, investment would decline until the capital–labour ratio reached again level *c*. It follows that the *steady state* capital–labour ratio is at k^*. Neither a capital–labour ratio of k_0 or k_1 in the figure would be an equilibrium. With the steady state capital–labour ratio k^*, output rises at the same rate as the population, leaving output per worker constant, i.e. output per worker is also in steady state at y^*.

Should the rate of savings rise then the rate of economic growth would rise only in the short run. The long-run level of the capital–output ratio and output per capita would increase but the long-run growth rate of output would not. This is illustrated in Figure 10.6 with the savings rate increase shown by a movement upwards in the savings function, from s_1Y to s_2Y. Savings have now risen in relation to investment needs to maintain a constant capital–labour ratio. The level of investment needed to keep the capital–labour ratio constant at k_1 is shown by point *g* but savings are now at a higher level. As a consequence, the capital stock per worker will rise until point *h* is reached – at k_2. Now the higher amount of saving is just sufficient to maintain the higher stock of capital. Note that at point *h* there is a higher capital–labour ratio and a higher output per worker than before the rate of savings increased, *but the economy has returned to its steady state growth path*. The increase in the growth rate of output has been transitory, i.e. there has only been a *one-off* increase in output per worker which has resulted in a short-term increase in the rate of economic growth. At *h*, the capital–labour ratio is again constant. With the labour force growing at the constant rate *l*, constancy of the capital–labour ratio implies that the capital stock and national output *must* be growing at the same constant rate *l*.

Hence, despite the increase in the marginal propensity to save (from s_1 to s_2) the long-run rate of growth of output (income) and the capital stock remains what it was before the rise in the savings rate.

This leads to an important conclusion.

> In the *neoclassical growth model*, the growth rate of the economy (i.e. economic growth) and the capital stock are *independent* of the savings rate over the *long-run*.

This analysis can be extended to look at the effects of a decline in the rate of savings, more depreciation, less investment and changes in population growth. For example, an increase in the rate of population growth will reduce the level of capital per worker and output per worker. Therefore, the faster the growth in the population, the theory suggests the need for higher investment and therefore capital accumulation if economic growth is not to suffer. Equally, the theory suggests that if two economies had the same growth in population, the same savings rate and the same production function, they would both eventually arrive at an identical income level. Neoclassical growth theory is consistent with the notion of growth *convergence*. In cases where the two countries had different savings rates but identical population growth, everything else being equal, they would arrive at different levels of income but their steady state growth rates would be the same.

This discussion of neoclassical growth theory has not considered technological progress. Suppose now that technological progress occurs over time, a not unreasonably assumption. Suppose that it occurs at rate *t* and is in the form of *labour-augmenting technical progress*; that is to say, it raises labour productivity. Now the expansion of the labour force is effectively not *l* but $l + t$ and therefore in the above discussion lK becomes $(l + t)K$. Since the labour force is now rising effectively by $l + t$, so must capital and output grow to maintain capital per worker and output per worker.

Endogenous growth model

An alternative model to neoclassical theory is associated with Paul Romer of Stanford University. In the neoclassical model economies with the same population growth and same technological progress will converge to the same steady state growth path. However, it is clear that differences in growth rates *do* persist across economies over many years.

Endogenous growth theory, as the name suggests, attempts to make the growth rate endogenous or determined within the theory. One way would be to make the rate of technical progress endogenous. For example, higher research and development expenditure might lead to higher economic growth and higher economic growth could lead to more research and development spending.

Another approach is to assume there are constant rather than diminishing returns to capital accumulation at the economy level. In the neoclassical model, diminishing returns are assumed, as reflected in the slope of the function $y = f(k)$ in Figures 10.5 and 10.6. Romer argues that investment may have externalities or spillovers. Whereas the continuous application of more capital in a given firm could be expected to lead to diminishing returns (if this did not occur the firm would continuously expand until it accounted for the economy's entire production), this might not be true at the level of the entire economy. Investment by firm A might lead to higher output in not just firm A but in other firms B, C, etc. because these other firms gain from firm A's investment, i.e. investment has beneficial externalities. This investment might be in physical capital but it could also be in human capital (a more productive labour force for a given physical capital stock). In these circumstances, all firms in the economy might expand together and have constant, not diminishing, returns to the total capital stock.

We can show this effect more formally as follows. Suppose that output per worker (y) is proportional to capital per worker (k) and assume there is no technical progress. In this case the production function is simply:

$$y = ak$$

where a is a constant

This states that output per worker is directly proportional to capital per worker or the capital–labour ratio. To simplify the explanation also assume a constant savings rate out of income (sY), constant population growth (l) and no depreciation of the capital stock. The latter assumption means that all savings increase the capital stock (K). Thus:

$$\Delta K = sY = s(aK)$$

or

$$\Delta K/K = sa$$

where a is a constant

Now the savings rate affects the growth rate of capital ($\Delta K/K$) and as output (Y) is proportional to capital, it follows that the growth rate of output is equivalent to:

$$\Delta Y/Y = sa$$

Hence, in endogenous growth theory the higher the savings rate out of income, the faster the economic growth rate. In other words, the steady state growth path is now affected by the rate at which capital accumulation occurs.

> The *endogenous growth* model suggests that if policy could raise the savings rate there would be a permanent increase in the economic growth rate.

Moreover, any policy that caused a one-off rise in the parameter a in the function $y = ak$ – for example, improved production processes – the result would be a permanent increase in the economic growth rate, everything else being equal. In endogenous growth theory growth rates between countries may diverge rather than converge.

Figure 10.7 illustrates the principles of endogenous growth theory. In this case, capital does not experience diminishing returns, the production function shifts upwards (from y_1 to y_2, etc.) and output per worker and capital per worker grow along the ak line – without limit.

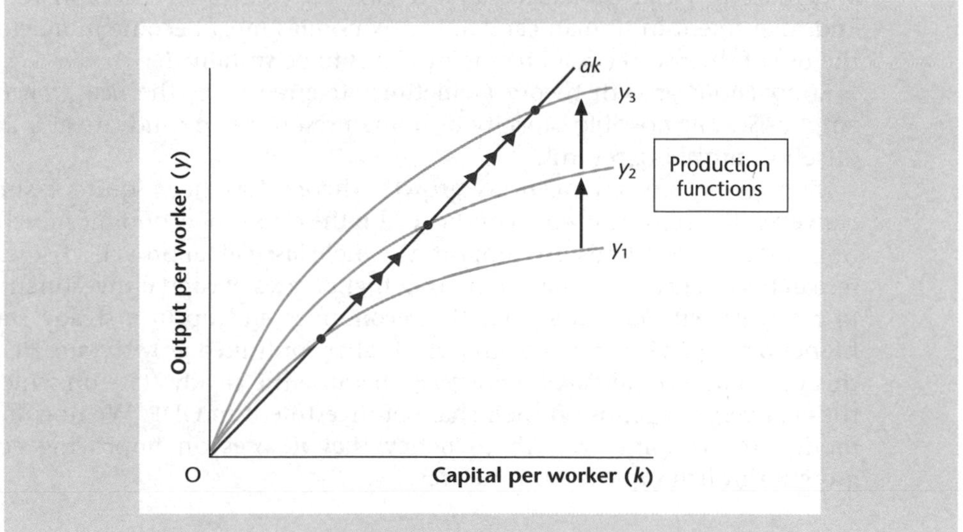

Figure 10.7 Endogenous growth theory

Endogenous growth theory has altered the way economists look at economic growth. To begin with the theory suggests a more obvious role for government policy to stimulate the economic growth rate. As firms may neglect the externalities from their investments, government intervention (e.g. investment subsidies or more investment in education and training), might work to raise economic performance. Equally, so might the share of government spending in GDP affect economic growth, either favourably or unfavourably.

However, the endogenous growth model is erected on the construct of constant returns to capital accumulation. Critics of the theory argue that constant returns are unlikely over the long term and even if they did exist, the history of government economic intervention to promote growth is one of wasted resources and mistimed interventions.

Growth theories compared

Which is the more appropriate theory for understanding economic growth in modern economies – the classical growth theory, the neoclassical theory or endogenous growth theory?

It is clear that no single theory can provide all the answers concerning the determination of long-term economic growth.

The classical theory views population growth as a function of economic growth such that economic growth can be expected to fluctuate as real GDP per worker increases and decreases in line with population growth. It fails to recognise that population can be *independent* of economic growth. It also fails to incorporate the effects of capital accumulation and technological progress.

The neoclassical theory emphasises the diminishing returns to capital investment so that an economy cannot simply maintain growth by accumulating more and more physical capital. Economic growth requires advances in technology and investment in human capital, i.e. economies must become more creative in the use of their scarce resources if growth is to be sustained.

Endogenous growth theory (sometimes referred to as the *new growth theory*) emphasises the possible capacity of human resources to innovate at a pace that offsets diminishing returns.

In recent years endogenous growth theory has been quite fashionable. However, the empirical work conducted on the causes of economic growth, while not unanimous, tends to support the neoclassical approach. For example, research by Robert Barro has found that higher rates of capital investment do lead to faster growth *for a time*, but that economies end up in a steady state with higher per capita income though not a higher continued growth rate. He refers to this outcome as *conditional convergence*, because the steady state on which countries converge depends on their share of investment in GDP. We now turn from models of economic growth to policy that focuses on improving economic growth through supply-side measures.

Application 10.1

The importance of high productivity

High productivity is the key to fast economic growth. Productivity can be measured in various ways, but the two most common measures are:

- labour productivity or output per worker or man hour;
- total factor productivity or output in relation to all factor inputs (total factor productivity is the *residual* growth in output not explained by labour, capital and other factor inputs).

Closing the productivity gap helps to deliver greater economic prosperity and rising living standards. In today's global economy, high productivity is important in determining international competitiveness.

The figure below shows output per worker in four major economies. It is clear that the USA leads in terms of labour productivity. The USA is often said to have the most 'flexible' labour force and that this is a significant cause of its higher productivity.

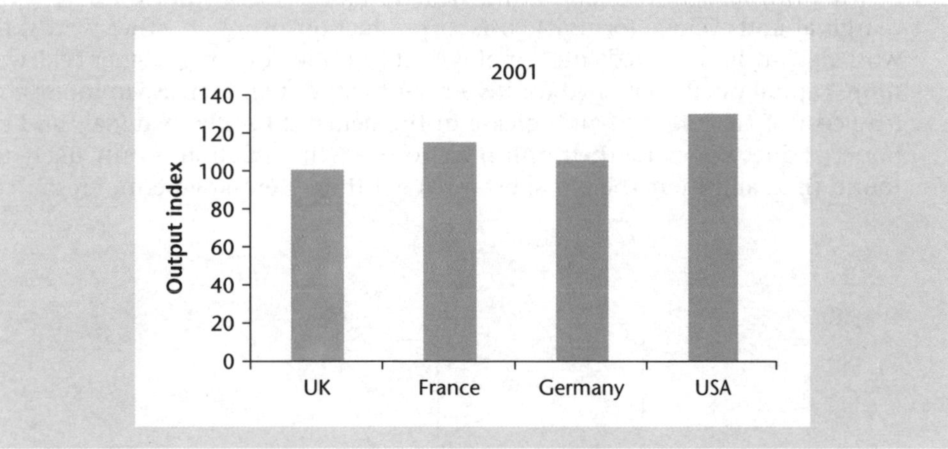

Source: Office for National Statistics

Activity

How does high productivity contribute to economic growth? What supply-side measures might be used to raise productivity in the UK, France and Germany to the level of the USA?

The principles of supply-side economics

In essence, *supply-side economics* is concerned with increasing aggregate supply so that more expenditure in the economy can be accommodated without inflation.

An economy's aggregate supply consists of the various amounts of total real output that producers are able and willing to produce at various price levels. Therefore, an economy's aggregate supply curve reflects the relationship between the volume of production in the economy at different prices. As we saw in Chapter 5, in principle the aggregate supply curve can be horizontal, upward sloping or vertical, depending upon the precise relationship between rising prices and output (since producers are most unlikely to supply more at lower prices, the supply curve will presumably not be negatively sloped). These possible shapes are illustrated in Figure 10.8.

Which of these aggregate supply curves is most likely to occur at any given time will reflect current economic conditions. A horizontal aggregate supply curve, such as AS_1 in Figure 10.8, suggests that supply will increase without a rise in the price level in the economy – which implies that output can rise without marginal and average (or unit) costs of production rising. In other words, more workers can be attracted into employment without offering higher real wages, more capital can be obtained for investment without an increase in interest rates (the cost of capital), and an increase in the demand for raw materials and components does not cause their unit price to rise. This situation is only likely to be found (if at all) where there is substantial existing unemployment of resources.

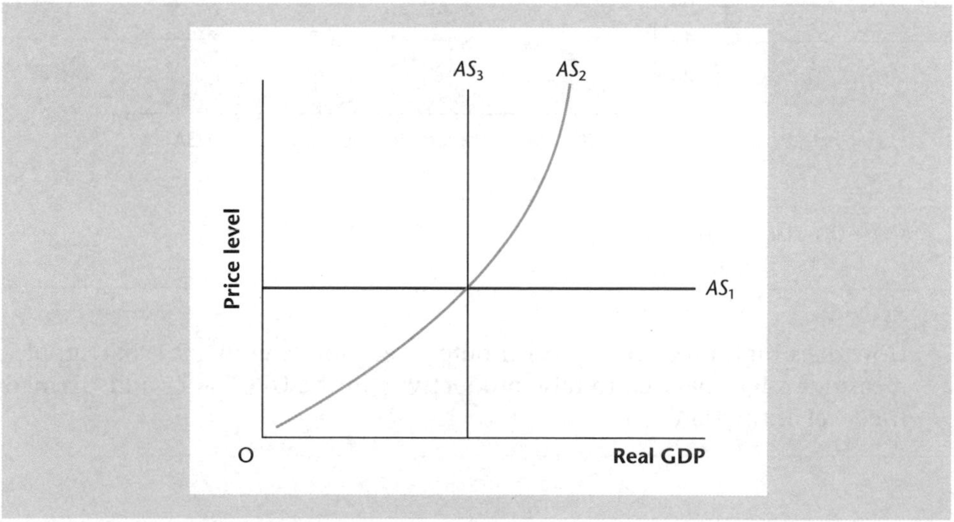

Figure 10.8 Aggregate supply curves

In contrast, an upward sloping aggregate supply curve, such as AS_2 in Figure 10.8, implies that higher units of output are associated with a higher price level. Higher prices are necessary to induce firms to produce more. Increased output means more demand for factors of production, especially labour and capital, which may raise their unit prices and therefore firms' unit production costs. As the economy gets closer to Keynesian full employment (or from a monetarist perspective, the 'natural rate of unemployment', see pp.245–246 and 294–296) so prices are driven higher for each proportionate increase in output, i.e. the slope of the *AS* curve increases.

Lastly, a vertical aggregate supply curve, such as AS_3 in Figure 10.8, means that output (in real or volume terms) cannot rise. Keynesians associate the vertical aggregate supply curve only with a fully employed economy, but some monetarists argue that, since workers appreciate the meaning of purchasing power, a mere increase in *money* wages does not lead to more employment and therefore output will not rise. For example, if workers are offered $10 per week more to attract them into employment or to work overtime, but this is completely offset by rising prices, then no more labour will be supplied since *real* wages or the real purchasing power of wages will not have changed. Similarly, insofar as firms increase output in response to the lure of higher real profits, a doubling of profits alongside a doubling of prices will have no effect on their decision to supply (this behaviour is in keeping with the extension of monetarist principles referred to as *rational expectations theory*, see pp.277–278). Consequently, a vertical aggregate supply curve indicates that output is unaffected by (i.e. is independent of) the price level. At best, there may be only a temporary rise in output when prices rise, until such time as workers and firms realise that the increases in wages and profits do not amount to real increases. In other words, output rises only until expectations about further inflation adapt to the actual price rise. It is for this reason that monetarists are more sceptical than Keynesians about the scope for fiscal measures to increase aggregate demand and therefore employment permanently.

The precise nature of the aggregate supply curve is important in appraising the value of Keynesian demand management techniques, for the following reason. If the aggregate supply curve is horizontal, an increase in aggregate demand resulting from an injection of government spending or a reduction in taxation will lead to more output and therefore more employment, without the emergence of inflation. This is shown by the shift in aggregate demand from AD_1 to AD_2 in Figure 10.9 with the price level remaining at P_1 but output rising from Y_1 to Y_2.

Even when the aggregate supply curve is upward sloping, although more demand produces some rise in prices (i.e. inflation), the volume of output and hence employment will still increase. In Figure 10.10 this is shown by the increase in aggregate demand from AD_1 to AD_2 with prices rising from P_1 to P_2 and output from Y_1 to Y_2. Which rises the most – output or prices – depends on the *elasticity* of the aggregate supply curve, i.e. the responsiveness of aggregate supply to price changes.

Both of these possibilities, therefore, imply that Keynesian demand management techniques can boost production and employment. Where, however, the aggregate supply curve is vertical, more aggregate demand merely spills over into

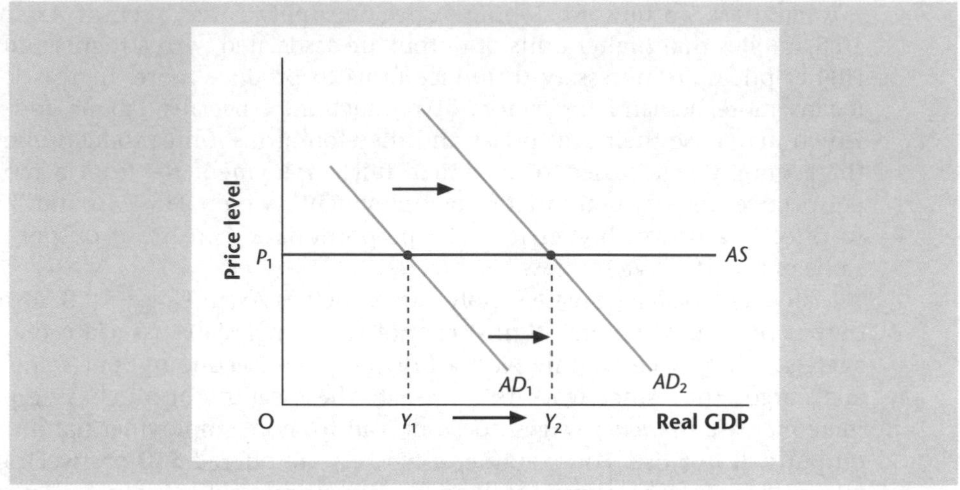

Figure 10.9 Increased aggregate demand and a horizontal aggregate supply curve

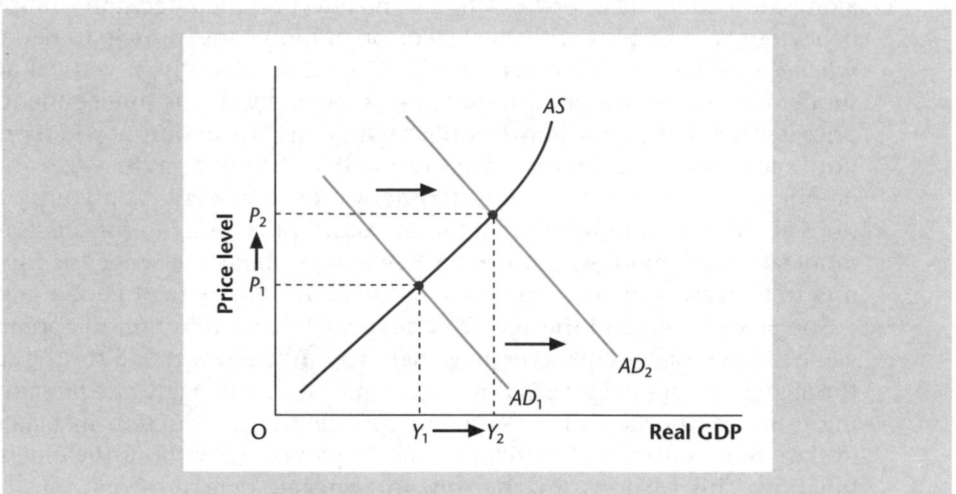

Figure 10.10 Increased aggregate demand and an upward sloping aggregate supply curve

inflation with no beneficial effects on production and employment because supply is fixed. This is shown in Figure 10.11 with a rise in aggregate demand from AD_1 to AD_2, leading to a corresponding rise in prices from P_1 to P_2 with output remaining stationary at Y. Therefore, in this situation increasing aggregate demand is simply inflationary and does not stimulate real output and employment.

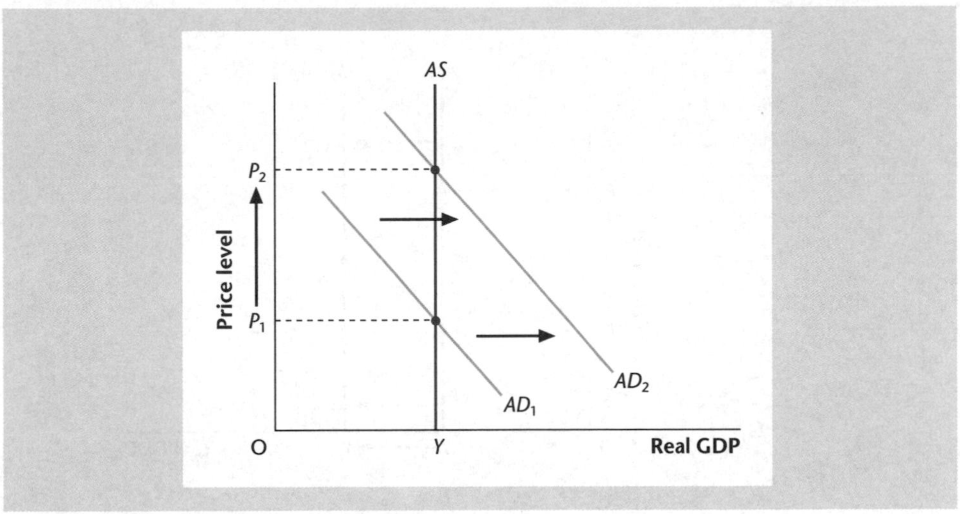

Figure 10.11 Increased aggregate demand and a vertical aggregate supply curve

Shifting the aggregate supply curve

According to supply-side economists, who tend to believe that Keynesian measures can, at best, only have short-term benefits, the solution to unemployment lies in measures that will shift the aggregate supply curve to the right (e.g. from AS_1 to AS_2 in Figure 10.12). This is equivalent to shifting the production possibility curve in Figure 10.1 outwards so that more goods and services are now produced. This can be achieved by either (or both) of the following:

- increasing the availability or quantity of economic resources used in production, i.e. more labour, capital or natural resources;
- changes in technology and other methods of increasing the productive efficiency with which the available economic resources are used in the economy, i.e. increasing productivity.

Since the availability of economic resources changes slowly over time (e.g. the population normally rises slowly) and few changes in technology produce immediate and dramatic effects on output, it follows that shifting the aggregate supply curve to the right is a gradual process. Supply-side economists argue, however, that governments can take measures to encourage the more efficient use of the existing resources and to encourage investment and technological change, leading to faster economic growth over the longer term. Technical progress raises economic growth in both the neoclassical and endogenous growth theories, while endogenous growth theory identifies scope for increasing the economic growth rate by promoting a higher rate of saving and therefore investment.

In Figure 10.12 the aggregate supply curve is assumed vertical, although the existence of an upward sloping curve would not substantially alter the following argument. The effect of supply-side policies is to shift the curve from AS_1 to AS_2.

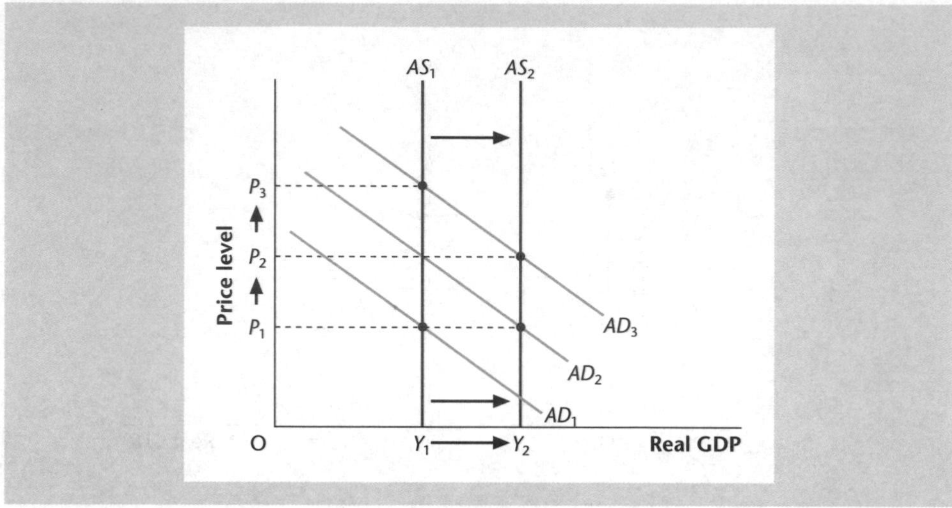

Figure 10.12 Shifting the aggregate supply curve

If aggregate demand remains unchanged (AD_1), the result would be a rise in real output (from Y_1 to Y_2) alongside a fall in the price level (to below P_1). In practice, however, the purpose of shifting the aggregate supply curve is to raise income and permit aggregate demand to rise without inflation. This is illustrated by the rise in aggregate demand from AD_1 to AD_2. Note that real output has risen from Y_1 to Y_2 but that prices have stayed constant at P_1. If aggregate demand was permitted to rise faster than aggregate supply, to AD_3, then prices would rise to P_2, but by less than if aggregate supply had remained fixed at AS_1 (the rise would have been from P_1 to P_3).

Increasing aggregate supply, therefore, permits a higher level of demand in the economy, leading to more employment while suppressing inflation. This helps to explain why the study of supply-side economics has become so popular. Supply-side policies, especially when combined with a 'sound' monetary policy, appear to offer a means of tackling both high inflation and low economic growth (and, consequently, rising unemployment), i.e. the problem of 'stagflation'.

Having studied the theory which lies behind supply-side economics, we now consider specific supply-side measures adopted by governments in many parts of the world in recent years. These measures are promoted by international agencies such as the IMF, World Bank, World Trade Organisation (WTO), OECD and, to a degree, the European Commission.

Supply-side economics in practice

After its election in 1979 the Conservative government in the UK largely shunned the aggregate demand management policies of previous governments in favour of supply-side policies, which encouraged private enterprise. This development amounted to a profound shift in macroeconomic policy and was mirrored by similar policy changes in other countries during the 1980s including the USA, initially under President Reagan.

Governments introduced a large number of supply-side measures aimed at improving productivity in their economies and encouraging private investment. They can be grouped into three broad categories.

Supply-side policies

- Improving the flexibility of the labour market.
- Improving economic incentives by reducing taxation.
- Deregulation of markets to promote competition and privatisation of public enterprises and services.

We now deal with each of these policies in detail.

Improving the flexibility of the labour market

Various policy measures to increase the flexibility of the labour market have been and are currently being implemented by governments in different countries. These are associated with:

- reducing the so-called *natural rate of unemployment*;
- eliminating the *poverty trap*;
- trade-union reforms.

The natural rate of unemployment

In a highly competitive labour market, wages will find their free-market level. This level is where the demand for labour by firms equals the supply of people willing to work at a given wage rate. Once all of those wanting to work at the going real wage rates are employed then there is no *involuntary* unemployment (although some people may remain 'voluntarily' unemployed as they hold out for jobs offering higher real wages).

No economic subject is more emotive and controversial than unemployment. Economists argue over what is the optimal unemployment rate that will maximise aggregate demand without spilling over into inflation. Politicians, whose task it is to choose and implement economic policy, worry also about what rate of unemployment is socially and politically acceptable. Particularly controversial is the notion of so-called *natural rate of unemployment* discussed in more detail later (see pp.245–246 and 294–296).

The *natural rate of unemployment* is defined as that rate of unemployment which exists when the demand for labour equals the supply of labour that is willing to work at the wage rates on offer.

These wage rates are the *real* (inflation-adjusted) wage rates and reflect the real cost to business of employing workers (ignoring other employment costs such as social security contributions). Other things being equal, when real wages rise the cost of employing labour increases and so fewer people are employed. Similarly, if real wages fall, industry will demand more labour and so more people are employed. The natural rate of unemployment is that rate of unemployment which an economy can expect to achieve without triggering inflationary pressures in the labour market. The 'natural' rate is also referred to as 'the non-accelerating-inflation rate of unemployment' or NAIRU.

The natural rate of unemployment is associated with a particular level of *voluntary* unemployment at any particular time, reflecting the relative benefits of working and not working (leisure time). It is important to note that those voluntarily unemployed are not necessarily social welfare scroungers or cheats – they have simply made a choice not to work given the current wages on offer and their preference for leisure over work. However, insofar as state welfare benefits make it easier to turn down low-wage jobs, some economists believe that a generous state welfare system raises the level of voluntary unemployment. When welfare benefits rise in real terms, the relative costs and benefits of working or not working change. More people can be expected to reject low-paid jobs: they decide (rationally) that they are 'better off' living instead on state welfare benefits.

Not all economists are happy with the concept of a natural rate of unemployment while others, although accepting the general idea, find difficulty in applying it. What is the market-clearing real wage? Can we estimate it? Does it always follow that the rate of unemployment is responsive to changes in state welfare payments? Even if it is, is cutting welfare benefits a socially or morally acceptable way of reducing unemployment? Are there better ways? These are but a few of the questions that arise in trying to address this issue.

The poverty trap

The extent to which unemployment benefits and other welfare payments create inflexibility in the labour market is controversial. But no doubt overgenerous payments do dull incentives among the unemployed to seek jobs. A high *replacement ratio* (the ratio of income received out of work to income received in work) will have a marked disincentive effect, leading to what has been termed an *unemployment trap* or *poverty trap*, in which it does not pay people to take jobs because of the resulting loss of welfare benefits.

Particular measures introduced by governments to limit the poverty trap include indexing social security benefits to retail prices rather than earnings (earnings grow more quickly than prices reflecting underlying productivity growth in the economy, thus the replacement ratio declines over time), reforms in social security, and making the obtaining of benefits more difficult, especially for school leavers. Other actions include raising the level at which poor families pay income tax on employment earnings. Such policy initiatives may relieve the unemployment trap and thereby promote employment over relying on welfare benefits. Alongside other government initiatives, such as the promotion of training and retraining schemes and housing and regional reforms, to facilitate the geographical movement of labour, the labour market can be made more responsive to demand and supply signals and therefore more 'flexible'. Another approach is to tackle labour market rigidities caused by trade unions.

Trade-union reforms

In the 1980s, some countries (such as the UK) adopted anti-union policies. Convinced that trade unions destroy jobs by raising wages above the levels employers can afford if their firms are to remain competitive in world markets, governments introduced employment and trade union legislation to curb union power, such as requiring compulsory ballots of members before strike action can take place and declaring 'secondary picketing' illegal. Secondary picketing occurs when union members hold demonstrations outside premises other than those in which the strike action is occurring so as to increase the disruption to business. Other state action has involved reducing or removing statutory minimum wages (although not in the UK where a statutory minimum wage was introduced, controversially, in the late 1990s).

A final reform aimed at increasing labour market 'flexibility' worth mentioning is reducing the power of professional bodies. By insisting on unnecessarily high entry qualifications, professional bodies may reduce the movement of workers between jobs in response to market signals.

Improving economic incentives by reducing taxation

In addition to reforming welfare payments and addressing the ability of unions and professional bodies to determine non-market wage rates, governments may attempt to increase flexibility in the labour market by reducing the burden of taxation so as to make working more worthwhile for taxpayers. The policy of reducing taxes may also act as a spur to savings, investment and private enterprise. A main claim of supply-side economists is that high tax rates create major disincentives to work, save, invest and create new businesses. As the UK Chancellor of the Exchequer noted in March 1986:

> Reductions in taxation motivate new business and improve incentives at work. They are the principal engine of the enterprise culture, on which our future prosperity and employment opportunities depend.

The Laffer curve

The idea that there is a significant relationship between tax rates and the willingness to work was popularised by the *Laffer curve*, reputedly conceived on the back of a restaurant table napkin by the American economist Professor Arthur Laffer.

> The basis of the *Laffer curve* is the belief that there is an optimal tax rate which will maximise government revenue.

When the tax rate is zero there is, of course, no tax revenue. Equally, if the tax rate was set at 100 per cent, presumably tax revenue would also be zero because there would be no incentive to work, save or invest at all and, hence, there would be no income to tax. It follows, therefore, that somewhere between these two extreme rates there must be a tax rate which maximises tax revenue. Although the precise shape of the Laffer curve can be expected to vary depending upon the nature of the labour market, it is conventional to draw it with a smooth slope and with one peak, as in Figure 10.13.

As the tax rate is increased from zero to T_1 in Figure 10.13, government tax revenues rise, as shown by the Laffer curve *TT*. Beyond T_1, however, raising tax rates is counterproductive. The disincentive effects of high taxation reduce the tax base (e.g. hours worked, income invested) so that, although the amount out of each dollar taken in tax rises, the number of dollars earned falls more quickly and therefore less tax is recovered. In other words, if the current tax rate is above T_1, it would pay a government aiming to maximise its tax revenues to *reduce* the tax rate. The tax revenues would then rise.

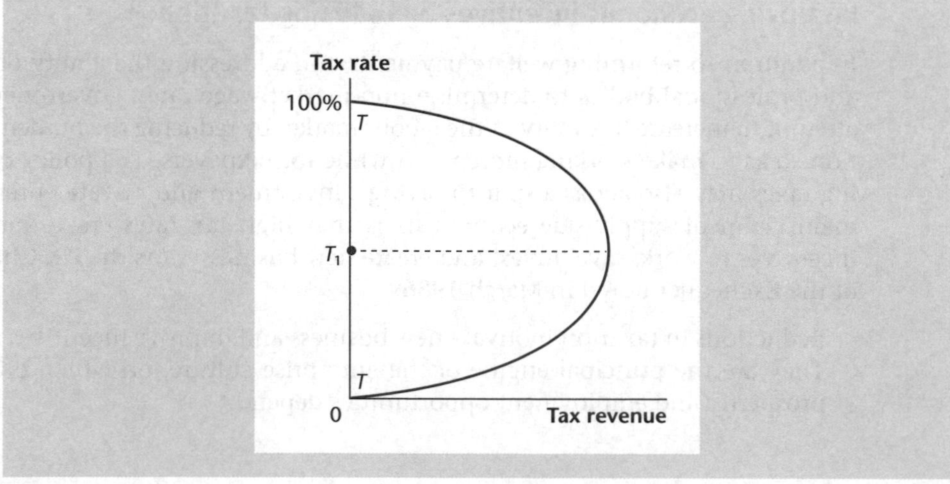

Figure 10.13 The Laffer curve – tax rates and tax revenues

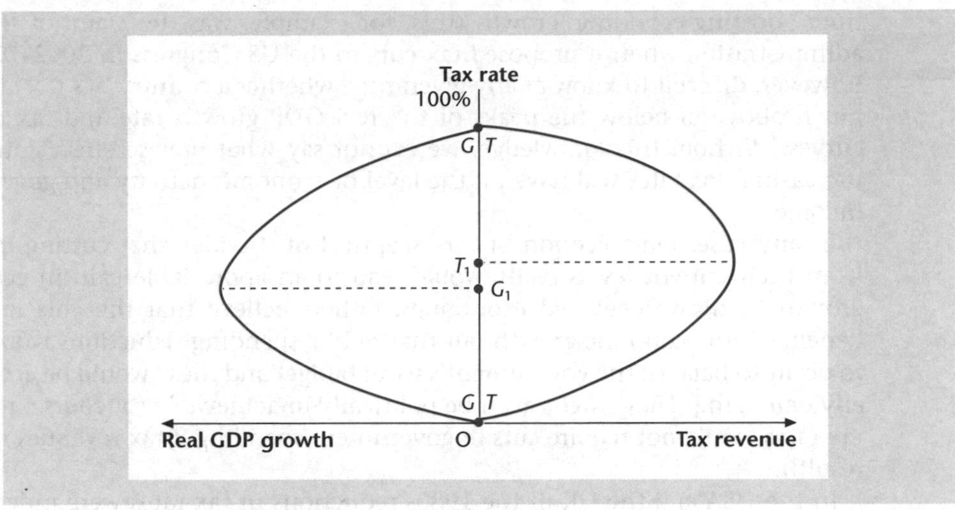

Figure 10.14 Tax rates, tax revenues and economic growth

A so-called *Gutmann effect* is also likely to reinforce the Laffer curve effect, leading to a greater rise in tax revenues as a result of a cut in direct tax rates. This occurs because people may feel that failing to declare taxable income is no longer worth the risk at lower tax rates.

The Laffer curve analysis can be extended to illustrate the possible effect of tax changes on the rate of economic growth. The right-hand side of Figure 10.14 reproduces the Laffer curve from Figure 10.13. On the left-hand side of the diagram, the curve *GG* marks out the rate of growth in real GDP per annum at different tax rates. Once again a single peak is assumed, at G_1. Below G_1 a rise in the tax rate is associated with higher economic growth. The provision of certain public services financed from taxes, for example defence, law and order, roads and perhaps rail links are conducive to private investment. Without them there would be insufficient security to produce and inadequate communications to distribute products at low cost. Above G_1, however, government spending and, more specifically, the related taxation are associated with a lower economic growth rate because of the disincentive effects of high taxes on work, savings and investment.

Note that there appears to be no reason why G_1 and T_1 should be at the *same* tax rate. In other words, the rate of tax that maximises tax revenues to government may not be the same as that which maximises economic growth. In Figure 10.14, G_1 is below T_1, suggesting that the tax rate that maximises the growth in real GDP is less than that which provides the largest government tax revenue. In this case government has a choice to make when setting the tax rate between maximising its own income and maximising the economy's growth rate.

The Laffer curve is an interesting concept and has proved influential in North America and elsewhere since the 1970s. It draws attention to the possibility that reducing tax rates might actually benefit government revenues, while at the same time boosting economic growth (this, for example, was the claim of the Bush administration when it proposed tax cuts to the US Congress in 2002–03). It is, however, difficult to know at any given time whether a country has tax rates that put it above or below the peaks of the real GDP growth rate and tax revenue curves. Without this knowledge, we cannot say what precise effect cutting (or increasing) tax rates will have on the level of economic activity and government income.

In any case, some economists are sceptical of the idea that cutting tax rates from their current levels really would lead to an appreciable gain in economic growth in most developed economies. Others believe that the cuts might be beneficial for economic growth but that public spending reductions would have to occur to balance the government's fiscal budget and these would be economically damaging. They might even be politically unachievable (of course, reducing tax rates would not require cuts in government spending if tax revenues rose as a result!).

In the USA and the UK in the 1980s reductions in tax rates were indeed associated with both a rise in economic growth and more government tax receipts. The causation, however, is not clear. Economists who support tax cuts point to this experience as proof of the Laffer effect. Others, however, suggest that faster economic growth *produced* higher incomes, which in turn generated higher tax receipts, but the tax rate cuts were not responsible for the higher growth rates achieved.

Income and substitution effects

In assessing the likely consequences of tax changes, economists distinguish between what are called *income* and *substitution effects*. In terms of income tax, the income effect depends upon the *average rate of tax* (*art*), which is equal to the tax paid (T) divided by the *tax base*, i.e. in this case income (Y). Thus:

$$art = T/Y$$

The substitution effect, by contrast, is associated with the *marginal rate of tax* (*mrt*) which is equal to the change in tax paid (ΔT) divided by the change in income (ΔY). That is:

$$mrt = \Delta T/\Delta Y$$

When deciding to increase hours of work or work effort, individuals are concerned with small or marginal changes in working time. Therefore, it is the *mrt* rather than the *art* that matters because this specifies what percentage of the *extra* income earned goes in tax. This also applies to a reduction in employment, where the *mrt* determines the net of tax income forgone by not working. This means, for example, that a cut in the income tax rate creates a greater incentive to work additional hours by increasing the marginal benefit of work (in terms of after-tax income), compared with the option of more leisure time or unemployment. That is to say, the 'take home pay' from additional work effort rises. At the same time, however, a cut in the income tax rate could provide an offsetting disincentive to work because the amount of work needed to produce a given after-tax income is reduced. If people work to earn a target income (e.g. to cover housing costs, food costs, motoring expenses, etc.) and discover that, after the tax rate reduction, they can achieve this desired income with less work than previously, they may decide to work *fewer* hours and take more leisure. Therefore we can conclude:

A reduction in the tax rate will result in a net incentive to increase work only if the *substitution effect* of a tax rate dominates the *income effect*.

Thus, a tax cut will create a net incentive for work over leisure only if a worker's incentive to work additional hours or with more effort as a result of the tax cut (which will be reflected in the *mrt*) outweighs the fact that the target income can now be achieved working fewer hours or with less effort (reflected in the *art*).

Given the existence of substitution and income effects of tax rate changes, it can be difficult to deduce in advance what overall effect a tax change will have on the incentive to work and, by similar logic, incentives to invest, save and establish new businesses. Therefore, as in the case of the Laffer curve, we are able to conceptualise the effect of tax changes, but this does not take us much further forward in deciding on the precise results in any specific case. Instead, the effects of a specific tax change need to be empirically assessed. In other words, the experiences of tax changes need to be observed and their effects tested.

Research has looked at the effects of tax cuts (and tax increases) across a range of economies. In general, the results are mixed, varying from case to case depending on the level and scope of the tax change and the income groups most affected. Often, higher income earners, with a higher *mrt*, are associated with the larger incentive effects of tax cuts, as we would expect. However, neither theory nor the empirical evidence based upon studies of the effect of taxation on work, investment and savings provides strong grounds for believing that modest tax changes will lead to an appreciable change in economic growth.

At the same time, there is no reason to be complacent about the effects of high taxation on the economy. Presumably the logic behind the Laffer curve holds and at *some* tax rate economic growth will suffer. It is argued that the high levels of income tax in parts of the EU (notably the Scandinavian economies), coupled with their generous welfare benefits, do act as a disincentive to work and invest.

Deregulation and privatisation

A third major strand of recent supply-side reforms involves measures to make markets work better by removing barriers to competition, including those introduced by the state. Most economists believe that competition is the key to higher productive efficiency, wider consumer choice and lower prices. Therefore monopolies, including state-owned monopolies protected by statute, should be dissolved or at least their conduct should be carefully regulated through *competition policy*.

There are two main parts to this reform programme: one concerns introducing competition to provide services in markets previously highly regulated and maintaining this competition through effective competition or anti-trust laws. The other involves the transfer of state-owned assets to the private sector. Here we shall use the terms *deregulation* and *market liberalisation* to describe introducing more competition and *privatisation* to describe the sale of state-owned assets to private sources.

Deregulation involves removing anti-competitive controls, such as the licensing of suppliers and other ways of limiting their numbers. For example, the airlines market and bus and coach transport have been opened up to more competition in many parts of the world in recent years. In some countries, stock markets and other financial activities where competition had been restricted by legal measures have been liberalised. In most of the EU the telecommunications and air travel markets have been opened up to competition and the European electricity and gas markets now face increasing competition due to EU directives. In the USA, telecommunications, airlines and road haulage were deregulated from the 1970s. At the same time, a number of countries have introduced tougher competition laws to outlaw the abuse of market dominance and restrictive and concerted practices. Restricted and concerted practices occur when firms act together to set prices or reduce competition in other ways – the most obvious example is the creation of a cartel.

Equally, many governments in both developed and developing economies have sold-off a number of their state-owned enterprises through programmes of *privatisation*. By the end of 2000, global privatisation receipts had risen to a record figure of $200bn. Industries particularly affected by privatisation have included telecommunications, electric power, airlines, the oil sector and banking. In addition to selling state assets, privatisation has involved central and local government departments outsourcing, to the private sector, some services previously provided by government employees (e.g. garbage collection and road maintenance services), usually through the use of a process of competitive tender. Academic studies of such privatised services in North America and Europe suggest cost savings for taxpayers commonly of between 5 and 20 per cent.

A desire to raise the efficiency with which goods and services are delivered has driven governments' privatisation programmes, although other aims, notably widening share ownership and financing government spending through receipts from assets sales, have also been important. In the main, governments have justified privatisation by pointing to higher *allocative* and *productive efficiency* in the private sector. That is to say, prices in the private sector more closely reflect the true economic costs of supplying particular services than in the state sector (where sometimes there are no user charges at all), leading to higher *allocative efficiency*, and supply costs are reduced because of higher labour, capital and total factor productivity in the private sector, leading to more *productive efficiency*.

As in the case of the disincentive effects of taxation and welfare benefits, however, the policy of privatisation is supported more by rhetoric than hard evidence. Recent surveys of the international evidence on the impact of privatisation have found that privatisation leads to efficiency improvements when coupled with market liberalisation measures. This places the emphasis on promoting competition as the key to improved economic growth and not simply on changing the ownership of assets.

Also, an emphasis on privatisation could detract from proper recognition of the role of the state in promoting economic growth. Market economies rely upon a sound and stable set of institutions, involving property rights, commercial and contract laws, courts, police, etc. without which few would be willing to save, invest and trade. Education, health programmes and infrastructure schemes (e.g. roads, ports, airports, public transport) also contribute to economic growth. In some fast-growing Asian economies, for example China, Singapore, Taiwan and Malaysia, governments have adopted various degrees of state planning and investment. Achieving higher economic growth may not, therefore, simply be a matter of achieving less government, but rather of achieving *better* government.

Application 10.2

Privatisation – still going strong

Mrs Thatcher is remembered for privatising telecommunications, gas, electricity, water, British Airways, British Aerospace, Rolls Royce, and much more. In total over £60bn of industrial assets were transferred from the state to the private sector under the Conservative Governments of Margaret Thatcher and John Major.

More recently, privatisation activity in the UK has slowed down. In part this is because of the election of a Labour Government, and in part because there is relatively little state enterprise left to sell. In spite of Labour's traditional hostility to privatisation the air traffic control system has been partially sold off and private capital has been introduced into the London Underground.

Outside the UK, privatisation activity continues to grow. The year 2000 may have seen the largest value of privatisation sales so far, breaking the previous record of $160bn worth of asset disposals. In Europe there have been major share sales in telecommunications (e.g. in Telia of Sweden and Deutsche Telekom). In Portugal a very active market exists for 'public private partnerships' (PPPs) in the financing, operation and maintenance of roads, rail and water services. Other countries are also experimenting with PPPs, particularly the UK, to finance roads, schools, hospitals and other public infrastructure.

▶

Application 10.2 continued

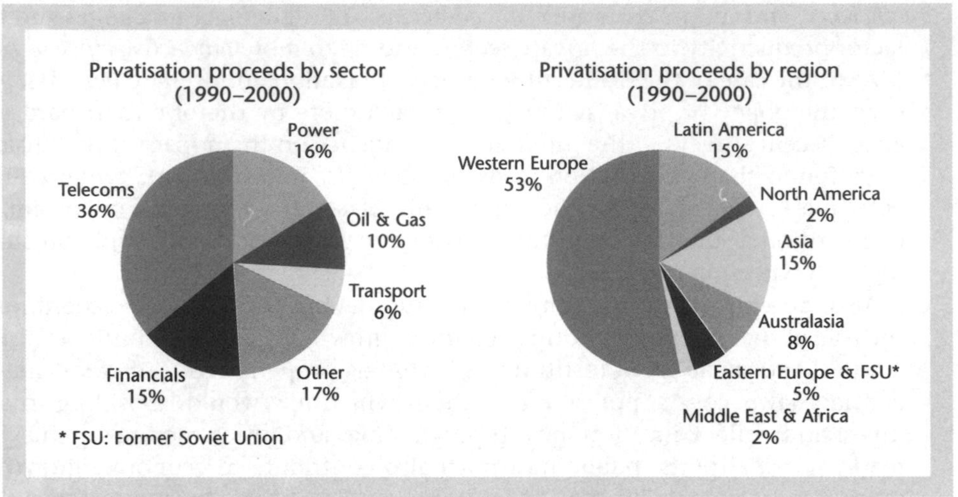

Source: *Privatisation International*, October 2000, Issue no. 145, p.7, with permission from Thomson Financial

As the left-hand pie chart shows, telecoms dominates international privatisation, accounting for around 36 per cent of all sell-offs. Both the costs of financing modern telecommunications and the opportunity to make telecommunications markets more competitive and raise efficiency are driving governments across the globe to privatise. Similar forces are causing governments to sell state enterprises in the power, oil and gas, financial and transport sectors.

To date over one-half of all privatisations by value have occurred in Western Europe (see right-hand pie chart above). But as privatisation continues to grow in popularity, it is to be expected that the balance will shift in favour of the other regions. So far privatisation has made very little impact on the economies of the Middle East and Africa, in spite of the need for considerable industrial restructuring in these countries.

Acknowledgement: *Economics Today*, Vol 8., No 3.

Activity

Why might privatisation improve the supply side of the economy?

Concluding remarks

This chapter has looked at economic growth and supply side economics. Three major growth models have been reviewed, the classical and neoclassical growth models and the endogenous (or new) growth model. Classical theory is pessimistic about long-term growth and its predictions are not consistent with developments in the world economy since the eighteenth century. The neoclassical growth model suggests that the growth rate of output is independent of the savings rate over the long run but endogenous growth theory argues that if policy could raise the savings rate there would be a permanent increase in the rate of economic growth. The models, therefore, have different implications for policy. The discussion also looked at the importance of technical progress as a driver of economic growth.

Supply-side economics is concerned with creating the optimal economic conditions for the promotion of economic expansion. In this context, sometimes unfavourable comparisons are made between the flexible labour markets in the USA and the more regulated labour markets of Europe and Australasia. Similar unfavourable comparisons are made between tax and state spending in Europe and Australasia and the lower levels of tax and the smaller government sector in the USA. It is sometimes argued that government policy in Europe and Australasia needs to focus more on promoting flexible labour markets and competition and reducing the size of the government sector and government tax rates if economic growth is to be increased. Similar supply-side reforms are also put forward for lower income, developing economies in Latin America, Africa and Asia, by international organisations such as the International Monetary Fund, World Bank and World Trade Organisation.

Where there is scope to improve the efficiency and performance of the economy by making markets more flexible and competitive and by reducing taxes and privatising industries, there is a strong case for supply-side measures of the types discussed in this chapter. However, as we have seen, while such measures are aimed at promoting economic growth and hence higher production, the precise relationship between them and economic growth is uncertain.

Finally, most economists agree that an attention to supply-side economics, while important, should not be allowed to detract from continuing concern with the level of aggregate demand in the economy. It is aggregate demand and aggregate supply *together* that determine production, employment and price levels. This is a subject to which we return in the next chapter, in a detailed discussion of the nature and causes of inflation.

Key learning points

- *Economic growth* is concerned with increases in real GDP.
- *Growth accounting* seeks to quantify the contribution to an economy's growth in output made by factor inputs.
- *Growth models* relate the causes of economic growth to factor inputs, namely labour, capital, technology and land resources.
- In the *classical model*, economic growth is only a temporary phenomenon and is dependent on population growth; in the *neoclassical model* the savings rate does not affect the steady state growth rate; in *endogenous growth theory* policy that raises the savings rate can lead to a permanent increase in the growth rate.

- The neoclassical and endogenous growth models recognise the importance of *technical progress* in promoting economic growth.
- *Supply-side economics* is concerned with policies to promote higher economic growth (increases in real GDP).
- Lowering tax rates may lead to more incentives for households to work and save and for industry to invest and produce.
- The *Laffer curve* shows the relationship between tax rates and government revenues and allows identification of the optimal tax rate to maximise government receipts.
- The *Gutmann effect* refers to an increase in tax revenues as a result of a cut in direct tax rates because of reduced tax evasion at lower tax rates.
- The incentive effects of tax cuts depend critically upon the response of individuals and businesses to tax changes and this in turn depends upon the response to changes in the *average rate of tax* (*art*) and *marginal rate of tax* (*mrt*).
- *Promoting competition* is another supply-side reform aimed at stimulating economic growth. A related reform is market liberalisation or deregulation.
- A further supply-side reform is concerned with *privatisation* or the transfer of the production and supply of goods and services from state-owned firms to private-sector firms.

? Topics for discussion

1. What are the main distinguishing features of the classical, neoclassical and endogenous growth models? What does each imply for economic policy?
2. Why might lowering your country's or state's tax rates stimulate economic growth? Under what circumstances may lower taxes *not* have the desired effect on economic growth?
3. Why might we expect a teacher on a fixed annual salary to respond differently to a cut in the rate of income tax compared with a bricklayer paid according to the number of bricks laid?
4. How might labour markets be made more flexible in your country or state?
5. What are the limitations of the Laffer curve as a tool of government policy formulation?
6. What is the case for having an effective national competition policy?
7. What is the economic argument for deregulation?
8. Why might privatisation improve economic performance?
9. Compare and contrast the likely effects of privatising (a) a textile manufacturer and (b) a water and sewerage supplier. Does privatisation make equal sense in both cases as part of government policy to promote economic growth?
10. Why should both aggregate demand and aggregate supply be considered when formulating government macroeconomic policy?

Chapter 11

INFLATION – CAUSES, CONSEQUENCES AND POLICY IMPLICATIONS

Aims and learning outcomes

This chapter deals with a central macroeconomic objective of governments across the world, namely, to control inflation. In general terms, inflation refers to any increase in the price level within the economy. However, in the context of the macroeconomy, we are more concerned about a *sustained* rise in prices over time rather than a one-off increase at a point in time. Also, at the outset it is important to appreciate that inflation may be caused by a number of different factors stemming from both the demand side and the supply side of the economy. We shall provide a detailed analysis of the sources of inflation and the consequences for individuals, firms and macroeconomic policy in this chapter.

A particularly important theme that has been examined over many years concerns the extent to which a trade-off may exist between the rate of inflation and the level of unemployment in an economy. This theme has grown in significance in recent years as countries such as the USA and UK have reported lower rates of inflation combined with low levels of unemployment. The underlying research concerning the relationship between inflation and unemployment derives from the so-called *Phillips curve*. We fully explain the importance of the Phillips curve relationship and highlight its implications for macroeconomic policy.

The chapter also discusses the various policy options open to governments to control the rate of inflation. It is important to note that a policy will only be effective if it targets the actual cause of rising prices. Given that inflation may have a number of possible causes, the appropriateness of policy responses becomes critical.

In the following sections the following issues concerning the causes, consequences and policy implications with respect to inflation are considered:

- measurement of inflation;
- causes of inflation;
- consequences of inflation;
- the relationship between inflation and unemployment;
- policy implications of inflation.

While the discussion below is concerned with the problems and policies associated with inflation, some economies may experience periods of deflationary pressures usually leading to a fall in the general level of prices – giving rise to the less common phenomenon of 'deflation' (or possibly 'disinflation'). We also deal with this issue and its associated consequences and policy implications in this chapter.

Learning outcomes

After studying this material you will be able to:

- Understand the meaning of inflation and how it is measured.
- Recognise the various possible causes of any inflation stemming from both the demand and supply sides of the economy.
- Appreciate the consequences of inflationary pressures for individuals, firms and governments.
- Understand the relationship between unemployment and inflation and the significance of the *short-run* and *long-run Phillips curves.*
- Identify a range of possible policy responses to inflationary pressures.
- Appreciate the economic implications of deflation or a fall in the level of prices.

Measurement of inflation

Inflation is a sustained increase in the general level of prices over time. *Creeping inflation* refers to small and gradual rises in prices over time while *hyperinflation* describes a situation of large and accelerating prices rises.

The rate of inflation is the percentage change in an economy's price level from one time period to the next, usually expressed as an annual rate. A common approach to measuring the rate of inflation is based on changes in the *consumer price index (CPI)*, which measures the level of prices for a wide range of goods and services bought by consumers in a country at a point in time. (In the UK this index is known as the *retail price index* (*RPI*); exclusion of mortgage interest payments from this index gives rise to the concept of *RPIX*, the 'underlying' or 'core' measure of inflation.) It should be noted that a range of other inflation indices are published by most governments, referring to the prices of goods and services bought by consumers, by firms, by the government and relating to foreign trade. The most comprehensive measure of the rate of inflation is one that covers *all* goods and services produced in the economy and included in the total for GDP – this is known as the *GDP deflator* (see pp.35–36).

Using any of these indices of price levels, the appropriating inflation rate is calculated as follows:

Calculating the rate of inflation

$$\text{Inflation rate} = \left(\frac{\text{Price index in this period} - \text{Price index in the previous period}}{\text{Price index in the previous period}}\right) \times 100$$

For example, if the CPI this month is recorded at 120 and in the same month last year it was 110, then the annual inflation rate is calculated as:

$$\text{Inflation rate} = \frac{120 - 110}{110} \times 100 = 9.09\%$$

It is important to understand that the inflation indices used may not be perfect measures of the true underlying inflation in an economy. There are a number of sources of possible bias in inflation indices. Some may lead us to believe that the inflation rate is over-estimated (or even under-estimated). The main sources of bias relate to:

- errors in data collection and estimation;
- bias caused by the introduction of new goods and services;
- bias introduced by quality improvements over time;
- changes in the typical basket of goods and services purchased.

We comment briefly on each of these sources of bias in turn.

Errors in data collection and estimation

Like all official statistics, inflation indices are calculated by statisticians based on a sample of goods and services. It is important that the sample and sampling techniques employed provide an accurate representation of consumption behaviour. Errors can arise in the collection of data and in the estimation of the inflation rate, particularly since some price data may be unintentionally excluded especially when patterns of consumer spending are changing very quickly. Furthermore, the choice of the reference (or base) period is important and may lead to a distortion in the computed inflation rate.

Bias caused by the introduction of new goods and services

Over time, many goods and services become unfashionable. Consider the speed of change with respect to most consumer durable goods – cars, televisions, kitchen appliances, etc. As the 'old' goods and services are replaced by new goods and services, a difficulty arises in comparing price levels from one time period to the next. For example, personal computers (PCs) have replaced manual typewriters. Since the former are more expensive than the latter, this creates a potential upward bias in the inflation rate if we include PCs rather than typewriters in the basket of goods and services used to measure inflation. This would clearly give a misleading impression of the 'true' rate of price increases for a *standard* basket of goods and services.

Bias introduced by quality improvements over time

Part of any rise in the price of goods and services may be due to a physical quality improvement or technological enhancement, as well as a pure inflation effect. For example, new television and car models will have extra features and therefore are likely to cost more than the older models which they replace – although it is possible that greater efficiency in the production of new models, using new technologies, may drive down unit costs and result in *lower* prices. The inflation measure may conceal the consequence of the product improvement and therefore exaggerate the true underlying rate of inflation.

Changes in the typical basket of goods and services purchased

Over time consumers change their pattern of spending. This may take place in two ways:

- by switching from purchasing one commodity to another, for example buying more pre-packed and pre-washed vegetables and less unprocessed foods, with the former more expensive than the latter – this is referred to as *a product substitution bias*;
- by switching to purchasing from large discount stores with competitive prices rather than local and generally more expensive convenience stores, leading to lower prices for the same goods – this is referred to as *an outlet substitution bias*.

For all of the reasons explained above, a certain degree of scepticism is required when interpreting 'official' statistics. However, in the absence of any more reliable estimates of inflation, the official figures represent the best information available upon which to base decisions concerning policy responses, wage bargaining and business planning.

Application 11.1

Measuring inflation

Read the following extract:

> In his assessment of the UK's suitability for entry into the euro, the Chancellor announced that the inflation target would switch in November 2003 from RPIX to the Harmonized Index of Consumer Prices (HICP), the system used

Application 11.1 continued

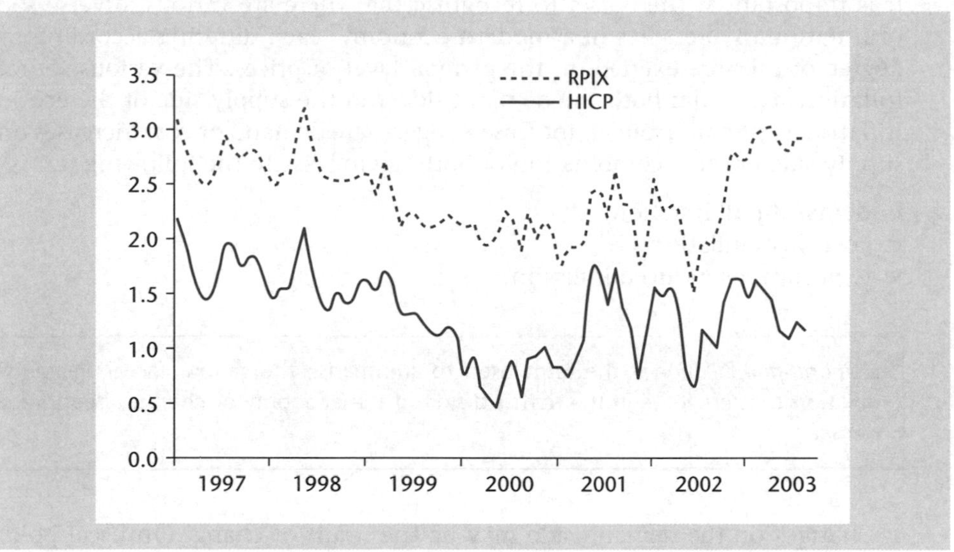

UK inflation (12-month percentage)

Source: ONS

in the Euro Area. The HICP measure is generally regarded as a technically superior measure of inflation to RPIX, which is often criticised for exaggerating inflationary pressures when house prices are moving sharply.

The June data showed RPIX edging down to 2.8 per cent, while the HICP dropped back to 1.1 per cent. There are two main reasons for the difference between the two measures. First, the treatment of owner-occupied housing costs which are included in RPIX but largely excluded from the HICP – this has been the reason for the widening of the gap in recent years but it should narrow as house price inflation eases. Second, the HICP uses a geometric average whereas RPIX uses an arithmetic average – this has accounted for roughly 0.4–0.5 per cent of the difference over the past decade. Hence this is consistent with a new HICP target of 2.0 per cent, a switch that is unlikely to have any significant impact on the immediate outlook for interest rates.

Source: CBI *Economic Bulletin*, July/August 2003.

Activity

Consider how switching from one inflation measure to another can cause confusion about an economy's true inflation rate and the possible consequences.

Causes of inflation

It is important at the outset to recognise that there are various, diverse sources of inflationary pressures in a modern economy, each differing according to the degree of pressure exerted on the general level of prices. The various sources of inflation stem from both the demand side and the supply side of the economy. Inflation can result from an increase in aggregate demand or cost increases on the supply side or some combination of both, giving rise to the following terms:

- demand-pull inflation;
- cost-push inflation;
- expectations-induced inflation.

> *Demand-pull inflation* is the term used to summarise the various factors leading to inflation that originate in the demand side of the economy or changes in aggregate demand.

Changes on the demand side may be the result of changes in fiscal policy or monetary policy.

> *Cost-push inflation* is a term used to describe cost pressures due to supply-side factors that cause changes in aggregate supply.

Changes on the supply side may originate from the domestic economy, for example, in terms of higher wages, or from the international economy, in terms of higher import prices.

> In addition, inflationary pressure may result from an *expectations-induced* effect – if prices or costs of production are expected to rise this may trigger demand and supply-side responses in advance and thus, in effect, cause (i.e. induce) inflation.

Figure 11.1 highlights these various possible sources of inflationary pressure. We comment on each of these in more detail below.

Demand-pull inflation

An increase in aggregate demand due to changes in consumption, investment, government spending or net exports can lead to inflationary pressures. However, to appreciate the underlying cause of demand-pull inflation it is important to identify what causes these changes in demand. In particular, increased

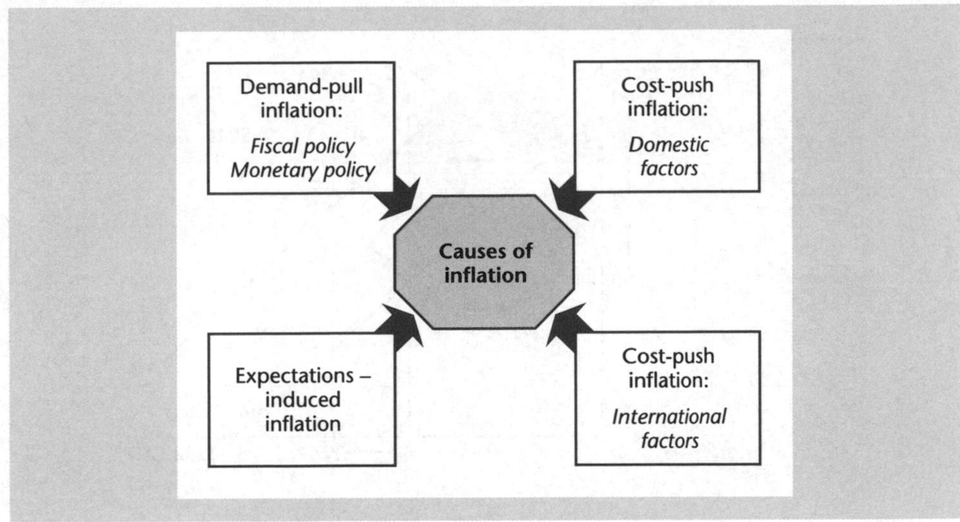

Figure 11.1 **Causes of inflation**

consumption and higher investment expenditure may result from an expansion in the money supply and lower interest rates. In Chapter 8 we looked in detail at the *quantity theory of money* and explained how an increased money supply could lead to higher prices. Another causal factor could be changes in fiscal policy, namely an increase in government purchases or a reduction in taxation.

Figure 11.2 illustrates the effect of an increase in aggregate demand (AD) on prices. With the initial aggregate demand of AD_0 and a given short-run aggregate supply (SRAS) schedule, macroeconomic equilibrium exists with a real GDP of Y_0

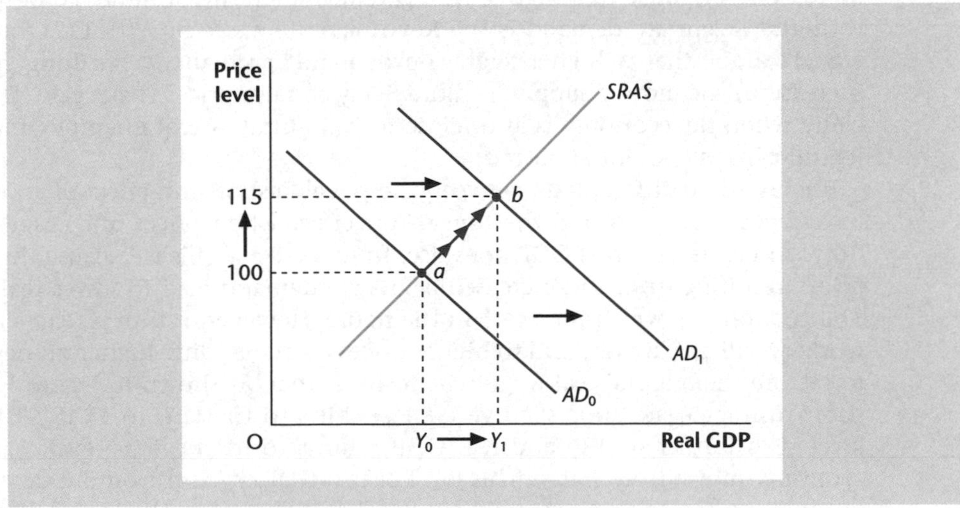

Figure 11.2 **Demand–pull inflation – short-run effect**

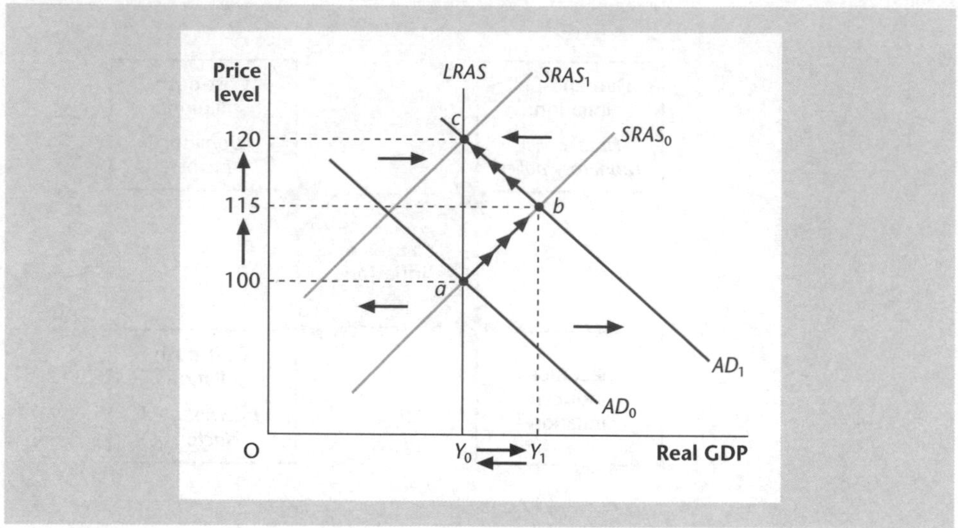

Figure 11.3 Demand–pull inflation – long-run effect

and the price level at 100. The increase in aggregate demand to AD_1 leads to a higher level of GDP (at Y_1) but also a higher level of prices (at 115 or a 15 per cent rate of inflation over the time period concerned). It should be obvious that the more *inelastic* the SRAS curve – i.e. the less responsive is real GDP to higher prices – the more the higher aggregate demand will impact on prices rather than real GDP or output. In the short-run, the SRAS curve can be expected to be inelastic because it takes time to increase supply – although where there are slack resources in the economy, including high unemployment, output rather than prices may increase in response to a higher aggregate demand. This stimulus to output due to higher aggregate demand is the Keynesian view (see pp.110–112), but monetarists argue that a higher aggregate demand, particularly resulting from an increase in the money supply, is more likely to raise prices than real GDP, especially when the economy is at or close to its natural rate of unemployment (i.e. its full capacity potential output).

It is useful to differentiate between the possible short-run effect of an increase in aggregate demand and the longer-run effect when prices and wages adjust fully. In Figure 11.2 real GDP does rise, from Y_0 to Y_1. This is because the higher prices resulting from the increased aggregate demand lead to lower real wages. The economy moves from *a* to *b* in the figure. However, it is to be expected that workers will quickly respond to higher prices by demanding higher money wages to restore the original real wage. The result is that, as shown in Figure 11.3, the short-run aggregate supply curve ($SRAS_0$) shifts to the left, to $SRAS_1$. The price level rises further to 120 and real GDP returns to its previous level, Y_0, as the economy moves from *b* to *c*. This level of real GDP, Y_0, is the output determined by the long-run aggregate supply curve (*LRAS*). Therefore, the long-run effect of the increase in aggregate demand is an increase in prices and not real GDP.

Persistent attempts to stimulate aggregate demand using fiscal and monetary policy measures will only lead to ever rising inflation if the economy is at its full capacity production – or on its long-run aggregate supply curve, LRAS, in Figure 11.3. The effect of demand stimulation will be to create a *price–wage–price spiral*. Monetarists associate this spiral with continued increases in the money supply and argue that in the long-run inflation can only be controlled by controlling the growth in the money supply (for a fuller discussion, see pp.199–206).

Cost-push inflation

An alternative set of causes of inflation may originate from the supply side of the economy, giving rise to the notion of *cost-push inflation*. Cost-push inflation is associated with a rise in the costs of production, which will lead to a leftward shift in the short-run aggregate supply curve. There are two possible main sources of cost-push inflation relating to *domestic* and *international* factors (as shown in Figure 11.1 above). These are:

- excessive wage demands;
- an increase in the price of imported raw materials and fuels.

In the case of a rise in wages, excessive wage demands may result from successful trade-union pay bargaining to which employers may respond by raising prices and cutting output – giving rise to the phenomenon commonly referred to as 'stagflation'. A rise in import prices may be the result of a general rise in the price of commodities, such as oil, in the global economy or a fall in the economy's exchange rate against other currencies resulting in more expensive imports.

The short-run and long-run effects of both domestic and international cost factors on prices and real GDP are illustrated in Figures 11.4 and 11.5 respectively. In Figure 11.4 the leftward shift in the short-run aggregate supply curve

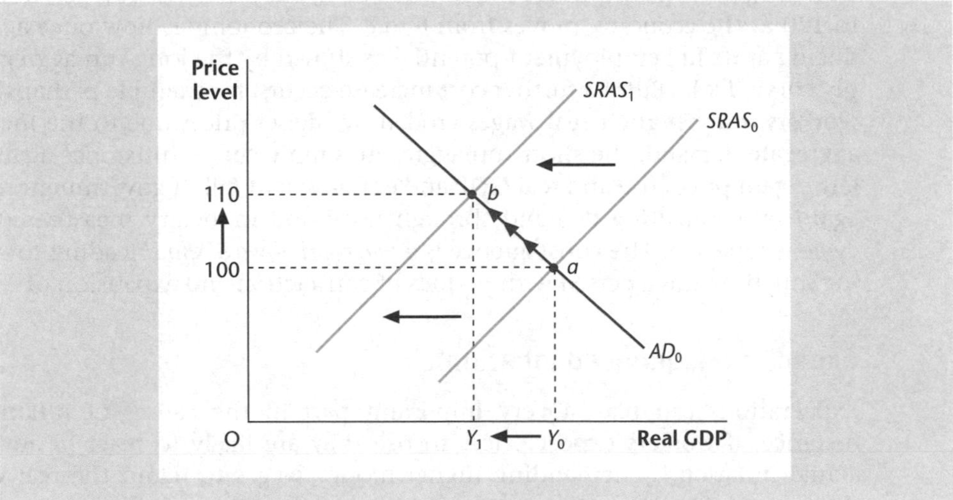

Figure 11.4 Cost-push inflation – short-run effect

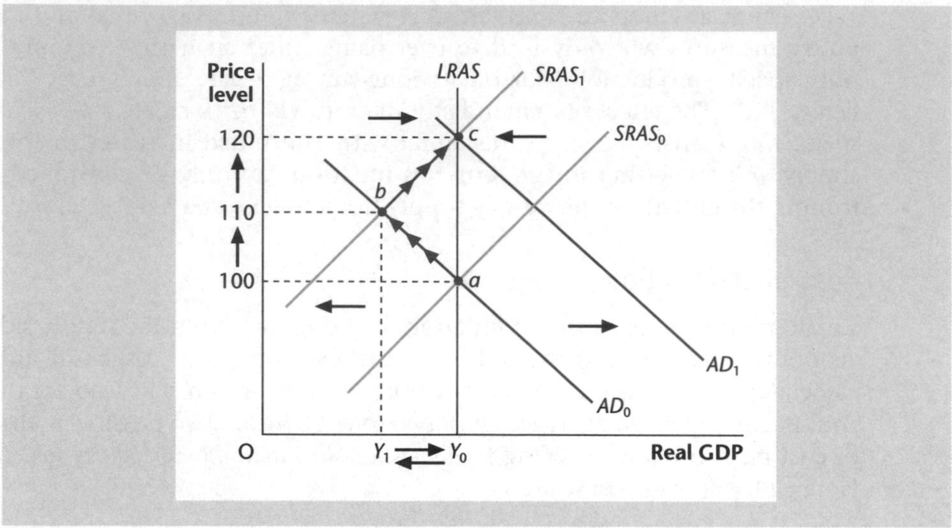

Figure 11.5 Cost–push inflation – long-run effect

(from $SRAS_0$ to $SRAS_1$) leads to a price rise from 100 to 110 and a fall in output from Y_0 to Y_1 as the economy tracks from *a* to *b*. It is important to note that like most forms of cost-push inflation, this is a once and for all price rise and should not lead to continuing inflation.

However, in practice, governments often respond to the fall in output and the consequent rise in unemployment by attempting to raise aggregate demand. In Figure 11.5 the government's response through expansionary (i.e. reflationary) fiscal and monetary policy changes causes the aggregate demand curve to shift from AD_0 to AD_1. Output is now restored to Y_0 but prices rise further, in this case to 120 as the economy moves from *b* to *c*. The economy is now once again producing at its full employment potential as shown by the long-run aggregate supply curve, *LRAS*. But if a further cost increase occurs, for example perhaps because workers now see their real wages eroded by higher prices due to the increase in aggregate demand, the short-run aggregate supply curve shifts once again to the left. Again prices rise and real GDP and employment fall. If government responds again by stimulating demand through fiscal and monetary measures then the cycle is repeated. The consequence is a *wage–price–wage spiral* leading to continuing inflation, interspersed with periods of contraction and expansion of real GDP.

Expectations-induced inflation

Expectations can play a very important part in the causes of inflation. For instance, if workers expect prices to rise they are likely to react in advance of actual inflation by demanding higher money wages to retain the real value of their wages. Similarly, if firms expect inflation then they are likely to respond by

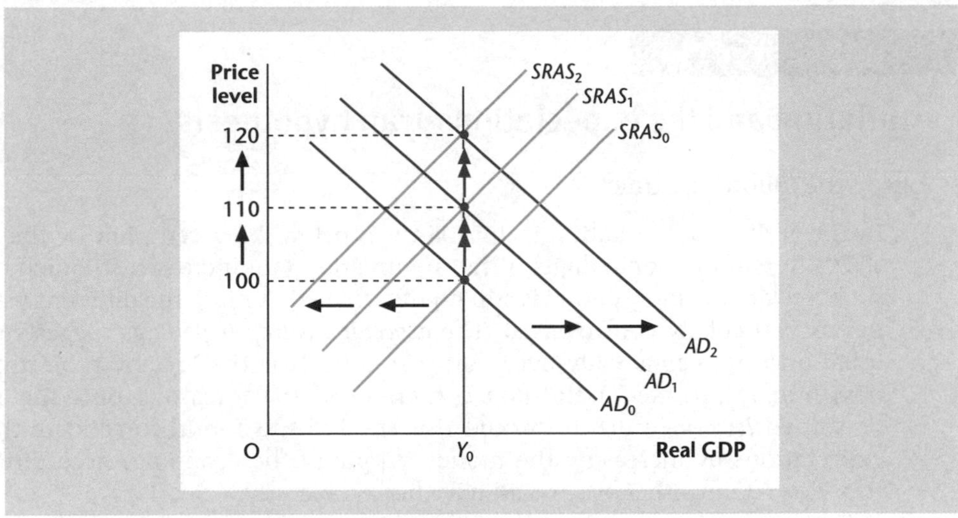

Figure 11.6 Expectations-induced inflation

building in inflationary expectations into their price planning and government may anticipate higher costs of running public services and raise taxes in advance. Also, consumers expecting goods to be more expensive in the future may buy now rather than delay their spending. The overall consequence is that the expectation of inflation can *induce* inflationary pressures both on the supply and demand sides of the economy.

An expectations effect is illustrated in Figure 11.6. Suppose that there is an expectation of an increase in aggregate demand from AD_0 to AD_1 and that workers anticipate correctly the resulting increase in prices (P). Workers can then be expected to demand a rise in their money wages (W) to retain their current real wage (W/P). This causes the short-run aggregate supply curve to shift leftwards from $SRAS_0$ to $SRAS_1$. The consequence is that real GDP is unchanged at Y_0, but the price level jumps from 100 to 110. If aggregate demand is expected to rise still further, from AD_1 to AD_2, this will spark off another demand for higher wages – resulting in a further leftward shift of the aggregate supply curve from $SRAS_1$ to $SRAS_2$. Real GDP will remain unchanged at Y_0 but the price level will rise from 110 to 120.

This is a similar effect to the one discussed earlier, but is occurring more rapidly because the inflation is expected. Of course, only if the increase in aggregate demand is *correctly anticipated* will the economy follow the precise path set down in Figure 11.6. For example, if aggregate demand rises by more than expected then there will be *unanticipated inflation*.

Expectations can also cause an increase in aggregate demand or a rightward shift in the AD curve. This occurs, for instance, when consumers expect goods to have higher prices in the future and therefore bring forward their purchases.

Application 11.2

Inflation and the expectations-trap hypothesis

Read the following extract:

In the early 1960s, inflation in the USA was below 2 per cent, but by the late 1970s, it was in double digits. Why the inflation rate increased so much over such a relatively short period is still highly debated. Among the different views, one is particularly controversial. The *expectations-trap hypothesis* suggests that inflation rose dramatically over that period because the Fed, by projecting a dovish image, painted itself into a corner: for whatever reasons, once the public started *believing* inflation would rise, the Fed was forced to validate those expectations by increasing the money supply in the economy. According to this view, doing otherwise would have been too costly.

The expectations-trap hypothesis is controversial because it implies that the same set of economic fundamentals, such as industrial production and the unemployment rate, can lead to a drastically different inflation rate, depending on how the public interprets the data and their effects on future inflation. One practical implication of the expectations-trap hypothesis is that it becomes very difficult for theorists and forecasters to predict inflation rates because any inflation rate can be rationalised from a given set of economic news.

The World According to A W Phillips

To understand what may have gone wrong in the 1970s, we first have to take a small detour to the world of British economist A W Phillips, who, in the late 1950s, published an article that would come to heavily influence policymaking and theoretical economics. His research documented a simple inverse relationship between the rate of growth in nominal wages and the unemployment rate in the UK. Subsequently, a similar relationship was found between the rate of growth of the prices of goods and the unemployment rate in many different countries. This empirical relationship became known as the Phillips curve, and it led many academics and policymakers to believe that a lower rate of unemployment could be achieved by tolerating a higher inflation rate.

As one example of the great power of good theorising, Milton Friedman in the late 1960s argued that a long-run trade-off between the inflation rate and the unemployment rate was pure fiction. He predicted that, in the long run, people would come to anticipate changes in monetary policy, adjust their expectations of future inflation rates, and thus neutralise monetary policy's effect on the real economy. In his view, only unanticipated changes in the money supply could affect output.

Suppose the central bank wants to lower interest rates to boost the economy. To achieve that goal, the Federal Reserve would reduce the federal funds rate, which is the rate banks charge one another for overnight loans. Although most

Application 11.2 continued

people are not directly affected by the federal funds rate, the goal is to change very short-term interest rates, such as the federal funds rate, which then affect long-term real interest rates, which, in turn, do influence people's decisions to buy a car or a house or to save. The real interest rate affects people's decisions to spend or save because it dictates the trade-off between consuming goods today or consuming them in the future. An increase in the real interest rate motivates people to increase their savings, which translates into a lower level of consumption today, but a higher one in the future.

To lower the federal funds rate, the central bank would typically need to increase the money supply, which tends to generate inflation. Since the nominal interest rate is the sum of the real interest rate and the rate of expected inflation, a fall in the nominal interest rate would bring about a corresponding fall in the real interest rate only if the public does not expect a change in inflation in the future. But, with time, the public would come to realise that, to keep interest rates low, the central bank needs to increase the money supply, an action that tends to be inflationary. The obvious consequence is that the public would then adjust upward its expectations about the rate of inflation. People would then demand to earn a higher nominal rate of interest on their savings to compensate them for the higher expected inflation, which erodes the value of their savings in the future. Similarly, because of higher expected inflation, borrowers would be willing to pay a higher nominal interest rate. This process ultimately leaves the real interest rate unchanged, since rising nominal interest rates offset the increase in expected inflation. As a result, monetary policy will lose its ability to affect components of the real economy, such as output, once the public comes to anticipate the change in monetary policy.

Obviously, this is more likely to happen as time passes. In the short run, there may be a trade-off between inflation and unemployment, but given time, people can gather more evidence that the Fed has instigated a change in policy and can adopt their expectations accordingly. Therefore, in the long run, a strategy of pursuing an expansionary monetary policy that creates inflation to lower the unemployment rate will not work. An expansionary policy will indeed increase the rate of inflation, but because it fails to lower real interest rates, it will leave the unemployment rate unchanged at its so-called natural rate.

What Friedman really pointed out is the importance of inflation expectations for the way changes in monetary policy are transmitted through the economy. His argument implies that monetary policy will lose its ability to stir the economy if the public comes to anticipate changes in policy and alters its inflation forecasts and that policymakers need to keep surprising the public for monetary policy to have some bite. If the central bank announces a policy of price stability (zero inflation) in the future, no-one will believe it. If the public

Application 11.2 continued

does believe the central bank and expects prices to stay constant in the future, the central bank would have an incentive to generate a little bit of inflation to lower the rate of unemployment. Obviously, no one would be fooled by such a policy for very long and the public would start taking into account this possibility when forming their expectations.

The main problem facing this hypothetical central bank is that its policy of price stability lacks credibility. To gain credibility a central bank must have a clear anti-inflation mandate and be shielded from political influences that will often be too willing to raise inflation in the hope of lowering the unemployment rate.

Proponents of the expectations-trap hypothesis argue that credibility is exactly what the Federal Reserve was missing in the 1970s.

The story of the expectations trap usually goes as follows. Suppose there is a sudden rise in expected inflation. The central bank could adopt a more restrictive monetary policy and raise the federal funds rate to fight the increase in expected inflation, but this action has a cost. If there is indeed a short-run trade-off between inflation and unemployment (that is, a Phillips curve), a rise in the federal funds rate will also lead not only to a lower inflation rate but also to a higher rate of unemployment. A dovish central bank, which assigns too much weight to output growth and not enough to inflation, may not be willing to pay that price. Instead, it would simply accommodate (and validate)

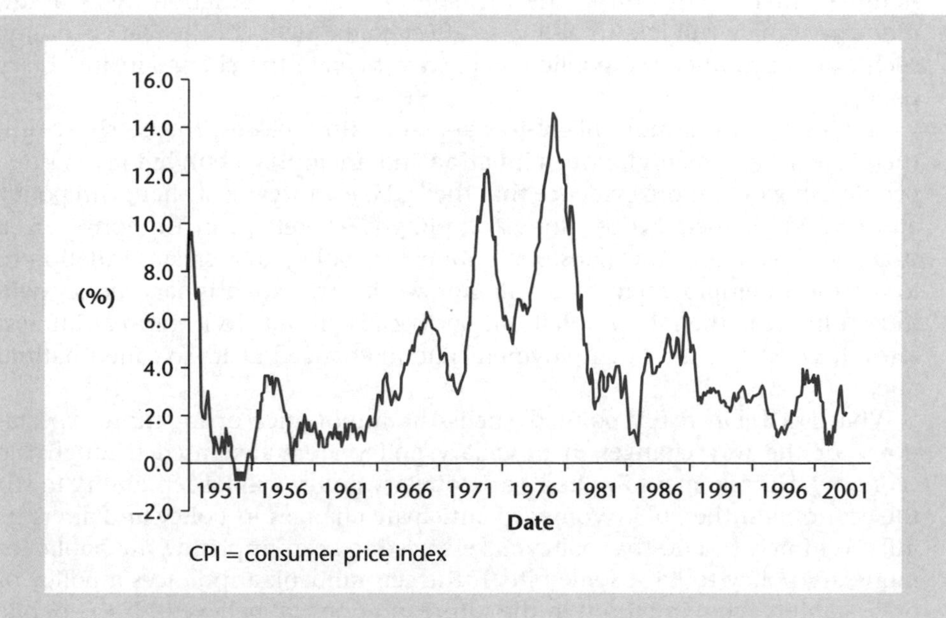

CPI = consumer price index

Application 11.2 continued

the rise in expected inflation by leaving nominal interest rates unchanged. The expectations-trap hypothesis dictates that a sudden increase in expected inflation can therefore lead to a long-run rise in the inflation rate because the dovish central bank ends up validating the initial rise in expected inflation. Proponents of this view argue that the Fed was probably caught in such a trap in the 1970s.

Source: Edited extract from Leduc, S, 'How Inflation Hawks Escape Expectations Traps', *Business Review*, First Quarter 2003, Federal Reserve Bank of Philadelphia.

Activity

On the basis of this discussion, explain why expectations are so important in understanding policy responses to inflation and unemployment.

Consequences of inflation

As noted above, inflation can either be *anticipated* or *unanticipated*. The economic costs of inflation can be expected to differ depending upon whether or not economic agents correctly expect the resulting rate of inflation. There will also be consequences for a country's international competitive position as a result of higher domestic inflation in relation to other countries. We discuss each of these consequences below.

Fully anticipated inflation

If inflation is fully anticipated then all individuals and firms in the economy expect it and thus are able to gain full compensation for any consequential effects. In this situation, the inflation will have no significant effect on the overall wealth of the economy or on the distribution of income between the various sectors of the economy. Banks may compensate for anticipated inflation by adjusting nominal interest rates on savings to ensure that real returns are not diminished. Similarly, governments may adjust tax thresholds to ensure that there is no *fiscal drag* effect resulting from inflation. The term fiscal drag refers to the extent to which tax revenues increase automatically due to a nominal rise in incomes. Also, governments may raise the level of transfer payments (e.g. pensions and other welfare payments) to ensure that recipients receive the same real level of income.

In the case of fully anticipated inflation there will be no *inflation* (or *money*) *illusion* on the part of workers and employers. In other words, workers do not confuse nominal and real wages (the real purchasing power of wages), such that they demand full compensation in terms of higher nominal wages to offset any anticipated inflation. This introduces the importance of how inflation expectations are formed in the economy with implications for wage bargaining and employment. We shall return to this issue later in the chapter in a discussion of the *Phillips curve*.

It should be noted that even when inflation is correctly anticipated and there is full compensation for it, as described above, some economic costs may still be incurred. There are two particular such costs, which can be significant particularly in times of *hyperinflation*. Hyperinflation is loosely defined as 'run away inflation' and sometimes more precisely as prices rising by at least 50 per cent per month. In such cases the consequential economic costs relate to so-called *shoe leather costs* and *menu costs*.

Shoe leather and menu costs

In times of high and accelerating inflation (i.e. hyperinflation) people tend to spend considerable time and effort searching for the lowest possible prices of goods and services – thereby using resources without any consequent increase in output. Such resource costs are commonly labelled *shoe-leather costs*.

Organisations, such as restaurants and shops, need to alter advertised price lists more frequently because of the rapid inflation. Again, this represents a use of economic resources without a resulting increase in the economy's output – such costs are commonly referred to as *menu costs*.

Although these costs certainly exist at times of very high inflation rates, it would be wrong to exaggerate their extent, especially in the case of fully anticipated inflation.

Unanticipated inflation

If the actual inflation rate is not fully anticipated then the real level of wages, interest rates, taxes and transfer payments may be affected (also, real wages may be affected even when the inflation is anticipated simply because workers and their trade unions are unable, given the state of the labour market, quickly to enforce nominal wage increases to fully compensate for the expected inflation). There are two main consequences of unanticipated inflation, namely *redistribution effects* and *uncertainty* (see Box 11.1).

Inflation and international competitiveness

Whether inflation is fully anticipated or not, there is likely to be a cost to an economy in terms of international competitiveness. This is most obviously the case where an economy is pursuing a fixed exchange rate policy. A country experiencing a faster rate of domestic inflation than that experienced by its trading partners is likely to suffer a deterioration in the price competitiveness of its

Box 11.1

Main consequences of unanticipated inflation

Redistribution effects

There are a number of ways in which unanticipated inflation can have redistribution effects:

- *From lenders to borrowers* – in times of unanticipated inflation, the nominal rate of interest on loans may be less than the inflation rate leading to a negative real interest rate. Additionally, the real value of debt falls with inflation to the benefit of borrowers and to the detriment of lenders. As, in general, savers tend to be amongst the older generations and borrowers tend to be younger, there will be a redistribution of wealth across generations in society.
- *From those on fixed incomes to those whose incomes adjust in line with inflation* – those relying on fixed incomes (e.g. rents, fixed-interest investments) will experience a fall in the real value of their incomes as a result of inflation. In addition, we can also expect a redistribution of national income as those workers with less bargaining power to raise their wages see a decline in real incomes relative to those workers with strong bargaining power in the labour market (e.g. strongly-unionised workers).
- *From taxpayers to the government* – as noted above, inflation leads to a *fiscal drag* effect. As a result of a movement into higher tax bands as nominal incomes rise to compensate for inflation, the tax burden will increase unless tax thresholds (i.e. the level of nominal income at which various tax rates are levied) are appropriately adjusted. Of course, the government may decide to spend this extra tax revenue thereby returning income to the private sector.

Uncertainty

Unanticipated inflation makes business forward planning more difficult with respect to future prices, wages, profits, etc., thus creating uncertainty. Such uncertainty may in turn discourage investment expenditure by the private sector with negative consequences for output and long-term economic growth.

exports and domestic products will become less price competitive compared to imports. This situation can be expected to lead to a deterioration in the current account of the balance of payments.

In the case of a freely floating exchange rate regime, the country with the higher inflation rate is likely to experience a depreciation in the exchange rate of its currency compared to the currencies of its trading partners. As a result, many economists are of the view that the costs associated with inflation are less where there is a freely floating exchange rate because the depreciation of the currency can compensate for the loss of price competitiveness across exports and imports. However, even with a floating exchange rate significant economic costs can still arise if currency depreciation results in even higher inflation due to rising import costs and this in turn leads to further currency depreciation. The result can be an inflationary spiral, especially because the freedom to depreciate the currency to prevent a current account deficit may remove a necessary incentive for governments to fight inflation. In addition, inflation in the context of a floating exchange rate may lead to greater currency speculation in the foreign exchange market, leading to considerable instability in the international value of currencies with a potentially damaging effect on international trade and capital flows.

It will be appreciated from the discussion above that governments and central banks are usually very concerned about inflationary pressures – especially the threat of hyperinflation – and have therefore made the control of inflation one of their major macroeconomic policy objectives. However, a critical question that has arisen over many years concerns whether or not it is possible to achieve a sustained low inflation rate while at the same time achieving and sustaining a low rate of unemployment. This question lies at the heart of the Phillips curve analysis, which we now discuss.

The relationship between inflation and unemployment

From our discussion earlier in this chapter concerning the demand-pull and cost-push causes of inflation, we can expect that as the economy approaches its full-employment output (e.g. illustrated by the long-run aggregate supply curves, LRAS, in Figures 11.5 and 11.6 above), the greater the inflationary pressure that is likely to exist in the economy. This is the result of the lack of spare capacity and hence bottlenecks in the availability of factors of production, notably labour. Conversely, it may be expected that in the presence of high unemployment, inflationary pressures will be subdued as a result of slack in the labour market and therefore reduced wage pressures. This raises the question as to whether or not there exists a reliable trade-off or inverse relationship between the level of unemployment (U) and the rate of money wage inflation (W). This question has been at the heart of a disagreement between the Keynesian school of thought and the monetarist school of thought for many years. The question has become a critical issue in recent times as governments have sought to control inflationary pressures and achieve sustainable, long-term economic growth.

The Phillips curve

In an article published in 1958, A W Phillips indicated on the basis of UK data for the period 1861–1957 that there was a strong negative relationship between the rate of change of money wages and the level of unemployment. The statistical analysis indicated that the relationship had been markedly stable for a continuous period of almost a hundred years with a higher unemployment rate being associated with a lower rate of growth of money wage rates. Soon after the original research was completed, it was argued that there was also a significant and stable negative relationship between the rate of change of prices (i.e. inflation) and the level of unemployment. This is not really surprising since wage increases not paid for out of higher productivity are likely to be passed on to consumers in the form of price increases. Hence the correlation between wage and price inflation is likely to be statistically high.

The Phillips curve

The *Phillips curve* shows the statistical relationship between inflation and unemployment over time.

A Phillips curve is shown in Figure 11.7.

The work of Phillips seemed to offer government a range of policy choices. It suggested that governments could *trade-off* a particular level of unemployment against a particular rate of inflation. For example, if aggregate demand were stimulated (say, via tax cuts and/or an expansion of government spending), this would reduce unemployment but at the expense of a higher rate of inflation and vice versa. In other words, governments could 'fine-tune' aggregate demand and push the economy up and down the Phillips curve (say from *A* to *B* and then back to *A* again). Furthermore, it was suggested that unemployment could not be reduced below the rate shown as point *A* in Figure 11.7, without triggering inflationary pressures. This rate is associated with equilibrium in the labour market where the demand for labour at a given real wage rate is equal to the supply of labour.

For much of the 1960s some governments actively attempted to manage their economies on the basis of the Phillips curve relationship. It provided an attractive

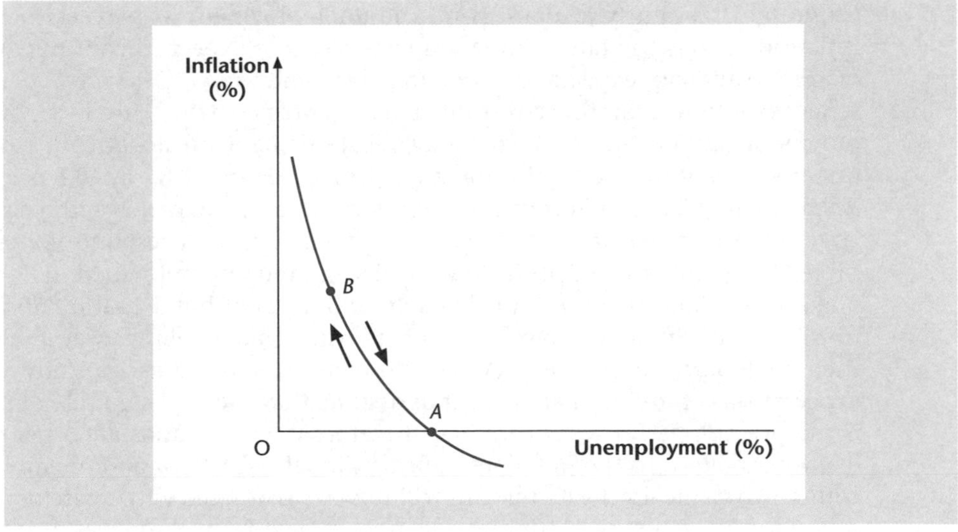

Figure 11.7 **The Phillips curve**

policy choice that could be triggered at appropriate times (perhaps reducing unemployment in the run-up to elections). However, towards the end of the 1960s the relationship began to look unstable as unemployment, wages and prices all began to rise together. During the late 1970s and early 1980s there was, in fact, a marked outward shift in the relationship with stagflation being a prominent feature of a number of industrial economies (rising unemployment associated with growing inflation).

Breakdown of the Phillips curve

With the stability of a trade-off between unemployment and inflation called into question, monetarist economists mounted a successful assault upon the Phillips curve. They argued that lower unemployment could be achieved only by accepting an ever-rising rate of inflation. Thus the relationship between inflation and unemployment was not stable as the Phillips curve implied. Monetarists maintained that Keynesian demand expansion initially raises prices and thereby lowers real wages (W/P). This increases the demand for labour. Unemployment falls but soon employees bargain for money wage increases to offset the fall in real wages experienced. The resulting increase restores real wages but threatens to cause a return of unemployment as employers shed labour. If the government reacts in a Keynesian fashion and stokes up demand to prevent a rise in unemployment, prices rise again and real wages fall until such time as workers successfully press, again, for a restoration of real income. As each of these price-wage cycles leads to a higher level of prices, Keynesian techniques prove inflationary.

This approach to the Phillips curve is illustrated in Figure 11.8. In the diagram, U^* is the 'natural rate of unemployment', where the level of inflation is anticipated and real wages are determined by demand and supply conditions in the labour market. For simplicity assume no productivity growth and that the economy is currently at point *A* on the unemployment axis experiencing zero inflation. This is the rate of inflation which people expect to continue; in other words inflationary expectations (P^e) are 0 per cent.

Suppose now that the government is dissatisfied with this level of unemployment and decides to increase aggregate demand in an attempt to reduce unemployment from U^* to U_1. Inflation rises, in Figure 11.8, say to 5 per cent – a *demand-pull* inflation effect due to increased aggregate demand on the part of the government. Wages are contractual and generally do not respond immediately. More labour is employed at the lower real wage and unemployment falls to point *B* along the Phillips curve, with P^e equal to 0 per cent but actual inflation rising to 5 per cent. In time, however, workers will demand higher wages to restore their real purchasing power. What happens now depends critically on how expectations of inflation adjust. Let us assume that the expected rate of inflation is the present rate of 5 per cent and therefore wage demands are 5 per cent. As real wages return to the initial level, firms will release labour and unemployment will return to the level U^* – but this will now be associated with a rate of inflation of 5 per cent. Thus, the economy has now moved from *B* to *C*, and not from *B* back to *A*, in Figure 11.8.

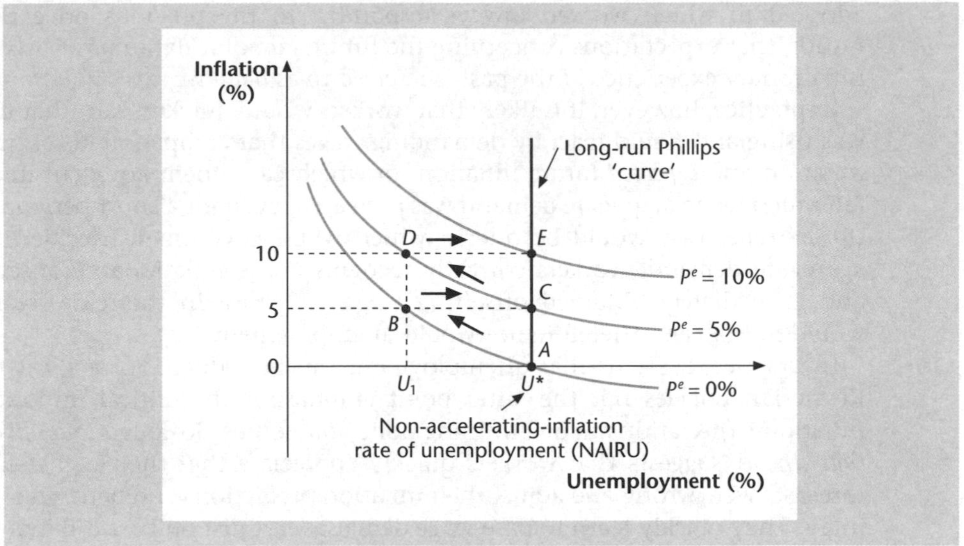

Figure 11.8 The long-run Phillips curve

Suppose the government now increases aggregate demand again in an attempt to lower unemployment from U^* to U_1. Once more prices rise, say from an inflation rate of 5 per cent to 10 per cent – more demand-pull inflation. Real wages fall again but this time causing a movement along the new Phillips curve associated with inflationary expectations of 5 per cent (i.e. $P^e = 5\%$), from point *C* to *D*. Workers respond with a corresponding 10 per cent wage demand which restores real wages and there is a movement from point *D* to *E*. Unemployment rises back to U^* but it is now associated with an inflation rate of 10 per cent. In other words, every round of increase in aggregate demand leads to a temporary fall in unemployment but a ratcheting up of the inflation rate and inflationary expectations. The economy returns to a rate of unemployment U^* but at an increasingly higher inflation rate. This gives rise to the so-called vertical *long-run Phillips curve*. Thus, however much the rate of inflation is increased, unemployment will have a natural tendency to return to U^*. There is only the possibility of a *short-run* trade-off between unemployment and inflation. It follows that in the *long run* there is no trade-off. Thus the level of unemployment represented by U^* has become known as the *natural rate of unemployment* (NRU) or the *non-accelerating-inflation rate of unemployment* (NAIRU). The way to reduce unemployment permanently is to reduce the 'natural rate' through supply-side reforms that make the labour market more flexible (see pp.244–251).

The role of expectations

The careful reader will have noted that the above mechanism depended upon how inflation expectations changed. In the example, a simple approach was adopted in which workers always responded to the previous price rise. The notion that expectations concerning the future rate of inflation are based on the inflationary experience of the past is referred to as *adaptive expectations*.

In practice, however, it is likely that workers would quickly learn that inflation was rising and would react by demanding wages that compensated for both past inflation and *expected* future inflation, in which case unemployment might not fall much when aggregate demand was increased, even for a short period. Indeed, the extreme case would be one in which when government decided to raise aggregate demand, workers correctly recognised the inflationary consequences and immediately obtained offsetting wage increases. In this case, real wages would not fall and therefore nor would unemployment.

In practice, it seems that unemployment can be reduced for a short time by Keynesian policies but the latter point emphasises the critical importance of inflation expectations in determining policy outcomes. So-called *rational expectations theory* suggests that workers quickly appreciate that their earlier inflation forecasts were wrong and adjust their inflation predictions and behaviour accordingly. They quickly learn to base wage demands not just on past inflation but on *all* information available to them regarding future inflation. Workers do not persistently underestimate the inflation rate.

Having examined the causes and consequences of inflation, and the relationship between inflation and unemployment, we now turn to describe the various policy alternatives open to governments attempting to control inflationary pressures.

Policy implications of inflation

As we stressed at the beginning of this chapter, it is important to appreciate that the choice of the appropriate policy to tackle inflation depends directly on identifying the underlying cause or causes of inflation. The main policy options can be placed under the following headings:

- monetary policy;
- fiscal policy;
- prices and incomes policy.

Monetary policy

If the monetarist school of thought is correct and the long-run Phillips curve is vertical at the natural rate of unemployment, then the appropriate policy response to bring down inflation must be to keep a tight control of the money supply. This has been a dominant approach to tackling inflation taken by many governments in recent decades. Controlling the money supply to bring down the inflation rate should, over time, lead to lowered inflationary expectations. This in turn should lead to lower actual inflation, for example as workers moderate their wage demands in the face of lowered inflation expectations – assuming, of course, that workers are always rational!

As discussed in Chapter 9, monetary policy involves the use of short-term interest rates by the central bank to influence the amount of money (liquidity) in the economy and therefore aggregate demand. The central bank may also choose directly to control liquidity by restricting the capacity of commercial banks to create credit. Monetary policy has been particularly effective in some countries as a result of the achievement of specific monetary growth or inflation targets set by central banks – thereby impacting upon inflationary expectations.

To bring down a high inflation rate to the target level may require a period of painful, short-term economic adjustment. A monetary squeeze leading to high real interest rates can be expected to cause a fall in economic activity until inflationary expectations are reduced. This adjustment process can also be expected to arise where fiscal measures are used to reduce inflation.

Fiscal policy

A reduction in government spending and/or an increase in taxation – i.e. a deflationary fiscal policy – will directly reduce aggregate demand in the economy. This is the preferred policy response to inflation adopted by Keynesian economists, although it is important to emphasise that such an approach is likely to result in transitional higher unemployment and perhaps even a recession. Using the Keynesian 45° line diagram introduced in Chapter 4, we can illustrate the impact of a decline in planned aggregate expenditure on the level of economic activity. In Figure 11.9, the fall in planned aggregate expenditure from AE_1 to AE_2 leads to a fall in real GDP from Y_1 to Y_2.

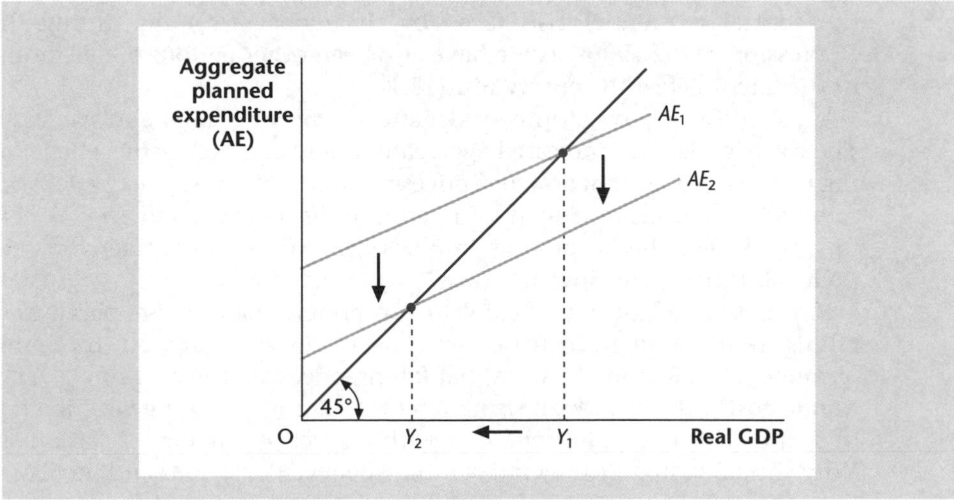

Figure 11.9 Effect of a deflationary fiscal policy

Prices and incomes policy

Whereas monetary and fiscal policies attempt to control inflation by restricting the growth in aggregate demand, prices and incomes policies tackle inflation by influencing cost factors and especially wage rates. The emphasis here is placed on the role of trade unions in wage negotiations. This type of policy can take a number of forms involving :

- the setting up of a prices and incomes control board to monitor and regulate price and wage rises on behalf of government;
- government requiring firms to avoid 'unjustified' price rises and trade unions to avoid 'unjustified' wage demands;
- voluntary agreements from employers and employees to keep the rise in prices and incomes within certain set norms;
- the passing of legislation to regulate or even freeze prices and wages.

Prices and incomes policies may have some short-term beneficial effect in moderating inflationary pressures and inflationary expectations on the costs side, but experience in many countries of their operation has shown that they are likely to break down in the longer term. This is because they do not address inflationary pressures coming from the demand side of the economy. They also involve governments directly regulating prices and wages, a measure which is contrary to the operation of a market economy and can lead to price and wage distortions. The result is likely to be a growing misallocation of resources.

Deflation

While the discussion above has focused on inflation, an emerging phenomenon in some countries today is deflation – i.e. a fall in the general price level. This was the central economic crisis faced by the global economy during the Great Depression of the 1930s. There have also been other periods of deflation, such as in the late nineteenth century in the UK.

We can identify two forms of deflation: *benign deflation* and *malign deflation.* The former relates to increased aggregate supply and productive efficiency allowing unit costs of production and prices to fall. In contrast, *malign* deflation refers to a lack of aggregate demand – referred to as *a deflationary gap*, as defined on pp.84–85. This has profound implications for economic activity, economic policy, business planning and wage bargaining.

In times of deflation, the real value of money balances *rises* because prices are falling, resulting in an increased purchasing power for any given nominal stock of money. While it might seem that falling prices are a good thing given the economic costs associated with rising prices, deflation can bring with it a reluctance to spend. This is certainly the case with respect to a malign deflation situation. Why should customers buy today if they believe that goods and services will cost less tomorrow? Such psychology can create a long-period of economic recession, such as occurred in Japan during the 1990s. In addition, if prices are falling then expectations of future inflation can be expected to decline with implications for wage negotiations – even cuts in nominal wages may occur.

Just as policy measures to curb inflation may involve contractionary fiscal and/or monetary policies, attempts to reduce the threat of (malign) deflation are likely to centre on policies to expand aggregate demand. However, in this context it should be noted that the effect of monetary policy may not be symmetrical, in the sense that while rises in interest rates will eventually curb spending, cuts in interest rates may be insufficient to stimulate demand. The impotency of monetary policy in a deflationary, malign-deflation environment has been likened to 'pushing on a string'. By contrast, raising interest rates in an inflationary environment has been described as 'pulling on a string'. The potential ineffectiveness of monetary policy during periods of malign deflation results from a lack of confidence on the part of consumers and firms to borrow and spend even at low or maybe zero real short-term interest rates.

Given the disadvantages and costs associated with both inflation and deflation, most economists would conclude that the ideal economic environment is one in which prices rise in a predictable manner and at a slow rate – perhaps between 1 per cent and 3 per cent per annum. It is argued that this outcome provides stability for longer-term planning and therefore the achievement of sustainable economic growth. Also a slow rise in prices year by year will reflect improvements in the quality of goods and services produced over time.

Application 11.3

Inflation to deflation

The rebirth of deflation?

Until a few years ago, deflation appeared to be an economic illness of the past. The deflation virus had devastated the world economy in the 1930s, but, thanks to the medicine developed by John Maynard Keynes in the wake of this experience, it had ceased to be seen as a serious menace. However, this perception changed when Japan fell into deflation in the second half of the 1990s and was unable to free itself again from this predicament. Deflation seemed to have made a powerful come-back in our time.

The appearance of deflation in Japan coincided with the demise of inflation in the rest of the world. Hence, what would probably have been welcomed as a final victory over inflation soon began to appear as a mixed blessing. Concerns began to rise when the Asian and Russian crises in 1997–98 boosted financial market instability and the burst of the internet bubble in 2000 caused stock prices to fall on a worldwide scale. An increasing number of financial markets participants now fear that the virus will spread from Japan to the rest of the world.

Before assessing the danger of a rebirth of deflation, we need to distinguish between two forms of deflation: a *malign* form and a *benign* form.

▶

Application 11.3 continued

The malign form of deflation is characterised by a fall in the general price level and aggregate demand. This is what has afflicted Japan in recent years. The benign form of deflation is characterised by a falling price level and rising demand. This may occur when technical progress or an improvement in the terms of trade causes a fall in prices that stimulates real demand. Benign inflation can be observed in a few Asian countries, such as China, Hong Kong, Singapore, Taiwan, and Thailand, where negative or very low positive inflation rates have been accompanied by robust GDP growth.

Does benign deflation raise the risk of malign deflation? Not necessarily. In an environment of benign deflation, where productivity growth is high or terms of trade improve, economic growth is robust and real interest rates are positive. Unless the price level falls at a very fast pace – which is unlikely in normal circumstances – positive real interest rates require positive nominal rates. Moreover, government revenues are likely to grow at a healthy rate while cyclical effects dampen spending growth. Hence, both monetary and fiscal policies have room for manoeuvre in case of a negative demand shock. Consumers are accustomed to a falling price level and hence are unlikely to suddenly change behaviour and hoard liquidity when a negative demand shock occurs. All this suggests that there is little reason to worry about benign deflation. But should the world be worried about the re-emergence of the malign form of deflation?

Risk of deflation in Euroland

The experience of Japan during the 1990s points to three important sources of deflation risk in its malign form:

- a plunge in asset prices;
- a sudden and sharp appreciation of the exchange rate;
- a fragile banking system.

Each of these events alone or, more likely, a combination of these events could have the power to push an already weak economy into deflation.

Recently, concerns have been growing that the German economy, which is particularly weak, could fall into deflation and drag the rest of Euroland with it.

Activity

Based on the three sources noted above, assess the risk of deflation in Euroland.

Concluding remarks

In this chapter we have looked at the causes, consequences and policy implications of inflation. We have seen that inflation has a number of possible causes, which are commonly grouped under the headings of demand-pull and cost-push inflation. Expectations have been shown to play a central role in the creation of inflationary pressures, as encapsulated particularly in the Phillips curve analysis.

Today it is clear that central banks in many developed countries place considerable emphasis upon the management of inflationary expectations. This is evidenced by the use of inflation and monetary targets and by the care taken in official statements not to stir up fears of higher future inflation. As part of this process, central banks are tending to place much greater reliance on more frequent and smaller adjustments in short-term interest rates, to constantly maintain a low inflation environment and steady economic growth.

The chapter has also touched on the subject of deflation, where the price level falls rather than rises. General economy-wide deflation can result from a lack of aggregate demand (malign deflation) or from the growth in aggregate supply outpacing the growth in aggregate demand (benign inflation). Deflation, like inflation, can have economic costs. As a consequence, a low inflation environment is probably the most conducive environment for consumption and investment and therefore economic growth.

Key learning points

- *Inflation* is defined as a sustained increase in the general level of prices over time, commonly measured using an official index, such as the consumer (or retail) price index.
- Official inflation indices may be biased for a number of reasons involving: errors in data collection and estimation; the introduction of new goods and quality improvements over time; and changes in the typical basket of goods and services purchased.
- Inflation may stem from both the demand-side and supply-side of the economy, giving rise to the terms *demand-pull* and *cost-push inflation.*
- *Demand-pull* inflation is the term used to summarise the various factors that lead to inflation which originate from changes in aggregate demand, i.e. it is the result of excess demand or an *inflationary gap* in the economy.
- Increases in aggregate demand and therefore the cause of demand-pull inflation may be the result of fiscal and/or monetary policies, leading to a rightward shift in the aggregate demand (AD) schedule.
- *Cost-push* inflation is the result of cost pressures due to supply-side factors that cause changes in aggregate supply – a leftward shift in the AS schedule. This may be due to higher wages leading to higher costs of production or due to higher import prices, which also raise supply costs.
- *Expectations* play a central role in the analysis of inflation. Where individuals expect higher inflation in the future, they will tend to demand higher wages and to bring forward purchases before prices rise, thereby creating inflationary pressures.

- The *economic costs of inflation* differ depending whether or not the inflation is *anticipated* or *unanticipated.*
- In the case of *fully anticipated inflation* there will be no significant damaging effects on the economy or the distribution of income, other than so-called *shoe leather* and *menu costs.*
- *Unanticipated inflation* will have important consequences in terms of redistribution effects and uncertainty.
- *Redistribution effects* take place from lenders to borrowers, from those with fixed incomes to those whose incomes adjust in line with inflation, and from taxpayers to the government.
- *Uncertainty* occurs because unanticipated inflation makes business planning more difficult with damaging implications for corporate investment, output and long-term economic growth.
- Inflation may also have important implications for *international competitiveness* through its effects on the prices of exports and imports and therefore international trade. The precise effects will vary depending upon whether an economy pursues a fixed or floating exchange rate regime.
- The *Phillips curve* shows an inverse relationship between the rate of inflation (of prices or wages) and the level of unemployment and therefore the impact of unemployment levels on inflation.
- *Monetarist economists* argue that there is only the possibility of a short-run trade off between unemployment and inflation – emphasising that in the long run there is no trade off at the *non-accelerating-inflation rate of unemployment (NAIRU).*
- The *long-run Phillips curve* leads to a focus on improving economic performance through supply-side reforms rather than aggregate demand management, especially if the economy is already at or close to its potential full-capacity working.
- *Adaptive expectations* refers to the notion that expectations of future inflation are based on past experiences.
- So-called *rational expectations* theory suggests that workers quickly adjust their inflation expectations and their behaviour – they quickly learn to base wage demands not just on past inflation but on all information available to them on future inflation.
- The main *policy options* to tackle inflation are: monetary policy, fiscal policy and prices and incomes policy.
- *Monetary policy* is concerned with influencing aggregate demand and therefore inflationary pressures through the use of short-term interest rates and measures to affect the level of liquidity (money supply) in the economy.
- *Fiscal policy* involves changes in government spending and/or taxation with a view to altering aggregate demand and therefore inflationary pressures.

- *Contractionary monetary and fiscal policies* to reduce inflation are likely to result in transitional higher unemployment and perhaps even an economic recession.
- *Prices and incomes policies* are sometimes used to tackle inflation and involve governments directly intervening in the setting of wages and prices in the economy.
- *Deflation* is defined as a situation of a falling price level due to either a lack of aggregate demand, resulting in *malign* deflation, or increased aggregate supply (*benign* deflation).
- In an environment of deflation monetary policy or cutting interest rates may be insufficient to stimulate aggregate demand – and has been likened to *pushing on a string*.

? Topics for discussion

1. Is inflation necessarily a bad thing? Justify your answer.
2. What role do expectations play in an inflationary environment and in determining the economic consequences of inflation?
3. Using appropriate diagrams compare and contrast cost-push and demand-pull inflation.
4. It is sometimes said that while cost-push factors can lead to higher prices and therefore an initial round of inflation, inflation can only be sustained by demand-pull factors. Explain this point of view.
5. An economy is suffering from higher inflation that is attributed to rising consumer demand outstripping the economy's ability to supply. Consider the appropriate macroeconomic policies that the government and its central bank could adopt to reduce inflationary pressures.
6. Is zero unem ployment achievable with stable prices? Is it desirable?
7. What do you understand by the term the term NAIRU? Using an appropriate diagram, show how attempts by government to reduce unemployment below this rate by expanding aggregate demand may only lead to higher inflation, especially in the longer term.
8. Why do some economists tend to argue that deflation, just like inflation, is bad?

Chapter 12

EMPLOYMENT AND UNEMPLOYMENT – MEASUREMENT AND POLICY

Aims and learning outcomes

In this chapter we are concerned with another major area of macroeconomic policy, namely employment policy and measures for tackling unemployment. As we saw in Chapter 10, the labour supply or employment level in an economy is an important input in national production and in determining the rate of economic growth. A failure to utilise fully the existing stock of labour available at any time means that an economy is not maximising its potential output, or potential real GDP. When unemployment occurs, an economy will be operating below its production possibility frontier (see p.9), implying a waste of economic resources, i.e. *actual GDP is less than potential real GDP.*

Achieving full employment of the labour force is, therefore, an important policy objective with respect to maximising output and, over time, the economy's growth rate (the growth of real GDP). At the same time, the labour force could be fully employed and yet the economy may fail to produce on its production possibility curve. This occurs when the labour force is *underutilised*. Workers may be employed but may have too little work to do or, because of poor management, they may 'slack' at work. For example, they may take prolonged 'rest breaks' or ration out the available work over the working day. Another consideration relates to the *hours of work*. Technically, the available labour force in an economy, say, per week, is the number of workers available for work (N) times the average hours worked (h). The labour force is therefore Nh. Hence, lengthening the working day increases the effective labour supply, while shortening the working day reduces it. If the output per employee or labour productivity per hour remains the same as hours of work are affected, then changing working hours will affect real GDP and the economic growth rate (everything else remaining equal). It has been argued, however, that reducing the hours worked does not necessarily lower real GDP because workers become more productive in the hours they work (i.e. they are more fully utilised per hour worked or able to work more efficiently because they are less tired).

A further consideration when discussing the labour force is its 'quality' or productivity. Developing countries usually have fast population growth, but lacking education, training and capital investment, workers are far less productive than in the more-developed economies. The USA, for example, has the highest levels of labour productivity of any economy. When discussing the labour force, we need to take account not only of its quantity but its *quality*, as reflected in educational attainment, training and skills.

In the remainder of this chapter we are going to be mainly concerned with the quantity of employment and unemployment. The chapter is concerned with:

- measurement of employment and unemployment;
- the relationship between employment and unemployment;
- types of unemployment and unemployment policy;
- costs of unemployment.

The discussion will focus mainly on the numbers of workers employed and unemployed rather than hours of work and the quality of the labour force. This is not to say that the latter are unimportant. In general, however, they change only slowly over time and in response to supply-side policies (see Chapter 10) rather than demand-side (fiscal policy, monetary policy) measures.

Learning outcomes

After studying this material you will be able to:

- Understand the meaning of the terms *employment* and *unemployment*.
- Identify the difference between the population and the workforce and the implications of changes in the workforce for policy.
- Recognise the different ways in which unemployment may be counted.
- Appreciate the different *types of unemployment* that exist and how they might best be tackled.
- Grasp the meaning of *full employment*.
- Understand the *economic and social consequences* of unemployment.

The chapter begins by looking at the measurement of employment and unemployment.

Measurement of employment and unemployment

The labour force is a sub-set of an economy's total population. The *potential workforce* will always be less than the total population because the population includes children below working age, those too sick to work, those in institutional care (e.g. prisoners and those too ill to work) and those above retirement age. Clearly, in countries with many compulsory years of schooling, well-funded state sickness benefits and compulsory retirement ages, the potential labour force will be lowered. Another consideration when defining the potential workforce is the percentage of women of working age who are seeking work. Over the last 50 years or so, there has been a gradual rise in the percentage of women working in developed economies as a result of more female job opportunities and less time spent rearing children due to a lowered birth rate. Also important have been increased educational opportunities for young women, which has opened up career opportunities outside of the home, leading to increased female *participation rates* in the workforce of many countries.

The *potential* workforce and the *actual* workforce will vary at any time depending upon the willingness to work and the availability of work. In particular, the actual workforce will be less than the potential workforce when:

- there is an economic recession and reduced jobs on offer;
- there is a fast-rising potential labour force but a slower growth in job opportunities;
- potential workers choose not to make themselves available for work, preferring instead leisure time, a decision perhaps supported by generous state welfare benefits (see pp.246–247 and especially the discussion of the *poverty trap* and the *replacement ratio*).

The term *unemployment rate* refers to the percentage of the workforce that is unemployed at any given time, i.e.:

$$\textit{Unemployment rate} = \frac{\text{Number of people unemployed}}{\text{Workforce}} \times 100$$

The true workforce is the potential workforce. However, official figures may simply calculate the workforce as the sum of the numbers of people in work and the numbers registered as unemployed. Thus, excluded are those unemployed but not registered (or counted – see below) as unemployed. Another two terms commonly used in employment policy are the *activity rate* and the *employment-to-population ratio*. They are defined as:

$$\textit{Activity rate} = \frac{\text{Workforce}}{\text{Working-age population}} \times 100$$

$$\textit{Employment-to-population ratio} = \frac{\text{Number employed}}{\text{Working-age population}} \times 100$$

Two broad methods are used across countries to measure the degree of unemployment. The first method is based on a *population survey*, the second on a *claimant count*.

Population survey of unemployment

A population survey is usually carried out by the government's statistical service and involves a survey of households across the economy. For example, in the UK the government's Office of National Statistics undertakes what is called the Labour Force Survey. Households are asked about the background of members of their household, including age, gender, qualifications, ethnicity, and about whether they have been seeking employment. The survey, therefore, provides information to estimate both the potential labour force (and its make up) and the actual labour force.

ILO and OECD surveys of unemployment

The International Labour Organisation (ILO) and the Organisation for Economic Cooperation and Development (OECD) also use a survey-based approach to estimate unemployment figures on a country-by-country basis. This produces a 'standardised' unemployment rate for international comparisons, whereby the unemployed are recorded as persons who are out of work and:

- are available to commence work within two weeks; and
- have actively sought work in the last four weeks; or
- are wanting to take up a job.

Claimant count of unemployment

This method counts the number of persons who are registered unemployed with state agencies (e.g. the employment service) and who are usually receiving state unemployment benefit. Additional conditions may be included, such as evidence of a clear effort to find employment. This method, unlike the population survey method, is more subject to manipulation by governments by altering the eligibility rules for state unemployment benefits or the criteria to be included in the count. It is also possible for the claimant count to show a falling rate of unemployment, while the population survey shows the opposite. For example, women seeking work after bringing up their children may be ineligible for unemployment benefit, and therefore fail to register in the claimant count, but show up as unemployed in the population survey.

A further categorisation sometimes used when discussing employment and unemployment issues is the *economically active* and the *economically inactive*. The economically active is equivalent to the workforce. The economically inactive represents the remainder of the population, including children, pensioners, those too ill to work, etc. Those economically active and in work may be in full-time or part-time employment. Those in part-time work but seeking full-time employment will not be included in the claimant count.

The relationship between employment and unemployment

Figure 12.1 highlights the flows of people into and out of the workforce and the relationship between employment and unemployment. It will be seen that

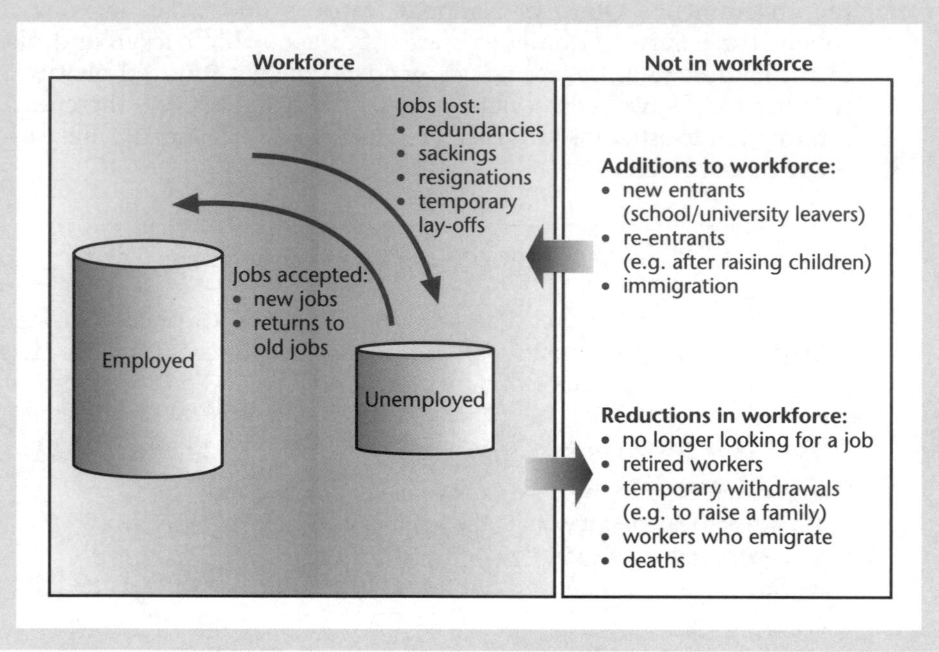

Figure 12.1 **Employment, unemployment and the workforce**

additions to the workforce result from new entrants as well as re-entrants who are actively seeking employment – although this does not guarantee that they will all find jobs. At the same time, reductions in the workforce take place for a variety of reasons – including death. Hence, the total size of the workforce is fluid. Likewise, the proportion of the workforce employed and unemployed also changes for a variety of reasons as illustrated in the figure.

The level of employment depends upon the numbers of people seeking work (the supply of labour) and the numbers of jobs available at any given time (the demand for labour). A main determinant of an equilibrium or balance between the supply and demand for labour in an economy is the *real wage rate*. As noted in earlier chapters, the real wage rate is the money wage rate or the amount paid (W) divided by the economy's price level (P); it represents real purchasing power. As real wages (W/P) rise we would expect more people to seek work and the reverse as real wages fall. Equally, over time real wage rates should alter in different sectors of the economy to reflect labour demand and supply in different occupations. We return to the role of real wage rate adjustments in determining the level of unemployment later in this chapter.

Figure 12.2 illustrates the roles of labour demand and supply in the context of employment (and unemployment), i.e. the labour market. New entrants into the labour force – perhaps attracted by the level of wages relative to prices given by $(W/P)_1$ – increase the pool of available workers or the potential workforce (e.g.

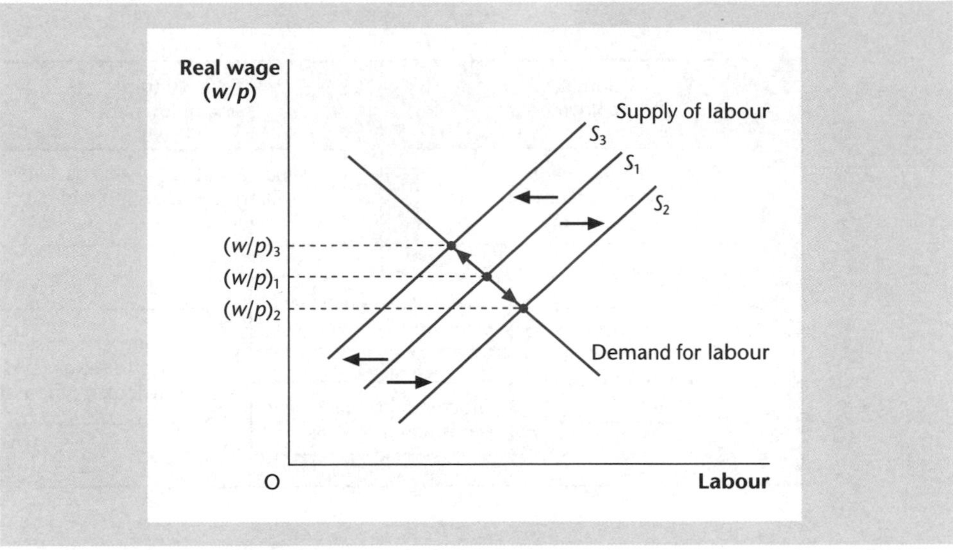

Figure 12.2 The labour market

retired persons seeking part-time work). The labour supply curve shifts to the right (S_1 to S_2) and consequently, the real wage falls to $(W/P)_2$. In contrast, people retiring or for other reasons no longer seeking employment reduce the potential workforce – the labour supply curve shifts to the left (S_1 to S_3) and real wages rise to $(W/P)_3$.

Types of unemployment and unemployment policy

Unemployment can occur for a number of reasons. As illustrated in Figure 12.1, in an economy people are constantly both entering and leaving employment. Whenever there is an imbalance at any time between the supply of labour seeking work and the demand for labour in the economy, unemployment will change. This unemployment may be short-term and disappear quickly as people successfully search out the available jobs. Or long-term unemployment may occur, where people are out of work for months and maybe even years.

Economists normally classify unemployment under the following broad headings:

- frictional unemployment;
- structural unemployment;
- classical unemployment;
- demand-deficient unemployment.

Figure 12.3 provides a useful overview of these classifications and distinguishes between those who are the *voluntary* and *involuntary* unemployed

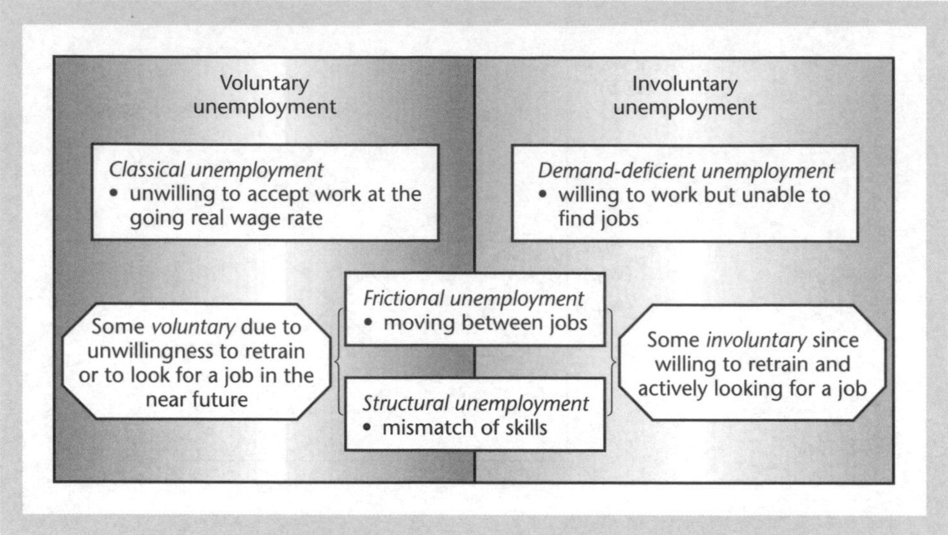

Figure 12.3 Types of unemployment

Frictional unemployment

Frictional unemployment is the term used to describe that unemployment which occurs temporarily as people change jobs. This is also sometimes referred to as *transitional unemployment*.

A dynamic economy is associated with people switching jobs according to demand and supply and real wage signals in the labour market. For example, a shop assistant may be made redundant in one store and register as unemployed until a new retail sales position becomes available. Provided that a new position arises quickly, which is likely in an expanding economy, the period of unemployment is short term. The length of frictional unemployment is reduced by having flexible labour markets that allow people to change jobs smoothly and employment agencies (private and state agencies) to assist people to find new, suitable employment quickly. As frictional unemployment is a necessary consequence of a dynamic, changing economy it should be seen as normal and unavoidable.

Structural unemployment

In contrast to frictional unemployment, *structural unemployment* is associated with rigidities in labour markets.

This occurs when particular industries and occupations suffer from an excess supply of labour. Where there is an excess supply of labour (insufficient demand for a type of labour) then real wage rates should adjust downwards for that type of labour. A lower real wage encourages unemployed labour to seek jobs in an alternative occupation, which now has a relatively higher real wage, and firms will have an incentive to take on more of this type of labour because it is less costly to employ.

In reality, real wages may take time to adjust to an excess supply of labour, i.e. wages may be 'sticky' in a downward direction. This will be so especially if government regulations prevent real wage reductions or trade unions and professional associations successfully oppose wage cuts. The result may be long-term unemployment in particular occupations, even whole industries. For example, recently there has been an excess supply of steel-making capacity internationally. This has led to lower steel prices and the closure of steel plants. The end result has been structural unemployment in the steel industry.

Structural unemployment is often associated with *regional unemployment* because industries tend to be located in specific geographic areas. A collapse in the number of jobs in an industry can lead to a whole area or region of the economy suffering from falling employment. For example, when steel workers are made unemployed they have much less to spend, leading to a contraction of aggregate demand and growing unemployment in the local community.

Structural unemployment should *eventually* disappear as real wages adjust downwards and workers move to other industries and other geographic regions seeking work. However, this may take a long time to occur. Workers may find it difficult to switch jobs because they lack the appropriate education and skills for the jobs available, leading to *occupational immobility* of labour. Also, people may be very reluctant to move geographically because of family ties and higher house prices in areas where work is available, leading to *geographical immobility* of labour. Also, immigration controls restrict geographical mobility between countries.

The most appropriate policies to deal with structural unemployment involve the use of retraining schemes and schemes to improve access to necessary education and training. Where structural unemployment is associated with regional unemployment, government might introduce financial incentives for firms to relocate to areas of high unemployment. Such incentives may include privileged tax rate regimes, such as tax free zones, and investment and employment incentives through direct government subsidies.

Classical unemployment

Both frictional and structural unemployment are associated with some *voluntary* unemployment and some *involuntary* unemployment as shown in Figure 12.3 above.

> *Voluntary unemployment* is defined as unemployment that results because people choose not to accept the jobs available.

Such people may decide to refuse work because they prefer leisure or because they are better off living on welfare benefits (i.e. the pay for the jobs available is not attractive compared to the state welfare benefits that are received while unemployed – a high *replacement ratio*).

> *Involuntary unemployment* occurs when people are actually seeking work but are unable to obtain it.

The higher the degree of voluntary unemployment, the longer people will be out of work, leading to higher frictional unemployment. Structural unemployment might be largely involuntary, but there could be some workers who choose not to switch to jobs on offer in the local community or some distance away (and even overseas).

Classical unemployment is entirely voluntary. Free-market economists would argue that provided people are willing to accept adjustments downwards in the real wage rates (W/P) they are prepared to accept, they will be able to obtain work. In particular, provided real wages do fall sharply when there is an over-supply of labour, at the industry or occupation level, or in the economy as a whole, the demand for labour and the supply of labour should move back into equilibrium. In classical unemployment, named because of its origins in the writings of nineteenth century so-called 'classical economists', the free market removes involuntary unemployment over time. Involuntary unemployment can only occur in the short term until real wages adjust to bring the supply of and demand for labour across the economy back into balance. The remaining unemployment is voluntary, representing workers who are unwilling to work at the market-clearing real wage rates. To tackle classical unemployment, government policies should be aimed at removing rigidities in the labour market so that real wages adjust more quickly. Voluntary unemployment is tackled by removing incentives not to work, notably generous state welfare benefits to the unemployed, and removing other rigidities to real wage reductions, for example trade-union wage bargaining.

Classical unemployment is related to a concept in economics introduced in the previous chapter known as the *natural rate of unemployment*, or alternatively referred to as the *non-accelerating-inflation rate of unemployment (NAIRU)*.

> The *natural rate of unemployment* is that level of unemployment which occurs when demand and supply are equal in the labour market, given the existing structure of the labour market, i.e. it is the unemployment rate that occurs when all labour markets across the economy are in equilibrium.

Given greater barriers to real wages adjusting quickly, for example trade union restrictions on wage reductions and state unemployment benefits, then the

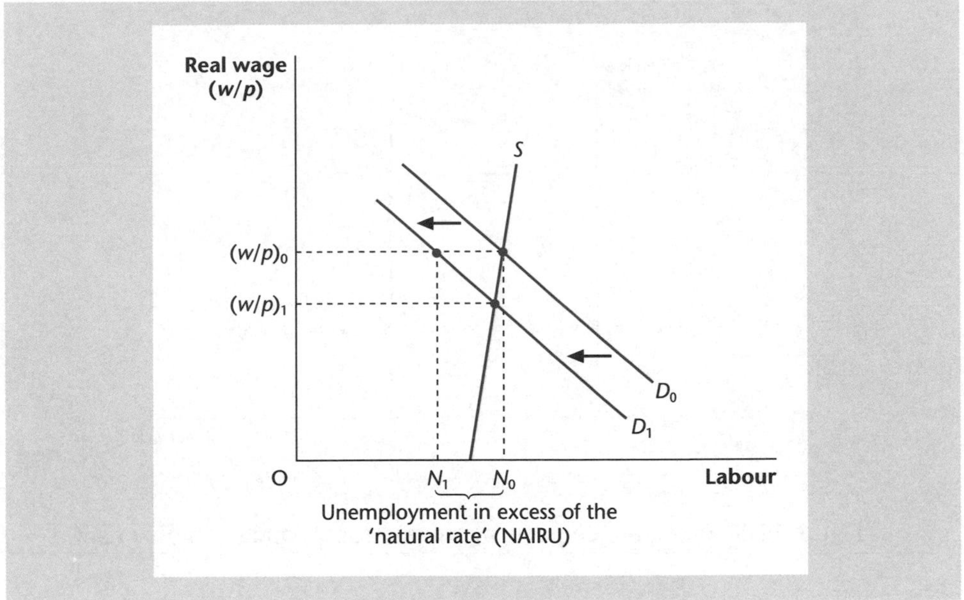

Figure 12.4 **Real wages and unemployment**

higher is the expected natural rate of unemployment. The alternative term *NAIRU* arises because this is the rate of unemployment that produces a stable (unchanging) inflation rate (we discussed this concept in some detail on p.277, in our discussion of the *Phillips curve*). The appropriate policy response is to introduce measures to make the labour market more 'flexible' or adaptive to changes in demand and supply conditions. Flexible labour markets are discussed in Chapter 10.

The concept of the natural rate of unemployment is controversial because, for the unemployed at least, the result may seem anything but 'natural' and certainly will not seem *just*. It arises from structural and frictional unemployment linked to voluntary decisions to postpone accepting work given the real wage on offer. The natural rate of unemployment can be expected to change as the flexibility of the labour market alters. Fast demographic and technological changes may also lead to periods of excess supply of labour, thereby raising the natural rate or NAIRU until labour markets fully adjust.

Figure 12.4 builds on Figure 12.2 and shows particular demand (*D*) and supply (*S*) curves for labour in the economy (although a similar diagram could be drawn for an industrial sector or region of the economy). The labour supply curve, *S*, is shown as relatively inelastic (steeply sloped) because the size of the potential workforce changes only slowly over time. It is not entirely inelastic, however, because more people can be expected to accept job offers the higher the real wage rate (*W*/*P*) – those previously not seeking work may now do so because of the higher real wage. The D_0 curve slopes downwards suggesting that employers

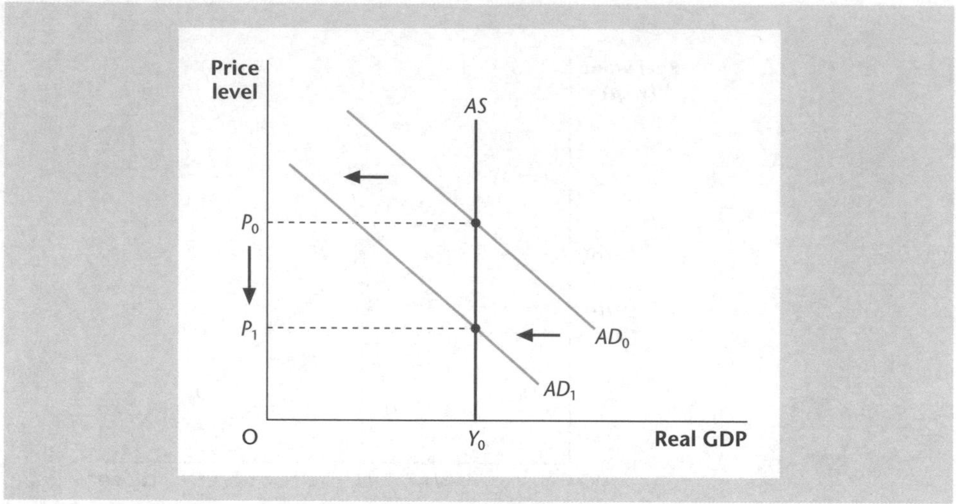

Figure 12.5 Aggregate demand, aggregate supply and unemployment

will wish to employ more workers the lower the real wage rate. The equilibrium, market-clearing real wage rate is $(W/P)_0$ and N_0 workers are employed. From a classical unemployment perspective, there is no involuntary unemployment because no workers are seeking work and are unable to obtain it (shown by the S curve) and no unfilled jobs are available (as shown by the D_0 curve). Suppose now that the demand for labour falls, perhaps because of an economic recession; the D_0 curve shifts to D_1 and the equilibrium real wage *should* fall to $(W/P)_1$. However, if the real wage rate is unable to adjust and remains at $(W/P)_0$ then there will be N_1N_0 unemployed (in excess of the natural rate of unemployment, NAIRU). At $(W/P)_0$, N_0 wish to work but only N_1 jobs are on offer.

Figure 12.4 illustrates how classical unemployment is the result of a disequilibrium in the labour market. Using the natural rate or NAIRU labels, with the original demand curve for labour, D_0, the natural rate of unemployment is given by the total workforce minus the number who are actually employed (N_0). But with the new lower demand for labour, D_1, the natural rate will be *higher* by the number of workers indicated by N_1N_0. We can show the same effects using the aggregate demand and aggregate supply curves introduced in Chapter 5. In Figure 12.5 the aggregate demand (AD) curve shows the total demand in the economy and the resulting levels of prices and real GDP. The aggregate supply (AS) curve is inelastic reflecting the inability to increase supply at higher prices given inelasticity in the supply of labour – labour is the most important input into production in the short-run because the capital stock takes much longer to alter. If the AD curve shifts leftwards from AD_0 to AD_1, reflecting an economic recession, prices will fall from P_0 to P_1. The result is a rise in the real wage (W/P) paid to workers in the absence of workers accepting a lower nominal wage (W) to offset fully the price fall. The result will be higher unemployment.

Application 12.1

Euroland's employment challenge

Potential growth rate of output

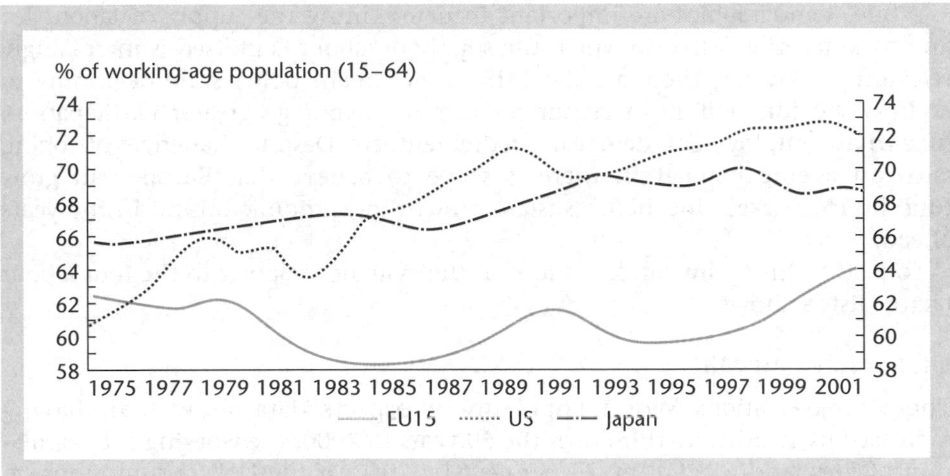

Employment rates in the EU, the US and Japan, 1975–2001
Source: European Commission

The chart shows that employment rates in the USA are well above those in both Japan and the EU. By the end of 2001 around 72 per cent of the working-age population in the USA were in employment, compared with just over 68 per cent in Japan and 64 per cent in the EU.

It is well known that the USA has favourable demographics compared to the 12 countries in the EU that belong to the euro (i.e. Euroland). In the 1990s annual labour force growth averaged 1.4 per cent in the USA against just half that rate in Euroland. Such strong growth in the labour force provides a significant growth advantage to the US economy. The potential growth rate of output of an economy is determined by the availability of capital and labour as well as total factor productivity (see Chapter 10). Concerning labour input, or more specifically potential growth of hours worked, in the 1970s the total hours worked in Euroland fell by an average of 0.4 per cent a year. This rate of decline eased in the 1980s to 0.1 per cent and turned marginally positive during the 1990s (+0.1 per cent). Is it likely that this improvement will continue during the next decade despite the unfavourable demographics? To answer this, we must focus on each of the labour inputs:

Application 12.1 continued

- labour force growth;
- employment growth;
- structural unemployment;
- average hours worked per employee.

While demographics are important in determining the supply of labour for an economy, the degree to which the supply of labour is utilised is increasingly relevant. In Europe, there are signs that government policies are beginning to address the functioning of labour markets to encourage greater participation, incentivise employment, deter early retirement, etc. Despite challenges of coping with an ageing population there is scope to believe that Europe can grow total hours worked, and hence sustain growth in economic output in the years ahead.

To justify this optimism, let us look at the evidence relating to the four labour factors listed above.

Labour force growth

The United Nations World Population Prospects data show that, having increased by nearly one third over the 50 years to 2000, the working age population of Euroland will fall by 27 per cent by 2050. If the UN's assumptions on migration are ignored the fall could be 34 per cent. These forecasts are the basis of concern about the long-term solvency of public pension systems across Europe. The greatest deterioration is set to take place between 2010 and 2030. Having grown by 2.6 per cent in the ten years to 2000, the working age population is expected to fall 0.5 per cent in the ten years to 2010. Thus, in the medium term, Euroland is faced with a demographic profile that is more challenging than in the 1990s. Based on demographics alone – and keeping all other factors unchanged – labour input is set to fall by 0.05 per cent *per annum* in 2003–10.

Employment growth

Euroland has seen a significant rise in its participation rate – the percentage of the working age population who are either in work or are actively seeking work – over the last 20 years. The rate has risen from a steady 65 per cent in the 1970s to just under 70 per cent by 2002. Europe has been increasingly addressing inherent inflexibilities of its labour markets and the employment-unfriendly tax and social security systems so we should expect participation to rise further in the years ahead as reforms take effect.

However, raising the participation rate alone does not benefit output. A higher participation rate means more of the working age population are willing to work – the labour force increases – but what determines output is whether the increase in supply of labour is effectively utilised.

Application 12.1 continued

Structural unemployment

Labour market structures and frictional unemployment inevitably mean that a certain portion of the potential labour force remains structurally unemployed. The problem with Euroland is that it has a higher rate of structural unemployment than the USA and UK. Structural unemployment can occur for many reasons, such as the geographical immobility of labour, hysteresis, the relative bargaining power of trade unions versus non-unionised labour, etc. The OECD estimates that the structural unemployment rate for Europe was 8.1 per cent in 2002. The USA and the UK, on the other hand, have reported considerably lower structural unemployment rates. Completely eliminating unemployment is unlikely as even a flexible and well-functioning labour market will generate a certain amount of frictional unemployment. Nevertheless, Euroland can reduce its structural rate. Labour market reforms in Europe include policies directed at reducing structural unemployment, for example by reducing the attractiveness of unemployment welfare benefits to make working financially attractive or to encourage the unemployed to travel further for work.

Average hours worked

Having considered participation rates and structural unemployment rates, consideration must be given as to how many hours each individual employee works. OECD data shows that in the early 1970s the average business sector employee worked approximately the same total annual hours in Euroland as in the USA or the UK. Although hours worked declined in all three economies during the 1970s, hours worked in the USA and UK levelled off in the 1980s (with the UK at a lower level than the USA) while in Euroland there has been a continuous decline. A business sector employee worked 15 per cent fewer hours in Euroland in 2002 than in the USA (10 per cent fewer than a UK employee). Hours worked have fallen an average of 0.5 per cent each year in the ten years to 2002 in Euroland versus 0.0 per cent in the USA and only 0.1 per cent in the UK.

Fortunately this downward trend in Euroland is not expected to continue – governments aim to halt the decline in hours worked over the medium term.

Putting it all together . . .

On the basis of the above discussion and the emerging evidence concerning government policy measures, it seems reasonable to expect that growth in total hours worked in Euroland will be faster this decade than last, meaning greater economic growth, all other factors remaining constant. There are further reasons to believe that the utilisation of labour may improve even more than outlined above. For example, pension policies are attempting to discourage early retirement. Increasing the effective age of retirement will, in the transition

▶

Application 12.1 continued

period, boost participation (and hence hours worked). Similarly, improved efficiency of the education system could reduce time spent in education and provide a temporary boost to participation rates. Hopefully, Euroland's unfavourable demographics situation can be checked. The implications for long-term economic growth will be even more positive if the ongoing reform measures also succeed in raising the productivity of the labour force.

Activity

The above optimistic conclusion relies heavily on 'everything else remaining unchanged'. What could change – in Euroland or elsewhere – to destabilise this scenario?

Demand-deficient unemployment

Whereas classical unemployment is associated over the longer term with voluntary unemployment, *demand-deficient unemployment* is associated with unemployment that is entirely *involuntary*. This is also often referred to as *Keynesian unemployment*.

Demand-deficient unemployment can be expected to occur under two general circumstances, namely conditions of *cyclical unemployment* and *general unemployment*.

Cyclical unemployment

Cyclical unemployment occurs during the business cycle when the economy goes into recession. Since the Industrial Revolution there has been a tendency for economic activity to fluctuate in cycles of generally around five to seven years (although other cycles of even up to 50 years have been identified by some economists, referred to as *Kondratief* or *long-wave* cycles). In some years the economy booms and real GDP grows quickly, while in other years the economy may slump and real GDP may grow very little or may even decline. Such recession periods lead to cyclical unemployment. The unemployment exists because of the stage of the business cycle reached and may be expected to disappear when the economy recovers. We look at business cycles in more detail in Chapter 17.

General unemployment

General unemployment is a term that was used in the 1930s to describe years of protracted unemployment resulting from a deficiency of aggregate demand.

This type of unemployment has been rare since the 1940s but, in principle, could return. Both general and cyclical unemployment might be tackled using Keynesian demand management techniques. We have described the principles of Keynesian economics in earlier chapters. Using fiscal policy measures – higher government spending and/or lower taxes – and through the national income *multiplier* effect, aggregate demand might be restored to a full employment level. For instance, returning to Figure 12.5, supposing aggregate demand fell from AD_0 to AD_1, leading to unemployment, government might step in and use fiscal policy to raise aggregate demand back to AD_0 and remove the unemployment problem.

It should be noted that while real wages adjusted downwards, through wage cuts, to restore full employment in the earlier discussion of classical unemployment, in Keynesian economics wages are not directly cut but demand is restored. Keynesian economists argue that wage reductions take too long to take effect, leading to years of unemployment and social deprivation. In other words, they act too slowly to be an effective policy measure and, while wage reductions may occur in the long-run, in Keynes' memorable words 'in the long-run we are all dead'! Keynesians also argue that reducing wages deflates consumer spending and therefore exacerbates the lack of aggregate demand in the economy, therefore perhaps worsening unemployment. At the same time, however, the Keynesian prescription may lead to a lower real wage because of price rises in response to a higher aggregate demand in the economy. Higher prices mean that with a fixed nominal wage (w), the real wage (w/p) declines.

The meaning of full employment

It is commonly an objective of government to maintain full employment in the economy. As discussed at the start of this chapter, an economy that is operating with unemployment is not producing on its production possibility curve and real GDP is therefore not being maximised. Unemployment is also a major cause of social deprivation and poverty and can lead to rising crime, social unrest and perhaps, even, social and political breakdown. Nevertheless, the term 'full employment' needs to be used with care – as we have seen, a dynamic economy needs people to switch jobs in response to changes in demand and supply in the labour market. Therefore, zero unemployment – the literal meaning of full employment – even if attainable, might not be desirable. Also, a fast-growing economy can expect to have pockets of structural and regional unemployment. It is most unlikely that all industries and all regions will expand at the same fast rate. Increasing aggregate demand using Keynesian methods might reduce pockets of unemployment but at the cost of creating serious inflationary pressures elsewhere in the economy. Moreover, business cycles are an endemic aspect of market economies, for reasons we explore in Chapter 17. Hence, some unemployment will always exist and the degree of unemployment can be expected to vary, sometimes sharply, over the short term as the labour market adjusts.

It is for these reasons that economists often use the terms the natural rate of unemployment and the NAIRU. These terms recognise the continued existence of unemployment, the amount being dependent upon the structure of the labour market.

Thus *full employment* refers to the condition that exists in an economy when the unemployment rate is equal to the natural rate of unemployment.

Costs of unemployment

There are three main costs commonly associated with unemployment which may be categorised under the headings of:

- economic costs;
- social costs;
- unemployment and hysteresis.

Economic costs

These arise in terms of the loss of national output that occurs because fewer members of the potential workforce are productively employed. This represents underutilised resources, with the cost disproportionately carried by the unemployed workers themselves in terms of lost income. However, some of the economic costs are borne by society in general because the unemployed may stop paying taxes and instead receive welfare benefits or other transfer payments from government.

A measure of the economic cost of unemployment in terms of national output is provided by *Okuns' law*.

Okuns' law states that a one percentage point of cyclical (demand-deficient) unemployment is associated with a loss that is equal to 2.5 per cent of full-employment output.

It should be noted that the loss of national output estimated on the basis of Okuns' law not only reflects the direct impact of increased unemployment, but other labour market developments that arise during periods of demand deficiency (as in an economic recession), including shorter working weeks, a reduced labour force participation and lower labour productivity. The loss of national output estimated on the basis of Okuns' Law is possibly excessive – but there is no escaping the reality that unemployment does produce a significant economic cost.

Social costs

These costs of unemployment arise in terms of the personal or psychological cost faced by unemployed workers and their families. These social costs will be particularly severe as the time out of work extends. The long-term unemployed are likely to lose job skills and self-esteem as time passes and may suffer from bouts of stress.

The economic and social costs of unemployment will be offset, to some extent, if unemployed workers take up economically productive activities, such as acquiring new skills. The acquisition of new skills represents an investment in human capital and should lead to an offsetting increased output in the future. Of course, we should not forget the fact that unemployment also provides the unemployed with more time for leisure activities! This time may be spent visiting friends, looking after children, working around the house, and so on. The benefits of these leisure activities must be weighed against the economic and social costs associated with unemployment – although they are unlikely to represent full compensation for most individuals.

Unemployment and hysteresis

A particular cost has been identified by economists in the context of countries which have experienced persistently high rates of unemployment over many years. Such countries also tend to report high levels of *long-term* unemployment. Examples are often associated with particular countries in the European Union, such as France, Italy, Spain and Portugal. These countries are often described as suffering from the problem of *hysteresis* (from the Greek word which means 'to be behind'). The problem arises because prolonged periods of unemployment can make people less employable – they lose the technical and social skills needed to work efficiently. In addition, countries experiencing hysteresis are likely to suffer a decline in capital formation and technological development can be expected to lag behind as a result. Job opportunities will become even more scarce when policies to stimulate the economy are put into effect. Consequently, the natural rate of unemployment will rise over time.

> *Hysteresis* means that the natural rate of unemployment depends on the actual rate of unemployment, *rising* if the actual rate is *above* the current natural rate and *falling* if the actual rate is *below* the current natural rate.

A situation of hysteresis can, however, be reversed by boosting productivity growth.

Application 12.2

Unemployment in the USA, Ireland and Japan

The following are short commentaries on unemployment in three countries.

The USA

In the USA the February unemployment figures caused a surge on the Wall Street stock exchange. The Dow Jones index rose by 268 points after it was revealed that unemployment increased slightly from 4.3 per cent to 4.4 per cent. Some 15,000 jobs were lost in the clothing industry, the automobile industry lost 8,000 jobs, 6,000 jobs went in the aircraft industry, the metals sector lost 6,000 jobs and 7,000 jobs went in the industrial machinery sector.

The financial markets in the USA were pleased that unemployment had risen.

Ireland

Unemployment in Ireland fell in February. The Live Register figure for unemployment was 207,600 – just under 7 per cent of the labour force. Enterprise Trade and Employment Minister Mary Harney welcomed the figures. Harney said the next push would be to get unemployment below the 5 per cent level.

What sort of wages and quality of jobs were obtained by those who left the Live Register is not clear. The Irish National Organisation of the Unemployed (INOU) believes that many of the people who left the register have been put onto government employment schemes and are therefore not really employed.

Japan

In Japan unemployment has risen to its highest level in 50 years. The percentage of the labour force without jobs has risen to 4.3 per cent; 2.98 million people are without work. The Japanese government is implementing a package to pull its economy out of recession.

Activity

1. Explain why the financial markets in the USA might be happy to see higher unemployment? Will this always be true?
2. Do government employment schemes, as in Ireland, simply mask the true employment rate or can they be economically beneficial?
3. What sort of 'package' could the Japanese government implement 'to pull its economy out of recession'?

Concluding remarks

In this chapter we have discussed the important subjects of employment and unemployment. As we have seen, the maximisation of real GDP depends upon full utilisation of the potential workforce. However, we have had cause to distinguish between the potential workforce, which is dependent upon demographics, and the actual workplace, which depends upon the desire to work. This led to the distinction being made between voluntary and involuntary unemployment. We have also noted that unemployment can be categorised into different types with different policy prescriptions, namely frictional, structural, classical and demand-deficient unemployment. Although full employment is a laudable goal, true full employment is unlikely ever to occur because economies and therefore their labour markets are constantly adjusting in response to demand and supply changes. The concepts of the natural rate of unemployment and the non-accelerating-inflation rate of unemployment (NAIRU) have been introduced to identify the unemployment rate that will occur when the labour market is in equilibrium.

Finally, the chapter has considered the economic and social costs of unemployment, including the concept of hysteresis. Long periods of unemployment may lead to higher natural rates of unemployment.

Key learning points

- The *potential workforce*, while less than the population, is usually higher than the actual workforce.
- The *unemployment rate* expresses the number of people unemployed as a percentage of the potential workforce.
- Unemployment can be measured using a survey method, e.g. Labour Force Survey, or through a claimant count (a count of the numbers claiming unemployment benefits from government).
- The *rate of unemployment* depends upon the demand for labour by employers or job availability and the supply of labour seeking work.
- Unemployment is usually divided by economists into different types, namely: *frictional* unemployment, *structural* unemployment, *classical* unemployment and *demand-deficient* unemployment.
- Each type of unemployment requires its own set of policy responses; for example, while Keynesian techniques may be appropriate for tackling demand-deficient unemployment (cyclical and general), they are not appropriate for tackling the other types.
- Under conditions of *classical unemployment*, the appropriate policy response is a direct reduction in real wage rates (w/p) to price people into jobs.
- *Frictional unemployment* is best tackled using policies to help people switch jobs quickly and without experiencing long periods out of work.

- *Structural* (including regional) *unemployment* requires policy responses targeted at the industry (or regional) level (e.g. retraining programmes).
- The *natural rate of unemployment* is that level of unemployment which occurs when the demand for labour equals the supply of labour in the labour market, given the existing structure of the labour market. An alternative name for this is the *NAIRU* (*non-accelerating-inflation rate of unemployment*).
- The *costs of unemployment* are both economic and social.
- The concept of *hysteresis* suggests that persistently high rates of unemployment are self-reinforcing because the longer people are out of work the more difficult they find it to be offered work. This leads to a higher natural rate of unemployment in the economy.

? Topics for discussion

1. What do you understand by the term 'full employment'? Is the attainment of full employment necessarily desirable?
2. Distinguish between the terms 'full employment' and the 'natural rate of unemployment'.
3. An economy has an average *national* unemployment level of 4 per cent but an unemployment rate of 12 per cent in its *north-west region*. The government has announced that it intends to cut national taxes and boost spending on the national education system to reduce unemployment in the north-west. Comment on the efficiency of this policy initiative.
4. An economy has high nationwide unemployment. Discuss and critically appraise the government's policy options.
5. What do you understand by the terms: (a) NAIRU and (b) hysteresis?
6. How might cyclical unemployment be tackled?
7. There is evidence of widespread voluntary unemployment. If people prefer leisure to working, should this be of any concern to government?
8. 'All unemployment is voluntary.' Discuss the economic basis for this assertion.
9. How might government best tackle (a) structural unemployment and (b) frictional unemployment?
10. According to a labour force survey the rate of unemployment is 8 per cent. However, according to the claimant count the unemployment rate is 5 per cent. How might this difference in the rate of unemployment be explained? What dilemma does the difference create for government?

Chapter 13

INTERNATIONAL TRADE – THEORY AND POLICY

Aims and learning outcomes

So far we have focused largely on issues and policies relating to the domestic economy. This has involved the measurement of economic activity (national income accounting), the determination of national income, the impact of various policy measures (fiscal, monetary and supply-side policies) upon the performance of the national economy and a discussion of inflation and unemployment. We now consider the impact of external factors upon the economy, thereby widening the analysis and understanding of macroeconomics to include the reasons for and benefits from international trading relationships. The study of international trade has a long tradition within economics. The subject has attracted the attention of the leading economists of the past three centuries and, to a large extent, their work on international economic problems has produced some of the most important tools of analysis used by modern economists. For example, early versions of the *quantity theory of money* (pp.199–202) were developed in the eighteenth century to explain the effects of gold flows linked to foreign trade on the level of domestic prices.

International economics has demanded greater attention from economists and businesses alike as the extent of world economic integration and interdependence has increased. Over the past three decades, the economies of North America, the European countries, Japan and the developing nations have become more and more dependent upon each other as sources of supply (e.g. raw materials) and as markets for goods and services. Inevitably this has meant that governments are less able to formulate national macroeconomic objectives in isolation from the influence of macroeconomic policy in the rest of the world. The links between policies are even more significant in terms of the world's financial and capital markets, as witnessed every day when the reverberations on any one stock market are felt across the globe.

In this chapter, the following issues are covered:

- the law of comparative advantage;
- further arguments for free trade;
- protectionism in international trade, including the main forms of trade restrictions;
- arguments in favour of protectionism;
- gainers and losers from free trade.

The growth of international trade allows each participating national economy to use its resources more efficiently by concentrating production on those activities to which it is best suited and from which it gets the benefits of economies of scale. In this way, international trade raises real incomes in each country in the same way that specialisation in production by an individual or firm or the 'division of labour' generates greater returns. Trade is beneficial in other ways; for example, improvements in technology originating in one country are shared with other countries through trade in goods embodying the technological advances. Such *technology transfer*, which is also associated with the growth of the transnational corporation, is an increasingly important vehicle for economic development across the world.

All firms are affected either directly or indirectly by international trade. The effects of this trade are felt in many forms: competition between firms for global or national market shares, availability of imported raw materials, the price of goods, investment opportunities worldwide, capital availability, employment prospects, and so on. At the same time, these effects themselves are directly influenced by other forces, not least the effect of exchange rates on trade and competitiveness. This chapter provides an overview of international trade theory. In particular, we examine the gains to be obtained from international trade for individual countries and the implications for economic development. In reality, of course, not all countries aspire to *free* trading relationships, in the sense of trading without state interference. Protectionist policies including restricting imports and promoting exports exist, to some degree, in all countries. Over the last 50 years the world has seen a gradual reduction in trade barriers. Conducting international business activities necessitates a clear understanding of the motives for different international trade policies. Hence, in this chapter we examine the arguments for and against both free trade and trade protection.

Learning outcomes

After studying this material you will be able to:

- Understand the main economic arguments for international trade free from state imposed restrictions.
- Appreciate the assumptions that lie behind the 'law of comparative advantage', which is the main economic argument for free trade.
- Recognise the economic advantages that arise from international specialisation in production at the economy level.
- Identify the main ways in which governments might attempt to influence trade patterns.
- Understand the different effects of tariffs and quotas.
- Realise when protectionist measures might have some economic justification.

We begin by explaining in formal terms why most economists believe that substantial economic gains arise from trade between nations.

The law of comparative advantage

Historically, countries began to trade with each other in order to make available to consumers in one country goods that were only produced in other countries. This is an over-simplification of trade today, however, since in practice the vast majority of goods and services traded are produced in many countries across the globe. This suggests that a more fundamental explanation for international trade exists today. The fact is that not all countries produce goods with the same efficiency. This gives rise to the *law of comparative advantage*.

> The *law of comparative advantage* demonstrates that international trade is potentially beneficial to the economic welfare of countries if each country specialises in the production of those goods and services in which it has a comparative advantage (i.e. the greatest *relative* efficiency). The law of comparative advantage is also sometimes referred to as the *law of comparative cost*. It dates back to the early nineteenth century and the writings of David Ricardo, an English economist.

The law of comparative advantage can be readily illustrated by means of a simplified numerical example, highlighting the gains for all countries participating in international trade. While the example is very simple and stylised, it does illustrate the main advantages of international specialisation in production.

Pre-trade situation

Suppose two countries, A and B, both produce and consume two goods, say wheat and cars. Suppose that when both countries use all of their resources efficiently to produce only wheat, country A is able to produce 1,000 tonnes and country B 2,000 tonnes per day. If all resources are switched to car production, both A and B are able to produce 500 cars each per day. This information is shown in Table 13.1.

If we make the simplifying assumptions that factors of production are able to move freely and without cost between the production of wheat and cars within each country and that production of both products can be varied without affecting average costs of production (i.e. constant cost production exists), then the production possibility frontiers facing A and B are as shown in Figure 13.1.

Table 13.1 Pre-trade output levels

	Wheat (tonnes)		*Cars*
Country A	1,000	or	500
Country B	2,000	or	500
Total world output	3,000	or	1,000

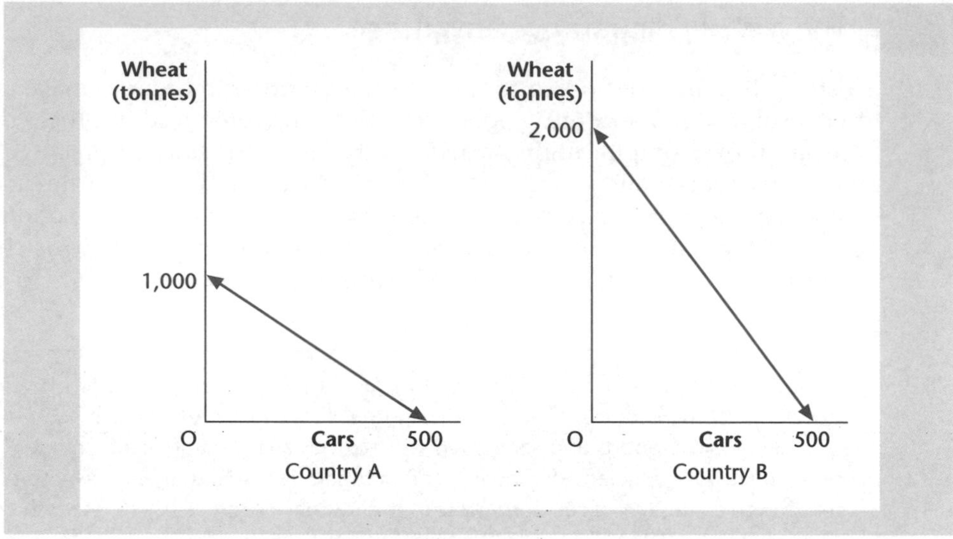

Figure 13.1 Pre-trade production possibility frontiers

Unlike the production possibility curve shown in Figure 1.2 (p.9), it will be observed that the curves here are represented as straight lines. This arises from the assumption of constant cost production, introduced merely to simplify the discussion, whereas in Chapter 1 more realistic diminishing returns are assumed. To examine whether or not there will be any gains for both countries from trading with each other, we must consider each country's *opportunity cost of production*, i.e. what it forgoes by producing more of one of the goods and less of the other.

In the case of A, resources can be used to produce either 1,000 tonnes of wheat or 500 cars. Thus, the opportunity cost of producing one extra tonne of wheat is 0.5 of a car. Similarly for B, 2,000 tonnes of wheat or 500 cars can be produced so that the opportunity cost of producing one extra tonne of wheat is 0.25 of a car. It is clear that country B is able to produce wheat at a lower *real* resource cost (in terms of cars) than country A. Therefore country B is said to have a *comparative advantage* in wheat production. Conversely, if A produces one more car, the opportunity cost is 2 tonnes of wheat, while in the case of B it is 4 tonnes. Thus, A is said to have a comparative advantage in car production.

Now let us assume initially that resources are divided equally to produce both wheat and cars, giving the outputs in each country as shown in Table 13.2 – with, as yet, no trade taking place between the countries.

Table 13.2 Pre-trade output levels without specialisation of production

	Wheat (tonnes)		*Cars*
Country A	500	and	250
Country B	1,000	and	250
Total world output	1,500	and	500

Table 13.3 Pre-trade output levels with specialisation of production*

	Wheat (tonnes)	*Cars*
Country A	0	500
Country B	2,000	0
Total world output	2,000	500

*With country A specialising in car production and country B in wheat production, based on the law of comparative advantage.

Suppose now that an agreement to establish trading links is reached. Under what international *terms of trade* will it be beneficial for both countries to agree to this trading link? In other words, what would have to be the exchange rate of wheat for cars to entice both countries to specialise in production, according to the law of comparative advantage, and trade with each other to meet their consumption needs? Since for country A the opportunity cost of producing 1 car is 2 tonnes of wheat, then presumably it will be happy to produce cars and exchange these for wheat provided the international terms of trade exceed 2 tonnes of wheat for 1 car, i.e. provided A gets at least 2 tonnes of wheat for each car it sells. For B, the opportunity cost of producing 1 tonne of wheat is 0.25 of a car. Hence, presumably B will be happy to produce wheat and exchange it for cars as long as the international terms of trade are less than 4 tonnes of wheat per car, i.e. provided the purchase of each car from A costs B less than 4 tonnes of wheat. If both countries agree to terms of trade of, say, 3 tonnes of wheat per car, then both will gain by specialising and trading. The outputs under specialisation, before trade takes place, are as shown in Table 13.3.

Post-trade situation

It should be noted that, comparing Tables 13.2 and 13.3, the total output of wheat from A and B combined ('world output') has increased by 500 tonnes with car production unchanged, hence there has been a net gain in 'world' output from countries A and B specialising in production according to comparative advantage, implying a higher economic welfare internationally. If A now exports 250 cars to B at an exchange rate of 1 car = 3 tonnes of wheat, then the two countries will be able to enjoy the consumption of the amounts of both goods as shown in Table 13.4.

Table 13.4 Pattern of consumption after trade*

	Wheat (tonnes)		*Cars*
Country A	750	and	250
Country B	1,250	and	250
Total world consumption	2,000	and	500

*Terms of trade: 1 car = 3 tonnes of wheat.

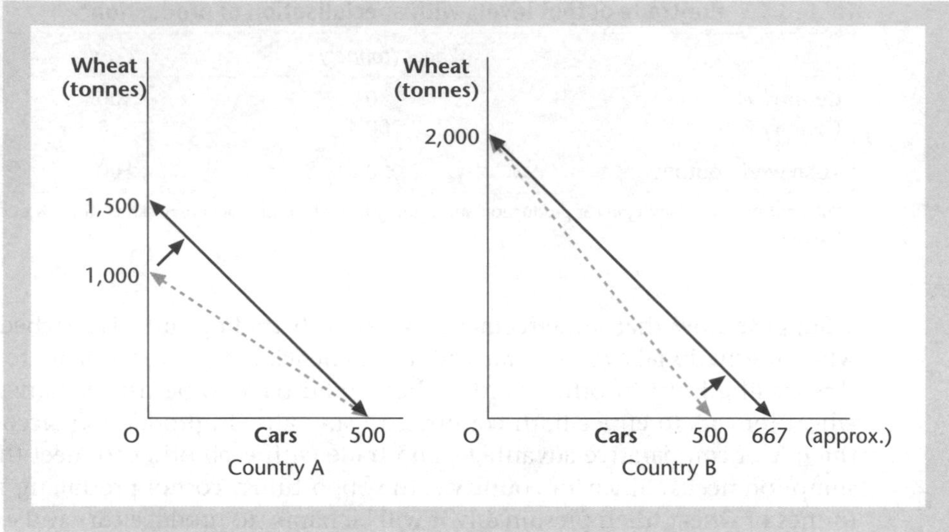

Figure 13.2 Gains from trade – post-trade production possibility frontiers

Compared with the pre-specialisation and pre-trade position shown in Table 13.2, both countries have gained in terms of additional consumption – A and B each have 250 tonnes more wheat and the same number of cars. Hence, there is a larger world output and a rise in economic welfare, as reflected in higher consumption of wheat in both of the countries. There has been an economic gain from international specialisation in production and free trade between countries. This is the central conclusion of the law of comparative advantage.

The gains from trading can also be demonstrated by redrawing the production possibility curves shown in Figure 13.1. These are shown in Figure 13.2. It will be seen that in both countries the curves have pivoted outwards following specialisation according to the law of comparative advantage, representing a gain in welfare. These frontier curves, as before, are drawn on the basis of the amount of wheat *or* the number of cars produced and consumed if specialisation of production and trade takes place. For example, the 500 cars produced by A are equivalent to 1,500 tonnes of wheat (with terms of trade of 1 car = 3 tonnes), while the 2,000 tonnes of wheat produced by B are equivalent to about 667 cars.

Relative and absolute advantage

Obviously, this example, which has been used to illustrate the law (or principle) of comparative advantage and the gains from trade, has been greatly simplified – for example we have ignored transport costs. Nevertheless, it provides a useful insight into why countries should specialise in production and trade. This applies even when some countries are more efficient in *absolute* terms in producing every type of good. In our example country B is superior to A at producing wheat and has the same efficiency in producing cars (see Table 13.2). Even had country B

Table 13.5 Changing the terms of trade*

	Wheat (tonnes)		*Cars*
Country A	625	and	250
Country B	1,375	and	250
Total world consumption	2,000	and	500

*Terms of trade: 1 car = 2.5 tonnes of wheat. Based on a revised production of wheat and cars in B (1,000 tonnes of wheat and 333 cars) prior to specialisation and trade.

been able to produce say, 333 cars rather than 250, it would have paid B to specialise in the production of wheat and purchase its cars from country A. This is so provided that the terms of trade are now less than 1 car equals 3 tonnes of wheat (rather than 4, as previously). For B the opportunity cost of producing 1 tonne of wheat is now 0.333 of a car. The opportunity cost to A of producing cars is, of course, unaffected. Hence, the terms of trade would now need to lie between 1 car equals 3 tonnes of wheat and 1 car equals 2 tonnes of wheat. With a terms of trade of 1 car equals 2.5 tonnes of wheat, the result of specialisation and trade would be as in Table 13.5.

Country A has clearly gained from trade because it now has the same number of cars to consume and more wheat (625 tonnes, as against 500 tonnes). Country B has more wheat to consume (1,375 tonnes, as against 1,000 tonnes) but a lower number of cars (250, as against 333). However, the loss of 83 cars consumed is equivalent to 249 tonnes of wheat given B's internal opportunity costs of production of 1 tonne of wheat = 0.333 of a car. The gain in wheat consumption is greater than 249 tonnes, namely 375 tonnes, confirming that B too has benefited in terms of economic welfare from trade and specialisation. Hence, although B has an absolute advantage in producing both wheat and cars compared to country A, it still pays B to specialise in the output in which it has a *competitive*, or *relative*, advantage and import the other product.

The message is, therefore, that countries should specialise in producing those goods in which they have a *comparative advantage* and trade. In addition, the law of comparative advantage supports 'free trade', i.e. trade without government restrictions on imports or exports. If import controls (see below) existed then this might prevent A or B, or both, from specialising and trading fully to their mutual advantage. Free trade combined with specialisation in production results in an increase in the world's output, arising from the more efficient use of the world's resources. This in turn has important consequences for economic development and business expansion.

Further arguments for free trade

The law of comparative advantage, as outlined above, is the central argument used by economists in support of free trading relationships between countries. There are, however, other, supportive arguments for international trade that we need to bear in mind, namely:

- *Economies of scale in production:* International trade, by creating larger markets for goods and services, benefits business through economies of scale in production. In our example above, to keep the arithmetic simple, we assumed constant cost production. In practice, we would expect specialisation in production to lead to economies of large-scale production, producing even greater gains from specialisation and trade.
- *Competition and product differentiation:* International trade increases competition between producers, thereby helping to ensure that markets are not dominated by any single producer, that production costs are minimised and that consumers get the best possible deal, not only in terms of price but also in terms of choice (e.g. product differentiation).
- *Efficient allocation of resources:* International trade leads to the development of international capital flows and encourages a more efficient allocation of investment funds internationally.
- *International co-operation:* International trading links are likely to foster greater economic and political co-operation between nations with implications for world economic growth, peace and stability.

Protectionism in international trade

Although the arguments in favour of free international trading relationships are powerful, countries sometimes adopt measures to restrict international trade. In this section we describe the most common forms of trade barrier and assess the arguments that have been put forward in favour of protecting domestic industries from imports and providing some sort of state assistance, either directly or indirectly, to exporters.

Trade restrictions can be applied by governments in a variety of ways, some of which may be openly identified while others may be 'hidden'. Restrictions are categorised as follows:

- embargoes on imports;
- quotas on imports;
- tariffs or customs duties;
- other import restrictions;
- subsidies;
- exchange controls;
- exchange rate policy.

We describe each of these briefly in turn.

Embargoes on imports

These are the most extreme forms of restriction on international trade, representing a total ban on the importation of certain types of goods or all goods from a particular country. The motives are often political or linked to international politics, for example, as in the case of the international trading restrictions imposed on Iraq by the United Nations after the 1991 Gulf War. From an economic viewpoint, embargoes deprive consumers of choice and lower prices and domestic industry ends up paying more for its raw materials and components. The principle of trade according to the law of comparative advantage is undermined and the overall result is likely to be a lower rate of world economic development.

Quotas on imports

These are *volume* restrictions on imports whereby specific limits are set on the quantity of particular products than can be imported from one or more countries. However, while the immediate effect is to limit the volume of imported goods, domestic consumers face a limited supply which, if demand is strong, tends to force up the price of the affected imports (and domestic substitutes), resulting in both higher profits for the producer or seller and lower consumer welfare. This has indeed been the experience in the past with imported Japanese cars sold in Europe affected by 'voluntary' quotas (see below) with distributors often in the position of being able to sell at full retail price with little or no discount to customers. Similarly, US restrictions on microchip imports from Japan in the late 1980s served mainly to support the profit margins of the Japanese producers. American computer manufacturers lost out through higher prices for a basic component.

Tariffs or customs duties

These are taxes on imported goods which have the effect of *directly raising the selling price* to the domestic consumer with the tariff revenue going to the government. Note, in contrast, that under quotas the restricted supply of imported goods leads to higher prices and hence higher profits to the producers or sellers of the goods. Tariffs may be *specific* (i.e. lump sum) in nature, or *ad valorem* (i.e. proportional to the value of the good). As with quotas, they can be applied to individual goods from individual countries or they can be applied more generally. The aim of tariffs is to discourage domestic residents from consuming particular imported goods by raising their price (although from the government's standpoint, the additional tax revenue may be an added incentive for their use). In the sense that consumers can still buy imports even though they are more expensive because of the tariffs, tariffs are less distortionary of trade than quotas. Quotas are restrictions on the volume of imports and therefore prevent consumers from having access to the goods.

The effect of imposing tariffs on the domestic economy is illustrated in Figure 13.3. The curve *D* represents the demand for cars in the domestic market, *S* represents the supply curve for cars produced domestically and *P* is the 'world price' of cars (i.e. the price at which cars can be imported from other countries). Under free trade, *P* will be the prevailing price in the domestic market as a result of competitive pressures. At this price, quantity Q_0 cars will be produced domestically, domestic consumption (demand) will be Q_3 and $Q_3 - Q_0$ will be imported.

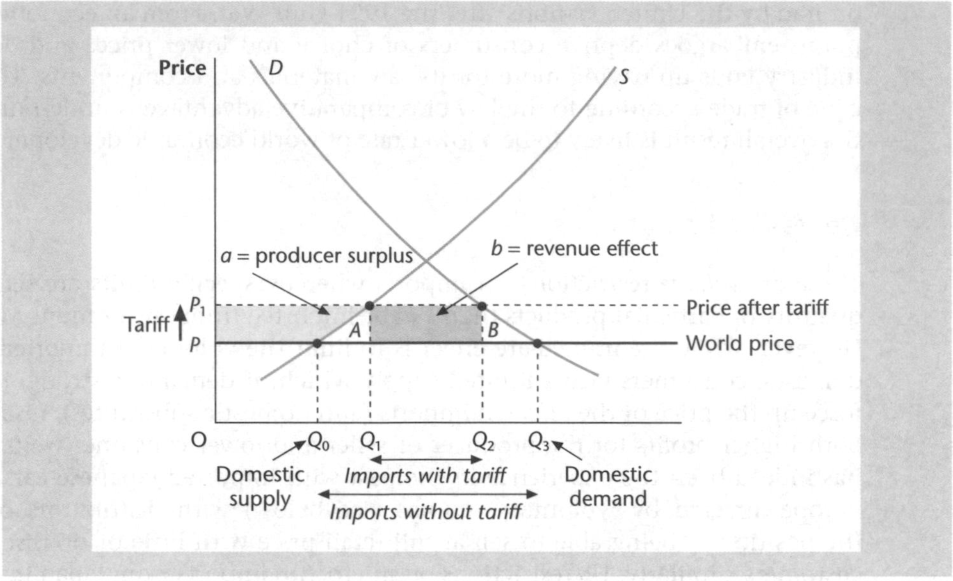

Figure 13.3 Effects of a tariff

Now suppose that the domestic authorities impose a specific tariff duty of PP_1 on each car. Importers must now pay the world price *plus* the tariff and will have to sell cars at the higher price of P_1. At this price, domestic demand will fall from Q_3 to Q_2, while domestic production will rise from Q_0 to Q_1 – this was presumably the point of levying the tariff. With higher domestic car production but lower domestic demand, imports will fall to $Q_2 - Q_1$, as shown.

Note that the elasticity (i.e. responsiveness) of the demand and supply curves will be critical in determining by how much a tariff will reduce imports. If demand and supply are inelastic, a tariff will have a fairly small effect on import volumes.

Who gains and who loses from the implication of this tariff? The direct effects are as follows:

- *Revenue effect:* There will be an increase in customs (tariff) receipts to the government equal to the shaded area *b* in Figure 13.3 (i.e. Q_1Q_2 units of imports times the PP_1 tax per unit). This is not of course a net gain from a national standpoint, since this tariff revenue is being paid by domestic buyers of cars.
- *Protective effect*: The increase in domestic production from Q_0 to Q_1 offers protection to some domestic firms who would not have been able to compete at the lower world price, *P*, but are now able to cover costs and survive at the higher price, P_1.
- *Consumption effect*: There is a reduction in domestic demand for cars from Q_3 to Q_2.
- *Redistribution effect*: There has been a transfer of income from consumers to companies as a result of the tariff. The marginal producer, located at Q_1, has

production costs that are just covered by P_1, and is only just able to survive with the tariff protection. But every other firm in the domestic industry is receiving more than needed to cover production costs (including a *normal profit*). The increased profit represents a transfer of *consumer surplus* into *producer surplus* (i.e. extra profit), shown by the shaded area *a* in Figure 13.3.

- *Export effect*: There is likely to be an export effect since the imposition of the tariff is likely to lead to retaliatory measures by other countries in the form of higher duties on the domestic country's exports – thereby depressing exports eventually.

Assuming the tariff is passed on in the form of higher prices to domestic buyers and demand is elastic, the consequence of the tariff will be that:

- domestic consumers buy fewer cars;
- domestic producers supply more cars to the market;
- foreign suppliers provide less cars to the market;
- the government earns some tax revenue.

However, to ascertain the *net welfare effect* of the tariff, we need to deduct the gain to producers and government from the loss to consumers. When we do this we are left with the triangles *A* and *B* in Figure 13.3. These two areas combined represent the *deadweight loss* to welfare from the tariff. Effectively area *A* is a deadweight loss from (inefficient) overproduction of domestic cars in place of cheaper imported cars and *B* is a deadweight loss resulting from the higher price of cars after the tariff, leading to a lower domestic demand for cars. It should be clear that the larger the tariff, the larger will be the deadweight welfare loss.

Other import restrictions

Apart from tariffs and quotas, governments may restrict the flow of certain imports by imposing a whole range of complex import regulations and import documentation requirements. Excessively high safety standards may be demanded of imported goods or just sheer bureaucracy may be used to slow down the volume of goods coming into the country. For example, exporters to Japan in the 1980s criticised the Japanese authorities for what were believed to be unnecessary delays in processing import documentation. Both the USA and the EU have been criticised for adopting product health and safety standards designed, at least in part, to assist their domestic producers against imports, for example EU restrictions on imports from the USA of genetically modified crop products.

During difficult trading conditions, countries may turn to the use of 'voluntary' import restrictions. Tariffs and quotas often conflict with international trading agreements, notably those introduced by the World Trade Organisation (WTO) and previously under the General Agreement on Tariffs and Trade (GATT) – see Chapter 16 for a discussion of the role of these international institutions. Such agreements exist to extend and protect free trade by ruling against import protection. Voluntary controls on trade subvert the spirit of these agreements without necessarily contravening their terms because they are 'voluntary'. A main victim of these controls in the 1980 and 1990s was Japan, which felt obliged, in the face of its balance of trade surplus with other industrial countries, to accept voluntary curbs on its exports. In particular, and as mentioned above, from the 1970s a voluntary quota applied to the importation of Japanese cars into the EU. This effectively limited the share of all Japanese manufacturers in much of the EU car market. One result was that Japanese manufacturers, such as Honda, Nissan and Toyota, built plants within the EU to circumvent such restrictions.

Subsidies

By subsidising the production of goods for domestic consumption as well as goods for export, governments attempt to maintain or increase the competitive position of domestic firms in the international marketplace. Subsidies may be clearly identified (e.g. government regional development grants and other investment incentives) or they may be more hidden (such as relaxed tax regulation for export producers). Exporters may be supported by government-backed guarantees against bad debts for overseas sales and may even receive direct financial assistance to export. Such forms of subsidy ultimately help to lower the price of goods produced by domestic firms (although at a cost to taxpayers) and hence reduce competition from imports and assist exports. This only applies, however, provided other countries do not adopt similar and offsetting trade practices. Often, in fact, they do. One outcome – and this applies to the use of tariffs and quotas too – is 'tit-for-tat' or 'beggar-my-neighbour' policies, which counter -balance each other, leaving no country at a particular net advantage in trading terms but with international specialisation and economic welfare damaged.

Exchange controls

Governments may exercise control over the importation of certain commodities by imposing exchange control regulations. For example, exchange controls may limit the use of a country's foreign currency reserves to the importation of 'essential' goods and services only, thereby, in effect, blocking the importation of 'luxury' or non-essential goods (this policy is commonly adopted by developing countries to economise on the use of foreign currency reserves). Exchange controls may also be implemented as an emergency measure in order to stem a sudden outflow of investment capital from a country, as in the case of Malaysia following the 1997 Asian financial crisis.

Exchange rate policy

Perhaps less obvious than the methods above, a government may attempt to influence trade flows by devaluing the currency, thereby making imports more expensive in domestic markets, while making its exports more attractive to foreigners. Such a policy is described as a *competitive devaluation*. Clearly, the extent to which the policy will be successful in stemming the flow of imports and boosting exports depends, among other things, on the sensitivity of, or more correctly the *elasticity of demand* for exports and imports to changes in their price and the extent to which the devaluation is unilateral. If two countries devalue their currencies by the same amount against each other, relative prices will remain unchanged. At the same time, the rise in the domestic price of imports can be expected to have an adverse effect on domestic production costs because imported raw materials and components cost more. This may lead to a rise in the general rate of inflation in an economy and, over time, lowered price competitiveness. The role of exchange rates in international trade is pursued further in the next chapter.

To complete our discussion of trade restrictions, it is important to note the significance of the *most favoured nation principle* (see Box 13.1).

Box 13.1

The most favoured nation (MFN) principle

Whenever import and export controls are applied, they can be applied against just one or a few named countries or all countries equally. Similarly, when a government reduces its economy's trade barriers, this may be done to favour imports from named countries or all countries. The *most favoured nation (MFN) principle* in foreign trade states that restrictions on foreign trade should be applied equally across countries so as to minimise trade distortions. However, in many parts of the world – an obvious example is the EU where there is internal free trade but some protectionist barriers to imports from outside the member states – the principle is not fully applied. In Chapter 16 we look at some examples of free trade areas and what are sometimes referred to as 'customs unions'.

Application 13.1

Agricultural protection and free trade

Read the following extract:

> The European Union must shortly decide on how to reform the Common Agricultural Policy. We must choose between continuing to support our farmers in a way which distorts global trade and helping our farmers to create a modern and sustainable future for EU agriculture. From a development perspective, it means we must decide whether we want to offer a fairer deal to developing countries. EU reform of its Common Agricultural Policy (CAP) is essential to meet the needs of a modern society. CAP reform does not mean the end of the

Application 13.1 continued

sort of high-quality national food production of which many EU member states are rightly proud. The European Commission's proposals for reform will not endanger quality production. By linking payments to farmers to environmental standards and rural development – rather than simply rewarding them for quantity of production – reform should actually improve quality. After all, quantity does not always mean quality.

Today, over a billion people live in abject poverty. Few of their countries have the opportunities they need to grow their economies and trade their way out of poverty. The OECD spends $310bn every year to support its agriculture sector. This often leads to overproduction which again requires funding for export subsidisation from taxpayers and higher prices for consumers. OECD countries' support for their farmers is approximately equivalent to the whole of sub-Saharan Africa's GDP.

Poor countries pay dearly for this protectionism. Africa's share of world trade has nearly halved from 4.4 per cent in 1983 to 2.3 per cent in 2000. We must tackle this in order to maintain progress towards the 2015 Millennium Development Goals. Multilateral trade liberalisation is indispensable for development: it provides countries with increased opportunities to trade, generating income and employment. It also contributes to higher economic growth, greater stimulus to domestic reforms and, therefore, faster poverty reduction.

Source: Edited extract from Baroness Amos (2003) 'Why are we waiting?', *Developments: The International Development Magazine*, Issue 22, published by the Department for International Development, London.

Activity

In the light of your understanding of the law of comparative advantage, set out the economic argument against the protection of European farmers from cheap food imports.

Arguments in favour of protectionism

In spite of the clear economic advantage of free trade, there are arguments sometimes put forward in favour of protecting domestic producers and exporters. They generally fall under one of the following headings:

- protection of infant industries;
- protection against 'unfair' competition;
- support for declining industries;
- support for strategic industries;
- retaliation;
- correction of balance of payments problems.

It should be appreciated, however, that the forces pressing for protectionism at any given time – namely, affected firms, investors and their employees – are more likely to be motivated by self-interest than the public interest. At the same time, consumers who lose out from protectionism, through restricted choice and higher prices, are usually less well organised and vocal. Protectionism can therefore increase because of the power of vested interests – vested interests who attempt to veil their self-seeking actions by justifying their case using the arguments below.

Protection of infant industries

It is sometimes argued that industries in the early stages of development – referred to as 'infant' or 'sunrise' industries – need protection from competition in order that they can grow to a stage at which they achieve economies of scale and can compete on equal terms. This type of argument is generally accepted by economists as a valid reason for some of the restrictive measures described above, especially for new industries in developing economies. There is, however, a real danger that protecting infant industries makes them over-reliant on state support, leading to sluggishness and inefficiency. Hence, the protection becomes permanent and the infant industry never matures. Equally, industries may be established behind tariff walls in countries where they have no long-term comparative advantage. Consequently, economic development becomes distorted and scarce resources are wasted.

Protection against 'unfair' competition

Producers often complain about unfair competition from firms in low-cost labour countries or because of subsidies granted to foreign producers by their governments. One particular form of 'unfair competition' that attracts much hostile comment from producers involves *dumping,* defined as the selling of goods abroad at 'uneconomically low' prices or below their production costs. For example, from time to time both the USA and the EU have introduced import duties on what they have called 'dumped' steel imports to protect their own steel producers.

Dumping results in domestic consumers paying lower prices for the goods that are being imported and in this sense 'dumping' actually benefits consumer welfare ('consumer surplus') in the countries affected by it. However, this benefit needs to be weighed against the loss of jobs in domestic industries unable to compete with these lower prices. In other words, consumers gain but some producers and their employees lose out. Therefore, the issue of dumping, like the issue of importing from cheap labour sources, largely becomes a question of balancing the effects on domestic employment with the effects on domestic prices. In practice, this involves not simply a dispassionate economic evaluation of costs and benefits, but politicians deciding whether or not protectionist measures are politically and socially necessary. It should also be appreciated that, from an economic perspective, cheap labour countries *should* specialise in producing goods which need abundant low-cost labour, for that is where their comparative advantage lies. This may be bad news, for example, for the textile industry in Western Europe and North America as they face competition from low-cost labour economies such as India and China, but the resources tied up in this industry would probably earn a higher return utilised in the production of other goods and services.

Support for declining industries

Just as a rationale for protectionist measures is support for newly-established industries, so protection is also sometimes proposed to ease the burden associated with 'declining' industries (such as steel, shipbuilding and textiles in the EU and North America). These are often referred to as 'sunset' industries. Most economists would argue, however, that protection in these circumstances should be avoided or, if used, should be short-lived – otherwise the trade protection arrests the decline of no longer competitive industries and the reallocation of economic resources to more productive uses, in accordance with changes in comparative cost advantages in production. Also, protection reduces the incentive for firms to restructure and become more efficient to survive. Arguably, if adopted, protection should be directed at easing the burden of adjustment associated with unemployment (especially regionally-concentrated unemployment), while assisting the switching of resources into new industries and skills over a longer period of time.

Support for strategic industries

Certain industries, such as defence and aerospace, may be classified as being of strategic importance from a military perspective. Also, certain high-tech industries are sometimes classified as strategic because they are perceived to be of long-term importance to a country's economic development. Consequently, protectionist measures may be adopted to safeguard the future of such industries even if there are no immediate short-term benefits to be derived. This argument, however, contains many dangers, not least who decides what is a strategically important industry? In the early 1970s, UK toy producers reputedly called for protection from imports citing strategic arguments. They argued that the industry's production processes could be readily switched to munitions in wartime. Perhaps not surprisingly, the government was unimpressed! Moreover, if an industry really is vital to a country's economic development, it would surely be expected to flourish in a free market.

Retaliation

An obvious argument in support of protectionism is that of retaliation against protectionist measures imposed by another country. The danger here, however, is a rapid escalation of protectionism on such a scale that world trade is curtailed – with severe consequences for world economic development. It would be much better if the countries concerned could find a way of dismantling the existing protectionist barriers rather than adopting self-defeating, retaliatory measures.

Correction of balance of payments problems

Protectionist policies are often seen as a quick and easy means for a country to reduce an imbalance between exports and imports or its balance of trade deficit. Trade embargoes and quotas will be immediate in their effect. Tariffs and currency devaluation also affect trade flows, although they are likely to take more time to affect the pattern of demand for imports and exports because they act through relative price changes. The ultimate success of such measures will be dependent on the responsiveness of demand to changes in relative prices, an issue we take up in the following chapter. Again, affecting imports and exports through protectionist measures risks retaliatory action by other countries. Moreover, all of the above arguments for trade protection need to be weighed against the economic advantages that result from specialisation of production, as set out in the law of comparative advantage reviewed at the start of this chapter.

Application 13.2

The World Bank and free trade

The World Bank's 2003 annual report on global economic prospects argued that cutting agricultural and industrial tariffs to a maximum of 10 per cent in developed countries and 15 per cent in developing ones could increase incomes by almost $350bn in the former economies and $170bn in the latter by 2015. If services were also liberalised, controls on the movement of skilled labour relaxed and customs controls simplified, even bigger economic gains would result. The World Bank also argued that developing countries, and especially middle-income ones, impeded their own economic growth through trade protection and should take the lead in removing trade barriers.

The figure below shows the World Bank's forecasts for economic growth in the high-income economies and the developing world. Within the latter grouping, the fastest growth, of around 6.7 per cent per annum, is predicted for south-east Asia and the Pacific region.

Malaysia: an example

Malaysia has adopted a fairly liberal trade policy since it embarked on its export-oriented industrialisation in the late 1960s. Nevertheless, it is a good example of

Application 13.2 continued

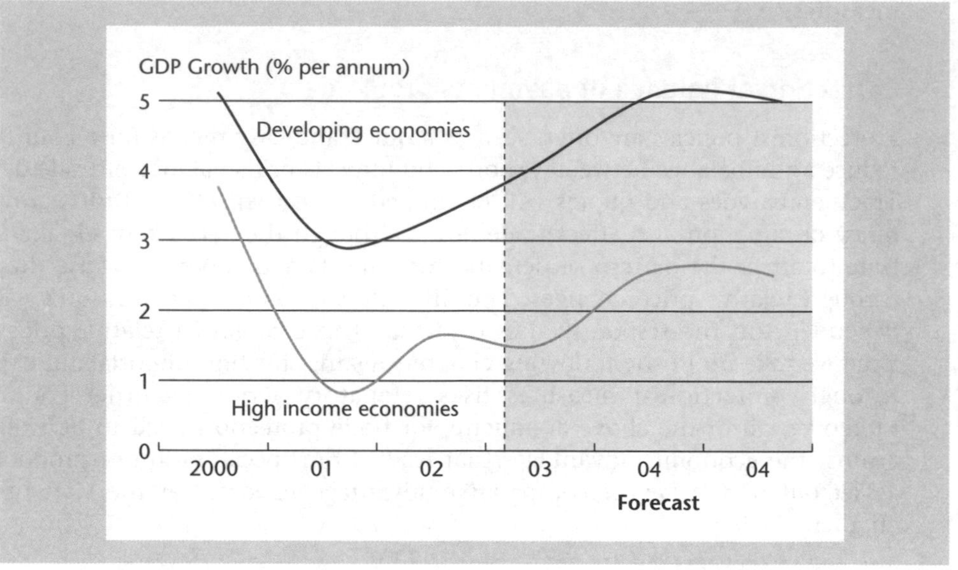

Gradual recovery from the global downturn

Source: World Bank data and projections

a middle-income country that continues with the trade protection which the World Bank criticises in its 2003 report. High import duties exist for a number of industries on 'infant industry' grounds; for example, heavy industries such as automobiles, steel and cement. The two national automobile companies – Perusahaan Otomobil Nasional Bhd (Proton) and Perusahaan Otomobil Kedua Sdn Bhd – maintain a market share of 75 per cent within Malaysia. This is largely due to tariffs of between 42 per cent and 300 per cent on imported vehicles.

Activity

Why do you think the World Bank promotes free trade as part of its economic development strategy for low and middle-income economies? Why might some governments disagree and prefer to retain import controls?

Gainers and losers from free trade

Throughout this chapter we have recognised that free trade, while beneficial overall, does create 'losers'. Losers include workers in domestic industries damaged by imports, who lose their jobs, and investors in these same firms, who see profits

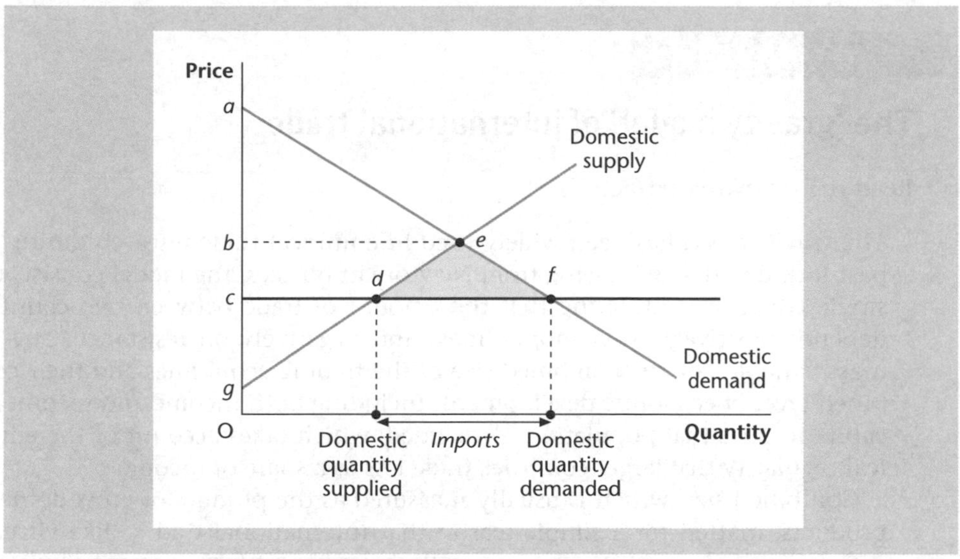

Figure 13.4 Welfare gains and losses from free trade

reduced because of lower-priced imports. Gainers are consumers who can now buy goods and services at lower prices. We illustrate this result in Figure 13.4. Assume one good is traded, then without free trade its price would be at the level determined by the intersection of the domestic supply and demand curves. With international trade, more of the good is supplied into the domestic market by importers. The result is that the price falls to the level in the rest of the world ('the world price'), ignoring transport and other transaction costs. The result is a fall in domestic supply with the difference between domestic demand and domestic supply met by imports.

The fall in price leads to a rise in consumer welfare ('consumer surplus') from *abe* before trade to *acf* after trade. By contrast, the welfare of producers ('producer surplus') declines, from *beg* before trade to *cdg* after trading. However, if we compare the gain in consumer welfare with the loss of producer welfare, we record a net gain. The loss of producer surplus is the area *bedc*, while the gain in consumer surplus is the area *befc*. Free trade has, therefore, led to a rise in net economic welfare equivalent to the shaded triangle *efd*. In principle, consumers could compensate those workers and investors who are losers and still retain a net welfare gain. In practice, of course, there is no guarantee that this compensation will be paid. This is a matter for government fiscal and welfare policies.

Application 13.3

The 'gravity model' of international trade

Read the following extract:

> The *gravity model* has been widely used in empirical trade research during the past four decades. Borrowing from Newtonian physics, the model consists of a single equation postulating that the amount of trade between two countries depends positively on economic mass and negatively on resistance. The key mass variables are the combined size of the trading economies and their combined level of economic development. Including both income and income per capita implies that population is included, which takes account of the empirical regularity that larger countries trade less as a share of income.
>
> Combined size, which is usually measured as the product of gross domestic products, matters for a simple reason that international trade – like virtually any other economic activity – generally increases with the overall size of the economy. The combined level of development, which is usually measured as the product of incomes per capita, is included because bilateral trade tends to rise more than proportionally as economies get richer. In particular, the demand for variety – goods that differ slightly in design, materials or technology – increases with income, which leads to two-way or intra-industry trade in similar goods because the production of differentiated goods remains specialised, reflecting increasing returns to scale.
>
> The main resistance factor in the gravity model is transport costs, which are usually proxied by geographical variables. The primary geographical variable is the absolute distance between the two trading countries, with closely located country-pairs generally trading more than country-pairs that are far apart. Recently, some theoretical models of trade have suggested that relative distance (i.e. the distance between two trading partners relative to the distances between them and other trading partners) matters more than absolute distance. In line with this insight, some recent empirical studies have included relative distance instead of absolute distance, or added a measure of remoteness like the average distance of each trading partner.
>
> Other proxies for transport costs are the number of landlocked countries in a bilateral trade relationship, the surface areas in both economies (both associated with higher transport costs), and the existence of adjacent land borders (which lowers transport costs). In particular, being landlocked is associated with large negative trade effects. Historical and cultural similarities, including colonial links and common language, tend to reduce cross-border search and communications costs because of familiarity with customs, institutions, and legal systems, thus facilitating trade.
>
> Besides the 'natural' frictions, there are artificial – especially policy-related – frictions. Most obvious among these are trade policies, including tariffs, quotas

Application 13.3 continued

and regional preferential trade agreements. Other important policy barriers are exchange and capital controls, which affect trade through a variety of channels, including the domestic price of imports and transaction costs.

The gravity model has proven to be highly successful in explaining bilateral trade flows. Its popularity has been enhanced by research showing that the gravity equation can be derived from some simple theoretical models of trade.

Source: Extract from IMF, *World Economic Outlook*, September 2002, p.122.

Activity

The growth of trade blocs is an important development in international relations. What insights does the gravity model offer in assessing the implications of this development?

Concluding remarks

This chapter has been concerned with the economic rationale for countries specialising and freely trading to meet their consumption needs. The law of comparative advantage is the centre piece of this rationale. The law, which dates back to the early nineteenth century and the writings of the English economist David Ricardo, explains how, when countries specialise and trade according to their comparative cost advantage, economic welfare is raised. Whereas it is obvious why a country imports goods it cannot produce itself or could only produce with great difficulty (e.g. Scandinavian countries and the supply of oranges and lemons), the law of comparative cost identifies that countries should import all goods (and services) in which they have a comparative or relative cost disadvantage and pay for these by exporting goods (and services) in which they have a comparative cost advantage.

In spite of the economic rationale for free trade, protectionist measures are widely adopted. In this chapter we have reviewed the main measures used, such as tariffs, quotas and export subsidies, and the main arguments for their use, e.g. the infant (sunrise) industry argument and protecting declining (sunset) industries. The conclusion reached is that while protectionist measures may have a role to play in trade policy from time to time, they should be used cautiously because they distort resource allocation and can reduce long-term economic welfare.

In the next chapter we turn to studying the outcome of international trade as recorded in the balance of payments accounts.

✔ Key learning points

- *International trade* improves international resource allocation and therefore economic welfare by allowing countries to specialise in producing those goods and services in which they have the greatest comparative advantage.
- The *law of comparative advantage* (or comparative cost) establishes the conditions under which specialisation and international trade are advantageous.
- Countries can gain by specialising in producing those goods and services in which they have the greatest relative comparative advantage even if they have an absolute cost advantage in producing all goods traded.
- *Specialisation* in production and free trade (in the sense of free movement of exports and imports between countries) can maximise economic welfare.
- *Protectionist measures* are used by countries and take the form of quota restrictions or restricting the volume of certain imports, tariffs (taxes) on imports, import regulations, export subsidies, exchange rate policy and foreign exchange controls.
- *Import restrictions* raise prices to domestic consumers and reduce consumer choice and thereby reduce *consumer welfare.*
- *Export subsidies* benefit export producers at a cost to taxpayers.
- Both import restrictions and export subsidies distort trade based on the principle of comparative cost advantage leading, potentially, to reduced economic welfare. They also risk retaliation by other countries, leading to a possible downward spiral in world trade.
- The main arguments for import protection and/or export subsidies include: (a) protection of infant industries; (b) protection against 'unfair' competition; (c) support for declining industries; (d) support for strategic industries; (e) retaliation; and (f) correction of balance of payments problems.
- These arguments may make a case for trade protection as a short-term measure as markets adjust. Longer-term trade protection risks distorting markets, leading to lower economic welfare, for example 'infant industries' may never grow up!

? Topics for discussion

1. Since the early 1980s China has opened up its economy to market forces and international trade after 30 years of central planning. In 2002 it became a member of the World Trade Organisation (WTO) and agreed to remove various import protection measures. In the light of the law of comparative advantage, how would you expect production and trade in China to alter over the coming years and why?
2. China maintains that some of its industries (e.g. motor car manufacture) need protection because they are 'infant industries'. Comment on the soundness of this argument and its likely economic consequences.

3. Country X produces 800 units of bananas and 400 units of steel when it divides its economic resources equally between these two types of products. Country Y produces 400 units of bananas and 400 units of steel under the same conditions. Identify which goods both countries should specialise in producing and the relevant terms of trade, assuming constant cost production.

4. The USA decided in 2002 to introduce tariffs on imported steel to protect its own steel producers from what it deemed to be 'dumping' by foreign steel producers. The EU threatened to retaliate by introducing tariffs on exports of US goods to Europe. Comment on the EU's response and its probable economic consequences.

5. Some Japanese electronics companies claim that Chinese-produced TVs are destroying Japan's domestic TV manufacturing capability and that the trade is unfair because Chinese wage rates are under a tenth of those paid in Japan. What would be your advice to the Japanese government?

6. Your country has decided to protect temporarily a major industry that is declining in the face of international competition. The options are to use quotas or tariffs on imports. Discuss the relative merits of using quotas or tariffs.

7. What do you understand by the term 'beggar-my-neighbour' policies in the context of international trade? Provide examples of this practice.

8. In the light of the analysis presented in this chapter, critically appraise the case for agricultural protection as practised in many parts of the world, including North America, the EU and Japan.

9. Given the economic arguments for free trade, why do you think agriculture and some other industries are still subject to protection from imports in many parts of the world?

Chapter 14

BALANCE OF PAYMENTS

Aims and learning outcomes

The last chapter reviewed the economic case for international trade based on the law of comparative advantage and arguments surrounding the use of protectionist measures by governments to influence the level of imports and exports.

In this chapter we turn to the related issue of the balance of payments. As has already been argued, international trade based on the law of comparative advantage can be beneficial to all countries that take part in it. However, even armed with protectionist measures, international trade can present countries with balance of payments difficulties arising from a persistent mismatch in the flow of exports and imports. Countries with persistently large balance of payments current account deficits are likely to see their economic growth slow down as part of their national income flows to other countries, unless internally generated growth can compensate for this. At the same time, those countries with persistently large balance of payments surpluses on current account, representing net injections into the circular flow of national income, may overheat as their economies reach capacity limits, unless new capacity can be developed or part of the surplus is invested overseas (a strategy that has been followed, for example, by the Japanese through their huge investments in Europe, North America and many parts of the Far East).

In this chapter we look at the composition of the balance of payments. The balance of payments account, in part, reflects the inflows and outflows of a country's imports and exports, respectively. But this represents only one part of the account. The balance of payments also reflects a country's inflows and outflows of capital and details how any deficits or surpluses in one part of the account may be offset by opposite movements in other parts of the account. Ultimately, the balance of payments account must balance, hence its name!

The following topics are discussed in this chapter:

- international trade and the balance of payments;
- balance of payments account;
- causes of changes in the balance of payments;
- management of current account imbalances.

At the outset, it is important to point out that balance of payments statistics are often subject to significant revisions. Given the scale and scope of the information being collected, it is inevitable that errors will arise – sometimes very large and erratic. As a general principle, therefore, the data for any one month or relatively short time periods should be interpreted with caution and greater reliance should instead be placed on longer-term trends.

Learning outcomes

After studying this material you will be able to:

- Understand the structure and content of a typical country's *balance of payments account*.
- Differentiate between a *balance of trade*, a *current account balance* and the *overall balance of payments*.
- Distinguish between the *current* and *capital accounts* of the balance of payments.
- Understand how current account deficits are financed and how surpluses are reflected in the accounts.
- Appreciate the policy options available to governments in their attempts to correct imbalances.
- Distinguish between *automatic adjustment* and *discretionary policy* in the context of deficits or surpluses.

International trade and the balance of payments

As discussed in the previous chapter, international trade based on the principle of comparative advantage can be beneficial to all countries that take part in it. However, international trade can present countries with balance of payments problems arising from a persistent mismatch in the flows of exports and imports, resulting in surpluses or deficits in the value of goods and services exchanged.

A number of potential problems arising from persistent deficits can be readily identified:

- Since a deficit between the value of exports and imports represents a *leakage* from the circular flow of income, there is a danger that economic growth will be retarded, unless growth is stimulated by internal (domestic) factors to compensate (such as government or investment expenditure).
- A persistent deficit is likely to put downward pressure on the value of the currency in the foreign exchange market as confidence in the currency is weakened and as demand for it, relative to other currencies, in general, falls.
- A depreciating exchange rate will mean that the price of imports in domestic terms will be rising, which will contribute to domestic inflationary pressures with consequence effects for wage demands and unemployment.

The potential problems arising from persistent surpluses are not so readily identified – it is reasonable to assume that countries would prefer to have

Application 14.1

The global current account discrepancy

In principle, since one country's export is another country's import, current account balances across the world should sum to zero. In practice, however, this is not the case. Indeed, since 1997, the world as a whole has apparently been running an increasing current account deficit – the so-called *global current account discrepancy*. The value of this discrepancy is now estimated to be about 2 per cent of global imports. Clearly, this poses problems for the analysis of global trade positions and imbalances. For example, it raises the question how much of the huge current account deficit reported by the USA year after year is simply the result of measurement errors? In addition, even if the USA current account deficit is correctly measured, the discrepancy means that a significant portion of the recent increase has no counterpart in the rest of the world.

Econometric research concerning the size of the global current account discrepancy suggests that four particular factors offer an explanation:

- *transportation lags*, if exports are recorded in one year, while the corresponding imports are not recorded until the next;
- *under-reporting of investment income*, partly related to tax evasion and the growth of off-shore centres;
- *asymmetric valuation*, where the export and import of the same good are valued at different prices;
- *data quality issues*, especially for transportation services and workers' remittances.

It is important to note that the global current account discrepancy is far from the only statistical problem facing balance of payments analysts. Measurement of international investment positions, which have grown rapidly in recent years, is also a serious problem. The quality of the official data on investment positions put together using surveys and capital flows is improving, but remains imperfect. Many industrial countries have only recently begun to compile data and methodologies differ – in particular, the foreign direct investment position is variously measured at book value, historic cost, or market prices. The data are also subject to large revisions, particularly when benchmark surveys are conducted.

Source: Extract from IMF, *World Economic Outlook*, September 2002, p.70.

Activity

Are there any economic consequences arising from a large global current account discrepancy?

persistent surpluses rather than deficits! However, problems can emerge and will pose challengers for the surplus country:

- A surplus of the value of exports over imports represents an *injection* into the circular flow of income, which may result in an *overheating* of the economy if domestic production is already at full capacity.
- Overheating will tend to reflect itself in upward pressure on prices as total demand for goods and services (domestic and foreign) exceeds total domestic supply.
- Surpluses are likely to put upward pressure on the exchange rate which will push up the price of exported goods and services in foreign markets. This gives rise to the possibility that the surplus will decline.

Before exploring the options open to governments concerning the management of deficits or surpluses and the problems which arise, we first explain the terminology and structure of the balance of payments account.

Balance of payments account

> The *balance of payments account* is a systematic summarised statement of a country's international trade in goods and services and capital transactions with all other countries combined over a specific period of time.

All international transactions automatically give rise to two offsetting entries in the balance of payments, referred to as:

- a *current account* transaction;
- a *capital and financial account* transaction.

For example, a surplus of imports over exports might be financed by a reduction in official reserves or by international borrowing; in other words, by a fall in external assets or a rise in external liabilities. Similarly, a surplus of exports over imports might lead to a rise in foreign currency reserves, new overseas investments or a repayment of past borrowings, leading to a rise in external assets or a fall in external liabilities. Media reports of a balance of payments deficit or surplus, therefore, should be clarified: they refer only to the situation on the *current account*. It is this part which reflects the difference between the value of goods and services imported and exported by the country during a given time period.

Current account

> The *current account* includes the value of all transactions related to the purchase and sale of goods and services.

Transactions involving *goods* are commonly (and correctly) referred to as *visible trade* or *merchandise trade*. The visible trade balance is thus the difference between the value of exported goods from the country and the value of imported goods into the country, and is known as the *balance of trade*.

Transactions involving *services* are referred to as *invisible trade* consisting of the sale and purchase of services between the country and the rest of the world including net receipts in the form of interest, profits and dividends, and other income transfers. These transactions give rise to the *invisible balance*. In more detail the invisible balance includes

- *Services*: These include transport services (such as shipping and aviation), royalties, banking services and other financial services (such as insurance) as well as estimated net receipts from other private and government services.
- *Income receipts*: These represent income receipts which arise from assets owned by domestic firms in foreign countries (as well as payments to foreigners arising from foreign ownership of assets in the domestic economy). These assets may be in the form of direct investments in companies overseas, stocks and shares held as securities overseas, as well as net interest earned on lending abroad by banks. Also included are government payments of a similar nature.
- *Unilateral current transfers*: These represent grants, subscriptions, overseas pensions, etc., paid and received by government and certain private remittances and other transfers.

Adding together the visible balance, the invisible balance gives the overall *current account balance* which may result in overall deficit or surplus which must be financed – and so we turn to the *capital account*.

Capital and financial account

The other part of the balance of payments account comprises the *capital account* (including the *financial account*) and reflects changes in a country's external assets and liabilities over a given time period, usually a year, i.e. transactions related to the international ownership of financial assets. It is subdivided as follows:

- *Changes in external assets held abroad*: These cover resident holdings of foreign currency or shares and other investments in overseas companies, loans by resident banks to overseas borrowers and changes in official reserve assets.
- *Changes in external liabilities*: These cover all investments in the country by overseas residents as well as borrowing from abroad by residents of the country and changes in official reserves in the form of liabilities.

The capital account is comprised of a country's private sector transactions and official reserve transactions, which are the result of the central bank's activities. It should be noted that while the assets and liabilities are recorded in the *capital and financial account* of the balance of payments for the period during which they have arisen, any eventual income or payment stream in the form of interest, profits and dividends appears under 'invisibles' in the current account. It is important to appreciate this point as it highlights the 'cost', for example, in

Table 14.1 US balance of payments account, 2002

Current account	***Credits***	***Debits***
(1) Exports, of which:	*+1,229.6*	
Merchandise	+681.9	
Services	+292.2	
Income receipts	+255.5	
(2) Imports, of which:		*–1,651.6*
Merchandise		–1,164.7
Services		–227.4
Income Receipts		–259.5
(3) Net unilateral transfers		–58.9
Balance (1) + (2) + (3)		**–480.9**
Capital and financial account	***Credits***	***Debits***
(4) Non-market capital asset transfers:		–1.3
(5) Increase (–) in US assets held abroad, of which:		*–179.0*
Official reserves		–3.7
Other assets		–175.3
(6) Increase in foreign assets held in US, of which:	*+707.0*	
Official reserve assets	+94.9	
Other assets	+612.1	
Balance (4) + (5) + (6)	**+526.7**	
Statistical discrepancy (i.e. ***balancing item*****)**		**–45.8**

terms of potential outflows on the current account in future years arising from foreign capital inflows today, as well as the potential future inflows from investments overseas made today.

Table 14.1 shows selected balance of payments data for the USA (although it should be noted that the presentation of such data will vary across countries), based on the structure described above. The table shows two categories which we have not yet described: transactions in *official reserves* and a *statistical discrepancy*.

Transactions in official reserves

Transaction in official reserves consist of drawings on or additions to the country's official reserves (mainly gold and convertible foreign currencies), normally held by a country's central bank. When the country has a net surplus inflow of foreign currencies from current and other capital account transactions, the official reserves of foreign currencies at the central bank will rise. They will fall when current and other capital account transactions lead to a net outflow of foreign currencies from the official reserves. In other words, an increase/decrease in official reserves is equivalent to an overall balance of payments surplus/deficit.

Statistical discrepancy

At the bottom line of Table 14.1 appears an item referred to as the *statistical discrepancy*. This relates to discrepancies between the total value of recorded transactions and the actual flow of currencies in and out of the country. In principle, there should not be a discrepancy but in practice errors and omissions arising in recording trade and capital movements will mean that a *balancing item* (reflecting the errors and omissions) will arise within the balance of payments accounts. Its value is known because the central bank records show the net result of all foreign currency transactions. A positive value indicates that there have been unrecorded net inflows and a negative figure that there have been unrecorded net outflows. The size of the balancing item for any one year can be large, highlighting the difficulties in accurate data collection. Indeed, it is probably fair to say that the balance of payments is usually subject to more error than most other items of the national accounts, especially in economies with large flows of trade and capital not conducted by government.

Importance of balance of payments records

While the existence of statistical discrepancies, as reflected in the balancing item, may call into question the reliability of information for any single year, nevertheless longer-term trends in the overall account and its counterparts provide useful indicators of economic performance and changes in a country's structure of international trade.

If a country has a surplus on its current account year after year, it might invest the surplus abroad or add it to official reserves. The balance of payments position would be strong. There is the problem, however, that if one country which is a major trading nation (e.g. Japan) has a continual surplus on its balance of payments current account, other countries must be in continual deficit. These other countries can run down their official reserves, perhaps to zero, and borrow as much as they can to meet the payments overseas. Eventually, however, they will run out of reserves and credit entirely and be unable to pay their debts. Every country must have a reasonably 'sound' balance of payments position if international trade is to prosper. It could therefore be argued that a country has a good balance of payments position if, in the longer term, it has neither a surplus nor a deficit on its current account.

Deficits on the current account must be financed by a run-down of official reserves, or by borrowing from overseas. But a country cannot finance deficits in this way indefinitely. Its official reserves will run out completely one day. Clearly if a country has a persistent long-term deficit, its balance of payments position will be very weak, and it must eventually take action to improve the position. The policy options available to governments are explored later in the chapter. First, let us examine the possible causes of changes in the balance of payments account.

Application 14.2

The UK's improving trade balance

The UK has run a trade deficit for many years, reflected in the decline of its manufacturing base. However, in July 2003 the trade deficit narrowed strongly. This appears to have resulted from a recovery in the global economy, which raised external demand for UK goods. The trade deficit fell from £4.5bn in June to £3.3bn in July.

In this overall trade deficit, there was a trade surplus with the USA of £600m, though a deficit with the rest of the EU of £1.5bn. The EU accounts for around 55 per cent of the UK's exports of goods. Alongside the trade deficit in July, strong income inflows from corporate profits and interest meant that the current account was favourable.

Activity

With reference to the structure of the balance of payments account, distinguish between a trade deficit and a favourable current account position on the balance of payments. Explain why the UK trade deficit narrowed when the global economy improved, making reference to relevant macroeconomic theory.

Causes of changes in the balance of payments

A change in the balance of payments account may be caused by:

- a change in assets or liabilities, i.e. the capital and financial account; or
- a change in the current account.

A change in assets and liabilities

A number of factors may result in a movement in the assets and liabilities of the capital and financial account. These are:

- *A change in interest rates*: Higher real interest rates in one country relative to another will attract more capital (in the form of portfolio investments) into the country (and vice versa in the case of lower real interest rates).
- *An expected change in exchange rates*: If overseas investors expect the value of a country's currency to fall in the foreign exchange market, they will probably sell assets denominated in the currency in order to prevent or minimise their expected future capital loss – this can give rise to significant capital outflows (as occurred during the currency crises in the Far East in 1997, in Russia in 1998 and in Argentina in 2001).

- *Prospects for economic growth and stability*: If overseas firms consider that a country is economically stable and has good prospects for sustained economic growth, they might be persuaded to make substantial direct investments. The government's economic policies will help foreign investors to assess the country's prospects. Direct investment might also be attracted by the offer of government grants, subsidies or other assistance in setting up operations in that country.
- *Exchange control regulations*: The abolition of exchange control regulations makes it possible for residents of a country to invest abroad without restriction. Consequently, this can result in substantial outflows of capital in the form of private investments overseas with implications for the capital and financial account.
- *Current account movements*: If a country is selling more goods and services overseas it can expect an overall decrease in its liabilities to non-residents.

A change in the current account balance

A country's current account balance is determined by factors such as:

- the price of exports;
- the volume of demand for exports in the overseas markets, which in turn is dependent on:
  - the price of goods in the domestic currency;
  - the quality and design of goods for export; and
  - the general economic conditions in the export markets;
- the volume of demand for imports, which in turn is dependent on:
  - the price of goods expressed in the importing country's currency;
  - the quality and design of imported goods;
  - the general domestic economic conditions;
- the length of the delivery period for exports and imports.

The relative importance of each of these factors will vary from country to country and over time. While price itself is likely to be the more significant factor generally, the importance attached to *non-price* factors (quality, design, after-sales-service, etc.) should not be underestimated in global, competitive markets. Non-price factors emphasise the supply-side aspects of international trade.

Management of current account imbalances

The discussion so far demonstrates the so-called *balance of payments identity*:

Current account balance + Capital account balance + Financial account balance = 0

We now turn to the consequences for a country that is expecting a persistent balance of payments current account deficit or surplus and consider what actions can be taken to correct the imbalance. This discussion provides a natural introduction to the analysis of exchange rates in the next chapter.

An imbalance with regard to the balance of payments will have the following implications. In the case of a deficit, the country will face a drain on its foreign currency reserves at the central bank and is likely to find itself getting more and more into debt with overseas monetary authorities. Countries may borrow foreign reserves from central banks of other economies and they may draw on arranged loan facilities with organisations such as the International Monetary Fund (IMF) and, in the case of developing economies, the World Bank (for fuller details see the coverage of international financial institutions in Chapter 16).

This type of situation cannot, of course, persist indefinitely since a country's own foreign currency reserves and sources of borrowing are both, ultimately, limited. In contrast, a country experiencing a continuous balance of payments current account surplus will be accumulating reserves at the expense of deficit countries. Consequently, it may be experiencing inflationary pressures in its domestic economy as the net inflow of currency boosts the domestic money supply (foreign currency inflows will ultimately be converted into domestic currency), although these may be stabilised by government debt sales (open market operations to soak up the excess money supply – see Chapter 9 on monetary policy).

As we mentioned earlier, a deficit on the balance of payments current account will also tend to exert downward pressure on the country's exchange rate while a surplus will exert upward pressure. Whether or not the authorities permit the exchange rate to change at all and, if so, by how much, depends on the particular exchange rate policy that is being pursued. We discuss the nature of exchange rate movements and the different exchange rate regimes that countries may adopt in the next chapter, Chapter 15.

Given these consequences of balance of payments current account imbalances, there are four possible courses of action that governments can take to correct them. Any or all of these courses could be implemented to varying degrees at the same time. They are:

- protectionist measures;
- demand management policies;
- supply-side policies;
- exchange rate policy.

Protectionist measures

We described in detail in Chapter 13 the range of protectionist measures that a country may adopt to influence or direct international trade flows. In summary, these include:

- tariffs or customs duties;
- non-tariff barriers;
- import quotas and embargoes;

- subsidies for domestic producers;
- exchange controls;
- exchange rate policy.

Demand management policies

The most common approach to dealing with current account problems (deficits or surpluses) is the adoption of demand management policies involving *contractionary* fiscal or monetary policies to reduce overall aggregate demand and therefore the demand for imports through the marginal propensity to import, *mpm* (the *mpm* represents the addition to expenditure on imports resulting from a unit change in income – for full details see p.89). For example, with a value of 0.3 for the *mpm*, a $1bn contraction in aggregate demand (due perhaps to cuts in government expenditure and/or higher taxes) will lead to a $300m fall in expenditure on imports. This might help to correct a balance of payments current account deficit. This is especially so because the net balance of payments effect may be expected to be in excess of $300m as domestic exporters attempt to compensate for sluggish markets at home by increasing their efforts to export.

Moreover, contractionary measures could also reduce domestic inflationary pressures, thereby increasing the competitiveness of exports in world markets. Unfortunately, contractionary (i.e. deflationary) measures might also lead, in the short-term at least, to a reduction in industrial output and loss of jobs in the country's economy. Certainly, the country must accept a lowering of its standard of living if severe deflationary steps are taken and if the export growth effect is weak. In contrast, a current account surplus could be reversed by pursuing expansionary fiscal and monetary policy measures. These will draw in imports dependent on the *mpm* and may lead potential exports to be switched to satisfying domestic demand.

In summary, therefore, the purpose of deflationary measures in the context of the balance of payments may be any or all of the following:

- to reduce the aggregate demand for goods and services at home, and so reduce expenditure on imports;
- to encourage domestic firms to switch to export markets as a result of a fall in domestic demand.
- to tackle domestic inflation, which might be undermining the beneficial effect for exports of a depreciating exchange rate by raising the prices of exported goods in terms of the domestic currency.

The need for a reduction of aggregate demand for goods and services at home stems from the fact that if a country's rate of economic growth is faster than the average growth rate of its trading partners, then this will tend to cause imports to rise faster than export through what economists call the *absorption effect*: the economy 'absorbs' more imports.

To highlight the importance of this concept, recall that aggregate demand is measured by the total expenditure on goods and services by households, firms, the government and foreigners. Allowing for the expenditure on imports, we arrive at the familiar equation for aggregate demand (AD):

$$AD = C + I + G + X - M$$

where:
C = consumption expenditure by households
I = investment expenditure by firms
G = government expenditure
$X - M$ = expenditure on exports minus expenditure on imports

It will also be remembered that, by definition, national income must be equal to national output which must be equal to national expenditure. Thus, with Y representing the size of the economy in general (total output) then we have:

$$Y = C + I + G + X - M$$

By rearranging terms, it will be seen that:

$$Y - (C + I + G) = X - M$$

This view of the economy suggests that when the domestic components of demand ($C + I + G$) exceed the total output of the economy (Y), then the difference between exports and imports ($X - M$) increases as imports are *absorbed* into the country to satisfy the shortfall between Y and ($C + I + G$). In other words:

$$Y - A = X - M$$

where:

$A = (C + I + G)$ = *the absorption effect*

As noted above, deflationary demand management measures may also lead, at least in the short term, to a reduction in industrial output and an increase in unemployment as well as lower economic growth and living standards, especially if the squeeze on aggregate demand is severe.

Similarly, expansionary demand management measures to reduce a current account surplus (by increasing the absorption of imports) may stimulate inflationary pressures with consequent effects for wages and competitiveness.

Supply-side policies

As we saw in Chapter 10 the rate of economic growth and hence the nation's output growth is affected by changes in productivity and other supply-side measures. It might be the case that a current account deficit has arisen because of a lack of competitiveness on the part of domestic firms in the world marketplace, resulting in a falling demand for exports and a rising demand for imports, which substitute in the eyes of consumers for inferior or more expensive domestic goods. This is a view commonly put forward to explain the current account deficits experienced by the UK and USA from time to time since the 1970s. Supply-side reforms may reverse this trend, although the process is likely to take many years. In the meantime, competitors are unlikely to be standing still.

Exchange rate policy

Finally, a current account deficit might be tackled by devaluing the currency against the currencies of international trading partners. This may arise as a result of a 'managed' fall in the exchange rate by the authorities (giving rise to the term 'devaluation') or the currency may be allowed to 'float freely' downwards faced with persistent current account deficits (giving rise to the term 'depreciation'). In either case, devaluation or depreciation, the result will be to make exports relatively cheaper to foreign buyers, and so the demand for exports should rise, assuming of course that changes in exchange rates are translated into changes in the prices of goods and services. The extent of the increase in export revenue due to a fall in the value of the currency will depend on:

- the elasticity of demand for the goods in export markets, i.e. the extent to which demand for exports increases as their (foreign) price falls as a result of devaluation or depreciation;
- the extent to which industry is able to respond to the export opportunities by either producing more goods, or switching goods from domestic to export markets.

The cost of imports will rise because more domestic currency would be needed to obtain the foreign currency to pay for imported goods. The volume of imports should fall, although whether or not the total *value* of imports falls will depend on the price elasticity of demand for imports:

- if demand for imports is *price inelastic*, the volume of demand will fall by less than the rise in price, so that the total value of imports will rise.
- if demand for imports is *price elastic*, the total value of imports will fall since the fall in volume will outweigh the increase in price.

Because the effect of depreciation or devaluation depends on price elasticities of demand in this way, it might be the case that depreciation of the currency on its own would be insufficient to rectify the balance of payments current account deficit unless an extremely large depreciation takes place. The reason is that when currencies depreciate, it may take time for people to adjust their patterns of consumption and to change their investment plans. For example, households and firms may continue to buy what they regard as high-quality imports, despite the fact that a fall in the value of their country's currency may have pushed up import prices. At the same time, foreigners may not respond immediately to the fall in the value of the currency by placing immediate orders for the country's goods – again, tastes and preferences take time to change. Thus, the initial

Box 14.1

Marshall-Lerner Condition

In the simplest form, the *Marshall-Lerner condition* states that the (absolute) value of the price elasticity of demand for exports, $|E^{exports}_{demand}|$, plus the (absolute) value of the price elasticity demand for imports, $|E^{imports}_{demand}|$, *must sum to more than 1* if a fall in the exchange rate is to lead to an improvement in the current account.

Symbolically:

$$|E^{exports}_{demand}| + |E^{imports}_{demand}| > 1$$

where | | denote absolute values (i.e. ignoring + or – signs).

Elasticity is simply a numerical measure of the proportional change in demand volumes with respect to proportional price changes (arising in this case as a result of changes in exchange rates).

responsiveness (i.e. *price elasticity*) of demand for both imports and exports as a consequence of changes in currency value may be quite low. This raises an important question: under what conditions will depreciation (or devaluation) of the exchange rate lead to an improvement in the current account?

The condition for this improvement is summarised by the so-called *Marshall-Lerner* condition (see Box 14.1).

The rationale for this condition is easily grasped. When the exchange rate falls, export prices fall (denominated in foreign currency terms) and so we would expect export volumes to rise – as long as demand for exports is sufficiently elastic. Likewise, when the exchange rate falls, import prices rise (in domestic currency terms) and so import volumes can be expected to fall – again, as long as demand for imports is sufficiently elastic.

Elasticity is simply a numerical measure of the responsiveness of demand with respect to a change in price.

If the (absolute) price elasticity of demand for exports plus the (absolute) price elasticity of demand for imports exceeds unity, then the increased cost of imports (in domestic currency value) is *outweighed* by the value of the growth in exports. Hence the current account of the balance of payments improves.

The logic underlying the Marshall-Lerner condition can easily be illustrated in diagrammatic form as shown in Figure 14.1.

The left-hand side of this figure shows the domestic demand for imports (expressed in domestic currency terms). Prior to devaluation (or depreciation) the demand for imports is Q_1, the unit price is P_1, and the total cost of imports is

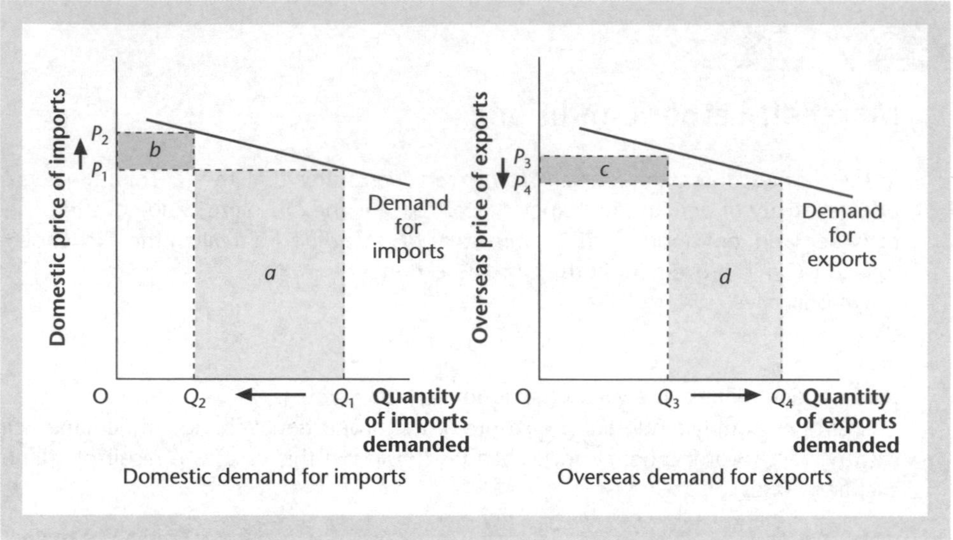

Figure 14.1 Marshall-Lerner condition

given by the rectangle $OP_1 \times OQ_1$. After a fall in the exchange rate, demand for imports is now Q_2, the domestic price is now P_2 and the total cost of imports is given by the area $OP_2 \times OQ_2$. If the reduction in expenditure on imports due to a fall in the volume demand (given by the shaded area *a*) is greater than the extra spending on the reduced volume (shaded area *b*), then the demand for imports is said to be *elastic*, i.e. an elasticity value greater than unity.

The right-hand side of Figure 14.1 shows the overseas demand for exports. After a fall in the exporting country's exchange rate, the overseas price of exports falls from P_3 to P_4, resulting in increased demand – from Q_3 to Q_4. The demand for exports is said to be *elastic* (i.e. an elasticity value greater than unity) since the area *d* is greater than area *c*.

Combining the two parts of Figure 14.1 provides us with the Marshall-Lerner condition described above. However, if the Marshall-Lerner condition is not satisfied then, as the currency of a deficit country falls in value, the initial effect may be a *worsening* in the balance of payments. Also, given that the volumes of imports and exports are likely to remain unchanged in the short-term initially, the total import bill (valued in domestic currency terms) will be rising faster than the total revenue from exports (valued in domestic currency terms) as the currency depreciates. Indeed, if exports are originally priced in the domestic currency, then with demand unchanged the domestic currency revenue will stay the same. Hence, initially, the current account can deteriorate sharply, as illustrated in Figure 14.2.

However, as Figure 14.2 also suggests, in time the balance of payments position is likely to improve as demand for the now cheaper-priced exports expands (assuming that the foreign price of the exported goods is reduced to reflect the depreciation) and as demand for the now more expensive imports falls. In other

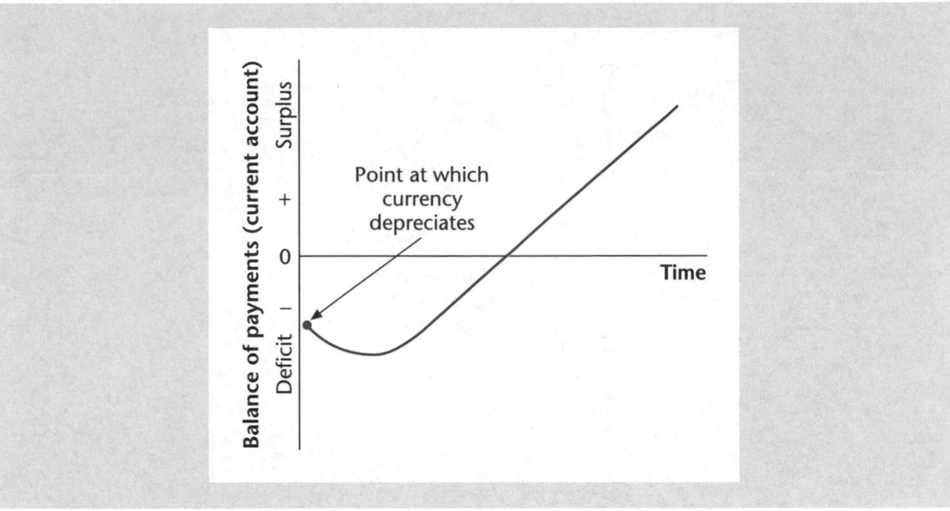

Figure 14.2 J-curve effect

words, depreciation can be expected eventually to lead to an improvement in the current account, giving rise to the *J-curve effect* as shown in the figure.

> **J-curve effect**
>
> The *J-curve effect* illustrates the tendency for a country's current account deficit to initially worsen following a devaluation (or depreciation) in its currency before then improving and, perhaps eventually, moving into surplus.

Economists have estimated that, for some countries, it may take on average around 18 months for the balance of payments to start to improve following a depreciation (or devaluation) of the domestic currency.

Of course, the opposite logic applies in the case of surplus countries facing an appreciation in their currencies. In the short term, if demand is sluggish to respond to relative price changes, appreciation is likely to boost the current account surplus further. Eventually, however, it is to be expected that the volume of imports and exports will respond to the price changes. This is known as the *inverted J-curve effect*, and is illustrated in Figure 14.3.

It should be noted that despite a general fall in the external value of a currency against other currencies, trade performance sometimes deteriorates. This suggests that factors other than relative prices are important in determining the extent to which a current account deficit can be reversed. Indeed, some economists argue that price considerations are often given too prominent a place in explanations of trade flows. They stress a number of other non-price reasons for the weakness

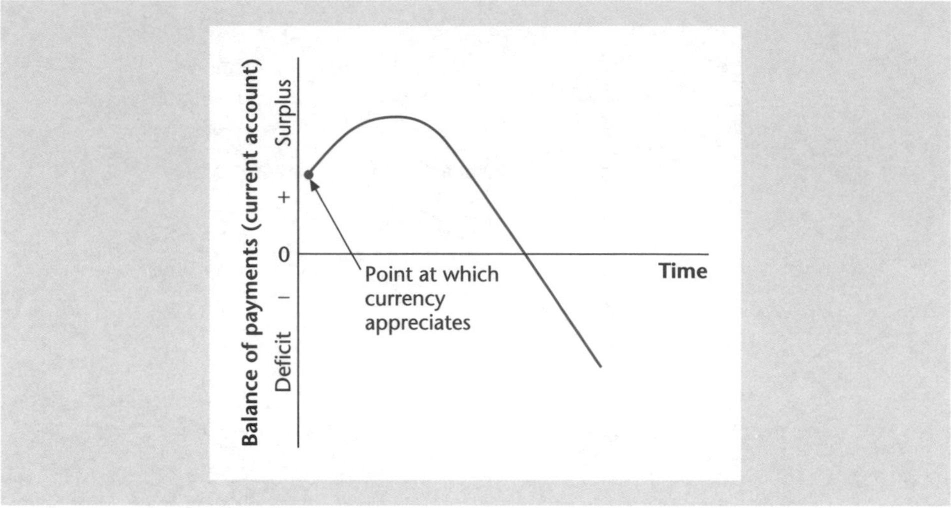

Figure 14.3 **Inverted J-curve effect**

in a balance of payments position, such as poor-quality products and low-technological change. In addition, supply-side constraints may exist, i.e. a country may not have sufficient capacity to satisfy a growing demand for its exports, no matter how competitive it is.

Automatic versus discretionary adjustments to the balance of payments

As we have seen so far in our analysis of how balance of payments problems can be rectified, adjustments to (changes in) the balance of payments might occur automatically, as a consequence of 'market forces'. On the other hand, adjustments might be instigated by action on the part of the government (and central bank).

- *Automatic adjustments* are those which occur to rectify a balance of payments imbalance without government interference.
- *Discretionary adjustments* are deliberate actions by the government (or central bank) to rectify the balance of payments imbalance.

In practice, there is likely to be a mixture of automatic and discretionary adjustments taking place, without any clear distinction between the two being possible. For example, one consequence of a balance of payments current account deficit might be higher interest rates to attract more foreign capital. This adjustment might be automatic, but it will probably be supported as well by the government's interest rate and exchange rate policies.

Automatic adjustments to a current account deficit might be:

- lower prices for home-produced output, and lower wages;
- a fall in demand for imported goods as these become relatively more expensive;
- a fall in the exchange rate of the domestic currency where the currency is freely floating;
- a fall in the total volume of goods purchased, both imported and home-produced;
- an 'efficiency drive' in the country's manufacturing industries as they try to become more competitive through lower unit costs, better quality and more reliable delivery dates.

Discretionary adjustments to correct a current account deficit might be:

- a managed depreciation of the currency to reduce a current account deficit;
- a cut in government spending on imported goods or government expenditure overseas;
- higher taxation to reduce demand in the economy, and so reduce the volume of imports;
- government subsidies to assist exporters.

The success of measures to rectify a balance of payments current account deficit will depend on retaliatory measures by other countries, and also on the

Application 14.3

The US trade deficit

The following commentary links the US trade deficit to the decline in value of the dollar in the foreign exchange market. (We look at exchange rates in detail in the next chapter.) Here we are concerned with trade deficits.

The most obvious reason for the dollar's depreciation is the widening of the US trade deficit, to some 5 per cent ($500bn) of its economy last year. The deficit is on course to reach around $540bn this year and around $600bn by 2005 (see the chart) despite dollar weakness.

Five years ago, the US current account deficit was $200bn and ten years ago it was just $48bn. The change over this period means the USA now requires net capital inflows of around $1.5bn a day to fund its trade gap and keep the currency stable.

Unfortunately, the US equity market, like others in the rest of the world, has fallen by about 60 per cent from its peak three years ago. The US economy is still recovering from recession in 2001, the government bond market has very low yields and the USA has a widening budget deficit. With interest rates low (1.25 per cent against 2 per cent in the Eurozone), it has become much more ▶

Application 14.3 continued

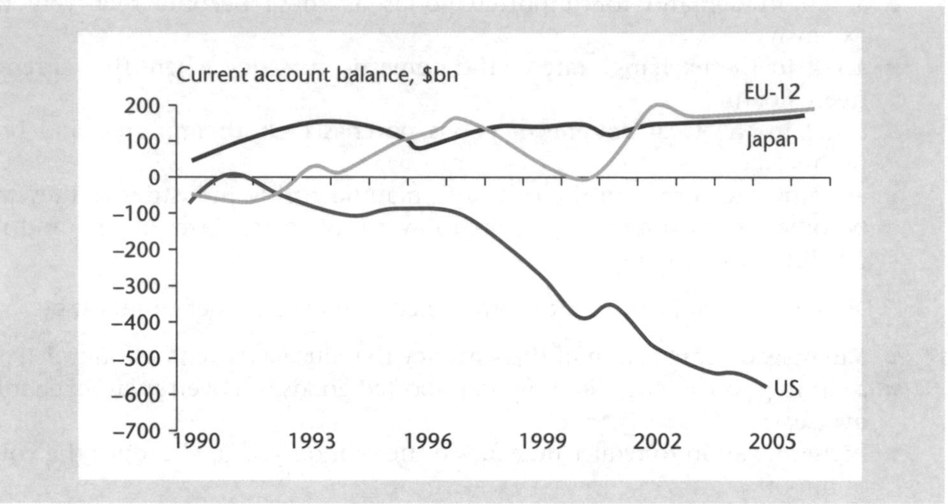

US current account deficit widens

difficult for the USA to attract the large share of net global investment flows that it needs to fund its trade deficit.

The reason for the widening trade deficit was the real – inflation adjusted – appreciation of the US currency during the 1990s, and faster growth in the US economy relative to that of its major trading partners. This made US exports more expensive and its imports cheaper as faster economic growth made it easier for foreign firms to sell into the USA, resulting in a widening US trade deficit.

But this trend did not lead immediately to a fall in the dollar, as financial markets concentrated on the faster growth rate of the USA relative to other economies. Moreover, with its equity market outperforming there was ample inflow of foreign investment to fund the US trade deficit. But typically financial markets become only really concerned about a trade deficit when it reaches around 5 per cent of GDP, as happened in the USA last year. Financial market concern can be particularly heightened if the external deficit is combined with a budget deficit, which may amount to 4 per cent of US GDP this year.

Source: *Lloyds TSB Economic Bulletin*, No. 45, June 2003, pp.10–11.

Activity

Consider why the financial markets may be concerned about the US 'double deficit', i.e. a trade deficit and a government budget deficit? What are the implications of a large US trade deficit for capital inflows to the USA and therefore interest rates and the state of the equity market?

price elasticities of demand for imports and exports (as discussed earlier). The measures used successfully by one country to correct a deficit may simply not work for another.

Concluding remarks

All businesses are affected by international trade whether directly, by being involved in importing and exporting, or indirectly, because of the impact that the balance of payments has upon domestic economic activity. One question which might run through a reader's mind at the end of this chapter is whether a current account imbalance matters.

There is no simple answer to this question, much depends upon what is happening to capital flows. Sustained imbalances in trade flows, unless offset by flows of capital, must eventually trigger changes in policy. If a country has a current account deficit which is financed by an inflow of investment funds from abroad then the imbalance is sustainable, especially if the capital inflow is long-term investment. (Short-term investment is much more of a problem because it can quickly flow out again – what is called a flight of *hot money*, precipitating a currency crisis.) The USA in the latter part of the nineteenth century ran current account deficits financed by inflows of capital (from Britain and elsewhere) that went, for example, into building America's railroads. Similarly, Japan maintained its large export surplus in the 1980s, without causing an even larger rise in the value of the yen against other currencies than took place, by investing large amounts of its surplus international earnings abroad.

In this chapter, we have made extensive reference to exchange rate movements in relation to the balance of payments. We now turn in the next chapter to look at the operation of exchange rates and provide a detailed assessment of the various types of exchange rate regimes and, in particular, the arguments for and against fixed and floating currencies.

Key learning points

- The *balance of payments* is the account that records a country's international trade in goods and services and its international capital account movements.
- The difference between a country's exports and imports of goods over a given time period is known as the country's *trade balance*.
- The *current account balance* is the difference between a country's exports and imports of *visibles* (merchandise or goods) and *invisibles* (services and income payments such as interest, profits and dividends and certain other transfers).
- The *capital and financial account balance* reflects changes in a country's external assets and external liabilities over a given time period and changes in official reserves.

- The *official reserves* are the country's foreign currency reserves normally held by the country's central bank.
- The current account deficit/surplus *plus* net capital inflow must equal *zero*, i.e. any current account deficit or surplus must be financed by an offsetting inflow or outflow of capital and changes in the level of official reserves.
- Countries may attempt to manage their balance of payments on current account using protectionist measures, demand management policies, supply-side policies, and exchange rate management policies to influence the level of exports and imports of goods and services and international capital flows.
- The *Marshall-Lerner condition* states that a devaluation (or depreciation) in the exchange rate will reduce a current account deficit if the (absolute) values of the elasticities of demand for exports and imports sum to more than unity.
- The *J-curve effect* illustrates the tendency for a country's current account deficit to initially worsen following a devaluation (or depreciation) of its currency before then moving into surplus.
- The *inverted J-curve effect* illustrates the tendency for a current account surplus to initially improve and then to decline due to an appreciation in the currency.
- *Automatic adjustments* are those which occur to rectify a balance of payments imbalance without government interference.
- *Discretionary adjustments* are deliberate actions by the authorities to rectify a balance of payments imbalance.

? Topics for discussion

1. Distinguish between a trade deficit and a current account deficit.
2. A developing country operates a trade deficit because of large imports of capital equipment. Explain how this country might sustain this deficit over time.
3. Is a balance of trade surplus necessarily a 'good thing'?
4. A country has a current account deficit. Advise (a) on its economic implications and (b) how the deficit might be tackled.
5. The USA has persistently reported large current account deficits on its balance of payments.
   (a) How is the USA able to sustain this position?
   (b) What problems (if any) does this situation pose for:
      (i) the USA?
      (ii) the rest of the world?
6. Analyse the effects of a current account surplus in a country pursuing:
   (a) a fixed exchange rate, or
   (b) a floating exchange rate.

Chapter 15

EXCHANGE RATES

Aims and learning outcomes

Whereas the previous chapter was concerned with the nature of the balance of payments, in this chapter we turn to consider the operation of exchange rates. A country's exchange rate can have a significant effect on the ability of domestic firms to compete in international markets with implications for the balance of payments. Moreover, countries with long-term deficits on the current account of the balance of payments are likely to see the value of their currencies decline in the foreign exchange market and those with a current account surplus are likely to see the value of their currencies rise in relation to the value of the currencies of their trading partners. However, the movements of exchange rates today, especially short-term movements, are most often dominated by international capital flows rather than trade flows. For this reason, a country with a current account deficit may actually see its exchange rate rise due to inflows on capital account. Similarly, a country with a surplus might see its exchange rate decline due to capital outflows. These international capital flows take the form of what is sometimes referred to as 'hot money', representing capital that moves from one international financial centre to another and is invested in bank accounts, stocks and shares with a view to achieving the highest possible return. This return will reflect the interest rate or yield on the investment and any change in the underlying value of the capital invested due to exchange rate movements. We discuss this in detail later in the chapter.

Countries may adopt different types of exchange rate policies, from allowing their exchange rate to freely fluctuate or 'float' depending upon the demand for and supply of their currency in the foreign exchange market, to adopting a fixed exchange rate regime. In the latter case the central bank is required to maintain the exchange rate at a given level, or within a given band, through operations in the foreign exchange market. In this chapter we look at the different types of exchange rate policy that might be adopted and the consequences for economic policy.

The following topics are discussed in the chapter:

- the meaning of exchange rate;
- purchasing power parity theory;
- exchange rate systems;
- fixed versus floating exchange rates;

- the determination of exchange rates;
- exchange rates and the balance of payments;
- exchange rates and business.

Learning outcomes

After studying this material you will be able to:

- Understand the meaning of an *exchange rate*.
- Appreciate how exchange rates are determined.
- Understand how central banks may influence exchange rates.
- Distinguish between *fixed* and *floating exchange rate regimes* and their economic implications.
- Recognise how the type of exchange rate regime adopted and changes in exchange rates affect the wider economy.
- Appreciate the relationship between the balance of payments and the exchange rate.
- Understand the meaning of the concept 'purchasing power parity'.

The meaning of exchange rate

An *exchange rate* is the price at which the currency of one country is exchanged for the currency of another country in the foreign exchange market (e.g. the price of the euro in exchange for US dollars).

The major foreign exchange markets are New York, Tokyo and London, although there are many other smaller foreign exchange markets, including Singapore, Paris and Sydney. At any given time, the price of one currency against another will tend to be the same across all of the world's foreign exchange markets – otherwise, there would be scope for profitable arbitrage, i.e. buying a currency in one market where it is cheaper and selling it into another market where it is priced higher. For this reason, we can for convenience and with some justification talk about *one* foreign exchange market – this is the approach adopted throughout the chapter.

Like all prices, the exchange rate is determined by the interaction of the forces of demand and supply. The demand for a currency at any given time reflects the amount of the currency that individuals and businesses wish to buy. This demand will be to finance foreign trade and foreign investment. Indeed, today the vast bulk of foreign exchange transactions are accounted for by investment needs. The world's financial institutions invest in portfolios of bank accounts, stocks and shares in different financial centres using the world's major currencies, notably the US dollar, the euro and the Japanese yen. By contrast, the supply of a currency in the world's foreign exchange market reflects the amount that individuals and businesses want to sell. Their alternative is to continue to hold the currency.

To highlight the significance of the market for foreign currencies, take a company like Cadbury Schweppes. The company imports cocoa to make chocolate products and thus needs foreign currencies to buy its cocoa. Equally, the company exports chocolate products, for which it earns foreign currencies. Cadbury Schweppes therefore both demands currencies from and supplies currencies to its banks and these currencies are traded in the foreign exchange market. In addition, if Cadbury Schweppes were to decide to make an acquisition of shares in another company, say an investment in the USA, it would need to buy dollars in the foreign exchange market to finance the acquisition. Apart from the foreign currency business transacted by companies, there are many millions of currency deals conducted by individuals for many different reasons. For example, when British people travel to France, they must purchase euros (since Britain is not part of the Eurozone), when Germans visit Japan, they must buy yen, and so on. The foreign exchange market reflect a vast number of minute-by-minute transactions in foreign currencies.

Looking at this more technically, the term *currency assets* (for example US dollar assets) refers to the net stock of financial assets denominated in US dollars held outside the US Federal Reserve and the US public sector. The current value of the US dollar therefore reflects the demand for and supply of these US dollar-denominated financial assets. The same applies to the other major currencies. It should be noted that many governments around the world (and not only the US government) borrow and raise funds in the international capital markets by issuing bonds denominated in US dollars. Also, the US dollar is used in many international trades including the buying and selling of oil and many other commodities and is held by central banks as part of their foreign currency reserve holdings. It is therefore sometimes referred to as a 'reserve currency'. Other important reserve currencies are the euro and the Japanese yen and again governments around the world issue bonds denominated in these currencies.

The quantity of US dollar assets demanded will increase in the foreign exchange market when the price of the dollar in terms of a foreign currency falls. Similarly, the demand for US dollar assets will decline when the price of the dollar in terms of a foreign currency rises. We can understand this if we take a simple example. Suppose that the US dollar increases in value from €1 = $1 to €1.2. Everything else remaining equal, the quantity of dollars demanded will fall for two broad reasons reflecting:

- *a transaction effect;*
- *a capital gains effect.*

The transaction effect

Whenever one currency is traded to buy another there is a transaction cost. Foreign exchange dealers charge a commission to cover their expenses and to make a profit (this may be as a direct charge or as a discounted value of the currency traded). By holding stocks of a currency such dealing costs are eliminated. Therefore, the larger the expected demand for a foreign currency in the near future, the more of it that will tend to be held (again, everything else being held constant). When a currency rises in value, in time the smaller will be the demand for the currency required to purchase the country's exports and the larger will be the flow of imports, and therefore the country's demand for foreign currency.

The capital gains effect

By correctly anticipating foreign exchange rate movements it is possible to make a capital gain – although incorrectly anticipating movements will produce capital losses. Suppose that the US dollar is currently trading at €1 = \$1, but you anticipate that the value will fall to €1 = \$1.2. By buying euros using dollars now and reselling when the price changes, there will be a substantial (20 per cent) capital gain (ignoring transaction costs).

For example, initially \$1m invested in euros will buy €1m. After the price of the euro has changed to \$1.2, the €1m can be sold to buy \$1.2m. Equally, suppose that you anticipate that the exchange rate will move against the euro, say from €1 = \$1 to €0.8 = \$1. Then by buying dollars and selling euros now a capital gain can also be made. For example, at the initial exchange rate, selling €1m will buy \$1m. After the fall in the exchange rate, \$1m will repurchase €1.25m.

It should be clear from this example why the foreign exchange market is subject to speculation or 'hot money' flows in favour of or against a currency, depending upon expectations about future prices. It should also be clear why the current exchange rate depends partly on the *expected* future exchange rate.

Figure 15.1 shows the relationship between the quantity of dollar assets demanded and supplied in the foreign exchange market and the price of the dollar expressed in terms of the euro. The demand curve is downward sloping because the lower the exchange rate of the dollar in terms of the euro the more likely it is that dollars will be demanded to purchase internationally competitive US exports – the *transaction effect*. Also, the lower the relative value of the dollar, the more likely that the next movement in the dollar exchange rate against the euro will be upwards, which means that holding dollar-denominated assets is more attractive – the *capital gains effect*. The supply curve is upward sloping suggesting that the higher the price of the dollar in terms of the euro, the more dollars will be supplied into the foreign exchange market (i.e. holders of dollars will be willing to supply dollars to the market as the price of the dollar against the euro rises). The *equilibrium exchange rate* in the foreign exchange market will be that at which the demand for dollar-denominated assets equals the supply of dollar-denominated assets (Q^*), namely at the exchange rate e^* in Figure 15.1.

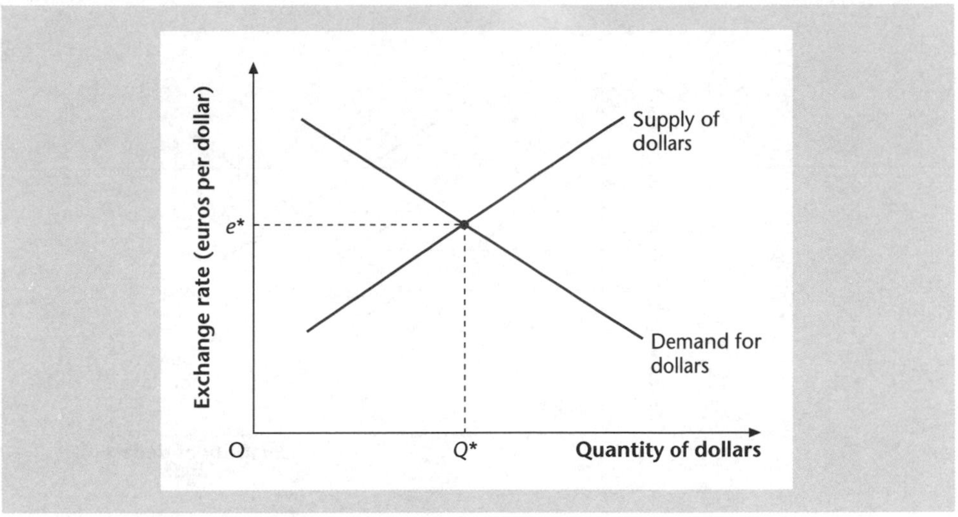

Figure 15.1 Determination of the exchange rate

Any change in the exchange rate causes a movement along the demand curve for dollars or dollar assets in Figure 15.1, reflecting transaction and capital gains effects. Changes in other factors impacting on the demand for a currency other than its current exchange rate will cause a shift in this demand curve. Important considerations affecting the demand for dollars will include:

- the volume of dollar-denominated payments, which in turn will reflect the size of the US economy or its GDP;
- the expected value of the dollar, for the reasons detailed above;
- the interest rate on dollar-denominated assets compared with the interest rate on assets denominated in other currencies, or what is termed the *interest rate differential*.

As investors want a return on their investments, the higher the relative interest rate on dollar-denominated assets, the more of these assets investors will wish to hold, everything else being equal. Changes in interest rates therefore affect the relative price of currencies. Of course, even a higher interest rate on dollar-denominated assets may not entice investors to buy them if they expect the value of the dollar to fall (perhaps as a result of a domestic economic or political crisis).

The supply of dollars in the foreign exchange market is also affected by the size of the government's budget deficit or surplus and the central bank's policy on buying and selling foreign currency assets. Whenever a government has a budget deficit, it finances this by borrowing through issuing bonds denominated (normally) in its own currency. The result is an increase in the supply of assets denominated in that currency. Similarly, if a government has a budget surplus, it can buy back bonds previously issued, leading to a fall in assets denominated in the country's currency. Equally, the central bank can operate in the foreign exchange market to influence the value of its currency by buying or selling assets

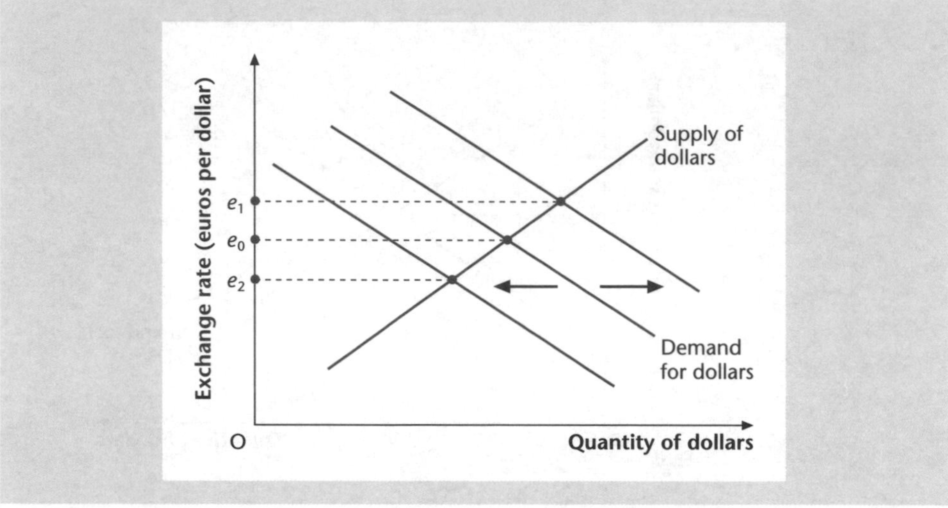

Figure 15.2 Shifting the demand curve and the exchange rate

denominated in its own currency. The central bank's attitude to influencing the market exchange rate will depend on the type of foreign exchange rate policy the country is following, which we discuss below.

However, before we do this, Figures 15.2 and 15.3 illustrate how changes in the demand for and supply of a currency, here the US dollar, affect the value of the currency in the foreign exchange market. An increase in the demand for dollars, for the reasons given above, will shift the demand curve for dollar-denominated assets rightwards, leading to a higher equilibrium exchange rate, e_1 rather than e_0; while a decrease in the demand for dollars will shift the demand curve leftwards,

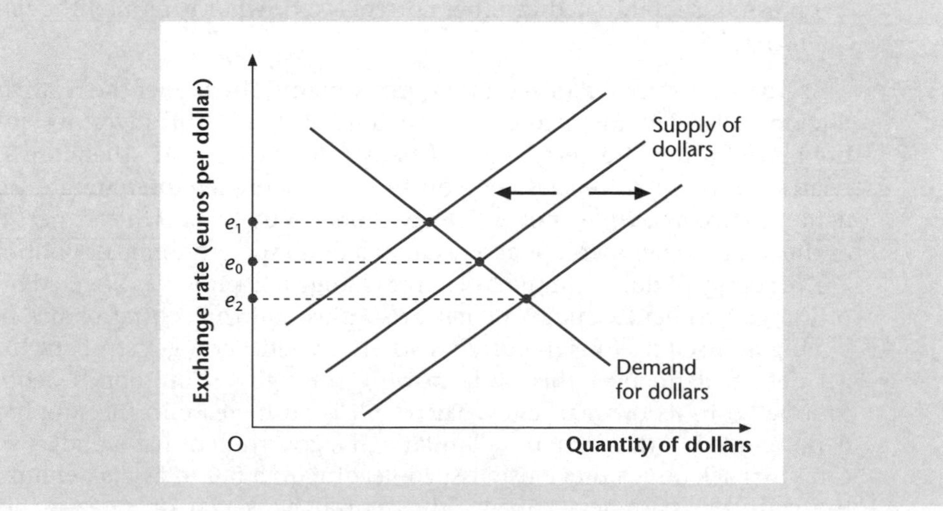

Figure 15.3 Shifting the supply curve and the exchange rate

producing a lower equilibrium exchange rate, e_2 rather than e_0, all other factors held constant. These movements are illustrated in Figure 15.2.

Similarly, in Figure 15.3 an increase in the supply of dollar-denominated assets will shift the supply curve to the right, reducing the equilibrium exchange rate from e_0 to e_2; while a decrease in dollar-denominated assets will shift the supply curve leftwards resulting in a higher exchange rate, e_1 rather than e_0, holding constant all other factors that may affect the exchange rate.

A country's central bank can attempt to influence the current exchange rate. Whether it chooses to do so or not will depend upon its attitude to the current exchange rate (is it the right rate for international trading purposes?) and the type of exchange rate regime the country is operating (e.g. fixed or floating). The central bank influences the exchange rate by buying or selling the currency (or currency-denominated assets) in the foreign exchange market. If it wants to depress the exchange rate it will sell its currency and buy foreign currencies. If it wants to push up the exchange rate, it will buy the currency using some of its foreign currency reserves. Central banks hold reserves of foreign currencies (and gold) to meet the needs of the country's financial system, to finance day-to-day trade and foreign investment needs in the economy and to intervene, if necessary, in the foreign exchange market.

In principle, it might be thought that the exchange rate should reflect the relative price of goods in different international markets. This leads to a theory of exchange rate determination known as *purchasing power parity theory*.

Purchasing power parity theory

Purchasing power parity (PPP) theory predicts that, under a floating exchange-rate system, the exchange rate of one currency against another currency will adjust to ensure that prices for identical goods in the two countries are the same.

Take the following example:

Suppose that a Volkswagen Golf car sells in Germany for €20,000 and in the US for $10,000. Then PPP theory indicates that, in the long run, the euro–dollar exchange rate would be €2 = $1. Logically, if there were no barriers to imports and exports and we ignore transaction costs, such as transport and insurance, then if the VW Golf sold in the US for $10,000 and in Germany for €20,000 and the current exchange rate were, say, $1=€1, then it would pay to arbitrage and buy VW Golfs in the US and ship them to Germany for resale at a profit. By so doing, the supply of VW Golfs available to customers in the US market would fall, raising their price there, and the supply in Germany would rise, lowering their price in that country. This trade would go on until the prices in the USA and Germany equalised (ignoring transaction costs such as shipping and insurance).

Of course, trade between countries occurs involving a wide range of goods and services and not just one product. Nevertheless, the same logic applies. If goods sell at a lower price in the USA than in Germany, it will pay importers to ship goods from the USA into Germany, paying for them in dollars. At the same time, German exporters will find it difficult to sell exports to the USA because of their lack of price competitiveness. The result will be a net demand for dollars using euros. This will lead to an appreciation in the value of the dollar expressed in euros until prices are equalised between the USA and Germany at the going exchange rate.

We can state, therefore, that based on purchasing power parity theory the price of goods in Germany (expressed in euros) should be equal to the price of goods in the USA (expressed in dollars) divided by the exchange rate of the dollar against the euro; i.e.

Germany *USA*

$$\text{Prices in euros} = \frac{\text{Prices in \$}}{(\text{Exchange rate : \$/€})}$$

In practice, however, day-to-day exchange rates are affected by a multitude of factors relating not just to relative prices in different countries and therefore trade flows, but also relating to foreign investment, speculation in the foreign exchange market and central bank intervention in the market. In addition, not all goods and services are internationally traded and therefore their prices do not affect PPP and in reality trade does involve transaction costs. For these reasons the current exchange rate of the dollar to the euro or any currency in terms of another may not accurately reflect the true PPP of the currencies. Nevertheless, over time, because of the impact of exchange rates on trade flows, we would expect PPP to be a good predictor of *long-run* exchange rates:

$$\text{Exchange rate: \$/€ (long-run)} = \frac{\text{Price index (\$)}}{\text{Price index (€)}}$$

Note the reference to a price 'index' – since trade involves a vast range of goods and services, we need a composite measure of all prices combined.

PPP theory therefore predicts that differential rates of inflation (based on changes in price indexes over time) leads to offsetting movements in exchange rate values. However, it should also be appreciated that the direction of causation could be in the opposite direction, i.e. it is possible that changes in exchange rates could lead to differential inflation rates. For example, if the demand for imports is relatively price inelastic, then a fall (depreciation) in the exchange rate will result in imported inflation which may impact on domestic inflation.

Exchange rate systems

There are a number of types of exchange rate systems that countries can adopt: the choice will be determined by the nature of the economic stance taken by governments and central banks and the problems they face. In essence, the systems may be categorised under three headings:

- a floating exchange rate system;
- a fixed exchange rate system;
- a managed exchange rate system.

The choice of exchange rate system is a major issue in economics today given the degree of international integration which has evolved in recent years as a result of the increasing globalisation of product and capital markets. Exchange rates have obvious and important implications for businesses, especially those involved in exporting and importing.

Floating exchange rates

Under a *floating exchange rate system*, a country's exchange rate is determined solely by the demand for and supply of its currency (or currency-denominated assets) in the foreign exchange market.

In other words, it is determined just like the price of any good or service in a free market – central banks do not intervene in the foreign exchange market to influence the exchange rate. A floating exchange rate system, by definition, therefore, results in an *equilibrium rate of exchange* that will vary continuously as the demand for and supply of the currency alters in the foreign exchange market. When a currency's exchange value rises as a result of market forces, the exchange rate is said to *appreciate*; when its value falls it is said to *depreciate*. These terms are quite distinct from *revaluation* and *devaluation* which are policy-determined changes in the value of a currency.

The process by which currencies float up or down is illustrated in Figure 15.4. Note that, unlike in Figures 15.1 to 15.3, we are now expressing exchange rates as *dollars per euro*. The horizontal axis therefore refers to the quantity of euros. Since currencies are commonly quoted in both directions (euros per dollar and dollars per euro) it is important to be familiar with the correct terminology and the use of appropriate diagrammatic analyses.

In Figure 15.4 (a) the initial equilibrium exchange rate for the euro in terms of the US dollar is shown as $1 and arises from foreign exchange transactions totalling q_1. Suppose now that the demand for the euro rises as a result of an increased demand for European exports. This is shown as a shift in the demand schedule for the euro from D_1D_1 to D_2D_2. In consequence, the euro appreciates from $1 to $1.20 because the amount of euros exchanged increases to q_2,

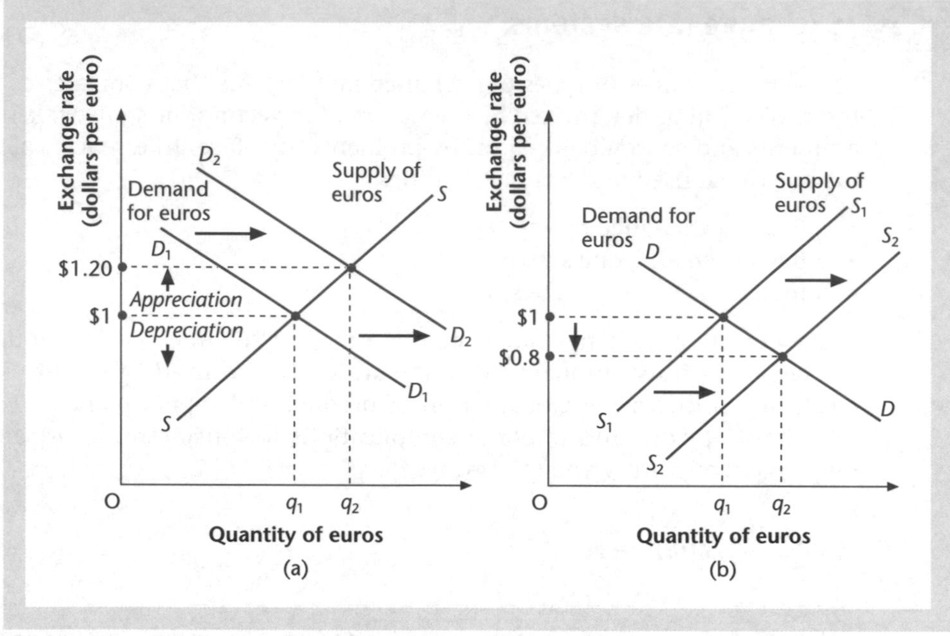

Figure 15.4 Floating exchange rates

everything else being equal. Note that had demand for the euro fallen, say due to a decline in demand for European exports, this would have caused the demand schedule for the euro to shift to the left, leading to a depreciation in the value of the euro expressed in dollars.

In Figure 15.4 (b), again the initial exchange rate is $1 = €1 but this time there is an increase in the supply of euros, from S_1S_1 to S_2S_2, to the foreign exchange market. This could arise, for example, if there was an increase in European demand for US goods. Everything else being equal, the $/€ exchange rate will depreciate to $0.8. Once again, it should be recognised that a reduction in the supply of euros in the foreign exchanges would have led to an appreciation in the value of the euro.

The above analysis of the determination of exchange rates is based upon the assumption that there is no central bank intervention in the foreign exchange market. The methods by which central banks and therefore governments can intervene are discussed below with reference to *fixed* and *managed* exchange rate systems. In other words, we have been concerned here only with *pure* or *freely floating* exchange rates. Also, it should be remembered that, although we have discussed the demand for and supply of currencies in terms of financing exports and imports, i.e. international trade, currencies are also bought and sold for many other reasons including speculation. A freely floating exchange rate could therefore be subject to some violent movements with damaging macroeconomic effects.

Fixed exchange rates

At the other extreme to a free floating exchange rate system lie *fixed exchange rates*. A government may pursue a policy of keeping the external value of its currency fixed at a stable rate by having its central bank intervene in the foreign exchange market.

Intervention is carried out using official foreign reserves to balance the demand for and the supply of the currency in order to maintain the particular exchange rate at a given level. For example, as illustrated in Figure 15.5, an increase in the demand for euros from D_1D_1 to D_2D_2 could be offset by the authorities augmenting the supply of euros from S_1S_1 to S_2S_2 (e.g. to buy dollar-denominated assets) in the foreign exchange market, in order to counteract the upward pressure on the value of the euro. Conversely, as can also be seen in Figure 15.5, a decrease in the demand for euros from D_2D_2 to D_1D_1 could be offset by the authorities, for example, restricting the supply of euros to the market, from S_2S_2 to S_1S_1. The end result of both of these actions is that the value of the euro is held at the fixed exchange rate of \$1.20 = €1.

The maintenance of fixed exchange rates in the manner just described requires that the authorities hold sufficient foreign currency reserves or have access to sufficient foreign currency loans for intervention purposes.

During the last century there have been two periods in which fixed exchange rate systems prevailed in the world economy. These are known as:

- the gold standard;
- the Bretton Woods system.

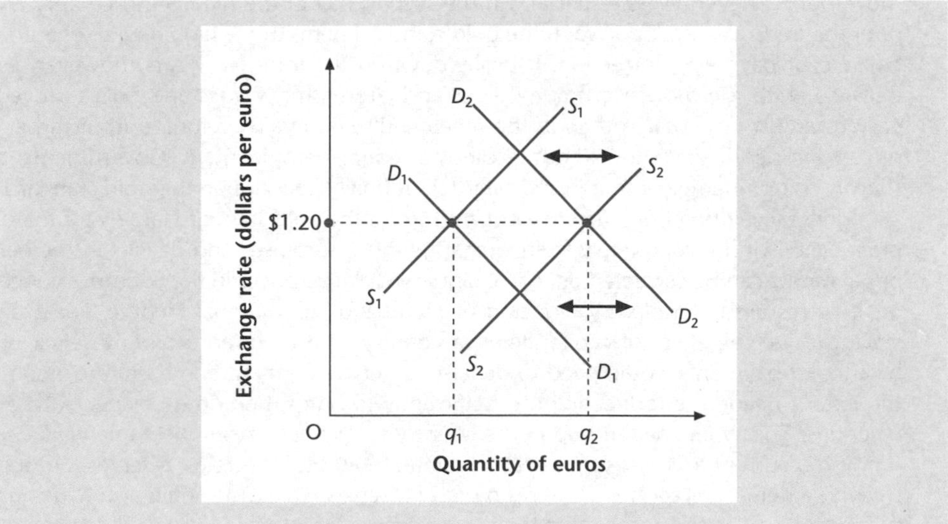

Figure 15.5 **Fixed exchange rates**

While these global systems are no longer in operation, many countries continue to pursue fixed-exchange policies on an individual basis for their own particular purposes. We summarise below the main features of the gold standard and Bretton Woods system in order to provide an historical context to understanding exchange rate systems in general.

Box 15.1

The gold standard

The gold standard lasted in one form or another up until the early 1930s. Under this system, the value of each currency was fixed in terms of an amount of gold. This necessarily meant that the value of any particular currency was fixed in terms of any other currency. In addition, international trade was primarily financed by gold shipments and the internal money supply was broadly determined by the amount of gold held by central banks. Basically, therefore, when exports exceeded imports, more gold flowed into the country than out. Consequently, the internal money supply rose, which in turn led to upward pressure on prices (see pp.199–202 and the discussion of the quantity theory of money for an explanation of the link between the money supply and prices), which in turn caused exports to become less competitive and imports more so. This process would continue until exports equalled imports and the gold inflow, therefore, ended. A similar mechanism operated in reverse when imports exceeded exports: gold would flow out of the country, the money supply would contract and prices would fall until, again, exports and imports were in balance.

It must be stressed that this is only a brief summary of the principles of the gold standard. In practice, occasional devaluations of currency values against gold occurred and central banks did intervene from time to time to ameliorate the economic effects of gold flows. Also, exchange rates were affected by inflows and outflows of gold reflecting capital movements. Nevertheless, especially in the second half of the nineteenth century and up until the outbreak of World War I, the gold standard permitted a high degree of automatic balance of payments correction. It broke down in the inter-war years, however, largely because, with the growth of trade unions and large firms, wages and prices proved less easy to adjust downwards than in the nineteenth century. Therefore, output rather than prices declined as gold flowed out leading to reduced employment. Governments facing sharply rising unemployment in the early 1930s finally abandoned the gold standard.

In general, economists today rule out a return to the gold standard largely for reasons of practicality. Under completely fixed exchange rates, surpluses and deficits in the balance of payments can be corrected only by changes in relative prices in the countries concerned or, if prices are inflexible, by reducing or increasing *real* national income. For example, leaving aside the effect of capital flows, a country with a current account deficit on the balance of payments would need to deflate aggregate demand and therefore incomes to the extent needed to reduce imports sufficiently to bring them into balance with export revenues. This would depend upon the country's *marginal propensity to import*. A country running a current account surplus can continue to add to its foreign reserves, but a country with a deficit will sooner or later run out of reserves. The same could apply to countries suffering from large net capital outflows. For every current account deficit of one country

Box 15.1 continued

there must be an equal and offsetting surplus in the current account of other countries. In principle, therefore, both deficit and surplus countries should act to correct current account imbalances. In practice, the burden of adjustment usually falls on the country running a current account deficit to deflate its national income.

Box 15.2

The Bretton Woods system

The second period of fixed exchange rates lasted from the end of World War II to the early 1970s. It emerged from a meeting of the allied powers at a conference at Bretton Woods, New Hampshire (USA) in 1944, and hence is often referred to as the *Bretton Woods system*. Following the collapse of the gold standard in the 1930s, countries had attempted to gain competitive advantage by devaluing their exchange rates, thereby making their exports relatively cheap and imports more expensive. Such action was primarily intended to boost employment prospects and was commonly referred to as a 'beggar my neighbour policy'. Ultimately, such measures damaged world trade.

At Bretton Woods it was agreed that fixed exchange rates should be restored but that a return to the gold standard was undesirable. A proposal advanced by the US delegation (called the *White Plan*) formed the basis of the scheme finally endorsed. Under this scheme, all currencies were assigned a fixed exchange rate against the US dollar (a *dollar parity*), which in turn was assigned a fixed value against gold ($35 per troy ounce for official transaction purposes). As a consequence, *cross exchange rates* between currencies were fixed. The link between the US dollar and an officially recorded volume of gold acted as a control mechanism on the printing of surplus dollars by the US government and therefore maintained confidence in the US dollar.

The Bretton Woods system was not entirely a fixed exchange rate regime since currencies were permitted a small degree of flexibility (±1 per cent against the dollar parity until 1971). Larger adjustments could take place but only in the event of 'fundamental disequilibria' in the balance of payments (i.e. persistent and large current account deficits or surpluses) and only by agreement with other countries (although this latter condition was not always met). The system was supervised by an international body also established at Bretton Woods, namely the *International Monetary Fund* (IMF) based in Washington (for a fuller description see pp.384–386). When countries suffered temporary current account deficits, governments were expected to intervene in the foreign exchange market to preserve the fixed parity using their foreign currency reserves. These reserves could be augmented by borrowing from the IMF up to agreed limits or from other countries' central banks. At the same time, countries were expected to correct balance of payments disequilibria by appropriate domestic fiscal and monetary policies – deficit countries deflating and surplus countries reflating their economies. In practice the burden fell mainly on the deficit countries because the surplus countries lacked the same pressure to act.

Box 15.2 continued

In the case of the UK the sterling exchange rate was devalued only twice during the Bretton Woods system – once in 1949, when sterling was devalued from $4.03 to $2.80, and again in 1967 when the parity was reduced to $2.40. This contrasts vividly with experience under floating exchange rates that the UK adopted in June 1972. After this date, the sterling exchange rate fluctuated widely against the dollar and other currencies. The same is true for other leading currencies, which also abandoned fixed exchange rates in the 1970s. Note that not all of sterling's fluctuation against the US dollar has been due to factors affecting the UK. Since the dollar has also floated up and down since the 1970s, movements in the $/£ rate often occur because the dollar itself is changing in value on the international markets. This point should always be borne in mind when interpreting movements of one currency against another. It also explains why, in the media, sterling is sometimes quoted in terms of a basket of leading currencies or, more correctly, the *sterling exchange rate index*, which is a trade-weighted average of major currencies. Movements in this rate are more likely to reflect fundamental changes in the external value of sterling. Other currencies have similar trade-weighted measures.

The Bretton Woods system broke down for a number of reasons. Briefly, there was a growing lack of international liquidity; the main currencies held in central bank foreign reserves were the US dollar and, to a declining extent, especially after the 1967 devaluation, sterling. World reserves could finance 48 weeks of exports in 1948 but only 14 weeks' worth by the mid-1970s. This was exacerbated by declining confidence in the US dollar. To expand international liquidity, central banks had to be willing to hold dollar-denominated assets in their foreign reserves. There were no difficulties while confidence in the dollar was maintained. However, rising US government expenditures overseas (e.g. the Vietnam War) as well as the financing of America's space programme and the establishment of its social welfare system (the 'Great Society' programme which commenced in the 1960s), led to a flood of dollars on to world markets and confidence sagged. In particular, dollars were traded for gold, which was considered to be a secure asset. At this time, however, gold had a fixed price under the Bretton Woods system of $35 per troy ounce, which the US government was committed to protect.

In 1968, following widespread conversion of dollar holdings into gold at the fixed rate by many countries, the USA had to concede defeat and a two-price system for gold was introduced. Under this two-price system central banks continued to transfer gold among themselves at $35 per troy ounce, while gold was allowed to find its own value in the free market for non-official purposes. However, with a worsening US balance of payments on current account this provided only a short respite. In August 1971, official dollar convertibility had to be suspended temporarily following renewed speculative activity. In December 1971 the so-called *Smithsonian Agreement* officially devalued the US dollar against other currencies and against gold (from $35 to $38 per troy ounce). Since other currencies were expressed in terms of the US dollar, this meant that new currency parities were established against the dollar. This agreement was then itself quickly overwhelmed by world economic events. Rising inflation aggravated by a quadrupling in world oil prices between 1972 and 1974, which undermined the balance of payments accounts of the leading industrial economies, meant that the Bretton Woods system finally collapsed. Governments turned to floating their currencies, usually in the form of a *managed float*.

Managed exchange rates

A *managed exchange rate system* or a *managed float* refers to a situation where exchange rates are determined in the main by the conditions of demand and supply, but central banks intervene from time to time to stabilise the rates or influence them in some way.

Thus, if a currency is depreciating in the foreign exchange market the authorities could sell foreign currency reserves and buy the currency, helping to reduce the downward pressure. Similarly, to reduce an appreciating currency value, the authorities could sell the currency and buy foreign currencies. In this way, intervention would help to smooth out the fluctuations in the exchange rate.

It should be noted that the degree to which the authorities are able to neutralise all fluctuations and hence keep the currency at a fixed rate, is limited. Central banks do not have unlimited foreign currency reserves or lines of credit to intervene over a long period in the foreign exchange market, especially given the huge volumes of currencies that are traded each day cross the world. Consequently, a degree of flexibility in the exchange rate may have to be accepted. Managed flexibility can take a number of different forms such as *dirty floating* and *joint floating*.

Dirty floating

In *dirty floating*, the decision as to when to intervene to support the currency and to what extent, depends on government discretion. The main objective, however, under dirty floating is to have reasonable stability in the exchange rate in order to maintain confidence in the currency – and perhaps in the government's general macroeconomic policy. The term 'dirty floating' arises because governments attempt to 'manage' the float through foreign exchange intervention. An alternative, and less pejorative term, is a *managed float*.

Joint floating

Following the collapse of the Bretton Woods system of fixed exchange rates, a number of European countries set up a *joint float* in 1972, which became known as the *snake*. Under the snake, currencies were pegged to each other but were allowed a maximum variation between any two of the participating currencies of $\pm 2^1/_4$ per cent. They were then allowed to float freely (or within a band) against other currencies. At first the snake was a joint float against the US dollar, although this link was broken in 1973 and it essentially evolved into a small 'club' or 'bloc' of European currencies shadowing the value of the deutschmark in the foreign exchange market.

In 1979, the snake arrangement was replaced by the *European Monetary System (EMS)*. This system played a major role in the development of the Single

European Market. Until 1993, member currencies were managed so that they remained within margins of ±2¼ against each other as well as against the *European Currency Unit* (ECU); the Italian lira and later the Spanish peseta and sterling had a wider margin of ±6 per cent. This arrangement was known as the *European Exchange Rate Mechanism (ERM)*. The ECU was a *basket* unit of account whose value was derived as a weighted average of EMS member currencies, including sterling. It should be noted that the UK did not participate in the ERM arrangements from its inception because of fears that membership might prove unsustainable. The value of sterling was especially volatile in the late 1970s and early 1980s when the UK achieved petro-currency status following North Sea oil discoveries. The UK joined the ERM in October 1990. Two years later, however, a sterling crisis led the UK to abandon the system. A similar crisis led the Italian lira also to leave the ERM, while, a few months later, a run on the French franc caused the permissible margins of fluctuation to be widened from ±2¼ per cent to ±15 per cent. The events of 1992–93 illustrated the difficulty of maintaining fixed (or semi-fixed) exchange rates in a world of large capital flows in and out of countries. An aim within Europe from the 1980s was eventual monetary union. In 1999, 11 of the 15 EU member states (excluding Denmark, Sweden and the UK) agreed to abandon their own currencies in favour of a common currency, the euro (Greece became the twelfth member when it adopted the euro in 2001). The ECU and ERM then became redundant.

Fixed versus floating exchange rates

In this section we set out the central arguments both in favour of and against the adoption of fixed or floating exchange rates. There is no simple answer as to which system is best: the choice will depend upon current economic conditions and, perhaps, the attitudes ruling at a given point in time ('free market' versus 'state intervention').

The case for floating exchange rates

The key arguments in support of a floating exchange rate system fall under four headings:

- a self-adjustment mechanism;
- independence of monetary policy;
- efficient resource allocation;
- insulation from imported inflation (but *only* in the case of an *appreciating* currency).

Self-adjustment mechanism

A floating exchange rate regime means that, by definition, the currency that is floating will be priced at the rate determined by market forces and, as such, will neither be overvalued or undervalued at any point in time. In addition, a floating exchange rate should ensure *automatic correction* of current account imbalances (but subject to the *Marshall-Lerner condition* and the *J-curve effect* – see pp.343–346)

For example, if a country is experiencing inflationary problems that lead to a current account deficit, then depreciation of its currency should compensate for a loss of price competitiveness in international markets and pull the current account of the balance of payments back towards equilibrium. Similarly, if a country is running a surplus on its current account, an appreciation in the exchange rate will increase the price of its exports in other countries and reduce the domestic price of its imports moving the current account back to equilibrium.

Independence of monetary policy

If floating exchange rates automatically rectify a current account problem, there will be less need for a country to pursue demand management policies to reduce incomes and therefore the demand for imports. The country will then be free to devote greater attention to solving internal problems. In particular, decisions concerning monetary policy can be taken *independently* of the exchange rate – interest rate policy is not a 'hostage' to the exchange but instead can be directed at domestic problems and the achievement of domestic objectives (such as low inflation). In this way, monetary sovereignty is ensured.

Efficient allocation of resources

At the same time, there will be less need for large foreign currency reserves to be held by the authorities because the exchange rate does not have to be supported. Financial resources can be allocated more efficiently to reflect shifts in demand patterns and comparative advantage in each country pursuing a floating exchange rate regime.

Insulation from imported inflation

A country experiencing a *rising* (i.e. appreciating) exchange rate will, to a degree, be insulated from higher import prices. For example, if the dollar price of oil increases, the price paid by Europeans in euros may remain stable if the value of the euro against the dollar also rises.

All of these arguments in favour of floating exchange rates only apply, however, provided an appreciation or depreciation of the currency is not managed by the authorities but reflects demand and supply pressures in the foreign exchange market. Also a floating system does not guarantee a current account balance because daily demand for and supply of leading currencies is affected by capital flows, including speculative activity relating to currency movements.

The case against floating exchange rates

There are three main drawbacks to the adoption of a floating exchange rate system involving:

- potential volatility and instability;
- a danger of destabilising capital flows;
- inflationary effects.

Potential volatility and instability

Leaving aside the possibility that floating exchange rates may reflect movements of capital rather than trade flows (indeed capital movements may have a perverse effect on the balance of trade through the exchange rate), their main drawback lies in the uncertainty created in international trading and investment. This is particularly important for businesses. For example, if a Japanese exporter invoices a foreign buyer in foreign currency, it will not be sure how much it will receive when this foreign currency is converted into domestic currency, i.e. yen. However, such exchange rate uncertainty can be mitigated – at a price – by the use of *forward exchange contracts*, discussed later in this chapter (p.375).

Danger of destabilising capital flows

Floating exchange rates could also discourage some investors from investing overseas – and could lead to exceptionally large capital movements. This is more likely to be the case when exchange rates move erratically, in large jumps, leading to possible large capital losses – as well as potential capital gains, of course – when the investor realises his or her investment or when interest, profits and dividends are remitted. The international investor faces exchange rate risk in addition to the usual risks attached to any investment activity. However, such risks are likely to be even greater when fixed exchange rates are unsustainable and do not reflect the 'real' economy – in which case, a voluntary or involuntary decision to float could result in massive capital inflows or outflows. Again, the use of forward exchange contracts may mitigate this uncertainty to some extent.

Inflationary effects

Above, we noted that an *appreciating* currency should help to reduce imported inflationary pressures. In contrast, a *falling* (i.e. depreciating) currency may increase imported inflation. For example, if the euro falls against the dollar then any rise in the dollar price of oil will result in a higher euro price being paid by Europeans in their domestic markets (if the price rise is passed on by oil importers and retailers). The danger of imported inflation is that it could lead to further falls in the value of the currency – and result in a vicious spiral of depreciation followed by higher inflation, leading to a further depreciation, etc. In addition, floating exchange rates may also promote inflationary monetary and fiscal policies because the need to set domestic policies, notably interest rates, to maintain a currency value is removed.

Application 15.1

A single currency for Europe

European Economic and Monetary Union

The European Union's historic project of economic and monetary union (EMU) got off the ground on 1 January 1999 with 11 member states taking part. At the Brussels Council meeting in May 1998, the governments had confirmed that EMU could begin as planned under the provisions of the Maastricht Treaty. The initial participants were the countries which had met the convergence criteria (relating to price and exchange-rate stability, interest-rate convergence and budget discipline). The UK and Denmark made use of the opt-out clause allowing them to stay outside. Greece joined EMU in 2001. Sweden decided against participation in a referendum on 14 September 2003.

The founding of EMU reflected the pursuit of both economic and political goals. From an economic standpoint the main issue was to set up a stability union, and anchor price stability and budget discipline in Europe on a permanent basis. Moreover, the objective was to complete the European single market by eliminating exchange-rate risks and to ensure a greater degree of planning certainty for trade and long-term investment. A large single European market for financial services was to create more favourable investment and financing opportunities. The EU also intended for the euro to promote transparency and competition and thus strengthen growth and employment in the single market. Finally, it was expected that EMU would give Europe new political stimuli to achieve further integration. All in all, the formation of EMU gave rise to a major economic area with a single currency which is only slightly smaller than the USA in terms of size and other indicators and considerably larger than Japan. The table below presents international comparisons for 2001.

International comparisons (2001)

	Unit	*USA*	*Euroland*	*Japan*
Population	M	285	307	127
GDP	EUR bn	8,701	6,824	2,920
GDP per capita	EUR	30,500	22,300	22,900
Share of world GDP	in %	27.2	21.3	9.1
Exports (goods and services)	% of GDP	9.9	19.8	10.7
Imports (goods and services)	% of GDP	13.5	18.7	10.1
General government deficit	% of GDP	0.5	1.5	6.1
General government debt	% of GDP	44.8	69.2	134.6
Current account balance	% of GDP	−3.9	−0.2	2.1

▶

Application 15.1 continued

The Euro as an international currency

Despite the fact that the Eurozone now rivals the USA in terms of size, it is notable that the European Central Bank's (ECB) declared policy is to refrain from promoting or hindering the use of the euro internationally as a unit of account, means of payment or store of value, and to leave this job to market forces instead.

The international role of a currency is predicated on a series of factors: a large, powerful economy with a significant share of world trade, unrestricted convertibility, confidence in the stability of value, highly sophisticated financial markets, good-quality economic policy and political stability. The US dollar established itself as the world's undisputed top currency on this basis after the second world war. As EMU largely fulfils the given prerequisites, it was widely anticipated in the run-up to its launch that the euro might one day seriously challenge the dollar's dominance. Since 1999 the following trends and facts have emerged in respect of official and private-sector use:

- The euro currently accounts for 13 per cent of total official *foreign-exchange reserves* worldwide, still a modest figure in comparison with the US dollar (68 per cent, both at end-2001). This share roughly matches that of the replaced currencies when one considers that the national central banks' foreign reserves held in those currencies – especially deutschmarks – lost their reserve status with the launch of EMU. Besides, the euro's statistical share suffered owing to the depreciation against the US dollar. The next statistics are likely to show the euro claiming a much high percentage of total official reserves.
- The euro is used as an *anchor currency* for exchange rate policy by about 50 – mostly small – countries which have close economic ties with the EU and are neighbours in the region. Given the orientation of their monetary regime to the euro these countries hold forex reserves in euros, for intervention purposes for instance.
- In *foreign exchange trading*, the US dollar and the euro are the currency pair bought and sold most frequently, at 30 per cent of the total (ahead of dollar–yen exchanges at 20 per cent).
- The euro has been well represented in *international bond issues*, accounting for nearly 40 per cent of the total, and the gap with the US dollar has narrowed considerably since 1998. The euro-denominated share of international debt securities outstanding rose by 3 percentage points to 29 per cent from 1999 to mid-2002, while the dollar's share fell to 44 per cent.

All in all, the euro has become the world's second most important currency, succeeding the deutschmark. It has not jeopardised the US dollar's leading role though. This is unlikely to change for the time being. Unlike the euro, the US

Application 15.1 continued

dollar has enjoyed the markets' confidence for decades and offers considerable economies of scale and network density. Anyway, a currency develops an international role in competition with its peers only slowly and gradually over a fairly long period. For example, the US dollar came to replace the pound sterling as reserve currency No. 1 between the two world wars.

Source: Edited extract from Deutsche Bank Research, *EMU Watch*, 28 March 2003.

Activity

The euro is growing in popularity as a global currency but what are the costs and benefits associated with its adoption by the individual member states of the European Union?

The case for fixed exchange rates

A fixed exchange rate system may be adopted by the authorities on the basis of three key arguments concerning:

- certainty and stability;
- adjustment pressures;
- anti-inflationary discipline.

Certainty and stability

By definition, a fixed exchange rate offers certainty and stability: everyone knows from day to day the value of the currency against other currencies. This certainty should help to promote international trade and investment by removing currency risk. To understand the significance of this benefit, imagine what would happen if the 50 states of the USA each had a separate currency and all 50 currencies floated freely against each other! It is clear that a single currency across the USA helps to promote integration and the free movement of goods and services. Indeed, this is the primary argument that has been put forward in support of single currency (the euro) within the European Union.

Adjustment pressures

Perhaps the strongest argument in favour of fixed exchange rates is that they impose some discipline on domestic monetary systems and force countries to adjust the 'real' economy to competitiveness. For example, if a country's exports become uncompetitive and there is a persistent current account deficit, the authorities will have to resort to deflationary policies to improve the country's international payments position. In addition, supply-side measures are also likely to be implemented, encouraging the restructuring of domestic industries. It has been suggested that the decline in a currency's value provides little incentive for uncompetitive industry to face up to the harsh reality of the need to restructure and invest in new plant and equipment. In other words, a currency depreciation may simply extend product life cycles and outmoded working practices and put off the inevitable structural adjustments needed in the economy.

Anti-inflationary discipline

Finally, insofar as a depreciating currency permits an exporter to pass on higher production costs, notably large wage settlements, a floating exchange rate system is not conducive to defeating domestic inflation. This is not the case with respect to a fixed exchange rate regime. If, at a given exchange rate, exports are not competitive, then the exporting firm will either have to cut costs and prices or go out of business. A fixed value for the currency offers no comfort to inefficient firms and, thus, should lead to lower domestic inflation.

The case against fixed exchange rates

There are three main arguments against a fixed exchange rate system involving:

- availability of reserves;
- burden of adjustment;
- loss of monetary control.

Availability of reserves

As discussed earlier, fixed exchange rates may be maintained by the authorities through intervention in the foreign exchange markets, but this requires large amounts of foreign currency reserves or immediate access to foreign currency loans. In practice, central banks have finite reserves and loan facilities. At the same time, as the world's capital markets have expanded and opened up in recent years, the extent to which any one government is able to intervene to counteract the huge volumes of capital that now flow around the world is extremely limited. Even the eight leading countries, known as the *Group of 8* or *G8* (USA, Japan, Germany, France, UK, Canada, Italy and Russia) acting in concert have not always been able to forestall currency movements. Ultimately, as the saying goes, 'you cannot buck the market'. Therefore, fixed exchange rates may be unrealistic today. The gold standard and the Bretton Woods system operated at a time when much smaller volumes of currency were traded daily internationally and a much larger proportion of foreign exchange transactions were trade-related. Even so, the Bretton Woods system collapsed because of widespread speculation against leading currencies, notably the US dollar.

Burden of adjustment

Under a fixed exchange rate system any changes in international competitiveness cannot be reflected in currency movements. Therefore, the burden of adjustment to improve competitiveness must fall on the domestic economy through industrial restructuring, wage restraint and deflationary policies. If adjustments such as these do not take place then there is a danger that an 'uncompetitive' economy (in terms of international trade) will suffer prolonged current account deficits on the balance of payments, falling output and higher unemployment, i.e. economic stagnation.

Loss of monetary control

Finally, in attempting to keep the exchange rate fixed in the face of market forces the authorities lose control over the domestic money supply. This occurs because the money supply has to accommodate the fixed exchange rate. For example, in order to halt an appreciation in the value of the currency, the authorities might intervene by selling the currency in the foreign exchange market. This currency, however, will then tend to find its way back into the domestic economy thereby boosting the money supply. This in turn will add to inflationary pressures. Alternatively, interest rates might be reduced to stem capital inflows into the country, but this will tend to encourage domestic credit expansion as people borrow more at the lower rates. Hence, the adoption of a fixed exchange rate system results in a loss of control over monetary policy. This partly explains the reluctance of Sweden, Denmark and the UK to join the Eurozone.

We have already explained why speculation in favour of or against a currency may occur with the objective of achieving a capital gain (or to avoid a capital loss). Currency speculation carries inevitable risk unless the direction of change in the exchange rate can be predicted with complete certainty. Under the Bretton Woods system of fixed rates, the likelihood of a currency revaluation was low while a currency under selling pressure might well be devalued. Speculation, therefore, was often 'a one-way bet'. Under floating rates, however, currencies can just as easily go up in value as down. From this brief discussion, it should be obvious why governments deny that they would like to see the value of their currency fall in international markets, while not intervening extensively to prevent a fall. Any suggestion that a government harboured a desire to see its currency decline in value would trigger a wave of speculative selling because the future movement of the currency would be more predictable.

The determination of exchange rates

So far we have been analysing different types of exchange rate system and the arguments for and against the adoption of each. A government, as a formal policy or on an *ad hoc* basis, may influence the value of its country's exchange rate relative to other currencies. Also, the exchange rate is affected by the flow of exports and imports of goods, services and capital into and out of a country. However, there are a number of other factors that interact within the economy to affect the external value of currencies and we now examine these.

The state of the macroeconomy

At the macroeconomy level, changes in national income have an impact upon the demand for imports as well as goods and services produced for the domestic market, which might otherwise be exported if demand for them did not exist in the home market. Changes in aggregate demand are therefore reflected in the demand for and supply of currencies on the foreign exchange market and, hence, in exchange rates. At the same time, supply-side factors play an important role. The ability of an economy to increase output and employment eventually has implications for its balance of payments and ultimately its exchange rate.

Apart from the general state of the macroeconomy, both on the demand side and on the supply side, there are two further economic variables that have a direct impact upon exchange rates. These are:

- the rate of domestic inflation relative to that in other countries;
- domestic interest rates compared with competing interest rates abroad.

The rate of inflation and the exchange rate

In general, differences in the rates of inflation between countries will be reflected in the exchange rates between their currencies. Countries experiencing higher rates of inflation will tend to experience depreciation in the external value of their currencies. The converse applies to countries experiencing lower rates of inflation than average, their exchange rates will tend to appreciate. These movements tend to occur gradually under freely floating exchange rates, but more slowly and falteringly where rates are managed or fixed because the authorities intervene to offset market movements, in ways already discussed.

Interest rates and exchange rates

A strong link is also evident between interest rates and exchange rates. For example, high interest rates in one country relative to other countries will tend to attract inflows of capital from these lower interest-rate economies (unless there are other factors acting as a disincentive to invest, for example political instability or a perception that the exchange rate of the country is about to fall). These capital flows will, in turn, raise the exchange rate of the recipient country. This relationship is particularly significant in the world's money and foreign currency markets today in equalising interest-rate differentials between the major international financial centres, as discussed in Box 15.1, which introduces the role of the *forward exchange market*.

The example above also highlights the extent to which speculation in foreign exchange can itself be a stabilising influence on exchange rate values. For example,

Box 15.3

The forward exchange market – an illustration

Capital is allowed to flow unhindered between the USA and Japan. Suppose that a three-month deposit of capital can earn a 4 per cent return in New York and a 1 per cent return in Tokyo. The 3 per cent margin between the returns will, everything else being equal, entice investors (speculators) to move yen from Tokyo to New York, investing perhaps in short-term US dollar deposit accounts. This action requires them to *sell* the yen and *buy* dollars at the current (or *spot*) exchange rate between the dollar and yen. As a consequence, the supply of yen will rise as the demand for the dollar rises, leading to an appreciation in the dollar's value and a fall in the value of the yen on the foreign exchange market. It should be noted that it is not necessary in practice for funds to move from Japan to the USA. The transactions occur in the major financial markets, which include Tokyo. It is also possible to trade in dollar-denominated assets in London. The City of London also contains the world's largest Eurocurrency trading market including the Eurodollar market. It is possible, therefore, to trade in US dollar-denominated amounts purely within the confines of the City of London.

During the three-month deposit period, it is possible that the value of the dollar could fall sharply (for whatever reason) against the yen. The consequent capital loss could then outweigh the greater return earned through the 3 per cent interest-rate differential. To protect against this possibility, the investor could cover the liability by dealing in the *forward exchange market*. That is, dollars could be bought against the spot exchange rate for the yen, and the investor could simultaneously agree to sell dollars against the yen *three months forward*. This is known as a *forward contract*. The difference between the quoted spot and forward exchange rates is known as the *forward premium* or *discount*, i.e. when the spot price of the yen rises above the forward price against the dollar, the yen is said to have a *forward discount* (when it falls below, a *forward premium*). It should be noted that the size of this premium or discount must exactly equal the difference between dollar and yen interest rates (in this case 3 per cent) otherwise an opportunity will exist for arbitrageurs to make money by buying or selling currency in the spot or forward markets. It follows therefore that *forward exchange rates are determined by interest rate differentials* rather than simply by market expectations of exchange rates in the future.

if a country has a current account deficit on its balance of payments account then there will be downward pressure on its currency. If speculators take the view that such a deficit is only temporary, then they may be tempted to buy the currency when it is falling in value and sell it when its value rises as the current account returns to surplus later – hoping, of course, to make a profit in the process, as detailed earlier in this chapter. In this way, any depreciation in the currency will be offset to some extent by the buying decisions of speculators.

In contrast, speculation may also be destabilising, particularly where the volumes of currencies being bought and sold are so huge that they lead to changes

Application 15.2

Determination of exchange rates

What factors are currently driving exchange rates?

It is well known in foreign exchange markets that consistently forecasting currency shifts accurately using economic models is virtually impossible. The best predictor of a shift in a currency's rate is its own most recent values. However, it may still be useful to at least understand what factors currency forecasters think are the most important influences on exchange rates. A recent survey from *Consensus Economics* has ranked the importance of seven key factors that were identified by forecasters as currently being key determinants of exchange rates.

The first six factors relate to economic variables and the seventh to some important 'other' factor, which may or may not be economic. These determining influences were assigned a score from 0 to 10, from no effect to maximum effect. The table below shows that the importance attached to the impact of these factors on some key exchange rates versus the US dollar varies between countries. A number of trends seem to emerge from the table.

Key exchange rate determinant (Score out of 10)

Currency, per US$	*Relative growth*	*Inflation differential*	*Trade/ current account trends*	*Short-term interest rate differences*	*Long-term interest rate differences*	*Equity market flow*	*Other factors*
Developed							
Japanese yen	4.8	2.5	5.8	1.7	2.7	5.2	8 Bond flows
Euro	5.9	2.6	4.6	3.9	3.7	5.9	9 Bond flows
Pound	5.3	2.7	3.4	4.9	4.7	5.1	
Swiss franc	4.6	2.6	4.4	4.2	4.6	5.4	
Asia							
Australia	6.3	2.9	4.6	5.4	4.5	6.3	8 Global risk aversion
New Zealand	6.6	3.0	4.8	5.3	4.3	5.6	8.5 Australian $
South Korea	6.8	4.2	7.2	6.6	5.0	7.2	8 Japanese yen
Singapore	6.8	3.3	5.0	6.3	4.5	6.3	8 Japanese yen
Eastern Europe							
Russian rouble	1.7	8.3	6.3	1.7	1.0	0.7	7 Foreign investment
Polish zloty	4.8	5.5	6.3	7.8	6.8	4.0	9 Privatisation
Czech koruna	4.3	4.8	4.5	6.8	6.0	4.3	9 Foreign investment
Hungarian forint	5.0	6.3	6.5	7.5	7.0	4.0	10 Foreign investment
Latin America							
Brazilian real	4.8	5.4	7.6	3.8	4.0	5.2	10 Politics & debt
Mexican peso	6.3	6.5	7.3	7.3	5.8	5.5	10 Foreign investment
Colombia	4.7	4.3	5.7	4.3	3.7	5.7	7 Brazilian real
Venezuelan bolivar	5.7	4.7	7.3	6.3	5.7	5.3	10 Politics
Other							
South Africa	5.5	5.3	5.3	4.6	4.3	6.5	8 Capital flows

Application 15.2 continued

One is that inflation is of low priority in the developed countries, at around 2.5 for the four countries in the table. This is true even in countries where the importance of inflation is given a higher score out of 10. It is given high prominence in Eastern Europe and Latin America for instance, but is still generally less important than other factors. Russia is the exception, where inflation is scored the most important factor impacting the exchange rate according to the survey.

Relative growth rates are important in all regions, though it seems least important for Russia. Relative growth is most important for the Asian currencies, ranging from 6.3 in Australia to 6.8 in South Korea and Singapore.

Russia also scores the lowest for equity market flows as a driver for the currency. But equity market flows seem important for the Asian economies including Australia and New Zealand. It is least important for Eastern Europe; perhaps reflecting the less mature nature of equity markets in the region and the relative lack of openness to international trade. For Latin America, equity market flows are scored around 5.5, but trade and current account flows are scored more highly, perhaps reflecting the area's high level of external debt. For the Western European countries, equity flows are the most important of the economic variables. Trade and current account differences are important for countries with large deficits, such as Poland and Brazil and for those with large surpluses, like Russia. The trade account scores well over 7 for Brazil, Mexico and Venezuela, matched only by South Korea in Asia on 7.2. Interest rate differentials are important for all countries other than the developed ones, where the average score is less than 5. For Russia, the score is 1.7 for the importance of short-term interest rate differentials and just 1 for long-term interest rates.

For all the countries in the table, the seventh variable is more important than any of the six key economic factors. That might explain why forecasting models that use these factors as principal drivers fail. The Australian currency scores 8 out of 10 for global risk aversion as a factor driving demand for it, but the most important economic factor scores just 6.3. In Latin America, politics has come to the fore and for Brazil and Venezuela it scores 10. In the case of Brazil, debt payment also scores 10 as a key concern. For South Africa, capital flows are judged key to the currency's trend, while privatisations are a key to understanding shifts in the Polish currency.

Source: Edited extract from Lloyds TSB *Economic* Bulletin, Number 44, November 2002.

Activity

Given the difficulty associated with forecasting exchange rate movements, how can speculators make money over the longer term?

in currency values that are not reflective of the underlying economic reality, i.e. exchange rates may *overshoot* or *undershoot* longer-run equilibrium levels. On balance, many economists would argue that excessive speculation is destabilising by creating uncertainty about currency values that damage world trade and growth. At the same time, this type of speculation is difficult to distinguish from sound commercial decisions by financiers, including corporate treasurers. If they believe a currency will shortly decline in value then it makes sense to sell the currency now. Recall, however, that the action of selling a currency, perhaps based upon a rumour in the markets that the currency is coming under pressure, can have the effect of *causing* the value of the currency to fall.

Exchange rates and the balance of payments

On several occasions we have noted, leaving aside possibly disruptive capital flows, that floating exchange rates can correct a current account imbalance: the adjustment should be automatic via the market mechanism. Demand for a surplus country's currency will be rising, pushing up its exchange rate and thus making its exports more expensive and its imports cheaper. In this way a current account surplus will tend to be eliminated, while the reverse process can be expected in the case of a deficit country.

As we explained fully in Chapter 14, in practice, this seemingly automatic mechanism does not always appear to work perfectly or, if it does, it takes time for the effects to become evident. This situation is typical of that which often faces countries. Despite a fall in their currency's exchange rate against nearly all other major currencies, the current account deficit may in fact grow and continue to be a problem for some time – due to a *J-curve effect*. The reason is that when currencies depreciate, it may take time for people to adjust their patterns of consumption and to change their investment plans. For example, households and firms may continue to buy what they regard as high-quality imports, despite the fact that a fall in the value of their country's currency may have pushed up import prices. At the same time, foreigners may not respond immediately to the fall in the value of the currency by placing orders for the country's goods – again, tastes and preferences take time to change. Thus, the initial responsiveness (i.e. *price elasticity*) of demand for both imports and exports as a consequence of changes in currency value may be quite low. Depreciation will lead to an improvement in the current account situation only if the sum of the price elasticities of demand for exports and for imports exceeds unity. This condition is known as the *Marshall-Lerner condition* (see p.343 for full details).

Some economists argue that price considerations are often given too prominent a place in explanations of trade flows. They stress a number of other non-price reasons for the weakness in a balance of payments position, such as poor quality products and low levels of technological change. It may also be the case that when a currency depreciates exporters chose to retain existing export prices (in foreign currency terms) and improve their profit margins, thus forestalling the improvement in price competitiveness that depreciation implies.

Exchange rates and business

Erratic changes in exchange rates can, as noted earlier, increase the uncertainty facing management in its decision making. Given the likelihood of a lengthy time period between winning an export order or placing an import order and the final delivery of the goods and the settling of accounts, exchange rate fluctuations can make all the difference between a profit or a loss on the transaction. In this way, floating exchange rates may discourage trade and investment decisions though, as discussed above, short-term risks can be overcome by the use of forward exchange markets, where firms can agree to buy and sell currency at a given future date at a contracted price. This will, however, involve transaction costs such as commission payments. Also, forward contracts cannot usually be negotiated for more than a year in advance, so they cannot be used to cover longer-term risks in international trade and investment. Other methods to reduce exchange rate risk include:

- use of *forecasts* of exchange rate movements;
- *risk-spreading* through having a range of overseas suppliers and export markets trading in different currencies, in the hope that this will provide some security;
- *hedging*, which is useful where there is no forward market: a corporate treasurer can deal in foreign currencies and deposit sums in different currencies as a hedge against currency fluctuations;
- *investing in foreign subsidiaries:* multinational companies can reduce exchange rate risk by sourcing and supplying in various countries. Exchange rate movements may also lead them to reallocate work between national plants to retain competitiveness and to protect profits.

Fluctuations in exchange rates require managers to make difficult economic decisions. This is illustrated by the following example.

Suppose a German firm is exporting a luxury car selling at €40,000 in Germany and, at an exchange rate of $1.75 = €1, at a price of $70,000 in the USA (ignoring freight and insurance charges, etc.). If the company currently sells 1,000 vehicles per annum in the USA, its total earnings there are $70m. If the euro exchange rate appreciates to US$2 = €1, the German manufacturer now faces two choices:

- to continue to sell in the USA at the existing price of $70,000 but receive only €35,000 ($70,000 ÷ $2) as against €40,000 per vehicle – in which case total receipts fall by €5m (€35m as against €40m).
- to raise the US price to compensate for the euro appreciation – in which case the price of vehicles in the USA would rise to $80,000. But at the higher price fewer cars are likely to be sold.

Which of the two options is chosen may well depend upon the price elasticity of demand for the vehicles in the USA. If they are price elastic, then raising the price to $80,000 might lead to *lower* sales receipts in euros than if the price had been left unchanged. For example, if vehicle sales fell to 750 per annum, total revenue in euros would be €30m (750 × $80,000 ÷ $2).

A similar managerial decision would have to be faced if the currency *depreciated*. In this case the question would be whether to reduce the overseas sales price by an equivalent amount or whether to sell at the same price but make a healthier profit margin in euro terms. Again, the price elasticity of demand for exports will be an important deciding factor. Also relevant are expectations as to how long the depreciation will last (there is no point in reducing prices today and then increasing them again next month), and whether the firm has sufficient capacity to produce more output for export (there is no point in stimulating export sales through price reductions which cannot be met by increased supply).

Concluding remarks

The discussion of exchange rates and exchange rate regimes in this chapter has highlighted why exchange rates fluctuate and their relationship to balance of payments current account surpluses and deficits. As we have seen, while over the long term a country with a balance of payments surplus on current account can expect its exchange rate to appreciate against that of its trading partners, and a country with a balance of payments deficit on current account can expect its exchange rate to depreciate, this is not necessarily so in the short term. Week-to-week, month-to-month and even year-to-year exchange rate movements are affected not just by the balance on the current account ('the balance of payments') but by the balance on the capital account. With large and liquid international financial markets trading vast amounts of foreign currencies daily, this foreign currency trading (and hence 'sentiment' in the financial markets about a currency's relative value) is a major determinant of a currency's short-term exchange rate.

Movements in exchange rates add a further and unwelcome element of risk and uncertainty in business decision making today. For this reason, many people in business demand greater exchange rate stability. But stable exchange rates have pitfalls as well as advantages. Without exchange rate flexibility, cost and price increases in excess of those experienced in competitor countries must eventually lead to a decline in exports and a rise in imports. The consequent deterioration in the current account will lead government to introduce economic measures designed to deflate demand and thus reduce economic growth to bring down inflation. This is likely to feed through into lower profitability, plant closures and unemployment.

At the same time, floating exchange rates may not be the answer. Floating rates may be inflationary, in the sense that they enable governments to postpone remedial action to reduce inflationary pressures, while depreciation increases the prices of imported goods, which adds to inflation.

In the next chapter we review some of the major institutions in the international economy that have an effect upon trade and capital flows and therefore on exchange rates.

Key learning points

- An *exchange rate* is the price of one currency expressed in terms of another.
- In a free market, the *equilibrium exchange rate* at any given time reflects the demand for and supply of a currency including currency denominated assets.
- The quantity of a currency demanded at any given time reflects (a) a *transaction effect*, and (b) a *capital gains effect*.
- The *transaction effect* reflects the demand, including expected demand, for currencies with respect to the purchase of imports and exports and for capital transactions purposes.
- The *capital gains effect* reflects the fact that in the presence of exchange rate movements capital gains (and losses) can be made in the foreign exchange market.
- *Purchasing power parity theory* relates the exchange rate between two (or more) currencies to the relative price levels in the two countries.
- In a *floating exchange rate system* the exchange rate appreciates and depreciates according to changes in the demand for and supply of the currency, relative to other currencies, in the foreign exchange market.
- Under a *managed float* central banks may intervene to influence the exchange rate by buying and selling currencies using their foreign reserves and loan facilities.
- In a *fixed exchange rate system* the exchange rate is pegged at a given (normally internationally agreed) level. A country's central bank is required to maintain the exchange rate at (or around) this level through foreign exchange market interventions until such time as a formal devaluation or revaluation of the currency is permitted.
- The *gold standard* was a fixed exchange rate system based on the value of gold and operated largely during the second half of the nineteenth century and until World War I.
- The *Bretton Woods system* was established at the end of World War II and introduced a fixed exchange rate regime internationally that was broadly maintained until the 1970s. It collapsed under the weight of speculative capital flows and high inflation internationally.
- From the 1970s the European Union countries developed a joint float, which became known as the 'snake', to provide for some exchange rate stability within Europe. This developed into the *European Monetary System* and later a common European currency, the *euro*.
- *Floating exchange rates* provide countries with more discretion over domestic monetary and fiscal policies, leaving the exchange rate to find its own level in the foreign exchange market in the light of domestic economic conditions. However, floating rates may remove an important restraint on governments that pursue inflationary economic policies and they can prove a disincentive

to trade and international investment because of the uncertainty created by frequently changing currency values.

- *Exchange rates* and *interest rate policy* tend to be linked because of the impact of changes in interest rates on international capital flows.
- The use of the *forward exchange market* can help to reduce the uncertainties for traders and investors caused by floating exchange rates.

? Topics for discussion

1. A developing country is reporting a trade deficit because of large imports of capital equipment to assist in its economic development. Explain how this country might sustain this deficit over time without provoking a large depreciation in its exchange rate.
2. How does a currency depreciation affect the balance of payments? When might a currency depreciation intended to correct a current account deficit fail?
3. Using relevant diagrams explain:
   (a) how a change in demand for a currency may cause the exchange rate of the currency against other currencies to fall
   (b) how a central bank might intervene in the foreign exchange market to prevent the decline in the exchange rate
   (c) why the decline in the exchange rate may initially cause a deterioration in the current account of the balance of payments.
4. Compare and contrast the relative advantages and disadvantages of adopting floating or fixed exchange rate regimes.
5. Why is purchasing power parity theory likely to be a defective explanation for the level of an exchange rate in the short run? Why is it likely to be a more effective explanation for long-run exchange rates?
6. 'The Far East Crisis of 1997 and the Argentinian peso crisis of 2001 proved that fixed exchange rates are unsustainable in a world denominated by global capital markets.'
   (a) How did fixed exchange rates contribute to these crises?
   (b) Why are fixed rates 'unsustainable in a world of global capital markets'?

Chapter 16

INSTITUTIONS IN THE INTERNATIONAL ECONOMY

Aims and learning outcomes

The last three chapters have looked at topics in international macroeconomics, namely international trade theory and policy, the balance of payments and exchange rates. We have seen how the law of comparative advantage underpins the economic case for free trade and have discussed the arguments for and against protectionism. We have also considered the composition of the balance of payments, balance of payments adjustments and the operation of the foreign exchange market. In this chapter we turn to review some of the major international institutions that play a key role in the international macroeconomy, impacting on trade and exchange rates. These institutions are mentioned frequently in the media and it is essential for anyone studying international aspects of the macroeconomy to understand their roles.

The discussion of each institution below must by necessity be brief for reasons of space. Each has been the subject of dedicated books covering many hundreds of pages. Nevertheless, we give the essence of their history, membership and functions below and we also provide website addresses for those who want to study each institution in more detail.

In this chapter the following international institutions are covered:

- the International Monetary Fund (IMF);
- the World Bank;
- the General Agreement on Tariffs and Trade (GATT) and the World Trade Organisation (WTO);
- the European Union (EU), including the European Central Bank (ECB);
- the North American Free Trade Agreement (NAFTA);
- Mercosur;
- the Association of Southeast Asian Nations (ASEAN);
- the Asian Development Bank;
- the Organisation for Economic Cooperation and Development (OECD).

The purpose of the chapter is to provide an understanding of these major international bodies.

Learning outcomes

After studying this material you will be able to:

- Understand the role of the IMF, its history and its main functions today.
- Appreciate the importance of the World Bank and its subsidiary organisations to economic development in low-income economies.
- Distinguish between the roles of the IMF and the World Bank.
- Recognise the work of the WTO in protecting world trade and its development out of the earlier GATT.
- Consider the nature and importance of the EU in the world economy and the case for a common currency.
- Understand the function of ASEAN in the Asia-Pacific region.
- Appreciate the role of Mercosur in Latin America.
- Understand the functions of the Asian Development Bank.
- Appreciate the role of the OECD.

The International Monetary Fund (IMF)

http://www.imf.org

The IMF was established at a meeting at Bretton Woods, New Hampshire in the USA, in July 1944. The aim was to add stability to the international economy and avoid the competitive currency devaluations of the inter-war years by providing emergency foreign currency loans to countries suffering from balance of payments problems. The IMF came into official existence on 27 December 1945 and commenced financial operations in March 1947. The Bretton Woods Agreement set up the regime of fixed exchange rates that operated up until the early 1970s (see pp.363–365). An international agency was needed to provide additional foreign reserves to those countries having temporary difficulty in maintaining their agreed exchange rates in the foreign exchange markets. Under the Bretton Woods Agreement countries with temporary balance of payments problems were not expected to devalue their currencies, although economies with more 'fundamental disequilibria' in their international trading accounts could devalue under IMF authority.

With the coming of more flexible exchange rates from the 1970s, the role of the IMF as a provider of emergency foreign reserves to countries with temporary balance of payments problems declined, although it continues. Major economies such as the USA and Japan are more likely to allow their exchange rates to alter in the foreign exchange market rather than resort to the IMF for loans. Since the 1970s the IMF has become involved to a much greater degree than previously in providing loans to low-income economies, alongside its sister institution the World Bank. Whereas the World Bank lends to these countries to finance long-term investments, such as in health, education and infrastructure, the IMF

Box 16.1

Activities of the IMF

- The IMF's *surveillance work* involves the monitoring of economic and financial developments and the provision of policy advice, aimed at preventing economic crises in the international economy.
- Its *lending activity* involves, as already noted, providing temporary loans to countries with balance of payments difficulties and providing loans to low-income countries to assist poverty reduction. Alongside the loans, the IMF provides policy advice to assist countries in their efforts to overcome their economic difficulties and may attach conditions to loans to achieve what it perceives to be necessary economic restructuring. Credit from the IMF is generally conditional on the adoption of appropriate policies to resolve a country's balance of payments difficulties or contribute to strong and sustainable economic growth.
- The IMF's *technical assistance* is concerned with providing economic expertise and training to governments.

lends to increase these countries' foreign reserves and thereby assist poverty reduction.

Another important function undertaken by the IMF is to act as a forum for finance ministers to meet and discuss international economic policy. The IMF therefore promotes international monetary cooperation, exchange rate stability and world trade.

The IMF undertakes three main types of activity, namely economic surveillance, lending, and technical assistance (see Box 16.1). It also publishes large amounts of data on the international economy.

In recent years, as part of its efforts to strengthen the international financial system and to improve its effectiveness at preventing and resolving economic crises, the IMF has developed standards and codes of good economic practice and has also endeavoured to strengthen financial sectors in economies affected by economic weakness. The IMF also operates a debt relief programme for low-income economies that suffer from crippling international indebtedness.

Loans to member countries are based on 'quotas'. Each member of the IMF is assigned a quota, which is based on a range of economic indicators for each country, including its GDP, current account transactions, and official reserves. The quotas are expressed in *special drawing rights* (*SDRs*), which are a unit of account within the IMF. A member's quota determines its maximum financial commitment to the IMF and its voting power. Total quotas at the end of January 2003 were SDR213bn (about $293bn). The largest member of the IMF is the USA, with a quota of SDR37,149.3mn. The USA therefore has the largest single vote in decision making within the IMF – 17.10 per cent of the total vote. The smallest quota is that for Palau, at SDR3.1mn. A member country is required to pay a subscription to the IMF based on its quota of which up to 25 per cent must be paid in reserve assets specified by the IMF (i.e. SDRs or international currencies such as the US dollar). The remainder can be paid in the member country's own currency.

The amount of financing a member country can obtain from the IMF is based on its quota. Under Stand-By and Extended Arrangements, for instance, a member can currently borrow up to 100 per cent of its quota annually and 300 per cent cumulatively. Access may be higher in exceptional circumstances and to meet specific problems. The IMF's Board of Governors conducts a general quota review at regular intervals, usually every five years. These reviews allow the IMF to assess the adequacy of quotas for both members' needs and to finance the activities of the IMF. There have been 12 general quota reviews to date and five have concluded that no increase in quotas was needed. The last quota adjustment occurred in January 1999, when a 45 per cent increase was sanctioned to reflect the growth of the world economy and the increased risk of financial crises. There was a financial crisis in Asia in 1997–98 that placed a strain on the IMF's resources. The IMF's resources for lending depend on the quotas of major currency foreign reserves and gold paid in by members (the IMF is still one of the largest official holders of gold in the world).

In 1969, the IMF created the SDR as an international reserve asset to supplement existing reserve assets made up of official holdings of gold, foreign exchange, and reserve positions at the IMF. SDR allocations are based on member countries' quotas. The SDR is valued on the basis of a basket of key international currencies and the daily price is posted on the IMF website. It serves as the unit of account of the IMF and a number of other international organisations. However, the role of SDRs as a reserve asset remains limited (accounting for a little more than 1 per cent of members' non-gold reserves at the present time). It is used almost exclusively in transactions between the IMF and its members. Member countries can exchange their holdings of SDRs for reserve currencies.

Today 184 countries are members of the IMF, membership having grown from under 50 in the mid-1940s (see Figure 16.1). The IMF is headed by a board of governors, an international monetary and financial committee, and an executive board. It employs about 2650 staff, recruited from some 140 countries and has its headquarters in New York.

The World Bank

http://www.worldbank.org

The World Bank is the name that is used for the International Bank for Reconstruction and Development (IBRD) and the International Development Association (IDA). Together these organisations provide low-interest loans, interest-free credit, and grants to developing countries to encourage their economic development. Around 10,000 people work in the World Bank's Washington DC headquarters and in its 109 country offices.

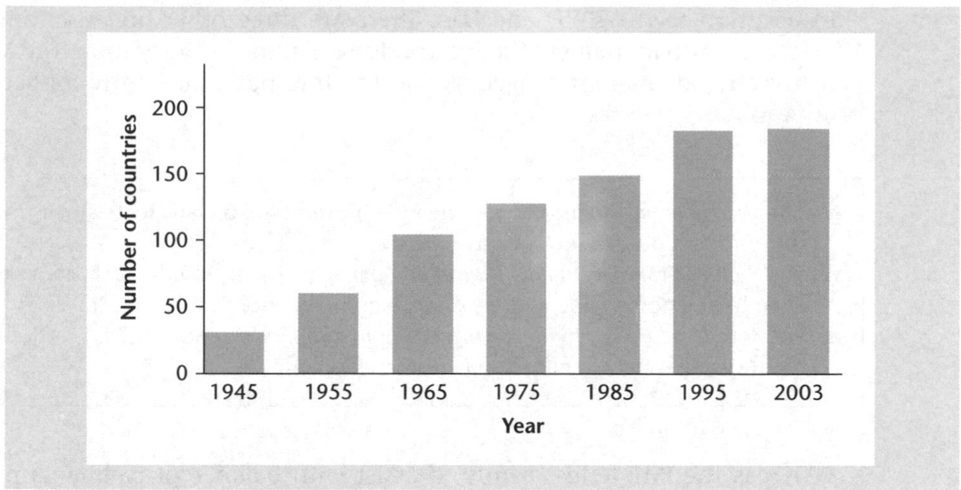

Figure 16.1 Growth in IMF membership, 1945–2003
Source: IMF

The World Bank was also established at Bretton Woods in 1944. It began life after World War II by assisting the reconstruction of the European economies, but since then its primary focus has been on raising the economic welfare of the poorest peoples of the world. Today it is one of the largest sources of development assistance internationally, providing finance and technical assistance to over 100 developing economies. In 2002 the World Bank provided $19.5bn to these countries.

In developing countries, 2.8bn people live on less than $700 a year and, of these, 1.2bn earn less than $1 a day. Alongside this desperate poverty, low-income countries generally find it difficult to borrow money in international markets and when they can borrow, it is often only at interest rates beyond their ability to service and repay. The World Bank provides direct financial grants, loans, and technical assistance. The loans have generous repayment terms, of 35 to 40 years, and there is usually a ten-year grace period before interest charges have to be met. The IDA provides interest-free credit and grants and is the world's largest source of concessional financing. Its funds come from some 40 rich countries, which make contributions every four years. In 2002 these countries made an additional $9bn available and an extra $6.6bn came from the World Bank's own resources.

The World Bank is involved in loans for infrastructure schemes, advising on economic restructuring, including trade liberalisation and privatisation, and providing education and health programmes. It currently finances 158 education projects in 83 countries and is actively involved in tackling the spread of AIDS, especially in Africa. The Bank raises much of its funds in the world's financial markets. It can borrow at much lower interest rates than poor countries because of its high credit risk rating. The World Bank has been active recently in debt relief to poor countries under the Heavily Indebted Poor Countries (HIPC) initiative.

In addition to the IBRD and IDA, there are three other organisations in the World Bank Group, namely the International Finance Corporation, the Multilateral Investment Guarantee Agency, and the International Centre for Settlement of Investment Disputes.

- The *International Finance Corporation* (IFC) promotes private sector investment by supporting high-risk sectors and countries.
- The *Multilateral Investment Guarantee Agency* (MIGA) provides political risk insurance to investors in and lenders to developing economies.
- The *International Centre for Settlement of Investment Disputes* (ICSID) settles investment disputes between foreign investors and countries.

Whereas the IMF lends mainly to assist with balance of payments problems and maintaining exchange rates, the World Bank is primarily concerned with financing economic development. However, as the IMF has become more involved in low-income economies, this has sometimes caused friction with the World Bank because of different policy stances on advancing loans to particular countries. The short extract from a book by Joseph Stiglitz presented in Application 16.1 below provides a critical insight into the operations of the IMF and World Bank, or what is sometimes referred to as 'the Washington Consensus'.

Application 16.1

The promise of global institutions

'The ideas and intentions behind the creation of the international economic institutions were good ones, yet they gradually evolved over the years to become something very different. The Keynesian orientation of the IMF, which emphasised market failures and the role for government in job creation, was replaced by the free market mantra of the 1980s, part of a new 'Washington Consensus' – a consensus between the IMF, the World Bank, and the US Treasury about the 'right' policies for developing countries – that signalled a radically different approach to economic development and stabilisation.

Many of the ideas incorporated in the consensus were developed in response to the problems in Latin America, where governments had let budgets get out of control while loose monetary policies had led to rampant inflation. A burst of growth in some of that region's countries in the decades immediately after World War II had not been sustained, allegedly because of excessive state intervention in the economy. The ideas that were developed to cope with problems arguably specific to Latin American countries have subsequently been applicable to countries around the world. Capital market liberalisation

Application 16.1 continued

has been pushed despite the fact that there is no evidence showing it spurs economic growth. In other cases, the economic policies that evolved into the Washington Consensus and were introduced into developing countries were not appropriate for countries in the early stages of development or early stages of transition.

To take just a few examples, most of the advanced industrial countries – including the USA and Japan – had built up their economies by wisely and selectively protecting some of their industries until they were strong enough to compete with foreign companies. While blanket protectionism has often not worked for countries that have tried it, neither has rapid trade liberalisation. Forcing a developing country to open itself up to imported products that would compete with those produced by certain of its industries, industries that were dangerously vulnerable to competition from much stronger counterpart industries in other countries, can have disastrous consequences – socially and economically. Jobs have systematically been destroyed – poor farmers in developing countries simply couldn't compete with the highly subsidised goods from Europe and America – before the countries' industrial and agricultural sectors were able to grow strong and create new jobs. Even worse, the IMF's insistence on developing countries maintaining tight monetary policies has led to interest rates that would make job creation impossible even in the best of circumstances. And because trade liberalisation occurred before safety nets were put into place, those who lost their jobs were forced into poverty. Liberalisation has thus, too often, not been followed by the promised growth, but by increased misery. And even those who have not lost their jobs have been hit by a heightened sense of insecurity.

Capital controls are another example: European countries banned the free flow of capital until the seventies. Some might say its not fair to insist that developing countries with a barely functioning bank system risk opening their markets. But putting aside such notions of fairness, it's bad economics; the influx of hot money into and out of the country that so frequently follows after capital market liberalisation leaves havoc in its wake. Small developing countries are like small boats. Rapid capital market liberalisation, in the manner pushed by the IMF, amounted to setting them off on a voyage on a rough sea, before the holes in their hulls have been repaired, before the captain has received training, before life vests have been put on board. Even in the best of circumstances, there was a high likelihood that they would be overturned when they were hit broadside by a big wave.

The application of mistaken economic theories would not be such a problem if the end of first colonialism and then communism had not given the IMF and the World Bank the opportunity to greatly expand their respective original mandates, to vastly extend their reach. Today these institutions have become dominant players in the world economy. Not only countries seeking their help,

Application 16.1 continued

but also those seeking their 'seal of approval' so that they can better access international capital markets must follow their economic prescriptions, prescriptions which reflect their free market ideologies and theories. The result for many people has been poverty and for many countries social and political chaos. The IMF has made mistakes in all the areas it has been involved in: development, crisis management, and in countries making the transition from communism to capitalism. Structural adjustment programs did not bring sustained growth even to those, like Bolivia, that adhered to its strictures; in many countries, excess austerity stifled growth; successful economic programs require extreme care in *sequencing* – the order in which reforms occur – and pacing. If, for instance, markets are opened up for competition too rapidly, before strong financial institutions are established, then jobs will be destroyed faster than new jobs are created. In many countries, mistakes in sequencing and pacing led to rising unemployment and increased poverty. After the 1997 Asian crisis, IMF policies exacerbated the crises in Indonesia and Thailand. Free market reforms in Latin America have had one or two successes – Chile is repeatedly cited – but much of the rest of the continent has still to make up for the lost decade of growth following the so-called successful IMF bailouts of the early 1980s, and many today have persistently high rates of unemployment – in Argentina, for instance, at double-digit levels since 1995 – even as inflation has been brought down. The collapse in Argentina in 2001 is one of the most recent of a series of failures over the past few years. Given the high unemployment rate for almost seven years, the wonder is not that the citizens eventually rioted, but that they suffered quietly so much for so long. Even those countries that have experienced some limited growth have seen the benefits accrue to the well-off, and especially the *very* well-off – the top 10 per cent – while poverty has remained high, and in some cases the income of those at the bottom has even fallen.

Underlying the problems of the IMF and the other international economic institutions is the problem of governance: who decides what they do. The institutions are dominated not just by the wealthiest industrial countries but by commercial and financial interests in those countries, and the policies of the institutions naturally reflect this. The choice of heads for these institutions symbolises the institutions' problem, and too often has contributed to their dysfunction. While almost all of the activities of the IMF and the World Bank today are in the developing world (certainly, all of their lending), they are led by representatives from the industrialised nations. (By custom or tacit agreement the head of the IMF is always a European, that of the World Bank an American). They are chosen behind closed doors, and it has never even been viewed as a prerequisite that the head should have any experience in the developing world. The institutions are not representative of the nations they serve . . .

Application 16.1 continued

For the peasants in developing countries who toil to pay off their countries' IMF debts or the businessmen who suffer from higher value-added taxes upon the insistence of the IMF, the current system run by the IMF is one of taxation without representation. Disillusion with the international system of globalisation under the aegis of the IMF grows as the poor in Indonesia, Morocco, or Papua New Guinea have fuel and food subsidies cut, as those in Thailand see AIDs increase as a result of IMF-forced cutbacks in health expenditures, and as families in many developing countries, having to pay for their children's education under so-called cost recovery programmes, make the painful choice not to send their daughters to school . . .

Globalisation itself is neither good nor bad. It has the *power* to do enormous good, and for the countries of East Asia, who have embraced globalisation *under their own terms*, at their own pace, it has been an enormous benefit, in spite of the setback of the 1997 crisis. But in much of the world it has not brought comparable benefits. For many, it seems closer to an unmitigated disaster.'

Source: Edited extract from Joseph Stiglitz (2002), *Globalisation and its Discontents*, Penguin Books, pp.16–20.

Activity

After reading this powerful critique of the policies of international bodies such as the IMF and World Bank since the 1980s, set out the changes that you feel should be made if the IMF and World Bank are to contribute better to global economic prosperity.

GATT and the World Trade Organisation

http://www.wto.org

The General Agreement on Tariffs and Trade (GATT) was established after World War II to promote international trade liberalisation. The global *Great Depression* of the 1930s had left a large number of tariffs and quotas in place that depressed world trade. Tariff negotiations began among the 23 founding GATT 'contracting parties' in 1946. This first round of negotiations resulted in 45,000 tariff concessions affecting trade worth $10bn or about one fifth of world trade at that time. These tariff concessions took effect in January 1948.

Since the 1940s there has been a series of international trade liberalisation rounds following meetings of the GATT signatories. Each has led to a significant reduction in import controls affecting manufactured goods. However, progress in reducing barriers to trade in agricultural products has made little progress because of determined opposition from farmers in Europe, North America and Japan.

Table 16.1 GATT Trade negotiation rounds

Negotiating round	*Year(s)*	*Number of participating countries*	*Agreed tariff reduction (%)*
Geneva	1947	23	–
Annecy	1949	13	–
Torquay	1951	38	73
Geneva	1956	26	–
Dillon	1960–61	26	–
Kennedy	1964–67	62	35
Tokyo	1973–79	99	33
Uruguay	1986–93	125	40

Table 16.1 shows details of the various rounds of GATT negotiations since 1947.

From the table it will be seen that the *Torquay Round* of 1951 resulted in a 73 per cent reduction in tariffs, on average – the largest percentage reduction to date. Other notable GATT trade rounds were the *Kennedy Round* in the mid-1960s, which included a new anti-dumping agreement, and the *Tokyo Round* during the 1970s, which led to an average one-third cut in customs duties on the manufacturers in the world's nine major industrial markets. This brought the average tariff on manufactured products down to 4.7 per cent compared with about 40 per cent at the time of GATT's creation. The tariff reductions were phased in over a period of eight years and the highest tariffs were reduced proportionately more than the lowest. The Tokyo Round also led to a series of agreements or 'codes' on non-tariff barriers, to which in the main only a relatively small number of mainly industrialised GATT members ascribed. These affected, amongst other things, subsidies, technical barriers to trade, import licensing procedures and government procurement.

The World Trade Organisation (WTO)

The *Uruguay Round* (1986–93) was the eighth multilateral trade negotiation held under GATT and led to the establishment of the *World Trade Organisation* (WTO). The WTO has taken over from GATT and serves as a judiciary with more extensive powers to police trade and penalise countries for adopting protectionist measures contrary to international agreement. The GATT codes on, for example, subsidies, technical barriers to trade, import licensing and anti-dumping are now multilateral commitments within the WTO agreement, extending to all member countries.

The WTO was created in 1995, producing the biggest reform of international trade since 1948. While GATT was an 'agreement' with a secretariat in Geneva, the WTO is a formal organisation (still based in Geneva). Furthermore, GATT dealt only with trade in goods, while the WTO agreements cover *services* and intellectual property (e.g. copyright and patents) as well. This has resulted in the *General Agreement on Trade in Services* (GATS), which is working to break down trade barriers, particularly in financial services, telecommunications, audio visual and maritime transport services.

The purpose of the WTO is to ensure that international trade flows as freely as possible by removing obstacles to trading. It has two main functions:

- to act as a forum for trade negotiations between countries;
- to settle disputes between countries on trade matters.

In April 2003 the WTO had 146 members, including all of the main international trading countries and over 100 developing countries; China is a recent member. The WTO has an agenda to assist economic development through expanding world trade.

The WTO has a 500-strong secretariat with a director general at its head and policy is set by member governments. All major decisions are made by the membership as a whole, either by ministers who meet every two years, or by government officials who meet regularly in Geneva. Decisions are normally taken by consensus. The day-to-day work of the WTO is supervised by a General Council, and numerous other committees and groups are involved in developing WTO policies.

The European Union

http://europa.eu.int

The European Union (EU) was established as the European Economic Community (EEC) in 1957. The name was changed to the EU following the *Maastricht Treaty* of February 1992. Six countries formed the original membership, namely Belgium, Germany, France, Italy, Luxembourg and the Netherlands. From the 1970s there have been four waves of accessions to the EU – in 1973 when Denmark, Ireland and the UK joined; in 1981 when Greece became a member; in 1986 when Spain and Portugal joined; and in 1995 with the addition of Austria, Finland and Sweden. There was a major expansion of the EU on 1 May 2004 when ten new members were admitted from central and eastern Europe (including Poland, Hungary and the Czech Republic) and Malta and Cyprus. This has created an economic area with a total GDP larger than that of the USA, encompassing a population of over half a billion people. Further expansion of membership is planned in the coming years – leading perhaps to over 40 countries inside the EU within a decade.

The main objectives of the EU go beyond promoting economic development through free trade between Member States to protecting human rights, ensuring freedom, security and justice, ensuring social progress within Europe and promoting Europe's interests within international organisations and meetings. In particular, the EU operates:

- a 'common external tariff', which applies to trade between Member States and the rest of the world;
- a Common Agricultural Policy to assist European farmers through subsidies and import controls;
- a Common Fisheries Policy.

There are also policies covering a wide range of other issues, such as food safety, regional development, education and training, health and the environment. Within the EU there is free movement of goods, services, people and capital. Recent years have seen progress in producing common policies on technical standards and trade in services such as banking and insurance.

The EU is run by five institutions:

- the *European Parliament*, which is elected by voters in each Member State;
- the *Council of the EU*, which is composed of representatives from the governments of the Member States;
- the *European Commission*, which is the EU's executive or civil service and is responsible for the development of new policy initiatives;
- the *European Court of Justice*, which overseas compliance with EU law;
- the *Court of Auditors*, which overseas the EU budget.

The EU also has other bodies, notably the *European Economic and Social Committee*, which considers economic and social issues in Europe; the *Committee of the Regions*, which overseas regional policy, the environment and education; the *European Ombudsman*, who deals with complaints from citizens about maladministration by an EU body; the *European Investment Bank*, which helps finance public and private long-term investments in the EU; and the *European Central Bank*.

The European Central Bank

The European Central Bank (ECB), based in Frankfurt am Main in Germany, is responsible for monetary policy and foreign exchange operations involving the euro, the EU's common currency. The ECB was founded on 1 June 1998, taking over from the European Monetary Institute (EMI) that had played a key role in preparing for the euro's launch on 1 January 1999. The ECB and the central banks of the countries that have adopted the euro make up a new entity known as the *Eurosystem*. As some Member States of the European Union (in 2003 the UK, Sweden and Denmark) have not adopted the euro, it is important to make a distinction between the Eurosystem of 12 countries and the *European System of Central Banks* (*ESCB*), which comprises all of the Member States. The central banks of Member States which do not participate in the euro meet to discuss monetary policy in Europe, but do not take part in decision making with regard to monetary policy for the euro area. This is the function of the ECB.

The ECB is independent of direct political control and works in close collaboration with the central banks of Member States to provide a sound monetary environment with low inflation in Europe. The ECB's primary objective is price stability, based on a target year-on-year increase in consumer prices across the Eurozone as a whole.

The main tasks of the ECB are to:

- define and implement the monetary policy of the Eurozone including setting interest rates;
- conduct foreign exchange operations as well as hold and manage the official exchange reserves of the countries of the Eurozone;
- issue euro notes;
- promote the smooth operation of payment systems.

The Governing Council is the ECB's highest decision-making body. It comprises the six members of the Executive Board and the governors of the 12 central banks of the Eurozone. It is chaired by the President of the ECB and the other five members of the Executive Board are appointed by the Member States for a non-renewable term of eight years.

In economics a *Customs Union* is a group of countries that have eliminated tariffs and sometimes other barriers that impede trade with each other, while maintaining a common external tariff. The EU is a customs union, although with policies extending well beyond economic matters and into the political and social spheres within Europe. This is what makes membership of the EU controversial, with some fearing the creation of a 'Federal Europe' and the loss of national control over economic, social and political policies, including foreign policy and defence.

Application 16.2

Europe's new draft constitution

'The European Convention has presented the final draft of a treaty establishing a constitution for Europe thus concluding 16 months of work. The draft consolidates and supplements the existing treaties. An intergovernmental conference must now decide on the final text of the treaty. The accession countries will also have taken their place and will be represented at the intergovernmental conference, just as they have already taken part in the European Convention. The treaty is to be signed in May 2004 . . . Some Member States have already expressed reservations about fully subscribing to the Convention's final draft. Thus, there is still the danger of another unproductive intergovernmental conference as seen in the past.

Since the new treaty establishing a constitution for Europe, which runs to some 338 articles, has to be ratified by the parliaments of 25 Member States, it will probably not enter into force until 2006 at the earliest. Besides, the

Application 16.2 continued

experience with the ratification process for the treaties of Maastricht and Nice has to be remembered: the fate of these treaty reforms was totally up in the air for a while owing to the negative outcome of referenda in Denmark and Ireland. Some Member States have announced their intention to hold again a referendum on the constitution. Since the new treaty can presumably, like its predecessors, only enter into force after it has been ratified by all Member States, delays cannot be ruled out.

The convention – a successful reform approach?

The decision to call a European convention was taken after the long and dissatisfactory negotiations at the summit of the European heads of state and government in Nice (December 2000). The outcome of the summit – although in force as the Treaty of Nice since last February – did not prepare the Union for the inclusion of another ten or more member states.

Expectations that the Convention would bring another quantum leap in integration – like those achieved by the Single European Act or the Maastricht Treaty – have admittedly not been met. But the present draft definitely goes way beyond cosmetic corrections to the existing treaties. The advances include:

- the consolidation of the existing treaties and the endowment of the Union with legal personality;
- a clearer distinction between the competences of the Union and those of the Member States, and a more transparent legislative procedure;
- the inclusion of the Charter of Fundamental Rights;
- improvements in the individual EU institutions' decision-making procedures and ability to act.

Despite all the proposed changes, the draft constitution keeps to the familiar, but only moderately effective, institutional structure. The attempt to reconcile fundamentally different views of the political finality of the Union did not succeed. The Convention was caught in a dilemma right from the start: it was expected to produce ambitious results, yet the results could not be too bold since the governments of the Member States have the final say on the constitutional treaty. And towards the end of the Convention the government representatives exerted pressure in favour of national interests – often at the expense of the community. Once again, many of the compromises were dictated by nation-state or small-state thinking, with the result that shortcomings in the functionality of the Union's institutions have been retained. In addition, many of the treaty provisions are not to take effect until after the European Parliament elections in 2009, which means that the enlarged Union will have to live with the present structures for another five years.'

The table below indicates the 'competencies' (responsibilities) for different policy areas within the EU.

Application 16.2 continued

Future allocation of competences

1. Exclusive competence of the Union
   - Monetary policy for EMU
   - Common commercial policy
   - Customs union
   - Conservation of marine biological resources
   - Conclusion of international agreements
2. Shared competence of Union and member states
   - Internal market
   - Area of freedom, security and justice
   - Agriculture and fisheries
   - Transport and trans-European networks
   - Energy
   - Aspects of social policy
   - Economic and social cohesion
   - Environment
   - Consumer protection
   - Common safety concerns in health matters
3. Supporting/coordinating action by the Union
   - Industry
   - Protection and improvement of human health
   - Education, vocational training, youth and sport
   - Culture
   - Civil protection

Source: Edited extract from Deutsche Bank Research, *EU Monitor*, July 2003, No. 3.

Activity

What do the negotiations on Europe's new draft constitution tell us about the difficulties of deepening economic and political integration? With reference to the above table, comment on the appropriate allocation of economic policies within the EU.

The North American Free Trade Agreement (NAFTA)

http://www.nafta-customs.org

The North American Free Trade Agreement (NAFTA) was signed by the USA, Canada and Mexico on 17 December 1992 and came into force on 1 January 1994. Full tariff liberalisation between Canada and the USA was achieved by January 1998. Most tariffs between the USA and Mexico and Canada and Mexico have now been removed.

NAFTA is not a customs union because it lacks a common external tariff. Its rationale is free trade between the member countries and therefore the creation of a 'free trade area'; although the agreement also provides for protection and enforcement of intellectual property rights (copyright and related rights, trademark rights, patent rights, etc.), something of importance to the USA in particular. The agreement also provides special provisions that permit continued government support for agricultural products, something important to US farmers. It should also be noted that some limitations remain in the USA, Canada and Mexico with regard to the equity ownership of certain strategic industries such as energy, maritime, civil aircraft, nuclear, airlines, fishing and broadcasting. Also, within NAFTA all three members maintain the right:

- to protect their domestic labour forces;
- to implement their own immigration policies;
- to guard their own borders.

The promoters of NAFTA in North America forecast that the agreement would lead to 200,000 new US jobs because of increased trade, higher wages in Mexico, environmental clean-up and improved health along the US–Mexico border. Critics argue that these benefits have not been achieved and are fearful that NAFTA poses a major threat to the US manufacturing sector (especially the car industry) and to investment expenditure in the USA.

Mercosur

http://www.rau.edu.uy/mercosur (in Spanish)

In 1960 under the Treaty of Montevideo, the *Latin American Free Trade Association (ALALC)* was established with the objective of removing trade barriers among member countries. In spite of some progress, frequent economic crises and nationalism within Latin America meant that a free trade area did not result. In 1978 it was agreed that change was needed and under a new Treaty of Montevideo, in 1980, the Latin American Integration Association (ALADI) was created as the successor to ALALC. Four countries went further on 26 March 1991, when Argentina, Brazil, Paraguay and Uruguay agreed to the establishment of *Mercosur* or the *Common Market of the Southern Cone*, effective from November 1991. The aim of Mercosur is to promote trade liberalisation through coordinated reductions in import duties and the imposition of a common external tariff. The Common External Tariff began in January 1995, although there are some continuing exceptions.

The Administrative Secretariat of Mercosur is based in Montevideo, Uruguay. In the past Bolivia has participated in some of Mercosur's technical meetings and there have been proposals that Chile should become a member. However, continuing economic difficulties in Latin America, most recently in Argentina, make rapid progress in advancing economic integration in that continent problematic.

Box 16.2

The Free Trade Area of the Americas (FTAA)

Since December 1994, all of the countries which make up North and South America (with the exception of Cuba) have met annually at the so-called *Summit of the Americas* to discuss and agree a plan for the creation of the *Free Trade Area of the Americas (FTAA)*. This would embrace 800 million consumers from Alaska to Cape Horn. The primary objective is to achieve free trade in the western hemisphere.

To achieve the goal of a FTAA, 11 working groups have been established to deal with issues concerning:

- tariffs and non-tariff barriers;
- customs procedures and rules of origin;
- investment;
- standards and technical barriers;
- sanitary and phytosanitary measures;
- antidumping and countervailing duties;
- problems of smaller economies;
- government procedures;
- intellectual property rights;
- services;
- competition policy.

It should be noted that negotiations on tariffs represent only part of one of the 11 working groups.

The Association of Southeast Asian Nations (ASEAN)

http://www.aseansec.org

The Association of Southeast Asian Nations was established on 8 August 1967 in Bangkok and had five original members – Indonesia, Malaysia, Philippines, Singapore and Thailand. Brunei Darussalam joined on 8 January 1984, Vietnam on 28 July 1995, Laos and Myanmar on 23 July 1997, and Cambodia on 30 April 1999. Today ASEAN covers a population of about 500 million.

The objectives of ASEAN are:

- to accelerate economic growth, social progress and cultural development in the region;
- to promote regional peace and stability.

Although ASEAN is essentially a political arrangement to preserve peace and security, it has adopted measures to promote intra-regional trade. One of these is the *Preferential Trading Arrangement* of 1977, which provides tariff preferences for trade among the ASEAN economies. In 1992 a scheme was launched to promote an *ASEAN Free Trade Area (AFTA)* and in 1997 the 'ASEAN Vision 2020' was declared to forge closer economic integration within the region. ASEAN has also promoted economic cooperation in investment, finance, transport and communications, energy policy, intellectual property rights and tourism. ASEAN meetings have produced some bold statements on regional economic integration (see for example, Application 16.3), although actual achievement has lagged behind.

Application 16.3

A Single Market for ASEAN?

At the ASEAN summit meeting in 2003, the ten leaders of the member states pledged to create a common market by 2020. The plan, called the Bali Concord II, is intended to create an integrated economic entity that will also embrace security and socio-cultural aspects.

The plans for an Asean Economic Community, paralleling the development of the European Economic Community in the past, represent an attempt to go beyond the current efforts to lower intra-regional tariffs on manufactured goods by eliminating non-tariff barriers and liberalising services industries.

As it moves towards a single market, ASEAN has agreed to complete the integration of 11 priority sectors including: automotives, electronics, wood, rubber, textiles, tourism and certain service industries (such as healthcare). The plans will also introduce new visa rules to allow the free movement of skilled labour and tourists within the region.

The leaders recognise that previous attempts at regional integration have been hampered by a lack of clarity concerning the precise changes that need to be made. The new agreement will establish a dispute resolution mechanism in order to minimise the risk of future disagreements that may impede integration.

Activity

Assess the implications of the establishment of a single market for the ASEAN region for:

(a) the region itself
(b) the global economy.

The Asian Development Bank (ADB)

http://www.adb.org

The Asian Development Bank is a multilateral development finance institution to reduce poverty in Asia and the Pacific region. It was established in 1966 and is owned by 61 member countries, mainly from the region, although European countries, the USA and Turkey are also members. It has its headquarters in Manila and has 24 other offices around the world. It employs over 2,000 staff from nearly 50 countries. Its function is to provide loans for projects that will contribute to raising economic growth and reducing poverty in the region.

The ADB carries out activities to promote economic growth, develop human resources, improve the status of women, and protect the environment. Other key development objectives include law and policy reform, regional cooperation, private-sector development and social development. The financial resources of the ADB consist of ordinary capital resources (subscribed capital, reserves and operating surpluses, and borrowed funds) and special funds, which consist mostly of contributions from member countries to ADB's concessional loan and technical assistance programmes.

Organisation for Economic Cooperation and Development (OECD)

http://www.oecd.org

Starting out life to assist in the reconstruction of Europe after World War II, today the OECD consists of 30 member countries with market economies, including most of the main trading countries with the major exceptions of Russia and China; members are listed in Table 16.2. Based in Paris, the OECD produces a large volume of publications and statistics on international economic and social issues. It is particularly known for its regular country surveys and commentaries

Table 16.2 OECD member countries, 2003

Australia	Austria	Belgium
Canada	Czech Republic	Denmark
Finland	France	Germany
Greece	Hungary	Iceland
Ireland	Italy	Japan
Korea	Luxembourg	Mexico
Netherlands	New Zealand	Norway
Poland	Portugal	Slovak Republic
Spain	Sweden	Switzerland
Turkey	UK	USA

and in recent years has been an active advocate of privatisation and market liberalisation policies. Its governing body is its Council made up of representatives from the governments of the member countries.

Concluding remarks

A large number of international organisations exist that impact on policies in the international macroeconomy. By its very nature this chapter has had to be selective in coverage. If you need information on any organisation not found in this chapter, you will normally find that it has its own website containing details of its policies and practices.

This chapter has looked at the IMF and its role in the foreign exchange market, as well as the role of the GATT and the WTO in reducing protectionism. It has also summarised the roles of the World Bank and the Asian Development Bank in terms of raising economic growth in low-income economies; and the EU, NAFTA, Mercosur and ASEAN as examples of important international trading blocs. Each of these institutions contributes to shaping the international economy, as does the OECD by advocating trade liberalisation policies.

✔ Key learning points

- The *IMF* was established at Bretton Woods, New Hampshire, USA, in 1944. Its main function is to provide emergency funding to countries suffering from temporary balance of payments problems and a shortage of foreign reserves. It also acts as an important international forum on economic matters.
- The *World Bank* was also established at the Bretton Woods meeting. Its primary objective is to provide financial assistance to low-income economies and promote economic development and poverty reduction. The World Bank Group includes the *International Bank for Reconstruction and Development*, the *International Development Association*, the *International Finance Corporation* and certain other bodies.
- The *General Agreement on Tariffs and Trade (GATT)* was signed immediately after World War II with the aim of reducing trade protection. It was responsible for a number of 'rounds' of reductions in import duties, including the Kennedy, Tokyo and Uruguay rounds.
- The *World Trade Organisation (WTO)* was created in 1995 and absorbed the GATT. It also has wider scope and powers than existed under the GATT, taking in trade in services, agricultural products and intellectual property rights, and having a trade dispute procedure. The WTO had 146 members in 2003.
- The *European Union* (EU) started life in 1957 as the *European Economic Community* with six Member States. The EU is a *customs union* with free trade between members and a common external tariff. Its policies extend today well beyond economic matters to political and social integration.

- The *North American Free Trade Agreement (NAFTA)* was signed by the USA, Canada and Mexico on 17 December 1992 and came into force on 1 January 1994. The objective is free trade between the three member countries. NAFTA is not a customs union because it lacks a common external tariff.
- *Mercosur* was established in Latin America on 26 March 1991, when Argentina, Brazil, Paraguay and Uruguay agreed to the establishment of the Common Market of the Southern Cone. The aim is to promote trade liberalisation through coordinated reductions in import duties and the imposition of a common external tariff. The common external tariff began in January 1995, although there are some continuing exceptions.
- *ASEAN* is the Association of Southeast Asian Nations established in 1967 with five original members. Today Indonesia, Malaysia, Philippines, Singapore, Thailand, Brunei Darussalam, Vietnam, Laos, Myanmar and Cambodia are members. ASEAN exists to accelerate economic growth, social progress and cultural development in the region and to promote regional peace and stability.
- The *Asian Development Bank* exists to reduce poverty in Asia and the Pacific region. It was established in 1966 and has 61 member countries. Its function is to provide loans for projects that will contribute to raising economic growth in the region.
- The *Organisation for Economic Cooperation and Development* consists of 30 of the main trading economies and concentrates upon publishing economic and social commentaries, statistics and the provision of policy advice.

? Topics for discussion

1. Compare and contrast the roles of the IMF and the World Bank. How does each contribute to a more prosperous international economy?
2. What do you understand by the term 'customs union'? Give an example of a free trade area that is a customs unions.
3. In what ways can financing from international bodies such as the World Bank and the Asian Development Bank contribute to reducing poverty in low-income economies?
4. Looking at the history of either the EU, Mercosur or ASEAN, discuss the difficulties that countries face in creating free trade areas and customs unions.
5. Why have some EU Member States not adopted the European common currency, the euro?
6. A number of countries are lining up to join the EU. What difficulties might be created within the EU from the accession of the lower-income economies of central, eastern and southern Europe?
7. What is the role of the OECD? How might the OECD contribute to the expansion of world trade?

Chapter 17

UNDERSTANDING BUSINESS CYCLES

Aims and learning outcomes

In the previous chapters of this book we have been developing our understanding of the different macroeconomic variables and policies, domestic and international, that impact on aggregate demand (AD) and aggregate supply (AS). We have explored how changes in AD and AS cause changes in the level of economic activity, i.e. changes in real GDP. In the main, we have been looking at how the level of economic activity shifts from one equilibrium to another equilibrium. The dynamics of economic activity, as the level of GDP changes, gives rise to the phenomenon of *business cycles*.

Business cycles are a recurrent feature of all economies, representing movements in national output over time. These cycles are alternatively referred to as *trade cycles*. This is an important topic in macroeconomics because an understanding of the causes and consequences of business cycles is fundamental to corporate strategic planning – with direct implications for business confidence, investment expenditure and employment decisions, output plans, pricing strategies, etc.

In this chapter we cover the principles of business cycles under the following headings:

- definition of business cycles;
- forecasting business cycles;
- causes of business cycles;
- theories of business cycles;
- consequences and policy responses.

The analysis of business cycles can be conducted from a highly mathematical standpoint. However, we will approach the subject using mainly diagrammatic representations, and particularly using the core principles developed earlier in the book based on the concepts of aggregate demand and aggregate supply.

Learning outcomes

After studying this material you will be able to:

- Understand the nature of business cycles in the context of the macroeconomy.
- Identify the causes of fluctuations in the level of economic activity over time.
- Appreciate the different theoretical explanations of business cycles.
- Understand the consequences of business cycles and the policy options available to governments with respect to the stabilisation of the cycles.
- Recognise the importance of business cycle forecasting for corporate strategic planning.

Definition of business cycles

A *business cycle* represents fluctuations in the level of economic activity (output) over time around the economy's *long-term* trend rate of growth.

Figure 17.1 illustrates a typical series of business cycles around the economy's long-term trend rate of growth.

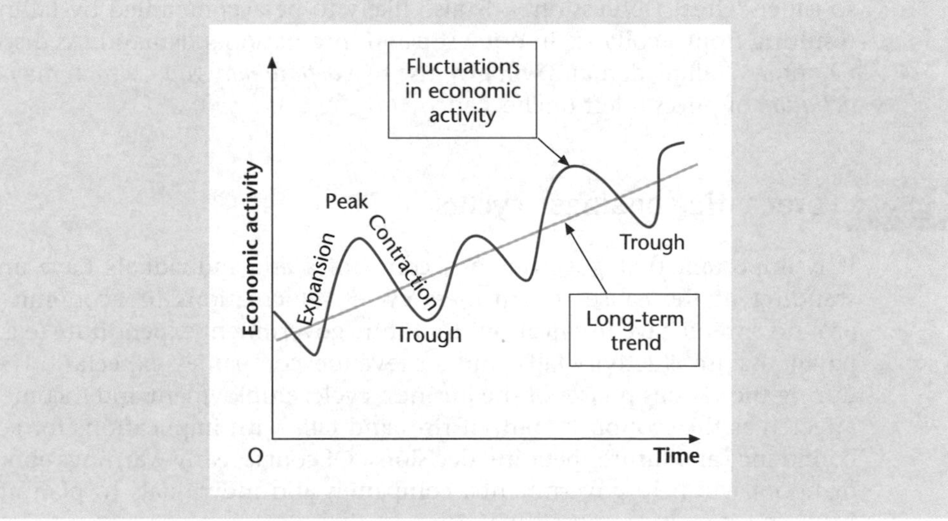

Figure 17.1 Phases of the business cycle

We can distinguish the four phases of a business cycle as follows.

- *Peak*: This represents a period when aggregate demand reaches a peak and, as a result, the economy's output is growing faster than its long-term (potential) trend and is therefore unsustainable.
- *Contraction*: A period when aggregate demand is falling accompanied by a decline in economic activity (and rising unemployment) leading to a recession.
- *Trough*: The phase when the level of economic activity is at its lowest point in the business cycle.
- *Expansion*: The phase after a trough when aggregate demand increases resulting in an expansion in output (and falling unemployment).

The various phases of a business cycle are often collectively referred to as a 'boom-bust' cycle. A *recession* is commonly defined as a situation when the level of economic activity has fallen for *at least* two consecutive quarters (i.e. at least two three-month periods). Note that this definition is based on at *least* two consecutive quarters. When an economy starts to recover after *only* two consecutive quarters, it is said to have experienced a *technical* recession. In addition, the term *growth recession* may be used to describe a situation when the economy is growing below its long-term trend but is *not* reporting an actual fall in output.

Finally, an economic *depression* describes a situation of a prolonged and severe period of low economic activity or a sustained trough in the economy accompanied by high unemployment levels. A depression, such as that of the 1930s – the so-called 'Great Depression' – is also likely to be accompanied by falling prices resulting from a collapse in domestic and international demand. As discussed in Chapter 4, falling demand will give rise to a *deflationary gap* – which may result in *deflation* of prices if left unchecked.

Forecasting business cycles

It is important that governments, companies and individuals have an understanding of the causes of business cycles. Fluctuations in economic activity around a trend have implications for future government expenditure (e.g. welfare payments rise as activity falls) and tax revenue; companies' expectations will vary during the various phases of the business cycle; employment and incomes will be affected as the economy's output rises and falls with implications for consumer confidence and future spending decisions. Of course, early warnings about a bust or boom will help governments, companies and individuals to plan ahead for future changes in economic activity.

There is a vast range of information available in most countries that can be, and is, used to tell us something about the current and future state of the

Box 17.1

Indicators of economic activity

Longer leading index

This index provides the earliest warning about a possible future upturn or downturn in the economy. Information which is likely to be included in such an index will involve data concerning new construction orders, housing starts, orders for new plant and equipment, as well as measures of business confidence. A longer leading index will turn up or down well in advance of the economy's change of direction – providing an early warning perhaps many months ahead (e.g. in the case of large-scale national infrastructural projects).

Shorter leading index

By definition, this index provides an early warning of upturns or downturns in economic activity, but the warning may be only a few months or even weeks ahead. Typically, such an index is based on data relating to changes in new car orders, movements in consumer credit figures, as well as consumer confidence indicators.

Coincident index

This indicator coincides with economic upturns and downturns and thus is not helpful as a *forecasting* technique with respect to business cycles. It may still be useful, however, if the information can be quickly collected and analysed. For example, timely information on cash withdrawals from bank accounts is likely to indicate a surge in spending almost immediately – and thus an increase in consumer demand with implications for corporate sales and economic activity.

Lagging index

This index is one which turns up or down *after* the economy has expanded or contracted – and thus is of no value whatsoever for forecasting purposes. Typically, figures for unemployment fall into this category – firms will generally attempt to avoid laying-off workers even when activity is reported to be slowing down. This arises from the high costs associated with hiring and firing staff.

economy. For example, new construction orders and housing starts may provide a reliable prediction of where the economy is heading, as may current retail sales figures. Generally, governments' statistical departments consolidate the information from many sources of data series into several distinct composite indicators of the state of the economic cycle. This gives rise to the indexes described in Box 17.1.

The methodology behind the generation of the above indexes is often quite complex. The components of each are smoothed, detrended, deseasonalised, etc., and then amalgamated using sophisticated statistical techniques of time series analysis. While such series do not offer any new information as such about the economy, they are useful means of combining information from a number of individual series to provide an overall, composite picture of where the economy may be heading.

Causes of business cycles

Given the importance of volatility in economic activity for everyone – governments, corporates and individuals – it is not surprising that considerable attention has been devoted to discovering the underlying causes of business cycles. However, the study of business cycles is a highly complex topic and, as yet, no-one has succeeded in developing one simple theory that fits all circumstances – this is not surprising given that economies are constantly changing and behaviour patterns are subject to a myriad of forces. Despite this, there is widespread agreement amongst economists on an analytical framework for examining the dynamics of the macroeconomy as a basis for explaining volatility in GDP. This framework is the aggregate demand (AD) and aggregate supply (AS) approach developed earlier in the book. This enables us to study the causes of business cycles with respect to changes in AD relative to the economy's growing productive capacity and supply response (i.e. AS). We shall adopt this approach in the next section when we describe the main theories that have been so far developed to explain business cycles.

As noted already in this chapter, business cycles are the result of up and down movements in economic activity that take place around a trend rate of growth for the economy. The question to be answered – before we can even begin to examine the various theories that have been put forward – is: 'What possible factors could cause cycles in economic activity to emerge?'

In general terms, the possible factors that cause business cycles may be grouped under three headings:

- political factors;
- international economic factors;
- domestic economic factors.

Political factors

Empirical evidence across many countries over many years shows some correlation between volatility in GDP and political or electoral cycles. It is often argued that *before elections* governments tend to adopt expansionary economic policies, while *after elections* contractionary policies are often implemented in the face of rising inflation and growing government budget deficits. For example, as an election winning strategy, the government in power may be tempted to implement tax cuts and increase government spending on welfare and infrastructure. If the government also has control over interest rates, it may decide to reduce the cost of borrowing – again for electoral purposes. Such measures could ignite an economic boom, leading to increased output and upward pressures on prices,

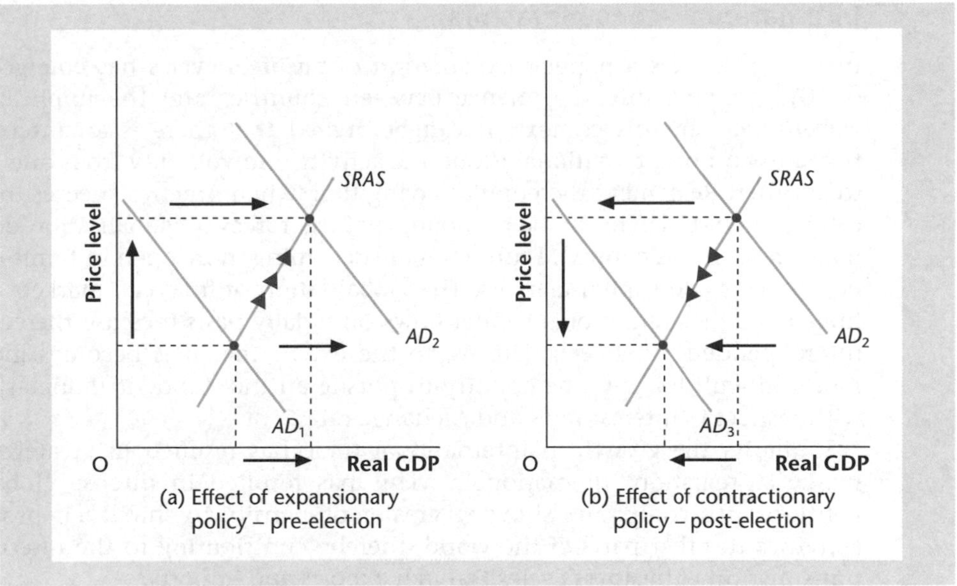

Figure 17.2 Political business cycles

depending on the degree of spare capacity in the economy. In other words, the government may stimulate aggregate demand in the short-run for political purposes. After the election, measures may have to be implemented to slow down the economy with the adoption of a tight monetary and/or fiscal policy stance. In this way contractionary policy may cause a recession.

Figure 17.2 illustrates before and after election situations using AD/AS analysis. Note that, in Figure 17.2(a), with a relatively inelastic short-run aggregate supply curve (SRAS), expansionary policy which shifts the aggregate demand (AD) curve to the right will lead to inflationary pressures. In contrast, Figure 17.2(b) shows how a contractionary policy, shifting the AD curve to the left, will cause a recession (a fall in real GDP) and, in this case, a falling price level. In practice, the outcome could be less extreme than as shown in Figure 17.2(b), leading to a fall in real GDP and a decline in the inflation *rate* rather than an absolute fall in prices (i.e. deflation).

The importance of political factors in causing volatility in real GDP has given rise to the term *political business cycles*. However, we would not wish to overemphasise this view of the business cycle. The view has some legitimacy, but it assumes that voters have short-term memories and can be 'fooled' into raising their spending before elections in response to fiscal and monetary measures, despite previous experiences of post-election contractionary policies. This would imply that voters do not use past information to shape their expectations of future economic outcomes, contrary to the underlying logic of *rational expectations theory* (for details of rational expectations theory, see p.278).

International economic factors

In recent decades a popular explanation of business cycles has emerged based on the growing interdependence between countries and the implications of *globalisation*. In this context, it can be argued that there is an international transmission of international economic activity and volatility from one country to another. Remember the popular saying that 'when America sneezes the world catches a cold'! There can be no doubt that the forces of globalisation do play a major role in this context. Economies are becoming more open in terms of product markets and capital markets. The globalisation of financial markets and the huge scale of international capital flows on a daily basis increase the economic interdependency between nations, to the extent that it is becomes more and more difficult for any one country to pursue an independent monetary policy with respect to interest rates and exchange rates.

Similarly, the growth in international trade has resulted in greater product market integration internationally. This has resulted in intense global competition with companies showing greater propensity to shift their production activities to other parts of the world, thereby contributing to the international transmission of business cycles through exports and imports.

International factors help to explain *how* business cycles are transmitted from one country to the next. However, these factors do not provide a convincing explanation of *why* business cycles begin in the first place. We still need to explain the initial fluctuations in domestic demand and output.

Domestic economic factors

The emergence of business cycles, resulting in sustained and irregular upward and downward movements in economic activity over time, suggests that there is sluggish adjustment within the economy to economic 'shocks'. These shocks may originally stem from political or international factors, as discussed above. Empirical evidence shows that at the domestic level business cycles reflect changes in aggregate demand when prices, employment and wages adjust in a sluggish fashion in the short term. Of all the components of aggregate demand (consumption, investment spending, government spending and net exports) that could be a source of 'shocks', one crucial variable stands out in all research on the causes of business cycles, namely *investment spending*.

The importance of investment spending in this context gives rise to the *multiplier-accelerator model*, drawing from Keynesian economics. Keynesians tend to argue that changes in investment spending represent a primary cause of business cycles, such that a slowdown in economic activity may result from a decrease in capital investment by firms (or government). This in turn will reduce aggregate demand, leading to a reduction in sales by firms – and a consequent fall in output as unsold stocks (inventories) of goods increase. This sequences may be described in more details as follows.

The multiplier-accelerator model

Consists of:

- *a multiplier effect* – whereby a change in investment spending (ΔI) causes a multiple change in national output (national income, ΔY);
- *an accelerator effect* – whereby a change in national output causes a further change in investment expenditure;
- *a combined multiplier-accelerator interaction* – whereby the multiplier and accelerator effects feed back on each other, as shown:

$$\underbrace{\Delta I \quad \rightarrow \quad \Delta Y}_{\text{Multiplier effect}} \underbrace{\quad \rightarrow \quad \Delta I}_{\text{Accelerator effect}} \ldots, \text{etc.}$$

Full details of both the multiplier and accelerator effects were provided in Chapter 4 (pp.87–97).

The insight of the interaction described above is that it takes an *accelerating* output growth to ensure continued increases in investment (as well as consumer) spending in the economy. As the economy tends towards full employment and hence as output growth slows down, investment spending slows down. Similarly, as output growth increases, investment spending increases too, everything else being equal. As a result of the multiplier effect, increased investment leads to a multiple rise in national income and output. The above multiplier-accelerator interaction means that a 'boom' will inevitably be followed by a 'bust'. This explanation of the business cycle suggests that it is changes in private sector investment spending that lead to volatility in the economy's output. It is for this reason that Keynesians advocate government intervention to reduce what they see as the inherent instability in capitalist economies. The model, however, is not a complete explanation of the causes of business cycles because if output kept rising and falling, as predicted, then firms would presumably act rationally and stop extrapolating past output growth to form assessments of future production and profitability. Over time, it can be assumed that firms will learn from the past and will adopt a more flexible production strategy than that implied by the multiplier-accelerator model.

That firms learn from the past and therefore adjust their production and stock levels accordingly suggests that business cycles should become less pronounced. *Stock adjustment* represents an important factor in the determination of business cycles. Holding stocks allows firms to meet short-term fluctuations in aggregate demand without incurring the expense of short-run fluctuations in output. For example, if demand is booming firms will not necessarily need to pay additional wages associated with overtime working if there are sufficient stocks to meet additional demand. Likewise, the result of holding stocks is that a fall in aggregate demand will be accompanied by a gradual process of output reduction as the stock of unsold goods builds up. Equally, once aggregate demand starts to recover the existence of stocks will mean that output will increase more slowly until firms' stock levels fall towards normal levels. The above discussion explains why changes in stock levels and stock adjustment represent a fundamental contribution to understanding business cycles and why the economy could spend several months or even years during the phases of recovery and recession.

Finally with respect to domestic factors, it is argued that the inevitable existence of 'ceilings' and 'floors' to economic activity represents another fundamental cause of business cycles. There is a constraint to aggregate supply as the economy approaches its full employment potential – this provides a 'ceiling', in the sense that real GDP cannot expand indefinitely. Likewise, there is a 'floor' in terms of aggregate demand. Aggregate demand cannot fall indefinitely because people need to consume food and to have other essentials to stay alive. Also, gross investment (including replacement investment) cannot become negative, and at some stage plant and machinery will have to be renewed.

As noted above, the AD–AS framework developed in Chapter 5 is commonly used to study the cause and effect of business cycles. All of the theories of the business cycle developed can be studied in terms of this framework. We set out the main theories on the following pages.

Application 17.1

What causes business cycles?

Read the following extract:

> 'What caused the Asian crisis, the recessions of the 1970s and 1980s, and even the Great Depression? According to many modern macroeconomists, shocks did. This unsatisfying answer lies at the heart of a currently popular framework for analysing business cycle fluctuations. This framework assumes that the macroeconomy usually obeys simple behavioural relationships but is occasionally disrupted by large 'shocks,' which force it temporarily away from these relationships and into recession. The behavioural relationships then guide the orderly recovery of the economy back to full employment, where the economy remains until another significant shock upsets it.
>
> Attributing fluctuations to shocks – movements in important economic variables that occur for reasons we do not understand – means we can never predict recessions . . . The greater the proportion of fluctuations we can classify as the observable and explainable product of purposeful economic decisions, the better chance we have of understanding, predicting, and avoiding recessions.
>
> While it will always be difficult to anticipate the particular event that precipitates a collapse, it is important to constantly assess the vulnerability of financial, product, and labour markets to potential shocks. Macroeconomists and forecasters tend to focus primarily on the overall health of the economy as measured by aggregate demand or by the unemployment rate; they may be

Application 17.1 continued

able to improve their economic models by incorporating vulnerability. Likewise, policy makers should be vigilant against vulnerability. To do so, they will need to develop new tools. In Asia, for example, policy makers should have had a better assessment of the ability of the financial system to absorb shocks to currency valuations. Many have blamed the bulk of recessions on monetary policy. But it is important first to distinguish the systematic response of monetary policy to existing conditions from policy regime shifts and exogenous policy shocks. To take a leading example, did the Fed cause the Great Depression by raising domestic interest rates to maintain the gold standard, or was the outflow of gold from the USA following Great Britain's abandonment of the gold standard the cause, and the Fed's 'business as usual' response to that triggering event? Such questions are very difficult to answer, but a careful attempt to do so must be made if we are to understand the role of monetary policy in cycles.

Most participants agreed that the Fed played a significant role in causing many of the recessions of the past century, largely in the pursuit of its goal of long-run price stability. The degree to which monetary policy did or could moderate the effects of cyclical downturns was less clear. Many pointed to the apparent diminution of the amplitude of business cycles in the postwar period as evidence of the Fed's ability to lessen the severity of contractions. Recently, some macroeconomists have advanced the idea that shocks to these supply-side or 'real' factors cause many, if not most, of the ups and downs in the economy. This idea contrasts sharply with the traditional macroeconomic notion that changes in aggregate demand cause most fluctuations, and the two views generate quite different policy implications.

Two real shocks need to be evaluated. One is a shock to the technological efficiency of firms' production of goods and services. Technological changes are very positively correlated with output and business cycles, a relationship that has led many observers to conclude that technology shocks cause fluctuations. The second real shock is a change in the desired distribution or allocation of economic resources across firms, industries and regions. Restructuring involves the costly and time-consuming reallocation of factors of production, especially workers, between firms, industries and regions through the processes of job creation and destruction. It also typically involves lower output, higher unemployment and often even recessions. In fact, job reallocation and job destruction rise sharply during recessions, leading some to surmise that shocks to the process of reallocation itself may be responsible for recessions and should therefore be taken into consideration by macroeconomic models.'

Source: Extract from Jeffrey C Fuhrer and Scott Schuh, 'Beyond Shocks: What Causes Business Cycles: An Overview', Conference Services (Proceedings), Federal Reserve Bank of Boston, June 1998.

Activity

What does this view of business cycles imply for government economic policy?

Theories of business cycles

All of the main economic theories that have been developed to date to explain business cycles can be examined on the basis of the assumptions made about the factors that cause aggregate demand and aggregate supply to fluctuate and the assumptions concerning the interactions between AD and AS. In essence, the theories can be classified as follows:

- demand-induced theories;
- supply-induced theories.

Demand-induced theories

Demand-induced theories of the business cycle have been developed over many years by a range of economists. Three main types of demand-induced theories are discussed here, namely:

- Keynesian theory;
- monetarist theory;
- rational expectations theories.

Keynesian theory

In traditional Keynesian economics the primary cause of the business cycle is a change in expectations concerning future sales and profits of firms. This change in expectations leads to a change in demand for new capital equipment and therefore investment. Keynes referred to a change in expectations as being the product of 'animal spirits', in the sense that firms' decisions concerning future investment expenditure are affected by rumours, 'gut feelings', hunches, intuition, etc., as well as real changes in aggregate demand. 'Animal spirits' can spark off a change in investment spending by firms representing the initial impulse which starts the multiplier-accelerator process described earlier.

Figure 17.3 illustrates a Keynesian view of the contraction (or recession) phase of the business cycle. It will be seen that the short-run aggregate supply curve (SRAS) is horizontal, suggesting that real GDP and not prices (including money wage rates) change in response to a fall in aggregate demand from AD_1 to AD_2. This implies that money wages are 'sticky' in a *downward* direction, perhaps because unions successfully resist wage cuts and some employees have fixed wage contracts. Therefore, with a fall in AD and no change in the money wage rate and the general level of prices (at least initially), the economy becomes stuck in a below full-employment equilibrium level of GDP (Y_2). In the absence of any further changes in AD or AS, the economy will stay in this position until 'animal spirits' cause investment and output to recover. This could take a long time – hence the Keynesian prescription of extra government spending and tax cuts to shift the AD curve back to the right (from AD_2 to AD_1) and to push the economy back to its full-employment equilibrium, Y_1. The long-run aggregate supply curve (LRAS) is, of course, vertical at the full-employment level of real GDP.

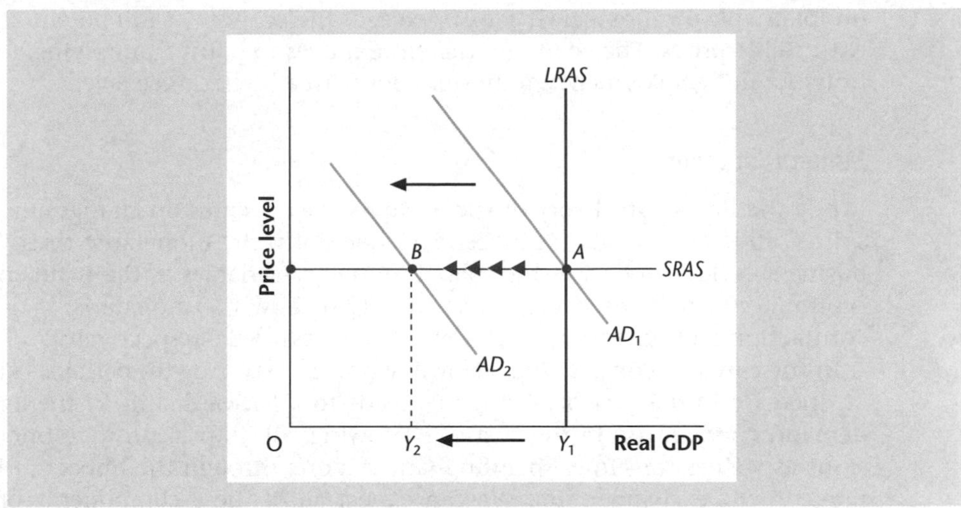

Figure 17.3 **A Keynesian economic contraction**

Figure 17.4 illustrates a Keynesian view of the expansion (i.e. recovery) phase of the business cycle. In this case wages and prices are not assumed to be 'sticky' in an *upward* direction. As aggregate demand shifts to the right, from AD_2 to AD_3, wages and prices can be expected to rise as demand rises, especially as the economy approaches its full-employment equilibrium, Y_1. The economy's adjustment path is shown by the smaller arrows in Figure 17.4, indicating that as AD shifts to the right, the short-run aggregate supply curve shifts upwards because of rising wages pushing up prices. Whereas with $SRAS_1$ the increase in AD would suggest a movement from point *B* on the diagram to point *C*, in practice, *C* is

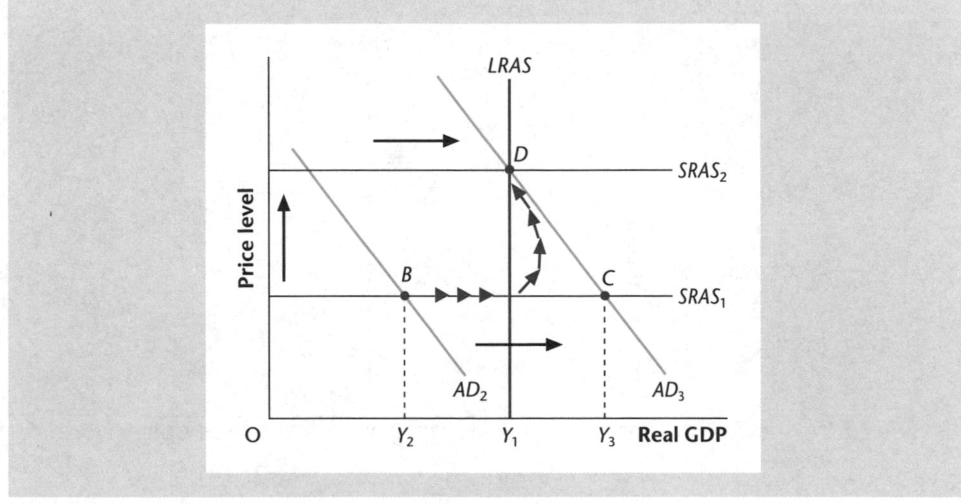

Figure 17.4 **A Keynesian economic expansion**

unobtainable because real GDP of Y_3 exceeds the economy's full potential output with stable prices. The economy therefore moves to point *D*, implying a restoration of a full-employment equilibrium but with a higher price level.

Monetarist theory

While the Keynesian theory of the business cycle focuses on changes in 'animal spirits' and their impact on investment decisions, the monetarist theory of the business cycles emphasises the role of monetary variables as the main source of economic fluctuations. Figures 17.5 and 17.6 show the monetarist view of the contraction and expansion phases of the business cycle, respectively.

In the case of a contraction, a slowdown in money growth, perhaps caused by an increase in the cost of borrowing, leads to a leftward shift in the aggregate demand curve. A rise in the cost of borrowing will impact on investment decisions as well as consumer spending (and exports through the impact of interest rates on the exchange rate). We can expect all of these components of AD to decline. Conversely, a rise in the money supply, and a consequent fall in interest rates, will tend to shift the AD curve to the right.

A fundamental difference between the Keynesian and monetarist views of the business cycle is concerned with the slope of the short-run aggregate supply curve. In the monetarist case, SRAS is upward sloping rather than horizontal. Monetarists consider that the money wage rate is only 'sticky' temporarily and will adjust as AD alters. Therefore, starting at point *A* in Figure 17.5, a fall in aggregate demand from AD_1 to AD_2, resulting from a slowdown in money growth, moves the economy initially from point *A* to point *B*, resulting in a contraction of real GDP from Y_1 to Y_2 – an economic recession. However, this will be

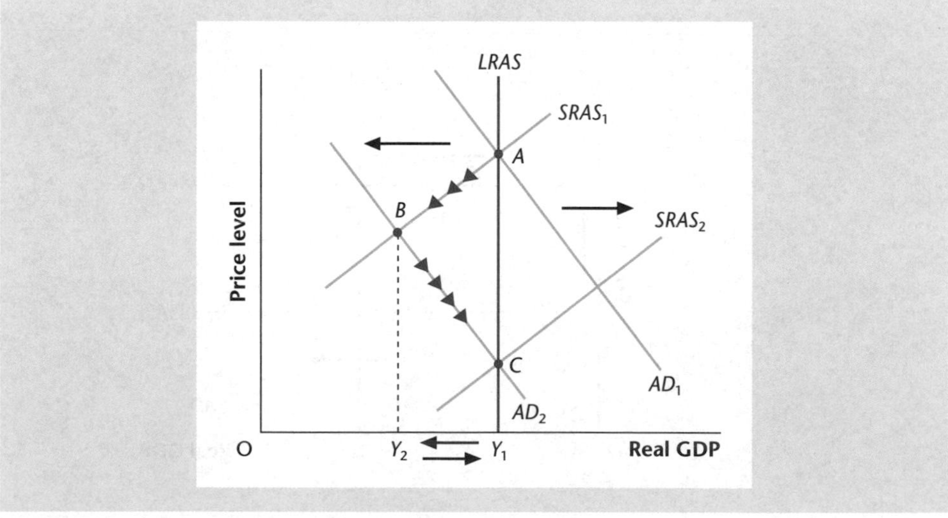

Figure 17.5 A monetarist economic contraction

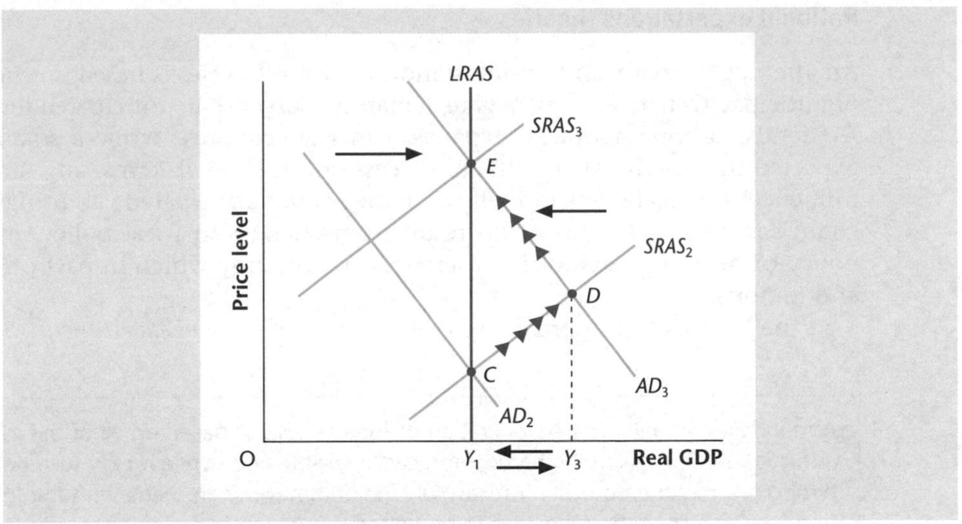

Figure 17.6 A monetarist economic expansion

short lived because in a recession there is a surplus of labour, which leads to a fall in money wage rates. As money wages fall, the short-run aggregate supply curve will shift rightwards from $SRAS_1$ to $SRAS_2$, restoring full employment – but at a lower level of money wages and prices. The smaller arrows in Figure 17.5 show the adjustment path of the economy, indicating a short-run recession at point *B* (real GDP of Y_2), and the restoration of full-employment at point *C* (real GDP of Y_1).

In Figure 17.6 the effects of an increase in the money supply and hence a fall in interest rates are shown. With the economy again at Y_1, at its full potential output given by LRAS, a rise in the money supply will shift aggregate demand rightwards from AD_2 to AD_3. This will result in an increase in both real GDP and the price level, as the economy moves from point *C* to point *D*. However, production at above sustainable full-employment output will quickly put upward pressure on wages leading to a rise in prices and a shift in the short-run aggregate supply curve leftwards from $SRAS_2$ to $SRAS_3$. The economy therefore moves from point *D* to point *E*, along the adjustment path indicated by the arrows, restoring full-employment equilibrium at Y_1, but at a higher price level than previously.

The monetarist theory suggests, first, that it is changes in the money supply that trigger the business cycle and, second, that movements of output (real GDP) away from full employment are only temporary. Business cycle recessions are therefore seen as caused by a slowdown in monetary growth, which, after a short time, is self-correcting. Similarly, business cycle expansions also come to an end following a monetary expansion. Government intervention to rectify 'booms' and 'busts' is therefore unnecessary and indeed could be destabilising. The monetarist view of business cycles also explains the role of central banks in using monetary policy to target inflation rather than real GDP.

Rational expectations theories

An alternative approach to understanding business cycles is based on the role of unanticipated changes in aggregate demand. A larger than anticipated increase in AD tends to bring about an expansion in the economy, while a smaller than expected increase in AD results in a recession. In general terms, any factor that influences aggregate demand whose change is not anticipated can bring about a change in real GDP. This could result from changes in fiscal policy, monetary policy or developments in the international economy which impact on exports and imports.

At the heart of this approach lies the concept of *rational expectations*.

> A *rational expectation* is an expectation or forecast that is based on all of the available information. This is simply the best forecast available and, while it may turn out to be wrong, at the time no other forecast which could have been made with the information available could be predicted to be better.

There are two theories of the business cycle that stem from the idea of rational expectations. Both theories are based on the notion that the money wage rate is determined by a rational, anticipated view of the future price level. The two approaches are referred to as:

- the New Classical theory;
- the New Keynesian theory.

In the case of the New Classical theory, economic fluctuations are the result of *unanticipated* changes in aggregate demand. Similarly, the New Keynesian theory puts unanticipated fluctuations in AD at the heart of an understanding of the business cycle, but also allows anticipated changes in AD to have an effect.

Unlike the other two demand-induced theories of the business cycle described above, in which we observed the impact of anticipated changes in aggregate demand, *rational expectations theories emphasise unanticipated changes*.

New classical theory

Figure 17.7 illustrates the essence of the New Classical theory of the business cycle. Assume that the economy is currently as shown by the aggregate demand curve AD_1 and the short-run aggregate supply curve $SRAS_1$ (with an anticipated price level of P_1). If aggregate demand is expected to increase such that AD_1 will shift to AD_2, this will result in a leftward shift in the aggregate supply curve from $SRAS_1$ to $SRAS_2$. The economy is expected to move along the adjustment path from *A*, to *B*, to *C*, in Figure 17.7 – based on an anticipated increase in aggregate demand from AD_1 to AD_2. The SRAS curve shifts leftwards from $SRAS_1$ to $SRAS_2$

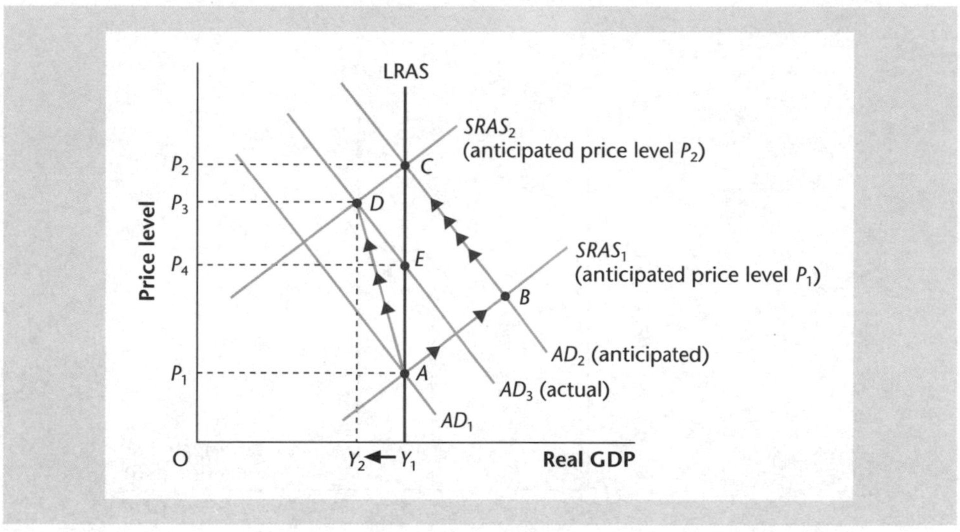

Figure 17.7 New classical theory – contraction

because of an expected price level, resulting from the increase in aggregate demand, of P_2. However, if the increase in actual aggregate demand is less than the expected increase, for example from AD_1 to AD_3, then the result will be a fall in real GDP from Y_1 to Y_2 and a rise in the price level from P_1 to P_3 (below P_2). The actual adjustment path is from *A* to *D*. The key to understanding this adjustment lies in changes in real wages (W/P). The anticipated increase in AD – which turns out to be incorrect – leads to a rise in money wages (W), which exceeds the actual rise in the price level (P_1 to P_3). This results in a higher real wage rate (W/P_3) which makes labour more expensive to employ, leading to a fall in output.

Note that in the New Classical theory real wages should quickly adjust downwards in response to unemployment, leading the economy to move back to full employment output Y_1, where AD_3 crosses the LRAS curve, at point *E*, with a lower price level as a result (P_4).

New Keynesian theory

In the case of the New Keynesian theory, the long-term nature of money wage contracts is emphasised. The money wage rate is 'sticky'. Also, both unanticipated and anticipated changes in aggregate demand lead to changes in real GDP. This is illustrated in Figure 17.8 by the shift in aggregate demand from AD_1 to AD_2. Even if AD shifts leftwards by more or less than shown in the figure, an economic contraction will still arise resulting from a downwardly inflexible wage rate. With inflexible money wages, the economy will move along $SRAS_1$ from point *A* to point *B*, leading to a recession. The economy remains on the same SRAS curve because money wages do not change (compare this with New

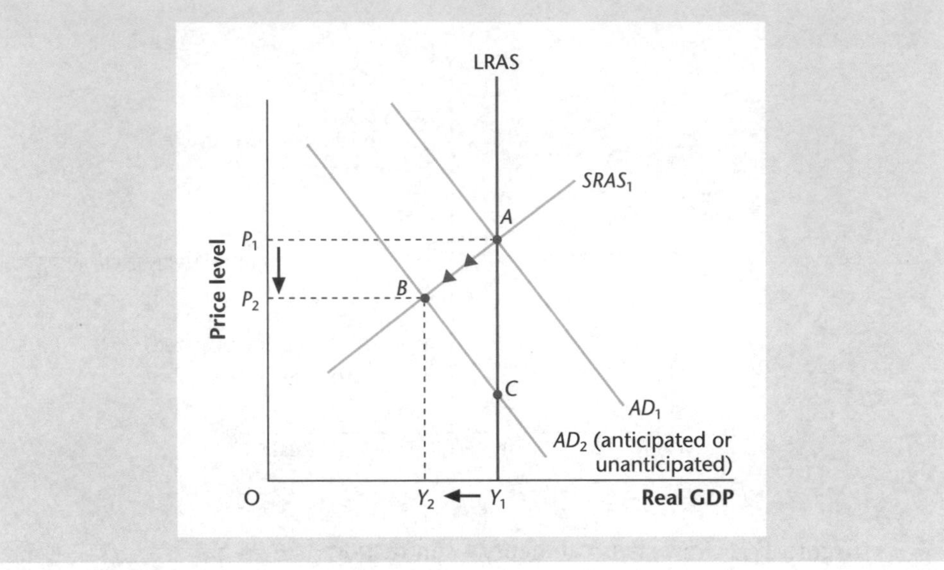

Figure 17.8 New Keynesian theory – contraction

Classical theory where wages do change and hence the SRAS curve shifts). The full employment equilibrium level of real GDP (Y_1) at point *C* will not be achieved. This movement along the $SRAS_1$ curve is caused by the inflexible money wages. The anticipated or unanticipated fall in AD leads to lower prices (from P_1 to P_2), leading to a rise in real wages (*W*/*P*). The result is unemployment.

This outcome contrasts with the earlier Keynesian theory of business cycles in which the short-run aggregate supply curve was horizontal rather than downward sloping. In New Keynesian theory prices do adjust to changes in aggregate demand, while money wages are inflexible or change more slowly than prices. In more traditional Keynesian theory, as illustrated in Figure 17.3, both money wages and prices (and therefore real wages: *W*/*P*) did not alter as aggregate demand fluctuated.

Supply-induced theories

The types of business cycle theories considered above are all based on fluctuations in aggregate demand, anticipated or unanticipated. However, we should not ignore the possibility of a supply-induced shock to the economy, which leads to a business cycle. The supporters of demand-induced theories regard aggregate supply shocks as rare rather than common events and hence argue that they are not a satisfactory explanation of the business cycle.

A particular supply-induced theory that has attracted considerable research and controversy in recent years is *the real business cycle theory*.

> *Real business cycle theorists* argue that a business cycle contraction can be caused by a major supply-side shock that reduces an economy's potential productive capacity. Similarly, an expansion may be the result of a supply-side event that causes the economy's capacity to produce to increase.

Supply side shocks or events that could trigger a business cycle include:

- *national disasters* (e.g. famines, floods, droughts and earthquakes);
- *international disturbances* (e.g. debt crises, wars and stock market collapses);
- *technological change* (e.g. resulting from new inventions and innovations leading to increased productivity).

The importance of such shocks in real business cycle theory can be traced back to the development of rational expectations theory, introduced by Robert E Lucas, Jr. Real business cycle theory today is now part of a wider research agenda called *dynamic general equilibrium analysis*.

Figure 17.9 shows the basis of the real business cycle theory. An adverse supply-side shock that reduces the capacity of the economy to produce is represented by a leftward shift of the long-run aggregate supply curve from $LRAS_1$ to $LRAS_2$. With aggregate demand given by AD_1, this will result in a movement in the economy from *A* to *B*, a rise in the price level from P_1 to P_2, and a fall in real GDP from Y_1 to Y_2, i.e. a recession (stagnation of output) combined with inflation, commonly referred to as *stagflation*.

Figure 17.9 also illustrates that there will be a consequent reduction in aggregate demand because as output falls, firms will reduce their demand for labour and

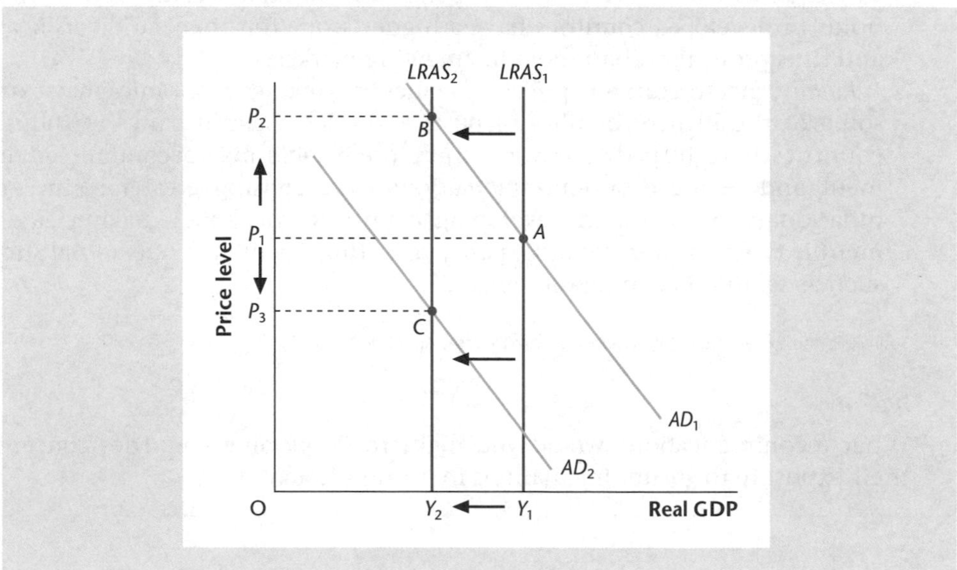

Figure 17.9 **Real business cycle theory – contraction**

Application 17.2

Business cycles in developing countries

Read the following extract:

> Empirical evidence clearly indicates that business cycles in developing countries are more severe and have more serious implications than those in the developed world. It has also been shown that consumption expenditure in developing nations fluctuates much more than GDP, while consumption in industrial countries fluctuates about the same as output. This indicates that households in the industrial countries can maintain consumption levels even in times of recession by running down assets accumulated in good times.
>
> Several explanations have been identified to explain the greater volatility in developing countries. *First*, emerging market economies are more vulnerable to commodity price shocks, given their dependency on primary product exports and imports (especially oil). Consequently, emerging market economies suffer greater fluctuations in the terms of trade (the ratio of export prices to import prices) than developed countries.
>
> *Second*, financial markets in the developing world are generally less sophisticated than those in industrial countries. Financial systems can help smooth economic fluctuations by making it easier to lend and borrow. Of course, it may also be argued that financial systems can fuel 'lending booms' which tend to increase volatility!
>
> *Third*, developing nations face greater asset price fluctuations with severe consequences for consumption expenditure through wealth effects. Households in developed countries have a higher scope for financial diversification and thus protection than those in emerging markets.
>
> *Finally*, macroeconomic policies in emerging market economies may explain some of the higher volatility of business cycles. Central banks in industrial countries have helped to create a more predictable macroeconomic environment and reduce economic fluctuations by exercising greater control over inflationary pressures. In developing countries, the policy-making environment is typically more volatile, partly reflecting the impact of external shocks, such as savings in commodity prices.

Source: Edited extract from IMF, *World Economic Outlook*, April 2002, p.125.

Activity

What recommendations would you make to developing countries concerning their exposure to greater fluctuations in economic activity?

scale back employment. A lower demand for labour will put downward pressure on money wages and, given the higher price level, real wages (w/p) will fall. With lower real wages household consumption can be expected to decline – aggregate demand shifts from AD_1 to AD_2 and the price level falls to P_3. This effect is reinforced by a likely decline in business confidence leading to reduced investment and a consequent decline in the production potential of the economy.

Supporters of the real business cycle theory point out that it is easy to confuse a demand-induced business cycle with a supply-induced cycle. Since both AD and LRAS shift in Figure 17.9, the fact that the initial change was on the supply-side may be overlooked. The crucial point in real business cycle theory is the correct identification of cause and effect; for example, a contraction in the money supply may be the result of a supply-induced shock, as firms demand less funds from the financial markets for capital spending purposes – rather than a reduction in the money supply being a policy response to an increase in aggregate demand to suppress inflation.

The real business cycle theory has attracted critics. They argue that supply-induced shocks are unlikely to lead to the scales of swings in output and employment seen over the years in many countries. Instead, they argue that such swings are more likely to be caused by fluctuations in aggregate demand.

Consequences and policy responses

As we have explored in this chapter, there are a number of competing theories of business cycles. However, there is no consensus as to which is the best theory to explain business cycles in modern economies. At the same time, it is important to take a view as to the most likely cause of any particular business cycle if we are to adopt appropriate policy responses.

If the 'old' or 'new' Keynesian theories are to be believed, then government intervention can be beneficial to help stabilise the economy and restore full employment. However, if these theories are incorrect then government intervention could, in fact, provoke greater instability into the economy – we consider the possible destabilising effect of Keynesian economics in more detail in Chapter 18.

In contrast, in the monetary and New Classical theories business cycles are temporary and self-correcting, through flexibility in money wages and prices. This supports a policy stance that generally favours free markets and argues against government intervention. The role of government (and central banks) is to provide an environment that is conducive to private enterprise, market transactions and wage and price flexibility.

Finally, defenders of the real business cycle theory raise the possibility that the business cycle is efficient. Recessions create the scope for beneficial resource reallocation from lower to higher productivity activities. They argue that the business cycle does not reflect an economy that is misbehaving. The policy implication of this view is that policy makers should not intervene at all on the demand-side of the economy. Instead, encouragement should be given to the development of technologies that support faster long-term economic growth.

Concluding remarks

This chapter has been concerned with the nature and causes of business cycles. Since the Industrial Revolution it has been observed that economic activity fluctuates from year to year, leading to the phenomenon of 'booms' and 'busts'. We have seen that there are a number of different theories of the business cycle, involving both demand-induced and supply-induced cycles. The cycles we have been concerned with are short-term cycles. In general, the period from peak to peak or trough to trough in these sorts of cycles is roughly around five to seven years, although this figure does vary across cycles. Some economists, however, have identified longer 'waves' of economic activity over 50 years or more. These 'long waves' are known as *Kondratieff waves* or *cycles*, after a Russian economist, which are said to occur because of the presence and eventual saturation of broad investment opportunities. For example, industrialisation in Europe during the first half of the nineteenth century, resulting from the development of steam power and development of the textile industry, has been described as a Kondratieff wave. More recently it has been argued that the period since 1945 has also followed a Kondratieff wave with investment opportunities in the electronics, chemicals, plastics, medicine, telecommunications and information technology sectors. However, the existence of clearly definable long-wave business cycles is very controversial. In any event, they do not reduce the importance of understanding the causes of the volatility of the economy over shorter, 'within wave', periods.

It is also important to understand that business cycles, while leading to occasional painful economic adjustments, do cause a 'shake out' of under-performing resources, which can then be used elsewhere in the economy. Some economists therefore argue that business cycles are beneficial and part of the natural adjustment process in capitalist economies. An attention to business cycles should not be allowed to divert attention away from the importance of achieving long-term economic growth.

Key learning points

- *Business cycles* represent movements in the level of economic activity (output) over time around the long-run, trend rate of growth in the economy.
- There are four phases of the business cycle: *peak, contraction, trough* and *expansion.*
- A *recession* is defined as a situation when the level of economic activity (real GDP) has fallen for at least two consecutive quarters.

- A *depression* describes a situation of prolonged, low economic activity.
- *Indicators of economic activity* fall into four main categories resulting in the creation of a number of indexes. These are referred to as: (a) the longer-leading index; (b) the shorter-leading index; (c) the coincident index; and (d) the lagging index.
- The *causes of business cycles* may be grouped under three headings: (a) political factors; (b) international economic factors; and (c) domestic economic factors.
- *Political factors* are generally associated with pre-election spending increases and tax cuts by governments and a reversal of these policies after an election.
- *International economic factors* focus on the international transmission of economic activity, including the globalisation of product and financial markets in general.
- The *multiplier-accelerator model* is central to an explanation of the business cycle based on domestic economic factors, with particular emphasis on stock (inventory) adjustment.
- There are a number of competing theories of business cycles, which may be classified as: *demand-induced theories*; and *supply-induced theories*.
- There are three main types of *demand-induced theories* of the business cycle. These are: Keynesian theory; monetarist theory; and rational expectations theories.
- Traditional *Keynesian theory*, sometimes referred to as 'old' Keynesian theory, of the business cycle focuses on changes in 'animal spirits' as the cause of the initial impulse that sparks off a business cycle with consequences for aggregate demand.
- The *monetarist theory* of the business cycle emphasises the role of monetary variables as the cause of changes in aggregate demand and therefore business cycles.
- A *rational expectation* is an expectation or forecast that is based on all available information at the time.
- There are two theories of the business cycle that stem from the idea of rational expectations, namely the *New Classical theory* and the *New Keynesian theory*.
- *The New Classical theory* highlights the importance of unanticipated changes in aggregate demand and the consequences for real wages and output.
- *The New Keynesian theory* is similar to the New Classical theory but highlights both anticipated and unanticipated changes in aggregate demand and considers money wages to be 'sticky' in a downward direction resulting from long-term employment contracts.
- A *supply-induced theory* of business cycles that has emerged in recent years is that referred to as 'real business cycle theory'.
- *Real business cycle* theorists argue that a business cycle expansion or contraction is caused by major supply-side shocks, which increase or decrease an economy's potential productive capacity.

- *Supply-side shocks* that may trigger a business cycle include natural disasters, international disturbances and technological change.
- The appropriate policy response to a business cycle depends upon which theory of the business cycle is favoured.
- *Kondratieff waves* or *cycles* are longer-term, 50-year fluctuations in economic activity associated with new breakthroughs in technology leading to the development of new industries.

? Topics for discussion

1. What do you understand by the term 'business cycle'? Compare and contrast 'long-wave' theory with the theories of shorter-term business cycles.
2. Compare and contrast the traditional (or 'old') and 'new' Keynesian theories of the business cycle with the monetarist theory of cycles.
3. Why may the 'supply-induced' business cycle theory be an inadequate explanation of most business cycles?
4. What do you understand by the term 'rational expectations'? Using appropriate diagrams, explain the differences between the two rational expectations theories of the business cycle discussed in this chapter,
5. What do you understand by the term 'real business cycle theory'? How does it contrast with demand-induced theories of the business cycle?
6. A recession is blamed on a fall in aggregate demand. Set out the appropriate policy response by government if (a) the monetarist theory of the business cycle is correct, or (b) the traditional Keynesian view of the business cycle is correct. Use appropriate diagrams to illustrate you responses.

Chapter 18

MARKET FORCES AND MACROECONOMIC MANAGEMENT

Aims and learning outcomes

This book is concerned with macroeconomic theory and its application. On a number of occasions we have looked at the actions governments and their central banks might take to stabilise economic activity, restore full employment and lower inflation using especially Keynesian techniques of demand management. However, since the 1970s Keynesian economic management has been attacked for leading to large and bureaucratic government, burdensome taxes and regulations, and for failing to achieve its goals of full employment and price stability. Instead, a number of economists have argued that economies function better with minimalist state intervention in the context of free markets. They argue that the macroeconomy needs little if any active economic management by government.

This chapter discusses some of the arguments for and against state intervention in the macroeconomy. It also considers whether, when governments do get involved, economic 'rules' are superior to governments having 'discretion' to shape policy. The chapter is not concerned with the superiority of capitalist over communist or 'command' economies. After 1945, Central and Eastern Europe developed as planned economies with state ownership of industry and much of commerce and agriculture; whereas Western Europe developed mainly with market economies and private enterprise. Economists rarely benefit from laboratory testing of their theories like chemists and physicists. However, the experiences of East Germany and West Germany developing side by side come fairly close to such a laboratory experiment. At the end of World War II the economy of Germany was ruined. East Germany under communist governments developed a highly state-planned economy after 1945. West Germany encouraged free enterprise and resource allocation through market signals. When the Berlin Wall fell in 1989, West Germany had incomes per head and productivity levels around three times as high as in East Germany. Clearly the market economy had proved much superior to state planning. Today it is hard to find any economist who argues for a fully state-planned economy. Rather discussions now centre on the extent to which governments should intervene in markets. This chapter focuses on this debate, in terms of macroeconomic management.

The following issues are discussed here:

- Keynesian economics and the market economy;
- information within government;
- motivation within government;
- rules versus discretion;
- the case for an independent central bank.

It should be understood that no economy operates without some government of some kind. All societies have laws, rules and conventions relating to human behaviour, both to shape that behaviour to achieve the common good or social welfare and to restrain individuals from infringing the rights of other individuals. In particular, market economies need laws to protect private property and to facilitate private contracting and exchange including conflict resolution. Society has developed legislatures, courts, police and defence forces to this end. These are all well-recognised services supplied by government. However, macroeconomic management by government goes beyond this minimalist role for the state, to embrace the active involvement of government in markets with a view to removing or at least reducing what are perceived to be socially costly outcomes, such as unemployment and inflation. This is much more controversial and depends upon markets failing and government intervention not failing or at least not failing as badly!

Learning outcomes

After studying this material you will be able to:

- Recognise the difficulties that can arise in applying Keynesian economic management principles and techniques.
- Understand why some economists favour a minimal role for the state in the economy.
- Appreciate the importance of both motivation and information within government.
- Identify the arguments for governments using 'rules' rather than 'discretion' in economic management.
- Understand the arguments for having a central bank which is free to operate independently of government.

Keynesian economics and the market economy

Keynesian economics developed out of the writings of the Cambridge economist John Maynard Keynes in the 1930s, a time of economic depression and high unemployment. Prior to Keynes, macroeconomic policy was dominated by the notion that markets would restore full employment without the need for governments to manage aggregate demand. Say's law of markets stated that 'supply creates its own demand'. For every dollar of production a dollar of income was created to purchase the output. Say's law maintained that there will always, or nearly always, be sufficient total demand or purchasing power in the economy to buy the full-employment level of output. As the Frenchman Jean Baptiste Say (1767–1832) explained:

> It is worthwhile to remark, that a product is no sooner created, than it, from that instant, affords a market for other products to the full extent of its own value. When the producer has put the finishing hand to his product, he is most anxious to sell it immediately, lest its value should vanish in his hands. Nor is he less anxious to dispose of the money he may get for it; for the value of money is also perishable. But the only way of getting rid of money is in the purchase of some product or other. Thus, the mere circumstance of the creation of one product immediately opens a vent [demand] for other products. (Say, 1821)

This statement ignores the possibility of savings or other leakages from the circular flow of income. Nevertheless, it formed the basis of classical and neoclassical approaches to macroeconomics up until the 1930s. Provided that interest rates varied to keep savings and investment expenditure equal, that trade balances were achieved so that imports and exports are equal and governments balanced their budgets, so that taxes were identical to government spending, then planned leakages from the circular flow of income would equal planned injections into the circular flow. In which case Say's law of markets appeared to hold true – *supply did create its own demand*. In reality the nineteenth century saw periods of economic boom and slump, but these were temporary and associated with imbalances in markets in the different phases of the business cycle. In the longer term, changes in demand and supply restored full employment through changes in real prices, wages and interest rates. The 1930s, however, saw an unprecedented, worldwide economic depression – the *Great Depression* – with record high unemployment and falling prices (deflation). Say's law of markets appeared to have broken down in the face of a sharp contraction in aggregate demand and the failure of real wages, prices and interest rates to adjust.

We have looked at Keynesian economics in detail in earlier chapters (see especially Chapters 6 and 7). Fiscal policy (changes in taxes and government spending) operating through the national income multiplier leads to changes in aggregate demand to maintain full employment and stable prices. We have also looked at the monetarist and supply-side economics critiques of Keynesian economics (in Chapters 8 to 10). Here we saw how Keynesian economics could lead to an over-expansion in the money supply leading to high inflation and how a neglect of the economic conditions for efficient production could lead to inadequate supply in the economy to meet demand. In the 1970s Keynesian economics was criticised for being too focused on demand over supply and for its inflationary consequences. It was also associated with 'big government'.

According to Keynesian economics, when the business cycle is heading into a downturn governments should cut taxes and raise their own spending. This fiscal injection reverses the decline in aggregate demand resulting from lower consumer and private investment spending. By contrast, in times when the economy is in a boom period governments should do the reverse to reduce inflationary pressures. Taxes should be increased and public spending should be reduced. Although governments did raise taxes from time to time from the 1950s, tax cuts were less common under Keynesian demand management policies. Equally, governments courted public popularity by spending more, such as on health and pensions, and were reluctant to cut state spending in boom periods because of the electoral consequences. The result was a *ratchet effect* under which government expenditure and taxes in Europe and North America increased over time. Only from the 1970s with the decline in support for Keynesian economics were serious attempts made to cut taxes and government spending as a share of GDP, for example in Australia, the USA, the UK and New Zealand.

Keynesian economics was therefore associated with 'big government'; something that in all probability John Maynard Keynes would have opposed. Keynesian demand management also failed to curb economic stagnation (resulting in growing unemployment) and inflation in the 1970s, i.e. *stagflation*. This resulted in a growth in interest in monetarist economics and supply-side economics as alternatives. The stagflation of the 1970s undermined support for Keynesian economics within governments. Moreover, even before the 1970s the track record of Keynesian economics was tarnished because of ill-timed government intervention in the economy. So-called 'lags' in government intervention meant that government action could destabilise rather than stabilise the economy. We can see how this could occur in the following example.

Example of destabilisation

Suppose that a downturn in the business cycle begins in January 2006. It will take time for government statisticians to collect the production and expenditure data to spot this downturn. Suppose that the statistics showing a downturn are circulated within government in April 2006. After due deliberation, in July of that year the government decides to take action to reverse the economic downturn. It must now alter taxes and/or state spending. Government investment expenditures cannot be altered quickly. It can take a number of years to construct a new road or hospital. Government current expenditure, such as on welfare benefits, can be altered more quickly. Suppose that the government decides to announce a rise in unemployment benefits. The decision will need to be discussed in the legislature and the social security department will need to prepare to make the higher payments. A few more weeks go by. Let us say that the higher unemployment benefit is at last paid out in October 2006. The additional income now enters the circular flow of income. But this is ten months after the downturn in the business cycle started. The extra government welfare spending may now be inadequate to reverse the growing recessionary tendencies in the economy. Alternatively, it is possible that the January statistics were mistaken and that the economy has not been going into recession. In which case the additional government spending will add to an already robust aggregate demand, perhaps leading to inflationary pressures.

In other words, to undertake Keynesian demand management in a timely and proportional fashion, governments need accurate economic forecasting and they need to be able to *respond very quickly* to forecasts by adjusting taxes and government spending. The alternative to fiscal policy measures, monetary policy, may also have slow effects. For example, changes in interest rates, while they can be introduced more quickly than tax and government spending changes, take time to influence consumers' willingness to borrow and to spend more and firms' willingness to borrow and to invest. Also, as with tax changes, households and firms may believe that the change is merely temporary and unsustainable and may therefore not change their spending behaviour at all.

In practice, government intervention operates only after time lags; for example, monetary expansion is commonly associated with an 18-month time lag before it changes the level of economic activity. However, this is a rough estimate and much will depend on the economic circumstances at the time, including the level of confidence in the economy. The result may be government policies that destabilise rather than stabilise the economy. The main time lags in formulating and implementing Keynesian policies are caused by:

- collecting macroeconomic data;
- analysing the macroeconomic data;
- making policy decisions within government;
- introducing the policy changes;
- the time taken for policy changes to impact on the economy.

Keynesian demand management, therefore, has a number of weaknesses relating to its inflationary effects, its tendency to lead to big government, and to the difficulty of introducing appropriate and timely policy changes. The case for Keynesian demand management is further weakened if we turn to consider the importance of both *information* and *motivation* within government.

Application 18.1

The noble vision

In March 1984 President Ronald Reagan made a speech to the Conservative Political Action Conference on the values of a free enterprise economy. The following are highlights from this speech:

Now, those who deal in a world of numbers cannot predict the progress of the human mind, the drive and energy of the spirit, or the power of incentives. We're beginning an industrial renaissance which most experts never saw coming.

Incentives laid the seeds for the great growth in venture capital which helped set off the revolution in high technology. Sunrise industries, such as computers,

Application 18.1 continued

micro-electronics, robotics, and fibre optics – all are creating a new world of opportunities. And as our knowledge expands, business investment is stimulated to modernise older industries with the newer technologies.

An opportunity society awaits us. We need only believe in ourselves and give men and women of faith, courage and vision the freedom to build it. Let others run down America and seek to punish success. Let them call you greedy for not wanting government to take more and more of your earnings. Let them defend their tombstone society of wage and price guidelines, mandatory quotas, tax increases, planned shortages and shared sacrifices.

We want no part of that mess, thank you very much. We will encourage all Americans – men and women, young and old, individuals of every race, creed, and colour – to succeed and be healthy, happy and whole. This is our goal. We see America not falling behind, but moving ahead; our citizens not fearful and divided, but confident and united by shared values of faith, family, work, neighbourhood, peace and freedom.

An opportunity society begins with growth, and that means incentives. My sympathies are with the taxpayers, not the tax-spenders. I consider stopping them from taking more of your earnings an economic responsibility and a moral obligation. I will not permit an antigrowth coalition to jeopardize this recovery. If they get their way, they'll charge everything on your 'Taxpayers Express Card'. And believe me, they never leave home without it.

As good conservatives, we were brought up to oppose deficits. But sometimes I think some have forgotten why. We were against deficit spending. Those who would be heroes trying to reduce deficits by raising taxes are not heroes. They have not addressed the point I made in the State of the Union: whether government borrows or increases taxes, it will be taking the same amount of money from the private economy and, either way, that's too much.

We must bring down government spending to a level where it cannot interfere with the ability of the economy to grow.

Combining these spending restraints with another key reform will make America's economy the undisputed leader for innovation, growth and opportunity. I'm talking about simplification of the entire tax system. We can make taxes more fair, easier to understand and, more important, we can greatly increase incentives by bringing personal tax rates down.

But economic opportunities can only flourish if the values at the foundation of our society and freedom remain strong and secure. Our families and friends must be able to live and work without always being afraid.

Activity

Set out the key principles of the 'free market' agenda, as put forward by President Reagan. What difficulties does the implementation of such an agenda face?

Information within government

That governments lack the necessary information to be able to intervene in economies and improve on the results of the free market is central to the criticisms of Keynesian demand management from so-called *Austrian economics*. The term Austrian economics now has no geographical significance, but rather applies to economists who follow the teachings of earlier Austrian-born economists, notably Ludwig von Mises (1881–1973), Joseph Schumpeter (1883–1950) and Friedrich von Hayek (1889–1992). The essence of Austrian economics lies in the process by which markets produce information about consumer wants and the costs of supplying consumers, and the ability of profit-motivated entrepreneurs to capitalise on this information by satisfying consumers. Hayek made clear the dynamic role of the price system as a mode of transmitting information in markets, writing that the competitive market economy exists to solve the 'central theoretical problem of all social science', namely:

> . . . how the spontaneous interaction of a number of people, each possessing only bits of knowledge, brings about a state of affairs. . . . which could be brought about by deliberate direction only by somebody who possesses the combined knowledge of all of these individuals. (Hayek, 1948)

In other words, for governments to be able to improve on market outcomes they need to possess the information that exists in the heads of the entire population – but, of course, this is impossible. In consequence, government intervention must always be second best to the results of individuals trading and exchanging voluntarily within markets.

Motivation within government

Governments may lack the necessary information that they need to intervene in markets and stabilise aggregate demand to produce full employment and low inflation. But even if they had this information, could we trust government to use it to maximise social welfare? Whereas some economists, notably from the Austrian school, emphasise the role of information as a decisive critique of government macroeconomic management, others point to the problem of motivation within government.

Ideally, politicians and civil servants should reflect the wishes of the electorate. If the electorate wants to have lower taxes or higher state pensions, the politicians and government officials should respond by designing such policy changes. In other words, politicians and civil servants should be 'disinterested' and should not have their own agendas. In practice, however, to assume entirely disinterested behaviour within government appears to be highly naïve. Politicians can be expected to operate economic policy so as to win elections. This leads to the notion of 'political' business cycles, as studied on pp.408–409. Political business cycles occur when economies are reflated ahead of elections to reduce unemployment and then taxes are raised and government spending promises reversed once the election is safely out of the way. Similarly, civil servants can be expected to support government policies that increase the number of civil service posts and enhance their salaries and status. In other words, some economists argue that, like the rest of us, politicians and civil servants can be expected to pursue their own ends or what economists call *utility maximising behaviour*. This self-seeking approach to the study of government and economic policy is referred to as *public choice theory* or alternatively *the economics of politics*. Whereas it may be over-cynical to assume that *all* politicians and *all* civil servants at *all* times pursue only their own utility, nevertheless it is probably at least equally as naïve to assume that they never put their own interests above the public interest.

> *Public choice theory* is concerned with *motivation* within government.

Coupled with the critique that governments lack the information needed to intervene in markets to maintain economic stability, public choice theory leads to the conclusion that Keynesian economics is doomed to disappoint. Indeed, with politicians courting votes at election time and civil servants welcoming the growth in their departments' budgets, the growth of 'big government' becomes easy to explain. Certainly, when the information and motivation critiques of government are combined, they produce a powerful explanation of why government intervention in markets may lead to lower rather than higher social welfare or what is referred to as 'state failure'.

Rules versus discretion

If politicians and civil servants may intervene with policies that are in their own interests rather than the public interest, perhaps governments should operate macroeconomic policies according to 'rules' rather than using 'discretion'.

> A *rule* lays down the action government must take under given conditions, whereas *discretion* allows government freedom of action.

An example of a rule-based policy is the policy laid down for the European Central Bank (ECB) to maintain inflation at 1 per cent in the Eurozone. Similarly, the Bank of England between 1997 and the end of 2003, had been required to operate monetary policy to maintain inflation (calculated on a different basis to that adopted in the Eurozone) at between 1.5 and 2.5 per cent. The 'golden rule' under which some governments agree not to run budget deficits over the entire business cycle is another example of a rules-based policy.

The argument for rules-based macroeconomic policy is based on a lack of confidence that governments can be trusted to adopt discretionary policies that improve social welfare. At the same time, however, a rules-based policy does limit freedom of movement in macroeconomic policy, which may be necessary at times of economic crisis. For this reason, governments usually retain powers to replace rules with discretionary policies if the economic circumstances dictate.

Application 18.2

Global market forces rule over government

Dr Greg Mills, national director of the South Africa Institute of International Affairs, talks about how globalisation has changed the world.

'European businesses battered by Asian fears', 'Cheap Asian imports could knock profits', 'JSE joins the global collapse', 'De Beers feels the Asian pain', 'Beijing shores up yuan as Asia takes heat'. These are just a sample of headlines in recent weeks. They reflect the integrated nature of today's global economy, where economic movements can immediately bring dividends in one area or, in another, exact punishment – witness the Asian currency crisis and the effects on emerging markets.

Globalisation is synonymous with this activity, describing the rapid acceleration of economic transactions across borders. With globalisation, knowledge has become increasingly mobile, so geographic location and time constraints are no longer major obstacles.

At its heart lies technological advance and information dissemination. The rapid development of technology has placed a premium on skills (and hence education) rather than resources as a national asset, while economic factors have focused attention on governments and systems of governance, and emphasised their weaknesses.

International best practice is now the benchmark for judging economies. This is a painful lesson the markets have taught southeast Asia and, now, southern Africa.

Governments are suddenly expected to facilitate rather than regulate economic activity.

While the rest of the world has been integrating, over the past 30 years Africa has been marginalising.

To take advantage of the benefits that globalisation offers, such as large private capital inflows (of which Africa receives less than 2 per cent of the global total), the continent's policy milieu will have to change substantially.

Even the relatively high global level of returns on investments in Africa (particularly in the areas of tourism and mining) have not proven sufficiently comforting to foreign capital.

▶

Application 18.2 continued

African governments' reputation for policy unpredictability has continued to deter investment.

Yet eastern Asia's woes and the effects on emerging markets worldwide do raise a number of questions about the sustainable nature of the global economy.

First, what kind of government does this new world need, and what are the consequences of deviating from global economic norms?

The fundamentals behind Asia's plummet are easy to identify. The combination of currency depreciation and fall in asset prices placed a large strain on countries which had poorly supervised, poorly functioning, badly regulated, corrupt and government-directed financial markets.

However, the continued fall in regional currency values would now appear to have little to do with bad economic fundamentals. Rather, there are fears that Asian political systems may be incapable of responding effectively to address financial reforms while maintaining power.

These tensions are proof for some that greatly different standards of governance and political systems cannot survive together in the face of globalisation and increasing expectations of a global commonality of styles and ethics.

There are fears that this ongoing crisis might ultimately produce a new paradigm in international relations – one that ends the era of increased global competition, where technological advances have raised productivity and kept down prices and inflation.

There is a danger, it is argued, that broken dreams in Asia will result in increased protectionism as a way to restore domestic economic and political confidence.

Of course, no-one believes such a strategy will solve any of Asia's economic problems. These can be rectified by restructuring systems of bank lending that have been incompetent, reckless and downright corrupt.

But still, given the political challenges that face the countries concerned in sorting out the banking systems, globalisation has proven an easier, politically popular target – just as in South Africa.

Second, in the light of the East Asian currency depreciation, can globalisation (and, more specifically, the most negative effects of the markets) be controlled or regulated?

At the time of the currency fall in September 1997, Prime Minister Mahathir of Malaysia attempted to shift the blame for the crash of the ringgit onto currency speculators, among them George Soros. Amid barely veiled accusations of global conspiracy, Mahathir went so far as to suggest a ban in dealing in the ringgit for purposes other than trade.

Soros initially retaliated by referring to Mahathir as a 'menace in his own country'.

Application 18.2 continued

More recently, he has suggested the need to reform the international financial system to avoid Asia-enforced global deflation, proposing the establishment of an international credit insurance corporation as a sister to the International Monetary Fund (IMF).

As the financier noted: 'What started out as a minor imbalance has become a much bigger one that threatens to engulf not only international credit but also international trade.'

In this vein, Malcolm Fraser, the former Australian prime minister, argues the IMF should work towards global 'economic equilibrium' through management of the global economy, and assistance to reduce the impact of crises.

In spite of these challenges, Africa has little to lose from globalisation, which offers ways both to reduce risk and the cost of doing so, as well as giving the continent access to capital flows.

Today, domestic policy is subject to the discipline of market forces which no-one controls – and where governments are increasingly redundant. This reality is an especially bitter pill for those countries which have traditionally relied on patronage to bolster weak systems of governance.

Source: http://www.btimes.co.za/98/0823/btmoney/money6.htm

Activity

In the light of the above discussion, consider the implications of globalisation for government economic policy and the management of market forces.

The case for an independent central bank

Recent years have seen a number of countries (e.g. New Zealand, the UK, the Eurozone countries) adopt an independent central bank. This occurred after research which suggested, tentatively, that greater central bank independence from political control led to lower inflation. For example, the Bundesbank in the former West Germany operated with a high degree of independence from the 1950s and was credited with the strength of the Deutschmark and Germany's relatively low inflation rates.

Central banks are normally state-owned and operate monetary policy as laid down by government. But if governments lack the information needed to operate a successful monetary policy and may be motivated to use monetary policy as part of the 'political' business cycle, there are economic benefits in having an independent central bank. An independent central bank operates according to rules, for example targets for inflation rates, laid down by government. In practice, governments often retain powers to overrule central bank decisions should they feel this necessary, although they will often be reluctant to do so, except where there are very good grounds, because of the likely adverse public reaction. It should be noted that there is still considerable disagreement over whether an independent central bank is economically advantageous.

Application 18.3

Causes of the Great Depression – Keynesian versus Monetarist views

Keynesian view

The Keynesian explanation for the Great Depression of the 1930s focuses on the central role of investment spending. Keynesians draw attention to the sharp increase in investment demand in the early 1920s. This increase was due to a number of factors. *First,* the rebuilding of much of Europe after World War I resulted in increased European demand for American goods. This growth in demand for exports resulted in increased US production and investment spending (on plant and machinery).

Second, domestic demand for goods and services in the USA also rose sharply in the wake of the War, further stimulating production and investment by American firms.

Third, optimism soared after the War, creating a 'feel good factor' that good times had arrived and would continue, driven by new technologies and leading to rising living standards. Some observers argue that this optimism encouraged US firms to expand productive capacity still further and to invest beyond the level that was required.

However, by the mid-1920s, many firms had excess productive capacity – leading to falls in investment demand. A negative *multiplier effect* came into play – an effect which began to accelerate as falls in output (GDP) led to falls in consumer spending, indicating even less need for productive capacity. In effect, the US economy fell into a vicious spiral of falling output, falling consumption and investment spending resulting in further falls in output, and so on.

In summary, the Keynesian view is that the Great Depression was caused by a reduction in investment spending which followed a prolonged investment boom.

Monetarist view

The monetarist explanation for the Great Depression focuses on the money supply and on government policies at the time concerning prices and wages. Investment expenditure is *not* seen as the destabilising factor – instead, investment itself was destabilised by monetary impulses.

Between 1929 and 1933 the US money supply fell by more than 25 per cent. This led to a sharp fall in aggregate demand and a consequent decline in real GDP.

Application 18.3 continued

The length of the Great Depression could have been shortened if, following the fall in the money supply, prices and wages had been allowed to fall to free-market levels. However, the US government pursued policies that propped up prices and wages. For example, price-fixing agreements among firms were permissible under President Roosevelt's National Recovery Act while labour legislation strengthened the power of trade unions in bargaining for wage increases.

Monetarists argue the combination of a monetary squeeze and the inflexibility of prices and wages made the Depression more severe and longer lasting.

Activity

Which of the above views do you support and why?

Concluding remarks

To be successful Keynesian demand management requires that governments intervene in the economy in a timely fashion and with appropriate policies to stabilise the economy at full employment with low inflation. In reality, governments are likely to face considerable difficulty in operating fully effective macroeconomic policies. This is so because of information problems and time lags in introducing policy changes, and because governments may not be disinterested policy makers. The result may be macroeconomic policies that, over time, destabilise rather than stabilise the economy.

At the same time, however, elected governments are held responsible by the electorate for the state of the economy. For this reason, governments will often not feel able to leave the level of economic activity to be determined solely by market forces. The reality is that governments are expected to adopt macroeconomic policies with the aim of improving economic performance. It is for this reason that this book has been concerned with understanding the operations of the macroeconomy and with the circumstances under which governments may help to bring about full employment, low inflation and economic growth.

✔ Key learning points

- *Say's law of markets* states that 'supply creates its own demand' and depends upon the smooth adjustment of real wages, prices and interest rates to changes in demand and supply.
- The 1930s saw an unprecedented economic depression with high unemployment. Keynesian economics was a response to this economic depression.

- Keynes advocated *fiscal policy* to restore a full employment level of aggregate demand.
- In practice, *Keynesian economics* has proved difficult to operate successfully and by the 1970s was associated with rising unemployment and high inflation or a condition of 'stagflation'.
- The failure of Keynesian economics has been put down to 'lags' in policy formulation and implementation; a lack of information within government about the true state of the economy and the response of markets to government measures; and the motivation of politicians and civil servants.
- *Public choice* theory is concerned with self-seeking behaviour within government, which may mean, for example, that Keynesian measures are introduced to achieve short-term political benefits, such as winning elections, over achieving longer-term economic prosperity.
- One policy response is to operate *rules-based* policies that limit the freedom of governments to use their discretion when formulating and implementing macroeconomic policies.
- Some economists favour having an *independent central bank* because this restricts the ability of government to interfere in setting monetary policy.

? Topics for discussion

1. Under what circumstances would you expect Say's law of markets not to operate to maintain full employment?
2. What difficulties face governments when they attempt to stabilise the economy using Keynesian policies?
3. Discuss the importance of forecasting in the context of successful macroeconomic policy formulation and implementation.
4. Compare and contrast the operation of Keynesian economics under the assumptions of both disinterested policy makers and policy makers who pursue self-seeking agendas?
5. What do you understand by the term 'public choice theory'? How does public choice theory undermine Keynesian economics?
6. Why favour 'rules' over 'discretion' in macroeconomic policy formulation? When might a rules-based policy prove problematic?
7. What are the arguments for and against having an independent central bank?

GLOSSARY

Absorption effect. The tendency for imports to rise faster than exports (causing a deficit in trade) due to a growth in aggregate demand and economic activity.

Accelerator effect. Explains how a change in the level of investment is determined by the rate at which national income in changing.

Adaptive expectations. The notion that individuals' expectations (e.g. about future inflation) are based on past experience and these modify as time passes.

Aggregate demand. The total amount of expenditure on domestic goods and services made up of $C + I + G + (X - M)$, where C represents consumer (or household) spending, I represents investment spending (including stock investment), G is government spending (both current and capital expenditure), X represents revenue from exports and M is expenditure on imports.

Aggregate demand curve. A graph showing the total amount of demand in the economy at different price levels.

Aggregate production function. The relationship between an economy's output and factor inputs (labour, land, capital as well as technology).

Aggregate supply curve. A graph showing the total amount of output at different price levels.

Aggregate supply. The total amount of output of goods and services produced in the economy.

Appreciation. See *Currency appreciation.*

ASEAN. The Association of Southeast Asian Nations established in 1967. Today Indonesia, Malaysia, Philippines, Singapore, Thailand, Brunei Darussalam, Vietnam, Laos, Myanmar and Cambodia are members. ASEAN exists to accelerate economic growth, social progress and cultural development in the region and to promote regional peace and stability.

Asian Development Bank. Exists to reduce poverty in Asia and the Pacific region. It was established in 1966 and has 61 member countries. Its function is to provide loans for projects that will contribute to raising economic growth in the region.

Automatic adjustments. Those which occur to rectify a balance of payments imbalance without government interference.

Automatic fiscal policy. A change in fiscal policy (tax revenue and government expenditure) that is triggered by fluctuations in economic activity (real GDP).

Autonomous expenditure. Those components of aggregate planned expenditure that are not influenced by real GDP.

Average propensity to consume (APC). The fraction of a given level of national income (Y) which is spent on consumption (C): $APC = C/Y$.

Average propensity to save (APS). The fraction of a given level of national income (Y) which is saved (S): $APS = S/Y$

Balance of payments. The account that records a country's international trade in goods and services and its international capital account movements.

Balance of trade. The value of exports minus the value of imports of goods (visibles). Note that trade in services (invisibles) is specifically excluded.

Balanced budget. Where government spending and taxation receipts are equal.

Balanced budget multiplier. The expansionary effect on national income even when government spending and tax revenues rise by the same amount.

Balancing item. A statistical adjustment to ensure that the two sides of the balance of payments account balance. It is necessary because of errors and omissions in compiling the statistics.

Bank credit multiplier. The amount of new deposits (money) created from an initial bank deposit, given by $1/RR$ where RR equals the reserve requirement ratio.

Black economy. See *Underground economy*.

Bonds. Debt issued by corporates or by governments in order to raise long-term finance. (Government bonds are commonly referred to as *gilts* or *gilt-edged* securities since the risk of default is virtually zero.)

Bretton Woods System. Established at the end of World War II and introduced a fixed exchange rate regime internationally that was broadly maintained until the 1970s. It collapsed under the weight of speculative capital flows and high inflation internationally.

Broad money. Includes money balances for transaction purposes and money held as a form of saving, which can be converted with relative ease without capital loss into spending on goods and services (e.g. M2 or M3 in the USA and M4 in the UK).

Budget deficit. The amount of government borrowing needed to fill the gap between government spending and tax revenue.

Budget surplus. The amount remaining when governments spend less than they raise in taxation.

Business cycles. Movements in the level of economic activity (output) over time around the economy's long-run, trend rate of growth.

Capital. The stock of plant, equipment, buildings and inventories of raw materials and semi-finished goods that are used to produce other goods and services.

Capital and financial account balance. Reflects changes in a country's external assets and external liabilities over a given time period and changes in official reserves.

Capital deepening. Increasing the quantity of fixed capital each worker has at his or her disposal (representing a key driver of productivity).

Capital depreciation. The decrease in the capital stock resulting from wear and tear and the scrapping of existing capital.

Capital gains effect. Refers to the fact that because of exchange rate movements, capital gains (and losses) can be made in the foreign exchange market.

Capital widening. Providing a growing workforce with additional capital so as to keep the capital: labour ratio constant.

Central bank. A bank's bank and a public authority charged with regulating and controlling a country's monetary policy and financial institutions and markets.

Ceteris paribus. A term derived from Latin meaning: *all other things remaining constant.* This is a convenient assumption used by economists to allow attention to be focused on certain key variables and how they respond to a change in one (or two) other variables.

Circular flow of income model. A simplified exposition of the way in which income flows around the economy in exchange for goods and services between the various sectors that contribute to overall economic activity.

Classical growth theory. A theory of economic growth based on the view that real GDP growth is temporary and that when real GDP per person increases above subsistence level, a population explosion brings real GDP back to subsistence level.

Classical unemployment. Entirely voluntary and is defined as unemployment that results because people choose not to accept the jobs available at the going wage rate.

Closed economy. An economy in which there are no flows of exports or imports, i.e. no foreign trade sector.

Coincident index. An indicator which coincides with economic upturns and downturns and thus is not helpful as a forecasting technique with respect to business cycles; however, data such as cash withdrawals from banks are likely to provide timely information about a possible imminent surge in consumer spending.

Commercial banks. Able to 'create money' even though they usually do not have the discretion to print bank notes. They do this through retaining only a proportion of any bank deposit as cash reserve in their vaults and as liquid investments and lending-out or 'advancing' the rest. This leads to the concept of the 'bank credit multiplier'.

Comparative advantage. A person or country has a comparative advantage in an activity if that person or country can perform the activity at a lower opportunity cost than anyone else or any other country.

Consumer price index (CPI). A weighted average of the prices of a general 'basket' of goods and services bought by final consumers. Each item in the index is weighted according to its relative importance in total consumers' expenditure.

Consumer spending. The proportion of national income or disposable income spent by households on final goods and services; it is the largest proportion of aggregate demand.

Consumer surplus. The value of consumption of goods and services to consumers in excess of the price that they have to pay to obtain them.

Consumption function. The relationship between planned consumer spending and disposable income. Its slope is given by the marginal propensity to consume (mpc). Changes in disposable income lead to changes in planned consumption, as shown along the consumption function. Changes in other factors which impact on consumer spending such as *wealth effects* lead to a shift in the position of the consumption function.

Contractionary fiscal policy. A decrease in government expenditures or an increase in tax revenues for the purpose of controlling aggregate demand.

Cost-push inflation. The result of cost pressures due to supply-side factors that cause changes in aggregate supply. This may be due to higher wages leading to higher costs of production or due to higher import prices, which also raise supply costs.

Crawling peg. A system whereby the government allows a gradual adjustment of the exchange rate.

Crowding-out effect. The tendency for a government budget deficit to drive up interest rates and thus cause a decrease in private sector investment expenditure.

Currency appreciation. A market-determined rise in the value of a currency relative to other currencies under a floating exchange rate regime.

Currency depreciation. A market-determined fall in the value of a currency relative to other currencies under a floating exchange rate regime.

Current account balance. The difference between a country's exports and imports of *visibles* (merchandise or goods) and *invisibles* (services and income payments such as interest, profits and dividends and certain other transfers).

Customs union. A free trade area with common external tariffs and quotas.

Cyclical unemployment. The fluctuations in unemployment over the business cycle.

Deadweight loss. The reduction in consumer surplus and/or producer surplus due to consumers having to pay a higher price for goods and services and inefficient production by firms respectively.

Deficit demand. A situation of disequilibrium where aggregate demand is less than aggregate supply. The outcome must be falling prices and rising unemployment.

Deficit financing. Refers to government expenditure financed by borrowing, i.e. the value of government spending exceeds the value of tax receipts thus adding to the country's national debt.

Deflation. Defined as a situation of a falling price level due to either a lack of aggregate demand, resulting in *malign* deflation, or increased aggregate supply arising from efficiencies in production (*benign* deflation).

Deflationary gap. Occurs when there is a deficiency in demand in the economy so that not all of the existing planned supply is bought. The result is economic deflation leading to higher unemployment, downward pressure on prices in the economy and possibly recession.

Demand for money. Refers to the desire to hold wealth and assets in liquid form, i.e. money balances, rather than using wealth to buy interest-bearing securities and goods and services.

Demand management policies. Demand-side policies (fiscal and/or monetary) designed to smooth out the fluctuations in the business cycle.

Demand-deficient unemployment. Disequilibrium unemployment caused by a fall in aggregate demand with no corresponding fall in the real wage rate. Also referred to as *cyclical* or *Keynesian* unemployment.

Demand-pull inflation. The term used to summarise the various factors that lead to inflation which originate from changes in aggregate demand, i.e. it is the result of excess demand or an *inflationary gap* in the economy.

Demand-side policies. Policies that focus on controlling or influencing aggregate expenditure in the economy.

Depreciation. See *Capital depreciation* and *Currency depreciation.*

Depression. A situation of prolonged low economic activity.

Devaluation. Where the government re-pegs the exchange rate at a lower level.

Diminishing marginal returns. As we apply more of one input (e.g. labour) to another input (e.g. capital or land), then after some point the resulting increase in output becomes smaller and smaller.

Direct controls. Controls on bank lending which may take both quantitative and qualitative forms, affecting the quantity and type of bank lending, respectively.

Direct taxes. Taxes imposed on any incomes paid directly to the tax collecting department by taxpayers or their agents.

Dirty floating. A system of flexible exchange rates but where the government intervenes to prevent excessive fluctuations or even to achieve an unofficial target exchange rate.

Discretionary fiscal policy. Changes in government expenditure and/or taxes for the purpose of directly controlling aggregate demand.

Disequilibrium. Occurs when the output that firms plan to produce and sell is *not* equal to the level of production that households plan to purchase.

Disinflation. A fall in the rate of inflation, in the extreme case leading to a fall in the price level, i.e. *deflation.*

Disposable income. The amount of current income available to households after payment of personal income taxes and national insurance contributions.

Dumping. The selling of goods in foreign markets at prices below their cost of production.

Economic growth. Concerned with increases in real GDP over time.

Economic objectives. Include: a high and sustained level of economic growth; full employment of resources, including labour; low inflation; and a sound balance of payments coupled with a stable currency value.

Economic policy options. Include: fiscal policy, monetary policy, exchange rate and trade policies, supply-side policies, prices and incomes policy, as well as employment policy.

Economic problem. The existence of scarce resources alongside insatiable demand for these resources; this leads to the concept of *opportunity cost.*

Elasticity. Calculated as the proportional (percentage) change in one variable divided by the proportional change in another variable.

Employment policy. Concerned with government efforts to create jobs and thereby reduce unemployment.

Endogenous growth theory. See *New growth theory*.

Equilibrium level of national income. The level of national income at which total injections is exactly equal to total leakages. This is given by the intersection of the aggregate expenditure schedule and the 45° line in the Keynesian 45° diagram.

Equilibrium price. The price at which the quantity demanded equals the quantity supplied.

Equilibrium quantity. The quantity bought and sold at the equilibrium price.

Euroland. Member countries of the European Union which have adopted the euro as their currency.

European Union (EU). Started life in 1957 as the *European Economic Community* with six Member States. Today the EU has 25 Member States with other countries at various stages of applying for membership. The EU is a *customs union* with free trade between members and a common external tariff. Today its policies extend well beyond economic matters to political and social integration.

Exchange rate. The rate at which one national currency exchanges for another. The rate is expressed as the amount of one currency that is necessary to purchase *one unit* of another currency (e.g. $1.50 = £1).

Exchange rate policy. Concerned with the degree of government and central bank intervention in the foreign exchange market to influence the level and direction of the external value of a country's currency.

Exchange rate regime. The system under which the government (or central bank) allows the exchange rate to be determined.

Exogenous. Describes a variable (e.g. investment) whose value is not determined within the system, i.e. it is set independently.

Expansion. A phase of the business cycle in which real GDP increases.

Expansionary fiscal policy. An increase in government expenditure or a decrease in tax revenues for the purpose of stimulating aggregate demand.

Expectations. These play a central role in the analysis of inflation. Where individuals expect higher inflation in the future, they will tend to demand higher wages and to bring forward purchases before prices rise, thereby creating inflationary pressures.

Expectations-augmented Phillips curve. A (short-run) Phillips curve whose position depends on the expected rate of inflation.

Expenditure method. In national income accounting, the sum of all the money values of expenditures on final goods and services produced in an economy.

Exports. The goods and services of one country that are sold to people in other countries.

Fine-tuning. The use of discretionary fiscal (or monetary) policy to counteract movements in economic activity.

Fiscal drag. The automatic tendency for tax receipts to change directly with changes in the national income as people move from lower to higher income tax brackets.

Fiscal policy. The term used to describe government macroeconomic policy that is concerned with changes in government expenditure and taxation.

Fixed capital. The nation's stock of building, machines and plant available for use in the production of goods and services.

Fixed exchange rate system. A regime in which a country's currency is pegged at a particular price (exchange rate) against other currencies.

Floating exchange rate. The value of currencies determined by the forces of demand and supply in the foreign exchange market.

Forward exchange market. A market which provides for the buying and selling of foreign currencies for delivery at some future point in time, thus helping to reduce the uncertainties for traders and investors caused by floating exchange rates.

Frictional unemployment. The unemployment that arises from normal labour turnover – people entering and leaving the labour force and from ongoing creation and destruction of jobs – also known as *transitional unemployment.*

Full employment. The full utilisation of all available labour (and capital) resources so that the economy is able to produce at the limits of its potential gross national product.

Full-employment level of national income. The level of national income at which there is no deficiency of demand.

GDP deflator. The weighted average of prices of all goods and services produced in an economy and purchased by households, firms, government and foreigners.

General Agreement on Tariffs and Trade (GATT). Signed immediately after World War II with the aim of reducing trade protection. It was responsible for a number of 'rounds' of reductions in import duties, including the Kennedy, Tokyo and Uruguay rounds.

Gold standard. A fixed exchange rate system based on the value of gold.

Government budget deficit. The deficit that arises when government expenditure exceeds the taxes collected.

Government expenditure. The term used to cover all forms of state spending at national or federal, state and more local levels. It is affected by many economic, political and social factors and thus it is conventional to treat government expenditure as *autonomous* of changes in national income in introductory Keynesian analysis.

Government intervention. May take place in market economies for a number of reasons involving: the provision of essential services; transfer payments; natural monopolies; social costs and benefits; support for industry and commerce; and the management of aggregate demand in the economy.

Great depression. A period (for example, from 1929–33) of sustained high unemployment and stagnant production throughout the world economy.

Gross domestic product (GDP). The total money value of all final goods and services produced in an economy over a given period of time (quarterly or annually). GDP can be measured in three ways: (a) the total value of final output or the sum of the value added by each industry in producing output (the *output* method); (b) the sum of factor incomes received from producing output (the *income* method); (c) the sum of expenditures on domestic output of goods and services (the *expenditure* method).

Gross investment. The total amount spent on adding to the capital stock and on replacing depreciated capital.

Gross national expenditure at factor cost. Equals gross national expenditure at market prices *minus* indirect taxes *plus* subsidies.

Gross national product (GNP). Equals GDP plus net property income from abroad. Net property income from abroad represents the balance of the inflow and outflow from an economy arising from the receipt and payment of interest, rent, dividends and profits.

Growth accounting. A method of calculating how much real GDP growth has resulted from growth of labour and capital and how much is attributable to technological change.

Guttman effect. Refers to an increase in tax revenues as a result of a cut in direct tax rates because people may feel that failing to declare taxable income is no longer worth the risk at low tax rates.

Hidden economy. See *Underground economy*.

Human capital. The skill and knowledge of people, arising from their education and on-the-job-training.

Hysteresis. The persistence of an effect even when the initial cause has ceased to exist. In economics, this refers to the persistence of unemployment even when the demand deficiency that caused it no long exists (i.e. after a recession has passed).

Imports. The goods and services bought from people in other countries.

Income method. In national income accounting measures the sum of all of the incomes received by the factors of production for their services.

Indirect taxes. Taxes applied to expenditure on goods and services or the value added to production.

Infant industry. An industry in the early stages of its establishment (sometimes referred to as a *sunrise* industry).

Infant industry argument. The proposition that protection is necessary to enable an infant industry to grow into a mature industry that can compete in world markets.

Inflation. Defined as a sustained increase in the general level of prices over time, commonly measured using an official index, such as the consumer (or retail) price index.

Inflationary gap. Occurs when there is excess demand in the economy that cannot be met through higher production; the result over time is rising prices (inflation).

Informal economy. See *Underground economy*.

Injections. Additions to the circular flow of income representing any expenditures on domestic goods and services which originate from outside the household sector, comprising investment expenditure, government expenditure and export revenues.

International Monetary Fund (IMF). Established at Bretton Woods, New Hampshire, USA, in 1944. Its main function is to provide emergency funding to countries suffering from temporary balance of payments problems and a shortage of foreign reserves.

It also acts as an important international forum on economic matters.

International trade policy. Involves measures taken by government, in addition to exchange rate policy, to influence the magnitude and direction of foreign trade.

Inventories. Goods held as unsold stocks (also referred to simply as *stocks*).

Inverted J–curve. Illustrates the tendency for a current account surplus to initially increase and to eventually decline due to an appreciation in the currency.

Investment. The production of items that are not for immediate consumption.

Investment demand. The relationship between investment expenditure and real interest rates, other influences on investment remaining constant.

Investment expenditure. Comprises *autonomous investment*, which is determined by factors other than the level of national income (such as interest rates and business confidence) and *induced investment*, which is investment brought about directly by changes in national income.

IS curve. Shows different combinations of real GDP and interest rates at which aggregate planned expenditure is in equilibrium (i.e. equilibrium in the 'goods' market).

J-curve effect. Illustrates the tendency for a country's current account deficit to worsen initially following a devaluation (or depreciation) of its currency before then moving into surplus.

Keynesian economics. Emphasises the use by governments of *discretionary fiscal policy* to smooth out business cycles and remove inflationary and deflationary gaps.

Keynesian theory of the business cycle. A theory that regards volatile expectations as the main source of economic fluctuations.

Kondratieff waves or cycles. Longer-term, 50-year fluctuations in economic activity associated with new breakthroughs in technology leading to the development of new industries.

Labour demand curve. A curve that shows the quantity of labour that firms plan to hire at each possible real wage rate.

Labour force. The total number of people available for employment in a country (i.e. the sum of the people who are employed and who are unemployed and seeking work).

Labour force participation rate. The percentage of the working-age population who are members of the labour force.

Labour supply curve. A curve that shows the quantity of labour that households plan to supply at each possible real wage rate.

Laffer curve. Shows the relationship between tax rates and government tax revenues and allows identification of the optimal tax rate to maximise government receipts.

Lagging index. An indicator which turns up or down after the economy has expanded or contracted and hence is of no value for forecasting purposes (figures for unemployment fall into this category).

Law of comparative advantage. Establishes the conditions under which specialisation and international trade are advantageous (also referred to as the law of *comparative cost*).

Law of diminishing returns. *See diminishing marginal returns.*

Leakages. Refer to that part of national income that is not spent by households on the consumption of domestically produced goods or services, comprising savings, taxes and expenditure on imports; also referred to as *withdrawals*.

Liquidity preference. The demand for holding assets in the form of money (cash).

Liquidity spectrum. Refers to the range of assets in an economy ranging from the most liquid to the least liquid (i.e. illiquid).

Liquidity. The ability to transform an asset or wealth holding into another form without loss of face value or delay.

LM curve. The different combinations of real GDP and interest rates at which the demand for money and the supply of money are in equilibrium (i.e. 'money' market equilibrium).

Longer leading index. The earliest warning about a possible future upturn or downturn in the economy (includes data such as new construction orders, housing starts, orders for new plant and equipment, as well as measures of business confidence).

Long-run aggregate supply curve. Relationship between the price level and real GDP, where real GDP reflects the economy's potential to produce given full employment of factor inputs and the available technology.

Long-run macroeconomic equilibrium. A situation that occurs when real GDP equals potential GDP – the economy is on its long-run aggregate supply curve.

Long-run Phillips curve. The relationship between inflation and unemployment when the actual inflation rate equals the expected inflation rate, and unemployment is at its natural rate.

Macroeconomic equilibrium. Occurs where aggregate demand equals aggregate supply so that there is no excess demand or excess supply in the economy. In the short-run, this equilibrium may or may not be at a full-employment level of real GDP.

Macroeconomic short run. A period during which real GDP has decreased below or increased above potential GDP.

Macroeconomics. Concerned with the workings of the wider economy, including the measurement and determination of national income, output and expenditure, and the consequences for employment and inflation.

Marginal propensity to consume (MPC). The fraction of an increase in national income (ΔY) which is spent on consumption (ΔC): $MPC = \Delta C/\Delta Y$.

Marginal propensity to import (MPM). The fraction of an increase in national income (ΔY) that is spent on imports (ΔM): $MPM = \Delta M/\Delta Y$.

Marginal propensity to save (MPS). The fraction of an increase in national income (ΔY) which is saved (ΔS): $MPS = \Delta S/\Delta Y$.

Marginal propensity to tax (MPT). The fraction of any change in national income (ΔY) which is taken in taxation (ΔT): $MPT = \Delta T/\Delta Y$ (i.e. the marginal rate of tax).

Marshall-Lerner condition. States that a devaluation (or depreciation) in the exchange rate will reduce a current account deficit if the (absolute) values of the elasticities of demand for exports and imports sum to more than unity.

Medium of exchange. The acceptability of money in exchange for goods and services.

Mercosur. Established in Latin America on 26 March 1991, when Argentina, Brazil, Paraguay and Uruguay agreed to the establishment of the Common Market of the Southern Cone. The aim is to promote trade liberalisation through coordinated reductions in import duties and the imposition of a common external tariff. The common external tariff began in January 1995, although there are some continuing exceptions.

Microeconomics. Involves the study of the individual parts of the economy with respect to individual market prices, individual firms' revenues and costs of production and the employment of factors of production at the individual firm or market level.

Monetarist. An economist who believes that fluctuations in the money stock are the main source of economic fluctuations and that 'inflation is caused by too much money chasing too few goods'.

Monetary base. Notes and coins held outside the central bank.

Monetary policy. Concerned with influencing aggregate demand and therefore inflationary pressures through the use of short-term interest rates and measures to affect the level of liquidity (money supply) in the economy.

Money illusion. When people believe that a money wage or price increase represents a *real* increase, i.e. they ignore or underestimate the effects of inflation.

Money supply growth. Determined by a range of factors, including the size of the government's budget deficit; domestic lending by banks to the private sector; official financing of a balance of payments current account deficit (or surplus); competition between domestic banks and other financial institutions, as well as foreign banks; the government's monetary policy; and banks' non-deposit liabilities.

Money transmission mechanism. Process by which a change in the money supply affects aggregate demand and, in turn, output and prices.

Money. Any good that is widely or readily accepted for the purpose of exchange, i.e. as a payment for goods and services. It has four main functions, namely: as a medium of exchange; a unit of account; a standard for deferred payment; and a store of value.

Multiplier effects. Show how an initial injection of extra spending leads to a multiple change in the level of national income, depending upon the size of the leakages from the circular flow of income.

NAIRU. See *Non-accelerating-inflation rate of unemployment.*

Narrow money. M0 (in the UK) or M1 (in the USA) representing very liquid assets which can be used immediately without capital loss in order to purchase goods and services (such as cash and cheques).

National debt. The total value of the stock of government debt at any given time. It is the product of the accumulated borrowing of government, less government debt repayments, over the years (also referred to as *gross public debt*).

National income. A statistical measure of the total money value of the output of goods and services produced by an economy over a specified period of time.

National income accounting. Based on three methods of measuring economic activity: output (or production) method, income method and expenditure method. In principle, estimates of national output, income and expenditure should be the same – but, in practice, discrepancies arise resulting from errors and omissions.

National income equilibrium. Occurs when aggregate supply equals aggregate planned expenditure.

Natural rate of unemployment (NRU). The unemployment rate which is consistent with a stable rate of inflation and when the economy is at full employment. There is no cyclical unemployment, all unemployment is frictional and structural. The term NRU is often used synonymously with the term *non-accelerating-inflation rate of unemployment (NAIRU).*

Neoclassical growth model. Indicates that the savings rate does not affect the steady state growth rate.

Net investment. Net increase in the capital stock, i.e. gross investment minus depreciation.

Net national product. Gross domestic product *minus* depreciation of the nation's capital stock.

Net property income from abroad. Net income in the form of interest, rent, profits and dividends to a nation's citizens from their ownership of assets abroad.

New classical theory. Highlights the importance of unanticipated changes in aggregate demand and the consequences for real wages and output.

New growth theory. A theory of economic growth which suggests that if policy could raise the savings rate there would be a permanent increase in the economic growth rate.

New Keynesian theory of the business cycle. A rational expectations theory of the business cycle that regards unanticipated fluctuations in aggregate demand as the main source of economic fluctuations but leaves room for anticipated demand fluctuations to play a role.

Nominal GDP. GDP valued in current prices (also referred to as *money GDP*).

Nominal interest rate. The rate of interest which does not take account of the rate of inflation.

Non-accelerating-inflation rate of unemployment (NAIRU). The rate of unemployment consistent with a constant rate of inflation. In monetarist analysis this is the natural rate of unemployment; the rate of unemployment at which the vertical long-run Phillips curve cuts the horizontal axis.

North American Free Trade Agreement (NAFTA). Signed by the USA, Canada and Mexico on 17 December 1992 and came into force on 1 January 1994. The objective is free trade between the three member countries. NAFTA is not a customs union because it lacks a common external tariff.

Official reserves. A country's foreign currency reserves normally held by the country's central bank.

Open economy. An economy with a foreign trade sector and, hence, a flow of exports and imports of goods and services.

Open market operations. The purchase or sale of government securities by the central bank in the open market in order to reduce (or increase) the money supply (liquidity) or to influence long-term interest rates.

Opportunity cost. The economic cost of using resources in one use rather than another and is defined as the *next best* or *alternative use forgone.*

Organisation for Economic Cooperation and Development (OECD). Consists of 30 of the main trading economies and concentrates upon publishing economic and social commentaries, statistics and the provision of policy advice.

Output gap. The difference between a country's (actual) real GDP and its potential GDP. A *negative* output gap exists when actual real GDP is below potential GDP, suggesting that the economy has spare capacity (in terms of labour and utilisation of resources generally). Also referred to as the *capacity gap*.

Output method. The sum of value added at each stage of production or the total value of the final output of goods and services produced in the economy over a specified period of time, giving rise to the *gross domestic product (GDP).*

Overheating. A combination of inflationary pressures and increasing import penetration resulting from aggregate demand growing faster than aggregate supply – thus putting upward pressure on domestic prices and increasing demand for imports.

Parallel economy. See *Underground economy*.

Phillips curve. A statistical relationship showing inverse relationship between the rate of inflation (of prices or wages) and the level of unemployment.

Policy goals. What the government is attempting to achieve over the longer run such as stable prices, full employment, strong and sustainable economic growth, a satisfactory balance of payments position, a stable currency and an equitable distribution of income and wealth.

Policy instruments. Include changes in taxation and government expenditure, changes in the level and structure of interest rates, credit restrictions and other monetary controls, manipulation of the exchange rate and measures to influence or control international trade flows.

Policy targets. Quantifiable aims set by governments and which governments (and other financial bodies, in particular central banks), attempt to achieve using policy instruments.

Potential GDP output. The value of production when all the economy's factors of production are fully employed. Unemployment is at its natural rate and the economy is at full employment.

Precautionary demand for money. Refers to the decision by people to keep money on hand or on deposit in the bank as a precaution for a 'rainy day' when it might suddenly be needed.

Prices and incomes policies. Examples of direct intervention by government in the working of a market economy and are concerned with directly influencing the setting of prices of goods and services and wage settlements.

Producer surplus. The additional earnings (profit) obtained by a producer from receiving a price for a good or service in excess of the price at which it would have been prepared to supply.

Production possibility curve. Shows the maximum output of two goods or services that can be obtained given the current level of resources and assuming maximum efficiency in production.

Progressive tax. A tax that takes a greater proportion of people's income as their income rises (e.g. income tax).

Proportional tax. A tax that takes a set proportion or percentage of income in tax.

Protectionist measures. Take the form of quota restrictions or restricting the volume of certain imports, tariffs (taxes) on imports, import regulations, export subsidies, exchange rate policy and foreign exchange controls.

Public choice theory. Concerned with self-seeking behaviour within government, which may mean, for example, that Keynesian measures are introduced to achieve short-term political benefits, such as winning elections, over achieving longer-term economic prosperity.

Purchasing power parity theory. Relates the exchange rate between two currencies to the relative price levels in the two countries.

Quantity theory of money. An identity that links total expenditure (M^SV) to the total value of output (PY).

Rational expectation. An expectation or forecast that is based on all available information at the time.

Real business cycle theorists. Argue that a business cycle expansion or contraction is caused by random supply-side shocks, which increase or decrease an economy's productive capacity.

Real gross domestic product (real GDP). The value of gross domestic product corrected for changes in the price level over time, i.e. GDP expressed in terms of *constant* prices.

Real interest rate. The nominal interest rate adjusted for inflation – the nominal interest rate minus the inflation rate.

Real money balances effect. States that with a lower price level the real purchasing power of the money stock in the economy rises, leading to higher demand.

Real output. The value of goods and services produced corrected for changes in the price level, i.e. the value expressed in terms of constant prices; see also *Real gross domestic product*.

Real wage rate. The money wage rate divided by the general price level (thus representing the purchasing power of the wages received).

Recession. A situation when the level of economic activity (real GDP) has fallen for at least two consecutive quarters.

Reflationary policy. Fiscal or monetary policy designed to increase the rate of growth of aggregate demand.

Regressive tax. A tax that takes a higher proportion of income from those least able to pay (e.g. tax on essential goods and services such as food and housing).

Reserve ratio. The fraction of a bank's total deposits that are held in reserve.

Saving. The amount of income remaining after meeting consumption expenditures.

Saving function. The relationship between saving and disposable income, other things remaining the same.

Say's law of markets. States that 'supply creates its own demand'.

Shadow economy. See *Underground economy*.

Shorter leading index. An early warning of upturns or downturns in economic activity, but the warning may be only a few months or even weeks ahead (includes data such as new car orders, movements in consumer credit, as well as consumer confidence indicators).

Short-run aggregate supply curve. A curve that shows the relationship between the quantity of real GDP supplied and the price level in the short-run when the money wage rate, other resource prices and potential GDP remain constant.

Short-run macroeconomic equilibrium. A situation that occurs when the quantity of real GDP demanded equals the quantity of real GDP supplied – at the point of intersection of the AD curve and the economy's short-run AS curve.

Short-run Phillips curve. A curve that shows the trade-off between inflation and unemployment, when the expected inflation rate and the natural rate of unemployment remain constant.

Speculative demand for money. Refers to the decision by people to hold money ready to take advantage of a profitable opportunity to invest in bonds which may arise (or they may sell bonds for money when they fear a fall in bond prices).

Stagflation. The combination of a rise in the price level (inflation) and stagnation (low growth and high unemployment).

Standard for deferred payments. Refers to money as an indication of the value that will be given in return at some future date for goods and services received now.

Stocks. See *Inventories*.

Stop-go policies. Alternate deflationary and reflationary policies to smooth the business cycle and to avoid rising inflation (in booms) and rising unemployment (in recessions).

Store of value. Refers to money as an asset that can be held and exchanged later for goods and services – as long as inflation does not erode its future purchasing power.

Structural unemployment. Associated with rigidities in the labour market representing the unemployment that arises when changes in technology or international competition change the skills needed to perform jobs or change the location of jobs.

Substitution effect. Identifies how changes in interest rates can lead to a substitution of current for future consumption (an *intertemporal substitution effect*) and how price changes can affect the demand for exports and imports (an *international substitution effect*).

Sunset industry. An industry (or sector) in structural decline.

Supply curve. A curve that shows the relationship between the price of a good or service and the quantity supplied when all other factors are held constant.

Supply-side economics. Government policies that are directed at tackling problems involving the growth and sustainability of a nation's total or aggregate supply of goods and services over time.

Tariff. A tax imposed by a country on imported goods and services.

Taxes. Levied to finance government spending and influence the allocation of resources and the distribution of income and wealth.

Terms of trade. The ratio of the price of exports to the price of imports, usually expressed as an index.

Total factor productivity growth. Output per unit of input indicating the productivity growth of the nation's capital stock and workforce.

Trade balance. The difference between a country's exports and imports of goods over a given time period; also referred to as the *visible balance.*

Trade cycle. See *Business cycles.*

Transaction effect. Reflects the demand, including expected demand, for currencies in order to purchase imports and exports and for capital transactions.

Transactions demand for money. Money held to meet day-to-day transactions.

Transfer payments. A one-way flow of funds (payments) from the government for which there is no provision or exchange of goods or services in return.

Transmission mechanism. See *Money transmission mechanism.*

Twin deficits. The tendency for a government budget deficit and a deficit on the current account of the balance of payments to move together.

Underground economy. Represents undeclared incomes and hence a loss of tax revenue to the government; also creates a distortion to official statistics relating to economic activity (alternatively referred to as the *hidden, shadow, informal, parallel* or *black economy*).

Unemployment rate. The number of people unemployed as a percentage of the potential workplace. The *rate of unemployment* depends upon the demand for labour by employers or job availability and the supply of labour seeking work.

Unit of account. Refers to money as a standard measure by which the value of different goods and services can be compared.

Velocity of circulation. The average number of times a unit of money is used annually to buy the goods and services that make up GDP.

Withdrawals. See *Leakages.*

Workforce. The number of people that are eligible to work.

World Bank. Established at the Bretton Woods meeting in 1944 with the primary objective today of providing financial assistance to low-income economies and promoting economic development and poverty reduction. The World Bank Group includes the *International Bank for Reconstruction and Development*, the *International Development Association*, the *International Finance Corporation* and certain other bodies.

World Trade Organisation (WTO). Created in 1995 and absorbed the GATT. It also has wider scope and powers than existed under GATT, taking in trade in services, agricultural products and intellectual property rights, and having a trade dispute procedure. The WTO had 146 members in 2003.

INDEX